T0178117

Lecture Notes in Computer Science 13313

More information about this series at https://link.springer.com/bookseries/558

Pei-Luen Patrick Rau (Ed.)

Cross-Cultural Design

Applications in Business, Communication, Health, Well-being, and Inclusiveness

14th International Conference, CCD 2022
Held as Part of the 24th HCI International Conference, HCII 2022
Virtual Event, June 26 – July 1, 2022
Proceedings, Part III

 Springer

Editor
Pei-Luen Patrick Rau
Tsinghua University
Beijing, China

ISSN 0302-9743   ISSN 1611-3349 (electronic)
Lecture Notes in Computer Science
ISBN 978-3-031-06049-6   ISBN 978-3-031-06050-2 (eBook)
https://doi.org/10.1007/978-3-031-06050-2

This Springer imprint is published by the registered company Springer Nature Switzerland AG
The registered company address is: Gewerbestrasse 11, 6330 Cham, Switzerland

Foreword

Human-computer interaction (HCI) is acquiring an ever-increasing scientific and industrial importance, as well as having more impact on people's everyday life, as an ever-growing number of human activities are progressively moving from the physical to the digital world. This process, which has been ongoing for some time now, has been dramatically accelerated by the COVID-19 pandemic. The HCI International (HCII) conference series, held yearly, aims to respond to the compelling need to advance the exchange of knowledge and research and development efforts on the human aspects of design and use of computing systems.

The 24th International Conference on Human-Computer Interaction, HCI International 2022 (HCII 2022), was planned to be held at the Gothia Towers Hotel and Swedish Exhibition & Congress Centre, Göteborg, Sweden, during June 26 to July 1, 2022. Due to the COVID-19 pandemic and with everyone's health and safety in mind, HCII 2022 was organized and run as a virtual conference. It incorporated the 21 thematic areas and affiliated conferences listed on the following page.

A total of 5583 individuals from academia, research institutes, industry, and governmental agencies from 88 countries submitted contributions, and 1276 papers and 275 posters were included in the proceedings to appear just before the start of the conference. The contributions thoroughly cover the entire field of human-computer interaction, addressing major advances in knowledge and effective use of computers in a variety of application areas. These papers provide academics, researchers, engineers, scientists, practitioners, and students with state-of-the-art information on the most recent advances in HCI. The volumes constituting the set of proceedings to appear before the start of the conference are listed in the following pages.

The HCI International (HCII) conference also offers the option of 'Late Breaking Work' which applies both for papers and posters, and the corresponding volume(s) of the proceedings will appear after the conference. Full papers will be included in the 'HCII 2022 - Late Breaking Papers' volumes of the proceedings to be published in the Springer LNCS series, while 'Poster Extended Abstracts' will be included as short research papers in the 'HCII 2022 - Late Breaking Posters' volumes to be published in the Springer CCIS series.

I would like to thank the Program Board Chairs and the members of the Program Boards of all thematic areas and affiliated conferences for their contribution and support towards the highest scientific quality and overall success of the HCI International 2022 conference; they have helped in so many ways, including session organization, paper reviewing (single-blind review process, with a minimum of two reviews per submission) and, more generally, acting as goodwill ambassadors for the HCII conference.

This conference would not have been possible without the continuous and unwavering support and advice of Gavriel Salvendy, founder, General Chair Emeritus, and Scientific Advisor. For his outstanding efforts, I would like to express my appreciation to Abbas Moallem, Communications Chair and Editor of HCI International News.

June 2022   Constantine Stephanidis

HCI International 2022 Thematic Areas and Affiliated Conferences

Thematic Areas

- HCI: Human-Computer Interaction
- HIMI: Human Interface and the Management of Information

Affiliated Conferences

- EPCE: 19th International Conference on Engineering Psychology and Cognitive Ergonomics
- AC: 16th International Conference on Augmented Cognition
- UAHCI: 16th International Conference on Universal Access in Human-Computer Interaction
- CCD: 14th International Conference on Cross-Cultural Design
- SCSM: 14th International Conference on Social Computing and Social Media
- VAMR: 14th International Conference on Virtual, Augmented and Mixed Reality
- DHM: 13th International Conference on Digital Human Modeling and Applications in Health, Safety, Ergonomics and Risk Management
- DUXU: 11th International Conference on Design, User Experience and Usability
- C&C: 10th International Conference on Culture and Computing
- DAPI: 10th International Conference on Distributed, Ambient and Pervasive Interactions
- HCIBGO: 9th International Conference on HCI in Business, Government and Organizations
- LCT: 9th International Conference on Learning and Collaboration Technologies
- ITAP: 8th International Conference on Human Aspects of IT for the Aged Population
- AIS: 4th International Conference on Adaptive Instructional Systems
- HCI-CPT: 4th International Conference on HCI for Cybersecurity, Privacy and Trust
- HCI-Games: 4th International Conference on HCI in Games
- MobiTAS: 4th International Conference on HCI in Mobility, Transport and Automotive Systems
- AI-HCI: 3rd International Conference on Artificial Intelligence in HCI
- MOBILE: 3rd International Conference on Design, Operation and Evaluation of Mobile Communications

List of Conference Proceedings Volumes Appearing Before the Conference

1. LNCS 13302, Human-Computer Interaction: Theoretical Approaches and Design Methods (Part I), edited by Masaaki Kurosu
2. LNCS 13303, Human-Computer Interaction: Technological Innovation (Part II), edited by Masaaki Kurosu
3. LNCS 13304, Human-Computer Interaction: User Experience and Behavior (Part III), edited by Masaaki Kurosu
4. LNCS 13305, Human Interface and the Management of Information: Visual and Information Design (Part I), edited by Sakae Yamamoto and Hirohiko Mori
5. LNCS 13306, Human Interface and the Management of Information: Applications in Complex Technological Environments (Part II), edited by Sakae Yamamoto and Hirohiko Mori
6. LNAI 13307, Engineering Psychology and Cognitive Ergonomics, edited by Don Harris and Wen-Chin Li
7. LNCS 13308, Universal Access in Human-Computer Interaction: Novel Design Approaches and Technologies (Part I), edited by Margherita Antona and Constantine Stephanidis
8. LNCS 13309, Universal Access in Human-Computer Interaction: User and Context Diversity (Part II), edited by Margherita Antona and Constantine Stephanidis
9. LNAI 13310, Augmented Cognition, edited by Dylan D. Schmorrow and Cali M. Fidopiastis
10. LNCS 13311, Cross-Cultural Design: Interaction Design Across Cultures (Part I), edited by Pei-Luen Patrick Rau
11. LNCS 13312, Cross-Cultural Design: Applications in Learning, Arts, Cultural Heritage, Creative Industries, and Virtual Reality (Part II), edited by Pei-Luen Patrick Rau
12. LNCS 13313, Cross-Cultural Design: Applications in Business, Communication, Health, Well-being, and Inclusiveness (Part III), edited by Pei-Luen Patrick Rau
13. LNCS 13314, Cross-Cultural Design: Product and Service Design, Mobility and Automotive Design, Cities, Urban Areas, and Intelligent Environments Design (Part IV), edited by Pei-Luen Patrick Rau
14. LNCS 13315, Social Computing and Social Media: Design, User Experience and Impact (Part I), edited by Gabriele Meiselwitz
15. LNCS 13316, Social Computing and Social Media: Applications in Education and Commerce (Part II), edited by Gabriele Meiselwitz
16. LNCS 13317, Virtual, Augmented and Mixed Reality: Design and Development (Part I), edited by Jessie Y. C. Chen and Gino Fragomeni
17. LNCS 13318, Virtual, Augmented and Mixed Reality: Applications in Education, Aviation and Industry (Part II), edited by Jessie Y. C. Chen and Gino Fragomeni

http://2022.hci.international/proceedings

Preface

The increasing internationalization and globalization of communication, business and industry is leading to a wide cultural diversification of individuals and groups of users who access information, services and products. If interactive systems are to be usable, useful, and appealing to such a wide range of users, culture becomes an important HCI issue. Therefore, HCI practitioners and designers face the challenges of designing across different cultures, and need to elaborate and adopt design approaches which take into account cultural models, factors, expectations and preferences, and allow to develop cross-cultural user experiences that accommodate global users.

The 14th Cross-Cultural Design (CCD) Conference, an affiliated conference of the HCI International Conference, encouraged papers from academics, researchers, industry and professionals, on a broad range of theoretical and applied issues related to Cross-Cultural Design and its applications.

Cross-cultural design has come to be a lateral HCI subject that deals not only with the role of culture in HCI and across the amplitude of HCI application domains, but also in the context of the entire spectrum of HCI methods, processes, practices, and tools. In this respect, a considerable number of papers were accepted to this year's CCD Conference addressing diverse topics, which spanned a wide variety of domains. One of the most prominent topic categories was interaction design, as seen from a cross-cultural perspective, exploring cross-cultural differences and intercultural design. Application domains of social impact, such as learning, arts and cultural heritage have constituted popular topics this year, as well as work conducted in the context of creative industries and virtual reality. Health, well-being, and inclusiveness were emphasized, as was business and communication, which are fields that were all challenged during the ongoing pandemic. Furthermore, among the contributions, views on contemporary and near-future intelligent technologies were presented, including those addressing mobility and automotive design, as well as design in intelligent environments, cities, and urban areas.

Four volumes of the HCII2022 proceedings are dedicated to this year's edition of the CCD Conference:

- Cross-Cultural Design: Interaction Design Across Cultures (Part I), addressing topics related to cross-cultural interaction design, collaborative and participatory cross-cultural design, cross-cultural differences and HCI, as well as aspects of intercultural design.
- Cross-Cultural Design: Applications in Learning, Arts, Cultural Heritage, Creative Industries, and Virtual Reality (Part II), addressing topics related to cross-cultural learning, training, and education; cross-cultural design in arts and music; creative industries and Cultural Heritage under a cross-cultural perspective; and, cross-cultural virtual reality and games.
- Cross-Cultural Design: Applications in Business, Communication, Health, Well-being, and Inclusiveness (Part III), addressing topics related to intercultural business

communication, cross-cultural communication and collaboration, HCI and the global social change imposed by COVID-19, and intercultural design for well-being and inclusiveness.

- Cross-Cultural Design: Product and Service Design, Mobility and Automotive Design, Cities, Urban Areas, and Intelligent Environments Design (Part IV), addressing topics related to cross-cultural product and service design, cross-cultural mobility and automotive UX design, design and culture in social development and digital transformation of cities and urban areas, and cross-cultural design in intelligent environments.

Papers of these volumes are included for publication after a minimum of two single–blind reviews from the members of the CCD Program Board or, in some cases, from members of the Program Boards of other affiliated conferences. I would like to thank all of them for their invaluable contribution, support and efforts.

June 2022   Pei-Luen Patrick Rau

14th International Conference on Cross-Cultural Design (CCD 2022)

Program Board Chair: **Pei-Luen Patrick Rau,** Tsinghua University, China

- Zhe Chen, Beihang University, China
- Kuohsiang Chen, Fozhou University of International Studies and Trade, China
- Na Chen, Beijing University of Chemical Technology, China
- Yu-Liang Chi, Chung Yuan Christian University, Taiwan
- Wen-Ko Chiou, Chang Geng University, Taiwan
- Xianghua Ding, Fudan University, China
- Paul L. Fu, Buckwheatt Inc., USA
- Zhiyong Fu, Tsinghua University, China
- Hanjing Huang, Fuzhou University, China
- Yu-Chi Lee, South China University of Technology, China
- Sheau-Farn Max Liang, National Taipei University of Technology, Taiwan
- Pin-Chao Liao, Tsinghua University, China
- Po-Hsien Lin, National Taiwan University of Arts, Taiwan
- Rungtai Lin, National Taiwan University of Arts, Taiwan
- Wei Lin, Feng Chia University, Taiwan
- Na Liu, Beijing University of Posts and Telecommunications, China
- Cheng-Hung Lo, Xi'an Jiaotong-Liverpool University, China
- Yongqi Lou, Tongji University, China
- Ta-Ping (Robert) Lu, Sichuan University – Pittsburgh Institute, China
- Liang Ma, Tsinghua University, China
- Xingda Qu, Shenzhen University, China
- Chun-Yi (Danny) Shen, Tamkang University, Taiwan
- Huatong Sun, University of Washington Tacoma, USA
- Hao Tan, Hunan University, China
- Pei-Lee Teh, Monash University Malaysia, Malaysia
- Lin Wang, Incheon National University, South Korea
- Hsiu-Ping Yueh, National Taiwan University, Taiwan
- Runting Zhong, Jiangnan University, China

The full list with the Program Board Chairs and the members of the Program Boards of all thematic areas and affiliated conferences is available online at

http://www.hci.international/board-members-2022.php

HCI International 2023

The 25th International Conference on Human-Computer Interaction, HCI International 2023, will be held jointly with the affiliated conferences at the AC Bella Sky Hotel and Bella Center, Copenhagen, Denmark, 23–28 July 2023. It will cover a broad spectrum of themes related to human-computer interaction, including theoretical issues, methods, tools, processes, and case studies in HCI design, as well as novel interaction techniques, interfaces, and applications. The proceedings will be published by Springer. More information will be available on the conference website: http://2023.hci.international/.

General Chair
Constantine Stephanidis
University of Crete and ICS-FORTH
Heraklion, Crete, Greece
Email: general_chair@hcii2023.org

http://2023.hci.international/

Contents – Part III

HCI and the Global Social Change Imposed by COVID-19

Intercultural Design for Well-being and Inclusiveness

Intercultural Business Communication

A Pilot Study on the Correlation Between Product Color and Olfactory Experience

Jun Chen[✉], Yifan Ding, and Rungtai Lin

Graduate School of Creative Industry Design, National Taiwan University of Arts,
New Taipei City 220307, Taiwan
cheesejune@qq.com, rtlin@mail.ntua.edu.tw

Abstract. The fragrance market is gradually igniting in the market due to the epidemic, the global economic depression and the changing consumer habits. Consumers were unable to go out shopping due to the epidemic and moved from offline to online shopping, while the five senses products can only be shown to consumers through visuals. How to trigger the senses of consumers, so that the product visually trigger consumer association, and influence consumer behavior, has become a common business and designer need to think about the problem. Sensory association breaks the boundaries of the senses and can give users a richer and better experience. This study analyzes color elements in the design of scented candles, aiming to understand the relationship between visual and olfactory experience through color imagery and mutual transformation and cooperation. Color, as the first representation of product appearance, is often widely noticed because it influences behavioral choices by affecting consumer psychology. In this study, we will discuss how consumers shop online when they cannot smell the odor and explore the correlation between product color and olfactory experience through the literature, and conceptualize the research plan. It is expected that the results of the follow-up study will be used to understand whether different colors of products affect consumers' judgment of olfactory experience and thus influence purchasing decisions. This will provide product designers with a design concept of visual and olfactory synaesthesia, which will allow them to emphasis more on synaesthetic design in future products.

Keywords: Home fragrance · Color imagery · Olfactory

1 Introduction

With the sudden strike of the epidemic, people's behavior and even lifestyles have changed, and with it, consumption patterns have also changed dramatically. The epidemic was so fierce that many people did not prepare for it in advance, causing consumers to move quickly from offline purchases to online shopping. In such a new era, it is becoming more and more common for consumers to make purchases without being able to smell the odor. In other words, how to include personal sensory phenomena in the design concept and process, and how to successfully attract consumers and facilitate the emotional connection between consumers and designers. Merchants can gradually develop sensory marketing, designers in design to link the senses, with the five senses to cause consumption. Krishna defines sensory marketing as marketing that appeals to consumers' senses and influences their perceptions, judgments and behaviors [1]. Many scholars have conducted studies on packaging design, but very few have explored the visual imagery and olfactory perception of the product, focusing on a single-sensory design is limited, and many studies have helped multi-sensory design to produce a better experience for consumers.

As a pilot study, this paper will comb through the relevant literature as much as possible, as well as analyze the relevant product designs, as a basis for subsequent research.

2   Literature Review

2.1   The Current State of Home Fragrance Products

Fragrance has a profound historical origin, in 4000 BC, ancient Egyptians have long learned to use the fragrance of spices in pursuit of beauty. Data shows that the current global perfume and fragrance market size of about 390.6 billion RMB yuan, and China only accounts for 2.5% of them, China's fragrance market has a very promising future development prospects. In recent years, China's fragrance market has also entered a phase of rapid development, many local fragrance brands are gradually emerging. In the highly competitive cosmetics market, China's fragrance market can be said to be a blue ocean, there is still a lot of consumer potential waiting for brands to explore.

With the advancement of modern analytical testing technology, people have come to understand the mechanism of the effect of fragrance products on human psychology and physiology [2]. In today's society, issues such as environmental protection, life stress, and modern civilization diseases are being taken seriously, and people are becoming concerned about the ingredients and quality of products, as well as how to create an atmosphere, have fun, and relieve stress in their lives. Fragrance products have become a must-have item in many homes, used to enhance the sense of family rituals and enhance the taste of life. With the improvement of scientific refining technology, the use of fragrance has become more widespread, the variety has become more diverse, and consumers have more choices. Home fragrance products are becoming popular among consumers for their stress-relieving, mood-creating and multi-functional decorations. Data show that during the epidemic, home fragrance sales have been soaring, and many consumers say they try to use fragrance products at home to relieve their emotions. With the upgrading of consumption, consumer demand for the product is gradually changing from demand-based consumption to satisfaction-based consumption. However, the wide range of goods on the market, the diversity and style of home fragrance design is really appreciated, and more motivated to explore [3]. The improvement in the standard of living of the public also makes the consumers' demand for products, no longer just the practical level, but also began to pay more attention to the pursuit of personalization, as well as the satisfaction of the emotional level of demand [4].

2.2   Color Imagery

The so-called imagery is an artistic image created by the unique emotional activity of the creator of an objective object. Simply put, it is an objective object that is used to put the subjective feelings. The formation of product imagery comes from the human perception of the product. Color imagery is formed through a combination of intuitive reactions, past experiences, and value judgments of the human psyche, and the unconscious psychological process of forming a mental sense of color [5].

Color associations sometimes have different connotations depending on cultural backgrounds and habits, and abstract associations increase with age [6]. Hong and Lin [7] interpreted color imagery as the different psychological or emotional feelings generated by different color qualities when the human eyes are exposed to color. Fragrance as a product with aesthetic characteristics and cultural symbols determines the wonderful individuality of the fragrance container shape. It is important to use different colors and visual shapes to reflect the different personalities of fragrance containers to attract consumers. In visual design, color is a function of identification and association, symbolic, and plays an important role in visual communication, and is one of the key elements of product design [8]. Users' product cognition mainly focuses on the grasp of perceptual elements such as product form, color and material. In the process of information dissemination, users use their existing knowledge and experience to send the information obtained by senses to the brain through the perception of the components of the surrounding products, and the brain acts on the information through thinking and other means and makes judgments, thus generating emotions about the products. According to human emotional needs, human sense of smell and the feeling of the container itself tactile, the design of the product shape should convey the language imagery [2]. Therefore, color matching is to choose the color for the purpose and function of the object, and also expect to achieve the communication effect of color imagery [9].

2.3   The Correlation Between Vision and Smell

The perception of people's favorite sensations of fragrance is often inseparable from the influence of vision and smell. The question of how visual stimuli, olfactory stimuli and the synergy between them affect people's olfactory perception of fragrance and product evaluation is in the exploratory stage in both theoretical and practical fields [10]. Ma and Qi [11] argued that both vision and smell are important senses in the human body, and through the action of the general sense, people's emotions can be fully mobilized. In some cases, olfaction can enhance the impression of visual images in daily life; for example, some odors can make food images more attractive, while unpleasant odors may make people look disgusting [12]. In conjunction with Amoore's classification of odors [13], in which life requires a person to describe olfactory experience in terms of color, some colors may be associated with odors, and many odors can be easily described by color. For example, reddish brown or golden brown may correspond to a musk; green may correspond to a mint; black may correspond to a putrid odor; yellow may be a lemon, etc. Color produces different responses in people's minds (biological, psychological, attention-grabbing objects) [14] and has a psychological impact on customers. Silva and Mazzilli [15] confirmed in their study that it is common to find an association between color and odor depending on the color of the raw material used in the perfume. Thus, it was found that color is able to influence consumers in establishing a relationship between color and scent.

Fragrance is a product that combines the objective image of the vessel with the subjective mind of the user into a product that carries a certain meaning and mood [16]. Many fragrance brands also attract the consumer's attention through different colors with the expectation of converting scent into vision, for example, the brands Dr. Vranjes, Atelier Cologne, Acqua Colonia, etc. (Table 1). By observing that these brands do not differ in terms of bottle appearance, all using the same shaped bottle and only changing in color, it is possible to find a number of cases in the market where certain colors are used to identify certain scents, which also proves that color plays an important role in the transmission of fragrance [15].

Table 1. Fragrance brands that use color to differentiate

Brands	Dr. Vranjes	Atelier Cologne	Acqua Colonia
Products			

From the fragrance products that use color to differentiate scents, it was also found that some scents use color based on the perception given by the consumer's previous olfactory experience. For example, for rose scents, pink and red are often used to represent the scent; for citrus scents, orange is often used; for lavender scents, purple is often used (Table 2). Fragrance brands also tend to use familiar things and colors to associate with scents, which helps consumers to perceive the product more quickly.

From the analysis of fragrance design in the market, in designers' design activities, synaesthesia allows designers to no longer be limited to a single sense, but to awaken another sense in people through the intercommunication of sense organs [17]. In order to understand the correlation between visual and olfactory senses, this study therefore proposes a visual and olfactory associative architecture diagram (see Fig. 1), from which patterns can be found to enable designers to more skillfully use visual and olfactory associative synaesthesia in their design approach. The three levels of external perception, imagery perception and internal feeling are used to establish a closer relationship between designers and consumers.

Table 2. Fragrance products that express scent with color

Properties	Fragrance Products
Rose	
Citrus	
Lavender	

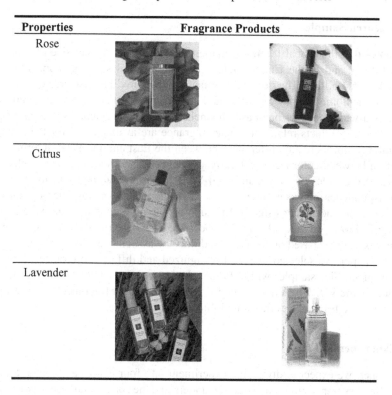

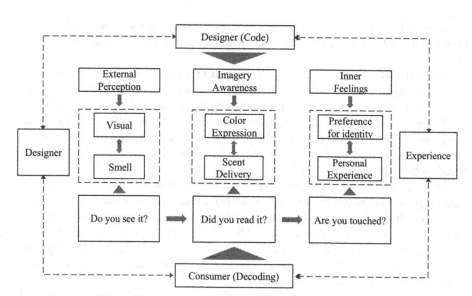

Fig. 1. Visual and olfactory cognitive architecture

3 Experimental Planning

3.1 Research Sample

Data shows that the global fragrance market has reached a market size of more than US$60 billion, and in the United States, the annual retail sales of home fragrances reached US$ 6.4 billion. The rise of the 'olfactory economy' has also created good conditions for the home fragrance market, and has given rise to many fragrance products, as well as a wide range of purchase channels, both in convenience stores and supermarkets where products related to home fragrance are available. So for the emerging Asian market, are there any differences between the East and the West in terms of the correlation between color and scent correspondence? Therefore, this paper selects the home scented candles of American brand VOLUSPA as a sample to analyze whether the correspondence between color and scent in the design of fragrance of European and American brands is consistent with Asian people in the Asian region where online shopping is developed, and whether it is possible to choose the scent that matches the olfactory experience based on the color and thus the associative synaesthesia.

In this paper, we selected five well-recognized and different fragrances to prepare the experiment. Five samples with different shades were selected according to the five fragrances in the VOLUSPA brand, and the adjectives of their fragrances were compiled according to the fragrance evaluation (Table 3).

3.2 Experimental Flow

In this paper, we expect to divide the experiment into four phases and match them by visual-olfactory transformation in order to understand the correspondence between them (see Fig. 2).

Phase I: Five fragrances with a large difference in the scent were selected, and the fragrance reviews of these five fragrances were used to compile an adjective for the scent.

Phase II: The visual to olfactory association experiment will be conducted first. Before the experiment, the subjects would not know anything about this brand and the product scent, and remove the text information on the product.

The subjects were allowed to conduct the experiment simultaneously in a distraction-free room, where the color corresponding to the scented candle packaging color and the picture of the scented candle were shown on a monitor, and the answers were given based on the questions (Table 4).

Phase III: The association experiment from smell to vision was conducted again, and subjects performed the experiment individually in a distraction-free room. The duration of the experiment was set for 15 min for each person, using 3 min duration for each fragrance note. Each scented candle would burn for one minute for the subject to smell and fill in the answer (Table 4), and two minutes time was provided for the subject to smell coffee beans to relieve the olfactory nerves and ventilate the room odor before continuing to smell the next scented candle.

Phase IV: Analysis and exploration of visual and olfactory correlations to understand consumers' preferences for color and scent combinations.

Table 3. Five types of fragrance notes and explanation.

Fragrance category	Explanation	Branded scented candles	Adjectives
Floral Notes	Most of the plant fragrance extracted from petals, flowers, flowers, etc.		Fragrant、Light and elegant
Fruity notes	Extracts the aroma composition of fruits.		Sweet、Sour
Green notes	The herbal flavor emitted by the plant is mostly extracted from leaves and green grass.		Fresh、Secluded
Oriental fragrance	The use of oriental trees or animal spices such as spices, resin, musk, etc.		Strong、Spicy
Woody fragrance	A dry woody scent consisting of sandalwood, patchouli, incense and cedar.		Cool、Mellow

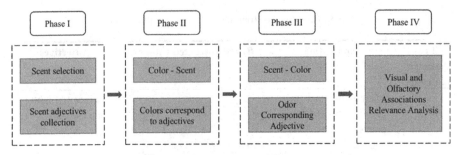

Fig. 2. Experimental flow

Table 4. Assessment framework for visual and olfactory association.

Properties	Visual-smell	Smell-visual
External perception	A1 Which smell do you associate with when you see this color? (In order of preference)	B1 Which color do you associate with this smell? (In order of preference)
Imagery awareness	A2 Which scent do you think corresponds to this color of scented candle?	B2 Which color scented candle does this smell correspond to?
Inner feelings	A3 How do you feel when you see this color?(Corresponding adjectives)	B3 How do you feel when you smell this smell?(Corresponding adjectives)
Overall evaluation	4 Overall, the color of this scented candle and its matching scent gave me a level of preference	

4   Results and Discussion

The present Morrot et al. also found in their study that the color of wine leads to the recognition of its odor, and suggested that color induces the formation of a psycho-visual image of an object with that color, and that the recognition of odor would come from the recognition of this psycho-visual image. The recognition of odor will come from the recognition of this psycho-visual image [18]. Kim moreover confirmed in his experiments that there is a strong correlation between vision and smell, and that the external color of perfume bottles and packaging can play an important role in assessing fragrance when consumers have inadequate or no olfactory experience of perfume [19]. The study found that the packaging design of fragrances tends to atmosphere two categories, one is the main fragrance brand image, regardless of the fragrance are presented in the same packaging. The other is to use different colors depending on the fragrance [3]. However, with the rapid development of e-commerce, how olfactory products can precisely attract consumers and grasp the new connection between consumers and products is a topic that needs to be studied in depth for the future development of e-commerce. The cross-modal products of visual and olfactory association should be designed to understand the consistency between stimuli and build a unified scent message [20]. And designers need to be able to understand consumers' intrinsic feelings in order to more effectively design packaging that meets their perceptions. Symbols, whether color, pattern, shape, etc., are likely to appeal to consumers who are looking for a fragrance with specific characteristics. In order to conduct a more objective study, this paper proposes a business development model for synaesthetic goods (see Fig. 3), which provides an implementable development direction for merchants and designers.

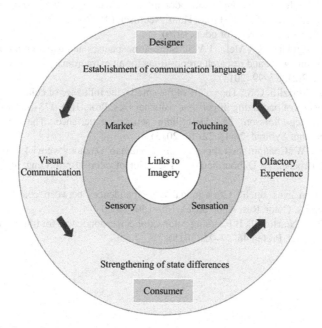

Fig. 3. United sense sympathetic commodity business development model

References

1. Krishna, A.: An introduction to sensory marketing. In: Sensory Marketing: Research on the Sensuality of Products, pp. 1–13. New York, NY (2010)
2. Li, C., Zheng, J.: Sweet atmosphere container design and user interaction emotional. Art Des. **9**, 226–228 (2010)
3. Lin, C.-H., Huang, Y.-C.: The preliminary study on package design of home fragrances in Taiwan. J. Commer. Des. **16**, 35–52 (2012)
4. Chu, Z.: Jiaju xiangxun chanpin de shichuan sheji yu xiujue qianghua. Master's thseis, LuXun Academy of Fine Arts (2018)
5. Chang, Z.-H., Huang, Y.-C., Chen, J.-H.: The Theoretical Discussion and Validation of Color Preference in Gender, vol. 15, pp. 57–76 (2011)
6. Hsu, S.: The visual images and color schemes of taiwan's fruit-flavored alcoholic drink aluminum can packaging. Master's thseis, Graduate Institute of Visual Communication Design Tainan University of Technology (2014)
7. Hung, P.-H., Lin, R.: A study of the correlation between color image and modeling design on virtual characters' personality. J. Ergon. Study **18**(1), 45–56 (2016)

8. Hung, W.-C., Wang, L.-T.: A study on the color and visual image for packages. Manag. Inf. Comput. **6**(2), 75–84 (2017)
9. Lin, J.Y.: Theory of Color, Sanmin, Taipei (1993)
10. Spence, C.: Multisensory packaging design: color, shape, texture, sound, and smell.Integr. Packag. Prod. Exp. Food Beverages 1–22 (2016)
11. Ma, M., Qi, Y.: Synaesthesia of vision and smell in perfume bottle design. Design 13 (2018)
12. Cook, S., et al.: Pleasant and unpleasant odorsinfluence hedonic evaluations of human faces: an event-related potential study. Front. Hum. Neurosci. (9), 661 (2015)
13. Amoore, J.E.: Molecular basis of odor (1970)
14. Farias, S.A., Aguiar, E.C., Melo, F.V.S.: Store atmospherics and experiential marketing: a conceptual frame work and research propositions for an extraordinary customer experience. Int. Bus. Res. **7**(2), 87–99 (2014)
15. Silva, C.A.P., Mazzilli, C.S.: The colors of the smells: the influence of culture and society in the visual design of packaging of perfume. Blucher Des. Proc. **1**(5), 373–378 (2014)
16. Paradis, C., Eeg-Olofsson, M.: Describing sensory experience. The genre of wine reviews.Metaphor Symbol. **28**(1), 22–40 (2013)
17. Wei, L., Ailiu, W.: Chanpin sheji zhong de tonggan tantao. Dazhong wenyi **4**, 130–131 (2010)
18. Morrot, G., Brochet, F., Dubourdieu, D.: The color of odors. Brain Lang. **79**(2), 309–320 (2001)
19. Kim, Y.J.: Can eyes smell? Cross-modal correspondences between color hue-tone and fragrance family. Color. Res. Appl. **38**(2), 139–156 (2013)
20. Schifferstein, H.N., Howell, B.F.: Using color–odor correspondences for fragrance packaging design. Food Qual. Prefer. **46**, 17–25 (2015)

Online Communication for Team Creativity in Tech Companies: Barriers and Tool Design

Yue Chen[1], Man Wu[2], and Qin Gao[2]([✉])

[1] East China University of Science and Technology, Shanghai 200237, China
[2] Tsinghua University, Beijing 100084, China
gaoqin@tsinghua.edu.cn

Abstract. Teams in tech companies collaboratively solve creative problems, and this team creative process increasingly occurs online. Despite many innovative tool designs to support collaborative creativity, many teams did not adopt them. This study aimed to identify the barriers to adoption and teams' needs for collaborative creativity support. We clarified the team creative process in practice by individual in-depth interviews with 15 employees in 12 different high-tech companies in China. The results suggested that the teams frequently shared information via communication tools or face to face, and many of them acknowledged the benefits of collaboration in team creativity. However, most of them ideated and evaluated ideas or solutions individually. The reasons for the low collaboration level included the features of their tasks, a lack of technical and managerial support for collaboration in the ideation and evaluation phase, and a lack of motivation for team creativity. Based on these findings, we outlined implications for designing tools to support team creativity and demonstrated a prototype of a communication tool with creative support features.

Keywords: Team creativity · Collaboration · Communication tools · Creativity support tools

1 Introduction

Technological innovation increasingly relies on teamwork, and creativity and innovation are generated from social interaction and information exchange [1, 2]. To solve problems without solutions, team members can collaboratively generate novel and useful ideas or solutions of, for example, products, services, processes, or steps [3]. This cognitive process is called creative problem-solving, and the outcome is called team creativity. Such a process is common in research, technology product development, and creative teams.

Modern teams inevitably office and perform creativity tasks online. Many research teams and technology companies are distributed geographically. Due to the COVID19 pandemic, increasing teams in research and technology companies work collaboratively on online communication applications, such as Slack, WeChat, and Feishu. However, on the one hand, these communication tools lacked support for team creativity. On the

P.-L. P. Rau (Ed.): HCII 2022, LNCS 13313, pp. 13–28, 2022.
https://doi.org/10.1007/978-3-031-06050-2_2

other hand, although many studies have proposed innovative designs of collaborative creativity support tools (CSTs) and proved their effectiveness, many of these tools have not been adopted by real teams yet.

Therefore, this paper aims to identify the reasons why teams adopt CSTs or not by studying their current team creative process. We individually interviewed 15 employees working in the teams in high-tech companies in China, including both new and small companies and big companies on the list of Fortune Global 500. We clarified their team creative process and use of communication tools and CSTs to further identify the barriers and their potential needs for these tools. Finally, we discussed and proposed a design of communication tools integrated with CST features to support team creativity.

2 Literature Review

2.1 Team Creative Process

The creative process usually consists of four phases: problem analysis, ideation, evaluation, and implementation [4]. In the problem analysis phase, individuals analyze and understand the current situation, and then find and formulate specific problems to be solved. In the ideation phase, individuals generate many new alternative ideas. In the evaluation phase, individuals evaluate and select among the alternative ideas. Finally, the chosen idea or solution will be implemented. This process is not linear or static but dynamic and recursive [5].

The ideation phase may distinguish creativity tasks from other problem-solving tasks, and many creativity research and CST designs focus on the ideation phase. Researchers suggested that the cognitive process of ideation is to establish semantic connections between existing knowledge [5, 6]. In the ideation phase, individuals have more divergent thinking, which is imaginative and less critical, opposite to convergent thinking. They also use various strategies to promote ideation, such as analogical reasoning and expansion or combination of existing ideas [7, 8].

At the team level, the creative process involves not only the cognitive process mentioned but also the social and motivational process [9]. The social process is the interactions among team members, such as information sharing and discussion. On the one hand, information flow among team members can increase the quality and flexibility of ideation and enhance team creativity [10, 11]. On the other hand, communication may also negatively affect ideation by increasing, for example, cognitive load, social loafing, and social anxiety [12, 13]. The motivational process is setting or maintaining members' motivation levels. Both intrinsic and extrinsic motivation can promote team creativity, but research suggests that intrinsic motivation is more important in the ideation phase [14]. These processes of team creativity can be affected group, task, and situational variables, including group members' features (e.g., knowledge and skills), group structure (e.g., group size and diversity), group climate (e.g., trust and conflict), and external demand (e.g., task structure and support for creativity) [9].

2.2 Creativity Support Tools

Creativity support tools/systems (CSTs/CSSs) are information systems that support creative processes such as product design, and ideation [15]. These tools are usually designed with the guidance of creativity theories and are widely used in the situations such as team creativity tasks, knowledge management, art design and decision making [16–18].

CSTs can be generally categorized into individual or team types [15]. At the individual level, Wang and Nickerson [18] conducted a literature-review study and proposed a design framework for individual CSTs. The framework suggested four types of features, including:

1. Motivating features by affective or achievement approaches.
2. Supports for the whole creative process, including task process control.
3. Supports for divergent thinking, such as stimulation for new ideas, memory retrieval facilitation, working memory assistance (e.g., by data visualization), and application of creativity techniques.
4. Supporting convergent thinking, such as labeling and classification support for evaluation.

Team-level CSTs can be generally categorized into four types [16, 19]: idea management systems, group support systems, computer-assisted creativity systems, and virtual team members.

Idea management systems are the systems that support collecting, evaluating, and selecting ideas. An example frequently used in video conferencing is the collaborative whiteboard applications, such as Mural of Microsoft Teams, which allows team members to co-edit shared whiteboards and post-it notes during online meetings. Another widely used tool is collaborative mind maps, such as Mind Master. Researchers have also proposed innovative designs to better organize and present ideas for evaluation, such as IdeaHound [20].

Group support systems are the systems that support team creativity by facilitating communication and coordination. For example, Sundholm et al. designed iLounge, a smart meeting room for co-located creative collaboration [21]. Kim et al. designed an application for collaborative prototyping, where distributed team members could collaboratively edit their prototypes and asynchronously interact with each other [22].

Computer-assisted creativity systems are the systems that assist the implementation of creative techniques as a coach. A major type is electronic brainstorming systems, such as Momentum [23]. These systems can apply brainstorming techniques to reduce the problems such as peer pressure, social loafing, and production blocking. Besides brainstorming, some systems incorporate other creative techniques, such as peripheral micro tasks [24], to facilitate ideation.

Virtual team members are the artificial intelligence that can help monitor human cognitive processes, simulate human creativity, or generate ideas like human team members. For example, AI conversational robots can play the role of facilitators, organize and coordinate complex tasks for team collaboration [25].

3   Method

3.1   Participants

We interviewed 15 employees individually. As shown in Table 1, they aged from 26 to 33 (M = 28.73, SD = 2.21). Six of them were females, and nine of them were males. They worked in 12 different technology companies. Six of the companies were in the IT industry. Other companies included manufacturing, transportation, finance, and the energy industry. Six of the participants (40%) worked in the R&D department. Their team size ranged from 3 to 30, with most between 6 and 10 (N = 8, 53%). All the teams had been formed for more than a year, and nine of them (60%) had been formed for more than two years. Most participants (N = 12, 80%) worked in a relatively stable team with low turnover rates. Eight participants (53%) worked in a fully co-located team. Some team members in the other seven teams (47%) worked in other cities in China.

Table 1. Summary of the participants.

Participants	Age	Gender	Industry	Department	Team size	Team was formed	Team turnover	Location
P1	26	F	IT, Big tech	R&D	7–8	<= 2 years	High	DT
P2	33	F	IT, Big tech	PD	7–8	<= 2 years	Low	DT
P3	31	F	IT, Small tech	PD	10	<= 2 years	High	DT
P4	25	M	IT, Unicorn	R&D	3–5	<= 2 years	High	DT
P5	29	F	TC, Big tech	R&D	7–8	>2 years	Low	CO
P6	27	F	IT, Unicorn	IT	20–30	>2 years	Low	CO
P7	28	M	IT, Big tech	IT	10	>2 years	Low	DT
P8	27	M	TP, tech	PD	3	>2 years	Low	CO
P9	28	F	TC, Big tech	R&D	17	<= 2 years	Low	DT
P10	27	M	IT, Big tech	R&D	12	>2 years	Low	CO
P11	32	M	IT, Small tech	R&D	5	>2 years	Low	CO

(*continued*)

Table 1. (*continued*)

Participants	Age	Gender	Industry	Department	Team size	Team was formed	Team turnover	Location
P12	28	M	FN, Large enterprise	PD	21	>2 years	Low	CO
P13	31	M	EG, Large enterprise	Testing	10	>2 years	Low	CO
P14	29	M	EG, Large enterprise	Testing	10	<= 2 years	Low	CO
P15	30	M	EG, Large enterprise	Testing	6	>2 years	Low	DT

Gender: F = female, M = male; Industry: IT = information technology, TC = telecommunication company, TP = transportation, FN = finance, EG = energy industry; Department: R&D = research and development, PD = product development, IT = information technology; Location: CO = co-located; DT = distributed but most members were co-located.

3.2 Data Collection

The individual interviews were semi-structured. We asked the following aspects during three different phases (i.e., problem analysis, ideation, and evaluation):

1. What was their team's typical team process in the three stages?
2. How did they use communication tools, and what was the impact of communication tools?
3. What did other creativity support tools their teams adopt?
4. What were the factors affecting the process and the potential challenges?

   Each interview lasted for around one hour and was audio-recorded and transcribed to texts later.

3.3 Data Analysis

The interview scripts were analyzed by thematic analysis [26] with NVivo 12. The scripts were coded iteratively for three rounds. In the first round, two researchers read the scripts and initially open-coded for each research question. In the first round of coding, researcher A generated 50 codes, and researcher B generated 54 codes, with 36 (69%) same or similar codes. Then, the two researchers discussed and generated an initial codebook. In the second round, researcher A modified and generated 54 codes, whereas researcher B generated 56 codes, with 51 (93%) same or similar codes. They finally discussed and generated a revised codebook with 54 codes. In the final round, Researcher A coded all the scripts.

4   Results

4.1   Team Creative Process

The teams generally experienced the team creative process as suggested in the literature, but we found differences in detailed phases. Overall, the creative process was more individual rather than collaborative, especially in the ideation and evaluation phases. However, team members shared much information in all the phases.

Problem Analysis. Their problems originated from the following sources: (1) team members' discovery (N = 11), (2) requests from other departments (N = 10), (3) feedback from the marketing department (N = 7), and (4) frontiers topics in their industry. After identifying a problem, most participants would analyze it individually (N = 7) or collaboratively (N = 4) with other members before reporting to the leaders. In this phase, though many participants analyze problems individually, most teams shared information, such as literature, knowledge, advice from experts, and reports about competitive products, by communication tools (N = 6) and face to face (N = 4).

Ideation. More than half of the participants (N = 8) said they usually generated ideas individually, and these ideas were evaluated and chosen by leaders later. Five participants said they generated ideas both individually and collaboratively. Only two participants (P14 and P15) said they generated ideas mainly in team meetings. The possible reason for less collaboration was that most teams explicitly decomposed their tasks, and each team member only concentrated on his/her own work. For example, P12 said,

> "We usually think and work individually... I will discuss with my leader only after I have figured out what to do, why to do so, and the logic." [P12, 28, male, finance industry]

For the same reason, only four participants said their teams brainstormed together and two of them said they seldomly brainstormed. The participants also gave negative comments on brainstorming. For example, P2 said many brainstormed ideas were not feasible and could not be implemented by their algorithms. P9 felt brainstorming was inefficient. In fact, the teams of the four participants did not conduct brainstorming carefully. For example, P2 said:

> "We brainstormed many times, but people chatted about irrelevant topics most of the time. We do not have a good moderator to control the process. If anyone comes out to be a moderator voluntarily, many other people will disagree with him/her. As a result, brainstorming is not an effective approach for our team." [P2, 33, female, IT industry]

Evaluation and Documentation. More than half of the participants (N = 9) said their ideas were evaluated mainly by their leaders though they could comment on the alternative ideas. Five participants said the ideas were evaluated by first their teammates and then their leaders. Overall, the evaluation and final decision were mainly made by leaders. After the project was finished, most teams would package and document their experience, the creative process, and the final products or solutions for further knowledge sharing in both teams and organizations. These documents were stored on cloud drives or wiki platforms and could be retrieved by categories and keyword tagging. However, many team members were not motivated to organize the information of the whole project and write the documents. As mentioned by P7,

"Many people are not motivated to document their projects carefully because documentation takes too much time and effort. Most people cannot be bothered to do it (because they have many other jobs)." [P7, 28, male, IT industry]

4.2 Communication Tools and Creativity-Support Tools

During the team creative process, the participants communicated with their team members via the following media: face-to-face communication, communication applications on smart devices, audio or video conferencing, emailing, phone calls, and short message service of mobile phones.

Table 2. Use of different media during team creative process.

Media	Number (percentage) of participants		
	Rarely use	Sometimes use	Frequently use
Face to face	0	2 (13%)	13 (87%)
Communication applications	1 (7%)	1 (7%)	13 (87%)
Audio or video conferencing	5 (33%)	2 (13%)	8 (53%)
Emailing	6 (40%)	0	9 (60%)
Phone calling	7 (47%)	0	8 (53%)
SMS on mobile phones	15 (100%)	0	0

As shown in Table 2, besides the face-to-face approach, the most frequently used media was communication applications such as WeChat, Feishu, and DingTalk in China. Their teams usually used these applications (1) to post notifications (N = 8), (2) when they could not meet face to face (N = 6), and (3) to carefully edit and convey complex messages (N = 3). Many participants said the communication applications were effective because:

1. They could record their discussions and any important information in these applications (N = 8).
2. They could accurately communicate with others (N = 5).
3. The applications were efficient (N = 2).

They usually use a mix of synchronous and asynchronous interaction approaches. They especially appreciated the editability and the data persistency of text-based communication applications, as well as the quick responses of synchronous video/audio-based approaches. As P7 said,

> *"We usually prepare and post a document on DingTalk (an application), and then have a call to discuss based on the document. The document can also be a record for accountability or contribution in the future." [P7, 28, male, IT industry]*

Regarding creativity support tools, most participants (N = 10) used mind map applications, especially in the problem analysis phase, but they usually drew maps individually. Five participants also used collaborative writing applications during the team creative process, such as Shimo and the collaborative writing function in Feishu. For example, P4 said their team kept a shared document in which team members could post their problems anytime. The problems in the document were discussed during their weekly meetings. In addition, some organizations provided creative training to help employees' ideation (by P5).

Some teams also used communication tools or knowledge sharing tools for peer review of ideas. For example, P4 said,

> *"Our team members can post their ideas every time they come up with an idea. The idea can be reviewed and liked by others. If an idea is liked many times, probably it will be feasible." [P4, 25, male, IT industry]*

As mentioned in Sect. 4.1, most shared knowledge was stored on cloud drives or wiki platforms. For example, P9's team collaboratively edited team wikis of previous projects. P7's organization kept a "knowledge base" website where teams could share their knowledge and documentation. Their organization sometimes held competitions to motivate employees and teams to contribute.

4.3 Challenges of Team Creative Process

Team Cognition. Five participants said their team members were diverse in majors and understood a problem from different perspectives. The different understandings, or the low level of shared mental model, may lead to conflicts among team members, as P2 and P8 mentioned. The conflicts sometimes could be intensified by personal emotions, as P15 said. In this situation, team members usually ask their leaders to moderate and make decisions. As P8 said, *"When we could not persuade each other, they would ask the leader to make decisions."*

Besides the shared mental model, three participants also mentioned barriers in building transactive memory systems. They said team members did not know much about others' expert knowledge domain or trust others' expertise. For example, P6, who majored in algorithms, said she could not evaluate the suggestions from people in other majors such as product design. However, P15 said their team members knew other members' expertise though they were experts in diverse domains, indicating a higher level of transactive memory systems. It may have also contributed to their higher level of collaboration in the creative process.

Social Factors. As the literature suggests, the development of team cognition and creativity require communication and social interactions. This importance of social interactions was also recognized by most participants. For example, P2 compared her previous team and current team to highlight the importance of social interactions (especially for transactive memory systems):

> *"My current team members are really social and like to interact with each other. We frequently meet and share information. On the contrary, my previous team members did not interact with each other much. For this reason, I did not know what others were doing, and the team efficiency was unsatisfying." [P2, 33, female, IT industry]*

However, as mentioned in Sect. 4.1, most participants tended to work individually and lacked interactions with their team members in the phases of ideation and evaluation.

Motivation. Some participants said they felt less motivated to contribute to team creativity. The major reason was the limited time for their work and projects mentioned by six participants. As P10 said, *"most requirements from other departments were very urgent."* Therefore, the participants tended to use their familiar problem-solving approaches to finish the tasks. The second reason was the lack of intrinsic motivation mentioned by five participants. Especially when the problem was difficult, team members took many efforts, but the outcomes may not meet their expectations, or they may not receive positive feedback (P5 and P8).

5 Discussion and Design Implications

5.1 Findings

This study conducted 15 interviews with employees in R&D, product development, and other departments of 12 tech companies in China. We found that **in most teams, ideation and evaluation was an individual rather than collaborative cognitive process**, with the following phenomena:

1. Most teams lacked communication and collaboration in the ideation and evaluation phases. It could impede the development of team cognitions, including shared mental models and transactive memory systems, which were beneficial to team creativity.
2. Most teams used various communication tools and knowledge-sharing platforms throughout the creative process, but few of them used collaborative CSTs. Many team members used mind maps individually but hardly shared them with others.

The interviews identified several reasons for the less collaborative ideation and evaluation. **First, a major reason was the urgent and well-decomposed features of their tasks.** Most teams had to immediately solve the problems to ensure the achievement of their organizations. To increase efficiency, most teams also explicitly broke their tasks into subtasks and distributed them to individual members, and the team leader would evaluate and make the final decision later. Therefore, members only concentrated on their own creative problem-solving tasks. This result was probably related to our sampling. Most participants of this study majored in science, technology, engineering, and mathematics, and most of them worked as engineers. Many tasks for them can be easier to break into subtasks and distribute than the tasks for other employees who worked on, for example, community supports and creative design.

Second, many teams lacked support (both technical and managerial support) for collaboration in the ideation and evaluation process. In fact, many participants acknowledged the benefits of communication and collaboration, as suggested in the literature about how team cognitions affected team creativity (e.g., [27, 28]). They also frequently shared information in the early phases and packaged documentation in the last documentation phase, indicating that their individual creative works relied on the team's explicit knowledge. However, in the ideation phase, many of them did not have efficient and convenient approaches to exchange information and could not conduct brainstorming well. It also took many efforts and time to organize documents for sharing at the end. As a result, many participants said that they had some difficulties in understanding others' expertise, thoughts, and activities; they could not collaboratively generate new ideas (i.e., collaborative ideation recommended by the literature [29, 30]).

Third, Several Teams were not Motivated for Higher Team Creativity. On the one hand, due to the limited time of their tasks, some participants had to consider how to deliver their solutions on time more than creativity. On the other hand, some of them rarely got positive feedback from team creativity; they felt that team creativity consumed much time and effort, but the input-output ratio was unsatisfying. Overall, the findings and reasons were covered by the previous research of team creative process and factors (e.g., [9]), but were highlighted by this study in the context of high-tech companies in China.

5.2 Design Implications

These findings of interviews suggested the following implications for the design of tools to support team creativity in tech companies. First, **integrate communication tools with collaborative CST features**, especially for tech companies in China. As mentioned in Sect. 5.1, many teams lack supports for collaborative ideation. They rarely use collaborative CSTs but frequently use communication tools. Therefore, teams can be easier to accept communication tools with CST features than other collaborative CSTs. Ideally, these features require less effort from team members but can significantly promote interactions and collaboration during the ideation phase. For example, the idea management features in collaborative CSTs [16, 19] can be embedded into group chatting, which means the ideas can be automatically gathered from the chatting messages or audio/video-recorded data.

Second, **mix synchronous and asynchronous interactions in the ideation and evaluation phases and increase data persistency**. As suggested by the interviews and consistent with the theory of media synchronicity [31], team members need synchronous interactions to get quicker response and reach mutual understanding and asynchronous interactions to prepare and elaborate their messages. Some team members even simultaneously use two types of approaches to discuss complex new ideas.

Team members also need functions to track their discussion later for accountability or contribution identification, which was also identified in previous research about collaborative writing [32]. Our study suggests that this could be a reason why team members choose to discuss via online applications instead of the face-to-face way. Though online applications naturally preserve users' interaction data, the awareness of members' contributions can be further enhanced by features such as reputation systems or integrative dashboards of contribution.

Third, **design features to motivate and facilitate social interactions and information exchange in the ideation and evaluation phases**. The interviews suggested several potential approaches. One approach to increase motivation is the aforementioned features that enhance the awareness of contribution and reputation. Previous social media research suggests that users may generate knowledgeable content to satisfy their needs for self-achievement and better reputations [33]. Similarly, communication tools may motivate team members to discuss more by the features highlighting their creative contribution to the team and organization. Another approach is reducing the efforts of social interactions by, for example, unfocused interaction features, such as one-click liking. These features can promote social interactions and gather voting data for later evaluation.

5.3   A Design to Support Communication and Team Creativity

Due to the low adoption of CSTs but frequently used communication tools, we explored the potential design to integrate communication tools with CST features to support team creativity in tech companies. Based on the findings of interviews, we determined the following design goals:

1. Cognitive goals: With the tool, users can easily and efficiently know others' ideas, share knowledge and the development of each idea, and, based on that, generate and evaluate new ideas.
2. Social goals: The tool can facilitate users to interact with others, increase their awareness of other members' contribution to team creativity, and create a social norm for sharing and collaboration.
3. Motivation goals: The tool can increase users' willingness to participate in the collaborative creative process.

For these goals, we proposed three major features on mobile devices. First, in the group chatting interface (which is available in most communication applications), users can chat and share information with their team members anytime, as shown in Fig. 1. Second, these chatting messages can be tagged, replied and liked by team members. In other words, the messages can be threaded. As shown in Fig. 2, members can tap a threaded message to check all the relevant information about this message, including the context, social interactions, and other threads with the same tag. Members can add different tags, such as ideas, previous cases useful to the current creativity task, and user requirements, as shown in Fig. 3. These two features may promote interactions during ideation and evaluation phases, support team cognitions, and create a collaborative atmosphere. They may also increase data persistency, highlight members' contributions, and thus increase motivation. Third, members can check the team badges and individual badges, as shown in Fig. 4. These features may create a social norm of both competition and cooperation and motivate team members, especially in ideation and evaluation phases.

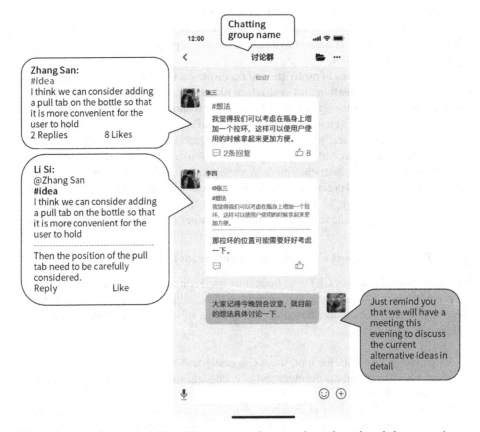

Fig. 1. Interface for group chatting. The group members can chat or have threaded conversations.

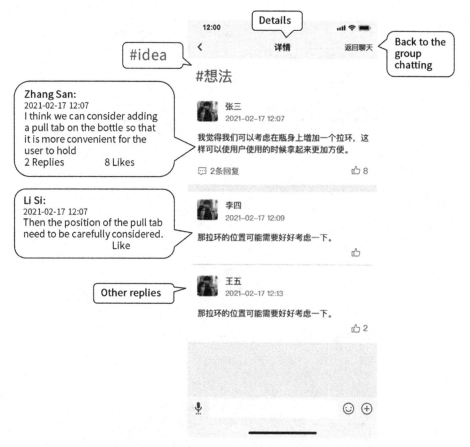

Fig. 2. Details of a threaded conversation.

5.4 Limitations

The major limitation was the sampling. Although we covered various types of tech companies in China, most participants worked as researchers or engineers. The features of their tasks can be different from those of other departments, such as community support and user experience design. Future research may enroll employees of other jobs in tech companies. In addition, based on the interviews, we proposed a design prototype, but it needs further evaluation.

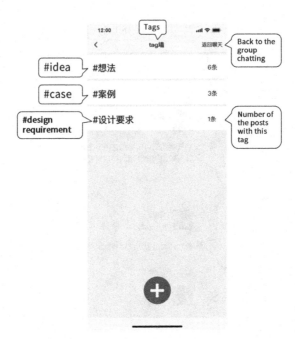

Fig. 3. The list of tags such as ideas and cases.

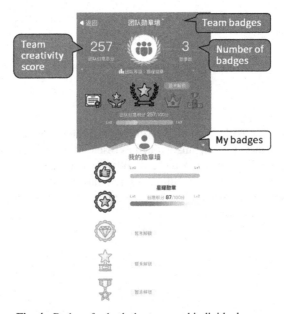

Fig. 4. Badges for both the team and individual users.

6 Conclusion

This study conducted in-depth interviews with 15 employees in high-tech companies in China and provided empirical data on the team creative process. The results suggested that most teams ideated and evaluated ideas or solutions individually instead of a collaborative process though they needed to share information throughout the creative process. The major reasons were the task features, a lack of support for collaboration in the ideation and evaluation phase, and a lack of motivation for team creativity. Finally, based on the interviews, we outlined implications for design to support team creativity and proposed a prototype of a communication tool with creative support features.

References

1. Sawyer, R.K., DeZutter, S.: Distributed creativity: how collective creations emerge from collaboration. Psychol. Aesthetics Creativity Arts **3**, 81 (2009)
2. Wuchty, S., Jones, B.F., Uzzi, B.: The increasing dominance of teams in production of knowledge. Science **316**, 1036–1039 (2007)
3. Shin, S.J., Zhou, J.: When is educational specialization heterogeneity related to creativity in research and development teams? Transformational leadership as a moderator. J. Appl. Psychol. **92**, 1709 (2007)
4. Howard, T.J., Culley, S.J., Dekoninck, E.: Describing the creative design process by the integration of engineering design and cognitive psychology literature. Des. Stud. **29**, 160–180 (2008). https://doi.org/10.1016/j.destud.2008.01.001
5. Lubart, T.I.: Models of the creative process: past, present and future. Creat. Res. J. **13**, 295–308 (2001)
6. Amabile, T.M.: How to Kill Creativity. Harvard Business School Publishing, Boston (1998)
7. Ward, T.B.: Cognition, creativity, and entrepreneurship. J. Bus. Ventur. **19**, 173–188 (2004)
8. Zeng, L., Proctor, R.W., Salvendy, G.: Creativity in ergonomic design: a supplemental value-adding source for product and service development. Hum. Factors **52**, 503–525 (2010)
9. Paulus, P.B., Dzindolet, M.: Social influence, creativity and innovation. Soc. Influ. **3**, 228–247 (2008)
10. Brown, S.L., Eisenhardt, K.M.: Product development: past research, present findings, and future directions. Acad. Manag. Rev. **20**, 343–378 (1995)
11. Drach-Zahavy, A., Somech, A.: Understanding team innovation: the role of team processes and structures. Group Dyn. Theory Res. Pract. **5**, 111 (2001)
12. Kratzer, J., Leenders, O.T.A., van Engelen, J.M.: Stimulating the potential: creative performance and communication in innovation teams. Creativity Innov. Manag. **13**, 63–71 (2004)
13. Maaravi, Y., Heller, B., Shoham, Y., Mohar, S., Deutsch, B.: Ideation in the digital age: literature review and integrative model for electronic brainstorming. RMS **15**(6), 1431–1464 (2020). https://doi.org/10.1007/s11846-020-00400-5
14. West, M.A., Sacramento, C.A., Fay, D.: Creativity and innovation implementation in work groups: the paradoxical role of demands. Creativity Innov. Organ. Teams 137–159 (2006)
15. Frich, J., MacDonald Vermeulen, L., Remy, C., Biskjaer, M.M., Dalsgaard, P.: Mapping the landscape of creativity support tools in HCI. In: Proceedings of the 2019 CHI Conference on Human Factors in Computing Systems, pp. 1–18 (2019)
16. Gabriel, A., Monticolo, D., Camargo, M., Bourgault, M.: Creativity support systems: a systematic mapping study. Think. Skills Creat. **21**, 109–122 (2016). https://doi.org/10.1016/j.tsc.2016.05.009

17. Remy, C., MacDonald Vermeulen, L., Frich, J., Biskjaer, M.M., Dalsgaard, P.: Evaluating creativity support tools in HCI research. In: Proceedings of the 2020 ACM Designing Interactive Systems Conference, pp. 457–476 (2020)
18. Wang, K., Nickerson, J.V.: A literature review on individual creativity support systems. Comput. Hum. Behav. **74**, 139–151 (2017)
19. Lubart, T.: How can computers be partners in the creative process: classification and commentary on the special issue. Int. J. Hum.-Comput. Stud. **63**, 365–369 (2005). https://doi.org/10.1016/j.ijhcs.2005.04.002
20. Siangliulue, P., Chan, J., Dow, S.P., Gajos, K.Z.: IdeaHound: improving large-scale collaborative ideation with crowd-powered real-time semantic modeling. In: Proceedings of the 29th Annual Symposium on User Interface Software and Technology, pp. 609–624 (2016)
21. Sundholm, H., Artman, H., Ramberg, R.: Backdoor creativity: collaborative creativity in technology supported teams. Presented at the 6th International Conference on the Design of Cooperative Systems, Hyères, France, 11–14 May 2004 (2004)
22. Kim, T.S., Kim, S., Choi, Y., Kim, J.: Winder: linking speech and visual objects to support communication in asynchronous collaboration. In: Proceedings of the 2021 CHI Conference on Human Factors in Computing Systems, pp. 1–17 (2021)
23. Bao, P., Gerber, E., Gergle, D., Hoffman, D.: Momentum: getting and staying on topic during a brainstorm. In: Proceedings of the SIGCHI Conference on Human Factors in Computing Systems, pp. 1233–1236 (2010)
24. Girotto, V., Walker, E., Burleson, W.: The effect of peripheral micro-tasks on crowd ideation. In: Proceedings of the 2017 CHI Conference on Human Factors in Computing Systems, pp. 1843–1854 (2017)
25. Tavanapour, N., Theodorakopoulos, D., Bittner, E.A.C.: A conversational agent as facilitator: guiding groups through collaboration processes. In: Zaphiris, P., Ioannou, A. (eds.) HCII 2020. LNCS, vol. 12206, pp. 108–129. Springer, Cham (2020). https://doi.org/10.1007/978-3-030-50506-6_9
26. Braun, V., Clarke, V.: Using thematic analysis in psychology. Qual. Res. Psychol. **3**, 77–101 (2006)
27. Ali, A., Wang, H., Khan, A.N.: Mechanism to enhance team creative performance through social media: a transactive memory system approach. Comput. Hum. Behav. **91**, 115–126 (2019)
28. Santos, C.M., Uitdewilligen, S., Passos, A.M.: Why is your team more creative than mine? The influence of shared mental models on intra-group conflict, team creativity and effectiveness. Creativity Innov. Manag. **24**, 645–658 (2015)
29. Nijstad, B.A., Stroebe, W.: How the group affects the mind: a cognitive model of idea generation in groups. Pers. Soc. Psychol. Rev. **10**, 186–213 (2006)
30. Paulus, P.B., Brown, V.R.: Toward more creative and innovative group idea generation: a cognitive-social-motivational perspective of brainstorming. Soc. Pers. Psychol. Compass **1**, 248–265 (2007)
31. Dennis, A.R., Fuller, R.M., Valacich, J.S.: Media, tasks, and communication processes: a theory of media synchronicity. MIS Q. **32**, 575–600 (2008)
32. Wang, D., Tan, H., Lu, T.: Why users do not want to write together when they are writing together: users' rationales for today's collaborative writing practices. Proc. ACM Hum.-Comput. Interact. **1**, 1–18 (2017). https://doi.org/10.1145/3134742
33. Ahmed, Y.A., Ahmad, M.N., Ahmad, N., Zakaria, N.H.: Social media for knowledge-sharing: a systematic literature review. Telematics Inform. **37**, 72–112 (2019)

Industrial Internet Enterprises' Talent Acquisition in China

Fei Guo, Ziyang Li, and Ang Zhang(⊠)

China Academy of Industrial Internet, Beijing 100102, China
zhang-ang-07@163.com

Abstract. The rapid growth of the Industrial Internet has brought concern in the shortage of high-quality talent. Under this circumstance, Industrial Internet enterprises spend more efforts on talent acquisition (TA). This study aims to explore TA issues of Industrial Internet enterprises in China. A questionnaire was designed and distributed to 45 participants from respective Industrial Internet enterprises. We identified 37 typical Industrial Internet positions and invited participants to rate them according to the degree of talent shortage. Results showed the top three positions with the greatest talent shortage were Industrial Internet platform architect, Industrial Internet solution engineer, and Industrial APP development engineer. Moreover, we investigated the main TA measures of related enterprises including college recruiting, experienced hiring, and internal hiring. We found Industrial Internet enterprises preferred experienced hiring and they faced a series of TA problems, such as small talent pool, incompetent graduates, rapid brain drain. At last, we made suggestions on those TA problems.

Keywords: Industrial Internet · Talent acquisition · Talent shortage

1 Introduction

Industrial Internet, also known as the Industrial Internet of Things (IIoT), describes a domain in which common industrial machines ubiquitously connect to the Internet by combining communication technologies with manufacturing [1, 2]. Apart from the application of the Internet, it also relates to common data platforms, industrial data processing, and complex security systems. Therefore, Industrial Internet has received increasing attention. The global Industrial Internet market was valued at USD 216.13 billion in 2020 and is expected to grow rapidly with 22.8% in the next five years [3].

The rapid growth of the Industrial Internet has raised concern in talent acquisition (TA) problems. Related enterprises are craving specialized talent. In this context, exploring the talent needs, finding typical positions and positions in talent shortage, and proposing development suggestions are significant to Industrial Internet enterprises. Therefore, this study explores the following questions: (1) What are the typical Industrial Internet positions and positions in talent shortage? (2) What are current TA strategies of Industrial Internet enterprises? (3) How can the TA situation be improved?

© The Author(s), under exclusive license to Springer Nature Switzerland AG 2022
P.-L. P. Rau (Ed.): HCII 2022, LNCS 13313, pp. 29–40, 2022.
https://doi.org/10.1007/978-3-031-06050-2_3

The remainder of this paper proceeds as follows. First, related literature is presented. Second, we identify the typical Industrial Internet positions and explore the positions in talent shortage through a questionnaire survey. Third, the findings on typical Industrial Internet positions, TA strategies, advice for related enterprises are illustrated in the Discussion section. The conclusions are presented in the last section.

2 Literature Review

2.1 Industrial Internet Talents

The Industrial Internet can control industrial infrastructure by collecting and leveraging industrial processing data and lead to optimal operations [4]. Accordingly, it generates benefits, such as quality improvement, efficiency increase, and cost reduction [5, 6]. Given the development prospects, many countries have pronounced their Industrial Internet strategies and strengthened their talent [7].

Talents are expected to take on more responsibilities for sustainability. Industrial Internet implementation involves artificial intelligence (AI), machine learning, cybersecurity, and other advanced skills, challenging traditional capabilities [8–10]. Accordingly, related enterprises crave specialized talent. Previous research revealed that Industrial Internet talents were expected to master information technology (IT), operation technology (OT), and communication technology skills (CT) [11]. Moreover, some institutes in China proposed specific Industrial Internet positions [12, 13], which are important references to our study.

2.2 Talent Acquisition (TA)

Talent acquisition (TA) is a long-term process for developing a talent pipeline and building a feasible talent pool [14]. It is related to human resource planning, employment management, and the training and development of employees [15, 16]. TA is distinguished from the concept of *recruitment*, understood as a subset of the former [17, 18].

Previous research has systematically proposed TA specific measures, including college recruiting, experienced hiring, and internal hiring. College recruiting is described as filling job vacancies with new college graduates [19, 20]. Factors such as college reputation, student capability, and internship coordination play an important role in the hiring process [20, 21]. Experienced hiring comes with full-time working experience [22]. Comparisons between the experienced and novice have been explored in various industries, such as cotton textiles [23], masonry [24, 25] and construction [26]. Moreover, internal hiring is related to on-the-job training, re-assigning, and promoting, gaining increasing attention recently [27, 28].

Investigating the TA issue is useful in understanding the talent demand of Industrial Internet enterprises. However, considering the differences between the Industrial Internet and traditional manufacturing [11], the applicability and peculiarity of TA measures still need further exploration.

3 Methodology

3.1 Data Collection

This exploratory study was conducted with Industrial Internet enterprises in China. We focused on technical and skilled talent and identified 37 typical Industrial Internet positions based on previous study [11–13, 29], such as Industrial Internet network architect, Industrial Internet identification architect, Industrial Internet solution engineer, Industrial APP development engineer, and Industrial Internet security development engineer. The 37 items and descriptions are provided in Appendix A. We designed a questionnaire including four parts to acquire TA situations. (1) Basic information of enterprises, including registration type (i.e., state-owned, limited liability, private enterprises, and others), business income and positioning strategy. (2) The number of technicians and skilled workers of the enterprises and their recruitment plans in 2022. (3) The 37 typical Industrial Internet positions and its degree of talent shortage. We explained the positions and invited participants to rate them according to the degree of talent shortage on a ten-point Likert scale (from 1 = "not at all" to 10 = "very much"). (4) Open questions of TA problems and advice in Industrial Internet, including "What problems does your company encounter in talent acquisition for Industrial Internet?" and "What is your advice for Industrial Internet talent acquisition?" (Table 1).

Table 1. Basic information of research sample.

Items	Category	Percentage
Enterprise type	State-owned enterprises	15.56%
	Limited liability company	48.89%
	Private enterprises	20.00%
	Collective enterprise, foreign-capital enterprise, etc.	15.56%
Business income	Less than 20 million (RMB)	28.89%
	20–400 million (RMB)	33.33%
	Above 400 million (RMB)	37.78%
Positioning strategy	Industrial internet network	22.73%
	Industrial big data processing	34.09%
	Industrial internet platform	34.09%
	Industrial internet security & protection	9.09%

3.2 Results

The research data were collected from 45 Industrial Internet enterprises in China. We reported the details of our survey results as follows.

Recruitment Plan. Research enterprises had a total number of 160,000 employees around. According to their recruitment plan, the number was expected to double to 320,000 in 2022. The annual average number of employee demand was about 3,500 per enterprise. The results showed that the Industrial Internet enterprises plan to rapidly expand their personnel next year.

The Degree of Talent Shortage. We listed 37 typical Industrial Internet positions and invited participants to rate them. Table 2 shows the data indicators regarding the degree of talent shortage of the positions, including mean (M) and standard deviation (SD). The positions are ranked in the descending order of the mean. The results showed that the top three positions with the greatest talent shortage were Industrial Internet platform architect, Industrial Internet solution engineer and Industrial APP development engineer.

Table 2. Indicators of the degree of talent shortage.

Ranking	Position	M	SD	Ranking	Position	M	SD
1	Industrial Internet Platform Architect	6.47	2.74	20	Industrial Internet Edge Computing Application Engineer	5.71	2.94
2	Industrial Internet Solution Engineer	6.29	2.82	21	Industrial Big Data Analyst	5.64	2.69
3	Industrial APP Development Engineer	6.27	2.81	22	Industrial Big Data Test Engineer	5.60	2.77
4	Industrial Internet Edge Computing Implementation Engineer	6.22	2.81	23	Industrial Internet Platform Test Engineer	5.56	2.60
5	Industrial Internet Application Development Engineer	6.18	2.70	24	Industrial Internet Security Architect	5.56	2.96
6	Industrial Internet Integration Engineer	6.11	2.54	25	Industrial Internet System Operation and Maintenance Engineer	5.47	2.75
7	Industrial Internet Platform Development Engineer	6.07	2.78	26	Industrial Internet Network Integration Engineer	5.38	2.84
8	Industrial Internet Operation Manager	6.04	2.75	27	Industrial Big Data Manager	5.38	2.71

(*continued*)

Table 2. (*continued*)

Ranking	Position	M	SD	Ranking	Position	M	SD
9	Industrial APP Productization Engineer	5.98	2.93	28	Industrial Internet Network Development Engineer	5.20	2.85
10	Industrial Internet Edge Computing Hardware Engineer	5.96	3.01	29	Industrial Internet Security Implementation Engineer	5.09	2.86
11	Industrial Internet Application Maturity Evaluation Engineer	5.96	2.89	30	Industrial Internet Identification Resolution System Integration Engineer	4.96	2.89
12	Industrial Internet Embedded Development Engineer	5.93	3.05	31	Industrial Internet Network Operation and Maintenance Engineer	4.96	2.71
13	Industrial Big Data Architect	5.89	2.88	32	Industrial Internet Identification Architect	4.91	3.05
14	Industrial Internet Edge Computing System Architect	5.89	2.96	33	Industrial Internet Identification Systems R&D Engineer	4.91	3.01
15	Industrial Internet Platform Operation and Maintenance Engineer	5.82	2.67	34	Industrial Internet Identification Operation and Maintenance Engineer	4.91	2.87
16	Industrial Internet Network Architect	5.80	3.27	35	Industrial Internet Identification Product Designer	4.89	2.92
17	Industrial Big Data Engineer	5.76	2.88	36	Industrial Internet Security Operation and Maintenance Engineer	4.80	2.74
18	Industrial Big Data Modeling Engineer	5.76	2.71	37	Industrial Internet Security Development Engineer	4.76	2.84
19	Industrial Big Data Application Engineer	5.71	2.73				

Problems and Advice. A percentage of 75% enterprises of our research sample indicated that they encountered TA problems. We selected keywords from the survey and classified the keywords into college recruiting, experienced hiring, and internal hiring. The detailed results are presented in Table 3.

Table 3. TA problems identified from the research sample.

TA measures	Keywords (mentioned frequency)	Descriptions
College recruiting	Competence (7)	College graduates lack technical competence
	Practice (3)	College graduates lack practical skills
	Adaptation Duration (3)	College graduates need a long time to adapt to new positions
Experienced hiring	Professionalism (12)	Experienced talents are familiar with traditional vocations rather than Industrial Internet
	Talent Pool (10)	There are few Industrial Internet talent storage
	Attractiveness (9)	Enterprises have little attractiveness to talents
Internal hiring	Brain drains (14)	Rapid brain drain in Industrial Internet enterprises
	Training system (5)	Enterprises have an unsound training system
	Cost (5)	Expenditure and time cost of internal training is high

Furthermore, participants had various advice on Industrial Internet TA. Several participants (35.56% of the sample) suggested that education should be improved to cultivate Internet application-oriented talents from the talent training perspective. Participants (20% of the sample) also indicated that enterprises could retain talents with more government support, such as talent subsidies and welfare.

4 Discussion

We have primarily analyzed the questionnaire results including basic information, recruitment plan, the degree of talent shortage, and TA problems of Industrial Internet enterprises. Afterwards, interviews (N = 16) were conducted to further understand our research questions. The explicit content is discussed as follows.

Typical Industrial Internet Positions. We identified **37 typical Industrial Internet positions** including Industrial Internet network architect, Industrial Internet identification architect, Industrial Internet solution engineer, Industrial APP development engineer, Industrial Internet security development engineer, etc. These positions were approved and rated by the participants at an average of 5.62 points. Additionally, most interviewees **indicated that** compound talents who have mastered IT and OT are commonly in shortage (10 out of 16 interviewees). However, Industrial Internet talents are too rare while technical and skilled works are hard to find. As participants said:

"The existing Industrial Internet employees mainly come from traditional industries. They still need to grow gradually in related projects to be the qualified talents. It takes time to become compound talents." (3 out of 16 interviewees)

According to the degree of talent shortage of the 37 typical positions, the top three positions scored above 6.27 points, including the Industrial Internet platform architect, Industrial Internet solution engineer and Industrial APP development engineer. These positions have high-quality requirements for professional knowledge, comprehensive ability, and mature communication skills. For example, some interviewees mentioned the "Industrial Internet platform architect is of great importance" (5 out of 16 interviewees). This position needed compound talents with both "practical experience in the production line and IT knowledge" to build Industrial Internet platforms. The more the professional and experienced engineers, the more products can meet customers' needs.

Current TA Strategies. We investigated current TA strategies of Industrial Internet enterprises. The main TA measures include college recruiting, experienced hiring, and internal hiring. However, experienced hiring is preferred by enterprises. Positions such as Industrial Internet platform architect and Industrial Internet solution engineer are seldom recruited from school. Its required "high educational background" (4 out of 16 interviewees) and "rich experience" (5 out of 16 interviewees), specifically "engagement in various business line for at least three years" (2 out of 16 interviewees). In the context of talent shortages, most enterprises implement Industrial Internet projects with teams consisting of an IT and an OT proficient employee.

A number of enterprises (4 out of 16 interviewees) have taken the initiative to start the internal hiring. They set up particular departments (also named *Enterprise Colleges*) to train new college graduates to improve their abilities quickly. The enterprises allocated professional internal lecturers and established systematic incentive regulations for teaching activities. When teaching Industrial Internet knowledge, IT and OT experts would jointly teach employees to cultivate compound talents.

Advice for Industrial Internet Enterprises. According to our study, Industrial Internet enterprises have three main TA problems. First, college recruiting is lagging because graduates lack technical competence. The lack of vocational and practical training in schools also leads to lack of practice and long adaptation duration of graduates. Second, experienced hiring is difficult for Industrial Internet enterprises. On the one hand, there is a large talent gap in Industrial Internet since existing employees have less matching experience and skills. More than one-third of the participants mentioned the keywords of *professionalism* and *talent pool*. On the other hand, Industrial Internet enterprises have little attraction to talents compared with IT and traditional manufacturing industries, affecting the supply of Industrial Internet talent to a certain extent. Furthermore, the high brain drain is also the main problem in related enterprises. Therefore, it is difficult to ensure long-term service of talents in the enterprise. It significantly increases the employment cost of Industrial Internet enterprises and leads to the lack of internal hiring. This situation is affected by local policies and development prospects.

We propose the following suggestions to facilitate TA for Industrial Internet enterprises. Industrial Internet enterprises are suggested to improve the salary of talents, clarify internal promotion directions, and establish equity incentives. Reduce brain drain rate by improving employee benefits and building an attractive enterprise culture. From a political perspective, policy reforms are necessary to improve TA situation, such as improving welfare, supporting development, and setting up subsidies for enterprises. From the tactical perspective, colleges and universities need to accelerate talent cultivation by integrating industry and education in the Industrial Internet. For example, introducing teachers with practical experiences is helpful. We suggest that colleges establish teaching teams with one IT and one OT discipline to teach Industrial Internet courses jointly.

This study makes several contributions to the literature. Theoretically, it extends the literature on TA by summarizing specific measures and validating them in the new context of Industrial Internet enterprises. Besides, we identified 37 typical Industrial Internet positions, providing an important reference for talent development. Moreover, the study explored existing TA problems and proposed improvement suggestions, which had a practical significance to Industrial Internet enterprises.

5 Conclusion

As Industrial Internet soars, related enterprises have an increasingly strong demand for technical and skilled talent. Qualified talents are expected to master IT and OT technologies, with comprehensive abilities and rich experience, which are difficult to acquire. This study explored the Industrial Internet enterprises' talent acquisition issues in China. Based on previous study, we identified 37 typical Industrial Internet positions and verified them. We conducted a questionnaire survey on 45 participants from Industrial Internet enterprises, in which the typical Industrial Internet positions were rated by participants according to the degree of talent shortage. Results showed the top three typical positions with the greatest talent shortage were Industrial Internet platform architect, Industrial Internet solution engineer and Industrial APP development engineer. Additionally, we investigated the main TA measures of related enterprises, including college recruiting, experienced hiring, and internal hiring. Considering the differences between the Industrial Internet and traditional industries, experienced hiring was preferred by related enterprises. However, the enterprises faced many problems in TA, such as small talent pool, incompetent graduates, rapid brain drain. Accordingly, we proposed improvement suggestions for related enterprises to promote TA issues. The government and colleges are also suggested to provide necessary supporting policies to facilitate the sustainable development of Industrial Internet.

Appendix A

Number	Position	Description
1	Industrial Internet Network Architect	Design internal and external networks, 5G private networks and industrial data exchange solutions of Industrial Internet enterprises
2	Industrial Internet Network Development Engineer	Design and develop internal and external networks, 5G private networks and industrial data exchange systems of Industrial Internet enterprises
3	Industrial Internet Network Integration Engineer	Engaged in the integration and implementation of internal and external networks, 5G private networks and industrial data exchange systems of Industrial Internet enterprises
4	Industrial Internet Network Operation and Maintenance Engineer	Engaged in the operation and maintenance of internal and external networks, 5G private networks and industrial data exchange systems of Industrial Internet enterprises
5	Industrial Internet Identification Architect	Design identification management and resolution systems, nodes and application scenarios
6	Industrial Internet Identification Systems R&D Engineer	Design and develop identification systems
7	Industrial Internet Identification Product Designer	Design of identification products
8	Industrial Internet Identification Operation and Maintenance Engineer	Responsible for the deployment and operation and maintenance of identification systems
9	Industrial Internet Identification Resolution System Integration Engineer	Responsible for system integration of identification resolution services
10	Industrial Internet Platform Architect	Design Industrial Internet platform construction and formulate operation schemes
11	Industrial Internet Platform Development Engineer	Design and develop industrial Internet platforms
12	Industrial Internet Platform Test Engineer	Test the function, performance and interface of Industrial Internet platforms
13	Industrial Internet Platform Operation and Maintenance Engineer	Responsible for operation, maintenance and optimization of Industrial Internet platforms

(*continued*)

(continued)

Number	Position	Description
14	Industrial APP Development Engineer	Design and develop Industrial APP
15	Industrial APP Productization Engineer	Responsible for market research, demand mining, development guidance, cost estimation and product promotion of Industrial APP
16	Industrial Big Data Architect	Design industrial big data construction, technical route, specifications and standards
17	Industrial Big Data Engineer	Engaged in industrial big data acquisition, desensitization, classification, storage and visualization
18	Industrial Big Data Application Engineer	Analyze industrial big data and design-related applications
19	Industrial Big Data Manager	Manage industrial big data processing, labeling, storage, etc
20	Industrial Big Data Analyst	Analyze and statistic industrial big data, deep mining and business prediction
21	Industrial Big Data Modeling Engineer	Design algorithm and mechanism model and formulate big data solutions
22	Industrial Big Data Test Engineer	Formulate industrial big data test scheme
23	Industrial Internet Security Architect	Design Industrial Internet security architecture and formulate security organization and management systems
24	Industrial Internet Security Development Engineer	Engaged in Industrial Internet security detection, Protection, audit, operation and maintenance management, developing related security products, tools, platforms and business systems
25	Industrial Internet Security Implementation Engineer	Implement security plan and implement joint commissioning
26	Industrial Internet Security Operation and Maintenance Engineer	Monitor Industrial Internet operation status manage Industrial Internet networks and platforms
27	Industrial Internet Edge Computing System Architect	Formulate technical route and design core code development of edge computing systems
28	Industrial Internet Edge Computing Hardware Engineer	Design intelligent sensor, intelligent gateway, intelligent controller, intelligent server, etc
29	Industrial Internet Embedded Development Engineer	Design and develop edge computing software

(continued)

(*continued*)

Number	Position	Description
30	Industrial Internet Edge Computing Application Engineer	Design edge computing algorithms and develop edge intelligent application software
31	Industrial Internet Edge Computing Implementation Engineer	Responsible for installation, commissioning and maintenance of edge computing products
32	Industrial Internet Application Development Engineer	Develop industry-oriented Industrial Internet software, cloud deployment and formulate overall solutions
33	Industrial Internet Application Maturity Evaluation Engineer	Evaluate Industrial Internet applications' level and implementation effect
34	Industrial Internet Solution Engineer	Formulate optimization solution planning for enterprise strategy and guide enterprises in intelligent transformation
35	Industrial Internet Integration Engineer	Responsible for the overall architecture design of the Industrial Internet system project and providing technical support
36	Industrial Internet System Operation and Maintenance Engineer	Responsible for intelligent product installation and configuration, performance and function test, software upgrade, patch installation, etc
37	Industrial Internet Operation Manager	Design overall operation scheme planning of Industrial Internet

References

1. Al-Turjman, F., Alturjman, S.: Context-sensitive access in industrial internet of things (IIoT) healthcare applications. IEEE Trans. Industr. Inf. **14**(6), 2736–2744 (2018)
2. Boyes, H., Hallaq, B., Cunningham, J., Watson, T.: The industrial internet of things (IIoT): an analysis framework. Comput. Ind. **101**, 1–12 (2018)
3. Industrial Internet of Things Market Size Report, 2021–2028. https://www.grandview research.com/industry-analysis/industrial-internet-of-things-iiot-market/toc. Accessed June 2021
4. Sisinni, E., Saifullah, A., Han, S., Jennehag, U., Gidlund, M.: Industrial internet of things: challenges, opportunities, and directions. IEEE Trans. Industr. Inf. **14**(11), 4724–4734 (2018)
5. Lade, P., Ghosh, R., Srinivasan, S.: Manufacturing analytics and industrial internet of things. IEEE Intell. Syst. **32**(3), 74–79 (2017)
6. Arnold, C., Kiel, D., Voigt, K.I.: How the industrial internet of things changes business models in different manufacturing industries. Int. J. Innov. Manag. **20**(08), 5–35 (2016)
7. Zhang, A., Guo, S.: Comparison of Chinese and foreign studies on skilled talents training for industrial internet. In: Rau, P.-L. (ed.) HCII 2021. LNCS, vol. 12771, pp. 547–560. Springer, Cham (2021). https://doi.org/10.1007/978-3-030-77074-7_41

8. O'Heir, J.: Filling the talent gap. Mech. Eng. **139**(01), 28–33 (2017)

9. Tian, Y., Li, T., Xiong, J., Bhuiyan, M.Z.A., Ma, J., Peng, C.: A blockchain-based machine learning framework for edge services in IIoT. IEEE Trans. Industr. Inf. **18**(3), 1918–1929 (2021)

10. Whysall, Z., Owtram, M., Brittain, S.: The new talent management challenges of Industry 4.0. J. Manag. Dev. **38**(2), 118–129 (2019)

11. Li, Z., Li, Z., Zhang, A.: Industrial internet talent cultivation in china from the perspective of undergraduate majors. In: Rau, P.-L. (ed.) HCII 2021. LNCS, vol. 12772, pp. 362–373. Springer, Cham (2021). https://doi.org/10.1007/978-3-030-77077-8_28

12. Industrial Internet Talents Competency Framework. https://www.miitec.org.cn/home/index/detail?id=293. Accessed 15 June 2020

13. Industrial Internet Talent White Paper, 2020. https://www.doc88.com/p-48139765974409.html. Accessed 19 June 2020

14. Tyagi, A.: Effective talent acquisition through e recruitment: a study. Int. J. Multidisc. Res. **2**(3), 302–312 (2012)

15. Chun, E., Evans, A.: The New Talent Acquisition Frontier: Integrating HR and Diversity Strategy in the Private and Public Sectors and Higher Education. Stylus Publishing, LLC, Sterling (2013)

16. Alashmawy, A., Yazdanifard, R.: A review of the role of marketing in recruitment and talent acquisition. Int. J. Manag. Account. Econ. **6**(7), 569–581 (2019)

17. Mangisa, C.A., Schultz, C.M., Van Hoek, L.: An analysis of transformational leadership, talent acquisition and talent retention of engineers at an energy provider in South Africa. SA J. Hum. Resour. Manag. **18**, 12 (2020)

18. Anita, R.: Effective strategic talent acquisition process-a conceptual study. Gavesana J. Manag. **11**(1), 42–51 (2019)

19. Rynes, S.L., Boudreau, J.W.: College recruiting in large organizations: practice, evaluation, and research implications. Pers. Psychol. **39**(4), 729–757 (1986)

20. Lockwood, D., Ansari, A.: Recruiting and retaining scarce information technology talent: a focus group study. Ind. Manag. Data Syst. **99**(6), 251–256 (1999)

21. Weible, R.: Are universities reaping the available benefits internship programs offer? J. Educ. Bus. **85**(2), 59–63 (2009)

22. Rynes, S.L., Orlitzky, M.O., Bretz, R.D., Jr.: Experienced hiring versus college recruiting: practices and emerging trends. Pers. Psychol. **50**(2), 309–339 (1997)

23. McHugh, C.L.: Earnings in the post-bellum Southern cotton textile industry: a case study. Explor. Econ. Hist. **21**(1), 28 (1984)

24. Alwasel, A., Abdel-Rahman, E.M., Haas, C.T., Lee, S.: Experience, productivity, and musculoskeletal injury among masonry workers. J. Constr. Eng. Manag. **143**(6), 5017003.1 (2017)

25. Ryu, J., Alwasel, A., Haas, C.T., Abdel-Rahman, E.: Analysis of relationships between body load and training, work methods, and work rate: overcoming the novice mason's risk hump. J. Constr. Eng. Manag. **146**(8), 04020097 (2020)

26. Min, S.N., Kim, J.Y., Parnianpour, M.: The effects of safety handrails and the heights of scaffolds on the subjective and objective evaluation of postural stability and cardiovascular stress in novice and expert construction workers. Appl. Ergon. **43**(3), 574–581 (2012)

27. DeVaro, J.: Internal hiring or external recruitment? IZA World of Labor (2020)

28. Bertheau, A.: Employer search behavior: reasons for internal hiring. Labour Econ. **73**, 102064 (2021)

29. Industrial Internet Encyclopedia. https://www.miit.gov.cn/jgsj/xgj/gzdt/art/2021/art_3cffba8810be4ec68bc3d1051a0c0453.html. Accessed 27 Sept 2021

The Influence of Strategic Agility on Product Design Organizations' Operations and Cultures

Yen Hsu[(⊠)] [iD] and Jin-Chun Lai [iD]

The Graduate Institute of Design Science, Tatung University, Taipei, Taiwan
yhsu@gm.ttu.edu.tw

Abstract. Responding to the uncertainties in a more volatile and ever-changing external environment, in recent years concepts, such as strategic agility, have been introduced in the management field to improve the flexibility and effectiveness of internal decision-making in an enterprise and to promote the performance of new product development while maintaining product innovation. However, compared with the business model innovation, few studies in the management field focus on product design and development, which is an area that emphasizes practice and strategy execution. Therefore, this study discusses the key considerations of early-stage development decisions analyzed in the existing literature on strategic agility and combines these key considerations with the theory of design strategy, which has a key impact on new product development performance, in order to explore the relationships between them. Based on an empirical analysis of 130 manufacturing industry firms, strategic agility was found to have a complete mediating effect between design strategy and new product development performance as well as a positive impact on design strategy operation. The preliminary model established in this study suggests that design and development organizations can use more flexible and elastic decision-making mechanisms to cope with the rapidly changing external environment. This study has theoretical significance for the development of design strategy research and has practical significance for the management of product design organizations under the current chaotic environment.

Keywords: Strategic agility · Design strategy · Design development organization · NPD performance

1 Introduction

The U.S. Army War College in the late 1990s predicted a very "volatile, uncertain, complex, and ambiguous" (VUCA) world. Today, VUCA has become a common term in the management field to describe any chaotic, turbulent, and ever-changing business environment, as companies and organizations around the world are facing a more severe test of survival.

The growing diversity and intensity of sources of change and dynamism in the modern business environment have made organizations and managers aware of the importance of agility as a means for enterprises to constantly adapt to external threats and opportunities (Weber and Tarba 2014). This is similar to Sullivan's (2012) view that problems often

P.-L. P. Rau (Ed.): HCII 2022, LNCS 13313, pp. 41–57, 2022.
https://doi.org/10.1007/978-3-031-06050-2_4

involve many incomprehensible causes and mitigating factors (both inside and outside the organization), and this complexity increases the volatility of change, the lack of past factors for prediction, and the difficulty of decision-making. It leads to confusion, which may bring about ambiguity as well, and so organizations also make corresponding changes in agility when they make decisions.

Strategic agility is defined as the ability of an organization to make strategic commitments while remaining agile and flexible and is considered a means by which an organization transforms and remolds itself, adapts, and ultimately survives (Doz and Kosonen 2010). There are many different research areas that analyze and examine agility in specific organizational conditions, focusing mostly on knowledge-intensive companies and manufacturing. According to a literature review and collection, most existing strategic agility research centers on organizations, such as large multinational corporations, but pays little attention to small- and medium-sized enterprises (SMEs) and startups with different backgrounds. These companies often have different characteristics from those large corporations, and thus the meaning of agility could be different accordingly (Xing et al. 2020).

The decisions and deployments of companies' senior executives often involve new product development performance. It is, therefore, crucial to make correct decisions at the early stage of product development as they help justify and are sometimes detrimental to future decisions (Octaviano Rojas Luiz et al. 2019). Therefore, in order to efficiently develop new products and launch them into the market, it is necessary to formulate a complex and sophisticated strategy and associate it with organizational factors concerning executive decisions, project management, cross-functional coordination, actual production, and development practice, until reaching the final completion of new product development as one factor of corporate performance.

For the requirement of new product development, a project organizer is involved in a dynamic decision-making process in which the company's list of active new product projects is regularly updated and revised. During this process, new products are evaluated, selected, and prioritized; existing projects can be accelerated, terminated, or reduced in priority; and resources are allocated or reallocated to active projects (Cooper et al. 2001). The external markets and changes can also affect organization management and decision-making, resulting in strategy adjustment. All these phenomena and actions demonstrate that strategic agility has become an important ability for companies have in order to respond quickly to potential threats and opportunities.

A large number of studies exploring the successful factors of new product development indicates that design is one of the important factors, and they all emphasize a strong and positive correlation between industrial design and company performance in industries with well-established industrial design investment strategies (Cool and Schendel 1987; Walsh et al. 1992; Baden-Fuller and Stopford 1994; Gemser et al. 1996; Gemser 1999). Therefore, when enterprises make decisions and deployments, proper planning of product innovation, a corresponding design strategy, and a good design of product development are necessary, as they are important driving forces for the improvement of corporate performance (Claybaugh et al. 2015; Urban and Hauser 1993).

In summary, it can be concluded that both the strategic agility of a company's management organization and the design strategy in actual operations are important factors for leaders to consider during the process of new product development, and these factors will eventually affect the performance of new product development. However, in the actual implementation of strategic agility inside an organization, decision-making and relevant actions take on different strategic forms due to different management considerations. From the design and development department as an example, in addition to the design strategy of a design itself within the organization, it is also necessary to cope with changes in the external environment and to reasonably manage a project portfolio and flexibly allocate resources when many projects run in parallel. As to what impacts will these factors have on the design strategies of the design and development department, and whether they will cause conflicts leading to the performance fluctuation of final products, there are no studies on the coordination between different decision-making strategies.

Based on the above discussion, the main objectives of this study are as follow. (1) Explore the correlation between strategic agility and design strategy. (2) Investigate the questions of how to coordinate the operation of design strategy with strategic agility, as a flexible means of responding to external changes, so as to influence the performance of new product development in enterprises, and whether strategic agility plays a mediating role in such process. Attempts will be made to probe the potential adjustment factors that may exist when design organizations implement these decisions. (3) Examine how the design and development organization or department in enterprises can flexibly use design strategies to improve the performance of new product development in the face of an unaccustomed rapidly changing VUCA market and external environment.

2   Literature Review

2.1   Strategic Agility in a Turbulent Environment

Business Model Innovation (BMI) can be regarded as an organizational innovation that changes the way companies create and capture value for their stakeholders (Masanell and Zhu 2013). The proposal of this concept is an innovation and supplement to hot business model issues in the field of management so as to respond to today's turbulent environment where technological developments and customer preferences are rapidly changing (Brown and Eisenhardt 1997; Chong et al. 2016). The turbulent environment creates continuous opportunities and crises in the market (Haleblian and Finkelstein 1993), in which the operation of a company requires not only a rapid response to changing market conditions but also proactive forecasting and flexible adjustment of the company's strategy deployment (Chong and Zhang 2016). In such external changes, the dynamic capability of a company (a high-level capability that can shape and deploy the resource to meet current market demands and future expectations) can give an advantage to a company via more active changes in the organization system (Leih et al. 2015; Sambamurthy et al. 2003). Therefore, the concept of strategic agility was put forward by scholars and defined as the ability of an organization to make strategic commitments while remaining agile and flexible, by which an organization transforms and remolds itself, adapts, and ultimately survives (Doz and Kosonen 2010). In the setting of the business model, Doz and Kosonen established three distinct dynamic capabilities for strategic agility as below.

(1) Strategy sensitivity

Strategy sensitivity is defined as "a sharp perception of strategy development, the awareness and the intensity of attention to strategy development" (Anna et al. 2017). Other scholars also believe that scenario planning and forecasting, critical evaluation from an external perspective to judge a company's business model, and generating alternative plans can also supplement the cognition of strategy sensitivity (Clauss 2021).

(2) Leadership unity

Leadership unity refers to the ability of senior management to make bold and rapid decisions under collective commitment and support, without interference from personal political struggles (Anna 2017; Clauss 2021). This can play a crucial role in the internal operation of a company in a turbulent environment to ensure the smooth implementation of senior management's decisions.

(3) Resource fluidity

Resource fluidity refers to the ability to reallocate resources, including knowledge and capabilities within a company, and to deploy them rapidly (Anna 2017; Doz and Kosonen 2010).

2.2 Product Innovation and Design Strategy

In a study focusing on more than 220 new product development projects of UK companies, Roy and Riedel (1997) proved that the small changes in design innovation can lead to the success of new product development projects. Many researchers have emphasized that industrial design and technological innovation play a key role in improving the competitiveness of products, enterprises, and the national economy (Rothwell et al. 1983; Berger 1989; Wray 1991; Utterback 1994; Sheldon 2004; Marxt and Hacklin 2005). The strategy of design innovation is considered useful because it provides a guideline for industrial design and research (Baxter 1995, Wandeback et al. 2002; Vidal 2004; Booker et al. 2005).

2.3 Influencing Factors of New Product Development Performance

Corporate performance in new product development is generally evaluated by financial and non-financial means in numerous studies (Lee 1992; Barczak 1995; Cooper and Kleinschmidt 1995; Hendricks et al. 1996; Robert and Carolyn 2003). For example, Ulrich and Eppinger (2000) proposed five specific criteria to evaluate the performance of product development, including product quality, product cost, development time, development cost, and development capability. Cooper and Press (1995) emphasized the non-price value of design such as uniqueness, reliability, ease of use, durability, and company image (e.g., product presentation, demonstration, packaging, and sales promotion), which can improve product quality.

A patent in direct corporate performance is an effective means to protect competitive company assets such as products, technological processes, and services, and it is also an important measure of technological innovation ability and industrial technological competitiveness. Studies on the relationship between research and development (R&D)

capability and patentability are extensive, in-depth, and generally positive (Artz et al. 2010; Lin et al. 2006; Reitzig and Puranam 2009; Romijn and Albaladejo 2002; Somaya et al. 2007;). In order to measure new product development (NPD) performance, Tai (2017) adapted four reflective projects from the literature on NPD and operation management (e.g., Hilletofth and Eriksson 2011; Bendoly et al. 2012; Thomas 2013; Gao and Tian 2014; Stark 2015). NPD performance is constructed by items that indicate the extent to which a company can achieve its new product target: (a) time-to-market, (b) innovation, (c) market performance, and (d) customer satisfaction. Respondents are asked to evaluate the performance indicators of new products launched in the previous three years.

By combining the above viewpoints, this paper also divides product development performance into financial performance and non-financial performance. Financial performance includes factors of time-to-market and market performance (sales volume of new products, turnover of new products, and profit of new products). Product innovation focuses on discussing the company's patent R&D and degree of innovation, which constitutes the evaluation standard of non-financial performance with customer satisfaction after the launch date of products.

3 Theoretical Assumptions

3.1 Design Strategy and NPD Performance

In addition to product innovation, innovation in design and design strategy can help improve competitiveness no matter how the industry develops. Numerous studies have stressed the strong and positive correlation between industrial design and corporate performance in industries with well-established industrial design investment strategies (Cool and Schendel 1987; Walsh et al. 1992; Baden-Fuller and Stopford 1994; Gemser et al. 1996; Gemser 1999). Cooper (1998) assumed that product innovation strategy closely relates to performance. The market, products, and technology selected by a company, as well as the direction of product innovation, significantly affect the success and profitability of the company. A survey conducted by Nystrom and Edvardsson (1980) on industrial product companies also found a close relationship between strategy and performance. Additionally, Allen and Hamilton (1982) noted that a new product strategy evidently links the NPD process to companies' targets and provides a focus for the generation of ideas and the development of appropriate screening criteria. Therefore, Hsu (2009) pointed out that NPD performance provides an appropriate standard for evaluating the adequacy of product strategy. This paper thus presents the first hypothesis:

H1: Design strategy positively affects NPD performance.

3.2 Strategic Agility and NPD Performance

Strategic agility has been shown in many studies to increase companies' competitive advantage and thus improve performance. Kumkale (2016) regarded strategic agility as a means to provide a competitive advantage. She considered that companies should constantly review their internal and external environments, rapidly collect and use information, and quickly respond to market changes to ensure strategic agility. When companies become agile, they can gain competitive advantages and improve performance.

In the management of tourism and hospitality industries, studies have shown that strategic agility can actively adjust the influence of absorptive capacity on company performance and help companies make corresponding decisions on operation performance by rapidly updating information and strategies (Kale et al. 2018). Ofoegbu and Akanbi (2012) found that strategic agility has a significant impact on business performance, and it is a key resource for companies to obtain competitive advantages. Talon and Pinsonneault (Kale et al. 2018) found a positive relation between agility and company performance. According to the above studies, the next hypothesis is presented:

H2: Strategic agility positively correlates with NPD performance.

3.3 Design Strategy and Strategic Agility

Product innovation adjusts performance in different NPD settings (Aronson et al. 2008; Salomo et al. 2007). For example, it can moderate the impact of process form on the success of new products, and so process form has a greater impact on the success of developing high-innovation products than low-innovation products (Salomo 2007). Furthermore, product innovation moderates the impact of new product profitability on NPD speed, and specifically the impact of high-innovation products' speed on NPD profitability is greater than that of low innovation products (Langerak and Hultink 2006). This is especially true in innovation-oriented design development organizations, where a series of design measures formulated on the basis of product development have been used as strategic management tools by companies to improve product competitiveness in the market (Mozota 1990; Poter 1985). In other words, design strategy is incorporated with the focus of companies' early decision-making stage.

When organizations make decisions, problems often involve many incomprehensible causes and mitigating factors (both inside and outside the organization). This complexity increases the volatility of change, the lack of past factors for prediction, and the difficulty of decision-making (Sullivan 2012). It also leads to confusion, which may bring about ambiguity as well. Previous studies on NPD management show that the front end of NPD is usually dynamic and interactive (Akbar and Tzokas 2013). This stage is characterized by complex information processing (Khurana and Rosenthal 1997; Debrentani and Reid 2012), temporary decision-making (Montoya and O'Driscoll 2000), and conflicting organizational pressures caused by, for instance, high complexity and uncertainty."

The above research all shows in the current turbulent and uncertain business environment that the formulation and execution of strategies for product innovation and development need more agility. The view of strategic agility strengthens very well the ability for companies to actively cope with external changes and to transform their organizational structure. A lot of literature on strategy has indicated that strategic agility can improve corporate performance by producing an effect on the scope and intensity of strategic actions (Tallon and Pinsonneault 2011; Ofoegbu and Akanbi 2012; Kumkale 2016; Kale et al. 2018). Therefore, it can be concluded that strategic agility correlates with the design strategy of the design organizing department, thus leading to the next hypothesis:

H3: Design strategy positively correlates with strategic agility.

3.4   The Mediating Role of Strategic Agility

The chaotic, turbulent, and ever-changing external business environment brought about by the VUCA era has created even greater difficulty and uncertainty in decision-making (Weber and Tarba 2014). Agility is increasingly important in more rapidly changing and diverse business competition, and more organization leaders and business managers have taken strategic agility in decision-making systems to enhance self-innovation and have injected ideas of innovation into organizations and product development to seek new opportunities. Design capability, which plays the same significant role in innovation, is also a key part of decision-making during initial development. The idea of strategic agility is to help the design and development organization consider the sensitivity of strategy, organizational commitment, and flexible allocation of resources in addition to the original consideration of design strategy. As hypothesized above in this study, the idea of strategic agility will prompt the organization department to carry out effective product innovation and development in a turbulent environment and highly uncertain market. This serves as a good guidance for organization managers to make decisions and implement them into actual design and development, so as to improve the agility and effectiveness of design strategy, which in turn influences the outcomes and performance of NPD in companies (as shown in Fig. 1). The above discussion leads us to the fourth hypothesis:

H4: Strategic agility adjusts the relationship between design strategy and NPD performance.

Fig. 1. A hypothetical model of the mediating effect of strategic agility on design strategy and NPD performance.

4   Methodology

4.1   Data Collection and Samples

This study's samples consist of survey data collected from China Import and Export Fair in 2021. The products at the fair were mostly household appliances and for daily consumption use, with some precision machineries and technological innovation products. Since China is a big manufacturing country with huge market demands, has a complex and changeable business environment, and has a fierce product competition that requires rapid innovation, this study focused on daily consumption and household appliances in the manufacturing industry. Trade fairs can be considered as an important communication forum for companies in certain industries, and exhibitors can be representative of the entire industry at large international fairs (Amit and Zott 2012). To ensure that the respondents could fill in the questionnaire accurately, the purpose and scope of this study were concisely explained, and a specific explanation was made about the design strategies on the first page of the questionnaire.

The tested group came from exhibitors at the fair, and their titles included department manager, R&D director, design director, and company leader. Some senior business personnel also participated in the survey. They all have attended decision-making meetings and have a deep understanding on their companies' products, related strategies, and operations, so bringing them into the sample allows for richer perspectives.

During the questionnaire distribution and filling out, 200 paper questionnaires and links to the electronic questionnaires were provided. At the end of the survey, 145 questionnaires were collected, and 130 applicable questionnaires were obtained after eliminating incomplete and incorrect ones and those sent by the same IP address (see Table 1 for details).

Table 1. Sample description

Descriptive features	Frequency	%		Frequency	%
Position					
Director	51	39.2	Business	55	42.3
Department manager	15	11.5	Others	9	7.0
Industry					
Daily consumption	52	40	Furniture decoration	30	23.1
Electronics & household electrical appliances	37	28.4	Others	11	8.5
Scale					
10–50	25	19.2	300–500	18	13.9
50–300	56	43.1	Above 500	31	23.8

4.2 Measurement

All scales in this study derived from the test items were used in relevant literature. All test items and scales were pre-tested by 10 representatives from academia and industry at the beginning of the survey to ensure structural integrity and eliminate semantic errors. All variables in the questionnaire were measured by the 7-point Likert Scale (1: Strongly disagree, 7: Strongly agree). The questionnaire was tested from three aspects: design strategy, strategic agility, and NPD performance.

In the measurement of design strategy, 20 industrial design innovation strategies summarized by Chang and Hsu (2003) in the survey of the electronics and computer industries in Taiwan were used as measurement indicators in the form of scale. The subjects were asked to judge the importance and degree of application of these strategies in the operation of a company according to the company situation and personal experience.

The strategic agility theory proposed by Doz and Kosonen (2010) was employed herein, and the three dimensions of strategy sensitivity, united leadership, and resource mobility were followed. Moreover, this study referred to the questionnaire revised by Hock, Clauss, and Schulz (2016) to ensure the effectiveness and credibility of the test items.

Many studies divided NPD performance into financial performance and non-financial performance (Lee 1992; Cooper and Kleinschmidt 1995; Robert and Carolyn 2003). This study followed the same method to evaluate NPD performance. For financial performance, factors including generic new product sales, new product turnover, and new product profit were taken into consideration. For non-financial performance, Tai (2017) adopted four evaluation measures: time-to-market, innovation, market performance, and customer satisfaction. As these four categories were also consistent with the financial and non-financial evaluation standards, this study incorporated time-to-market, innovation, and customer satisfaction into the non-financial indicator. It has been noted that technological innovation is an important source of competitive advantage for companies (Tidd and Bessant 2009), and patents are a direct demonstration of the correlation between R&D and performance (Minseo et al. 2017). As a result, this study accepted the views of Minseo et al. (2017) on the influence of technological innovation on patents and NPD and cited some items from them as considerations in non-financial performance.

4.3 Data Analysis/Measurement Evaluation

Before data analysis, this study conducted reliability analyses and validity tests on the questionnaire to check the overall measurement quality. According to the reliability standard suggested by DeVellis (1991), Cronbach's α between 0.70 and 0.80 indicates fairly good reliability, while Cronbach's α between 0.80 and 0.90 indicates very good reliability.

Table 2. Reliability statistics

Observation item	The Cronbach's α	Number of item
Design strategy	.862	20
Strategic agility	.775	9
NPD performance	.834	7

This study analyzed the reliability of the design strategy scale with a total of 20 questions, and the result shown in Table 2 indicated that the internal concordance coefficient of Cronbach's α was 0.862, which is acceptable. The reliability analysis of the strategic agility scale with a total of nine questions indicated that the internal concordance coefficient of Cronbach's α was 0.775, which is acceptable. The analysis result of the NPD performance scale with a total of 7 questions indicated that the internal concordance coefficient of Cronbach's α was 0.834, which is also acceptable. As to the validity of the questionnaire, all the item scales used in this study derived from well-established scales that have been validated and widely cited in previous literature. Aside from that, the scales have been pre-tested by ten professionals before data collection, and the test results suggested considerable distribution and reliability, indicating that the scales have credible validity.

5   Results

5.1   Characteristics and Naming of Product Design Strategy Group

In virtue of factor analysis, this study reduced the dimensions of 20 previous product design strategies, simplified the factor components, and attempted to clarify these factor groups. The factors are named by their characteristics, so as to generalize flexible and elastic design strategies that conform to the current VUCA era.

Table 3. Results of Bartlett's Sphericity Test

KMO and Bartlett test		
Kaiser-Meyer-Olkin		.802
Bartlett's sphericity test	Approximate chi-square distribution	913.636
	Degree of freedom	190
	Statistical significance	.000

The results of the Bartlett's sphericity test show that the variables are related to each other ($X^2 = 771.953$, df $= 136$, p < 0.001), and the value of KMO is 0.838, indicating that the data are suitable for factor analysis (see Table 3).

Table 4. Factor analysis (principal component analysis) of product design strategy (rotated)

	Factor loadings					
	Factor 1	Factor 2	Factor 3	Factor 4	Factor 5	Factor 6
Factor name	management improving	innovation and technology	market insight	product optimizing	R&D focusing	marketing promoting
Emphasis social and cultural performance	.846	.062	.076	.092	-.023	.026
Design good man–machine interface	.734	.011	.148	.026	.158	-.068
Improving design and development process	.673	.159	.284	.061	.034	.224
Uplift the investment of R&D	.654	.324	.042	.143	-.046	.253
Develop special product form features	.117	.817	.103	.065	-.085	.236
Upgrade company's product design image	.130	.764	.213	.241	-.020	.018
Reinforce technical cooperation	.305	.398	.380	.165	.017	.239
Reinforce the labour division of the same trade	.178	.391	.173	.386	.124	.269
Reinforce marketing information gathering and adaptation ability	.248	.136	.679	.026	-.032	.419
Increasing product added values	.216	.169	.619	.216	-.112	.183
Developing new target markets	.046	.524	.618	-.011	.280	-.127
Consider environmental design	.338	.077	.506	.497	-.030	.000
Uplift product brand image and popularity	.003	.084	.368	.771	.005	.107
Upgrade product quality level	.001	.078	-.047	.639	.456	.178
Developing unique product functions	.235	.389	-.078	.615	.004	.134
Reduce the production cost	-.098	-.174	.212	-.137	.766	.138
Meet the requirements of safety and regulations	.074	.015	-.038	.177	.753	-.079
Easy to manufacture and maintain	.133	.107	-.161	.093	.690	.242
Reinforce promotion effectiveness	.098	.037	.112	.122	.278	.773
Add product variety	.095	.308	.209	.216	.017	.697

According to the principle that the eigenvalue is greater than 1 (Robert and Wortzel 1992), six factors should be intercepted. As can be seen from the factor loading matrix shown in Table 4, these six factors were extracted by the principal axis, and orthogonal rotation was executed on them by varimax (Lin 1992). From the type matrix chart, it can be found that the first factor contains four topics, which mostly relate to the operation of internal product management, and so this factor group was named "management improving type". The second factor contains four topics, which are mostly about innovation and technology, and so it was named "innovation and technology type". The third factor contains four topics, mainly composed of market orientation, and so it was named "market insight type". The fourth factor contains three topics, mainly referring to product function and image, and so it was named "product optimizing type". The fifth factor contains three topics, mainly composed of manufacturing and standardization, and so it was named "R&D focusing type". The sixth factor contains two topics, mainly composed of promotion and product diversification, and so it was named "marketing promoting type". These six factors explain 64.6% of the variation, and the correlation among the six factors is shown in the factor correlation matrix table in Table 4.

5.2 Model Analysis and Hypothesis Testing

In order to determine the mediating effect of strategic agility between design strategy and NPD performance, four different path models were established using regression analysis, and the results are shown in Table 5.

Table 5. Regression analysis of mediating effect among design strategy, strategic agility, and NPD performance

	Strategic agility	NPD performance		
	Model 1	Model 2	Model 3	Model 4
Design strategy	.47***	.35***		.12
Strategic agility			.55***	.49***
R^2	.222	.127	.305	.317
Adj R^2	.216	.120	.300	.306
F	36.46***	18.61***	56.17***	29.46***
df	(1,128)	(1,128)	(1,128)	(2,127)

Notes: The values in the table are standardized regression coefficients (β). *p < .05, **p < .01, and ***p < .001

The results of Model 1 show that the design strategy has significant explanatory power on strategic agility (β = .47, p < .001), and so H1 is accepted. In Model 2 the design strategy has significant explanatory power on NPD performance (β = .35, p < .001), and so H2 is accepted. Similarly, in Model 3 strategic agility also has significant explanatory power on NPD performance (β = .55, p < .001), and so H3 is accepted.

In Model 4 when considering the explanatory power of both design strategy and strategic agility on NPD performance, it was found that the explanatory power of design strategy was not significant ($\beta = .12$, $p = .13$), whereas the strategic agility was significant ($\beta = .49$, $p < .001$). According to the criteria of Baron and Kenny (1986), the mediating effect was proved, and strategic agility had a full mediation relationship between design strategy and NPD performance, so H4 is accepted. The results of structural path analysis are shown in Fig. 2.

Fig. 2. Results of path analysis on hypothetical models. Note: All paths in the graph are normalized. *p < .05, **p < .01, and ***p < .001.

5.3 Discussion and Conclusion

Strategic agility has a very important role in the operation and decision-making of companies. The execution of corporate strategies is also affected by environmental uncertainty and thus changes rapidly. This study has preliminarily explored and verified the influence of the execution of design strategy on NPD performance and the mediating role of strategic agility as a new decision-making mechanism in this influence.

Confirmatory factor analysis shows that although turbulent and changing environmental factors aggravate the difficulty and uncertainty of decision-making, the design strategy should still be the focus of the company's initial decision-making. According to this study, the strategic approaches of companies can currently be divided into six groups; i.e., management improving type, innovation and technology type, market insight type, product optimizing type, R&D focusing type, and marketing promoting type, which are significantly different from the previous generalization of the practices of innovation strategies in industrial design (Chang and Hsu 2003). Moreover, the key role of design strategy in promoting NPD performance has been reconfirmed (Walsh 1992; Cooper 1998; Hsu 2009).

This study has further verified the theoretical hypothesis that strategic agility can adjust the relationship between design strategy and NPD performance. In the path hypothesis considering the influence of design strategy and strategic agility on NPD performance, it is found that design strategy has no significant influence on NPD performance, while strategic agility is still significant and has a full mediation relationship. These results show that organization managers can implement the agility thinking of decision-making into actual design and development activities and improve the flexibility and effectiveness of design strategy execution, so as to reduce the negative impact of disorder caused by rapid changes in the external environment on NPD, thus improving corporate performance. In addition, the results of this study re-emphasize the importance of strategic agility in the relevant literature (Weber and Tarba 2014; Doz and Kosonen 2010).

This study casts new topics and more practical information for related research in the fields of design strategy and management in the past. In this VUCA era, enterprise transformation and decision upgrading need more specific and effective strategy approaches. The introduction of agility in the management field can be a good way to explore flexible response measures for companies to cope with the intense and chaotic competitive environment. This study confirms the critical role of agility for design developing organizations in implementing design decisions.

There are some limitations in this study since the questionnaires were collected in a short period of time, and the samples were not rich enough. As there are many factors involved in this study, a more reasonable amount of samples (above 200) should be collected to test our theoretical models by high-order methods, such as a structural equation model, and thus reduce the resulting bias caused by the limited data volume. Moreover, the observations of this study were carried out at the same international trade fair, and all the invited units were domestic high-quality manufacturing companies. Hence, there may be a certain deviation in the selection of the samples that cannot cover the whole situation of the industry, as some companies that are too small or focus on local development were not included in the samples.

The other limitation is that the theoretical framework proposed in this study has not been explored in detail. One example covers the different influence of different dimensions of strategic agility on design strategy during the operation of specific cases. In order to coordinate with strategy execution to improve NPD performance, for the dynamic changes among dimensions, how they could be flexibly combined in practice to meet the implementation of the strategy should be explored. Aside from that, this study has confirmed that strategic agility has a mediating effect on design strategy, which therefore fills the gap in the literature and provides new ideas for traditional research on design strategy and management. More novel research is needed to clarify the concepts related to design strategy and agility and to examine the agile practices of current business owners in NPD, especially in the execution of design strategies.

References

Akbar, H., Tzokas, N.: An exploration of new product development's front-end knowledge conceptualization process in discontinuous innovations. Br. J. Manag. 24(2), 245–263 (2013)

Arbussa, A., Bikfalvi, A., Marquès, P.: Strategic agility-driven business model renewal: the case of an SME. Manag. Decis. 55(2), 271–293 (2017)

Aronson, Z.H., Reilly, R.R., Lynn, G.S.: The role of leader personality in new product development success: an examination of teams developing radical and incremental innovations. Int. J. Technol. Manage. 44(1–2), 5–27 (2008)

Artz, K.E., Norman, P.M., Hatfield, D.E., Cardinal, L.B.: A loungitudinal study of the impact of R&D, patents, and product innovation on firm performance. J. Prod. Innov. Manag. 27(5), 725–740 (2010)

Baden-Fuller, C., Stopford, J.M.: Rejuvenating the Mature Business. Harvard Business School Press, Boston (1994)

Barczak, G.: New product strategy, structure, process, and performance in the telecommunications industry. J. Prod. Innov. Manag. **12**, 224–234 (1995)

Baron, R.M., Kenny, D.A.: The moderator–mediator variable distinction in social psychological research: conceptual, strategic, and statistical considerations. J. Pers. Soc. Psychol. **51**(6), 1173 (1986)

Baxter, M.: Product Design: A Practical Guide to Systematic Methods of New Product Development. Chapman and Hall, London (1995)

Bendoly, E., Bharadwaj, A., Bharadwaj, S.: Complementary drivers of new product development performance: cross-functional coordination, information system capability, and intelligence quality. Prod. Oper. Manage. **21**(4), 653-667.1 (2012)

Booker, J.D., Swift, K.G., Brown, N.J.: Designing for assembly quality: strategies, guidelines and techniques. J. Eng. Des. **16**(3), 279–295 (2005)

Hamilton, B.-A.: New Product Management for the 1980s. Booz-Allen and Hamilton, New York (1982)

Brown, S.L., Eisenhardt, K.M.: The art of continuous change: linking complexity theory and time-paced evolution in relentlessly shifting organizations. Admin. Sci. Q. **42**, 1–34 (1997)

Casadesus-Masanell, R., Zhu, F.: Business model innovation and competitive imitation: the case of sponsor-based business models. Strateg. Manag. J. **34**(4), 464–482 (2013)

Chang, W., Hsu, Y.: A study on the product design strategy Taiwan home appliance manufacturers adopted after Taiwan joined WTO. In: Journal of the Asian Design International Conference, University of Tsukuba Institute of Art and Design, Japan, CD title (2003)

Chang, W., Hsu, Y.: A study of the product design related strategy of Taiwanese home appliance industries dealing with entering WTO. J. Des. **9**, 1–13 (2004)

Chong, W.K., Bian, D., Zhang, N.: E-marketing services and e-marketing performance: the roles of innovation, knowledge complexity and environmental turbulence in influencing the relationship. J. Mark. Manag. **32**(1–2), 149–178 (2016)

Clauss, T., Abebe, M., Tangpong, C., Hock, M.: Strategic agility, business model innovation, and firm performance: an empirical investigation. IEEE Trans. Eng. Manag. **68**(3), 767–784 (2019)

Claybaugh, C.C., Ramamurthy, K., Haseman, W.D.: Assimilation of enterprise technology upgrades: a factor-based study. Enterpr. Inf. Syst. **11**(2), 250–283 (2015)

Cool, K.O., Schendel, D.E.: Strategic group formation and strategic skills: a longitudinal analysis of the US pharmaceutical industry, 1963–1982. Manage. Sci. **33**(9), 1069–1207 (1987)

Cooper, R., Press, M.: The Design Agenda: A Guide to Successful Design Management. Wiley, New York (1995)

Cooper, R.G., Kleinschmidt, E.J.: Benchmarking the firm's critical success factors in new product development. J. Prod. Innov. Manag. **12**(5), 374–391 (1995)

Cooper, R.G.: Product Leadership: Creating and Launching Superior New Products. Perseus Books, New York (1998)

Cooper, R.G., Edgett, S.J., Kleinschmidt, E.J.: Portfolio management for new products (2001)

De Brentani, U., Reid, S.E.: The fuzzy front-end of discontinuous innovation: Insights for research and management. J. Prod. Innov. Manag. **29**(1), 70–87 (2012)

De Vellis, R.F.: Theory and Applications. Scale Development. SAGE Publications, Newbury Park, pp. 24–50 (1991)

Doz, Y.L., Kosonen, M.: Embedding strategic agility: a leadership agenda for accelerating business model renewal. Long Range Plan. **43**(2–3), 370–382 (2010)

Doz, Y., Kosonen, M.: The dynamics of strategic agility: Nokia's rollercoaster experience. Calif. Manage. Rev. **50**(3), 95–118 (2008)

Doz, Y.: Fostering strategic agility: How individual executives and human resource practices contribute. Hum. Resour. Manag. Rev. **30**(1), 100693 (2019)

Gao, T., Tian, Y.: Mechanism of supply chain coordination cased on dynamic capability framework-the mediating role of manufacturing capabilities. J. Ind. Eng. Manage. **7**(5), 1250–1267 (2014)

Gemser, G.: Design innovation, and value appropriation. Unpublished doctoral dissertation. Erasmus University, Rotterdam (1999)

Gemser, G., Leenders, M.A.A.M., Wijnberg, N.M.: The dynamics of inter-firm networks in the course of the industry life cycle: the role of appropriability. Technol. Anal. Strat. Manag. **8**(4), 439–453 (1996)

Haleblian, J., Finkelstein, S.: Top management team size, CEO dominance, and firm performance: the moderating roles of environmental turbulence and discretion. Acad. Manag. J. **36**(4), 844–863 (1993)

Hauser, J.R., Urban, G.L., Weinberg, B.D.: How consumers allocate their time when searching for information. J. Mark. Res. **30**(4), 452–466 (1993)

Hendricks, J.A., Defreitas, D.G., Walker, D.K.: Changing performance measures at caterpillar. Strategic Finance **78**(6), 18–23 (1996)

Hilletofth, P., Eriksson, D.: Coordinating new product development with supply chain management. Ind. Manage. Data Syst. **111**(2), 264–281 (2011)

Hock, M., Clauss, T., Schulz, E.: The impact of organizational culture on a firm's capability to innovate the business model. R&D Manag. **46**(3), 433–450 (2016)

Hsu, Y.: Comparative study of product design strategy and related design issues. J. Eng. Des. **17**(4), 357–370 (2006)

Hsu, Y.: Exploring design innovation and performance: the roles of issue related to design strategy. J. Eng. Des. **20**(6), 555–569 (2009)

Kale, E., Aknar, A., Başar, Ö.: Absorptive capacity and firm performance: the mediating role of strategic agility. Int. J. Hosp. Manag. **78**, 276–283 (2018)

Khurana, A., Rosenthal, S.R.: Integrating the fuzzy front end of new product development. IEEE Eng. Manage. Rev. **25**(4), 35–49 (1997)

Kim, M., Kim, J.E., Sawng, Y.W., Lim, K.S.: Impacts of innovation type SME's R&D capability on patent and new product development. Asia Pacific J. Innov. Entrepreneurs. **12**(1), 45–61 (2018)

Kumkale, I.: Organization's tool for creating competitive advantage: strategic agility. Balkan Near East. J. Soc. Sci. **2**(3), 118–124 (2016)

Langerak, F., Jan Hultink, E.: The impact of product innovativeness on the link between development speed and new product profitability. J. Prod. Innov. Manag. **23**(3), 203–214 (2006)

Lee, J.Y.: How to make financial and nonfinancial data add up. J. Account. **174**, 62–65 (1992)

Leih, G.L., Teece, D.J.: Business model innovation and organizational design: a dynamic capabilities perspective. Oxford University Press, New York, USA, pp. 24–42 (2015)

Lin, B.W., Lee, Y., Hung, S.C.: R&D intensity and commercialization orientation effects on financial performance. J. Bus. Res. **59**(5), 679–685 (2006)

Lin, C.: Statistics: psychology and education. Donhwa Book, Taipei (1992)

Lin, M.J., Lee, Z.: The study of the relationship with product development strategy, market information processing, and new product performance. J. Sci. Technol. Manag. **5**, 79–104 (2000)

Luiz, O.R., de Souza, F.B., Luiz, J.V.R., Jugend, D., Salgado, M.H., da Silva, S.L.: Impact of critical chain project management and product portfolio management on new product development performance. J. Bus. Indust. Mark. **34**(8), 1692–1705 (2019)

Marxt, C., Hacklin, F.: Design, product development, innovation: all the same in the end? A short discussion on terminology. J. Eng. Des. **16**(4), 413–421 (2005)

Montoya-Weiss, M.M., O'Driscoll, T.M.: From experience: applying performance support technology in the fuzzy front end. J. Prod. Innov. Manag. **17**(2), 143–161 (2000)

Nilsen-Hamilton, M., Hamilton, R.T., Allen, W.R., Potter-Perigo, S.: Synergistic stimulation of S6 ribosomal protein phosphorylation and DNA synthesis by epidermal growth factor and insulin in quiescent 3T3 cells. Cell **31**(1), 237–242 (1982)

Nystrom, H., Edvardsson, B.: Research and Development Strategies for four Swedish Farm Machine Companies. Institute for Economics and Statistics, Sweden (1980)

Ofoegbu, O.E., Akanbi, P.A.: The influence of strategic agility on the perceived performance of manufacturing firms in Nigeria. Int. Bus. Econ. Res. J. **11**(2), 153–160 (2012)

Amit, R., Zott, C.: Creating value through business model innovation. MIT Sloan Manage. Rev. **53**, 41–49 (2012)

Reitzig, M., Puranam, P.: Value appropriation as an organizational capability: the case of IP protection through patents. Strateg. Manag. J. **30**(7), 765–789 (2009)

Robert, E.M., Carolyn, A.S.: Business performance and dimensions of strategic orientation. J. Bus. Res. **56**(3), 163–176 (2003)

Robert, M.L., Wortzel, L.H.: New life style determinants of women's food shopping behaviour. J. Mark. **43**(3), 28–29 (1979)

Romijn, H., Albaladejo, M.: Determinants of innovation capability in small electronics and software firms in southeast England. Res. Policy **31**(7), 1053–1067 (2002)

Rothwell, R., et al.: Design and the Economy, the Role of Design and Innovation in the Prosperity of Industrial Companies. Design Council, London (1983)

Roy, R., Riedel, J.C.: Design and innovation in successful product competition. Technovation **17**(10), 537–594 (1997)

Salomo, S., Weise, J., Gemünden, H.G.: NPD planning activities and innovation performance: the mediating role of process management and the moderating effect of product innovativeness. J. Prod. Innov. Manag. **24**(4), 285–302 (2007)

Sambamurthy, V., Bharadwaj, A., Grover, V.: Shaping agility through digital options: reconceptualizing the role of information technology in contemporary firms. MIS Q. **27**(2), 237–263 (2003)

Sheldon, D.F.: A review on the relevance of design science in a global product development arena. J. Eng. Des. **15**(6), 541–550 (2004)

Somaya, D., Williamson, I.O., Zhang, X.: Combining patent law expertise with R&D for patenting performance. Organ. Sci. **18**(6), 922–937 (2007)

Stark, J.: Product Lifecycle Management: 21st Century Paradigm for Product Realisation. Springer, London (2015)

Sullivan, J.: VUCA: the new normal for talent management and workforce planning (2012). https://www.ere.net/vuca-the-new-normal-for-talent-management-and-workforce-planning/. Accessed 23 Nov 2020

Tai, Y.M.: Effects of product lifecycle management systems on new product development performance. J. Eng. Tech. Manage. **46**, 67–83 (2017)

Tallon, P.P., Pinsonneault, A.: Competing perspectives on the link between strategic information technology alignment and organizational agility: insights from a mediation model. MIS Q. **35**(2), 463–486 (2011)

Thomas, E.: Supplier integration in new product development: computer mediated communication, knowledge exchange and buyer performance. Ind. Mark. Manage. **42**(6), 890–899 (2013)

Tidd, J., Bessant, J.: Managing Innovation: Integrating Technological, Market and Organizational Change, 4th edn. John Wiley & Sons, New York, NY (2009)

Ulrich, K.T., Eppinger, S.D.: Product Design and Development. McGraw-Hill, New York (2000)

Vidal, R., Mulet, E., Gomez-Senent, E.: Effectiveness of the means of expression in creative problem-solving in design groups. J. Eng. Des. **15**(3), 285–298 (2004)

Walsh, V., et al.: Winning by Design: Technology, Product Design, and International Competitiveness. Blackwell Business Publishing, Oxford (1992)

Wandeback, F., Wahlborg, P.J., Soderberg, R.: Use of measurement data in computer-aided tolerance management. J. Eng. Des. **13**(1), 63–76 (2002)

Weber, Y., Tarba, S.Y.: Strategic agility: a state of the art introduction to the special section on strategic agility. Calif. Manage. Rev. **56**(3), 5–12 (2014)

Wray, G.R.: Design or decline – a national emergency. Proc. Inst. Mech. Eng. Part B **205**, 153–170 (1991)

Xing, Y., Liu, Y., Boojihawon, D.K., Tarba, S.: Entrepreneurial team and strategic agility: a conceptual framework and research agenda. Hum. Resour. Manag. Rev. **30**(1), 1–10 (2020)

Effects of Animation-Guided Mindfulness Meditation on Flight Attendants' Flow Ergonomics

Chao Liu[1]([✉]), Wen-Ko Chiou[2]([✉]), Hao Chen[1]([✉]), and SzuErh Hsu[2]([✉])

[1] Business Analytics Research Center, Chang Gung University, Taoyuan City, Taiwan
174673015@qq.com, victory666666@126.com
[2] Department of Industrial Design, Chang Gung University, Taoyuan City, Taiwan
wkchiu@mail.cgu.edu.tw, h410@hotmail.com

Abstract. This study investigated whether animated guided mindfulness meditation can increase Flow Ergonomics in flight attendants. Due to the relationship between the working environment and the nature of work, the psychological state of flight attendants has always been negative. Mindfulness practices are often used to reduce anxiety levels and stress. Therefore, this research team used grounded theory method to collect data from qualitative re-search interviews, and obtained seven dimensional models of individual Flow Ergonomics. Theoretical framework regard Flow Ergonomics as the core category, containing oneness beyond, flow concentration, positive emotions and meaning, negative emotions, happiness life, environment connection and accept, and design a set of mindfulness meditation animation based on Flow Ergonomics, and use the Flow Ergonomics scale to assess whether mindfulness meditation animation can increase the Flow Ergonomics of the flight attendants. In this study, 60 flight attendants were recruited, 30 in each group, and divided into two groups, one was the experimental group and the other was the control group. Before and two weeks after the intervention, the experimental group and the control group were pre-tested and post-tested with the Flow Ergonomics scale, respectively, to understand the impact of the intervention of mindful animation on flight attendants before and after the intervention. This study expected that the 8-week interventional training could: (1) improve the level of mindfulness and Flow Ergonomics of flight attendants in the experimental group; (2) It can partially promote the positive change of cognitive emotion regulation strategies of the experimental group. The animation of mindfulness meditation can provide new ideas and methods for self-health education and clinical treatment.

Keywords: Flow ergonomics · Mindfulness meditation · Animation-guided

1 Introduction

The relationship between the working environment and the nature of the work makes the psychological state of flight attendants always in a negative state. For example, the working environment is easy to cause hypoxia and noise, and it is necessary to deal with all

© The Author(s), under exclusive license to Springer Nature Switzerland AG 2022
P.-L. P. Rau (Ed.): HCII 2022, LNCS 13313, pp. 58–67, 2022.
https://doi.org/10.1007/978-3-031-06050-2_5

kinds of problems of passengers during the work. Therefore, it is the reason that affects the positive psychological state. In addition, due to the uncertainty of flight, it is easy to cause fear and anxiety, which has affected the mental health of flight attendants to a certain extent. Mindfulness practices are often used to reduce anxiety levels (Andreasen et al. 1997) and stress Shapiro et al. (2005) to achieve a peaceful and joyful state of mind. Therefore, this research team used grounded theory method to collect data through qualitative research interviews to obtain the model of individual flow ergonomics. Theoretical framework regard flow ergonomics as the core category, containing a oneness transcendence, mindfulness and flow, positive emotion and meaning, negative emotion, pleasant life, environmental connection and acceptance, and design a set of mindfulness meditation animation through the core value, and our team develop the flow ergonomics scale to assess whether or not that mindfulness meditation animation can increase the flow ergonomics of the flight attendants.

2   Literature Review

2.1   Flight Attendants

The relationship between the working environment and the nature of the work makes the psychological state of flight attendants always in a negative state. For example, the working environment is easy to cause hypoxia and noise, and it is necessary to deal with all kinds of problems of passengers during the work. Therefore, it is the reason that affects the positive psychological state. In addition, due to the uncertainty of flight, it is easy to cause fear and anxiety, which has affected the mental health of flight attendants to a certain extent. Weatherford and Brown (1986) pointed out that irregular shifts were one of the main factors affecting the health of flight attendants. Irregular working hours not only limited their private lives, but also caused work-family conflicts. Ballard et al. (2006) found that most flight attendants reported poor health status, and those with poor health status had low job satisfaction and experienced passenger harassment. Psychological distress was significantly related to low job satisfaction, nervous relationship with colleagues and taking care of children. A number of studies have shown that the physical and mental health of flight attendants is closely related to work stress. Therefore, improving the physical and mental health of flight attendants is a topic worthy of much attention.

2.2   Flight Attendants Flow Ergonomics

In the past, human factors were mainly divided into physical human factors, cognitive human factors, and organizational human factors. physical human factors are about the human body's response to the physical and physiological demands of work. Repetitive strain injuries caused by repetition, vibration, force and posture are the most common types of problems and therefore have design significance. It deals with the anatomical, anthropometric, physiological and biomechanical characteristics of the human body related to physical activity. Related topics include work posture, material handling, repetitive movements, work-related musculoskeletal disorders, workplace layout, safety and health. Cognitive ergonomics focuses on mental processes, such as perception, memory, reasoning, and motor responses, because they affect how humans interact with other elements of the system. According to the International Human factors Association, organizational human factors deal with the organization of work systems, including their organizational structure and processes (Bedny et al. 2001). Since organizational human factor engineering involves the design of work systems suitable for human nature (Hendrick and Kleiner 2002), Duffy (1999) shows that the re-ward structure for rebuilding team communication and communication quality is significantly correlated with organizational performance. This means that companies using team work structures should adopt various ways to promote effective communication between team members and establish a balanced reward structure that improves organizational effectiveness.

Flow is a kind of pleasant experience that can be obtained when one's mental energy and attention are fully invested and immersed in the current ongoing task (Csikszentmihalyi 1975). The concept of flow comes from the realm of peak experience. In 1968, Maslow began to study peak experience. Maslow believed that very few people achieve the highest level of self-actualization; However, this peak experience can be experienced by anyone. Although little is known about these experiences, Maslow's research confirms that peak experiences do exist and contribute to the development of human psychology and mental health.

The concept of flow stems from research on the optimal human state (Seligman 2002). The concept of flow proposed by Csikszentmihalyi in the late 1970s (1975–1990) shares many qualities with the concepts of peak experience and self-actualiztion (Privette 1983). Flow is a state of mind in which a person is completely immersed in the current activity, in which the individual seems to forget everything except what they are doing, losing self-awareness and any worrying or negative thoughts (Wright et al. 2006), They usually report a feeling of being one with the activity (Nakamura and Csikszentmihalyi 2005). Focusing on tasks, the sense of oneness of mind and body comes together to create a present state of consciousness, which brings the intense enjoyment of fluid experiences (Jackson 2000). The ability to focus on the task at hand is a catalyst for creating opportunities for experiencing flow states (Csikszentmihalyi 1978; Swann et al. 2012). Flow can be experienced by anyone performing different activities (Fritz and Avsec 2007). According to the elaboration of Flow by Csikszentmihalyi (1990), flow experiences occur when attention is freely engaged to achieve goals. Csikszentmihalyi (1991) describes the conditions required to achieve flow: activities with clear goals, a balance between challenge and skill, and clear and real-time feedback on effectiveness and progress. The balance between challenge and skill is the most critical element of flow experience. For an individual, any task should be challenging to a certain degree, regardless of the type of activity, what is important is the balance between the challenge of the task and the individual's ability. Jackson and Csikszentmihalyi (1999) transformed this idea into a two-dimensional flow model. Other concepts are included in the model to explain requirements and capabilities in different scenarios. When one's abilities are much higher than the challenge of a task requires, the individual will feel bored, but when the demands on one's abilities are too high, anxiety will follow. Jackson and Csikszentmihalyi (1999) summarized the characteristics of flow into nine dimensions: (1) challenge-skill balance; (2) Focus on the task at hand; (3) the fusion of action and consciousness; (4) Clear mission objectives; (5) Tasks provide timely feedback; (6) Sense of complete control over tasks; (7) The perception of time changes (becomes faster or slower); (8) Loss of self-awareness; (9) Independent experience. Flow has been described as a positive psychological state and has been shown to increase human well-being (Fritz and Avsec 2007).

"Physical human factor", "cognitive human factor" and "organizational human factor" reinforce the people-oriented and user-centered concept from three aspects of physiology, cognition and organizational relations respectively. However, the seemingly complete theory still has shortcomings. Although the products or services designed based on the existing human factors theory are becoming more and more user-friendly, they still cannot relieve the psychological pressure faced by modern humans. This is because the existing theory of human factors still stays at the material level and solves problems at the material level. Psycho-pharmacology in humans, on the other hand, is a problem of the mind, and psychopharmacology has historically been distinguished from other medical diseases because they affect higher cognitive processes known as "the mind" (Andreasen 1997).

Therefore, "flow ergonomics" refers to the theory category of new human fac-tors that can relieve the psychological pressure faced by modern human beings and solve the spiritual level rather than the material level. In the past, the team has constructed this model and developed scales. The Chinese scale has also passed reliability and validity tests.

2.3 Animation-Guided Mindfulness Meditation

Animation Teaching Agents are animated images designed for teaching and entertainment, suitable for all ages. Sometimes referred to as edutainment, serious teaching, or other information, delivered in a playful animation (Yusuf and Afolabi 2010). Animation as a teaching method can strengthen students' participation in learning. One study reviewed more than 300 studies on the effectiveness of using animation to improve student achievement (Soe et al. 2000). They found evidence that animation works for language learning, history and physics education.

Many previous studies have shown that mindfulness training can promote positive emotions (Hill and Updegraff 2012). A mindfulness training enhanced the positive emotions of those prone to depression (Geschwind et al. 2011). A previous study on the influence of animation-guided meditation on promoting creativity, flow and emotion (Chen et al. 2021) showed that animation-guided mindfulness meditation has a positive correlation with positive emotion, flow and creativity. Therefore, this study takes flight attendants as experimental objects to observe the degree of flow.

3   Methods

The study recruited 60 flight attendants, 30 in each group, and divided them into two groups, one experimental group and one control group. Experimental group will with mindfulness meditation animation as a basis for the intervention, the experimental group employees intervened mindfulness meditation with animation in a total of 4 weeks, once a week, every time 3 min. Those in the control group either did none of these exercises at the same time, or simply read. Before and two weeks after the implementation, the experimental group and the control group were pre-tested and post-tested with the flow ergonomics scale, respectively, to understand the impact of the intervention of mindful animation on flight attendants before and after the implementation, and to verify the effect of the intervention of mindful animation on the mental health of flight attendants. Finally, SPSS statistical software was used to conduct t-test analysis on the pre-test and post-test data, so as to examine the possibility of the intervention of mindful animation and the impact of the intervention of mindful animation on the actual behavior of flight attendants. This study was approved by the IRB Review Board of Chang Gung Hospital to ensure the safety and confidentiality of each subject.

4 Results

This study conducted nine 2 (Time: Pre, Post) × 2 (Group: Audio, Animation) ANOVA with repeated measures on flow (DFS), mindfulness (MAAS), spirituality (SAIL), life satisfaction (SWL), positive affect (PA), negative affect (NA), subjective well-being (SWB), merciful (MERCY), and oneness (ONE). The p-values of Box's test and Mauchly's test were all greater than 0.05, showed that the observed covariance matrices of the dependent variables are equal across groups, indicating that these data were suitable for ANOVA. The descriptive statistics are presented in Table 1, and the results of the ANOVA are presented in Table 2.

Table 1. Descriptive statistics.

Group	Measure	Mean (SD)	
		Pre	Post
Animation	DFS	3.104 (0.862)	3.663 (0.723)
	MAAS	3.298 (0.714)	3.913 (0.599)
	SAIL	3.713 (1.090)	4.191 (0.927)
	SWL	2.820 (0.957)	3.268 (1.038)
	PA	2.900 (0.912)	3.577 (0.861)
	NA	2.477 (1.144)	1.870 (0.965)
	SWB	3.243 (2.402)	4.973 (1.950)
	MERCY	4.883 (1.053)	5.550 (0.871)
	ONE	5.736 (1.711)	7.188 (1.146)
Control	DFS	3.289 (0.702)	3.322 (0.609)
	MAAS	3.276 (0.823)	3.293 (0.691)
	SAIL	3.837 (0.966)	3.913 (0.786)

(*continued*)

Table 1. (*continued*)

Group	Measure	Mean (SD)	
		Pre	Post
	SWL	3.162 (0.753)	3.151 (0.770)
	PA	3.140 (0.774)	3.110 (0.669)
	NA	2.203 (0.683)	2.343 (0.8651)
	SWB	4.099 (1.395)	3.918 (1.092)
	MERCY	5.027 (0.883)	4.819 (1.173)
	ONE	5.864 (1.510)	6.046 (1.789)

Table 2. ANOVA results.

Measure	Variable	F	p	η2
DFS	Time*	5.842	0.019	0.092
	Group	0.325	0.571	0.006
	Time × Group*	4.602	0.036	0.074
MAAS	Time*	5.450	0.023	0.086
	Group*	6.972	0.011	0.107
	Time × Group*	4.855	0.032	0.077
SAIL	Time	3.561	0.064	0.058
	Group	0.203	0.654	0.003
	Time × Group	1.885	0.175	0.031
SWL	Time	1.707	0.196	0.029
	Group	0.518	0.474	0.009
	Time × Group	1.886	0.175	0.031
PA	Time*	4.731	0.034	0.075
	Group	0.596	0.443	0.010
	Time × Group*	5.650	0.021	0.089
NA	Time	1.923	0.171	0.032
	Group	0.342	0.561	0.006
	Time × Group*	4.922	0.030	0.078
SWB	Time*	5.088	0.028	0.081
	Group	0.106	0.746	0.002
	Time × Group**	7.746	0.007	0.118
MERCY	Time	1.529	0.221	0.026
	Group	2.642	0.109	0.044
	Time × Group*	5.571	0.022	0.088

(*continued*)

Table 2. (*continued*)

Measure	Variable	F	p	η2
ONE	Time[**]	9.265	0.004	0.138
	Group	2.862	0.096	0.047
	Time × Group[*]	5.599	0.021	0.088

Note. *p < 0.05; **p < 0.01; ***p < 0.001.

According to the results of ANOVA, animation-guided meditation can significantly improve participants' flow, mindfulness, positive affect, subjective well-being, and oneness. Animation-guided meditation had no significant effect on spirituality, life satisfaction, negative affect and merciful. However, for negative affect and merciful, there was a significant interaction effect (Time × Group), indicating that animation guided meditation has certain influence on these two variables.

5 Discussion

First of all, MM animation has the function of purifying negative emotions, so purification means to break through the original psychological hurdle and improve the spirit. If the long-term emotional workers of relaxation wear can not break through the obstacles, because there were already a lot of psychological disorders, the reflection of consciousness, about the psychology of many of the daily experience, such as melancholy and anger, impatience, etc., the majority of these psychological problems, the past negative experience of confirmed poor adaptation model habitual reaction. MM animation is a warm cleanser of negative emotions. Second, because MM animation plays a role in developing positive emotions, according to Fredrickson's positive emotion extension constructive theory, positive emotions can expand the attention span of cabin crews and enhance cognitive flexibility; MM animation training can effectively break the inertial link of bad emotions and MM animation training effectively breaks the inertial links of bad emotions and reinforces positive emotional patterns. In particular, it dissolves resentment, which is particularly damaging to the body and mind, relieves mental and physical stress and builds up the power of positive emotions. Developing these positive emotions will, over time, lead to greater happiness and satisfaction. With practice, sensitivities arise and it becomes easier to approach and inspire positive emotions at work and in everyday life. Finally, MM animation played a role in improving life satisfaction, as participants became more focused and immersed in the process of communicating love, creating a positive perception of selflessness and non-self-centredness. MM animation directly cultivates the four immeasurable minds: compassion, sorrow, joy and reverence. In this way, the effects of parenthood are fostered and become self-evident. In fact, MM animation developed the four immeasurable minds to counter the four immeasurable minds of anger, cruelty, jealousy and clinginess; MM animation fosters a positive perception of people and oneself, which increases kindness to others and increases life satisfaction. By conveying compassion to oneself, the practitioner creates a safe space and establishes a positive non-defensive attitude to embrace the experience, and the practitioner adopts an accepting attitude to embrace the experience. Because MM animation plays an important role in connecting with others, MM animation encourages the practitioner to use warm and compassionate feelings towards others and to respond to distress (e.g. Hostility, greed, stress, depression) with a kind-hearted attitude of warmth and acceptance. Practicing MM animation fosters a positive attitude towards others and increases the likelihood that the practitioner will be altruistic. In order to improve MM animation and to play a role in the transcendental linkage, the practitioner gradually moves from his own angle to the angle of sentient beings, thereby cultivating and enhancing the flow human factors.

6   Research Limitations and Future Studies

The job of a cabin attendant may be psychologically stressful for certain professions. Therefore, the aim of this study is to investigate whether MM animation can increase the flow human factors of cabin attendants. The results showed that MM animation can increase the flow human factors of cabin crew. Therefore, airline managers should properly promote MM animation interventions to enhance flight attendants' stress tolerance and autonomy, improve flight attendants' flow human factors, and increase the overall service level of the airline and the market competitiveness of air transport.

This study has the following research limitations: (1) since the sample is entirely from airlines, due to the constraints of the number of airline employees, research funding and the nature of flight attendants' work, the sample size in this study is relatively small and the sample composition is female. (2) the results of this study may not be suitable for dissemination to other groups of cabin crew due to the nature of their working environment and work, and the universal value of the study results is not high.

Future research will further explore whether there are common characteristics of MM animations by expanding the scope of the sample collection, increasing the sample survey of cabin crew from other airlines, and studying the flow factors of cabin crew. The impact on other sample groups to test the generality of the findings of this study. Future research will further elucidate the mechanisms by which MM animation promotes flow human factors.

7   Conclusions

The study concluded that the experimental group employees who received the mindfulness meditation animation intervention training scored higher on the flow ergonomics than the control group employees who did not receive the flow App training. This study expected that the 4-week intervention training, the following conclusions can be drawn: (1) App could improve the level of mindfulness and flow ergonomics of flight attendants in the experimental group; (2) It can partially promote the positive change of cognitive emotion regulation strategies of the experimental group, such as self-blame and catastrophitization. The animation of mindfulness meditation can provide new ideas and methods for self-health education and clinical treatment.

Our study revealed that MM animation elicited a significant increase in flow human factors. This result clarified the psychological effects of MM and suggested a possibility of clinical use. The mechanisms which underlie the effects of the MM on mindfulness, spirituality, SWB, and other psychological constructs require further elucidation.

References

Andreasen, N.C.: The evolving concept of schizophrenia: from Kraepelin to the present and future. Schizophr. Res. **28**(2–3), 105–109 (1997)

Ballard, T.J., et al.: Self perceived health and mental health among women flight attendants. Occup. Environ. Med. **63**(1), 33–38 (2006)

Bedny, G., Karwowski, W., Bedny, M.: The principle of unity of cognition and behavior: implications of activity theory for the study of human work. Int. J. Cogn. Ergon. **5**(4), 401–420 (2001)

Chen, H., Liu, C., Hsu, S.E., Huang, D.H., Liu, C.Y., Chiou, W.K.: The effects of animation on the guessability of universal healthcare symbols for middle-aged and older adults. Human Factors. 00187208211060900 (2021)

Csikszentmihalyi, M.: Flowing: a general model of intrinsically rewarding experiences. J. Human. Psychol. (1975)

Csikszentmihalyi, M.: Attention and the holistic approach to behavior. In: Pope, K.S., Singer, J.L. (eds) The Stream of Consciousness. Emotions, Personality, and Psychotherapy. Springer, Boston, MA (1978). https://doi.org/10.1007/978-1-4684-2466-9_13

Csikszentmihalyi, M.: Flow: The Psychology of Optimal Experience. HarperPerennial, New York (1991)

Csikszentmihalyi, M., Csikzentmihaly, M.: Flow: The Psychology of Optimal Experience, vol. 1990. Harper & Row, New York (1990)

Duffy, V.G.: The impact of organizational ergonomics on work effectiveness: with special reference to concurrent engineering in manufacturing industries. Ergonomics **42**(4), 614–637 (1999)

Fritz, B.S., Avsec, A.: The experience of flow and subjective well-being of music students. Horizons Psychol. **16**(2), 5–17 (2007)

Geschwind, N., Peeters, F., Drukker, M., van Os, J., Wichers, M.: Mindfulness training increases momentary positive emotions and reward experience in adults vulnerable to depression: a randomized controlled trial. J. Consult. Clin. Psychol. **79**(5), 618 (2011)

Hill, C.L., Updegraff, J.A.: Mindfulness and its relationship to emotional regulation. Emotion **12**(1), 81 (2012)

Jackson, S.A.: Joy, fun, and flow state in sport (2000)

Jackson, S.A., Csikszentmihalyi, M.: Flow in Sports. Human Kinetics (1999)

Karwowski, W.: The discipline of human factors and ergonomics. Handbook Human Factors Ergon. **4**, 3–37 (2012)

Hendrick, H.W., Kleiner, B.M.: Macroergonomics: Theory, Methods, and Applications. Lawrence Erlbaum Associates Publishers, Mahwah (2002)

Nakamura, J., Csikszentmihalyi, M.: Engagement in a profession: the case of undergraduate teaching. Daedalus **134**(3), 60–67 (2005)

Privette, G.: Peak experience, peak performance, and flow: a comparative analysis of positive human experiences. J. Person. Soc. Psychol. **45**(6), 1361 (1983)

Seligman, M.E.: Positive psychology, positive prevention, and positive therapy. Handbook Positive Psychol. **2**(2002), 3–12 (2002)

Shapiro, S.L., Astin, J.A., Bishop, S.R., Cordova, M.: Mindfulness-based stress reduction for health care professionals: results from a randomized trial. Int. J. Stress Manage. **12**(2), 164 (2005)

Swann, W.B., Jr., Jetten, J., Gómez, Á., Whitehouse, H., Bastian, B.: When group membership gets personal: a theory of identity fusion. Psychol. Rev. **119**(3), 441 (2012)

Soe, K., Koki, S., Chang, J.M.: Effect of Computer-Assisted Instruction (CAI) on Reading Achievement: A Meta-Analysis (2000)

Weatherford, G.D., Brown, F.L.: New Courses for the Colorado River: Major Issues for the Next Century. University of New Mexico Press, Albuquerque (1986)

Wright, J.J., Sadlo, G., Stew, G.: Challenge-skills and mindfulness: an exploration of the conundrum of flow process. OTJR: Occup. Participation Health **26**(1), 25–32 (2006)

Yusuf, M.O., Afolabi, A.O.: Effects of computer assisted instruction (CAI) on secondary school students' performance in biology. Turkish Online J. Educ. Technol. TOJET **9**(1), 62–69 (2010)

Evaluating the Attractiveness Factors of Internet Celebrity Products Using Survey Data

Xiaolin Tan[1,2], Saihong Han[1], and Runting Zhong[1(✉)] 📵

[1] School of Business, Jiangnan University, 1800 Lihu Avenue, Wuxi 214122, Jiangsu, People's Republic of China
zhongrt@jiangnan.edu.cn

[2] School of Economics and Management, Southeast University, 2 Southeast Avenue, Nanjing 211189, Jiangsu, People's Republic of China

Abstract. In this study, we developed an instrument to measure the attractiveness of Internet celebrity products. An online survey was conducted on 306 consumers (mean age = 24 years). Via exploratory factor analysis and regression analysis, a model of the attractiveness source of Internet celebrity products was constructed based on the survey and interview. The results showed that the attractiveness of Internet celebrity products was mainly affected by products' practical value, hedonic value, and Internet celebrity product purchase experience, with regression coefficients of 0.710, 0.164, and 0.193, respectively. This instrument offers a method to understand what attributes of Internet celebrity products attract consumers. Targeted optimization suggestions were also presented for product providers and consumers.

Keywords: Attractiveness · Internet celebrity products · Influencing factors

1 Introduction

The *2018 China Internet Celebrity Economic Development Insight Report* showed that as of May 2018, the total number of Chinese Internet celebrity fans exceeded 588 million, and the economic scale generated by the Internet celebrity product market reached 2 trillion yuan [1]. According to the *2021–2027 China Internet Celebrity E-commerce Market In-depth Survey and Future Prospect Forecast Report*, by the end of 2020, the number of short video users had reached 873 million, and the domestic social e-commerce market sales had exceeded 370 million [2]. The development of fan scale dissemination channels has paved the way for the emergence of hot-selling Internet celebrity products. Internet celebrity products refer to products that gain public attention on online platforms by virtue of their own characteristics or Internet celebrity marketing and achieve traffic aggregation and high-speed dissemination in a short period [3–5].

With the improvement of residents' living standards and the development of the Internet, Internet celebrity products are showing an explosive growth trend. For example, Genki Forest, a beverage brand focusing on 'zero sucrose', has sold more than 2.5 billion bottles in four years and has become a pioneer in the industry. Compared to ordinary

P.-L. P. Rau (Ed.): HCII 2022, LNCS 13313, pp. 68–81, 2022.
https://doi.org/10.1007/978-3-031-06050-2_6

products, Internet celebrity products are usually developed according to the preferences of young people [6]. They are widely promoted online through live streaming and social media, which brings them high traffic and hot sales quickly [7, 8]. However, the quality and service of these products are often easily overlooked. Hence, the short-term success of some Internet celebrity products cannot last [8].

Despite the popularity, not all people think that Internet celebrity products' performance lives up to their expectations. Some consider Internet celebrity products *"appealing in visuality but disappointing in quality."* For example, an American Internet celebrity cosmetics brand, Kylie Cosmetics, has a dissatisfying consumer rating of 1.61 stars from 203 reviews [9]. Consumers complaining about Kylie Cosmetics most frequently mention customer service, quality, and price. However, there still are satisfied consumers. Some enjoyed these products because they *"can enhance your confidence"*. Therefore, it is necessary to evaluate the attractiveness of Internet celebrity products for different people.

This study aims at developing an instrument consisting of multiple key constructs to measure the attractiveness of Internet celebrity products. The results provide a method to gain insight on what attributes of Internet celebrity products attract consumers significantly.

2 Literature Review and Hypothesis

2.1 Models for Evaluating Product Attractiveness

To evaluate product attractiveness of Internet celebrity products, many models with key factors were constructed [10–13]. The Kano model is a theoretical basis for assessing product attractiveness [10]. It defines five categories of perceived quality: must-be quality (attributes expected to be at a sufficiently good level), one-dimensional quality (the quality of performance of current needs), attractive quality (attributes which surprise and delight customers), indifferent quality (attributes causing neither satisfaction nor disaatisfaciton), and reverse quality (attributes causing consumer dissatisfaction) [11, 14]. One study adopts the so-called analytical Kano model to measure the computer keyboard attractiveness using two parameters: the importance index and the satisfaction index [12]. Kansei Engineering is a tool translating customers' feelings into product parameters, and one of its crucial processes is Kansei evaluation [15, 16]. Several Kansei evaluation models were developed to assess customer attribute preferences of products, and they generally focused on consumers' psychological needs and personal taste [16–20]. Another model for measuring the form attractiveness of passenger cars was developed [21]. It suggests the use of a five-factor instrument in terms of aesthetic sensibilities, novelty-and-fashion, identity suitability, apparent function, and symbol of its form design. Another evaluation method for product-form attractiveness based on Miryoku Engineering was also proposed [13]. These models gave insights into the influencing factors affecting product attractiveness.

2.2 Factors Affecting Product Attractiveness

The attractiveness of a product is defined as the degree to which the product value is perceived by consumers [22]. Based on prior studies, factors affecting product attractiveness can be: functional value (commodity quality [23], core functions [24]), cost value (price, promotion [25]), service value (service quality [26], personnel [26], context [23]), and design value (form design [13], aesthetics [27], visual appeal [28, 29]). Under the Internet celebrity economy, the dissemination value (Internet celebrity marketing [30]) and Internet celebrity value (celebrity effect [31]) can also be involved. To further classify these indicators, the products' practical and hedonic values are introduced [32]. This study classified these factors into four categories: practical value, hedonic value, Internet celebrity product purchase experience, and demographic information. These factors are shown in Fig. 1.

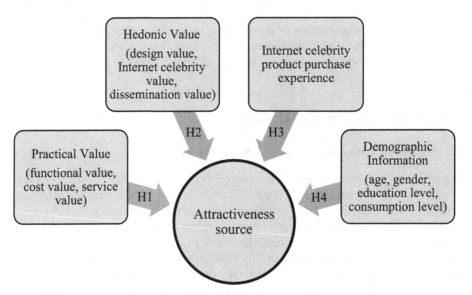

Fig. 1. Influencing factors based on literature.

Practical Value. Practical value of Internet celebrity products includes product functional value [23, 24, 33, 34], cost value [25, 33, 35, 36], and service value [23, 26, 33, 37]. It can mainly be reflected through function utility value, positively affecting customer satisfaction and behavior [38]. A similar study shows that product attractiveness is affected by consumers' recognition of core functions, satisfaction with the product form, and product added value [24]. Another study states that practical value (the services, convenience, and quality of the grocery retailer) positively influences customer satisfaction [39]. In addition, when measuring the attractiveness of retail products, factors including stock availability, price, store design, personnel service, and atmosphere should also be considered [26]. Therefore, we proposed the following hypothesis:

H1: Product practical value positively affects the attractiveness of Internet celebrity products.

Hedonic Value. Hedonic value focuses on the perceptual experience of consumers and often includes design value [40–43], dissemination value [23, 44] and Internet celebrity value [23, 45–47]. In the pursuit of aesthetics and emotional resonance, consumers are often not guided by economic practicality but products' design merits and emotional value [40]. Other product attributes related to visual appeal, such as shape and color, affect product attractiveness [41, 42]. For example, package color properties varied in hue, brightness, and saturation. Warmer, saturated, less bright packages are more attractive and less healthy, enhancing sensory expectation and perception [42]. In addition, Internet celebrities greatly impact product attractiveness, and consumers also have greater purchase impulse towards products with Internet celebrity value [45]. Therefore, we proposed the following hypothesis:

H2: Product hedonic value positively affects the attractiveness of Internet celebrity products.

Internet Celebrity Product Purchase Experience. A prior study shows that consumers' perceived attractiveness of products is affected by their familiarity with the products [23]. Therefore, we also discussed whether consumers with different purchase experiences have differences in the perceived attractiveness of Internet celebrity products. Therefore, we proposed the following hypothesis:

H3: Consumers' purchase experience of Internet celebrity products positively affects the attractiveness of Internet celebrity products.

Demographic Information. The individual differences of consumers in terms of age, gender, income, etc., impact their different practical and hedonic values, as well as online shopping behaviors [48]. Therefore, we proposed the following hypothesis:

H4: Demographic variables including consumer age, gender, consumption level, and education level have a significant impact on the attractiveness of Internet celebrity products.

3 Method

3.1 Interview

After literature review, we preliminarily interviewed 10 participants about their purchase experience and product attractiveness source. The response indicated that purchase experiences may impact customer perceived attractiveness. Three out of ten respondents had few Internet celebrity product purchase experiences. Expression of *"misrepresented"*, *"exaggerated"*, and *"marketing gimmicks"* frequently occurred among them. In contrast, two respondents frequently bought Internet celebrity products, saying they *"must buy some of these products every month."* They mentioned *"try"* and *"popular"* with a positive attitude. We then constructed survey items before conducting the consumer survey. The questionnaire was surveyed online for data collection and then for factor, correlation, and regression analyses. A multi-factor model was extracted to develop the instrument.

3.2 Survey

The dependent variable was attractiveness, and the independent variables were practical value, hedonic value, purchase experience, and demographic information (see Fig. 1). The scenario simulation method was adopted, allowing participants to read the scenario description first: "The 618 Shopping Festival is approaching, you want to choose a snail powder/drink/sneaker. Among many product recommendations on the shopping platform, you happen to see the popular Internet celebrity product Li Ziqi snail powder/Genki Forest/Li-Ning...." The questionnaire was designed in two parts. The first part consists of 28 questions to investigate attractiveness sources of Internet celebrity products, where the Likert scale is used (1 = completely disagree, 5 = completely agree). The second part contains nine questions about participants' demographic information and purchase experience. The survey items of the first part are shown in Table 2.

Table 1. Survey items of the first part.

Dimensions	Survey items
Attractiveness	Generally speaking, I am interested in this Internet celebrity product [49]
	I would consciously browse the recommendations of such internet celebrity products [49]
	I am more focused when a product is embedded with "Internet celebrity" [49]
Functional value	I think this Internet celebrity product is of good quality [34]
	I think this Internet celebrity product has good craftsmanship [34]
	I think this Internet celebrity product is very useful [34]
	I think this Internet celebrity product is very durable [34]
Cost value	This Internet celebrity product has a reasonable price [35, 36]
	This Internet celebrity product is low in price [35, 36]
	This Internet celebrity product meets my need at a reasonable price [35, 36]
	The price and function provided by this Internet celebrity product match [35, 36]
Service value	The logistics and distribution of this Internet celebrity product are highly time-efficient [37]
	The customer service of this Internet celebrity product responds quickly to customer requirements [37]
	The after-sales service of this Internet celebrity product is satisfying [37]
	Employees of this Internet celebrity product show good self-cultivation and ability [37]
	The tangible service facilities of this Internet celebrity product are exquisite and complete [37]

(continued)

Table 1. (*continued*)

Dimensions	Survey items
Design value	This Internet celebrity product is beautifully packaged and eye-catching [43]
	This Internet celebrity product has beautiful appearance and unique design [43]
	This Internet celebrity product has a good color match and is suitable for taking pictures [43]
	This Internet celebrity product helps me to build a distinctive personal image [43]
	This Internet celebrity product can reflect my personal achievement or taste correctly
Internet celebrity value	I think I would be more willing to buy this Internet celebrity product when it is endorsed by Internet celebrities [46, 47]
	I think I would project my liking for the Internet celebrity to the Internet celebrity products [46, 47]
	I think it is a good decision to purchase what Internet celebrity promoted [46, 47]
	I think buying this product recommended by the Internet celebrity is a pleasure [46, 47]
Dissemination value	I can see the evaluation or recommendations of this Internet celebrity product on Weibo, Bilibili and other platforms [44]
	I can become familiar with and purchase this Internet celebrity product easily [44]
	Many people around me are discussing and sharing this Internet celebrity product [44]

3.3 Sampling

We distributed e-questionnaires to consumer groups in China, giving each participant 1 yuan for feedback. A total of 325 questionnaires were sent and collected. After eliminating questionnaires with incomplete responses or completion time shorter than 1.25 mins [50], 306 questionnaires were valid for data analysis, with an effective rate of 94.15%. The age of the respondents ranged from 12 to 55, with an average of 24 and a standard variation of 7.8 years. 50.33% of them had a bachelor's degree, and 27.45% had a master's degree. More than half of the respondents' monthly consumption was between 1001–2500 yuan (63.73%). There were 142 males (46.41%) and 164 females (53.59%). Among Internet celebrity products, respondents preferred food (51.96%), clothes (37.58%), and cosmetics (25.82%). They also preferred to purchase online through e-commerce platforms (79.41%). Only 11.11% of the respondents had never bought any Internet celebrity products.

3.4 Analysis Method

Cronbach's alpha of the 306 valid questionnaires was 0.894, which revealed that the questions had good internal consistency and the questionnaire was reliable. To determine the internal factors that influenced Internet celebrity product attractiveness, this study conducted exploratory factor analysis (EFA) with 28 items and then did a hierarchical regression with the common factors identified by factor analysis. The regression results indicated the main variables that built the attractiveness model of Internet celebrity products. A significance level of 0.05 was used, and all the procedures were conducted with SPSS v20.

4 Results

4.1 Factor Analysis

The Kaiser-Meyer-Olkin (KMO) measure of sampling adequacy was 0.962, and Bartlett's test of sphericity rejected the H_0 hypothesis ($\chi^2 = 8479.669$; $p < .001$), which means that there were internal factors among these questions and it is appropriate to do an EFA [51, 52]. In the factor extracting and screening phase, the following rules were used: using a minimum eigenvalue of 1 as a cutoff value for extraction; deleting items with factor loadings less than 0.5 on all factors or greater than 0.5 on two or more factors; a simple factor structure [53, 54]. As a result, items Q12-Q16 (service value) and Q20-Q25 (Internet celebrity value) were deleted during the process. Finally, 14 items were retained, and the component matrix was obliquely rotated to acquire a meaningful explanation of the model. The 14 items so obtained were composed of two factors and explained 73.084% of the total variance. The two factors and their corresponding items are in Table 3. They are named: practical value and hedonic value.

Table 2. Rotated component matrix of EFA.

Item code	Description	Factor	
		1-Practical value	2-Hedonic value
Q04	This Internet celebrity product is of good quality	0.809	
Q05	This Internet celebrity product has good craftsmanship	0.849	
Q06	This Internet celebrity product is very useful	0.828	
Q07	This Internet celebrity product is very durable	0.847	
Q08	This Internet celebrity product has a reasonable price	0.816	
Q09	This Internet celebrity product is low in price	0.792	

(*continued*)

Table 2. (*continued*)

Item code	Description	Factor	
		1-Practical value	2-Hedonic value
Q10	This Internet celebrity product meets my need at a reasonable price	0.760	
Q11	The price and function provided by this Internet celebrity product match		0.855
Q17	This Internet celebrity product is beautifully packaged and eye-catching		0.855
Q18	This Internet celebrity product has beautiful appearance and unique design		0.870
Q19	This Internet celebrity product has a good color match and is suitable for taking pictures		0.890
Q26	I can see the evaluation or recommendations of this Internet celebrity product on Weibo, Bilibili and other platforms		0.756
Q27	I can become familiar with and purchase this Internet celebrity product easily		0.610
Q28	Many people around me are discussing and sharing this Internet celebrity product		0.634

* Likert scale was used. 1 = completely disagree. 5 = completely agree.

In the further reliability test, Cronbach's alpha of the dependent variable was 0.862, the internal consistency reliability of practical value was 0.951, and the internal consistency reliability of hedonic value was 0.909. The factor aggregation was basically in line with the expected categories.

4.2 Regression Analysis

The correlation analysis showed that age ($r = 0.230$), monthly consumption level ($r = 0.164$), practical value ($r = 0.815$), hedonic value ($r = 0.632$) and purchase experience ($r = 0.524$) were positively correlated with the attractiveness of Internet celebrity products ($ps < 0.01$).

Then we constructed a regression model of the attractiveness source of Internet celebrity products. The dependent variable was the attractiveness of Internet celebrity products. The independent variables were consumer age, gender, education level, monthly consumption level, practical value, hedonic value, and Internet celebrity product purchase experience. The stepwise method was used to screen variables. The final regression model contained three factors: purchase experience, practical value, and hedonic value. The Analysis of Variance (ANOVA) indicated that the regression model was significant ($ps < 0.001$), and these three factors explained 69.7% of the total variance. The regression results are shown in Table 4.

Table 3. ANOVA results of the regression model.

Items added	Adjusted R square	R square change	F change	Sig. F change
Practical value	0.663	0.664	601.174	0.000
Hedonic value, practical value	0.688	0.260	235.503	0.000
Hedonic value, practical value, purchase experience	0.697	0.010	9.975	0.002

The coefficients indicated that all three factors positively influenced the attractiveness of Internet celebrity products (see Table 4). The practical value ($\beta_1 = 0.710, p = 0.000$) is the most important factor in their attractiveness. People tend to choose Internet celebrity products with strong functional utility and cost-effective performance. The second most important factor is consumers' Internet celebrity product purchase experience ($\beta_2 = 0.193$, $p = 0.002$). The rich and frequent shopping experience of Internet celebrity products is conducive to attracting consumers. The third factor is the hedonic value ($\beta_3 = 0.164$, $p = 0.000$). Product design and marketing play a unique role as consumers pursue diverse experiences in the Internet age.

Table 4. Coefficients of predictor variables in regression analysis (N = 306).

Model	B	Std. error	Beta	t	Sig.
Constant	−0.101	1.863		−0.632	0.528
Practical value	0.710	0.046	0.657	15.479	0.000
Hedonic value	0.164	0.052	0.135	4.100	0.000
Purchase experience	0.193	0.047	0.152	3.158	0.002

The regression equation was constructed as:

Internet celebrity product attractiveness
$$= -0.101 + 0.710 \text{ } Practical \text{ } value + 0.164 \text{ } Hedonic \text{ } value$$
$$+ \text{ } 0.193 \text{ } Internet \text{ } celebrity \text{ } product \text{ } expeirence$$

All the Variance Inflation Factor (VIF) values of the equation variables were less than 5, the eigenvalues were not 0, and the conditional indices were all less than 30, proving that the multicollinearity problem of the regression model was not serious. The model to evaluate the attractiveness of Internet celebrity products is shown in Fig. 2.

Practical Value. H1 was partially supported. Practical value, specifically functional value and cost value, has a significant impact on the attractiveness of Internet celebrity products ($\beta1 = 0.710$), in line with prior studies [24, 38]. Prior studies usually used

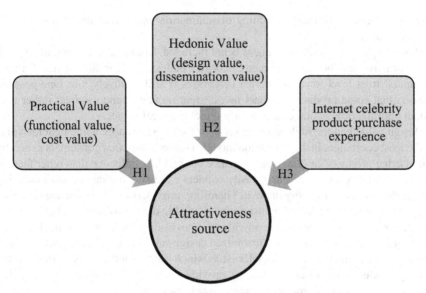

Fig. 2. Attractiveness model of Internet celebrity products.

function utility to describe the practical concept [23, 24, 33, 38]. In this study, we broadened the concept by using practical value, which covers more practical factors such as cost value.

Service value was not included because its influence was not significant, which indicated that consumers focus on the product itself more than its customer service when evaluating its attractiveness. Another reason is that the convergence of service quality in the Chinese Internet celebrity product market has weakened the influence of customer service. However, service quality is still very crucial to customer satisfaction.

Practical value explained 66.3% of the total variance and had the largest coefficient in the regression model, indicating that consumers prioritize products' function utility and cost-efficiency. Practical values such as good quality, craftsmanship, and durability are the most important factors in consumers' perceived attractiveness. Therefore, product quality should be guaranteed first for Internet celebrity product providers. Especially when products' sales go up, it is urgent to standardize production and seek stable suppliers to ensure quality control capabilities and good response. If quality control is poor, reviews on social media will quickly take bad effect. Besides, consumers are attracted to quality products at a reasonable price, i.e., Internet celebrity products with low-cost advantages are more attractive. In addition, consumers' perceived attractiveness of Internet celebrity products is likely to increase when product providers launch products with well-known brands, which is another way to elevate the attractiveness.

Hedonic Value. H2 was partially supported. Hedonic value, specifically design value and dissemination value, plays a positive role in the attractiveness of Internet celebrity products ($\beta2 = 0.164$), in line with some previous research where hedonic value generally acknowledged the effect of visual appeal and design [38, 42]. In this study, the concept of hedonic value is enriched by adding dissemination value to it, and it refers to the marketing advantage.

However, Internet celebrity value was not included. Consumers do not think a product is attractive just because Internet celebrities endorse it. It indicated that Chinese consumers' trust level towards Internet celebrities is still relatively low. One possible reason is that some product providers invest great money in endorsement rather than product optimization, which causes poor product practical value.

Design value had the highest mean score in the questionnaire, while hedonic value had the least coefficient in the regression model. This indicated that consumers generally acknowledge products' aesthetic performance but had less influence than other factors. The reason may be that consumers easily connect excessive packaging and marketing with exorbitant price or quality distrust. Therefore, providers need to excavate customer needs and customize products for customers. Using big data, providers can better understand customers' characteristics. It provides the possibility for future improvement and customized functions or services. Customized design surprises customers, and delighted customers can even share it on social media, which contributed greatly to the Internet celebrity product attractiveness. Product providers should also follow the marketing trend and invest wisely in endorsement and live streaming.

Internet Celebrity Product Purchase Experience. H3 was supported. The purchase experience of Internet celebrity products has a significant impact on the attractiveness of products ($\beta3 = 0.193$). Prior studies mentioned the effect of purchase context on product attractiveness, which is part of the purchase experience [23]. For example, a good website design can leave a good impression, thereby increasing product attractiveness for customers. This study showed that respondents with more Internet celebrity product purchase experience are more likely to be attracted by them again. As a result, product providers should attract consumers to make the first attempt by clearly illustrating products' practical and hedonic value. More importantly, customers' own impression, as well as of other customers, influence their purchase choices. Consumers would read others' reviews first to get familiar with the product and then decide whether to purchase or not. Hence, providers should actively collect feedback and respond quickly to facilitate positive reviews.

Demographic Information. H4 was not supported. Consumers' demographic characteristics, including age, gender, education level, and monthly consumption level, do not significantly impact the attractiveness of Internet celebrity products. The reason may be that our sample was a little homogenous, which provides possibilities for future research. 82.35% of the participants were younger than 40, and 77.78% graduated from college or above. However, we simulated Internet celebrity products fit for both women and men in the survey, so gender's effect was insignificant. In the future, we can also simulate Internet celebrity products whose prices differ greatly, which may better reveal the influence of consumption level.

5 Conclusion

In this study, we developed an instrument to measure the attractiveness of Internet celebrity products. Via exploratory factor analysis and regression analysis, a model of the attractiveness source of Internet celebrity products was constructed. It verified that the practical value, hedonic value, and purchase experience of Internet celebrity products positively affect their attractiveness. This instrument offers a method to understand what attributes of Internet celebrity products attract consumers and gives insight into product providers and consumers. Quality control, customized functions and services, Internet celebrity endorsement, and social media marketing are recommended.

References

1. iResearch: 2018 China Internet Celebrity Economic Development Insight Report (in Chinese)
2. Intelligence Research Group: 2021–2027 China Internet Celebrity E-commerce Market In-depth Survey and Future Prospect Forecast Report (in Chinese)
3. Sun, J., Wang, X.: Wanghong and Wanghong economy—a review based on celebrity theory. Foreign Econ. Manag. **41**, 18–30 (2019)
4. Liu, B., Zhang, H., Luo, C.: A big data analysis of the e-word-of-mouth of internet celebrity ventures. J. Guangxi Univ. Natl. **40**, 118–126 (2018)
5. Shen, G.: The new era of internet celebrities: the productization of internet celebrities and internet celebrity products (in Chinese). China Advertising. 121–123 (2019)
6. American Association of Adevertising Agencies: Celebrity Endorsers Have More Impact on Young Consumers (2016)
7. Chen, Z., Benbasat, I., Cenfetelli, R.: Grassroots Internet Celebrity Plus Live Streaming. In: Activating IT-Mediated Lifestyle Marketing Services at e-Commerce Websites. ICIS 2017 Proceedings (2017)
8. Yin, S.: How do Internet Celebrity Products Win Changhong Word of Mouth (in Chinese) (2021). http://mp.weixin.qq.com/s?__biz=MzA4OTIyMjUyOQ==&mid=2654667035& idx=4&sn=dd0f28baf3ea36df7364aba434bd1b4e&chksm=8bd19df5bca614e3aa27e183481 99d2a2f47945a563122119d15dd07e8cb10c4c02d2d2ec6b7#rd
9. Kylie Cosmetics Reviews - 1.4 Stars. https://www.sitejabber.com/reviews/kyliecosmetics. com. Accessed 24 Jan 2022
10. Kano, N.: Attractive quality and must be quality. Hinshitsu (Qual. J. Japanese Soc. Qual. Control). **14**, 39–48 (1984)
11. Robinson, J., et al.: Using internet content as a means to establish live social networks by linking internet users to each other who are simultaneously engaged in the same and/or similar content (2012). https://patents.google.com/patent/US8117281B2/en
12. Turisova, R., Sinay, J.: Ergonomics versus product attractiveness. Theor. Issues Ergon. Sci. **18**, 1–13 (2017). https://doi.org/10.1080/1463922X.2015.1126382
13. Dong, W.: The evaluation method for product form attractiveness based on Miryoku engineering. Appl. Mech. Mater. **44–47**, 86–90 (2011). https://doi.org/10.4028/www.scientific. net/AMM.44-47.86
14. Sharif Ullah, A.M.M., Tamaki, J.: Analysis of kano-model-based customer needs for product development. J. Syst. Eng. **14**, 154–172 (2011). https://doi.org/10.1002/sys.20168
15. Schütte*, S.T.W., Eklund, J., Axelsson, J.R.C., Nagamachi, M.: Concepts, methods and tools in Kansei engineering. Theoret. Issues Ergon. Sci. **5**, 214–231 (2004). https://doi.org/10.1080/ 1463922021000049980
16. Su, Z., Yu, S., Chu, J., Zhai, Q., Gong, J., Fan, H.: A novel architecture: using convolutional neural networks for Kansei attributes automatic evaluation and labeling. Adv. Eng. Inform. **44**, 101055 (2020). https://doi.org/10.1016/j.aei.2020.101055
17. Chou, J.-R.: A Kansei evaluation approach based on the technique of computing with words. Adv. Eng. Inform. **30**, 1–15 (2016). https://doi.org/10.1016/j.aei.2015.11.001

18. Lee, S., Harada, A., Stappers, P.J.: Pleasure with products: design based on Kansei. Pleasure with Products: Beyond Usability (2002).https://doi.org/10.1201/9780203302279.ch16
19. Yanagisawa, H.: Kansei quality in product design. In: Fukuda, S. (ed.) Emotional Engineering: Service Development, pp. 289–310. Springer, London (2011). https://doi.org/10.1007/978-1-84996-423-4_16
20. Yan, H.-B., Huynh, V.-N., Murai, T., Nakamori, Y.: Kansei evaluation based on prioritized multi-attribute fuzzy target-oriented decision analysis. Inf. Sci. **178**, 4080–4093 (2008). https://doi.org/10.1016/j.ins.2008.06.023
21. Chang, H.-C., Lai, H.-H., Chang, Y.-M.: A measurement scale for evaluating the attractiveness of a passenger car form aimed at young consumers. Int. J. Ind. Ergon. **37**, 21–30 (2007). https://doi.org/10.1016/j.ergon.2006.09.014
22. Martinez, L.M., Rando, B., Agante, L., Abreu, A.M.: True colors: consumers' packaging choices depend on the color of retail environment. J. Retail. Consum. Serv. **59**, 102372 (2021). https://doi.org/10.1016/j.jretconser.2020.102372
23. Schnurr, B., BrunnerSperdin, A., StokburgerSauer, N.E.: The effect of context attractiveness on product attractiveness and product quality: the moderating role of product familiarity. Mark. Lett. **28**(2), 241–253 (2016). https://doi.org/10.1007/s11002-016-9404-3
24. Yao, H.: Effective Marketing Series Talk ③——Establishing Effective Marketing Ideas for Dis-tribution Operation (in Chinese). China Marketing. 78–79 (2001)
25. Peng, L., Zhang, W., Wang, X., Liang, S.: Moderating effects of time pressure on the relationship between perceived value and purchase intention in social E-commerce sales promotion: considering the impact of product involvement. Inf. Manag. **56**, 317–328 (2019). https://doi.org/10.1016/j.im.2018.11.007
26. Lindquist, J.D.: Meaning of Image: A Survey of Empirical and Hypothetical Evidence. (1975)
27. Blijlevens, J., Carbon, C.-C., Mugge, R., Schoormans, J.P.L.: Aesthetic appraisal of product designs: Independent effects of typicality and arousal. Br. J. Psychol. **103**, 44–57 (2012). https://doi.org/10.1111/j.2044-8295.2011.02038.x
28. Bloch, P.H.: Seeking the ideal form: product design and consumer response. J. Mark. **59**, 16–29 (1995). https://doi.org/10.1177/002224299505900302
29. Creusen, M.E.H., Schoormans, J.P.L.: The different roles of product appearance in consumer choice*. J. Prod. Innov. Manag. **22**, 63–81 (2005). https://doi.org/10.1111/j.0737-6782.2005.00103.x
30. Park, H.J., Lin, L.M.: The effects of match-ups on the consumer attitudes toward internet celebrities and their live streaming contents in the context of product endorsement. J. Retail. Consum. Serv. **52**, 101934 (2020). https://doi.org/10.1016/j.jretconser.2019.101934
31. Luo, M., Sima, F.: Research on the online marketing strategy and the trend of developing of "internet celebrity live broadcast" for shoes and clothes enterprises. Front. Soc. Sci. Technol. **2**, 1–17 (2020). https://doi.org/10.25236/FSST.2020.021307
32. Gao, P.: Analysis of e-commerce agricultural product comment based on data mining Take "Sanzhisongshu" Tmall's Pecan Product as Example. Office Informatization. **25**, 40–42 (2020)
33. Ainsworth, J., Foster, J.: Comfort in brick and mortar shopping experiences: examining antecedents and consequences of comfortable retail experiences. J. Retail. Consum. Serv. **35**, 27–35 (2017). https://doi.org/10.1016/j.jretconser.2016.11.005
34. Dodds, W.B., Monroe, K.B., Grewal, D.: Effects of price, brand, and store information on buyers' product evaluations. J. Mark. Res. **28**, 307–319 (1991). https://doi.org/10.1177/002224379102800305
35. Sánchez, J., Callarisa, L., Rodríguez, R.M., Moliner, M.A.: Perceived value of the purchase of a tourism product. Tour. Manage. **27**, 394–409 (2006). https://doi.org/10.1016/j.tourman.2004.11.007

36. Sui, L., Li, Y., Cheng, X.: A study on the value differences of tourists visiting cultural heritages in both China and western countries-a case study of tourists in Xi'an. Tourism Tribune. **25**, 35–41 (2010)
37. Zeithaml, V.A., Berry, L.L., Parasuraman, A.: The behavioral consequences of service quality. J. Mark. **60**, 31–46 (1996). https://doi.org/10.1177/002224299606000203
38. Li, L.-Y., Lee, L.-Y.: Experiential consumption and customer satisfaction: moderating effects of perceived values. Int. J. Mark. Stud. **8**, 32–40 (2016)
39. Martínez-Ruiz, M.P., JiménezZarco, A.I., IzquierdoYusta, A.: Customer satisfaction's key factors in Spanish grocery stores: evidence from hypermarkets and supermarkets. J. Retail. Consum. Serv. **17**, 278–285 (2010). https://doi.org/10.1016/j.jretconser.2010.02.005
40. Wang, L.C., Baker, J., Wagner, J.A., Wakefield, K.: Can a retail web site be social? J. Mark. **71**, 143–157 (2007). https://doi.org/10.1509/jmkg.71.3.143
41. Singh, S.: Impact of color on marketing. Manag. Decis. **44**, 783–789 (2006). https://doi.org/10.1108/00251740610673332
42. Tijssen, I., Zandstra, E.H., de Graaf, C., Jager, G.: Why a 'light' product package should not be light blue: Effects of package colour on perceived healthiness and attractiveness of sugar- and fat-reduced products. Food Qual. Prefer. **59**, 46–58 (2017). https://doi.org/10.1016/j.foodqual.2017.01.019
43. Homburg, C., Schwemmle, M., Kuehnl, C.: New product design: concept, measurement, and consequences. J. Mark. **79**, 41–56 (2015). https://doi.org/10.1509/jm.14.0199
44. Li, Z.: Research on the Impact of Online Opinion Leaders on Consumers' Purchasing Behavior in Social E-commerce Platform (2018). https://kns.cnki.net/kcms/detail/detail.aspx?dbcode=CMFD&dbname=CMFD201802&filename=1018231044.nh&uniplatform=NZKPT&v=2I0B3jtlFt1EPxeu3-vwen-mFP8aPA3cYLJystbEyuh4360er-3lW-l2BnsqVud5
45. Chen, T.Y., Yeh, T.L., Lee, F.Y.: The impact of Internet celebrity characteristics on followers' impulse purchase behavior: the mediation of attachment and parasocial interaction. J. Res. Interact. Mark. **15**, 483–501 (2021). https://doi.org/10.1108/JRIM-09-2020-0183
46. Ohanian, R.: Construction and validation of a scale to measure celebrity endorsers' perceived expertise, trustworthiness, and attractiveness. J. Advert. **19**, 39–52 (1990). https://doi.org/10.1080/00913367.1990.10673191
47. Meng, F.: Research of Opinion Leaders' Impact on Purchase Intention Under Social Commerce Context (2012). https://kns.cnki.net/kcms/detail/frame/list.aspx?dbcode=CDFD&filename=1012373669.nh&dbname=CDFD1214&RefType=1&vl=l8LTLYMCfA6qBInUyxy6b8jhqMopR1wTjG4WeBUIk0sdyDo7f8ejt2hdZy30qsZo
48. Jiao, S.: Research on the influencing factors of online shopping based on hedonic shopping and practical shopping (in Chinese). J. Commer. Econ. 67–68 (2015)
49. Wei, P.-S., Lu, H.-P.: An examination of the celebrity endorsements and online customer reviews influence female consumers' shopping behavior. Comput. Hum. Behav. **29**, 193–201 (2013). https://doi.org/10.1016/j.chb.2012.08.005
50. Konstan, J.A., Simon Rosser, B.R., Ross, M.W., Stanton, J., Edwards, W.M.: The story of subject naught: a cautionary but optimistic tale of internet survey research. J. Comput.-Mediat. Commun. **10**, 00 (2005). https://doi.org/10.1111/j.1083-6101.2005.tb00248.x
51. Williams, B., Onsman, A., Brown, T.: Exploratory factor analysis: a five-step guide for novices. Australasian J. Paramed. **8**, 1–10 (2010). https://doi.org/10.33151/ajp.8.3.93
52. George, D., Mallery, P.: SPSS for Windows Step by Step: A Simple Study Guide and Reference, 17.0 Update. Allyn & Bacon, Boston (2009)
53. Horn, J.L.: A rationale and test for the number of factors in factor analysis. Psychometrika **30**, 179–185 (1965). https://doi.org/10.1007/BF02289447
54. Wang, Y.-S.: Assessment of learner satisfaction with asynchronous electronic learning systems. Inf. Manage. **41**, 75–86 (2003). https://doi.org/10.1016/S0378-7206(03)00028-4

Personal Information Protection Behaviors of Consumers in Different Country Context and User Interface Designs

Tianlan Wei[1], Cong Cao[1]([⊠]) [iD], and Yangyan Shi[2] [iD]

[1] Zhejiang University of Technology, Hangzhou, China
congcao@zjut.edu.cn
[2] Macquarie University, Sydney, Australia

Abstract. Internet information security is getting more attention. Users are adopting more and more ways to protect their information when browsing the web and shopping online, and more users are choosing not to disclose personal information to websites. Many factors influence consumers' privacy disclosure intention. This study innovatively introduces consumers' country background and website user interface design to explore their influence on behavioural intention. We developed a model of factors influencing consumers' intention to disclose personal information, organized experiments to collect data, and conducted an empirical study using partial least squares structural equation modeling (PLS-SEM). The study results showed that consumers' general trust in companies is influenced by many factors and significantly affects consumers' intention to disclose information. Corporate reputation significantly affects consumers' intention to disclose information directly and indirectly. Consumers' privacy concerns can also have a significant impact. Country context and user interface design also influenced consumer behaviour, but not as much as corporate reputation and consumer privacy concerns. Research provides targeted development recommendations for consumers, businesses, and legislators.

Keywords: Data disclosure · Privacy concerns · E-commerce · Trust · User face design · PLS-SEM

1 Introduction

Many data and phenomena indicate that the digital economy and e-commerce are growing unprecedented. According to the United Nations Conference on Trade and Development, global Internet bandwidth grew by 33% in 2020. Monthly global data traffic is expected to grow from 230 bytes in 2020 to 780 bytes in 2026 [1]. E-commerce is also growing at an unprecedented rate, significantly when the COVID-19 outbreak shifted more and more transactions online. The United Nations Conference on Trade and Development counted e-commerce in countries such as China, the United States, and South Korea, which account for 65% of the global B2C e-commerce volume. The report [2] shows that online retail as a percentage of total retail sales in these countries increased

© The Author(s), under exclusive license to Springer Nature Switzerland AG 2022
P.-L. P. Rau (Ed.): HCII 2022, LNCS 13313, pp. 82–98, 2022.
https://doi.org/10.1007/978-3-031-06050-2_7

by 3% in 2020 (16% to 19%), a percentage that was 2% in 2019; most likely due to the epidemic, total retail sales in these countries decreased by 1% in 2020, while total e-commerce retail sales increased by 22%. Similarly, according to Insider Intelligence, global e-commerce sales grew by 25.7% to 4.213 trillion USD in 2020, compared to total global retail sales of about 24 trillion dollars, a decline of 2.8% [3].

With the digital economy and e-commerce, the Internet has been integrated into many aspects of modern life. Every day, many users shop, place orders and check information through websites and mobile applications. Websites inevitably need users' personal information, and merchants will collect users' behavioural habits. As a result, personal information data security has received attention, and scholars in various fields have analyzed data security's technical and legal aspects.

On May 25, 2018, the General Data Protection Regulation issued by the European Parliament and the Council of the European Union came into force [4]. This regulation includes stringent data protection provisions. As it extends to all websites related to E.U. residents, most companies will first design their web pages and implement appropriate data protection practices according to this standard. The General Data Protection Regulation (GDPR) requires websites to obtain users' consent or refusal to collect user information, so privacy solicitation notices will not be turned off outright [5]. However, different websites may design different information collection pop-ups. The screen-to-body ratio, colour, button distribution, and other features of these pop-ups may affect users' choices.

New development issues are emerging in privacy policies, national environments, and the rapid growth of e-commerce. The E.U.'s General Data Protection Regulation and national privacy and information security regulations require companies to consult with consumers before collecting their information. Consumers will make choices based on their habits and understanding. At the same time, many factors can influence consumers' decisions to disclose personal information. Therefore, we proposed the following research questions.

- What kind of privacy protection behaviour do people from different regions, cultures, and educational backgrounds use websites?
- What are people's reactions to website privacy protection agreements?
- How does the design of different information collection pop-ups affect users' willingness to disclose personal information?

In this study, we first analyzed the legal and public opinion environment of personal information protection in Europe, Australia, and China through legal comparison and literature review to outline the legal background of each region. By summarizing historical research, we proposed factors influencing consumers' intention to disclose personal information during online consumption, proposed research hypotheses, and design models.

We then built a mock-up webpage to recreate a scenario of a consumer buying a high-end sports camera online. The webpage is compliant with strict GDPR standards. The shopping site applied to collect consumers' preferences to provide personalized services and improve the quality of services, such as the customer's hobby sports and frequently browsed photography equipment. The authorization of personal information will help to improve the consumer's user experience. We observe and record volunteers shopping in an experimental scenario and collect their behaviour of providing personal information or not.

The website was open to volunteers worldwide, so it helped us analyze the impact of different country contexts on consumers' disclosure of personal information. We analyzed the behavioural choice of whether consumers ultimately agree to disclose personal information to the website by processing the data using the partial least squares structural equation modeling (PLS-SEM) method to verify whether the model assumptions hold.

2 Theoretical Background and Hypotheses Development

Studies of consumers' intention to disclose personal information often use Privacy Calculus Theory. This theory suggests that customers are willing to disclose personal information when fair procedures protect their privacy [6]. Moreover, people face a tradeoff between perceived benefits and expected costs of privacy abuse and misuse when deciding whether to provide personal information to a service provider [7]. Users generally decide whether to provide personal information in response to a privacy solicitation request based on the expected benefits and the potential losses.

These findings are consistent with Social Exchange Theory, a classical sociological theory that states that people will only engage in exchanges if the expected outcome is positive relative to the expected cost [8]. When consumers are faced with the choice of whether to provide personal information, they will only disclose personal data when the perceived benefits outweigh the associated risks [9]. Kokolakis believes consumers may see disclosure as a quid pro quo for service providers to provide personalized services, i.e., "You tell me, and I tell you." (Fig. 1) [10] .

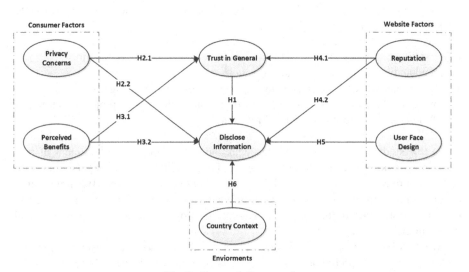

Fig. 1. Research framework.

2.1 Trust in General

Establishing consumer trust is one of the critical issues in the current development of e-commerce. For the definition of trust, scholars in new fields give different explanations. Psychology believes that trust is a relatively stable personality trait that people gradually form through social learning [11]. The field of sociology considers trust as a cycle between individuals based on risk and behaviour and as a subjective assessment of risk by individuals [12].

Many studies of consumer trust have been conducted by scholars in e-commerce, with specific definitions and understandings of consumer trust. Corritore and Kracher define online trust as a relationship in which an individual trusts a particular transaction or website [13]. McKnight et al. summarized previous research and definitions of the dimensions of trust, measuring trust in five dimensions: structure, personality, perception, intention, and behaviour [14]. Yuan summarized previous studies to classify and summarize the factors influencing consumer trust into consumers' factors, commerce vendors' factors, and security [15].

Many scholarly studies have shown that trust may be the most influential factor in consumers' willingness to disclose personal information [16–19]. Some studies of interpersonal interaction contexts also confirm trust as a prerequisite for the provision of personal information, as it reduces the risks associated with the provision of personal information [20]. Wakefield's research found that user trust and privacy beliefs create incentives for consumers to disclose personal information online. This effect is more pronounced for users with high Internet security concerns [21]. When consumers believe that a website will protect their personal information well and not over collect or misuse it, consumers' perceived risk is lower. Therefore, trust in the website is generated. Consumer trust is likely to impact consumers' behavioural intentions directly. Therefore, it is inferred that trust will influence consumers' information disclosure behaviour. Our study, therefore, proposes the following hypothesis.

Hypothesis 1: Consumer trust in general for the website has a significant positive impact on users' willingness to disclose information.

2.2 Consumer Factors

Privacy concerns are associated with people's perceptions after receiving specific information [22] and are a salient dispositional belief [23]. Smith et al. consider privacy concerns "the degree to which an individual believes that a high potential for loss is associated with releasing personal information to a firm" [24]. Some scholars have studied and validated the impact of online privacy concerns on consumers' online shopping behaviour. Dinev and Hart conducted an empirical survey of 422 respondents to investigate the factors influencing consumers' online privacy concerns and behavioural intentions to transact online [25]. Eastlick et al. found that consumers' privacy concerns negatively affect consumers' purchase intentions directly and indirectly through trust when studying the effects of consumers' privacy concerns and perceived merchant reputation on consumers' trust and other feelings [26]. In short, people's perception of the risk of misuse or abuse of personal information may affect their trust in companies and their intention to disclose personal information. Therefore, this study proposes the following hypothesis.

Hypothesis 2.1: Privacy concerns significantly negatively impact users' trust in general.

Some studies have also confirmed that consumers' privacy concerns about online information have a negative effect on their intention to disclose personal information. For example, Sheehan and Hoy's study found that the greater the consumer's concerns about the privacy of online information, the lower the consumer's online registration rate and the more they choose to provide fake, or incomplete, personal information and reduce their trust in the website [27]. Dinev et al. found that privacy concerns had a significant adverse effect on the intention to provide information when studying the factors influencing the intention to provide information in online transactions [28]. At the same time, consumers may be reluctant to give companies excessive information permissions if they do not know how they will use their information [29]. Therefore, this study proposes the following hypothesis.

Hypothesis 2.2: Privacy concerns significantly negatively impact users' willingness to disclose information.

On the other hand, privacy concerns do not always prevent consumers from disclosing personal information online. A phenomenon is known as the "privacy paradox" [30] because the perceived benefits of the consumer self may offset the perceived costs. In this model, an individual's perception of the value gained by disclosing personal information is the perceived benefit. Fernandes T. et al. analyzed perceived benefits by splitting them into perceived utilitarian and hedonic benefits [31]. From a utilitarian perspective, consumers are concerned with purchasing a product or service efficiently and timely; hedonic values satisfy consumers' need for escapism, entertainment, or emotional release [32]. Studies have more often used utilitarian values to measure consumers' perceived usefulness. However, perceived hedonic benefits can play an important role [33]. Although privacy issues have been relatively well studied in some literature, more insights are needed regarding the impact of hedonic and utilitarian interests on the data disclosure decision process [34]. Synthesizing the findings of previous studies, we can assume that perceived interests motivate people to disclose personal information, even if they claim to care about privacy. Therefore, this study proposes the following hypothesis.

Hypothesis 3.1: Perceived benefits have a significant positive impact on users' trust in general.

Hypothesis 3.2: Perceived benefits have a significant positive impact on users' willingness to disclose information.

2.3   Website Factors

Reputation is the degree to which the public perceives that the company is honest, caring, and fulfilling agreements with consumers [35]. The literature [35, 36] suggests that reputation positively affects trust in traditional markets and online environments. Burke et al. argue that reputation not only creates a "halo effect" for quality firms but can even reduce consumers' price sensitivity and directly attract consumers to choose [37]. The literature [38] found that consumers will be more likely to give information to a reputable business when confronted with a privacy information solicitation notice.

At the same time, the reputation of a company and its website have a broad impact, and what people are saying about the web page will influence the choice of more new users. Our study, therefore, proposes the following hypothesis.

Hypothesis 4.1: Website reputation has a significant positive impact on users' trust in general.

Hypothesis 4.2: Website reputation has a significant positive impact on users' willingness to disclose information.

Web pop-ups displaying privacy agreements are essential for companies to solicit personal information from users. This study will focus on the user interface design of pop-ups to analyze the impact of human-computer interaction interfaces on consumer choice - the strict requirements of the E.U. General Data Protection Regulation has led to a dramatic change in webpage cookie request pop-ups, requiring that webpage cookie request pop-ups must not be directly closed and require users to agree or reject [4]. Through interviews with library users, Imler et al. found that only 16% of users would seek services through pop-up windows [39], which reflects those pop-ups have a limited impact on users. Companies need to use reasonable ways to increase users' attention to pop-ups, especially when the content of pop-ups is must-know information security information. A clear and reasonable design of pop-ups may increase users' trust incorporate web pages. In contrast, the design of the pop-up interface for personal information solicitation requests is likely to have an implicit impact on consumers' choices and ultimately influence users' willingness to disclose personal information. Therefore, this study proposes the following hypothesis.

Hypothesis 5: Quality of user interface design has a significant positive impact on users' willingness to disclose information.

2.4 Environments

When consumers make decisions, they may not be determined exclusively by rational calculations based on expected costs and benefits; other elements independent of objective tradeoffs may also influence individual intentions [40]. Some scholars have argued that rationality has a limited impact when people make privacy disclosure choices after developing economic models. Acquisti and Grossklags point out that "in the presence of complex, ramified consequences associated with the protection or release of personal information, our innate bounded rationality limits our ability to acquire, memorize and process all relevant information, and it makes us rely on simplified mental models" [41]. That is, consumers' intention to disclose information is influenced by cognitive biases. Barth and De Jong thus propose, based on the privacy paradox, that "to a greater extent, decision-making takes place on an irrational level rather than on a rational one" [42]. Scholar Quinn applied habit as a process gratification to media usage scenarios and argued that habit and other benefits could impact consumers' privacy concerns [43]. In summary, users' consumption habits affect their trust in general. In contrast, the information disclosure habits formed by consumers in the past can influence consumers' current disclosure intentions, along with a lack of concern for information security issues. Therefore, we proposed the following hypothesis.

Therefore, we believe personal context may also potentially impact consumers' privacy disclosure intentions. This phenomenon is particularly pronounced in different national contexts. Our study is conducted with consumers from multiple countries, including China, Australia, and the European Union, and volunteers will have different national backgrounds, education levels, and online shopping habits. Therefore, we proposed the following hypothesis.

Hypothesis 6: Country Context has a significant positive impact on users' willingness to disclose information.

3 Methods

3.1 Research Methodology

The experiment was conducted online, and all volunteers could perform the simulation and answer the questionnaire through our virtual website. In addition to personal information, all questions in the questionnaire were measured by the 7-point Likert scale. The scale design in the questionnaire was based on proven scales from similar studies in the past. Volunteers were asked to rate the questions on a scale of 1 to 7, depending on their situation, with 1 indicating strong disagreement and 7 indicating strong agreement. Participants participated voluntarily and were assured of complete confidentiality to reduce common method bias [44].

In the experiment, we designed a virtual online shopping website. We invited participants to simulate the purchase of high-end sports cameras on the website. We observed the participants during the simulated shopping to exploring their intention to disclose personal information and related information protection behaviours. After the mock shopping was completed, we asked the participants some questions to satisfy the data collection needs. After the virtual website and questionnaire design were completed, we conducted a small-scale test in the relevant areas. We collected 30 experimental results to check whether the experimental process was scientific and feasible and whether the reliability and validity met the research needs and made appropriate adjustments based on the participants' suggestions. As a result, we obtained a formal experimental system.

After the initial experimental data collection, we used the PLS-SEM statistical technique for data processing and analysis, using the SmartPLS 3.3.5 software to address possible non-normality issues, allowing non-parametric tests [45]. Furthermore, we used this method for data evaluation because the PLS-SEM technique is less restrictive to experimental data and better suited to the conditions of this study. Another advantage of this method is that it can efficiently handle reflective and formative measurement models without identification problems.

3.2 Sampling and Data Collection

The demographic profile of respondents is shown in Table 1. The experimental participant volunteers were evenly distributed between males and females, with young and middle-aged adults aged 25 to 45 years accounting for 85.93% of the study participants. The age group of participants was mainly concentrated between 25 and 35 years, accounting for

58.52%. All of the participants had received or were currently pursuing higher education, with 65.93% of them pursuing a bachelor's degree and the remainder a master's degree and higher.

In this study, participants were restricted to be 24 years of age or older and have a high education level. These restrictions are motivated by the concern for cross-border e-commerce consumers. In cross-border e-commerce, consumers often need to have the necessary knowledge and financial foundation and experience online shopping. Therefore, the participants in the experiment are more in line with the current consumer profile of online shopping platforms, which can improve the experiment's credibility to a certain extent.

Table 1. Demographic profile of respondents, $N = 135$.

Measure	Category	N	Percent
Gender	Male	65	48.15%
	Female	70	51.85%
Age	25–35	79	58.52%
	36–45	37	27.41%
	46–55	13	9.63%
	Over 55	6	4.44%
Education	Undergraduate	89	65.93%
	Postgraduate	46	34.07%

4 Results

4.1 Measurement Model

After data collection, we used internal consistency reliability to determine the reliability of each construct measurement method. Cronbach's Alpha, Composite Reliability, Average Variance Extracted (AVE) three parameters were used to assess the validity and reliability of the scale. According to the measurements in Table [2], the values of Composite Reliability (CR) are all higher than 0.900, which far exceeds the value of 0.798 recommended by Hair et al. [46]. Meanwhile, Cronbach's Coefficient α (CCA) [47] is more significant than 0.7 for each structure, as suggested by Hair et al. [48] and Nunnally and Bernstein [49]. Average Variance Extracted (AVE) exceeds the recommended 0.5 [50, 51]. These data indicate that the measurements of each structure in this study have good internal consistency (Table 2).

On the other hand, we analyze the construct validity of the study using three coefficients: content validity, convergent validity, and discriminant validity. Their content validity is guaranteed since the relevant questions in the study are adapted from the existing literature. As shown in table [3], the square root of the AVE for any construct in the model is greater than the corresponding correlation values for the other constructs. Moreover, as shown in table [4], the standardized outer loadings for all indicators in the constructs are more significant than 0.820. The AVE for the different constructions is

Table 2. Descriptive statistics for the constructs

	CCA	CR	AVE
Trust in General (Trust)	0.937	0.970	0.941
Disclose Information (Infor)	0.917	0.960	0.923
Reputation (Reput)	0.933	0.952	0.833
User Face Design (Desig)	0.887	0.930	0.816
Privacy Concerns (Conce)	0.931	0.951	0.830
Perceived Benefits (Benef)	0.935	0.958	0.885
Country Context (Count)	0.949	0.966	0.906

also known to be greater than 0.5 [52]. Therefore, it can be considered that the measurements of the different constructions in this study have sufficient judgmental validity (Table 3 and 4) [51].

Table 3. Correlations among constructs and the square root of the *AVE*.

	Trust	Infor	Reput	Desig	Conce	Benef	Count
Trust	**0.970**						
Infor	0.912	**0.961**					
Reput	0.734	0.768	**0.913**				
Desig	0.864	0.857	0.788	**0.903**			
Conce	0.257	0.245	0.009	0.250	**0.911**		
Benef	−0.277	−0.331	−0.324	−0.343	−0.739	**0.941**	
Count	0.467	0.424	−0.014	0.290	0.614	−0.374	**0.952**

Note: Bold number represent the square roots of the AVEs.

Table 4. Factor loadings and cross loadings.

	Trust	Infor	Reput	Desig	Conce	Benef	Count
Trust.1	**0.971**	0.895	0.726	0.838	0.234	−0.246	0.435
Trust.2	**0.969**	0.874	0.699	0.839	0.265	−0.292	0.471
Infor.1	0.892	**0.962**	0.737	0.836	0.275	−0.322	0.430
Infor.2	0.860	**0.960**	0.738	0.810	0.196	−0.314	0.385

(*continued*)

Table 4. (*continued*)

	Trust	Infor	Reput	Desig	Conce	Benef	Count
Reput.1	0.711	0.715	**0.912**	0.733	0.000	−0.253	0.029
Reput.2	0.674	0.713	**0.923**	0.741	−0.028	−0.264	−0.059
Reput.3	0.655	0.694	**0.913**	0.711	0.005	−0.323	0.018
Reput.4	0.639	0.680	**0.902**	0.691	0.058	−0.348	− 0.039
Desig.1	0.847	0.825	0.761	**0.932**	0.253	−0.329	0.288
Desig.2	0.779	0.775	0.717	**0.905**	0.218	−0.300	0.244
Desig.3	0.709	0.717	0.654	**0.871**	0.203	−0.301	0.253
Conce.1	0.279	0.262	0.028	0.274	**0.943**	−0.697	0.588
Conce.2	0.219	0.214	0.031	0.200	**0.922**	−0.668	0.533
Conce.3	0.244	0.218	−0.038	0.228	**0.926**	−0.674	0.623
Conce.4	0.179	0.190	0.010	0.196	**0.849**	−0.656	0.477
Benef.1	−0.280	−0.317	−0.322	−0.344	−0.697	**0.943**	−0.364
Benef.2	−0.254	−0.326	−0.272	−0.296	−0.710	**0.946**	−0.371
Benef.3	−0.246	−0.289	−0.324	−0.329	−0.677	**0.933**	−0.319
Count.1	0.468	0.445	−0.023	0.294	0.608	−0.359	**0.970**
Count.2	0.367	0.310	−0.069	0.201	0.556	−0.337	**0.921**
Count.3	0.479	0.432	0.037	0.313	0.585	−0.370	**0.964**

Note: Bold number indicate outer loading on the assigned constructs.

4.2 Structural Model

In this study, the statistical significance of the t-values of the path coefficients in the model was tested using bootstrapping of SmartPLS 3.3.5. The number of samples obtained for the experiment was 135. After data collation and calculation, the individual path coefficients of the model and the statistical significance test results are shown in Fig. 2. In the model building process, we proposed nine hypotheses. The analysis results showed that seven of them met the statistical significance test: the effect of trust in general on disclosure intention, the positive effect of privacy concerns and reputation on users' trust and disclosure intention, the effect of user face design on disclosure intention, and the effect of country context on disclosure intention. Two additional hypotheses did not meet the statistical significance test in our study: the effect of consumers' perceived benefits on trust and intention to disclose information. The analysis also revealed that the degree of influence of different factors on consumers' privacy disclosure intentions was different: website reputation had a very significant effect on the formation of consumers' overall trust, followed by consumers' privacy concerns, and overall trust had the most significant influence on consumers' information disclosure intentions. Country environmental context and user interface design are positive. However, the strength of the influence is weaker compared to other factors.

Among the data analysis techniques used in this study, the coefficient of determination (R^2) is often used to assess the model's predictive ability. It is the most commonly used coefficient when evaluating the structural model [53]. The value of R^2 is between 0 and 1, with higher values implying a more vital predictive ability of the hypothesis. In this study, the R^2 of the experimental data was 0.870, indicating that the model has enough explanatory power of the factors influencing consumers' privacy disclosure intentions [51].

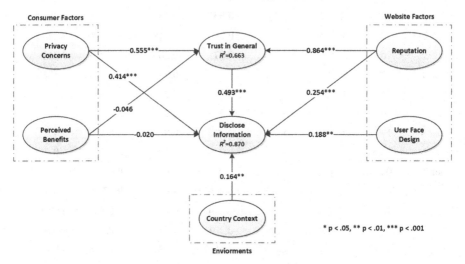

Fig. 2. PLS-SEM analysis results.

5   Discussion and Implication

5.1   Summary of Results

This study focuses on customers' information protection behaviour in cross-border e-commerce when making online purchases and seeks and verifies the factors influencing consumers' intention and behaviour to disclose their personal information. By compiling and analyzing existing studies, we categorized the relevant influencing factors into factors of companies and their websites, consumers themselves, and the influence of the national environment on consumers. After experimenting, the research team used PLS-SEM techniques to evaluate the research model and hypotheses. The results showed that many elements influence contemporary consumers' privacy disclosure behaviour when online cross-border purchases. The experimental data demonstrated that consumers' privacy concerns, corporate input, user face design, and national environmental context directly or indirectly influence consumers' intention to disclose personal information.

Based on the empirical study, we can conclude that the consumer's country context and the user page design of the webpage have a significant influence on the consumer's information protection behaviour. However, the influence of these two factors is limited, and they influence consumers' behaviour and intention to disclose personal information but do not play a decisive or critical role. Among the influential factors verified in this study, the degree of consumers' privacy concern and corporate reputation, which directly or indirectly influence consumers' intention to protect privacy to a greater extent, is the most significant influential elements. Some factors directly influence consumers' privacy protection behaviour and indirectly influence consumers' privacy disclosure intention by affecting consumers' trust in service providers. Therefore, there are more reasonable ways for companies to build consumers' trust in the company's services in general, thus facilitating trade closure. In actual cross-border e-commerce transactions, consumer trust-building has become an increasingly important part of a company's external development. It can contribute to sustainable business development in many ways [54].

However, the research experiment results do not validate all of our proposed hypotheses. Consumers' perceived benefits in this study do not influence their intention to disclose personal information, nor do they help companies build their trust in them. After comparing different studies, we believe that some differences in the experimental design may make it challenging to test our hypotheses. In some studies in history, scholars would indicate to experiment participants or questionnaire fillers that if they provided their personal information, they would be able to receive some money or enjoy some discounts in shopping. In our experiments, we do not increase consumers' perceived benefits more intuitively, such as through money. To better recreate the current state of information collected on the web in general, we only informed participants that we would be able to improve the quality of our services through the personal information they provided, for example, by pushing them personalized products that are more suitable for them. The experiment results do not support our hypothesis, so we believe there is value in conducting a more in-depth study on the issue of the impact of perceived benefits, from which perhaps companies will find new ideas for development.

In summary, among the factors influencing consumers' privacy disclosure intention, the indirect influence of corporate reputation through building consumer trust formation is significant. Consumers' privacy concerns can significantly impact consumers' choices from both direct and indirect perspectives. We focus on these two aspects while combining the context of the consumer country environment and the user interface design of the service website to find new development paths that can help enhance the development of cross-border e-commerce while better protecting consumer privacy.

5.2 Implication for Theory

Around the beginning of the 21st century, as e-commerce began to develop, scholars began to study users' factor concerns in the Internet world and focus on what factors affect users' intention to disclose privacy. Many of them were developed based on consumers' perceived benefits and risks in previous experiments. Our study's innovative analysis of the effects of country context and user interface design on privacy-preserving behaviour enriches the research.

The experiment went well, and the hypotheses of the study were validated. The results show that consumers' national environmental background can influence their privacy protection behaviour. Such influence can come from many sources, such as legal background, ethnic habits, and news reports. When the media in a particular region frequently report the risk or privacy information leakage, users may act more to protect their privacy due to the regional influence of culture [55]. Differences in objective conditions in different countries may also influence consumers' privacy protection behaviours. For example, in China, well-established courier transit stations allow consumers to obtain adequate courier services by simply providing the address of the transit station, so many people use this method to protect their address information. More regional differences in the environment can have different effects on consumer behaviour. On the other hand, a cleaner, clearer user interface design in the experiment can increase consumers' intention to provide personal information. Compared to previous studies, these findings are innovative and enrich the existing theoretical research on consumers' information protection behaviours.

The study results show that corporate reputation and consumer privacy concerns remain the most important factors affecting consumer trust and privacy disclosure intention. Building a good reputation and consumer trust has been the most crucial concern for the companies concerned. Our study found that consumers' perceived benefits were not effective in influencing their privacy protection behaviour, which is inconsistent with previous research theories. We believe that the main reason for this phenomenon is that the perceived benefit we give in our experiments is "better service" rather than money. This may also be since consumers' privacy concerns are more pronounced, and the threshold of expected benefits is higher as their online shopping experience increases due to the growing sophistication of cross-border e-commerce. These issues deserve in-depth study.

In conclusion, this study enriches the theoretical study of consumer privacy protection behaviour by expanding on existing research to explore the design of national environments and privacy information solicitation pop-up windows. The study also provides new ideas for future theoretical and practical development.

5.3 Implication for Practice

Internet companies often want to grasp more information about their users, whether their personal information, browsing preferences, or shopping habits. The mastery of information can help companies grasp user characteristics, provide personalized services to users through algorithms better, and conduct in-depth marketing campaigns through extensive data analysis and other means. These development needs have become the motivation for companies to collect more personal information from consumers.

This study experimentally identifies factors that influence consumer privacy protection behaviour. By changing these conditions, companies can better create a secure environment and provide reliable services to consumers, prompting them to form trust and be willing to provide the necessary information.

Consumers' trust is the most important factor influencing consumers' privacy disclosure intentions. Moreover, there are many ways to build consumer trust. Creating a good reputation, providing reliable service to customers, and ensuring good product quality can all help companies build consumer trust. Furthermore, building consumer trust facilitates access to more data, and it has benefits in many ways, such as expanding the reach and increasing profits [56]. Building consumer trust is essential and worthwhile for companies. In addition, companies need to pay special attention to building a good reputation because reputation directly influences consumer disclosure intentions and indirectly influences consumer behaviour by affecting consumers' trust in general.

It makes sense for consumers to maintain the necessary privacy concern. Simple improvement of service quality has become challenging to attract consumers to provide their personal information, which is beneficial to protect information security. At the same time, consumers should remain independent and rational when they are concerned about protecting their information and avoid being put at risk by the higher perceived benefits of induced visual design.

6 Conclusion

The development of the Internet and e-commerce has given related companies the ability to collect more consumer information and data. Ensuring that this data is not stolen or misused has become a common concern for consumers, businesses, and governments worldwide. Consumers will decide how to protect their personal information based on the environment, their own needs, corporate reputation, and other elements. Users' information protection behaviour, or privacy disclosure intention, is influenced by various elements. With the internationalization of e-commerce and the maturity of online shopping platforms, differences in national backgrounds are causing users to make different choices. In contrast, user interface design quietly influences consumer choices. This study adds these two factors to the formal study of consumers' intention to disclose personal information and analyzes their influence through an empirical study.

By setting up a virtual shopping website, observing experimenters' privacy-preserving behaviours during the simulated shopping process, and using PLS-SEM for post-data analysis, we validated a model of factors influencing consumers' intention to disclose personal information. The results show that consumers' trust, influenced by many factors, affects their intention to disclose information. Corporate reputation is a strong influence on disclosure intention both directly and indirectly. At the same time, consumer privacy concern is another critical factor. Consumers' national environmental background and the website's user interface design have a weaker influence than the above two factors. The study's findings enrich the existing theoretical research and provide suggestions for development for companies, consumers, and legislators.

Although this study discusses consumer country context and user interface design, the study is not thorough enough. In the experiment, we imposed significant restrictions on the scope of the subjects, such as limiting the age to 25 years or older. Although these restrictions helped improve the study's efficiency, they led to a lack of generalizability of the findings. There is a need to expand the range of subjects in future studies and obtain more generalizable findings.

At the same time, participants showed weaker responses to perceived benefits in our experiments. Future research is necessary to explore what leads to such a phenomenon. For example, it could be analyzed whether the sensitivity of contemporary consumers facing perceived benefits in e-commerce has decreased and whether the impact of perceived benefits has changed.

Acknowledgments. This study is supported by grants from the Zhejiang University of Technology Humanities and Social Sciences Pre-Research Fund Project (GZ21731320013), the Zhejiang University of Technology Subject Reform Project (GZ21511320030), and China's National Undergraduate Innovation and Entrepreneurship Training Program (File No. 202110337048).

References

1. UNCTAD: Digital economy report 2021. Tech. rep., United Nations Conference on Trade and Development, Palais des Nations, 8–14, Av. de la Paix, 1211 Geneva 10, Switzerland (2021)
2. UNCTAD: Estimates of global e-commerce 2019 and preliminary assessment ofcovid-19 impact on online retail 2020. Tech. rep., United Nations Conference on Trade and Development, Palais des Nations, 8–14, Av. de la Paix, 1211 Geneva 10, Switzerland (2021)
3. Huang, G.B.: Global ecommerce forecast 2021(2021). https://www.emarketer.com
4. Regulation, P.: Regulation (EU) 2016/679 of the European Parliament and of the Council. Regulation (EU), 679, (2016)
5. Voigt, P., Von dem Bussche, A.: The EU General Data Protection Regulation (GDPR). A Practical Guide, 1st edn., vol. 10, pp. 10–5555 Springer, Cham (2017). https://doi.org/10.1007/978-3-319-57959-7
6. Culnan, M.J., Armstrong, P.K.: Information privacy concerns, procedural fairness, and impersonal trust: an empirical investigation. Organ. Sci. **10**(1), 104–115 (1999)
7. Robinson, C.: Disclosure of personal data in ecommerce: a cross-national comparison of Estonia and the united states. Telematics Inform. **34**(2), 569–582 (2017)
8. Leach, E.: Social BEhavior: Its Elementary Forms. Harcourt, Brace (1961)
9. Martin, K.D., Murphy, P.E.: The role of data privacy in marketing. J. Acad. Mark. Sci. **45**(2), 135–155 (2016). https://doi.org/10.1007/s11747-016-0495-4
10. Kokolakis, S.: Privacy attitudes and privacy behaviour: a review of current research on the privacy paradox phenomenon. Comput. Secur. **64**, 122–134 (2017)
11. Punyatoya, P.: Effects of cognitive and affective trust on online customer behavior. Market. Intell. Plann. **37**(2018)
12. Huang, J.S., Pan, S.L.: China's suning: combining online and offline businesses units. In: Digital Enablement and Innovation in China: A Casebook, pp. 39–44. World Scientific, Beijing (2019)
13. Corritore, C.L., Kracher, B., Wiedenbeck, S.: On-line trust: concepts, evolving themes, a model. Int. J. Hum Comput Stud. **58**(6), 737–758 (2003)
14. Liu, Y., Tang, X.: The effects of online trust-building mechanisms on trust and repurchase intentions: an empirical study on eBay. Inf. Technol. People **31**(2018)
15. Liang, Y.: Research on factors affecting mobile E-commerce consumer trust. In: Zhang, R., Zhang, Z., Liu, K., Zhang, J. (eds.) LISS 2013, pp. 1023–1028. Springer, Berlin (2013). https://doi.org/10.1007/978-3-642-40660-7_153
16. Hoffman, D.L., Novak, T.P., Peralta, M.A.: Information privacy in the marketspace: implications for the commercial uses of anonymity on the web. Inf. Soc. **15**(2), 129–139 (1999)
17. Jarvenpaa, S.L., Tractinsky, N., Vitale, M.: Consumer trust in an internet store. Inf. Technol. Manage. **1**(1), 45–71 (2000)
18. Jarvenpaa, S.L., Knoll, K., Leidner, D.E.: Is anybody out there? Antecedents of trust in global virtual teams. J. Manag. Inf. Syst. **14**(4), 29–64 (1998)
19. Swaminathan, V., Lepkowska-White, E., Rao, B.P.: Browsers or buyers in cyberspace? An investigation of factors influencing electronic exchange. J. Comput. Mediat. Commun. **5**(2), JCMC523 (1999)

20. Steel, J.L.: Interpersonal correlates of trust and self-disclosure. Psychol. Rep. **68**(3 suppl), 1319–1320 (1991)
21. Wakefield, R.: The influence of user affect in online information disclosure. J. Strateg. Inf. Syst. **22**(2), 157–174 (2013)
22. Dinev, T., Hart, P.: An extended privacy calculus model for e-commerce transactions. Inf. Syst. Res. **17**(1), 61–80 (2006)
23. Bansal, G., Zahedi, F.M., Gefen, D.: Do context and personality matter? Trust and privacy concerns in disclosing private information online. Inf. Manag. **53**(1), 1–21 (2016)
24. Smith, H.J., Dinev, T., Xu, H.: Information privacy research: an interdisciplinary review. MIS Q. **35**, 989–1015 (2011)
25. Dinev, T., Hart, P.: Internet privacy concerns and social awareness as determinants of intention to transact. Int. J. Electron. Commer. **10**(2), 7–29 (2005)
26. Eastlick, M.A., Lotz, S.L., Warrington, P.: Understanding online B-to-C relationships: an integrated model of privacy concerns, trust, and commitment. J. Bus. Res. **59**(8), 877–886 (2006)
27. Sheehan, K.B., Hoy, M.G.: Flaming, complaining, abstaining: how online users respond to privacy concerns. J. Advert. **28**(3), 37–51 (1999)
28. Dinev, T., Hart, P., Mullen, M.R.: Internet privacy concerns and beliefs about government surveillance–an empirical investigation. J. Strateg. Inf. Syst. **17**(3), 214–233 (2008)
29. Yu, L., Li, H., He, W., Wang, F.K., Jiao, S.: A meta-analysis to explore privacy cognition and information disclosure of internet users. Int. J. Inf. Manage. **51**, 102015 (2020)
30. Bol, N., et al.: Understanding the effects of personalization as a privacy calculus: analyzing self-disclosure across health, news, and commerce contexts. J. Comput.-Mediat. Commun. **23**(6), 370–388 (2018)
31. Fernandes, T., Pereira, N.: Revisiting the privacy calculus: why are consumers (really) willing to disclose personal data online? Telematics Inform. **65**, 101717 (2021)
32. Sun, Y., Wang, N., Shen, X.L., Zhang, J.X.: Location information disclosure in location-based social network services: privacy calculus, benefit structure, and gender differences. Comput. Hum. Behav. **52**, 278–292 (2015)
33. Venkatesh, V., Morris, M.G.: Why don't men ever stop to ask for directions? Gender, social influence, and their role in technology acceptance and usage behavior. MIS Q **24**, 115–139 (2000)
34. Plangger, K., Montecchi, M.: Thinking beyond privacy calculus: investigating reactions to customer surveillance. J. Interact. Mark. **50**, 32–44 (2020)
35. Doney, P.M., Cannon, J.P.: An examination of the nature of trust in buyer–seller relationships. J. Mark. **61**(2), 35–51 (1997)
36. Ganesan, S.: Determinants of long-term orientation in buyer-seller relationships. J. Mark. **58**(2), 1–19 (1994)
37. Burke, P.F., Dowling, G., Wei, E.: The relative impact of corporate reputation on consumer choice: beyond a halo effect. J. Mark. Manag. **34**(1314), 1227–1257 (2018)
38. Earp, J.B., Baumer, D.: Innovative web use to learn about consumer behavior and online privacy. Commun. ACM **46**(4), 81–83 (2003)
39. Imler, B.B., Garcia, K.R., Clements, N.: Are reference pop-up widgets welcome or annoying? A usability study. Ref. Serv. Rev. **44**(3), 282–291 (2016)
40. Adjerid, I., Peer, E., Acquisti, A.: Beyond the privacy paradox: objective versus relative risk in privacy decision making. MIS Q. **42**(2), 465–488 (2018)
41. Acquisti, A., Grossklags, J.: What can behavioral economics teach us about privacy. Digit. Privacy Theory Technol. Pract. **18**, 363–377 (2007)
42. Barth, S., De Jong, M.D.: The privacy paradox–investigating discrepancies between expressed privacy concerns and actual online behavior–a systematic literature review. Telematics Inform. **34**(7), 1038–1058 (2017)

43. Quinn, K.: Why we share: a uses and gratifications approach to privacy regulation in social media use. J. Broadcast. Electron. Media **60**(1), 61–86 (2016)
44. Podsakoff, P.M., MacKenzie, S.B., Podsakoff, N.P.: Sources of method bias in social science research and recommendations on how to control it. Annu. Rev. Psychol. **63**, 539–569 (2012)
45. Ringle, C.M., Wende, S., Becker, J.M.: SmartPLS 3. SmartPLS GmbH, Boenningstedt. J. Serv, Sci. Manag. **10**(3), 32–49 (2015)
46. Sarstedt, M., Ringle, C.M., Hair, J.F., et al.: Partial least squares structural equation modeling. Handb. Market Res. **26**(1), 1–40 (2017)
47. Cronbach, L.J.: Coefficient alpha and the internal structure of tests. Psychometrika **16**(3), 297–334 (1951)
48. Hair, J.F.: Multivariate Data Analysis, 7th edn. Prentice Hall, Upper Saddle River (2009)
49. Nunnally, J.C.: Psychometric Theory 3E. Tata McGraw-Hill Education, New York (1994)
50. Forza, C.: Survey research in operations management: a process-based perspective. Int. J. Oper. Prod. Manag. **22**(2), 152–194 (2002)
51. Hair, J.F., Sarstedt, M., Ringle, C.M., Mena, J.A.: An assessment of the use of partial least squares structural equation modeling in marketing research. J. Acad. Mark. Sci. **40**(3), 414–433 (2012)
52. Barclay, D., Thompson, R., Higgins, C.: The partial least squares (PLS) approach to causal modeling: personal computer use as an illustration. Technol. Stud. **2** (1995)
53. Chin, W.W., Newsted, P.R.: Structural equation modeling analysis with small samples using partial least squares. Stat. Strat. Small Sample Res. **1**(1), 307–341 (1999)
54. Luhmann, N.: Trust and Power. Wiley, Chichester (2018)
55. Li, S.: Study on development of small and medium-sized enterprises cluster in china with view of regional cultural perspective. Sci. Res. **37**, 7–18 (2010)
56. Manchala, D.W.: E-commerce trust metrics and models. IEEE Internet Comput. **4**(2), 36–44 (2000)

Cross-Cultural Communication and Collaboration

Cosmonarrative and the Narrative Cosmos: Visual Narrative in Material-based Image

Zhonghao Chen[✉]

Xi'an Jiangtong-Liverpool University, Suzhou 215200, JS, China
Zhonghao.chen@xjtlu.edu.cn

Abstract. Visual narrative is an evolving interdisciplinarity that confronts the entanglement of narrative and visuality. The phenomenon of objective concretization (Simondon 2010) is increasingly apparent in both narrative and image domains. This deepening partitioning is self-limiting for interpreting the complexity of visual narrative among contemporary visual media and beyond. Cosmonarrative proposed is a theoretic framework for reinterpreting visual narrative in the realm of the material-based image by following Hui's (2019) cosmotechnics which acknowledges relativity, diversity and locality in the view of post-universality.

Keywords: Visual narrative · Material-based image · Cosmotechnics · Cosmonarrative

1 Introduction: The Question Concerning the Narrative Paradigm

Narrative has been an essential being that defines humans and their externalisation throughout the known histories. It ranges from oral myth literature, the trans-media narrative culture, to the phenomenon of digitalisation and virtualisation. Despite the diversity of narrative ecology, the permeation of linear story formula with descending exclusivity such as monomyth (Campbell 2003) exhibits its dominating algorithmic presence and unilateral development among our current landscapes of industrialisation and culturalization. In his enlightening essay "The question concerning technology in China an essay in cosmotechnics", Hui (2019) states the issues with the current technological recognition and introduces the term cosmotechnics. He questions the "universality", "globalisation", and "linearity" of technology. Further, he examines the features and evidence of techno diversity, specifically, its relationship with cosmic order and locality entangled with technological development. Cosmotechnics also critiques the "exclusive" nature of the contemporary technology culture and its linear progressiveness inherited from western logic and history, namely, colonialism and capitalism. Yuk expresses, "Preliminary definition of cosmotechnics as a unification between the cosmic order and the moral order through technical activities, to suggest that technology should be re-situated in broader reality, which enables it and also constraints it. The detachment of technology from such reality has resulted in the desire to be universalising and become the ground of everything. Following this view, narrative can also be seen suffering from similar situations and progression of institutionalisation and culturalization.

Joseph Campbell's (2003) brilliant journey into the mythic being of humankind is highly enlightening. After that, a delicate and universal formula was extracted out of the mythscape that materialised and fertilised generous allowance of applications across numerous media and expanding frontiers of narrative creation. The hero's journey has continually proved its essentiality through story, film, and new media such as games, interactive art, etc. This monomyth formula also incubates exchanging ground for trans- and cross-cultural communications, which unavoidably can be recognised as a global contribution and planetary achievement. Nevertheless, this formula and its "universality" progress unilaterally with consequences. Reminiscent of contemporary technology, story and narrative's detachment from its context and locality cascading into the constrain of formalistic configuration and functions as deductive information, to name particular phenomena such as formalism of arts and the visual art worlds, where content and context are stripped out to its essential elements for allowances of aesthetic impulse or intended outcomes (Bell 1969).

When I hear modern people complain of being lonely, I know what has happened. They have lost the cosmos.

--D.H. Lawrence, Apocalypse

Benjamin (1969) profoundly declaimed the impairment, even death of oral story-telling and depicted the decline of the story to mere information in his essay the storyteller. Furthermore, he illustrates the detachment of the body of the storyteller and the interactivity of the audience in terms of oral storytelling. The narrative and its individuation (Simondon 2013) transcend its organic and involving nature into a highly objectified utility where only self-containment is detectable and presentable—seeing the current spreadable mass media (Jenkins 2018) and expanding information capitalism. According to Benjamin's vision, it is alarming how accurate and predictable the evolution of narrative has been. With the advancement of practice and media, the inertia of obtaining an adequately orientated perspective of narrative recognition and reception lie in entropy. Moreover, the lack of conceptual and analytical tools or language for differentiating narratives of kinds today raises alarms.

ludonarrative dissonance, a term created by Hocking (2009), gained noticeable attention in his media critique of the well-known game "Bio Shock" regarding its narrative dissonance between the narrative tendency like theme and narrative facts generated by the ludological mechanism and technology such as a game console. In this context, the player as the main character confuses or even abandons their objectives as the saviour by endlessly indulging themself in the gameplay-generated narrative. These interactive or ludic facts distract thematic and moral ground with objectivism message betrayed in the story's actions. The narrative tendency such as theme and plot contradict the narrative facts of ludic activities, which to a certain degree renders the game Bio Shock as an obsolete piece of digital and interactive narrative work. This phenomenon can also be applied to other popular games, such as the legend of Zelda: Breath of the Wild. Similarly, in the Zelda tale, the player as the universal saviour tends to be endlessly attracted by the virtual exploration in this digital world sugarcoated by Zeldian goodies rather than saving the princess. The player manages to enjoy progressing along with the ludological/ interactive narrative of the game, such as fighting and mountain climbing, rather than following the storyline of the classical heroism.

Hence a new fairy tale of dissonance surfaces among the game communities: the bachelor prince.

The current dualistic debate of narratology vs ludology seems inefficient, out of context and irrelevant in the cases mentioned above. Yet, the phenomenon of ludonarrative dissonance resonates further with another significant sector of narrative: image-based visual narrative. Let us dive into the historically relevant formalism to visualise the issue better. The painting movement recognised as New York school and its timely context are top references, contextually speaking. As an informal group of artists loosely recognised as abstract expressionists. Their practice of painting/art confronts the urgency of painterly concerns and philosophical demands of their time. The individuality and heroic existence caught in the duration of the cold war and binary conflicts between the states and the USSR. With a loose glimpse of the works from this association, it is obvious to see the limitation of the term Abstract Expressionism implies for such a diverse body of works and creators (Leja et al. 1993).

Not only does the manifestation of the movement seem rigid, but also the primary theoretical and critical framing of its time. The main support and art critic of the group Greenberg (1939), the author of "Avant-garde and Kitsch 1939", confidently defines the painting as "canvas is canvas, paint is paint." The reductive manifestation again shuffles the diverse visual narrative styles, methods and painterly beings into a medium based formalism. This cultural gesture guaranteed the inevitability of the tragic staging of Zombie formalism (Hill 2016). On the contrary, located in USSR. Social realism sprouting out of nationally founded associations to create an opposing cultural and visual narrative. Of course, the narrative art applied here served as a form of propaganda rather than holistic visual storytelling (Groys 2019). It would be no surprise that recognition of zombie social realism has long been part of a narrative culture entangled somewhere somehow. In both cases, the tendency of "objectification" and "division" of both medium and message were anthropological phenomena where universalisation was attempted for the sake of illustrating deputised information and value. Tragically, in either scenario, the narrative potential is the subject of exploitation and regulation. The complex nature and co-existence of the medium, gesture, visuality and locality are ignored substantially for the sake of institutionalisation and culturalization.

Behind both the ludonarrative dissonance and medium debate mentioned above, self-limitation of the current narrative system and its evaluative glossary remains the critical problem. This problem also continually reveals cascading impacts of the dualistic quarrels within the narrative crisis.

2 Method: Cosmotechnicsc and Cosmonarrative

This textual exploration develops a methodology by introducing the cosmonarrative as a theoretic framework and conceptual tool for interpreting visual narrative's relative, eclectic and evolving nature in the domain of the material-based image. The work in progress, which qualitatively investigates the cross-cultural phenomenon of visual narrative, is accompanied by a systematic analysis of relevant cases. The examination and analysis are structured into four consecutive steps that will build on one another:

1. **Visual narrative: pictoriality and its narrative tendency.** In this section, a systematic study of pictorial narrative is conducted. The principles of pictorial storytelling are drafted out as a base of visual narrative;
2. **Interactive narrative: haptic and gestural.** Closer observations on material-based images such as painting reveal the traces of the craft (Leslie 1998), medium, and human presence. The configuration narrates haptically along the pictoriality of the images;
3. **Material narrative: visual narrative facts.** Cases' examinations in this section display the stories of materiality. The physical surroundings express and communicate to us through the material configuration. Paintings have been harvesting this feature of our physical world. Furthermore, it applies the materiality as part of the complex visual narratives;
4. **Cosmic as Locality: the worlds of creator and participator.** Revealing the cosmic being of cosmonarrative by extending the narrative beyond the material-based image itself into its locality, such as studio and viewers' orientation. The entanglement of locality informs the image-making as part of its medium, thus co-constituting the narrative fundamentally;

3 Examination and Analysis: Narrative Diversity

"The most elemental process of modern times is the conquest of the world as images."

--Martin Heidegger, Holzwege

In comparison to the formalist approach, London school, on the other hand, exhibits extremely versatile outcomes. Close examination of artists like Bacon and Kosseff reveals much secrecy of inspiration and complication.

…as if Bacon's paintings have gone feral.

--David Sylvester, Interviews with Francis Bacon

Bacon's painting forces the viewer to acknowledge the violence through pictorial reading and infusing the criminal compulsion into the body by tracing the gestural impasto stuck on the painting surface and soaked into the canvas. The desire to consume by destruction can be seen as a universality that breaks away from the virtuality and co-fabricates its narrative with an entangled and dialectic plurality. The non-traditional material and unconventional gestures provoke the observer's shivering and shuddering. The protective glass of the picture frame only makes all scenarios more unavoidable. The cracking and simultaneously shrinking surface yells out the illustrative arrangements composed by the artist without any reluctance. The self-definition or the tagging fashionably called these days is the minor concern of Bacon's representational materialisation.

Leon Kossoff is another vivid example. It appears that gravity was the only adversary of his painting universe. The artist sculpts away his canvas, where pigment is piled so thickly that supporting material has to be placed in between the strokes for holding the picture altogether from dripping down. The paintings depict the surrounding post-war landscape of London. Meanwhile, it refuses to be merely an image, but its paint scrape correlates to its locality with and beyond the painterly involvement.

Visual narrative in paintings mentioned above indicates love fairs of complications and entanglements of various narrative paradigms. This entangled narrative feast shackles the binary chains around it all the way.

3.1 Visual Narrative: Pictoriality and Its Narrative Tendency

Narrative art is one of the dominating paradigms that elucidates the known territory of pictorial storytelling. Narrative art, especially in the printing and the technical image (Flusser 2011), both aid the dematerialisation of visual narration. This is mainly due to the non-surface feature of the technical image and the sole focus on pictoriality. In the established discipline of image narrative investigation, such as art history, this tendency to interpret images detached from their what about and whereabouts has also been inseverable.

The specific properties of the pictorial narrative are built upon visual elements and principles (Klee 1964).

Besides the formalistic properties, tactics of representation are the reciprocal partner here. A large proportion of pictorial storytelling can be grouped into three categories (Diyong 2008).

- Pivotal Moment
- Simultaneous Arrangement
- Juxtaposition.

Pivotal Moment

Since pictorial art contains a large section of still image. The photographic being of capturing the pivotal moment is among the favoured tactics of image-makers. The pre-moving image mechanism is a powerful and suggestive way for evoking imagination and an evocative narrative setting. The sensation of trophy and triumph are always easily summonable in images of this kind (Fig. 1).

Simultaneous Arrangement

Close exanimation of Jackson Pollock's image, the sense of non-linearity dances with its exuberance. Traditional composition and the materialisation of time are merely the arte-facts of the past. We can receive all at once or scrutinise infinitely at one or multi-locations willingly and simultaneously. This "all over" mechanism plays with the essential image mechanism of simultaneous space and time intertwinement (Elkins 2018). It can also achieve a linear time scale by admitting ownership of the physically expansive picture plane (Fig. 2).

Fig. 1. A pivotal moment of the boxing game is depicted. "Dempsey and Firpo," by Bellow (1924).

Fig. 2. The works infinite ways of visual reading. "Number 31," by Pollock (1950).

The acknowledgement of the picture surface is not a unique feature of modernists. Numerous image-making cultures in the past were also masters of this aspect.

Tapping into the history further, various ancient cultures also adored this visual phenomenon, from cathedral murals to Thangka, the Tibetan Buddhist painting and Dunhuang paintings of Mogao Caves. The wisdom and sensitivity of our ancestors are crystally captured among these material-based images (Fig. 3).

Fig. 3. Bhutanese thanka of Mt. Meru and the Buddhist Universe. Thanka painting by Unknow Author, 19th century.

Juxtaposition

Riding along with technological progressions such as printing, photography and digital imaging. The enchantment of collage and its tactical depth quickly proves its spreadable vitality. Juxtaposition as a pictorial narrative and image-making tactics is one of the essential ways of narration. The modernist artist were the pioneers of this mechanism. Not only sophisticated formal play was introduced to the mass, but strong symbolic and innovative visual narratives were also investigated and practised. The Russian Avant-garde and Bauhaus both developed systematic methodologies and applications of visual narrative, which delves into the vast expanse of juxtaposed visuality (Fig. 4).

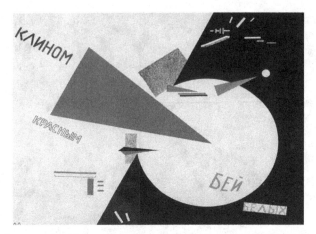

Fig. 4. "Bear the Whites with the Red Wedge," by E, Lissitzky, 1919–1920.

3.2 Interactive Narrative: Haptic and Gestural

Experience, which is passed on from mouth to mouth, is the source from which all storytellers have drawn. And among those who have written down the tales, it is the great ones whose written version differs least from the speech of the many nameless storytellers. Incidentally, among the last-named, there are two groups which, to be sure, overlap in many ways. And the figure of the storyteller gets its full corporeality only for the one who can picture them both.

--Walter Benjamin, The Storyteller

Interactivity has been gaining momentum along with digital media art and game design. However, the gestural and haptic properties are not new realisations of today's technology. On the contrary, both haptic and gestural features are essential narrative aspects and senses making out of our ontological surroundings. As Vilém (2011) describes the first stage of the material-based image is out of the material world where all dimension is ontologically conjunctive. Image existed during the exploration and interaction into the material environment.

In the context of painting, a primary type of interactive narrative occurs during the "tracing" and "resonating" with the maker's embodiment among materials and forms selected.

The French painter Soutine was very fond and obsessed with the surface of old paintings. He would demand painting surfaces of this kind aggressively for his image-making and refuse to work until the obtainment of such consumables otherwise. The extremely haptic surface of Soutine's painting creates a sense of touch upon touch. "shuddering" (Adorno 1997) expressed by Donald Kuspit (2001) in his Soutine's Shudder: Jewish Naiveté. A unique visual result is generated by intertwining the painted layers and their underlayers. This combination exposes a diverse narrative generation by the superimposed painterliness and images. During close observation, the viewer can imagine how Soutine carves and struggles through the "paintscape" with his hands while projecting his self-initiated paint-made utopia onto the surface. This confrontation constructs multiple narratives within a single image. The shuttering, the destructive, the reborn and as Deleuze called: the diagram (O'Sullivan 2009) (Fig. 5).

Fig. 5. Landscape painting by Soutine depicts scenery near his French residency. "View of Céret." By Soutine (1922).

Gerhard Richter's practice is consisted of dramatically and narratively different, even contradicting works. Among his most recognisable paintings, the smearing surfaces where the painter's body movements materialised into the uncountable layers of colour and pigment. Like a waltz dance between entropy and negentropy. The narrative is embodied through the frozen moments imbedded in the material and the remembrance of the lost and unpresented. Materialised time and emotions collide and expand cosmically from the painting. This narrative generative mechanism even multiplies its vitality among his more non-literal works. The smearing across the canvas over the painted figuration conveys a detailed message as human and meaningful as his so-called abstraction (Fig. 6).

Giacometti would constantly utilise a mechanism of adding/Plus and erasing/minus to capture the essence of his subjects. The painted figure is so intensely painted that the recognition of the face is physically recognised through the tracing of the marks rather than the actual visual information depicted on the canvas. Any detailed examination of the painting reveals stories of the painted and the painting entities. The loneliness and existential dialectics are not just an image or physical figuration of a pivotal moment but a constant struggle to succeed and fail at the cost and confusion of the individuation. It is

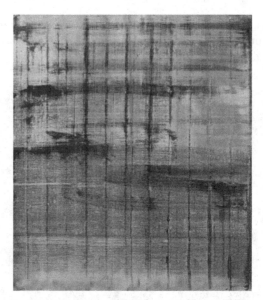

Fig. 6. "March (807)," by Richter and March (1994).

then exhibited as an image that subtly transcends into a thing that screams out solidarities of its being and surroundings (Wilson and Giacometti 2003) (Fig. 7).

Fig. 7. Diego, Giacometti's rendering of Caroline's face directly confronts the viewer's eye-line, taking on the scale of a real human head. "Caroline," by Giacometti (1961).

The literati painting in a scroll is another great case study for interactive and pictorial narrative. (Hockney 2001) The Chinese philosophy and its alignment with the cosmic order incubated an entirely different sense of technics and depiction of nature. The literati artists' priority was not to virtualise the chosen segment of the landscape but to externalise the natural and cosmic orders through the locally entangled materiality. The non-fixed point of view and perspective system further indicates the established practice of cosmotechnics in the context of image-based cultural practice.

Moreover, the related cosmonarrative interprets, evaluates and becomes. The viewing of the scroll painting bears contextual awareness instead of a universally approved exhibition where art objects are holistically displayed to satisfy the totalitarian and materialistic curiosity. The traditional Literati uses the form of Ya Ji/雅集 (Graceful Gathering), where like-minded personals would view small sections of the painting at a time while the scroll is continually revealed by the others that stimulated senses of a journey into the vast and diverse nature. More importantly, this nature is where we are part of and cannot conclude within a single paradigm of any categories (Fig. 8).

Fig. 8. "Nymph of the Luo River," by Gu Kaizhi (near 345–406), 345–406.

3.3 Material Narrative: Visual Narrative Facts

With narrative tendencies such as pictorial narrative and bodily involvement combined with technics, narrative diversity has rooted itself firmly among the paintings listed in this textual exploration. However, another aspect yet to be analysed is the story of materiality.

Alberto Burri, who is associated with matterism, created imagery surfaces with unconventional materials that bypassed the pictorial play almost completely and confronted the audience with haptic sensation and the recollection of bodily traces. Several works explored the existential trauma caused by the second world war by brutal manipulations of materials and destructive actions such as burning of the painted matters (Fig. 9).

"The words don't mean anything to me; they talk around the picture. What I have to express appears in the picture," he once remarked. "With the other elements, it involves a whole chain of pulls and tensions. But this is only the architectonic structure. For the rest, I have nothing to add (Artnet 2022)."

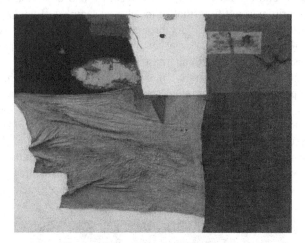

Fig. 9. "Sacco/SAck," by Burri (1952).

Lucia Freud's painted figures beautifully disturb the observer. The touch of the artist's hands is soon to be lost and covered by the skin of the pigment and the overwhelmingly detectable under paints upon close examination. This physical being of the coated and berried layers silently screams out the decay and mortality of our body through representation and situated pigment. The paint's skin intertwines with the contents of his painted human flesh. They dry and shrink unexpectedly on the picture surface. A narrative of inseparable visuality and materiality embodied in flesh figuration (Fig. 10).

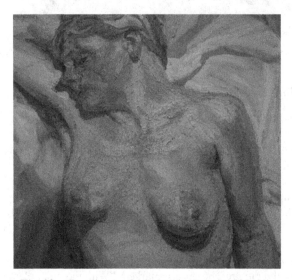

Fig. 10. "Standing by the Rags," by Freud (1988–89).

Zhonghao's paintings tend to converge the pictorial and the material plurally into a void of self-explanatory. Mostly, a fraction of recognisable motive uncomfortably poses itself in a crowded environment where pigment seems to be more than just an acting agency but a visualisation of the material reality. The shrinking paint skin caused by the thick and uneven drying process of oil paint simulates the dying beings located or abandoned somewhere inappropriately. Dripping colour with physicality actively hinting its correlation with bodylines. The material configuration accompanied by figuration sporadically suggests the narrative of the depicted subjects. In various works, the narrative was mainly expressed through the conditions of the medium. Among those paintings, not only the painting and the painter tells, but the paint itself screams out its world, and perhaps its story of mutilation and rebirth (Fig. 11).

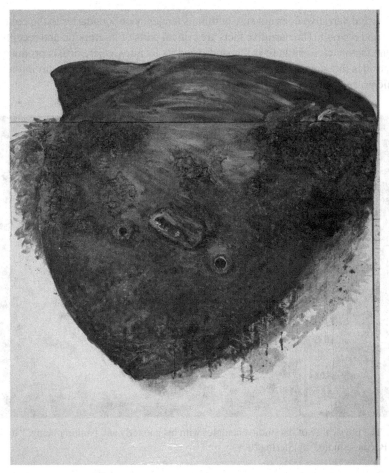

Fig. 11. An ocean being is trapped or displayed in the void. "Ocean Being," by Chen (2010).

Here, the material tends to tell its own stories autonomously and curatorially. Additionally, artist and their works in this section are also entangled with the neighbouring categories. This entanglement exactly elucidates the diversity and plurality of the visual narrative of painting and material-based image.

4   Cosmic as Locality: The Worlds of Creator and Participator

This is not wrong in so far as such externalisation and extension are considered as proceeding from what Leroi-Gaughan (Lenay 2018) called a "technical tendency." However, we still have to explain what he called "technical facts," which are different from region to region and from culture to culture.

--Yuk Hui, The Question Concerning Technology in China: An Essay in Cosmotechnics

The visual narrative does not stay within its tendency or boundaries in the context of painting and beyond. The narrative facts are critical parts of its creation and reception as well. One factual element here is the studio and its locality, where artists produce their works besides the materiality that infiltrates the maker's world. This studio influence is a holistic process with reciprocal nature, a cosmical infusion (Fig. 12).

Fig. 12. The physicality of his studio entangles with his painterly and painting being. "10 things Francis Bacon's studio," by Sterin (2009)

Artists were creating and being created in the environments. This locality is a supportive background and part of the becoming and narrative of the paintings made.

The out-of-print catalogues du MNAM "dear painter paints me" vividly captures the painting business by exhibiting a punctual selection of material-based images (Gingeras

2002). Those images illustrate the complicated nature of the visual narrative of contemporary painting and the phenomenon of contextualization accordingly. Following the logic of cosmonarrative, we can also claim that dear paint and dear cosmic surroundings "paint" me.

Cosmonarrative as a conceptual tool that acknowledges both the place of the creation and the location of the reception while the narrative is being viewed. A gallery space, textbook, screen-based platform would constitute various cosmonarratives for diverse reding of material-based images. As Yuk once said, "A thousand cosmotechnics."

5 Conclusion

In the technologically accelerating time of Anthropocene, linearity and the inertia of objective concretization continually push along the logic of detachment and desire for objectification. Within the horizontally expanding mediascape and material environment, insisted efforts and practice must continuously examine our narrative sphere intervened endlessly by digitalisation, technical image and virtualisation.

Cosmonarrative as a theoretical framework, conceptual tool and inclusive mechanism, aims to interpret the expanding visual narrative commencing material-based image where a new grounding of possibilities for recognising visual narrative and its gender of plurality and diversity.

References

Adorno, T.W.: Aesthetic Theory. A&C Black, London (1997)

Bell, C.: Significant form. Other books by the same author **339** (1969)

Benjamin, W.: The storyteller (1969)

Burri, A.: http://www.artnet.com/artists/alberto-burri. Accessed 22 Jan 2022

Chen, Z.H.: Ocean Being. Courtesy of the artist (2010)

Campbell, J.: The Hero's Journey: Joseph Campbell on His Life and Work. New World Library (2003)

Chabot, P.: The Philosophy of Simondon: Between Technology and Individuation. A&C Black, London (2013)

Diyong, L.: The emergence of spatial problems and the rise of spatial narratology. J. Shanghai Normal Univ. (Philosophy & Social Sciences Edition), **6** (2008)

Elkins, J.: The Domain of Images. Cornell University Press, Ithaca (2018)

Freud, L.: Standing by the Rags by profzucker is licensed under CC BY-NC-SA 2.0 (1988–89). https://www.flickr.com/photos/82032880@N00/24216111160. Accessed 4 Feb 2022

Flusser, V.: Into the Universe of Technical Images. University of Minnesota Press, Minnesota (2011)

Bellow, G., Dempsey, Firpo.: "NYC - The Whitney: Dempsey and Firpo" by Wallyg is licensed under CC BY-NC-ND 2.0 (1924). https://www.flickr.com/photos/70323761@N00/265558341 23. Accessed 27 Jan 2022

Sacco, B.A., Sack, S.: "IMG_2490A the contemporary art: the art that does not create the dream" by jean louis mazieres is licensed under CC BY-NC-SA 2.0 (1952). https://www.flickr.com/photos/79505738@N03/32987363592. Accessed 27 Jan 2022

Caroline, G.A., Giacometti, A.: Bob Ramsak is licensed under CC BY-NC-ND 2.0 (1961). https://www.flickr.com/photos/54981096@N00/5047392047. Accessed 7 Feb 2022

Greenberg, C.: Avant-Garde and Kitsch. In: Harrison, C., Wood, P. (eds.) Art in Theory. Blackwell, Cambridge (1990)

Gu, K.Z.: Nymph of the Luo River. (13th century Song Dynasty copy of original by Gu Kaizhi). https://commons.wikimedia.org/wiki/File:Luoshenfu_Gu_Kai_Zhi.jpg. Accessed 4 Feb 2022

Gingeras, A.M., Wien, K., Frankfurt, S.K.: "Dear Painter, Paint Me"--: Painting the Figure Since Late Picabia. Centre Pompidou (2002)

Grance, H.A.: Style and the art of Chaim Soutine: ethnicity, nationalism and geography in the critical reception and historiography. University of North Texas (2006)

Groys, B.: The cold war between medium and message. Javnost Public **26**(4), 363–369 (2019)

Hockney, D.: Secret Knowledge: Rediscovering the Lost Techniques of the Old Masters. Thames & Hudson, New York (2001)

von Herrmann, H.M., Holzwege, F.W.: Frankfurt am Main: v. Klostermann (1950)

Hill, W.: What is zombie formalism? Eyeline **84**, 19–23 (2016)

Hocking, C.: Ludonarrative dissonance in Bioshock: the problem of what the game is about. Well Played **1**, 255–260 (2009)

Hui, Y.: The Question Concerning Technology in China: An Essay in Cosmotechnics. MIT Press, London (2019)

Hui Y.: http://philosophyandtechnology.network/1266/interview-a-thousand-cosmotechnics/. Accessed 9 Feb 2022

Hui, Y.: https://www.tandfonline.com/doi/abs/10.1080/13596740701559720. Accessed 28 Aug 2021

Jenkins, H., Ford, S., Green, J.: Spreadable Media. New York University Press, New York (2013)

Kuspit, D.: Jewish Naiveté?: Soutine's shudder. Complex Ident. Jew. Conscious. Modern Art **12**, 81–99 (2001)

Krebber, A., Roscher, M. (eds.): Animal Biography: Re-Framing Animal Lives. Springer, Cham (2018). https://doi.org/10.1007/978-3-319-98288-5

Klee, P.: The Diaries of Paul Klee, 1898–1918. University of California Press, Berkeley (1964)

Lissitzky, E.: Beat the Whites with the Red Wedge. (1919–1920). https://www.flickr.com/photos/116153022@N02/14876525737. Copyright "Beat the Whites with the Red Wedge" by www.brevestoriadelcinema.org. Accessed 7 Feb 2022

Leslie, E.: Walter Benjamin: traces of craft. J. Des. Hist. **11**(1), 5–13 (1998)

Lenay C.: Leroi-Gourhan: Technical trends and human cognition. In: French Philosophy of Technology, pp. 209–226. Springer, Cham (2018). https://doi.org/10.1007/978-3-319-89518-5

Leja, M., Gottlieb, A., Newman, B., et al.: Reframing Abstract Expressionism: Subjectivity and Painting in the 1940s. Yale University Press, New Haven (1993)

Lawrence, D.H.: Apocalypse and the Writings on Revelation. Cambridge University Press, Cambridge (2002)

O'Sullivan, S.: From stuttering and stammering to the diagram: Deleuze, Bacon and contemporary art practice. Deleuze Studies **3**(2), 247–258 (2009)

Pollock, J.: Number 31 (1950). https://wordpress.org/openverse/image/7b5f9439-afc5-4138-bb43-f0662cb007a8. Copyright "Jackson Pollock, Number 31, 1950" by Detlef Schobert is licensed under CC BY-NC-ND 2.0. Accessed 1 Feb 2021

Richter, G.: March (807) (1994). https://www.flickr.com/photos/79505738@N03/40566110962. Copyright "IMG_5440 Gerhard Richter. 1932. March (807) 1994 Dresde. Gemälde Galerie Neue Meister. Albertinum. photography" by jean louis mazieres is licensed under CC BY-NC-SA 2.0. Accessed 5 Feb 2022

Soutine C.: View of Céret (1893–1943) (1922). https://www.sothebys.com/en/auctions/ecatalogue/2019/impressionist-modern-art-evening-n10067/lot.pr.9V5YX.html. Accessed 7 Feb 2022

Simondon, G.: The limits of human progress: a critical study. Cult. Polit. **6**(2), 229–236 (2010)

Unknow Author: Bhutanese thanka of Mt. Meru and the Buddhist Universe. (19th century). https://en.wikipedia.org/wiki/File:Bhutanese_thanka_of_Mt._Meru_and_the_Buddhist_Uni verse.jpg. Accessed 7 Feb 2022

Wilson, L., Giacometti, A., Giacometti, A.: Myth, Magic, and the Man. Yale University Press, London (2003)

10 Things Francis Bacon's Studio (2009). https://www.flickr.com/photos/14037991@N04/428 8949430. "10 things Francis Bacon's studio" by Sterin is licensed under CC BY-NC-ND 2.0. Accessed 7 Feb 2022

In Social Media We Distrust: Investigating Users' Hostile Media Perception of Facebook News Content

Helga G. Csarnó[1], Yi-Hsing Han[2(✉)], and Shih-Hsien Hsu[2]

[1] National Chengchi University, Taipei, Taiwan
[2] National Taiwan University, Taipei, Taiwan
paulhan@nccu.edu.tw

Abstract. The majority of internet users today find their news on social media (Gil de Zúñiga et al. 2017), however, media trust, and especially trust in social media is low. (Edelman 2019) In growing political polarization the effects of perceived media hostility are also gaining more importance. In this research internet users of international news participated in an online experiment to assess how issue involvement on the 2020 military conflict between the United States and Iran correlates with general trust in the media and with the credibility of the largest social media network, Facebook, as a news source. The current research investigated whether the hostile media effect still occurs in a purely social media context and results showed that partisans (those with a strong supporting or opposing opinion on the military conflict) perceive news content on Facebook as hostile along the same lines as they do in a traditional media context. Current study fills the literature gap of the hostile media effect in a social media context. Findings may also have implications for the news industry as to how journalist roles influence users' perceptions.

Keywords: Social media · Media trust · News credibility · Hostile media effect

1 Introduction

1.1 Research Background

From the mid-2000s to the early 2010s, journalistic practices started to shift to fit the new attention economy [1], resulting in the rise of perceived misleading headlines, sensationalism, and the birth of clickbait and listicle journalism. Online discussions were increasingly based around polarized clusters of opinion, forming echo-chambers [2] and resulting in a heavily divided environment of public discourse that is prevalent up to day. A major part (42%) of the American public has assessed national news media as too liberal [3], and populistic politics also profited from the rhetoric of biased and left-leaning news media, while those holding a populist worldview tend to have low trust in mainstream media and a preference for commercial and tabloid media [4]. As societies came to realize the political and social meddling power of misinformation in the mid- to late-2010s, higher than ever levels of media distrust set in.

P.-L. P. Rau (Ed.): HCII 2022, LNCS 13313, pp. 118–136, 2022.
https://doi.org/10.1007/978-3-031-06050-2_9

Recent surveys also describe changing patterns of news consumption: a "massive rise in news engagement" [5], where the rate of people disengaged from the news has fallen, and the ratio of those who actively share news is higher than ever. With tendencies to distrust social media, this might be cause for worry, however, the Reuters Institute [6] has also reported that concern about the quality of information caused people to seek out 'reputable' news sources (40% in the US), while 24% says they stopped using sources with questionable reputation altogether. The notion and impact of sharing news might also be changing, as the Reuters Institute observed a rise in using messaging apps such as WhatsApp and Line as a general tendency. They also describe a phenomenon where users are more likely to be in large group chats with people they do not personally know. Users are now more likely to be sharing news in these private environments than to post them publicly. Private and public Facebook groups are also prevalent, however, more so in certain countries than others.

In such a rapidly changing media landscape and in the light of rising polarization of opinion [7], current research aims to look into how issue involvement influences different media perceptions, such as bias perception (the hostile media effect) and media credibility. Since today's news consumption is so closely intertwined with social media use [8], the research investigates how those with strong opinions on controversial issues perceive the credibility of a specific SNS platform, Facebook. An attempt is made to look into the relationship between specifics of news content creation (the role the journalist takes on) and the perception of bias by the users. Looking into these media effects, perceptions, and content characteristics might offer insight into how social media contexts impact the users' relationship with news content, especially in case of high-involvement individuals – an important area of research in an extremely personalized, self- and peer-curated information environment that is prone to selective sharing, echo chambers and might enhance opinion polarization [2, 9, 10].

1.2   Research Purpose

This research aims to investigate how news content shared on the largest SNS, Facebook, is perceived by the users, and how partisanship (defined in this study as a strong supporting or opposing opinion on the 2020 U.S.-Iran military conflict) affects this perception. It looks into participants' perceived credibility of Facebook as a news source, as well as their general trust towards the media. To do so, an online experiment is conducted to investigate whether there is a difference between bias perception in case participants see a news post written by a journalist who employs the objective-normative role, versus when they employ the advocacy role.

This research contributes to hostile media perception literature in a strictly social media context, specifically for news content on Facebook. Effectively, this research can address whether the hostile media effect occurs even before Facebook users click to read a full article. Findings of the study may offer clarity to media practitioners and journalism studies scholars as to whether advocacy journalism in a social media context induces bias.

2 Literature Review

2.1 Hostile Media Effect

In a groundbreaking research article, Vallone et al. (1985) coined the term for the hostile media phenomenon (HMP, or hostile media effect, HME) [11]. Using an unbiased piece of reporting that aired on television covering the 1983 Beirut massacre, they observed that both pro-Israeli and pro-Arab partisans not only perceived the objective reports as biased, but they also perceived them to be biased against their own stance, hence the use of the word hostile. They called this "biased perception of media bias" [11]. Perloff, in a meta-analysis overarching 30 years of hostile media effect literature, defines the hostile media effect as "the tendency for individuals with a strong pre-existing attitude on an issue to perceive that ostensibly neutral, even-handed media coverage of the topic is biased against their side and in favor of their antagonists' point of view" [12].

This effect has been widely studied in communication science since then, but has also peaked the attention of public opinion and social science researchers [12]. Since Vallone et al. used a controversial issue with high relevance in their experiment, many others followed by repeating the experiment using different political and social issues and defining partisans as those who have high levels of issue involvement on the issue in question [11]. Other issues have also proven to cause this effect such as genetically modified food [13, 14], the 1997 United Parcel Service strike [15], the abolishment of the National Security Law in South Korea [16], the use of primates in lab testing [17] and sports coverage [18] just to mention a few examples. Research methods have overwhelmingly been laboratory experiments or survey research according to Perloff (2018), leaning on Hansen and Kim's (2001) meta-analysis, accounts for a medium effect size (r = .296) [19].

As for the objective content that triggers the HME, first hostile media studies made use of content that was unbiased to test the effect. The vast majority of these studies used the terms of neutral, evenhanded, or balanced content [12], with less regard to the generally accepted notion that unbiased reporting is not necessarily possible, or doubts raised by post-modernism whether an objectively valid reality exists. In their exploratory study, Vallone et al. (1985) defined their concept of unbiased reporting as reporting that in the eyes of an impartial reader would seem objective and unbiased [11]. However, recognizing that in practice objective reporting might not always be the case, since partisan leaning media has become a more common phenomenon, Gunther et al. (2001) designed a study with less objective material. They coined the term for relative hostile media effect, wherein "supporters and opponents of an issue perceive bias in a consistent direction (i.e., leaning toward one side), but each group perceives coverage as significantly more unfavorable to its own position relative to the other group" [5].

Partisanship
Involvement. A key moderator for HMP is involvement, however, the definition of involvement (just as the definition of the hostile media effect) is not coherent all throughout published research, also, there is no consensus in the necessity of issue-involvement or ego-involvement for HME to occur, as some studies, such as Arpan and Raney (2003) explicated this aspect as a prior attitude [18]. Hansen and Kim (2011) however concluded

that involvement is a moderating variable in the occurrence of HME [19]. Different types of involvement, such as value-relevant or affective involvement were investigated by Choi et al. (2009) and Matthes (2013) [16, 20]. Choi and colleagues built on meta-analysis by Johnson and Eagly (1990), and differentiated three types of involvement: value-relevant (other times called as ego-serving), outcome-relevant, and impression-relevant involvement, and out of these three, focused on value-relevant and outcome-relevant involvement [21]. Their results showed that value-relevant involvement (involvement that is rooted in one's important personal values) was a critically significant predictor of HMP, while outcome-relevant involvement (involvement in an issue that is relevant to one's current goals and outcomes) was not significant as predictor. Other than involvement, they also found media skepticism to be the strongest single predictor in their model. Matthes (2013) set out to investigate whether the hostile media phenomenon is more affected by cognitive or emotional (affective) involvement, and found that the latter was overwhelmingly supported by survey data [20]. Furthermore, the level of involvement of the audience was found significant no matter the reason of the type of involvement [22]. Hansen and Kim (2011) found that the extent of the hostile media effect is positively correlated to the level of issue-involvement: the more extreme the perceiver's views were, the more they perceived content to be hostile, or at least not supportive enough towards the issue in question – finding however significant hostile media perception under low involvement as well [19].

Social Identity. This leads us to the third key moderating factor of the HME, social identity. Social identity theory [23] describes that social groups and belonging are important aspects of the self, and involves stereotyping out-groups and striving to see our group, the in-group in a positive light. Through the third-person effect, this social theory is applicable to the hostile media phenomenon, whereby ego-involvement can render a story on a controversial issue highly relevant to social identity, and therefore cause the HME to occur [24]. Looking specifically into cases where the controversial reporting covered low-status groups or groups with which participants strongly identified, and therefore were more motivated to preserve a positive image of it, Hartmann and Tanis (2013) describe higher sensitivity to how they perceived the media [24]. In Tsfati (2007) perceived media bias by Israeli Arab citizens led to perceived media stigmatization, and a relationship with increased minority alienation was established [25]. Similar effects were observed in strong political group identification [26] where social in-group thinking was the theoretical framework of hostile perception of a political campaign; or religious groups [27]. The message source may also trigger the third-person effect: as in-group or out-group perceptions of the source come to affect, a social distance between the audience and the source is established, which affects hostility perception. This may cause for bias perception to be lower when the source is understood to be an in-group member than in case of an out-group member source [28, 29].

The underlying information processing mechanisms of the HME have been of scholarly attention from the very beginning. Vallone et al. (1985) speculated selective perception and selective evaluation may both explain the audience's bias [11], but since their data supported both processes, the question remained unexplained. Schmitt et al. (2004) proposed three information processing mechanisms that might explain the HME: selective recall (partisans disproportionately better remembering information they disagree with), selective categorization (the tendency for partisans to categorize more of the news content as unfavorable than moderates would), and different standards (thinking that counterarguments to our viewpoint are invalid or irrelevant) [30]. Running an experiment with the divisive issue of genetically modified food in the focus, they concluded that "selective categorization appears to be the one viable explanation for the hostile media effect," [30] while selective recall has not shown to have a significant relationship with the HME. This means that partisans have a tendency to perceive and categorize more of the media content as unfavorable than moderates would. However, there is no support that selective memory would mediate hostile media perceptions. In a separate study, Giner-Sorolla and Chaiken (1994) hypothesized that pre-existing negative attitude towards the media in general have a mediating effect on HME, calling it a cause for the hostile media judgments [31].

Outcomes and consequences of the hostile media effect for partisans include corrective action [32] – this describes the phenomenon where presumed strong influence of the perceived biased media coverage makes partisans voice their opinions in public spaces as if to correct the wrong coverage's effects. In other cases, related to the aforementioned effects of social identity and intergroup perceptions, minorities may self-perceive as having less political power than others, resulting in lower trust in the media and in the institution of democracy [33]. Hostile media effect is also theorized to be related to public opinion inference, a concept coined in Gunther (1993) [34]. Persuasive press inference is a phenomenon whereby people gather their perception of public opinion from what is being communicated by mass media. This happens through a generalization that the news content that they perceived as biased is similar to the rest of media content – and that media, perceived to be impactful, will influence others' opinions. This holds as a way of public opinion inference even though idea of media power has been disproven, showing that biased media coverage does not affect moderates' opinion, merely reinforces the opinion of partisans [22]. Partisans in particular are described to hold the belief that biased media content may affect others' opinions, however, findings on this are contradictory. Christensen et al. (2002) observed that while moderates do in part infer public opinion from their subjective understanding of the news content, partisans however, when triggered for hostile media effect, are also likely to project their own opinion on the public. In this scenario, partisans did not perceive the entire public opinion as hostile, only the specific piece of news content. [12, 15] notes that comparing the strength of projection and of persuasive press inference on perceptions of public opinion, the former is a more important factor.

The HME in the Social Media Context
Although the majority of HME literature was produced under mass-media logic and with traditional media content [19], with the growing weight of social media and its implications on information abundance [35] and on attitude towards news consumption [8] makes it an important and relevant area for hostile media perception research. Published research on HME under social media environments show these platforms of communication, that are furthering selective exposure as compared to traditional mass media [2], are perhaps deepening political and ideological polarization [12]. Partisans tend to selectively share news even when it's factual: Shin and Thorson (2017) found that partisans selectively share fact-checking messages that support their own candidate,

and selective sharing of news with a heightening sense of media hostility influences discussion and opinion polarization [10]. Perception of media hostility is also worsened by politicians' narratives on unfair media coverage and fake news – even following politicians on social media may lead to a heightened sense of media hostility. [12, 36] also notes that the tone of discussion on social media tends to be more vicious than previously observed in traditional media settings, and argues that relative hostile media effect might be a key aspect to look into.

Since most key factors – involvement, perceived reach, social identity, the third-person effect – are not specifically more limited under social media than in other media channels; and in fact the two main sources of public opinion inference, namely, inter-personal and mass media messages [37] come together on SNS; in this research it is hypothesized that the hostile media effect is likely to occur in a similar way and have similar consequences under a social media context like in a traditional media one. While the total reach of a particular social media post is only available to page managers and not to the public eye, SNS users may deduce potential reach by looking at aggregate user representations, that is, the number of likes and reactions, the number of comments, and the number of shares on a post.

Therefore it is hypothesized that the hostile media effect occurs in a purely social media context as well in the same way it does in online and traditional news media.

Hypothesis 1a: Pro-attack participants reading a balanced news story on the 2020 U.S.-Iran military conflict will perceive the content to be more hostile toward their personal position than moderates, those who are neither pro-attack or anti-attack.

Hypothesis 1b: Anti-attack participants reading a balanced news story on the 2020 U.S.-Iran military conflict will perceive the content to be more hostile toward their personal position than moderates, those who are neither pro-attack or anti-attack.

Research on the effect of partisanship on hostility perception showed that audiences are significantly more critical towards information that counters their beliefs, and less so against confirming information [13].

Hypothesis 2a: Anti-attack participants will perceive slanted information pre-sented as a slanted news story to be more biased in favor of the pro-attack position than pro-attack participants.

Hypothesis 2b: Pro-attack participants will perceive slanted information presented as a slanted news story to be more biased in favor of the anti-attack position than anti-attack participants.

News Credibility

Media credibility is an important indicator of successful communication – previous stud-ies have shown that if medium credibility is low, people are less likely to pay attention to it [38], while Wanta and Hu (1994) argue that the success of mass media communication altogether depends on credibility [39].

The concept of media credibility is a complex, multidimensional one that scholars began to study in the 1950s. There are two major branches of credibility research – one focuses on source credibility [40], analyzing the features of the communicator, while the other branch, medium credibility [41] focuses on how different channels of communication, for example, newspapers, television, radio, etc. influence perceived credibility.

Perceived credibility of news in a social media context is important because according to a 2018 Pew Research Center survey, almost two thirds (68%) of Americans used social media to get their news at least occasionally [42]. It is a unique medium in terms of audience perception – usually when a particular medium becomes widely popular, its perceived credibility will go up, [43] but, in the case of news on social media, many are skeptical about the information they are getting. (57% of respondents in Shearer & Matsa, 2018) This suggests a general low perceived credibility of news in a social media context, and, because of its widespread use, it might affect a large part of the population. For online news media, research initially measured the perceived credibility of online news to be between that of newspapers and television (a rating of 2.06 on a 0–4 Likert scale as written by Kiousis, 2001) [44].

It is unclear how the unique traits and segments of social media platforms influence source credibility. Because of the diversity of SNS platforms, it is not possible to talk about general medium credibility of social media, thus Schmierbach and Oeldorf-Hirsch (2012) focused on comparing news credibility in the context of a specific SNS platform with the credibility of online news in itself: in the case of Twitter, they found that the perceived credibility of a New York Times story shared as a tweet was lower than that of the original article itself [45]. Still about Twitter Westerman et al. (2014) found that more recent tweets were positively correlated with all factors of cognitive elaboration, and elaboration was in turn positively correlated with source credibility [46].

Involvement still seems to play an important role in perceived credibility. Arpan and Raney (2003) did an experimental study on sports fans and found that the source of the sports news affected perception of credibility [18]. Participants who supported their hometown team found the same article to be significantly more supportive towards the rival town's team if it was printed in a neutral town's or the rival town's newspaper, in contrast to their hometown's newspaper. As for the effect of involvement in an online news setting, Choi et al. (2009) asked partisan participants to evaluate the credibility of news coverage on the Iraq War, and found that anti-partisans (those who opposed the war) perceived the Internet as a news source to be less aligned with a pro-government position than traditional media, and simultaneously found the Internet as a news source more credible than did neutral respondents [16]. Therefore, there seems to be an enhancing effect of involvement of issue involvement on news credibility, but it is unclear in what specific way this effect unfolds in the case of different issues and communication platforms.

Considering this information this current research proposes a research question to investigate the relationship between partisanship and perceived credibility of Facebook as a source for news information.

RQ: What is the relationship between participants' strength of opinion about the 2020 U.S.-Iran military conflict and their perceived credibility of Facebook as a news source?

Journalistic Roles

Journalistic values and practices, which Deuze (2005) sums up as an occupational ideology, [47] reflect the fact that journalists see their work as a profession, rather than a job, and find their service to the public important – in fact, a significant factor in their occupational satisfaction derives from carrying out the public service role of journalism [48]. There are definitely more than one journalistic roles that media workers take on simultaneously, such as the interpretive, the disseminator, the adversarial, or the mobilizer roles, with the first two being the most prevalent, [49] and the latter two frowned upon under the objective-neutral media model of the United States [50].

These roles and values hold up under social media as well, journalists, pressured to keep up with Twitter and citizen journalists use social media to perform their journalistic roles [48, 51]. However, in social media environments, lines of professional and personal life have become blurry for media workers. Journalists use social media to varying degrees, for either, both, or neither private and professional purposes – important factors in their choices are their age, their outlook on their profession, and skepticism towards the platform. Many of them reported concerns about their objectivity versus opinionatedness in social media spaces [51].

Deuze (2005) talks about the process of normalization (originally of the blogosphere): the tendency for journalists to continue to apply their occupational values and practices to new and emerging platforms [47]. Larsorsa et al. (2012) argue that normalization continues well into social media. This platform might have first seemed like a "new tool for carrying out the traditional tasks" [48], but social media also seems to be greatly influencing the way journalists perform their roles, and the importance they give to different journalistic values and practices. The new environment is characterized by increased transparency of journalistic processes, and Singer (2005) concludes that social media is merely a new platform for journalists to display their professional identity and values [52]. However, Hedman and Djerf-Pierre (2013) argue that this performative environment leads to a need for news media to continuously justify itself in front of the public [48]. The perception of the role of a journalist in the community has also been influenced, namely, it has become more important in the new media news environment, as news consumers now have a closer, more interactive relationship with journalists [53].

Although a multitude of alternative models of journalism exist globally [54], the most prevalent ones in American journalism are the objective-neutral model in which journalists refrain to factual information and aim to balance their sources, [55] and the advocacy model, in which journalists may take one side of an issue, often advocating for social change [56]. Strictly speaking, advocacy is the difference in communication between public relations messages and journalism. However, many argue that the reality of the two models is less black and white [57, 58]. Fisher (2016) writes that today advocacy journalism exists on a continuum from subtle to overt, determined by macro, organizational, production and source factors, as well as personal factors on behalf of the journalist [58].

Although historically partisanship of newspapers was once accepted in the United States also, since the commercialization of legacy papers objectivity became the norm to better accommodate advertising and to raise credibility [57]. Some still argue that advocacy journalism is more transparent of the journalist's bias, and therefore it is more trustworthy and credible than strictly objective journalism, traditionally objectivism is considered to be more credible, as it has been specifically designed for this desired effect. In this research the objective-normative landscape of journalism is accepted, and it is hypothesized that advocacy journalism under a social media environment will result in higher bias perception than the objective-normative role.

Hypothesis 3: Advocacy journalism will result in higher perception of bias in a news post on Facebook than objective-neutral journalism.

3   Method

3.1   Online Experiment Design

A two-condition online experiment (Objective-normative journalist role v. Advocacy journalist role) was employed in the current study to test the effect of journalistic roles on HME. Participants were randomly assigned to read an objective-normative journalist role condition or an advocacy journalist role condition.

3.2   Stimulus Materials

Two images were created as stimulus material. The two variants represented the objective-normative journalist role and the advocacy journalist role to test about which of these roles will result in higher bias perception. These were also the content pieces that the hostile media effect was tested on, with the objective-normative condition representing a balanced piece of content, and the advocacy role a slanted one.

The images were designed as screenshots of a Facebook post – a fictional news post by Reuters news agency titled "The U.S. Orders Strike Killing Top Iranian General Qassim Suleimani" with description "Suleimani was planning attacks on Americans across the region, leading to an airstrike in Baghdad, the Pentagon statement said" and added text "Breaking News: The U.S. confirmed it was behind the strike that killed the powerful Iranian commander Qassim Suleimani, a major escalation in a conflict with Iran." The new post also came with a thumbnail image, and came with 21K likes, 7.1K comments, and 21K shares. This basic news post was unchanged under both conditions, as conditions were manipulated via a fictional journalist sharing this original post.

The post was designed as if shared by a fictional journalist named John Journalist. To manipulate for the journalistic role condition, two variants were created: one where John Journalist, taking on the objective-normative role, shared his views in a factual and objective manner, and one where he took on the advocacy role, sharing both facts and opinions from an anti-attack viewpoint.

The original news article post was selected after considering multiple controversial issues that would serve for testing the hostile media effect. After discussion, selecting on the 2020 U.S.-Iran military conflict served as a news story that had the potential to involve international audiences. For the selection of the original news post multiple major international news outlets' first (breaking news) social media posts about this issue were considered both on Facebook and on Twitter. After consideration, one of the breaking news posts on the issue by the New York Times was selected. The original Facebook post linked to a New York Times article [59], this interactivity was not provided during the experiment.

Manipulation was carried out by taking a screenshot of the original New York Times Facebook post, and carefully re-designing it to fit all above considerations, while also keeping aesthetically consistent with Facebook's layout as of February 2020.

3.3 Participants

Data was collected from international readers of English speaking international news media via Qualtric.com between May 18th 2020 and June 10th 2020. Participants were recruited through Facebook and a total of 342 respondents completed the online experiment. This led to final sample size of N = 339 (161 female, 177 males, 1 other, Median age group of 25–34). The majority of the sample has a bachelor degree or above (79.6%). Participants were of 22 different nationalities, with 131 (38%) respondents from Hungary, 96 (28%) from the United States, 20 (6%) from the United Kingdom, 15 (4.5%) from Taiwan, and 11 (3.2%) from Australia. The reason for selecting an international audience was that involvement on the issue selected for measuring partisanship (the U.S.-Iran military conflict of January 2020) is one of international interest. (Poushter, 2018).

3.4 Measurement

Partisanship. Following hostile media perception literature [11, 13, 25], this study treats partisanship as involvement on a divisive issue. Measuring issue involvement instead makes sure that participants' strength of opinion. The issue in question needs to be divisive and of international relevance. The issue of the 2020 military conflict between the United States and Iran was selected. This event at the time of data collection was the last installment of a long history of conflict between the two countries, one that had been drawing international attention for decades and captured worldwide attention in January 2020.

To assess partisanship a screening item adapted from Gunther and Schmitt (2004) [13] asked participants to give their opinion to the 2020 US-Iranian military conflict on a 7-point Likert scale (1 – I strongly oppose the U.S. military actions. 4 – I am strictly neutral on this issue. 7 – I strongly support the U.S. military actions) ($M = 3.81$, $SD = 1.86$). Please see Table 1. Those whose opinion takes the value of 1, strongly oppose, 2, oppose, 6, support, 7, strongly support, are to be considered partisans. Those whose opinion falls between 3 and 5 were considered moderates. In this research two different variables were created to conduct analysis on partisanship: one differentiated 2 groups, moderates and partisans, while another differentiated 3 groups, moderates, anti-partisans, and pro-partisans.

Hostile Media Perception. To measure their hostile media perception, participants are shown stimulus material and are asked to answer two items adapted from Gunther and Schmitt (2004) [13]. Would you say that the portrayal of the strike in this post is strictly neutral, or is it biased in favor of one side or the other? ($M = 2.56$, $SD = 1.17$) Would you say that the journalist responsible for this post was strictly neutral, or were

Table 1. Participants' partisanship ($N = 339$).

Opinion	Frequency (n)	Percentage (%)
I strongly oppose the U.S. military actions	42	12.4
I oppose the U.S. military actions	59	17.4
I somewhat oppose the U.S. military actions	39	11.5
I am neutral on this issue	95	28.0
I somewhat support the U.S. military actions	36	10.6
I support the U.S. military actions	23	6.8
I strongly support the U.S. military actions	45	13.3

they biased in favor of one side or the other? ($M = 2.30$, $SD = 1.09$) Answers were given on a 5-point Likert scale ranging from 1 – strongly biased against, through 3 – strictly neutral, to 5 – strongly biased in favor. These two items were combined into one variable, hostile media perception ($M = 2.43$, $SD = 1.04$).

Adapted from the same study, Gunther and Schmitt (2004) [13], participants estimate the percentage of the content that was favorable and unfavorable, respectively, on a scale with 10% increments ranging between 0% and 100% [13]. Please estimate what percentage of the Facebook post was favorable towards the U.S. military actions. ($M = 37.61$, $SD = 25.82$) Please estimate what percentage of the Facebook post was unfavorable towards the U.S. military actions. ($M = 53.03$, $SD = 29.19$).

News Credibility. The measure Facebook's credibility as a news source, a revised 11-item scale for online news credibility based on Gaziano and McGrath's (1986) credibility scale is adapted [41]. Items are adapted to fit the purpose as *Do you agree that news on Facebook...* with answers ranging on a 5-point Likert scale from 1 = strongly disagree to 5 = strongly agree, with 3 representing neutral. The scale measures three factors: 5 items for balance, 3 items for honesty, and 3 items for currency. These 11 items were combined into one variable to conduct analysis on Facebook's perceived credibility as a news source ($\alpha = .906$, $M = 3.05$, $SD = .79$).

4 Results

4.1 Testing the Hostile Media Effect

For H1a and H1b participants who were shown the objective journalist role condition stimulus material are considered, as this serves as a balanced news story. Running an independent-samples t-test shows that there is significant difference in terms of hostile media perception between pro-attack participants and moderate participants when they were shown a balanced news story, $t(112) = 2.69$, $p < .05$). Specifically, pro-attack partisan respondents ($M = 2.30$, $SD = 1.03$) perceived the objective stimulus material as more anti-attack than moderate respondents did ($M = 2.81$, $SD = .84$). Therefore, H1a is supported.

Also, there is a significant difference in terms of hostile media perception between anti-attack participants and moderate participants when they were shown a balanced news story, t (108.59) $= -2.30$, $p < .05$. Specifically, anti-attack respondents ($M = 3.11$, $SD = .88$) perceived the objective stimulus material as more pro-attack than did moderate respondents ($M = 2.81$, $SD = .84$). H1b is also supported.

For H2a and H2b we consider respondents who were shown the advocate journalist role condition stimulus material, as this serves as a slanted news story. Running an independent-samples t-test shows there is no significant partisan difference in terms of perceived pro-attack bias, therefore H2a is not supported. However, there is a significant partisan group difference in terms of perceived anti-attack bias, t (87.89) $= 4.20$, $p < .001$. Specifically, pro-attack partisans ($M = 1.46$, $SD = .83$) perceived the post to be significantly more in favor of the anti-attack position than anti-attack partisans ($M = 2.26$, $SD = .941$). H2b is supported. When asked to estimate the percentage to which the anti-attack slanted post was biased against the military actions, pro-attack participants ($M = 71.05$, $SD = 32.94$) answered with higher percentages than anti-attack participants ($M = 60.87$, $SD = 27.87$), but the difference did not reach significant level ($p = .135$).

4.2 Partisanship and Facebook's News Credibility

RQ seeks to answer what relationship is there between partisanship and Facebook's perceived credibility as a news source. Running an independent-samples t-test shows significant results. There is a significant difference in terms of perceived credibility of Facebook as a news source, t (328.17) $= 3.43$, $p < .001$. Specifically, participants with a stronger opinion on the U.S.-Iran military conflict ($M = 2.18$, $SD = .90$) perceive Facebook to be a less credible news source than moderate participants ($M = 2.50$, $SD = .77$).

Differentiating between partisan groups also shows significant results. Running an One-way ANOVA shows there is a significant difference between groups in terms of perceived credibility of Facebook as a news source, $F(2, 336) = 12.67$, $p < .001$). *Post hoc* analysis using *Tukey HSD* suggests that pro-partisan respondents ($M = 1.90$, SD $= .87$) perceive Facebook as a news source as less credible than moderates (M $= 2.50$, $SD = .77$) and anti-partisans ($M = 2.37$, $SD = .88$).

4.3 Impact of Journalistic Roles

H3 states "Advocacy journalism will result in higher perception of bias in a news post on Facebook than objective-neutral journalism." Running an independent-samples t-test shows that there is a significant group in terms of hostility perception (t $= 7.23$, $p < .001$). Specifically, those who were shown the advocacy journalism stimulus material ($M = 2.05$, $SD = 1.01$) perceived more bias than those who were shown the objective-neutral stimulus material ($M = 2.81$, $SD = .92$). H4 is supported.

5 Discussion and Conclusion

Considering that social media is a widespread source of news worldwide, and political polarization has been on the rise, this study built on hostile media effect literature to understand how issue involvement affects bias perception in a social media context. The research also sought to understand how partisanship affects news credibility and how journalistic roles affect bias perceptions.

5.1 Hostile Media Effect Under Social Media

The most important finding of this study is that the HME occurs under a strictly social media context. Participants were shown a Facebook news post about a divisive issue and then asked to assess how biased it was in favor and against the issue in question. Drawing from HME literature, we expected that partisan participants (those with a strong opinion for or against the issue in question) will perceive a piece of relatively objective reporting as biased. We expected that this effect would occur no matter which side of the issue the partisan is on. (H1a, H1b) Both these expectations were proven supported.

Existing literature on the HME also says that pro-partisans will perceive a truly biased piece of reporting as more biased in favor of the anti-partisans, than anti-partisans will. This phenomenon should also occur on both sides of the issue, meaning that anti-partisans will perceive a pro-partisan piece of content as more biased than those who are pro-partisans (H2a, H2b). H2 was partially supported – H2b showed that pro-partisans saw the anti-partisan news story as significantly more biased in favor of the anti-partisan side than did anti-partisans. H2a showed no significant results, as in, anti-attack participants did not show significant signs of the relative hostile media effect. This result might indicate that there was an overlap between partisan groups in this study and partisanship in the traditional sense of political leaning. It may have been the case that pro-partisans in this study, meaning those supporting the military actions, fell on the conservative or even Republican political spectrum, while those who were anti-partisans, and opposed the military actions, fell on the liberal, Democrat spectrum. Literature shows that there is a relationship with political partisanship and bias perception, Watts et al. (1999) found that the public is more likely to perceive liberal bias in the media, not because of the actual quality of the content, but because of the narrative of a liberally biased media became prominent during political campaigns in the 1990s [69]. A decade later Feldman (2011) running an issue involvement based study on the relative hostile media effect, also found that selective perception was more significant amongst the partisan group in her study that aligned with conservative political values [68]. Arguably more research would need to be done to fully understand why H2a was not supported. However, it is still an important finding that the hostile media effect occurs even in a strictly social media environment, effectively meaning that partisan participants did not have to read the actual article behind a Facebook post to perceive it as biased against their own point of view.

The relevance of this finding comes from the nature of SNS networks to cater to personalized needs, providing self-, peer-, and algorithm-curated flows of information, and resulting in extremely selective exposure [2]. This, combined with the general vicious nature of discussion that is prevalent in social media environments [12] may lead to extreme opinion polarization. HME may play an important role in this, as partisans may infer public opinion from both slanted and objective social media news content that they perceive as biased, [67] and as we have discussed, this may lead to outcomes such as corrective action, that is not always within the realm of democratic thinking [32].

5.2 Facebook's Credibility Among Partisans

The findings suggest that partisanship is negatively correlated to news credibility, as asked in RQ. In this study social media, such as Facebook, Twitter, YouTube, or Reddit was the second most popular main source for news (29.8%). Perceived credibility of Facebook as a news source was significantly lower among partisans than moderates.

The significance of the findings on Facebook's perceived news credibility is twofold – first, it is a direct investigation of this specific SNS platform's credibility as a news source, and second, it suggests that partisanship is negatively correlated with Facebook's credibility as a news source.

Facebook is still the most widely adapted SNS and a significant source for news, therefore its credibility is worthy of attention. Source credibility of SNS platforms is not widely researched, and results are hard to compare between platforms due to their layout and functional differences. Therefore, research about the credibility of news tweets on Twitter [45] is not necessarily indicative of Facebook's credibility of a news source. Some studies have shown that social media use worsens heterogeneity of discussion networks [62], while others [61, 63] argue that Facebook, or in general, SNS use exposes users to diverse views, and yet other research says that this exposure might lead to further polarization [64] – but in any of these cases it is an important finding that those with stronger opinions in general contribute lower credibility to Facebook as a source than moderates do.

5.3 Effects of Journalistic Roles on HME

As predicted in H3, bias perception under the advocacy role was significantly higher than under the objective-normative role. The novelty of this finding is that the perception of journalist roles performed in a social media context concurs with research about perception of journalistic roles under mass media logic. However, this result does not resolve the notion that in practice objective, dry content might contradict the logic of SNS platforms, where more engagement often leads to more exposure [9]. On the other hand, social media news content creation is a complicated ecosystem, in which not all journalists are adapting SNS platforms (determining factors being age, type of work, and professional attitude [48]), and not all news outlets have guidelines for journalists' social media participation, which makes news workers uncertain as of how to behave professionally in an SNS environment.

As objective-normative journalism was designed exactly with the purpose of raising news credibility to better accommodate advertising and generate more revenue, [57] it might be an important implication of this finding that this type of social media content might drive less bias perception and in turn possibly raise platform credibility. As social media trust is generally low [5], and lower perceived credibility of Facebook was observed in this current research, SNS platforms must be aware that these negative user perceptions might result in less attention paid to these platforms [38], and in consequence, gaining less revenue through social media advertising. As SNS platforms do not control their published content directly, particularly in the case of news and journalism, Facebook has made various efforts to fact-check, screen for misinformation, and promote quality journalism and trusted sources [60].

However, these findings underpin the value of objective-normative journalism in a social media context; that is, this journalistic role resulted in significantly lower perceived bias by both partisan and moderate participants of this study. That being said, this research on its own is not sufficient to perfectly model the experience of coming across a news article on Facebook, shared by a journalist behaving a certain way. For example, perception of the journalistic text in a traditional media context includes perception of the presenter, source of the news [22], while in this study we aimed to design a generic, anonymous fictional journalist. In a real-life scenario, it is arguably more likely that users will seek out or come across social media news content by journalists they are interested in, and might even agree with. Yet, it is important to note that, although this study did not focus on this particular bias, anti-partisans (those who are against the military strike) perceived anti-partisan slanted news content ($M = 2.26$, $SD = .94$) as significantly more biased against the attack, than how they perceived bias in objective content. ($M = 3.11$, $SD = .88$) (t (93.26) $= 4.63$, p $< .001$) This suggests that bias is recognized by partisans even when they receive content that shares their opinion.

Altogether, this study underlines that objective-normative journalism results in significantly lower perceived bias than advocacy journalism is, a potentially important consideration for news practitioners who produce news content for social media platforms. A practical implication for those who partake in social media news content production would be to develop codes of conduct for staff members regarding the tone and factuality of the social news content, while being mindful of the long-term professional goals and marketing targets of the given news outlet. Globally there exist a multitude of different journalistic mindsets – Hanitzsch and Vos (2018) specified 18 different roles that are valid under different cultural, contextual, political settings [54]. In this framework of globally diverse concepts of journalism it might not be of utmost importance for each and every news outlet to have an objective-normative performance, or to convey unopinionated information to their audience.

It has to be taken into consideration that this study focused on an international news outlet's international audience – on a culturally diverse news audience that cannot be characterized by one political or contextual setting. Implications therefore apply to news content producers who are primarily targeting this diverse demographic, which, in the age of the international news flow of social media, might be a growing chunk of the existing outlets. For these outlets, desired levels of bias perception must be discussed on an editorial level and social media guidelines might help journalists to navigate this new media environment.

5.4   Limitations and Future Research

Important findings aside, this research has limitations that need to be addressed. As Hypothesis 2a was not supported, further investigation would be necessary to determine whether anti-attack respondents would perceive a pro-attack slanted post as more biased towards the pro-attack side, than would pro-attack respondents. For this, it would possibly not be sufficient to present participants with either objective or slanted stimulus material, but the direction of the slant would also need to be specified, running the experiment with three variants of the stimulus material. In case this would not produce significant results either, further research would be necessary to understand what makes anti-attack respondents different from pro-attack respondents in their relative hostile media perception.

Other limitations include demographics and the time of data collection. For this study data was collected from an international sample as an effort to imitate a typical audience of international news outlets. This being the case, the majority of participants were nationals of the United States or Europe, therefore they might not be representative of a global international news audience. The time of data collection might also have been important. Soon after the military conflict was selected as the controversial issue in this study, the COVID-19 pandemic soaked up most of the international news audience's attention. Data was collected after the first waves of COVID-19 hit the Western hemisphere. However, this was still a short window after an exceptional time in history. During times of crisis research points out that expectations towards the media change, and readers are looking for more hard news, and less news analysis [65]. Therefore it is possible that results might have been influenced by this contextual environment.

Future research may also consider investigating different social media platforms, not only Facebook, as all SNS platforms are different in terms of their theme, user demographics, or even different focus [66]. In this study focus was merely on Facebook, but results might not be applicable to SNS platforms that are different in nature.

References

1. Nixon, B.: The business of news in the attention economy: audience labor and MediaNews Group's efforts to capitalize on news consumption. Journalism **21**(1), 1–22 (2017). https://doi.org/10.1177/1464884917719145
2. Thorson, K., Wells, C.: Curated flows: a framework for mapping media exposure in the digital age. Commun. Theory **26**(3), 309–328 (2016). https://doi.org/10.1111/comt.12087
3. Gallup. Media Use and Evaluation (2019). https://news.gallup.com/poll/1663/media-use-evaluation.aspx
4. Fawzi, N.: Untrustworthy news and the media as "enemy of the people?" How a populist worldview shapes recipients' attitudes toward the media. Int. J. Press/Polit. **24**(2), 146–164 (2019). https://doi.org/10.1177/1940161218811981
5. Edelman: 2019 Edelman Trust Barometer Global Report (2019). https://www.edelman.com/sites/g/files/aatuss191/files/2019-02/2019_Edelman_Trust_Barometer_Global_Report.pdf
6. Newman, N., Fletcher, R., Kalogeropoulos, A., Nielsen, R.K.: Reuters digital news report 2019. Reuters Institute for the Study of Journalism (2019)
7. Schaeffer, K.: Far more Americans see 'very strong' partisan conflicts now than in the last two Presidential Election years. Pew Research Center (2020)
8. Gil de Zúñiga, H., Weeks, B., Ardèvol-Abreu, A.: Effects of the news-finds-me perception in communication: social media use implications for news seeking and learning about politics. J. Comput.-Mediated Commun. **22**(3), 105–123 (2017). https://doi.org/10.1111/jcc4.12185
9. Oeldorf-Hirsch, A.: The role of engagement in learning from active and incidental news exposure on social media. Mass Commun. Soc. **21**(2), 225–247 (2018). https://doi.org/10.1080/15205436.2017.1384022
10. Shin, J., Thorson, K.: Partisan selective sharing: the biased diffusion of fact-checking messages on social media. J. Commun. **67**(2), 233–255 (2017). https://doi.org/10.1111/jcom.12284

11. Vallone, R.P., Ross, L., Lepper, M.R.: The hostile media phenomenon: biased perception and perceptions of media bias in coverage of the Beirut massacre. J. Pers. Soc. Psychol. **49**(3), 577–585 (1985). https://doi.org/10.1037/0022-3514.49.3.577

12. Perloff, R.M.: A three-decade retrospective on the hostile media effect. In: Advances in Foundational Mass Communication Theories, pp. 196–224. Routledge (2018). https://doi.org/10.4324/9781315164441-12

13. Gunther, A.C., Schmitt, K.: Mapping boundaries of the hostile media effect. J. Commun. **54**(1), 55–70 (2004). https://doi.org/10.1111/j.1460-2466.2004.tb02613.x

14. Gunther, A.C., Liebhart, J.L.: Broad reach or biased source? Decomposing the hostile media effect. J. Commun. **56**(3), 449–466 (2006). https://doi.org/10.1111/j.1460-2466.2006.00295.x

15. Christen, C.T., Kannaovakun, P., Gunther, A.C.: Hostile media perceptions: partisan assessments of press and public during the 1997 united parcel service strike. Polit. Commun. **19**(4), 423–436 (2002). https://doi.org/10.1080/10584600290109988

16. Choi, J., Yang, M., Chang, J.J.: Elaboration of the hostile media phenomenon. Commun. Res. **36**(1), 54–75 (2009). https://doi.org/10.1177/0093650208326462

17. Gunther, A.C., Christen, C.T., Liebhart, J.L., Chia, S.: Congenial public, contrary press, and biased estimates of the climate of opinion. Public Opin. Q. **65**(3), 295–320 (2001)

18. Arpan, L.M., Raney, A.A.: An experimental investigation of news source and the hostile media effect. Journal. Mass Commun. Q. **80**(2), 265–281 (2003). https://doi.org/10.1177/107769900308000203

19. Hansen, G.J., Kim, H.: Is the media biased against me? A meta-analysis of the hostile media effect research. Commun. Res. Rep. **28**(2), 169–179 (2011). https://doi.org/10.1080/08824096.2011.565280

20. Matthes, J.: The affective underpinnings of hostile media perceptions. Commun. Res. **40**(3), 360–387 (2013). https://doi.org/10.1177/0093650211420255

21. Johnson, B.T., Eagly, A.H.: Involvement and persuasion: types, traditions, and the evidence. Psychol. Bull. **107**(3), 375–384 (1990). https://doi.org/10.1037/0033-2909.107.3.375

22. Tsfati, Y., Cohen, J.: Perceptions of media and media effects: the third person effect, trust in media and hostile media perceptions. In: Valdivia, A.N. (ed.) The International Encyclopedia of Media Studies. Wiley-Blackwell (2012)

23. Tajfel, H., Turner, J.C.: The social identity theory of intergroup behavior. In: Political Psychology, pp. 276–293. Psychology Press (2004). https://doi.org/10.4324/9780203505984-16

24. Hartmann, T., Tanis, M.: Examining the hostile media effect as an intergroup phenomenon: the role of ingroup identification and status. J. Commun. **63**(3), 535–555 (2013). https://doi.org/10.1111/jcom.12031

25. Tsfati, Y.: Hostile media perceptions, presumed media influence, and minority alienation: the case of Arabs in Israel. J. Commun. **57**(4), 632–651 (2007). https://doi.org/10.1111/j.1460-2466.2007.00361.x

26. Duck, J.M., Terry, D.J., Hogg, M.A.: Perceptions of a media campaign: the role of social identity and the changing intergroup context. Pers. Soc. Psychol. Bull. **24**(1), 3–16 (1998). https://doi.org/10.1177/0146167298241001

27. Ariyanto, A., Hornsey, M.J., Gallois, C.: Group allegiances and perceptions of media bias. Group Process. Intergroup Relat. **10**(2), 266–279 (2007). https://doi.org/10.1177/1368430207074733

28. Bolsen, T., Druckman, J.N., Cook, F.L.: The influence of partisan motivated reasoning on public opinion. Polit. Behav. **36**(2), 235–262 (2013). https://doi.org/10.1007/s11109-013-9238-0

29. Reid, S.A.: A self-categorization explanation for the hostile media effect. J. Commun. **62**(3), 381–399 (2012). https://doi.org/10.1111/j.1460-2466.2012.01647.x

30. Schmitt, K.M., Gunther, A.C., Liebhart, J.L.: Why partisans see mass media as biased. Commun. Res. **31**(6), 623–641 (2004). https://doi.org/10.1177/0093650204269390
31. Giner-Sorolla, R., Chaiken, S.: The causes of hostile media judgments. J. Exp. Soc. Psychol. **30**(2), 165–180 (1994)
32. Barnidge, M., Rojas, H.: Hostile media perceptions, presumed media influence, and political talk: expanding the corrective action hypothesis. Int. J. Public Opin. Res. **26**(2), 135–156 (2014). https://doi.org/10.1093/ijpor/edt032
33. Tsfati, Y., Cohen, J.: The influence of presumed media influence on democratic legitimacy: the case of Gaza settlers. Commun. Res. **32**(6), 794–821 (2005)
34. Gunther, A.C.: Biased press or biased public? Attitudes toward media coverage of social groups. Public Opin. Q. **56**(2), 147–167 (1992). https://doi.org/10.1086/269308
35. Klinger, U., Svensson, J.: The emergence of network media logic in political communication: a theoretical approach. New Media Soc. **17**(8), 1241–1257 (2015)
36. Weeks, B.E., Kim, D.H., Hahn, L.B., Diehl, T.H., Kwak, N.: Hostile media perceptions in the age of social media: following politicians, emotions, and perceptions of media bias. J. Broadcast. Electron. Media **63**(3), 374–392 (2019)
37. Noelle-Neumann, E.: The spiral of silence: public opinion–our social skin. University of Chicago Press (1993)
38. Gaziano, C.: How credible is the credibility crisis? Journal. Q. **65**(2), 267–278 (1988). https://doi.org/10.1177/107769908806500202
39. Wanta, W., Hu, Y.-W.: The effects of credibility, reliance, and exposure on media agenda-setting: a path analysis model. Journal. Q. **71**(1), 90–98 (1994). https://doi.org/10.1177/107769909407100109
40. Hovland, C.I., Weiss, W.: The influence of source credibility on communication effectiveness. Public Opin. Q. **15**(4), 635–650 (1951). https://doi.org/10.1086/266350
41. Gaziano, C., McGrath, K.: Measuring the concept of credibility. Journal. Q. **63**(3), 451–462 (1986). https://doi.org/10.1177/107769908606300301
42. Shearer, E., Matsa, K.E.: News use across social media platforms 2018. Pew Research Center's Journalism Project (2018). https://www.journalism.org/2018/09/10/news-use-across-social-media-platforms-2018/
43. Flanagin, A.J., Metzger, M.J.: Perceptions of Internet information credibility. Journal. Mass Commun. Q. **77**(3), 515–540 (2000)
44. Kiousis, S.: Public trust or mistrust? Perceptions of media credibility in the information age. Mass Commun. Soc. **4**(4), 381–403 (2001). https://doi.org/10.1207/s15327825mcs0404_4
45. Schmierbach, M., Oeldorf-Hirsch, A.: A little bird told me, so i didn't believe it: Twitter, credibility, and issue perceptions. Commun. Q. **60**(3), 317–337 (2012). https://doi.org/10.1080/01463373.2012.688723
46. Westerman, D., Spence, P.R., Van Der Heide, B.: A social network as information: the effect of system generated reports of connectedness on credibility on Twitter. Comput. Hum. Behav. **28**(1), 199–206 (2012)
47. Deuze, M.: What is journalism? Journalism **6**(4), 442–464 (2005). https://doi.org/10.1177/1464884905056815
48. Hedman, U., Djerf-Pierre, M.: The social journalist. Digit. Journal. **1**(3), 368–385 (2013). https://doi.org/10.1080/21670811.2013.776804
49. Van der Wurff, R., Schoenbach, K.: Civic and citizen demands of news media and journalists: what does the audience expect from good journalism? Journal. Mass Commun. Q. **91**(3), 433–451 (2014)
50. Tsfati, Y., Meyers, O., Peri, Y.: What is good journalism? Comparing Israeli public and journalists' perspectives. Journalism **7**(2), 152–173 (2006). https://doi.org/10.1177/1464884906062603

51. Lasorsa, D.L., Lewis, S.C., Holton, A.E.: Normalizing Twitter. Journal. Stud. **13**(1), 19–36 (2012). https://doi.org/10.1080/1461670x.2011.571825
52. Singer, J.B.: The political j-blogger: 'normalizing'a new media form to fit old norms and practices. Journalism **6**(2), 173–198 (2005)
53. Nah, S., Chung, D.S.: When citizens meet both professional and citizen journalists: social trust, media credibility, and perceived journalistic roles among online community news readers. Journalism **13**(6), 714–730 (2012). https://doi.org/10.1177/1464884911431381
54. Hanitzsch, T., Vos, T.P.: Journalism beyond democracy: a new look into journalistic roles in political and everyday life. Journalism **19**(2), 146–164 (2018). https://doi.org/10.1177/146 4884916673386
55. Schudson, M.: The objectivity norm in American journalism. Journalism **2**(2), 149–170 (2001). https://doi.org/10.1177/146488490100200201
56. Janowitz, M.: Professional models in Journalism: the gatekeeper and the advocate. Journal. Q. **52**(4), 618–626 (1975). https://doi.org/10.1177/107769907505200402
57. Charles, M.: Advocacy journalism. In: Vos, T.P., Hanusch, F., Dimitrakopoulou, D., Geertsema-Sligh, M., Sehl, A. (eds.) The International Encyclopedia of Journalism Studies. Wiley (2019)
58. Fisher, C.: The advocacy continuum: towards a theory of advocacy in journalism. Journalism **17**(6), 711–726 (2016). https://doi.org/10.1177/1464884915582311
59. Crowley, M., Eric, H., Schmitt, E.: U.S. Strike in Iraq kills qassim suleimani, commander of Iranian forces. The New York Times, 2 January 2020. https://www.nytimes.com/2020/01/02/world/middleeast/qassem-soleimani-iraq-iran-attack.html
60. Facebook: How Facebook's fact-checking program works. Facebook (2019). https://www.facebook.com/journalismproject/programs/third-party-fact-checking/how-it-works
61. Kim, Y.: The contribution of social network sites to exposure to political difference: the relationships among SNSs, online political messaging, and exposure to cross-cutting perspectives. Comput. Hum. Behav. **27**(2), 971–977 (2011). https://doi.org/10.1016/j.chb.2010.12.001
62. Kim, Y., Hsu, S.-H., de Zúñiga, H.G.: Influence of social media use on discussion network heterogeneity and civic engagement: the moderating role of personality traits. J. Commun. **63**(3), 498–516 (2013). https://doi.org/10.1111/jcom.12034
63. Bakshy, E., Messing, S., Adamic, L.A.: Exposure to ideologically diverse news and opinion on Facebook. Science **348**(6239), 1130–1132 (2015). https://doi.org/10.1126/science.aaa1160
64. Bail, C.A., et al.: Exposure to opposing views on social media can increase political polarization. Proc. Natl. Acad. Sci. **115**(37), 9216–9221 (2018)
65. Costera Meijer, I.: The paradox of popularity. Journal. Stud. **8**(1), 96–116 (2007). https://doi.org/10.1080/14616700601056874
66. Mull, I.R., Lee, S.E.: "PIN" pointing the motivational dimensions behind Pinterest. Comput. Hum. Behav. **33**, 192–200 (2014)
67. Gunther, A.C.: The persuasive press inference. Commun. Res. **25**(5), 486–504 (1998). https://doi.org/10.1177/009365098025005002
68. Feldman, L.: Partisan differences in opinionated news perceptions: a test of the hostile media effect. Polit. Behav. **33**(3), 407–432 (2011). https://doi.org/10.1007/s11109-010-9139-4
69. Watts, M.D., Domke, D., Shah, D.V., Fan, D.P.: Elite cues and media bias in presidential campaigns. Commun. Res. **26**(2), 144–175 (1999). https://doi.org/10.1177/009365099026 002003

Realizing the Potential Effect of Interactable Concept Network for Idea Generation

Yi-Jing Lin(✉) [iD] and Yen Hsu [iD]

The Graduate Institute of Design Science, Tatung University, Taipei, Taiwan
una0903@gmail.com

Abstract. Idea generation is the foundation of creativity and innovation, and learning various ideation methods, such as mind-map, scamper, etc. is a critical capability in a design-thinking course. With emerging technologies, many data-driven conceptual design tools exist to provide designers with external inspirational stimuli for ideation. Compared to traditional ideation methods, the data-driven conceptual tools are time-saving for gathering information, and labor-saving for generating numerous, various and creative ideas. Moreover, designers are able to avoid individually experiential limitation, which may cause the fixation of ideation. However, most data-driven conceptual tools are biased towards the industrial engineering field, and are too complicated to intuitively use for novice designers. Hence, this study established the user-friendly ideation tool named Interactable Concept Network (ICN) by integrating the mind-mapping method, semantic network database, and human cognitive process, additionally investigated its effects on novice designers learning of design-thinking courses. We assume that there is a potential effectiveness to assist and inspire novice designers to develop more creative concepts by applying ICN tool. With a pre–post-test design, a brief design course-long experiment as pre-test was then conducted with the mind-map method to evaluate the initial learning motivation and creativity. At this current study stage, the pre-test results revealed that the recognition and delivery errors caused by the handwritten and inaccurate description influenced the score of creativity.

Keywords: Data-driven · Idea generation · Creativity · Semantic network database

1 Introduction

Conceptual idea generation is a critical foundation in the early stage of product development, more over wrong decisions even lead to the failure of the new project [4]. In view of the various semantic databases establishment, such as TechNet, ConceptNet and WordNet, a growing amount of research about applying data-driven to stimuli designers idea generation has been proposed [6, 13, 19, 20]. Compared with traditional ideation methods procedures, the data-driven approach ideation tools are more efficiency on time-saving and labor saving for gathering information, enhancing creativity and even avoiding the fixation of individually experiential limitation [6]. Moreover, the data-driven approach

P.-L. P. Rau (Ed.): HCII 2022, LNCS 13313, pp. 137–147, 2022.
https://doi.org/10.1007/978-3-031-06050-2_10

ideation tools provide the designers stimuli nodes based on existing semantic databases with a visualization network form for supporting "gathering overall information for the insights" [20], "expanding individual thoughts by information retrieval" [13], and "exploring unfamiliar issues".

Nevertheless, the computer-aid methods of concept networks are complexity to use, and more discussed in engineering fields. Also the existing concept network methods are based on keywords retrieval of the specific knowledgebase, it may exist stimuli fixation in the similar topic, and lack considering the interactable possibility between humans and computers. Therefore, we proposed the new interactable concept network (ICN), which is a ideation web application based on the ConceptNet with blending the familiar ideation method - mind map with intuitive operation.

The purpose of this study was to prove the effectiveness of the interactivity of the ICN application for novice designers generation conceptual ideas. The research introducing the ICN tool to the learning environment and using ANCOVA to analyze the pretest/posttest scores to realize whether it has the effect for students on learning motivation and creativity. In this paper, the results of the pre-test revealed that there's information missing and misunderstanding about recognizing and delivery caused by handwriting and inaccurate words. In the further post-test stage, in order to reduce the errors of information transferring, the experiments will be corrected with computer-aid and adding the annotation to the descriptions.

2 Related Work

2.1 Data-Driven for Generating Ideas

The researchers focus on applying a data-driven approach to designing in the concept generation stage at the front end of the product development procedure, and on providing external data to inspire designers ideation for new design concepts. In the literatures, there are a variety of databases used as design stimuli. For instance, Han et al. integrated B-Link database, which consists of human judgements, as well as TechNet, which contains over four million engineering terms, to generate stimuli with images [6]. Song et al. applied TechNet extracted the functional words from patent documents and created a semantic network based on word co-occurrences to insight core and peripheral functions for developing new family series of products [19]. You et al. proposed advertisements auto-generator by gathering and analyzing the rules of 13,000 advertisement images as a database [23]. Wodehouse et al. extracted affective words from user comments of a numerous electronic books and corresponded to the patent function as a database in heatmap form to offer designers user-centered experience design suggestions [22].

Most of the literature is discussing the establishment of databases with various types of sources and what retrieval results were provided for inspiring designers, such as patent documents [20], social media [8], and shopping websites [15]. Compared with traditional ideation methods, computer-aid data-driven approaches are not only time-saving but also providing efficiently information retrieval. In addition, due to the analyzing and collation of large amounts of data by AI algorithms, it brings to revolutionary design methods and design strategies for designers with suggestions of ideation, decision and evaluation. However, the data-driven platforms are mainly as an information retrieval tool that designers interact with rigidly and one-way interaction. Thus, this research tries to propose a new interactive way of mutual communication.

2.2 Semantic Network Mapping

There's various types and scopes of data, including texts, images and videos. Due to the universality of semantic extraction, the research is focused on discussing semantic databases. The primary phase of the generation knowledge database task is data processing and recognition with AI algorithms, which enable computers to recognize the structure of data and extract it into nodes from raw data. The knowledge databases are established by organizing the nodes into visualization graphs with meaningful relations or rules. For example, Luo et al. established the InnoGPS as an information map, which is reorganized the patent documents according to IPC system and visualized the nodes distribution with co-occurrence of tech-term semantics based on TechNet [13]. Moreover, the nodes extraction depends on the purpose of applying the semantic database, such as function-based extraction for family products development strategy [20]; technology-based extraction for engineering technology creation activity [17]. In this research keyword-based were utilized for its universality [12, 22].

To manifest meaningful organizing of the nodes as knowledge map, there's existed available semantic knowledge database for offering semantics relation as weights. For example, ConceptNet is a universal human cognitive semantic knowledge database using Wikipedia platform as data source by MIT Media Lab proposed [24]; TechNet is a technology semantic knowledge database obtained by extracting technology terms from patent documents by Sarica et al. proposed [18]; WordNet is a lexical database storing the structural relationships between words in English by George A. Miller proposed [14].

In particular, ConceptNet containing commonsense knowledge is suitable to be used for assisting designers generating conceptual ideation, cause the still data accumulating and similarity of linkage to human cognition approach. For instance, Han et al. built a design ideation tool called Combinator, which linked its core database from crawling internet through ConceptNet [9].

3   Method

3.1   Participant

One class of sophomore students (N = 19) from the Department of Product Design of a university in Taiwan were voluntary and solicited to be the participants in the experiment. All of the students had completed a full semester of design thinking courses and they understood the mind-map method before. Experts participated (N = 5) in the experiment to evaluate the students' creativity of concepts.

In the current stage (pre-test), all of the student participants generate ideas by conventional mind-map method without computer-aid. In the post-test stage, student participants are divided into equal-size of experimental and control groups of students with Randomized block design (RBD). The experimental group include 10 students (3 males and 7 females), who generate ideas utilizing the ICN tool. On the other hand, the control group consisted of 9 students (2 males and 7 females), who generate ideas using the mapping tools (kumu.io) with google search engine. The average age of the students in both groups is 20.

3.2 Instrument and Measures

To evaluate the effectiveness of the interactable concept network tool (ICN is as shown in Fig. 2) on novice designers, a quasi-experimental research was conducted on a brief course-long (1 h) in a classroom of a university. This research mainly includes the pre-test, post-test, learning motivation questionnaire for analyzing students' behaviors and creativity rubrics for measuring learning effectiveness on ideation competence, as shown in Fig. 1.

The questionnaires assessed students' learning behavior and creativity. Detailed descriptions are provided in the following paragraphs:

Learning motivation: An intrinsic value scale was applied to the Motivated Strategies for Learning Questionnaire (MSLQ) to measure learning motivation. Researchers have recommended using the intrinsic value scale when assessing students' goals and beliefs about the importance and interest of ideation work. The questionnaire was composed of seventeen items (see Table 1), all of which were rated using a seven-point Likert scale [16].

Learning Idea generation: This study adopted a creativity rubric for measuring students' learning effective on ideation competence with an extrinsic value scale. The extrinsic value scale has been recommended by researchers when assessing student organizational ability and creativity about the novelty, usefulness, and quantity of concepts. The assessment was referenced to the creativity metrics rubric [11], which refers to the consensual technique of creativity assessment [1] and rating with a group of "expert judges" [2]. The researchers developed a creativity rubric of six criteria: organization of mind map, concept novelty, Effectiveness, implementability, concept quantity and product description with 1–5 Likert type items (see Table 2).

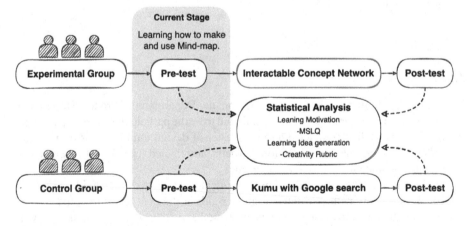

Fig. 1. The experimental process.

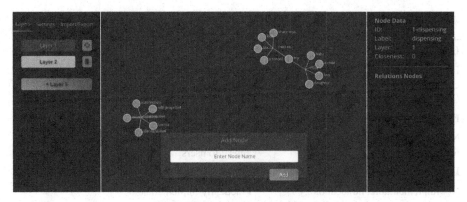

Fig. 2. The experimental process.

Table 1. Motivated strategies for learning questionnaire

Motivation

Value	Expectancy	Affect
Intrinsic goals	Control beliefs	Test anxiety
Extrinsic goals	Self-efficacy	
Task value		

Learning strategies

Cognitive and metacognitive strategies	Resource management
Rehearsal	Time study management
Elaboration	Effort regulation
Organization	Peer learning
Critical thinking	Help seeking
Metacognitive self-regulation	

Table 2. The creativity rubric

Measure score

Level 1/score:1/5	Level 5/score:5/5

Organization of mind map

Choppy and confusing	Well organized and logical development
Many key words and concepts are missing from the topic	All key words and concepts are related the topic in a meaningful way
Never manifest the cognitive process of Analogy or Combination	A great deal manifest the cognitive process of Analogy and Combination

(continued)

Table 2. (*continued*)

Concept novelty	
Entirely similar to existing design concepts, Copy of existing product	Entirely different to existing design concepts, Idea is a real surprise

Effectiveness (sub-metric of usefulness)	
Not meet the market demand, and useless for users	Accord with the market demand, and entirely appeal to users

Implementability (sub-metric of usefulness)	
Not implementable, no technology expertise exists for industrializing this product	Practically implementable There is established knowledge and technology expertise for industrializing this product

Concept quantity				
No concept is generated, or the concept does not match the topic	Generate 1 concept related to the topic	Generate 2 concepts related to the topic	Generate 3 concepts related to the topic	Generate more than 4 concepts related to the topic

Product description				
An attempt is made to explain the concept; however, it lacks significant details or is incomplete	The purpose and appearance of the design concept is presented but generally unclear and lacking in detail	The purpose and appearance of the design concept is generally clear and somewhat detailed	The purpose and appearance of the design concept is clear and generally detailed	The purpose and appearance of the design concept is clear and detailed Information about general size, shape, materials, and other important product features is included

3.3 Experimental Procedure

All participants were protected by keeping their personal information hidden through the experimental process. At the beginning of the course, the student participants are informed of the aim of the research and the experimental procedure.

These student participants have fully completed one semester design thinking course and have related knowledge of the mind map. To realize the effect of ICN tool, which is based mind map method, both groups of students (N = 19) took a pre-test experiment conducting individual ideation with the mind map method (shown a Fig. 3). In the further post-test stage, the experimental group of students will take ICN tool based on the available semantic network–ConceptNet to generate ideas, and the control group of students will take the mapping tool–kumu with google search for ideations.

At the current stage, all students are taught to use the combination [7, 10] and analogy [3, 21] cognitive to generate brief words of the mind map, which is about the topic of the post pandemic era, for 20 min of divergent design thinking. After the mind-mapping process, students used the mind-map to generate concept sketches as many as possible in the 30 min of convergent design thinking. To reduce information missing, students were asked to apply the FBS framework to describe concept, including function, behavior and structure (noting on the sketches directly) [5]. After this course experiment, all student participants were indicated to complete the pre-test questionnaire survey which consisted of intrinsic items related to their demographic background, learning motivation and learning strategies. On the other hand, the experts who include industry professionals (N = 3) and academics (N = 2) evaluated students' organizational capability and creativity of sketches as extrinsic items with a rubric form. The procedure of implementing the pre-test experiment is as shown in Table 3.

Table 3. The pre-test experimental course process.

Activity	Duration	Contents
Step1: Introduction	5 min	Introduce the experiment process Teach about how to organize and diverge by analogy and combination thinking
Step2: Divergence	20 min	Diverging ideas by organizing mind-map in the topic: The products or concepts for the post pandemic era
Step3: Convergence	30 min	Converging and generating ideas in sketches and descriptions, which include function, behavior and structure (FBS)
Step4: Questionnaire	5 min	Completing the MSLQ questionnaire
Step5: Judgement	No limits	Experts give ratings based on the rubric

In the post-test study, student participants will be divided into two groups which include an experimental group and a control group according to the result scores of the pre-test in randomized block design.

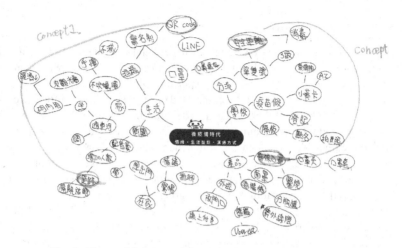

Fig. 3. The establishment of the mind map in pretest experiment.

The research data of the pre-test, the researchers used Pearson correlation analysis to determine the relation between the factors as the standard of the post-test and the basis for correcting the subsequent experiment.

In further work, the students in the experimental group will apply the ICN tool which is integrates semantic knowledgebase into the mind map method, and the control group will be able to use google search to retrieve related information for organizing thoughts with the mapping platform (kumu). The semantic database intervention is the main difference between the two groups. In order to evaluate the effect on their learning motivation and creativity with the data-driven method intervention. Both in the pre-test and post-test experiment, all student participants need to complete an MSLQ; and experts judge the concepts in the creativity rubric. The study will use one-way analysis of covariance (ANCOVA) with the post-test and pre-test scores of learning motivation and creativity as the dependent variable and covariate, respectively.

4   Results and Discussion

4.1   Analysis of Learning Motivation and Strategy

The current results show that most students were satisfied with the knowledge applied during the course, and also had a positive attitude with learning strategy to organize and use the skill to complete their further design work. Figure 4 shows that most participants of the learning motivation values, distributed on a 7 point Likert scales, are positive (higher than 4 scores) and have a mean of 5.42 scores; also the learning strategy values have a mean of 4.94 scores.

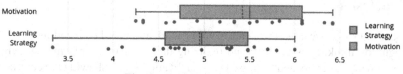

Fig. 4. The MSLQ of box plots.

4.2 Analysis of Ideation Competence

On the other hand, the ideation competence of students with traditional methods judged by experts is lower than expected, especially in creativity performance. Figure 5 shows that moderate performances (lower than 3 scores) on a 5 point Likert scale include organization (mean = 3.04), creativity (mean = 2.93), description (mean = 2.89) and quantity (mean = 2.9).

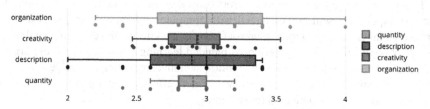

Fig. 5. The experts evaluation of box plots.

The correlation analysis between the factors shows the result, that description scores have impacts on creativity and organization as shown in Table 4. According to the experts' feedback, it is difficult to recognize the words and understand the meaning from descriptions. Hence, the result might be caused by the unrecognizable handwritten words and poor expression of the sketches. In addition, there's no significant correlation between the learning behaviors and the creation results.

Table 4. Pearson correlation analysis.

	Organization	Creativity	Quantity	Description	Learning motivation
Creativity	0.444				
Quantity	0.061	0.43			
Description	**.481***	**.757***	0.347		
Learning motivation	0.157	0.092	−0.193	0.351	
Learning strategy	0.076	-0.202	−0.293	−0.274	0.345

**correlation is significant at the 0.01 level (2-tailed).

5   Conclusion

At the current stage, we taught students to apply an ideation method blending mind-map and cognition thinking as pre-test; and realizing the mistakes of information delivery between novice designers and experts. The visualization graph showing the correlations in Fig. 6, it's revealed that the description scores have a critical influence on other factors. Hence, in order to focus on investigating the effect of ICN tools on novice designers, we will propose a post-test experiment that participants use web applications (such as ICN and Kumu) for ideation to reduce the interference of recognizing missing; adding brief annotation of descriptions for easy understanding. Further, the research will use ANCOVA in the pre-test and post-test scores of learning motivation and creativity as the dependent variables and covariates respectively, to investigate whether ICN tool, which the researcher proposed, is effective for assisting novice designers expanding their thinking, generating ideas efficiently and even increasing their learning motivation on design thinking courses.

In order to reduce the recognition errors caused by the handwritten description, the post-test experiment will be conducted with computer-aid applications, such as ICN (Experimental Group) and kumu (Control Group). In addition, the researchers will integrate ICN applications into the proposed blended learning environment to support co-design activities in the future. A study to follow will involve participants as design teams to further investigate the ICN effects to develop more effective and user-friendly ideation methods to support collaborative brainstorming.

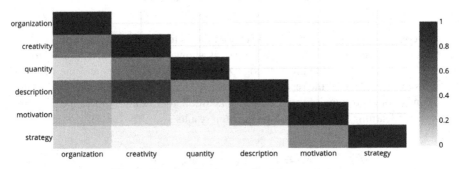

Fig. 6. The visualization graph of the correlations.

References

1. Amabile, T.M.: Creativity in Context. Westview Press, Boulder (1996). https://doi.org/10.4324/9780429501234
2. Baer, J.: Commentary: divergent thinking tests have problems, but this is not the solution. Psychol. Aesthet. Creat. Arts **2**(2) 89–92 (2008)
3. Chan, J., Fu, K., Schunn, C., Cagan, J., Wood, K., Kotovsky, K.: On the bene- fits and pitfalls of analogies for innovative design: Ideation performance based on analogical distance, commonness, and modality of examples. J. Mech. Des. **133** (2011)
4. Chen, L., et al.: An artificial intelligence based data-driven approach for design ideation. J. Vis. Commun. Image Represent **61**, 10–22 (2019)

5. Gero, J.S., Kannengiesser, U.: The situated function–behaviour–structure framework. Design Studies 25(4), 373–391 (2004). https://doi.org/10.1016/j.destud.2003.10.010. https://www.sciencedirect.com/science/article/pii/S0142694X03000735

6. Han, J., Forbes, H., Shi, F., Hao, J., Schaefer, D.: A data-driven approach for creative concept generation and evaluation. In: Proceedings of the Design Society: DESIGN Conference, vol. 1, pp. 167–176 (2020). https://doi.org/10.1017/dsd.2020.5

7. Han, J., Hua, M., Shi, F., Childs, P.R.N.: A further exploration of the three driven approaches to combinational creativity. In: Proceedings of the Design Society: International Conference on Engineering Design, vol. 1, pp. 2735–2744 (2019). https://doi.org/10.1017/dsi.2019.280

8. Han, J., Park, D., Forbes, H., Schaefer, D.: A computational approach for using social networking platforms to support creative idea generation. Procedia CIRP **91**, 382–387 (2020)

9. Han, J., Shi, F., Chen, L., Childs, P.R.: The combinator–a computer-based tool for creative idea generation based on a simulation approach. Des. Sci. 4 (2018). https://doi.org/10.1017/dsj.2018.7

10. Han, J., Shi, F., Park, D., Chen, L., Childs, P., et al.: The conceptual distances between ideas in combinational creativity. In: DS 92: Proceedings of the DESIGN 2018 15th International Design Conference, pp. 1857–1866 (2018)

11. Koronis, G., Silva, A., Kang, J.K.S., Yogiaman, C.: How to best frame a design brief to maximize novelty and usefulness in idea generation. In: Proceedings of the Design Society: DESIGN Conference, vol. 1, pp. 1745–1754 (2020). https://doi.org/10.1017/dsd.2020.77. https://www.cambridge.org/core/article/how-to-best-frame-a-design-brief-to-maximize-novelty-and-usefulness-in-idea-generation/BF14ECC7199C206E6B9A757AE4C09E1B

12. Lee, S., Yoon, B., Park, Y.: An approach to discovering new technology opportunities: keyword-based patent map approach. Technovation **29**(6–7), 481–497 (2009). https://doi.org/10.1016/j.technovation.2008.10.006

13. Luo, J., Sarica, S., Wood, K.L.: Guiding data-driven design ideation by knowledge distance. Knowl.-Based Syst. **218**, 106873 (2021)

14. Miller, G.A.: WordNet: An Electronic Lexical Database. MIT Press, Cambridge (1998)

15. Ozer, M., Cebeci, U.: Affective design using big data within the context of online shopping. J. Eng. Des. **30**(8–9), 368–384 (2019). https://doi.org/10.1080/09544828.2019.1656803

16. Pintrich, P.R., De Groot, E.V.: Motivational and self-regulated learning components of classroom academic performance. J. Educ. Psychol. **82**(1), 33 (1990)

17. Sarica, S., Luo, J.: Design knowledge representation with technology semantic network. Proc. Des. Soc. **1**, 1043–1052 (2021)

18. Sarica, S., Luo, J., Wood, K.L.: TechNet: technology semantic network based on patent data. Exp. Syst. Appl. **142**, 112995 (2020)

19. Song, B., Luo, J.: Mining patent precedents for data-driven design: the case of spherical rolling robots. J. Mech. Des. **139**(11) (2017)

20. Song, B., Luo, J., Wood, K.: Data-driven platform design: patent data and function network analysis. J. Mech. Des. **144**(2), 021101 (2019)

21. Srinivasan, V., et al.: Does analogical distance affect performance of ideation? J. Mech. Des. **140**(7) (2018)

22. Wodehouse, A., Vasantha, G., Corney, J., Jagadeesan, A., MacLachlan, R.: Realising the affective potential of patents: a new model of database interpretation for user-centred design. J. Eng. Des. **29**(8–9), 484–511 (2018)

23. You, W.T., Sun, L.Y., Yang, Z.Y., Yang, C.Y.: Automatic advertising image color design incorporating a visual color analyzer. J. Comput. Lang. **55**, 100910 (2019)

24. Zhao, Y., et al.: Mining affective words to capture customer's affective response to apparel products. Text. Res. J. **88**(12), 1426–1436 (2018)

A Novel Transformer-Based Model for Dialog State Tracking

Yu Miao, Kuilong Liu, Wenbo Yang, and Changyuan Yang[✉]

Alibaba Group, Hangzhou 311121, China
`changyuan.yangcy@alibaba-inc.com`

Abstract. Dialog state tracking (DST) is a core component in the task-oriented dialog systems. Many previous approaches regard DST as a classification task for a set of predefined slot-value pairs, but these approaches can not handle the situation of dynamic ontology. Other methods consider slot as span-based, while these methods are insufficient when the target slot-value cannot be found as a word segment in the dialog context. To mitigate these problems, we propose a Transformer-based model for DST. The proposed method can achieve the DST task by extracting the slot-value from the dialog context or classifying for the slot with limited values. Experimental evidence shows that our proposed model can achieve competitive performance on the WOZ 2.0 dataset while being 20× faster than the state-of-the-art model. To demonstrate the effectiveness of our proposed model on multi-domain, we experiment with the recently released MultiWOZ-2.0 dataset. The experiment shows that our model can achieve promising result.

Keywords: Dialog State Tracking (DST) · Multi-domain dialogue systems · Pretrained-model

1 Introduction

Task-oriented dialogue systems have received more and more attention in recent years. This type of dialog system refers to multi-turn dialogues driven by tasks. Generally, a task-oriented dialog system can be considered as a sequential decision-making process. The machine needs to maintain and update the internal dialog state by understanding user sentences during the dialog process, and then select the next optimal action according to the current state to help users to achieve their goals.

Dialog state tracking (DST) is a central constituent in task-oriented dialogue systems. It maintains the current dialog state, which is a cumulative semantic representation of the entire dialogue history, generally presented as a set of slot-value pairs. With the development of deep learning, many data-driven models have been proposed for the task of DST [2,5,8,11,15,19,20]. Despiting the promising performance, these methods still have certain limitations. Many approaches consider DST as a classification task for a predefined collection of slot-value pairs or to score the relevance of slot-value pairs to dialog context [8,11,15,19]. However, such methods are insufficient when the slot with non-enumerable values appears (e.g., values for the time slot can have Countless choices). The other approaches treat slots as span-based [2], where the values can be found through the span matching with the start and end positions in the dialogue context. However, such methods are inadequate to handle situations where the target slot-value does not appear as word segment in the dialog context. More recently, a hybrid state tracking method, HyST [5] has been proposed, which is based on hierarchical RNN and open-vocabulary generation. HyST can be regarded as a combination of class-based an span-based DST methods. However, in the inference stage, HyST needs to present the ensemble results of multiple models, which will increase the computational complexity.

Recently, several pre-trained models based on Transformer [16] such as BERT [4], ALBERT [9] and ELECTRA [3], have achieved the state-of-the-art results in many downstream tasks. The "pre-training + fine-tuning" mode has been widely used in the NLP field. In this paper, we propose a novel dialog state tracker. In the proposed model architecture, the pre-trained model is adopted to produce contextualized word representation of the dialog context. This method is applicable to a variety of pre-trained models, not just specific ones. When the slot-value is uncountable, the proposed method can extract the value from the dialogue context by span matching, and when the target slot-value does not appear in the dialog context, the method can also complete the task by classifying for the slot with limited values.

2   Pre-trained Models

In this section, we summarize several of pre-trained models and how they can be utilized to perform DST in our model.

2.1   BERT

BERT is a language representation model [4], which is composed of multi-layers of bidirectional Transformer [16]. BERT's input representation is a sequence of input token. The special classification token [CLS] is always the first token of each input sequence. The final hidden state of [CLS] is used as composite sequence representation, while the final hidden states of other tokens are used as the representations of their corresponding tokens.

During the pre-training stage, BERT is trained on two unsupervised tasks: masked language modeling (masked LM) and next sentence prediction (NSP). In the masked LM task, a certain percentage of the input tokens are randomly masked, and then BERT is trained to predict those masked tokens. In the NSP task, BERT is trained to predict whether one sentence is successive to another. The results show that BERT fine-tuned with one output layer can achieve promising performance for a wide range of downstream tasks [4].

2.2 ALBERT

ALBERT stands for A Lite BERT [9], which combines two parameter reduction methods to decrease the significant restrictions in optimizing pre-trained models. The first method is factorized embedding parameterization, which method separates the large vocabulary embedding matrix into two small matrices. The second is cross-layer parameter sharing, which prevents the parameter from increasing through the growth of the network layer. During the pre-training, ALBERT use a sentence-order prediction (SOP) loss to address the ineffectiveness [10, 18] of the NSP loss. The experimental evidence shows that ALBERT can achieve better results than BERT on many downstream tasks, while fewer parameters are needed.

2.3 ELECTRA

ELECTRA is a pre-training model [3], which can achieve higher accuracy on downstream tasks than BERT while train much faster. Unlike prior work, ELECTRA applies replaced token detection instead of masked LM. The pre-trained ELECTRA can be considered as a discriminator that predicts whether it is an original or a replacement for every token. The advantage of the discriminative task is that the model can learn from all input tokens instead of the small masked subset, which improves the computational efficiency.

2.4 Pre-trained Model for DST

Despite the differences, the above pre-trained models are all applications of Transformer, and their input and output representations are consistent. Therefore, we can use these models as dialog context encoders in the DST task. Figure 1 demonstrates the model architecture of our proposed approach. The proposed application of pre-trained models to DST is similar to the combination of sentence pair classification task and the Stanford Question Answering Dataset (SQuAD) task [13]. Table 1 shows the configurations of the pre-trained models applied to DST in this paper.

Table 1. The configurations of the pre-trained models discussed in this paper.

Model	Parameters	Layers	Hidden
BERT-base	110M	12	768
ALBERT-base	12M	12	768
ELECTRA-base	110M	12	768

3 Method

In this section, we describe the proposed model in detail. As shown in Fig. 1, the pre-trained model takes a turn of tokenized conversation content as input then

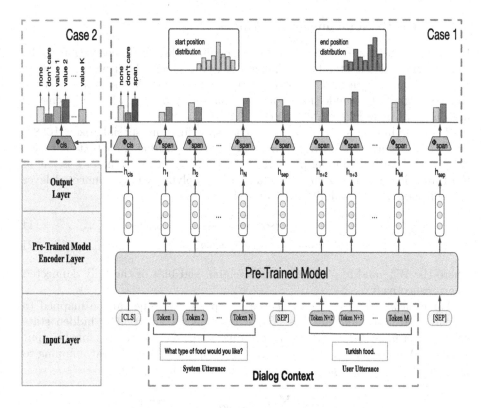

Fig. 1. Architecture of our proposed model for DST.

outputs the sentence-level and token-level hidden states. Like work proposed by [2], for a slot with non-enumerable values, the sentence-level representation is used to estimate the three associations (*none, don't care, span*) of the slot and the input dialog context, while the proposed model applies the token-level representations to predict the start and end positions of the target slot-value. For a slot with limited values, the sentence-level representation is used in the classification module to generate a distribution over $k+2$ types of corresponding values of the slot: *none, don't care, value 1, ..., value k*.

3.1 Dialog Context Encoder

We use the pre-trained model as the dialog context encoder. The input to the pre-trained model is composed of system utterance and user utterance. Same as the input format of the pre-trained models, the first token of the input sequence is [CLS], and the special token [SEP] is used to separate the system utterance and user utterance. The pre-trained model takes the input token sequence ($[x_0, x_1, ..., x_{M+1}]$) and then outputs the hidden state vectors ($[h_0, h_1, ..., h_{M+1}]$) corresponding to each input token.

3.2   Slot with Non-enumerable Values

In this case, the values of the slots are not enumerable, which means that in the test, the slot-value related to the dialog may never appeared during the training. Hence, we can not recognize slot-value by sentence pair classification. S is the collection of all informable slots. There is a subset S_n of S, in which all elements are slots with non-enumerable values.

The first hidden state vector h_{cls} corresponding the special token [CLS], which is the sentence-level representation for the input dialog context. For each $s \in S_n$, the proposed model predicts the probability of the value of s is one of the three classes (*area, food, price range*) by applying a fully connected layer and softmax. The probability is expressed as:

$$prob_{cls}^s = \text{softmax}\,(W_{cls}^s h_{cls} + b_{cls}^s) \tag{1}$$

$$slot\_value^s = \text{argmax}\,(prob_{cls}^s) \tag{2}$$

where the W_{cls}^s and b_{cls}^s represent the weights and bias of the fully connected layer, respectively.

For each $s \in \{s | s \in S_n, slot\_value^s = \text{span}\}$, its value can be mapped to a span with start and end position in the dialog context. The hidden state vectors after h_{cls} ($[h_1, ..., h_{M+1}]$) are the token-level representations for the input sequence. We use these vectors as input, and apply a two-way linear mapping to get a start distribution $prob_{start}^s$ and an end distribution $prob_{end}^s$:

$$[prob_{start}^s, prob_{end}^s] = W_{span}^s\,[h_1, ..., h_{M+1}]^T$$
$$+ b_{span}^s \tag{3}$$

$$start\_position^s = \text{argmax}\,(prob_{start}^s) \tag{4}$$

$$end\_position^s = \text{argmax}\,(prob_{end}^s) \tag{5}$$

where the weight matrix W_{span}^s and the bias term b_{span}^s are learnable model parameters.

3.3   Slot with Limited Values

In this case, the values of the slots are limited. We can still recognize the slot-value in the above span-based method. However, this method cannot handle the situation where the target slot-value does not directly appear in the context as a word segment. For example, the user utterance "My wife thinks she likes International but I don't want to take out a loan." implies a target slot-value price range=cheap, whose span cannot be defined. In addition, compared with the classification task, the sequence Tagging is more computationally intensive. Therefore, we apply the classification method to recognize the slot-values in this case. There is a subset S_l of S, in which all elements are slots with limited values. For each $s \in S_l$, the distribution over $k + 2$ types of values can be expressed as Eq. 1.

3.4 Dialog State Update Mechanism

We use an update mechanism to track the dialog states across turns. In each turn, only when the model's prediction value of a slot is not *none*, it will be used to update the dialog state.

3.5 Parameter Sharing

Although the proposed model is slot-specific, all slots are related to each other. Parameter sharing among related tasks reduces the number of model parameters and speeds up model inference, and it also improves the model's generalization ability. Like Bert-DST [2], we apply parameter sharing on the dialog context encoder across all slots.

4 Experiments and Results

4.1 Dataset and Metric

The Woz 2.0 dataset [17] and the MultiWOZ 2.0 dataset [1] are used to evaluate the proposed model. The Woz 2.0 dataset is a standard benchmark for a task-oriented dialog system in restaurant search domain. There are three informable slots (*area, food, price range*) that the user can utilize to restrain the search range. There are 1200 dialogues in the dataset, including 600, 200, 400 dialogues for *train, validate, and test* respectively. MultiWOZ 2.0 is one of the largest multi-domain dialogue corpus with 37 slots across 7 distinct domains and over 10, 000 dialogues. The data splits (train/valid/test) of MultiWOZ 2.0 are 8438, 1000 and 1000, respectively.

Similar to former work, we use *joint goal accuracy* [6] as the evaluation metric. It is worth noting that we did not apply output expansion during the test to handle other potentially valid output spans, which means that the output span of our model must be precisely the same as the label span to be considered correct.

4.2 Experimental Details

We employ the pre-trained model provided by Google Research (bert-base-uncased, albert-base-v2, ELECTRA-Base). The model parameters are updated by Adam [7] optimizer with an initial learning rate $2e-5$ in the training phase, We apply a warm-up strategy for Adam optimizer, the proportion for linear learning rate warm-up is set as 0.1. The batch size is set as 64. We apply early stopping according to the join goal accuracy on the validation set, and a fixed number of maximum epochs is set to 10. The maximum input sequence length of pre-trained models is set as 180.

4.3   Results and Inference Speed

Table 2 presents the property of different approaches on the standard WOZ 2.0 dataset. Our model achieves competitive results compared with the state-of-the-art model, which cannot handle unknown ontology.

The input to the state-of-the-art model is a combination of dialog context and a slot-value candidate [8], and then the model needs to traverse all the predefined slot-value candidates to achieve the DST task, which significantly increases the computational cost. In comparison, due to the input-output structures of our method, the input to the proposed model only contains dialog context, thus the model does not required to traverse all the slot-value pairs to achieve the competitive results.

As shown in Table 2, our proposed models are much faster than previous works. The state-of-the-art model [8] is based on BERT. The experimental results show that our BERT-based model is 16.9× faster on inference than the full BERT-based model proposed by [8] and 3.6× faster than their distilled model. Averagely, the fastest model we proposed (ALBERT-based) is 20× faster than their full model and 4× faster than their distilled model.

Table 2. The test accuracies of different models on the WoZ 2.0 dataset and their inference time on GPU (GeForce GTX 1080). We measured the average time required for each model to process one dialog turn (in milliseconds).

DST model	Joint goal accuracy	Inf. time on GPU (ms)
NBT-DNN [11]	84.4%	-
NBT-CNN [11]	84.2%	-
GLAD [19]	88.1 ± 0.4%	-
GCE [12]	88.5%	-
StateNet [15]	88.9%	-
BERT-DST [2]	87.7 ± 1.1%	-
Lai. full model [8]	**90.5%**	113
Lai. distilled model [8]	90.4%	24
Propose model (BERT)	89.6%	6.69
Propose model (ALBERT)	89.9%	**5.64**
Propose model (ELECTRA)	90.2%	6.72

According to the results on the WOZ 2.0 dataset, the ELECTRA-based model achieve the best result among all our proposed models. We apply the ELECTRA-based model to further experiment. Table 3 shows the experimental results on the MultiWOZ 2.0 dataset. The DSTQA model outperforms all baselines, while our model achieves a competitive result in a joint goal accuracy of 50.21%.

Table 3. The test accuracies of different models on the MultiWOZ 2.0 dataset.

DST model	Joint goal accuracy
MDBT [14]	15.57%
GLAD [19]	35.57%
GCE [12]	35.58%
JST [5]	40.74%
HyST [5]	44.24%
DSTQA [20]	**51.44%**
Propose model (ELECTRA)	50.21%

5   Conclusion

The problem of tracking user's state in a dialog is a significant work. In this paper, we propose a model based on pre-trained model for the task of DST. Our proposed model achieves competitive performance on the WoZ 2.0 dataset while being 20× faster on inference than the state-of-the-art model. The experiment on the Multi-WOZ 2.0 dataset show the effectiveness of the proposed model cross-domain, our model can obtain similar accuracy compared to the state-of-the-art model. In the future, we plan to investigate other transformer-based dialog models.

References

1. Budzianowski, P., et al.: MultiWOZ - a large-scale multi-domain wizard-of-Oz dataset for task-oriented dialogue modelling. In: Proceedings of the 2018 Conference on Empirical Methods in Natural Language Processing. pp. 5016–5026 (2018). https://doi.org/10.18653/v1/D18-1547, https://www.aclweb.org/anthology/D18-1547

2. Chao, G.L., Lane, I.: BERT-DST: scalable end-to-end dialogue state tracking with bidirectional encoder representations from transformer. In: Proceedings of Interspeech 2019, pp. 1468–1472 (2019). https://doi.org/10.21437/Interspeech.2019-1355

3. Clark, K., Luong, M.T., Le, Q.V., Manning, C.D.: ELECTRA: pre-training text encoders as discriminators rather than generators. In: International Conference on Learning Representations (2020). https://openreview.net/pdf?id=r1xMH1BtvB

4. Devlin, J., Chang, M.W., Lee, K., Toutanova, K.: BERT: pre-training of deep bidirectional transformers for language understanding. In: Proceedings of the 2019 Conference of the North American Chapter of the Association for Computational Linguistics: Human Language Technologies, pp. 4171–4186 (2019). https://doi.org/10.18653/v1/N19-1423, https://www.aclweb.org/anthology/N19-1423

5. Goel, R., Paul, S., Hakkani-Tür, D.: HyST: a hybrid approach for flexible and accurate dialogue state tracking. arXiv preprint arXiv:1907.00883 (2019)

6. Henderson, M., Thomson, B., Williams, J.D.: The second dialog state tracking challenge. In: Proceedings of the 15th Annual Meeting of the Special Interest Group on Discourse and Dialogue (SIGDIAL), pp. 263–272 (2014). https://doi.org/10.3115/v1/W14-4337, https://www.aclweb.org/anthology/W14-4337

7. Kingma, D.P., Ba, J.: Adam: a method for stochastic optimization. CoRR abs/1412.6980 (2015)
8. Lai, T.M., Hung Tran, Q., Bui, T., Kihara, D.: A simple but effective BERT model for dialog state tracking on resource-limited systems. In: ICASSP 2020–2020 IEEE International Conference on Acoustics, Speech and Signal Processing (ICASSP), pp. 8034–8038 (2020). https://doi.org/10.1109/ICASSP40776.2020.9053975
9. Lan, Z., Chen, M., Goodman, S., Gimpel, K., Sharma, P., Soricut, R.: Albert: a lite BERT for self-supervised learning of language representations. In: International Conference on Learning Representations (2020). https://openreview.net/forum?id=H1eA7AEtvS
10. Liu, Y., et al.: Roberta: a robustly optimized BERT pretraining approach. arXiv preprint arXiv:1907.11692 (2019)
11. Mrkšić, N., Ó Séaghdha, D., Wen, T.H., Thomson, B., Young, S.: Neural belief tracker: data-driven dialogue state tracking. In: Proceedings of the 55th Annual Meeting of the Association for Computational Linguistics, pp. 1777–1788 (2017). https://doi.org/10.18653/v1/P17-1163, https://www.aclweb.org/anthology/P17-1163
12. Nouri, E., Hosseini-Asl, E.: Toward scalable neural dialogue state tracking model. CoRR (2018). http://arxiv.org/abs/1812.00899
13. Rajpurkar, P., Zhang, J., Lopyrev, K., Liang, P.: SQuAD: 100,000+questions for machine comprehension of text. In: Proceedings of the 2016 Conference on Empirical Methods in Natural Language Processing, pp. 2383–2392 (2016). https://doi.org/10.18653/v1/D16-1264, https://www.aclweb.org/anthology/D16-1264
14. Ramadan, O., Budzianowski, P., Gašić, M.: Large-scale multi-domain belief tracking with knowledge sharing. In: Proceedings of the 56th Annual Meeting of the Association for Computational Linguistics, pp. 432–437 (2018). https://doi.org/10.18653/v1/P18-2069, https://www.aclweb.org/anthology/P18-2069
15. Ren, L., Xie, K., Chen, L., Yu, K.: Towards universal dialogue state tracking. In: Proceedings of the 2018 Conference on Empirical Methods in Natural Language Processing, pp. 2780–2786 (2018). https://doi.org/10.18653/v1/D18-1299, https://www.aclweb.org/anthology/D18-1299
16. Vaswani, A., et al.: Attention is all you need. In: Advances in Neural Information Processing Systems, pp. 5998–6008 (2017)
17. Wen, T.H., et al.: A network-based end-to-end trainable task-oriented dialogue system. In: Proceedings of the 15th Conference of the European Chapter of the Association for Computational Linguistics, pp. 438–449. Association for Computational Linguistics (2017). https://www.aclweb.org/anthology/E17-1042
18. Yang, Z., Dai, Z., Yang, Y., Carbonell, J., Salakhutdinov, R.R., Le, Q.V.: XLNet: generalized autoregressive pretraining for language understanding. In: Advances in Neural Information Processing Systems, pp. 5754–5764 (2019)
19. Zhong, V., Xiong, C., Socher, R.: Global-locally self-attentive encoder for dialogue state tracking. In: Proceedings of the 56th Annual Meeting of the Association for Computational Linguistics, pp. 1458–1467 (2018). https://doi.org/10.18653/v1/P18-1135, https://www.aclweb.org/anthology/P18-1135
20. Zhou, L., Small, K.: Multi-domain dialogue state tracking as dynamic knowledge graph enhanced question answering. arXiv preprint arXiv:1911.06192 (2019)

Annotation References for Facilitation Analysis in Intercultural Collaboration

Mizuki Motozawa$^{(\boxtimes)}$ iD, Yohei Murakami iD, and Mondheera Pituxcoosuvarn iD

Ritsumeikan University, Kyoto, Japan
is0380sr@ed.ritsumei.ac.jp

Abstract. In an intercultural children collaboration using machine translation, the children of low-resource languages have difficulties in participating and engaging in conversations due to inaccuracy of machine translation for the low-resource languages. In order to facilitate and motivate speech for these children, we have focused on the facilitator's utterances. To identify the facilitator's speech patterns that encourage the responses of low-resource language speaking children, we need to annotate the actual conversation logs. However, the existing annotation scheme cannot be applied to facilitation utterances completely because it is a classification of speech patterns for general problem-solving purposes. In this study, we have identified the problems that occurred when applying the existing annotation schemes. In addition, we proposed and evaluated a new annotation rule of the existing annotation scheme for facilitation analysis.

Keywords: Dialogue analysis · Intercultural collaboration · Facilitation

1 Introduction

The importance of respecting cultural diversity is emphasized in today's globalized society. To cultivate such an attitude, intercultural collaboration using machine translation is useful. For example, in "KISSY (Kyoto International Summer School for Youth)", a summer school program held by NPO Pangaea, a non-profit organization, children and adult facilitators from four countries (Japan, Kenya, Georgia, and Cambodia) formed multinational groups and discussed a solution to international problems using a multilingual chat tool with machine translation embedded [1]. However, due to the inaccuracy of machine translation for low-resource languages, children who speak the low-resource languages were not able to actively participate in the group discussions and did not speak up as much as they should [8,11]. To address this issue, we aim at examining the impact of the facilitator's dialogue act on the children's responses using real-world dialogue log data, with a focus on the fact that the number of children's statements varies depending on the type of facilitator utterance.

© The Author(s), under exclusive license to Springer Nature Switzerland AG 2022
P.-L. P. Rau (Ed.): HCII 2022, LNCS 13313, pp. 157–172, 2022.
https://doi.org/10.1007/978-3-031-06050-2_12

However, the applicability of existing annotation schemes based on speech acts and dialogue acts to facilitators' utterances is not clear as they are created for domain-independent and generic tasks, but not for facilitation. Therefore, we applied those annotation schemes to actual dialogue log data to clarify the problems in annotating facilitators' utterances and evaluated their applicability [3].

2   Dialogue Act Annotation

Speech tags for dialogue analysis have been designed based on the research on speech acts. A speech act is an action that is carried out by utterance. Austin classified the speech acts into three types: *locutionary act*, *illocutionary act*, and *perlocutionary act* [4]. *Locutionary act* is the act of uttering a sentence with a certain meaning using speech, words, sentences, or other linguistic expressions for the purpose of communication. *Illocutionary act* is an utterance by which the speaker is performing some other action, such as a command or a request, to the listener. Last, the *perlocutionary act*, is an utterance that affects the emotion, thought, or action of the listener. The forces performed by the illocutionary act are called *illocutionary forces*. The illocutionary forces are classified by Searle into five categories: *Verdictives*, *Exercitves*, *Commisives*, *Behabitives*, and *Expositives* [9]. In addition, Vanderveken developed a system of performative verbs based on the simplest performative verbs in each of Searle's five categories, by deriving other performative verbs by assigning specific conditions to them [10]. In other words, Vanderveken's system of performative verbs is more organized and defined hierarchically by subdividing Searle's classification of speech acts.

Based on these theoretical backgrounds in linguistics, several annotation schemes for dialogue analysis have been proposed. The multidimensional DIT scheme has been developed for information-seeking dialogs that do not depend on a specific domain [5]. Another example is the DAMSL scheme which is an application-independent multidimensional annotation scheme [2]. Furthermore, the DIT++ scheme is a comprehensive general-purpose annotation scheme that combines the DIT scheme with concepts from DAMSL and other schemes [5]. This DIT++ scheme introduces a number of subcategories of communication-related information, such as feedback information, turn allocation information, and voice management information.

The International Organization for Standardization (ISO) published a standard scheme for language resource management called ISO 24617-2 [6]. This scheme inherits the full set of communication features of DIT++ and adds several annotation items to support annotation of dialogue acts comprehensively. The additional annotation items include the following aspects. The first aspect is *Dimensions* which classify conversations involving multiple communicative functions when they occur concurrently. Second, *Qualifiers*, express whether a speech act is conditional, insincere, or performed with a specific emotion. Then, *Communicative functions* describe whether a speech act is a form of communication. *Functional and feedback dependences* indicate that an utterance is meaningless on its own, and depends on other utterances to be meaningful. Last, *Rhetorical relations* are used to annotate the relations that one utterance leads to another.

3 Motivation

In a preliminary experiment, we analyzed facilitators' utterances from 4 groups using Searle's utterance categories and Vanderveken's performative verbs, which were defined as a further subdivision of Searle's categories. Specifically, we defined our tag sets based on Searle's utterance categories and Vanderveken's performative verbs and annotated the facilitators' utterances in a children's intercultural collaboration with our tag sets. Since this study focuses on facilitators' utterances that elicit a response from the children, we employed Vanderveken's subdivision only for Searle's *Directive* utterances. The tag sets used in our analysis are shown in Table 1 and Table 2.

Based on these tag sets, we examined the facilitators' utterances that showed significant differences in the responses of low-resource language children. The results showed that *Request* utterances in directives conditional on addressee's consent facilitated the responses of low-resource language children, while *Tell* utterances in directives without addressee's consent tended to suppress the responses of low-resource language children compared to high-resource language children [7].

Table 1. Searle's five categories of illocutionary acts.

Category	Tag defnition
Assertives	Utterance aimed at expressing a state of affairs
Commissives	Utterance aimed at committing the speaker to a certain action
Directives	Utterance aimed at directing the listener to do a certain action
Expressives	Utterance aimed at expressing the speaker's feelings
Declarations	Utterance aimed at bringing a state of affairs into existence by declaring it

Table 2. Vanderveken's performative verbs.

Subdivision of directives	Tag definition
Request	Utterance aimed at directing the listener while allowing the listener to reject or not respond to the directions
Tell	Utterance aimed at directing the listener without allowing the listener to reject or not respond to the directions
Insist	Utterance aimed at increasing the degree of demand with persistent directions
Suggest	Utterance aimed at making the listener consider the performance of a certain action

The qualitative analysis of the preliminary experiment finds two annotation aspects that additionally needed to be taken into account. The first aspect is destination. In the dialogue log data, not all of the facilitators' utterances were directed to all the children, and some facilitators' utterances referred to a specific child by name. The facilitators' utterances that were made for a specific child by name were expected to be more likely to be responded to because they identified the respondent. However, our tag set does not provide any scheme to annotate which child each facilitator's utterance was meant for and from which child the response was expected. As a result, the rate of responses from children was calculated regardless of the direction of the utterance, and the effect of the facilitators' utterances could not be accurately evaluated.

The second aspect to consider is the chain structure of utterances. In the dialogue log data, when there was no response from any child to a facilitator's instruction, the facilitator often rephrased the instruction or explained it in more detail. Thus, it was expected that the effect of the same utterance category might vary depending on the utterance before and after it. However, since our tag set was intended to classify only a single utterance, it did not take into account the chain structure of the utterances. As a result, it was difficult to find a regularity in the classification of the same utterance, because some utterances lead to response(s) while others do not.

4   Facilitator's Utterances Tags

In order to analyze the findings from the preliminary experiments, in this chapter, we define the requirements of the tag set for annotation and describe the ISO tag set that satisfies these requirements.

4.1   Requirements

To count the number of no-response utterances accurately, it is necessary to consider who was expected to respond to the utterance. When the destination of an utterance is identified by name, it is inappropriate to count the number of no-response utterances by taking other participants into account, since they were not required to respond. Therefore, in order to indicate whether each facilitator's utterance was directed to all the children or to a specific child, we need an annotation item indicating the destination and the ID of the participant as a value of the item.

Furthermore, to evaluate the effects of the previous and following utterances, it is necessary to consider the chain structure of the utterances. By classifying not only individual utterances but also how they are related to each other, we can evaluate the effects of combinations of utterances. Therefore, we need an utterance ID to identify a specific utterance, and an annotation item to indicate the association with an existing utterance.

4.2   ISO 24617-2 (SemAF)

ISO 24617-2 is a standardized annotation framework for analyzing dialogue acts. In a dialogue act, there is a speaker, an agent who creates the dialogue act, and one more agent called the listener who receives the dialogue act. For example, in a dialogue between two people, there is one speaker and one listener in the dialogue act. In the case of dialogue among three or more people, in addition to the speaker and listener, there are various types of participants, such as those who are present but do not participate in the conversation, or those who participate only slightly. In a communication situation with multiple participants, the speaker may talk to one particular participant rather than the others; ISO 24617-2 defines the *addressee* attribute to designate the participant who is spoken to primarily. This *addressee* is an obligatory attribute that should be tagged to every utterance.

In the analysis of dialogue acts, relations between utterances such as explanations, causes, concessions, and so on, have been extensively studied and are called rhetorical relations or discourse relations. ISO 24617-2 defines the *rhetoRel* attribute to specify specific rhetorical relations between speech acts, and 19 rhetorical relations as its value. In this study, we focus on the facilitators' *Elaboration* and *Restatement* utterances, which were observed in the preliminary experiment, and use those two tags and *Other* to indicate other rhetorical relations. In addition, since not all utterances are related to the previous utterances, we used *Other* to indicate no relation as well as other relations, making a total of three classifications. Moreover, in order to identify which existing utterances have a relationship with the target utterance, the utterance ID of the existing utterance should be specified. The tag set of rhetorical relations between utterances used in this study is shown in Table 3.

ISO 24617-2 comprehensively defines tag classification of utterances as *Communicative Functions*. In order to unify the tag set used for annotation with the ISO annotation scheme, the tag set for utterance classification was also mapped from the tag set used in the preliminary experiment to the ISO 24617-2 tag set. . The new tag set for utterance classification and the tag set for subdivision of *Directives* are shown in Table 4 and Table 5, respectively.

Table 3. Rhetorical relations.

Relation	Tag definition
Elaboration	Relations that a target utterance elaborates on an existing utterance. e.g. "Your role is scriptwriter" followed by "the scriptwriter is in charge of the storyline of the clay animation"
Restatement	Relations that a target utterance restates an existing utterance. e.g. "Which movie do you want to see?" followed by "which movie are you more interested in?"
Other	No relation between a target utterance and any of the existing utterances, or any relationship other than the two tags above

Table 4. ISO communicative functions corresponding to utterance classifications.

Category	Tag definition
Information-providing	Utterance aimed at informing another of specific information. e.g. "I have to prepare my presentation"
Commissive	Utterance aimed at committing the speaker to the performance of a certain action. This category also includes utterances in which the speaker asks for the other person's consent to the action. e.g. "I will now serve as your facilitator"
Information-seeking	Utterance aimed at asking questions to elicit information from the listener. This category also includes a query to check the progress of a project or job. e.g. "How far along are you in the process?"
Directive	Utterance aimed at directing the listener to do a certain action. e.g. "What's your idea?", "What is your solution to the problem?"
Dimension-specific	Utterance aimed at performing social functions, such as greeting, thanking, apologizing, expressing emotions, interjections, and responding to previous utterances. e.g. "Good morning.", "Thank you"

Table 5. ISO directive functions corresponding to subdivision of directives.

Category	Tag definition
Request	Utterance aimed at requesting the other party to carry out an action only conditional on the other party's consent. e.g. "If anyone has a solution to this problem, please let me know"
Instruct	Utterance aimed at instructing the other person to feel obligated to perform an action without the other party's consent. e.g. "Please give me some ideas.", "Give me your opinion"
Suggestion	Utterance aimed at making the other party consider whether to carry out an action. This also includes the case that suggests the listener carry out the action together with the speaker e.g. "Let's go to the park together.", "Would you like to be a leader?"
Address offer	Utterance that addresses the offer previously made by the other party whether the speaker wants the listener to do or not to do something. e.g. A: "Shall I do it for you??" S: "Yes, please"

5 Facilitators' Utterances Annotation

5.1 Ambiguity in Annotation

Since ISO 24617-2 is domain-independent and created for general purpose, there existed two ambiguous tag classifications in annotating facilitators' utterances that were intended to facilitate discussion rather than accomplish tasks. The first is the questions that facilitators ask to elicit children's opinions in group work, for example, "Do you have any ideas?" and "What is your idea?". If we focus only on the content of the utterance, both can be classified as information-seeking utterances because the utterances are considered questions. The information-seeking tag is for an utterance in which the speaker tries to obtain information that the speaker wants to know by asking questions to the listener. However, considering the fact that it is an utterance from the facilitator, they can also be classified as direct utterances, because the facilitator was trying to direct the children to share their ideas with others. The ideas were not information that the facilitator that they themself wanted to know, but were meant to be shared with the group members for accomplishing the group goal. This case can be classified as directive speech.

The second is the facilitator's utterances for the group work facilitation. For example, if the facilitator says, "Let's decide the role assignments", this can be categorized as an information-providing utterance that provides the next agenda, or a directive utterance that instructs the group to discuss the role assignments or a commissive utterance that promises that everyone including the facilitator will discuss. Thus, several facilitators' utterances that are intended to facilitate discussion are difficult to classify into utterance categories.

5.2   Annotation Rules

In order to deal with the ambiguity of the tags assigned to the facilitator's utterances, it is necessary to define the criteria for annotation.

Questions asked by the facilitators to the children are classified according to whether they are uttered to accomplish the group work task or whether the facilitators themself want to know. For instance, questions to elicit children's opinions in group work should be classified as "directive" because they are not informed that the facilitator wants to know, but rather, they are utterances to facilitate discussion and promote group work. On the other hand, utterances like "What are we discussing now?", "Did you sleep well last night?" should be classified as "information seeking".

To classify facilitators' utterances for the group work facilitation, it is necessary to investigate the intention and the function of the facilitator's utterances and the children's responses before and after the target utterances. For example, if an utterance was intended to initiate group work, it will be classified as an "instruct" utterance because the group tended to start working following that specific utterance. On the other hand, if the utterance is simply an announcement about the contents of the group work, it is classified as an "information-providing" utterance. However, since the facilitator is in a position to support the promotion of group work, it is not appropriate to interpret it as a commissive utterance that the facilitator will work in a group together.

	A	B	C	D	E Utterance Type	F Directive Type	G Relation	H Related utterance ID	I Addressee	Confidence	Note
1	foreign_id	created	sender	en							
2	1410	2019/8/5 7:25	Facilitator	Let's talk from now							
3	1411	2019/8/5 7:25	Child:B	Kamera	Information-providing						
4	1420	2019/8/5 7:26	Facilitator	About role	Commissive / Information-seeking						
5	1426	2019/8/5 7:27	Child:G	photographer	Directive						
6	1427	2019/8/5 7:28	Child:C	Sculptor	Dimension-specific						
7	1430	2019/8/5 7:28	Facilitator	Please indicate which role you would like to be in charge							
8	1431	2019/8/5 7:28	Child:B	Kamera							
9	1432	2019/8/5 7:28	Child:A	soundcreater							
10	1440	2019/8/5 7:30	Child:C	Sculptor							
11	1449	2019/8/5 7:30	Facilitator	What does Kotaro want to do?							
12	1454	2019/8/5 7:31	Child:D	Editor							
13	1460	2019/8/5 7:31	Child:E	Scene Designer							
14	1465	2019/8/5 7:31	Facilitator	Now that everyone's role is decided							
15	1468	2019/8/5 7:31	Child:C	I want to do Sculptor							

Fig. 1. Excel form for annotations.

5.3   Design of Annotation References

For each tag definition, we have tried to be as concise as possible. We tried not to confuse annotators with over-complicated explanations for each tag category. However, the lack of brevity of the description may lead to a broad interpretation and differences in recognition among annotators. To address this problem, we have created the criteria and examples of utterances that are ambiguous and difficult to distinguish, as shown in the previous section. In addition, the instructions for ambiguous tags were included as well.

For the annotation, we created an Excel form using data from our dataset, as shown in Fig. 1. In this annotation form, we displayed adjacent pairs consisting of each utterance from the facilitators and the children's responses to it. In this way, the function of each utterance can be easily recognized. In addition, for the relation tag set, each utterance was given an utterance ID, since it is necessary to indicate which utterance it is related to with this classification tag. For the conversation log, we also attached an ID to each utterance to indicate the utterance owner and to recognize the flow of the dialogue.

In addition, the order of tags selection was also considered so that each utterance was first tagged with Searle's utterance classification, and only directive utterances were further classified with Vanderveken's subdivision tags. In order to clarify the relationship between agreement and confidence, we also instructed the annotators to rate their confidence level in each tagged utterance.

6   Annotation Experiment

6.1   Experiment Environment

We annotated the dialogue data using a tag set based on ISO24617-2. The data is the dialogue log of the participants collected from the chat for group work at

Fig. 2. Facilitator and children working in a group (Photo offer: NPO Pangaea).

KISSY workshop. This workshop focused on intercultural collaboration among children, and the group works were conducted by multinational children and adult facilitators, as shown in Fig. 2. Therefore, communication among the participants was conducted using a multilingual chat tool. Figure 3 shows the screen of the multilingual chat tool used in the workshop. With this tool, participants were able to chat in their first languages, which are then translated into the ones spoken by the other participants, so that every single utterance will be recorded in the log data in multiple languages. In this annotation, we used Japanese log data consisting of the original utterances in Japanese and the Japanese translations of utterances in other languages. The reliability of the annotation method was verified by conducting an annotation experiment with six Japanese native speakers on 15 utterances of the facilitators in the log data.

6.2 Evaluation

The total of 90 tags annotated by 6 annotators on 15 facilitators' utterances are shown in Tables 6, 8, 7 and 9.

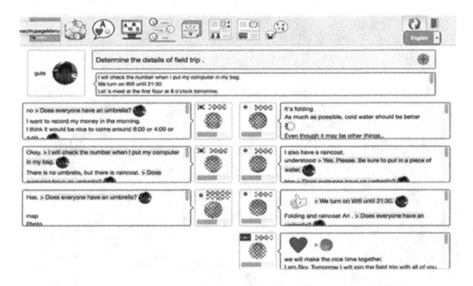

Fig. 3. Multilingual chat tool (Photo offer: NPO Pangaea).

Table 6. Annotation results of utterance classifications.

Category	Count
Information-providing	12
Commissive	12
Information-seeking	23
Directive	35
Dimension-specific	8
Total	90

Table 7. Annotation results for the subdivision of directives.

Category	Count
Request	11
Instruct	14
Suggestion	10
Address offer	0
Total	35

Table 8. Annotation results of rhetorical relation.

Relation	Count
Restatement	9
Elaboration	22
No relation (or other relation)	59
Total	90

Table 9. Annotation results of addressee.

Direction	Count
All the participants	79
A specific participant	11
Total	90

Reliability. The kappa coefficient of tagging among annotators is important. Therefore, we examined the inter-rater agreement rate using the kappa coefficient. In this paper, we employed the Fleiss' kappa coefficient because there were more than three raters and more than three categories of nominal scale items. The kappa values for each tag set are shown below.

Fleiss' kappa coefficient(k) for each annotation tag
> Utterance classifications: Kappa = 0.538
> Subdivision of Directive: Kappa = 0.344
> Rhetorical Relation: Kappa = 0.201
> Addressee: Kappa = 0.648

As a result, all of four annotation items were evaluated to be more or less consistent. Among them, the kappa coefficient is particularly high for the speech act classification and the addressee, which can be determined from the utterance itself. These results showed the consistency of these tag sets can be considered guaranteed.

On the other hand, for the instruction subdivision and the rhetorical relation, although there is more than a certain degree of agreement, it is conceivable that there are still some ambiguous tag classifications that do not match, and that there is room for improvement. The actual annotation results show that in the subdivision of directives, "Request" and "Suggest" were the most frequent tagging of the minority when the annotators were separated into several tags, so it is necessary to describe these tag definitions more clearly. As for the inter-speech relations, there were some utterances in which the tagging of "No relation (or other relation)" matched, but there were no utterances in which the tagging of "Restatement" and "Instruct" matched. As a feedback from the annotators, there were some cases where it was difficult to tag "other inter-speech relations" because it was not clear what other inter-speech relations existed, and it was

168 M. Motozawa et al.

unclear how to distinguish between "Restatement" and "Instruct". Therefore, it is thought that the tagging should be restricted to only those utterances that fall under the Restatement or Instruct category.

Tag Usages Distribution. In order to check for differences in the tagging of each annotator, the number of times each tag was used by each annotator was counted and a bar graph was created as shown in the Fig. 4. In this graph, the horizontal axis represents each annotation tag, and the vertical axis represents the number of times it is used. From this graph, we can see that there is not much bias in the usage rate of any annotator for "utterance classifications" and "addressee". On the other hand, there are some biases in the usage rate of "instruction subdivision" and "inter-speech relation". First of all, for the tag set of "subdivision of directives", the number of annotations to the category of "Request" is different among the annotators. Furthermore, when comparing the graphs for each annotator, we can see that the usage rate of each category tag in Annotator D, the yellow graph, is slightly different from the other annotators, suggesting that we may not have understood the tag definitions well. Furthermore, in the tag set of "inter-speech relations", there seemed to be a particular bias towards the tag of "Restatement". In addition, for the annotator that was not used in this "Restatement" tag, i.e., the number of times it was used was zero, it was used more than the other annotators in the "No relation (or other relation)" classification tag. The annotation results of "Restatement" and "No relationship (or other relationship)" may have been divided by the annotator.

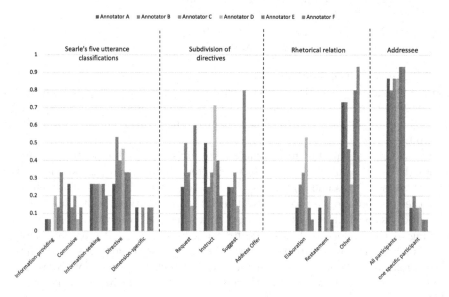

Fig. 4. Number of tags used for each annotator.

Annotation Difficulties. When the annotators were asked to perform these annotation tasks, they were asked to assign a number from 1 to 5 to indicate their confidence in tagging each utterance, with 1 representing not confident at all and 5 representing very confident.

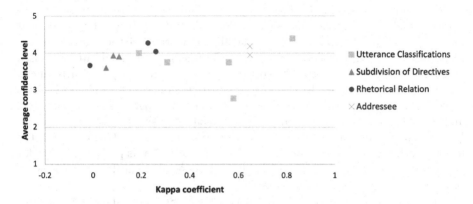

Fig. 5. Correlation chart for each tag.

Because low kappa coefficients in tag sets could be due to annotation difficulties, we examined the relationships between the kappa coefficient and the confidence level of each tag. Correlation coefficients and correlation plots calculated from the average of the agreement and confidence for each tag set are shown below. The absolute number of correlation coefficients in each tag set is greater than 0.7, indicating that there is a strong correlation. There was a positive correlation between the "directive" subcategories and rhetorical relations. Furthermore, the confidence level was higher for the categories with a high kappa coefficient, whereas the tag definitions for the categories with a low kappa coefficient were not always obvious. There was a positive correlation between the "directive" subcategories and inter-speech relations. Furthermore, the confidence level was higher for the categories with a high kappa coefficient, whereas the tag definitions for the categories with a low kappa coefficient were not always obvious.

Furthermore, some categories with low agreement and high confidence were included, even though they were not correlated with respect to the speech act classification. Therefore, these categories may have been interpreted differently by each annotator, and different tags may have been used to distinguish them from other categories, suggesting the need to describe discrimination criteria in the definition of each tag.

Correlation coefficient for each tag set
> Utterance Classifications: Correlation = 0.0900
> Subdivision of Directives: Correlation = 0.8817
> Rhetorical Relation: Correlation = 0.8767
> Addressee: Correlation = -

7 Discussion

First, in terms of utterance categorization, the categorizations with the lowest kappa coefficient were "Information-providing" and "Commissive", and these categorizations were often confusingly tagged among annotators. For example, "Information-providing", "Commissive", and "Directive" were often used to tag utterances about future actions, such as "let's discuss the story". This particular utterance can be interpreted as, the facilitator instructed the discussion, the facilitator informed that they would have a discussion, or the facilitator promised to have a discussion. In order to correctly annotate these types of utterances, firstly, utterances related to the upcoming discussion should not be classified as "Commissive" because the facilitator was not participating in the discussion, and secondly, subsequent utterances by the facilitator should also be examined. Unless it should be classified as "Information-providing". In addition to this, the agreement between the two subcategories of "Directive" was particularly low for "Request" and "Suggest". Therefore, it is necessary to clarify the criteria by providing examples of those utterances.

In addition, since there was no consistent for "Suggest" and the confidence level was low, it is necessary to improve the definition by increasing the number of utterances and providing more detailed definitions. For "Restatement" and "Elaboration" in relation, which had a low kappa coefficient, these were often confused with "no relation (or other relations)". Many annotators who did not know what other relations existed found it difficult to distinguish between them because they couldn't apply the elimination approach and didn't know what other relations were possible. Therefore, it would be better to present all the focused relations in the inter-speech relations and direct the annotators to select one of them if it applies to them.

In the category "Rhetorical Relation", the facilitator also supplemented the previous utterance with examples. Therefore, it is necessary to add the category called "Exemplification" in addition to the two existing relationships. The "Rhetorical Relation" tag set with the additional tags is shown in Table 10.

Regarding the addressee annotation, the overall agreement was high. However, there were some utterances with low agreement. When we checked those utterances, we found that those utterances occurred when a facilitator asked a question about an idea that a specific participant gave earlier. In most cases, this kind of utterance usually contains the addressee's name, but in some cases, the facilitator did not say the addressee's name. Therefore, the annotation results differed between the annotators who considered the flow of the utterances and the annotators who only considered the specific utterances. Therefore, the annotation manual should include instructions on how to annotate, as well as how to check the flow of conversation.

Table 10. Tag definition of an updated rhetorical relation.

Category	Tag definition
Elaboration	Relations that a target utterance elaborates on an existing utterance. e.g. "Your role is scriptwriter" followed by "the scriptwriter is in charge of the storyline of the cray animation"
Restatement	Relations that a target utterance restates an existing utterance. e.g. "Which movie do you want to see?" followed by "which movie are you more interested in?"
Exemplification	Relations that a target utterance gives an example related to an existing utterance e.g. In Shiritori game, you lose if your say a word ends in "n()" followed by "For example, if you say "mikan", you lose

8   Conclusion

To improve the discussion in children's multilingual collaboration, we found that it was difficult to apply the existing annotation schemes. Using those schemes, a number of issues were raised. From our annotation experiment, it was difficult for annotators to make decisions because of the lack of clarity among the utterance classification tags. In addition, information about the addressee of each utterance was necessary when counting the number of cases with and without response(s) to obtain the response rate to each classification. We conducted the annotation experiment using the existing tag set again, evaluated the uniformity of the tag set, and proposed a tag set with guaranteed uniformity by extracting and improving the tags that needed further improvement.

Acknowledgements. This research was partially supported by a Grant-in-Aid for Scientific Research (B) (21H03561, 2021–2024, 21H03556, 2021–2023) and a Grant-in-Aid for Early-Career Scientists (21K17794, 2021–2024) from the Japan Society for the Promotion of Sciences (JSPS).

References

1. Aiken, M.: Multilingual communication in electronic meetings. ACM SIGGROUP Bull. **23**(1), 18–19 (2002)
2. Allen, J., Core, M.: Draft of DAMSL Dialog Act Markup in Several Layers (2007)
3. Araki, M., Itoh, T., Kumagai, T., Ishizaki, M.: Proposal of a standard utterance-unit tagging scheme. J. Jpn. Soc. Artif. Intell. **14**(2), 251–260 (1999)
4. Austin, J.: How to Do Things with Words. Oxford, Oxford University Press (1975)
5. Bunt, H.: The dit++ taxonomy for functional dialogue markup. In: Heylen, D., Pelachaud, C., Catizone, R., Traum, D. (eds.) Proceedings of AAMAS Workshop "Towards a Standard Markup Language for Embodied Dialogue Acts (EDAML 2009), pp. 13–24 (2009)
6. ISO/TC37/SC4: Language resource management - semantic annotation framework (SemAF), part 2: Dialogue acts. Tech. rep., ISO (2010)

7. Motozawa, M., Murakami, Y., Pituxcoosuvarn, M., Takasaki, T., Mori, Y.: Conversation analysis for facilitation in children's intercultural collaboration. In: Proceedings of the 20th ACM Interaction Design and Children (IDC 2021), pp. 62–68 (2021)
8. Pituxcoosuvarn, M., Ishida, T., Yamashita, N., Takasaki, T., Mori, Y.: Machine translation usage in a children's workshop. In: Egi, H., Yuizono, T., Baloian, N., Yoshino, T., Ichimura, S., Rodrigues, A. (eds.) CollabTech 2018. LNCS, vol. 11000, pp. 59–73. Springer, Cham (2018). https://doi.org/10.1007/978-3-319-98743-9_5
9. Searle, J.: Speech Acts. Cambridge University Press, Cambridge (1969)
10. Vanderveken, D.: Meaning and Speech Acts: vol. 1. Principles of Language Use. Cambridge University Press, Cambridge (1990)
11. Yamashita, N., Ishida, T.: Effects of machine translation on collaborative work. In: Proceedings of the 20th Anniversary Conference on Computer Supported Cooperative Work, pp. 515–524 (2006)

Confidence Value Calculation for Cultural-Based Misunderstanding Warning in Multilingual Chat

Mondheera Pituxcoosuvarn[(✉)] [ID] and Yohei Murakami[ID]

Ritsumeikan University, Kyoto, Japan
ampere.scout@gmail.com

Abstract. Previously, the Cultural Difference Detection (CDD) concept had been introduced to predict possible misunderstandings when machine translation (MT) users communicate across cultures. CDD compared images that linked to a concept in two languages with the assumption that the low similarity of images can indicate cultural misunderstanding. Its result has been used for warning MT users of words that could possibly cause misunderstanding. However, how it should be applied in the warning system has not yet been studied. One of the complications with the warning system is the accuracy of CDD. This paper proposes a method to calculate *confidence value* and to use this value to predict the accuracy of CDD. This *confidence value* could be used to decide whether to warn or not to warn the user when a suspect word is typed in the text box. This *confidence value* is calculated from the similarity among the images used during the CDD calculation. To examine the proposed confidence value, we conducted an experiment by comparing the accuracy of CDD and the *confidence value*. The experiment confirms that our proposed confidence concept reflects the CDD accuracy as there is a strong correlation between the *confidence value* and the CDD accuracy.

Keywords: Intercultural collaboration · Cultural difference · Cultural misunderstanding

1 Introduction

In collaboration, diversity is an important factor for creativity, innovation, and performance [13]. Cultural diversity also plays a crucial role in organizations. It also positively impacts revenue, customers, market share, and relative profit [3]. As a consequence, intercultural collaboration would benefit teams and organizations. However, intercultural collaboration comes with barriers to communication including language barriers and cultural differences. There are several methods to help team members overcome the language barrier, such as using machine translation (MT) support tools and services for translation [6]. Despite MT's usefulness, it sometimes causes difficulties, for instance, conversation breakdown [9] and difficulties to establish mutual understanding [14].

P.-L. P. Rau (Ed.): HCII 2022, LNCS 13313, pp. 173–187, 2022.
https://doi.org/10.1007/978-3-031-06050-2_13

Improving the quality of translation can be one method to improve MT-mediated translation, but it cannot improve the failure to establish a common ground that is caused by cultural differences. Since people who speak a different language sometimes have different images on their minds [2,10], it is possible to use images to identify the cultural differences. For instance, the word '団子' (dan-go) refers in Japanese to a sweet dumpling made of rice flour and is translated into 'dumpling' in English, as shown in Fig. 1. Even though the translation is not wrong, the images of '団子' and 'dumpling' from image search are different and people from different cultures tend to have different mental images looking at each word. Based on this idea, a group of researchers [11] introduced a method to automatically detect words that possibly cause misunderstanding, or the Cultural Difference Detection (CDD), using an image database and automated image comparison technique.

Dumplings   団子 (Dango)

Fig. 1. Images of 'dumpling' and '団子' (dan-go, Japanese sweet)

Later, the idea of how the results of CDD can be used and the experiment focusing on human-computer interaction was published [12]. This work suggested warning the users when the users use words that could cause cultural misunderstanding based on CDD. However, how to determine which words the application should warn the user about and which words should be ignored, has not been studied, given that there are chances of the wrong prediction. The main contribution of this research is to fill this gap. This paper introduces *confidence value* to help with the decision-making process of cultural misunderstanding warning. We also the relationship between the proposed *confidence value* and the prediction accuracy of the CDD.

In the next section, we explain how CDD result are calculated and how they are used in existing study. Section 3 introduces our *confidence value* and the process to calculate it. Next, Sect. 4 describes our experiment to examine the relationship between accuracy and confidence value. The results will be discussed in Sect. 7 and concluded in Sect. 8 of this paper.

2 Related Work

There have been several methods proposed by different groups of researchers to detect cultural differences. Some groups of researchers focused on analyzing cross-national surveys [1,4,15], while some of them focused on analyzing available data, such as Wikipedia [16]. Later, unlike with the other methods, automated cultural difference detection or CDD had been introduced, so the cultural difference can be detected without spending human effort [11].

2.1 Cultural Difference Detection (CDD)

As proposed earlier, an images database can be used to identify cultural differences when they are linked to or tagged with keywords in different languages [11]. Figure 2 shows the overall process of CDD. The process starts with selecting a synset (set of synonyms) from Japanese WordNet [5]. Japanese WordNet is a concept dictionary containing lexical data in Japanese and English. It extends the original English WordNet, created by Princeton University [7]. A synset contains various information but CDD uses only one or two word(s) in English and one or two word(s) in Japanese depending on the availability. Each word is used as a keyword for searching several images. Then, each image is converted into feature vectors and the average feature vectors will be calculated. After that, two average vectors will be compared. The original paper used cosine similarity in this step. If the similarity is low or lower than a threshold, it is assumed that cultural differences exist. If the similarity is higher than a threshold, it is assumed that there is no cultural difference between the two language-speaking cultures.

Later, Nishimura et al. [8] proposed a method for calculating the optimal threshold to increase the accuracy of the detection. Using Japanese WordNet, they experimented by comparing the similarity of images with the result of human (Japanese) determination. They adjusted the threshold value to determine the ideal threshold.

2.2 Cultural Difference Warning

The results from CDD can be used as a reference for cultural differences or applied to collaboration technology, such as an MT-embedded chat system. It was used to warn MT users of cultural misunderstanding in an experiment [12]. The researchers aimed to create a system that warns its users when the word that could cause misunderstanding is typed in an MT-embedded chat system, as shown in Fig. 3. They studied how users react to cultural misunderstanding warnings by comparing controlled groups, which did not receive a warning, to an experimental group, which received the warning. They confirmed that cultural misunderstanding warnings did increase understanding. However, this study mainly focused on the interaction and understanding result. CDD accuracy and thresholds were not discussed in their paper.

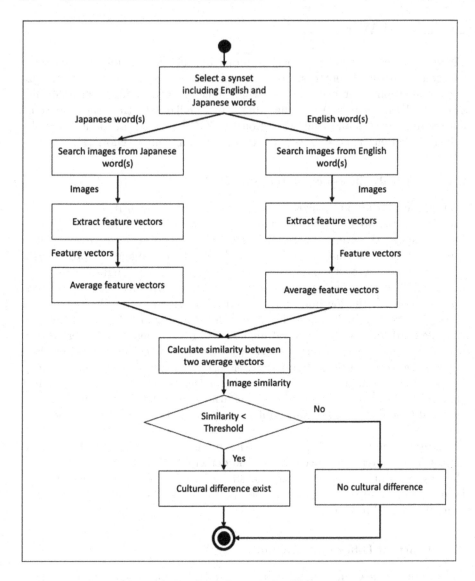

Fig. 2. A flowchart showing the CDD process

Fig. 3. An example of misunderstanding warning

3   Confidence Value

Since existing studies have not covered the issue of when should the system warn the user given that the accuracy of CDD has not yet been perfect for several reasons, this section introduces the idea of *confidence value* to help with the decision after CDD predict whether a particular word would cause misunderstanding or not.

3.1   Motivation and Concept

To further study the automated system to be used in the intercultural support tool, we recreated an experiment based on the original CDD. We observed that during image collection some sets of images contained similar images while some sets of images contained different images. Figure 4 displays images from Google image search of the word 'Leftover' and the word 'Globe'. 'Leftover' contains images of different types of food which associate with the keyword correctly. However, when this set of images is used to compare with images from different language keywords, the vector of English language 'Leftover' would be mixed up and, several times, lead to inaccurate similarity value. Whereas, some other keywords, for example, the word 'Globe' shows similar images, so when it is used in CDD calculation, the result is more reliable.

As a result, we suspect that there might be a correlation between the similarity of the images in the same set and the accuracy of the prediction from CDD.

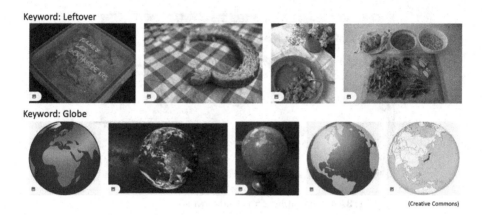

Fig. 4. Examples of keyword with different image search result (above) and keyword with similar image search results (below)

3.2 Confidence Value Calculation Process

To calculate the *confidence value*, the process displayed in Fig. 5 will be executed. For each word, the image set linked to that keyword, which is the same set of images for CDD calculation, will be loaded. The image will be converted into feature vectors, then the feature vectors will be compared by similarity calculation between two vectors for all possible pairs. The similarity values will be averaged and it is called a *confidence value*.

3.3 Confidence Value in CDD Calculation

To apply *confidence value* to CDD calculation, first, each keyword, or each word used in CDD calculation can be associated with one *confidence value*. However, some synsets contain more than one keyword that is used in CDD calculation. In that case, the *confidence value* between two keywords will be averaged. This averaged value could be used to indicate how certain the calculation is for each language in the same synset. In this paper, we focus on using *confidence value* to reflect the accuracy of the similarity between two languages, so the *confidence value* for each language will be averaged once again to indicate how certain each CDD result is.

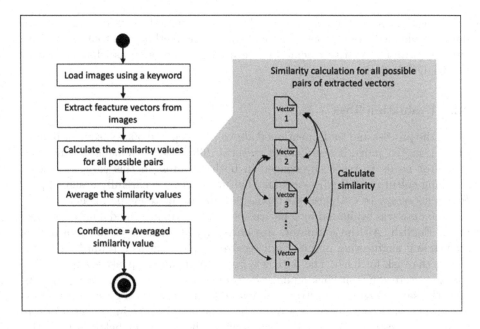

Fig. 5. Confidence value calculation process

4   Experiment

In the previous section, we have introduced the idea of calculating and using *confidence value*. In this section, we will explain the experiment we conducted to study the relationship between confidence value and the accuracy of CDD decisions.

4.1   Data Preparation

To prepare data for this experiment, we calculated the similarity between words in English and Japanese based on the CDD concept explained in Sect. 2.2. The Japanese WordNet was used as our database for words. The synsets are randomly chosen but limited to a synset under a category named 'physical entity' (an entity that has physical existence) to eliminate words that are too abstract. Google Custom Search was used for searching and downloading image data. In this experiment, 10 images were downloaded per keyword. To extract image features, we utilized a popular tool called VGG16[1] from Keras, and to calculate similarity we used cosine similarity.

---

[1] https://keras.io/applications/#vgg16.

For each synset, the *confidence value* was calculated using the same image data downloaded from Google Custom Search. The method and tools for feature extraction and similarity calculation we used are the same as what is used in our CDD calculation.

4.2 Evaluation Task

Using the process and tools mentioned above, we prepared 300 synsets for human evaluation. To judge if there exists cultural difference is challenging since the evaluator needs to truly be engaged in both cultures, in this case, Japanese-speaking culture and English-speaking culture. So that a carefully designed process is necessary to evaluate this type of culturally related experiment.

The data was evaluated by 3 native speakers of Japanese and 3 native speakers of English. All the evaluators are university students with an information science and engineering major. Each received a payment as a reward for working on the task for 6.5 h. The data sets given to Japanese speakers and English speakers were different, but among the same language speakers, the data sets were the same. Figure 6 illustrates an example of synset data given to the evaluator. The data and images are from the same synset. The image set above is from search results using English words while the image set below is from the Japanese words, however, the evaluators were not informed about the image source. First, the evaluators were asked to rate the similarity of two image sets using numbers 1 to 5: 1 for 'not at all', 2 for 'little', 3 for 'Medium', 4 for 'Much', and 5 for 'Very much'.

Then they were asked to rate the association between image sets and words in A, B, and C columns using the same scale. Words in A, B, and C are different between English and Japanese but they are all linked to the same synset. Column A contains a description that describes the synset while column B and column C contain words associated with the synset. In other words, both Japanese and English words in column B and column C are synonyms.

Since synsets are randomly selected from Japanese WordNet and the WordNet also includes a large number of technical terms. Some selected word does not make sense for general readers, even for educated native speakers, such as 'Dolobid' (nonsteroidal anti-inflammatory used to treat arthritis and other inflammatory conditions), transept (structure forming the transverse part of a cruciform church; crosses the nave at right angles), etc. As a consequence, we also instructed the evaluators to rate if they understood the description and those two words in their language.

	Synset and Images	Are two sets similar?	A	B	C	How well do you know/ you understand words A, B, and C?
For Japanese Speakers / **For English Speakers**	03002711-n		A long chair; for reclining	daybed	chaise	
	Image Set 1	4	5	5	5	5
	Image Set 2		3	3	3	
	03002711-n		長椅子	寝椅子	長椅子	
	Image Set 1	4	4	4	4	5
	Image Set 2		5	5	5	
*Rating	1: Not at all 2: Little 3: Medium 4: Much 5 : for Very much					

Fig. 6. Example of data given to English speaking evaluators and Japanese speaking evaluators

5 Accuracy Calculation Using Human Evaluated Data

5.1 Error Elimination

Before calculating the accuracy, the errors that were caused by or related to the knowledge of the evaluators were eliminated.

After the evaluation task had been completed, we first filtered out the synsets that could not be used because one or more evaluators did not understand the terms. The second type of error could happen when the image results are not correctly associated with the description or keywords. For example, there was a synset that contained the word 'biped' which means 'an animal that uses two legs for walking'. However, it is also a name of a popular video game for gamers. The popularity of this video game is greater than the popularity of using this word with its original meaning, so the image search result mainly showed the character from the game. When the evaluators or people who are not gamers see the image set and words from this synset, they cannot associate the images to the keyword even though the results are from the same language and the same keyword. In this case, it is not related to cultural differences between two language speakers, but it might appear as a cultural difference when using CDD. To eliminate this type of error, if the image search results for the English speaker side show that there is no strong relationship between the English description and word(s) (less than or equal to 3), the synset is filtered out. As well as for the Japanese speaker side, if the Japanese evaluator rates the relationship between the image set (from Japanese keywords) and Japanese words less than or equal to 3, the synset will not be used for calculation, because it shows the image set does not make sense to a native speaker.

5.2 Accuracy Evaluation Process

After making sure that the words and image set from the same language-speaking culture are related if the image set from the other language-speaking culture shows little relation to word(s) (less than or equal 3), this indicates that cultural differences exist to the evaluator. To illustrate, assume that Fig. 6 contains averaged ratings from 3 English speakers and 3 Japanese speakers. For English speakers, the first row of images (from English keyword(s)) are well associated with words in A, B, and C. However, when the second row of images (from Japanese Keyword(s)) shows little relation to the word(s). It can be implied that the cultural difference exists or cultural misunderstanding might happen when this word is used in multilingual communication.

For Japanese speakers, first, we needed to check if the image on the second row (from the Japanese keyword(s)) reflects Japanese words in A, B, and C correctly. In this case, the association is high so the synset is not needed to be eliminated. For Japanese, the first row of images (from English keyword) is also not strongly related to the words in Japanese. This implies that there exists cultural differences or cultural misunderstanding when this word is used.

Next, we labeled each synset with 'Yes' for the synset with cultural difference, or 'No' for the synset without a cultural difference, using the judgment explained earlier.

It is also necessary to set the threshold for CDD prediction. We set the optimal threshold using a method based on existing work [8]. For our data, the optimal threshold to judge whether there is a cultural difference or not is 0.54. Thus, the synsets in which CDD similarity was less than 0.54 were predicted as cultural differences having existed. Finally, we compared the prediction result from CDD to human evaluation.

6   Experiment Result

After comparing the CDD prediction result to a human evaluation in two languages, we calculate the percentage of correct prediction for each synset with a different range of confidence value, as shown in Table 1. The second column shows the correct percentage comparing English speakers' evaluation to CDD result while the third column shows the correct percentage comparing Japanese speakers' evaluation to the CDD result.

Table 1. Percentage of CDD accurate prediction for synsets with confidence value in each range.

Confidence	Percentage correct prediction for English	Percentage correct prediction for Japanese
0–0.1	N/A	N/A
0.1–0.2	80%	60%
0.2–0.3	67%	69%
0.3–0.4	71%	65%
0.4–0.5	90%	82%
0.5–0.6	90%	75%
0.6–0.7	100%	89%
0.7–0.8	100%	100%
0.8–0.9	N/A	N/A
0.9–1	N/A	NA

To illustrate the relationship between confidence value and accuracy, we plotted the percentage of correct prediction for each range of *confidence value* on a graph in Fig. 7. We observed that, for the synsets with high *confidence value*, the accuracy of prediction is also high. The correlation between accuracy for English and the confidence value is 0.843 and the correlation between accuracy for Japanese and the confidence value is 0.927. From this result, we can infer that the proposed confidence value is strongly correlated to the accuracy of CDD prediction.

7 Discussion and Future Work

7.1 Application of the Result

This research aims to calculate the confidence value to support the decision for the multilingual chat system to warn or not to warn the user. If the confidence of a synset is high and CDD predicts that using the word in each synset will cause cultural misunderstanding, the system should warn right away. As well as, when CDD predicts that no cultural difference exists, the system can ignore that word.

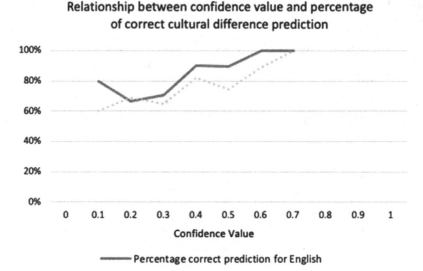

Fig. 7. Relationship between confidence value and percentage of correct cultural difference prediction by CDD

For the synset with low similarity, it is needed to use other methods together with CDD for confirmation. We are still researching several methods that can be used to detect cultural differences alone or with CDD, such as multilingual dictionary-based detection, etc.

7.2 Confidence Value Distribution

When we investigated the distribution of confidence value, as shown in Fig. 8, it is obvious that most synsets have a low confidence value with an average of 0.36. Low average confidence implies that most image search results are diverse. This could be the main cause of error detection when using CDD. Because high confidence can guarantee CDD prediction results, it is necessary to study the methods to overcome this image variety problem. One possible solution that could help to deal with this problem in the future is using fewer images or only one that represents each word correctly instead.

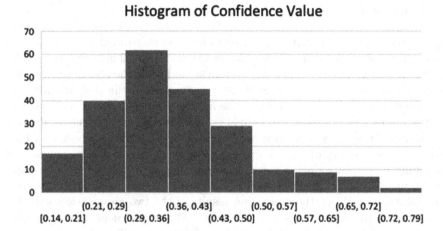

Fig. 8. Histogram of confidence value

7.3   The Eliminated Synset

During the data preparation step, we eliminated some synsets when the image search results, using one language as a keyword, do not match the description, or words in that language. We qualitatively analyzed the synset that we tagged as 'Error' and found that there are reasons why native speakers cannot associate the images with the given words. When there are several meanings associated with one word, in other words, some words have several homonyms. In this case, several types of images can represent each homonym. Some homonyms could be a specific name, such as the name of a famous person or a famous brand name. However, the popularity can be limited only to some locations, cultures, and some groups of people which causes people who are not in those areas or from those groups to be unable to recognize the association between the images and words. This raises another issue of cultural difference not between language speakers, but between subcultures. We also plan to investigate this issue further in the future.

7.4   Limitation

This paper focused on proposing confidence value to be used to support the decision of misunderstanding warnings in the multilingual chat system. However, there is still room for research to be conducted to improve this support system.

During the human evaluation process, the threshold (More than 3 and less than or equal 3) has been selected to judge whether a cultural difference exists or not. However, further study is needed to make sure that 3 is the optimal value for use as the criteria.

For simplicity, this research treats cultural difference as a discrete concept: exist or does not exist. It is also to treat cultural difference as a continuous concept.

8   Conclusion

This paper's main contribution is to provide a method to calculate *confidence value* for automated cultural different detection (CDD). This confidence value can be used to help decide when the system should warn the user about cultural misunderstanding when a suspected word is typed into the chat window. We conducted an experiment to evaluate the accuracy of the automated system by comparing the CDD judgment to human evaluation. However, human evaluation for cultural differences is challenging, because the evaluators needed to have a deep understanding of both cultures. Because of this problem, our second contribution is to introduce a method to evaluate cultural differences by using two groups of people. Each group only understands one language or is from only one culture. When the evaluation results of the two groups are combined, it is possible to identify cultural differences. Our experiment result confirms that there is a high correlation between the proposed *confidence value* and the accuracy of CDD prediction. *confidence value* can help to make fast decisions about what to warn or not to warn about for the high confidence synset, however; for the low confidence synset, we suggest that it is necessary to apply some other methods to CDD, for example, a dictionary-based prediction which also included in our future work.

References

1. Cho, H., Ishida, T., Yamashita, N., Inaba, R., Mori, Y., Koda, T.: Culturally-situated pictogram retrieval. In: Ishida, T., Fussell, S.R., Vossen, P.T.J.M. (eds.) IWIC 2007. LNCS, vol. 4568, pp. 221–235. Springer, Heidelberg (2007). https://doi.org/10.1007/978-3-540-74000-1_17
2. Deutscher, G.: Through the Language Glass: Why the World Looks Different in Other Languages. Metropolitan Books, New York (2010)
3. Herring, C.: Does diversity pay?: race, gender, and the business case for diversity. Am. Sociol. Rev. **74**(2), 208–224 (2009)
4. Hofstede, G.: Cultural dimensions in management and planning. Asia Pac. J. Health Manag. **1**(2), 81–99 (1984)
5. Isahara, H., Bond, F., Uchimoto, K., Utiyama, M., Kanzaki, K.: Development of the Japanese wordnet. In: Sixth International Conference on Language Resources and Evaluation (2008)
6. Ishida, T., Murakami, Y., Lin, D., Nakaguchi, T., Otani, M.: Language service infrastructure on the web: the language grid. Computer **51**(6), 72–81 (2018)
7. Miller, G.: WordNet: An Electronic Lexical Database. MIT Press, Cambridge (1998)
8. Nishimura, I., Murakami, Y., Pituxcoosuvarn, M.: Image-based detection criteria for cultural differences in translation. In: Nolte, A., Alvarez, C., Hishiyama, R., Chounta, I.-A., Rodríguez-Triana, M.J., Inoue, T. (eds.) CollabTech 2020. LNCS, vol. 12324, pp. 81–95. Springer, Cham (2020). https://doi.org/10.1007/978-3-030-58157-2_6
9. Pituxcoosuvarn, M., Ishida, T.: Multilingual communication via best-balanced machine translation. N. Gener. Comput. **36**(4), 349–364 (2018)

10. Pituxcoosuvarn, M., Ishida, T., Yamashita, N., Takasaki, T., Mori, Y.: Machine translation usage in a children's workshop. In: Egi, H., Yuizono, T., Baloian, N., Yoshino, T., Ichimura, S., Rodrigues, A. (eds.) CollabTech 2018. LNCS, vol. 11000, pp. 59–73. Springer, Cham (2018). https://doi.org/10.1007/978-3-319-98743-9_5
11. Pituxcoosuvarn, M., Lin, D., Ishida, T.: A method for automated detection of cultural difference based on image similarity. In: Nakanishi, H., Egi, H., Chounta, I.-A., Takada, H., Ichimura, S., Hoppe, U. (eds.) CRIWG+CollabTech 2019. LNCS, vol. 11677, pp. 129–143. Springer, Cham (2019). https://doi.org/10.1007/978-3-030-28011-6_9
12. Pituxcoosuvarn, M., Murakami, Y., Lin, D., Ishida, T.: Effect of cultural misunderstanding warning in MT-mediated communication. In: Nolte, A., Alvarez, C., Hishiyama, R., Chounta, I.-A., Rodríguez-Triana, M.J., Inoue, T. (eds.) CollabTech 2020. LNCS, vol. 12324, pp. 112–127. Springer, Cham (2020). https://doi.org/10.1007/978-3-030-58157-2_8
13. Talke, K., Salomo, S., Rost, K.: How top management team diversity affects innovativeness and performance via the strategic choice to focus on innovation fields. Res. Policy **39**(7), 907–918 (2010)
14. Yamashita, N., Inaba, R., Kuzuoka, H., Ishida, T.: Difficulties in establishing common ground in multiparty groups using machine translation. In: Proceedings of the SIGCHI Conference on Human Factors in Computing Systems, pp. 679–688. ACM (2009)
15. Yoshino, R., Hayashi, C.: An overview of cultural link analysis of national character. Behaviormetrika **29**(2), 125–141 (2002)
16. Yoshino, T., Miyabe, M., Suwa, T.: A proposed cultural difference detection method using data from Japanese and Chinese Wikipedia. In: 2015 International Conference on Culture and Computing (Culture Computing), pp. 159–166. IEEE (2015)

A Study of Cross-Cultural Communication in the NPD: Applying Piaget's Theory to Multidisciplinary Communication in the Three Validation Stages

Der-Wai Wang[✉] and Yen Hsu

The Graduate Institute of Design Science, Tatung University, Taipei, Taiwan
warrenwang.dw@outlook.com, yhsu@gm.ttu.edu.tw

Abstract. The importance of cross-functional and multi-disciplinary communication has been emphasized for new product development (NPD) in many researches. Many of them were discussed about the conflicts or problems among different R&D functions within NPD process. Whereas in product development practices, companies of ICT (information, computer, technology) industries have focused on quality issues in NPD with three stages as known as EVT, DVT and PVT. Dedicated R&D functions are assigned with specific targets to fulfill at each of the stages. The major reason to plan such process is to define clear development stages and thresholds so that the quality can be assured and risk can be reduced as getting into next stage. This process is in line with ISO 9000 quality system as well; it helps companies comply with an international quality system. It is valuable that companies can aggregate various opinions upon different development issues from different R&D functions for achieving common goals. The core of communication among R&D teams is to tackle multi-disciplinary or cross-cultural gaps. This study is applying meta-analytics to interpret Piaget's cognitive theory as non-technical skills (NTS) into the actions which R&D teams can take to reach better cross-cultural communication within EVT/DVT/PVT stages. The actions include: (1) In EVT stage, it needs to absorb inputs from different R&D teams, with assimilation attitude to utilize different ideas is the best approach. (2) Moving into DVT, because different ideas have been achieved upon common ground, adaption can help reach the best balance among sophisticated conditions. (3) Last in PVT, accommodating all considerations to fit in mass production is the best interest for companies.

Keywords: Piaget's theory · NPD (New Product Development) · ISO 9000 · EVT (Engineering Validation Test) · DVT (Design Validation Test) · PVT (Production Validation Test)

1 Introduction

New product development (NPD) is one of the major activities to propel product innovations and sustain the growth for companies (Im et al. 2013; Pugh 1991). This activity is

P.-L. P. Rau (Ed.): HCII 2022, LNCS 13313, pp. 188–201, 2022.
https://doi.org/10.1007/978-3-031-06050-2_14

like an electricity generator providing continuous and supportive power in many aspects. With this support, externally a company can perform corporate social responsibility, CSR (such as ESG, environmental, social and governance) and internally drive either advanced studies or development projects to accumulate competitive strength and elevate company's image (Fuente et al. 2021; Nirino et al. 2021; Yu and Luu 2021). Therefore, New Product Development is the very core activity within company's operation and management (Hales and Gooch 2004; Pahl et al. 2007b). Especially, by means of Engineering design in twenty-first century, NPD has been much more sophisticated and complicated than ever before; almost impossible to be accomplished by any single role of engineering functions. Therefore, collaboration and communication have been becoming a vital part all the way through the engineering design and development process (Edmondson and Nembhard 2009; Pessôa and Trabasso 2017).

In common and most cases, new product development is organized and managed in the form of projects, in which magnitude, complexity, novelty and production quantity are four major features identified by researches (Rodwell 1971). These four items depicted the opportunities and challenges a company would have while proceeding new product development projects (Hales and Gooch 2004). NPD projects are planned and scheduled by each individual company as dedicated procedures with its particular requirements and complicated issues, including various missions at different stages or the timing to have different R&D functions participating project teams for specific development issues, etc. It is a series of activities with knowledge-intensive, multi-disciplinary, precisely time-controlled, strictly progress-monitored and cross-cultural collaboration (Relvas and Ramos 2021).

This study is aimed at categorizing the distinctive needs in EVT/DVT/PVT stages and interpreting Piaget's cognitive theory into three measures that R&D teams can take as communication enhancement factors for reaching consensus more effectively and efficiently. As working together for projects, R&D teams have to not only express the professional knowledge in their points of view, bus also find out the best solutions within multi-disciplinary communication during the three validation (or verification) stages in NPD process. Furthermore, the communication is in the forms of cross-cultural (i.e., multidisciplinary) information sharing and conclusions making, to explicate Piaget's theory of cognitive communication—adaption, assimilation and accommodation can construct pathways toward common ground of mutual understandings within NPD process. The ultimate goals are just as Tjosvold's study (2008), by enhancing mutual understandings, the internal conflicts can be reduced and NPD progresses can be moved forward much more faster and smoother (Tjosvold 2008).

2   Process, Quality and Communication in the NPD Literature

2.1   NPD Process and Quality Control

In addition to those characterizing and influencing features for NPD process, such as the project size, complexity, innovation and production, delivery time and technical risk were two more features taken into consideration in researches as well (Hales and Gooch 2004). Delivery time can be regarded the best product-launch timing to gain better profits on one hand, project teams can complete the design and development tasks within soonest schedule to reduce the expenses on the other. Meanwhile, technical risk refers to how well the projects can be fulfilled into quality products. This item has been expanded as widely covered management topics of product quality for companies. Moreover, poor quality may cause the effort and expense invested in vain, on the contrast, good quality can make company's investment generate folds of value in return. Juran (1986) depicted that the most outward evidence of poor quality could cause loss of sales and huge cost. The actions for companies to improve product quality encountered certain non-uniformities (i.e., cross-cultural situations), for example, multiple functions, multiple hierarchical levels, multiple product lines, that should be well taken care of with certain solutions. In order to have quality issues managed explicitly, a systematic procedure named Quality trilogy was proposed for company's quality management. As the table described the contents below (Table 1):

Table 1. Basic process of quality trilogy (Juran 1986).

Quality planning	Quality control	Quality improvement
• Identify the customers, both external and internal • Develop product features that respond to customer needs (products include both goods and services) • Establish quality goals that meet the needs of customers and suppliers alike, and do so at a minimum combined cost • Develop a process that can produce the needed product features • Prove process capability-prove that the process can meet the quality goals under operating conditions	• Choose control subjects-what to control • Choose units of measurement • Establish measurement • Establish standards of performance • Measure actual performance • Interpret the difference (actual vs. standard) • Take action on difference	• Prove the need for improvement • Identify specific projects for improvement • Organize to guide the projects • Organize for diagnosis-for discovery of causes • Prove remedies • Prove that the remedies are effective under operating conditions • Provide for control to hold the gains

What Juran's quality trilogy covered are three basic phases for quality management, including quality planning, quality control and quality improvement, in which the procedures, targets and methods are all with quality-focused points of view (Juran 1986). In NPD extents, it needs steps further to engage with the complete NPD system. Applying quality trilogy into Cooper's (1990) influencing and classic stage-gate system can help companies or R&D functions always seize what targets to achieve and how well to complete in each stage (Fig. 1). The merits of evolving hybrid approaches creates certain strategic and tactical driving forces for these three phases, including to make products successful, to optimize organizations and processes, to make NPD approaches more agile (Cooper 2019).

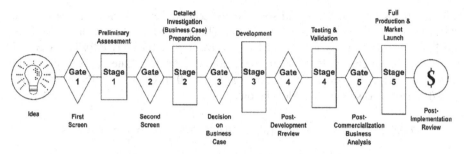

Fig. 1. Stage-gate system (Cooper 1990).

Furthermore, companies dealing with multi-national business would not only establish their own quality management systems internally, but also engage with international clients with same standards (i.e., to be in line internationally). ISO 9000 is an internationally recognized route for both internal and external parties. As ISO 9001:2015 articulates: the advantages to adopt ISO 9000 standards include: (1) a uniformity framework which bridges different quality management systems; (2) documentation alignments for different parties with clause structure of ISO 9000; (3) synchronization of specific terminology of ISO 9000 standards within the organization (ISO 2015). Putting into practices, companies have NPD process certified with ISO 9000 system, the overall quality management had been elevated and enhanced in many fields, such as supplier relationships, information and analysis, strategic quality planning and even human resource management as well, exhibited by results of empirical surveys (Rao et al. 1997). The survey results well resonated the ISO 9000 principles of quality management, for example, continuous improvement, system approach management, process approach…etc.

A research of quality system in Japan indicated that ISO 9000 principle has been specified and allocated into EVT, DVT, PVT stages. The guidelines in ISO 9000 are all accomplished in the common NPD process (Iwama 2001). However, to comply with ISO 9000 quality standards did not assure the successful business or greater competitiveness. It further depended on the maturity level of defining the quality targets and process (Pivka 2004). How to best use this framework is becoming a very key issue. Based on similar recognition, ICT companies in Taiwan, for example, had a distinctive collaboration arrangement by well using the merits of this framework and global deployment. An in-depth studies revealed that Taiwanese ODM manufacturers kept initial stages of product planning, EVT and up to DVT in Taiwan as a kind of competitive strength, and then allocated PVT and MP stages in offshore manufacturing sites (Chen 2004). Studies further showed, by well using the global value chain and inter-firm dynamics, Taiwanese contract (or ODM) manufactures of notebook PCs had reached certain milestones, which accounted for nearly 92% worldwide shipment in 2009 (Kawakami 2011). A survey in an EEU country which employed ISO 9000 quality system as another example did show the positive feedback on business, as well (Javorcik and Sawada 2018).

Within and between these three validation (or verification) stages, companies allocated and assigned members from suitable departments such as industrial design, R&D, quality control, procurement, etc. to work out and contribute for various topics or issues; so that during development procedures, team members do everything they can to fusion different fields of knowledge and solutions to accomplish company's goals (Iwama 2001; Javorcik and Sawada 2018; Porter and Tanner 2004). The ultimate goal may not be achieved all at once but fulfilled step by step at EVT/DVT/PVT stages and thresholds, in which ISO 9000 quality system melt into stage-gate as a complete and commonly adopted process. Corresponding ISO 9000 to Common NPD process and EVT/DVT/PVT as shown in Table 2 below:

Table 2. Mapping ISO 9000 with EVT/DVT/PVT in Common NPD process

Stage (Kawakami 2011)	**EVT** (engineering verification test)	**DVT** (design verification test)	**PVT** (production verification test)
ISO-9001 corresponded (Iwama 2001)	**Design review**	**Design verification**	**Design validation**
Host (Eng and Ozdemir 2014)	**R&D**	**R&D**	**R&D and production**
Objectives (Eng and Ozdemir 2014)	• Prototype developed • Use mock-up or eve T1 housing for pilot run • Key component functions workable • Identify the customers, both external and internal	• Use MP housing for pilot run • H/W fix • Reliability test	• Product should be very mature • Similar to MP Product • Factory tune production process for the preparation of MP
Output Requirements (Eng and Ozdemir 2014)	• EVT test report • EMC/safety submission • Block diagram/circuit explanation • Testing • Pd free parts check • Corrosion test	• DVT test report • Yield rate report • Component verification • Customer verification • Dust test • Choose control subjects-what to control	• PVT test report • Yield rate report • Failure analysis report • Golden sample • Online preparation list • Product spec • Prove the need for improvement

Note: Aggregated from different researches (Eng and Ozdemir 2014; Iwama 2001; Kawakami 2011).

Based on the researches interpreted above, to summarize the major actions and brief target items as the list below:

– EVT (Engineering Validation Test): to utilize inputs from different R&D teams; to prepare and test preliminary dummy (appearance) mock-ups and then working engineering Prototypes.
– DVT (Design Validation Test): to balance the needs and requirements from different R&D teams; to prepare and test minimum working samples (or minimum viable

products, MVP) with silicon soft tooling or 3D printing; and pilot run for product assembly.

- PVT (Production Validation Test): to fit in the encountered pros and cons; to prepare and test hard tooling (for production), trial run for product assembly in controlled quantities or batches.

2.2 NPD Process and Communication Activities

The review activities conducted as quality management measures at these three verification stages routinely or iteratively can be regarded as a kind of valuable events where the reviewers can assess whether the outputs of the design meet the targets and mature enough to be transferred to other functions or next stages. They can be taken place by short meetings typically or exist in many other ways (Johnson and Gibson 2014). The beneficial upsides of design reviews are composed of synchronizing understandings of project goals, developing multi-aspects and candid dialogues, identifying design proposals' weakness and strength, sharing experiences, advancing design…etc. The key aspects of overall design activities are sharing in many ways, for example, regular updates, reports, technical information, or meeting minutes as an exchange mechanism of information (Mattson and Sorensen 2020). With this mechanism, it shapes a process in which various, alternative concepts can be generated and the selection of a dedicated conceptual design all based on the well-organized and precisely-controlled convergence approaches (Pugh 1991). However, studies by Harvard business school and others showed there might be a limit of process-based thinking. How to keep out-of-box ideas rather let them vanish in the process? The information sharing and learning, i.e. rounds of communication, by the participants within NPD process is a must for contemporary management (Brown and Duguid 2000; Gidel et al. 2005).

A diagram, depicting information flows in Fig. 2, illustrated the holistic NPD process in a systematic way and indicated the flows between different functions with brevity. It analyzed holistic NPD process, from identifying the needs and wants of markets and users all the way through to the selling of the well-completed products (Pahl et al. 2007a). The dotted lines moving around the diagrams implied the information flows within NPD process. Design & development is the box with most dotted lines gathered together, in which a lot of information and ideas sparkling via communication with different parties. With complete and profound communication, project teams could have the products designed much better. So scheduling, planning, discussing, sharing, analyzing, even criticizing are the possible behaviors likely happened around NPD process (Browning et al. 2006; Gopsill et al. 2015; Sim 2004). Upon this subject, all topics and issues are dispersed within a wide variety of disciplines or function units so that cross-cultural communication is more than necessary.

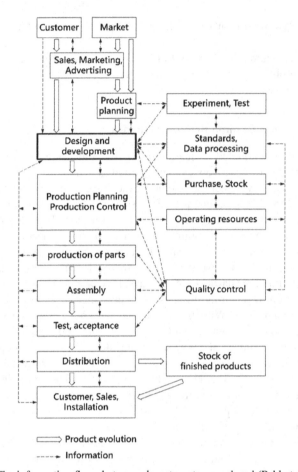

Fig. 2. The information flows between departments, re-colored (Pahl et al. 2007a).

3 Applying Piaget's Cognitive Theory to Cross-Cultural Communication

3.1 Meta-analytics as a Data Analyzing Approach

NPD process is a highly-organized and precisely-planned systematic process. This single generic process had been applied onto a very wide range of product categories, such as commonly seen quick-build products, customized products, platform products; or more sophisticated like process-intensive products, technology-push products, high-risk products, complex systems (Ulrich and Eppinger 2012). Because NPD process has a special characteristic: one process fitting many genres of products, to adopt meta-analytics as analyzing approach is a suitable option. The principles of meta-analytics enable designers to use systematic approaches with relatively broader possibilities or virtual infinity but without any huge revision in process, methodology, system design or test plan. Even though the situations or product definitions are going to be different, the time or expense invested previously can be kept and cumulated (Simske 2019). For example, a research well used merits of meta-analytics to provide significant results of team adaption for different situations within NPD process (Christian et al. 2017).

3.2 NTS: The Tips of Cross-Cultural Communication

Since the communication of NPD is across different perspectives of disciplines or cultures, the information of contents could be varied accordingly, it causes something not clear enough among each party, (i.e., uncertainties). Uncertainty is one of the major concerns in the cross-cultural communication (Hogg and Wagoner 2017). Furthermore, different disciplines refer to different cultures which result in epistemological differences (Dyer et al. 2021). In terms of human factors, it is about the information input and process, in which stimuli received by sensory system and then perceived and responded (Sanders and McCormick 1987). To put it into psychology aspects, it is very similar to cognitive process of recognition and reception to the cross-cultural (or multi-disciplinary) messages from the design concepts. Psychological aspects can be supportive factors which help designers well accomplish the information sharing within NPD of design (Wilpert 2007). A theoretical framework provided three intra-personal factors which play important roles for the outputs of creative performance (Amabile 1982; Amabile et al. 1990; Amabile and Pillemer 2012). These three factors, quoted form Amabile (1982), are as below:

- Domain-relevant skills: such as knowledge about and talent in the domain, which depend on innate abilities and training.
- Creativity-relevant skills: such as cognitive style, work habits, and knowledge of creativity heuristics, which depend on personality, characteristics and training.
- Task motivation: which depends on individual task preferences and socially imposed constraints.

To apply into NPD process, Domain-relevant skills, or domain knowledge, are the professional skills or knowledge possessed by each R&D team. As for the other two items, there are nothing to do with professional but personal. These two factors can be regarded as kinds of non-technical skills (NTS). For example, the personal ability of cognition or motivation has no direct links to professional expertise, but they may enhance the professional skills in another way around, such as elimination of possible communication error (Etheridge et al. 2021; Masaomi et al. 2020; Nicolaides et al. 2018). The non-technical skills have been widely used in medical fields and recognized as an effective approach for self-development of medical staffs coping with volatile environment (Abahuje et al. 2021; Doyen et al. 2019; Nicolaides et al. 2020). NTS consists with four non-professional factors, yet very helpful to enhance professional performance; which are task management, teamwork, situation awareness and decision-making (Flin et al. 2010; Mitchell et al. 2012). These factors reflect the tips of cross-cultural communication, for instance, teamwork reverberates cross-cultural collaboration, situation awareness echoes cognitive psychology…etc.

3.3 Piaget's Three Forms of Knowledge and Cognitive Theory

Except four factors of NTS can be supportive roles for professional performance and communication, Piaget's three forms of knowledge, which result from practices of cognition, can be helpful factors to eliminate uncertainties arising from cross-cultural communication within NPD process. A brief description of Piaget's three forms of knowledge as below (Piaget 1971):

- Physical experiences of external objects or anything related to them, relatively huge amount of knowledge from continuous learning behavior or practical intelligence.
- Knowledge structured inherently (or innate with hereditary programming), within extremely restricted category such as perceptual structures; kind of instinct capabilities varied from different individuals.
- Logic-mathematical knowledge acquired from scientific trainings, as extensive as physical experiences, remained independence of experience, coordinated to the actions conducted by the subject onto the objects around.

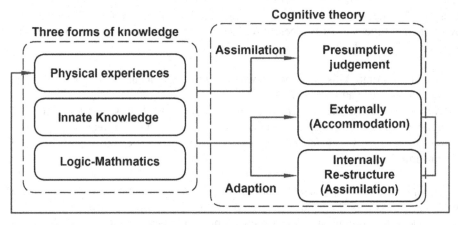

Fig. 3. Mechanism of Piaget's cognitive theory and three forms of knowledge

These three forms of knowledge were further interpreted by Piaget, some of personal experiences, innate knowledge or derived from science, can gather and be accounted for a metal model called assimilatory schemata in which justified certain information into one's personal knowledge or further becoming presumptive judgement; other information beyond being assimilated can be adapted in two complementary ways—externally (representation) or internally (thought). Externally, in forms of outward representations, such as learning, experimenting, and then to conclude into the physical experience or knowledge. This outside-in process is named as accommodation by Piaget. Internally, on the other hand, to re-structure or digest the information received through consciousness, or more precisely through reflective abstraction, and then to conclude into physical experiences or knowledge (Phillips 1971; Piaget 1971). The structure and flows of Piaget's three forms of knowledge and cognitive theory as illustrated in Fig. 3. In this manner, Piaget's three forms of knowledge and cognitive theory can act as NTS factors to strengthen the bedrock of consensus and accumulate basis of mutual understanding.

3.4 Piaget's Cognitive Theory on Three Verification Stages of NPD

The Piaget's research approaches have been analyzed relying on two theoretical pillars—constructivism and stage theory. Both of them embodied the development of core cognitive activities; a perceptual model to receive and perceive (Byrnes 2020; Carey et al. 2015). Although studies have kept evolving in cognitive, neuro-science and other related fields, the concepts of constructivism and stage theory are very suitable to interpret the cross-cultural communication among different R&D teams within NPD process.

The R&D project teams with various backgrounds and knowledge can be regarded as multi-cultural environment, the discussions and conversations for NPD projects are similar to the cross-cultural or intercultural communication (Cooper 2019; Tjosvold 2009; Ulrich and Eppinger 2012). Moreover, the contents of the discussions are mostly based on the professional knowledge and scientific researches. To be juxtaposed with Piaget's three forms of knowledge, the discussions in NPD were mostly in the Piaget's third category of knowledge—logic-mathematical knowledge. However, because there are many different R&D teams participated in NPD process, the professional fields varied, so did the information. Assimilation of Piaget's cognitive theory can help multi-disciplinary team members communicate the contents that have been agreed upon previously. On the other hand, accommodation can be a factor to help team members digest the information which had not been reached into mutual understandings. Piaget's cognitive theory acts such a moderation role to the communication within NPD process. Studies of mental development showed Piaget's assimilation and accommodation can form dynamic mental development (Block 1982). For difficult issues or complex information, the skills of adaption can be used to classify whether to experiment or learn externally or to digest internally. These actions can be treated as non-technical skills for cross-cultural communication as conducting new product development. In order to perform the best uses, NTS can be further distinguished by attributes and applied into different stages such as EVT, DVT, PVT.

4 Conclusions and Discussions

The conclusions are that the EVT stage mostly uses assimilation principle, the DVT stage overall needs both assimilation and accommodation (i.e., adaptation), and the PVT stage employs the accommodation principle. The results are shown as three separated items below.

(1) EVT (Engineering Validation Test): Using assimilation to integrate new ideas, technologies, or information which project teams received, learned or adopted

(2) DVT (Design Validation Test): Using Adaptation (both assimilation and accommodation) to adjust or modify existing design to fulfill product propositions and constraints.
(3) PVT (Production Validation Test): Using accommodation to fit into particular requirements such as production, quality, after service, etc.

Furthermore, the mechanism of Piaget's cognitive theory and three forms of knowledge was converted into the attitudes as NTS skills which R&D teams can adopt as co-working gestures within NPD. Each of them has been mapping with the necessary skills—utilize/balance/fit-in used in EVT/DVT/PVT stages. Please see the mappings in Table 3 below.

For more discussions, the three NTS skills or attitudes can be developed or varied into certain different gestures which can be factors to have NPD's cross-cultural communication faster or smoother. To explore more details or topics around NTS skills will be significantly helpful factors for industries.

Table 3. Mapping Piaget's theory to development stages and tasks

Phases tasks	**EVT** engineering validation (verification) test	**DVT** design validation (verification) test	**PVT** production validation (verification) test
Tasks to accomplish	To Prepare and test (1) Dummy appearance mock-ups (2) Working engineering prototypes	To Prepare and test minimum working samples (1) Soft tooling for tests of working samples (2) Product assembly trial	To prepare and test (1) Tooling for production (2) Produce products in batches
Targets	To integrate new ideas, technologies, or information which project team received, learned or adopted	To adjust existing design to fulfill product propositions and constraints	To fit in particular requirements such as production, quality, service etc.
NTS actions mapping to Piaget's theory	**To utilize with assimilation attitude**	**To balance with adaption attitude**	**To fit in with accommodation attitude**

References

Abahuje, E., et al.: Understanding barriers and facilitators to behavior change after implementation of an interdisciplinary surgical non-technical skills training program in Rwanda. J. Surg. Educ. **78**(5), 1618–1628 (2021). https://doi.org/10.1016/j.jsurg.2021.01.011

Amabile, T.M.: Social psychology of creativity: a consensual assessment technique. J. Pers. Soc. Psychol. **43**(5), 997–1013 (1982). https://doi.org/10.1037/0022-3514.43.5.997

Amabile, T.M., Goldfarb, P., Brackfield, S.C.: Social influences on creativity: evaluation, coaction, and surveillance. Creat. Res. J. **3**(1), 6–21 (1990). https://doi.org/10.1080/10400419009534330

Amabile, T.M., Pillemer, J.: Perspectives on the social psychology of creativity. J. Creat. Behav. **46**(1), 3–15 (2012). https://doi.org/10.1002/jocb.001

Block, J.: Assimilation, accommodation, and the dynamics of personality development. Child Dev. **53**(2), 281–295 (1982). https://doi.org/10.2307/1128971

Brown, J.S., Duguid, P.: Balancing act: how to capture knowledge without killing it. Harv. Bus. Rev. **78**(3), 73–80 (2000)

Browning, T.R., Fricke, E., Negele, H.: Key concepts in modeling product development processes. Syst. Eng. **9**(2), 104–128 (2006). https://doi.org/10.1002/sys.20047

Byrnes, J.P.: Piaget's cognitive-developmental theory. In: Benson, J.B. (ed.) Encyclopedia of Infant and Early Childhood Development, 2nd edn., pp. 532–539. Elsevier, Oxford (2020)

Carey, S., Zaitchik, D., Bascandziev, I.: Theories of development: in dialog with Jean Piaget. Dev. Rev. **38**, 36–54 (2015). https://doi.org/10.1016/j.dr.2015.07.003

Chen, S.-H.: Taiwanese IT firms' offshore R&D in China and the connection with the global innovation network. Res. Policy **33**(2), 337–349 (2004). https://doi.org/10.1016/j.respol.2003.09.003

Christian, J.S., Christian, M.S., Pearsall, M.J., Long, E.C.: Team adaptation in context: an integrated conceptual model and meta-analytic review. Organ. Behav. Hum. Decis. Process. **140**, 62–89 (2017). https://doi.org/10.1016/j.obhdp.2017.01.003

Cooper, R.G.: Stage-gate systems: a new tool for managing new products. Bus. Horiz. **33**, 44–46 (1990)

Cooper, R.G.: The drivers of success in new-product development. Ind. Mark. Manag. **76**, 36–47 (2019). https://doi.org/10.1016/j.indmarman.2018.07.005

Doyen, B., Van Herzeele, I., Maertens, H., Vlerick, P., Vermassen, F.: Non-technical skills in surgical disciplines: communication styles & attitudes towards uncertainty and risk in surgical staff, trainees and applicants: a comparative study. Eur. J. Vasc. Endovasc. Surg. **58**(6, Supplement 1), e31–e32 (2019). https://doi.org/10.1016/j.ejvs.2019.06.539

Dyer, L., Power, J., Steen, A., Wallis, L., Davison, A.: Uncertainty and disciplinary difference: mapping attitudes towards uncertainty across discipline boundaries. Des. Stud. **77**, 101055 (2021). https://doi.org/10.1016/j.destud.2021.101055

Edmondson, A.C., Nembhard, I.M.: Product development and learning in project teams: the challenges are the benefits. J. Prod. Innov. Manag. **26**(2), 123–138 (2009). https://doi.org/10.1111/j.1540-5885.2009.00341.x

Eng, T.-Y., Ozdemir, S.: International R&D partnerships and intrafirm R&D–marketing–production integration of manufacturing firms in emerging economies. Ind. Mark. Manag. **43**(1), 32–44 (2014). https://doi.org/10.1016/j.indmarman.2013.07.013

Etheridge, J.C., et al.: Virtual non-technical skills assessment training is an effective, scalable approach for novice raters. J. Surg. Educ. **79**(1), 51–55 (2021). https://doi.org/10.1016/j.jsurg.2021.08.008

Flin, R., Patey, R., Glavin, R., Maran, N.: Anaesthetists' non-technical skills. Br. J. Anaesth. **105**(1), 38–44 (2010). https://doi.org/10.1093/bja/aeq134

De laFuente, G., Ortiz, M., Velasco, P.: The value of a firm's engagement in ESG practices: are we looking at the right side? Long Range Plann. 102143 (2021). https://doi.org/10.1016/j.lrp.2021.102143

Gidel, T., Gautier, R., Duchamp, R.: Decision-making framework methodology: an original approach to project risk management in new product design. J. Eng. Des. **16**(1), 1–23 (2005). https://doi.org/10.1080/09544820512331325238

Gopsill, J.A., McAlpine, H.C., Hicks, B.J.: Supporting engineering design communication using a custom-built social media tool – PartBook. Adv. Eng. Inform. **29**(3), 269–756 (2015). https://doi.org/10.1016/j.aei.2015.04.008

Hales, C., Gooch, S.: Profiling the project. In: Hales, C., Gooch, S. (eds.) Managing Engineering Design, pp. 55–81. Springer, London (2004). https://doi.org/10.1007/978-0-85729-394-7_4

Hogg, M.A., Wagoner, J.A.: Uncertainty–identity theory. In: Kim, Y.Y., McKay-Semmler, K.L. (eds.) The International Encyclopedia of Intercultural Communication, pp. 1–9. Wiley, Hoboken (2017)

Im, S., Montoya, M.M., Workman, J.P., Jr.: Antecedents and consequences of creativity in product innovation teams. J. Prod. Innov. Manag. **30**(1), 170–185 (2013). https://doi.org/10.1111/j.1540-5885.2012.00887.x

ISO: ISO9001:2015. In quality management systems requirements. British Standards Institution, London (2015)

Iwama, H.: ISO9001 and reliability management program: ISO9001 and product development program. J. Reliability Eng. Assoc. Jpn. (REAJ) **23**(3), 288–293 (2001). https://doi.org/10.11348/reajshinrai.23.3_288

Javorcik, B., Sawada, N.: The ISO 9000 certification: little pain, big gain? Eur. Econ. Rev. **105**, 103–114 (2018). https://doi.org/10.1016/j.euroecorev.2018.03.005

Johnson, A., Gibson, A.: Communication for engineers. In: Johnson, A., Gibson, A. (eds.) Sustainability in Engineering Design, pp. 181–223. Academic Press, Boston (2014)

Juran, J.M.: Universal approach to managing for quallity: the quality trilogy. Qual. Progress 18–24 (1986). https://books.google.com.tw/books?id=1K6WYgEACAAJ

Kawakami, M.: Inter-firm dynamics in notebook PC value chains and the rise of Taiwanese orig-inal design manufacturing firms. In: Kawakami, M., Sturgeon, T.J. (eds.) The Dynamics of Local Learning in Global Value Chains: Experiences from East Asia. IS, pp. 16–42. Palgrave Macmillan, London (2011). https://doi.org/10.1057/9780230281783_2

Masaomi, Y., et al.: Continuing surgical education of non-technical skills. Ann. Med. Surg. **58**, 177–186 (2020). https://doi.org/10.1016/j.amsu.2020.07.062

Mattson, C.A., Sorensen, C.D.: Product development tools and techniques. In: Mattson, C.A., Sorensen, C.D. (eds.) Product Development: Principles and Tools for Creating Desirable and Transferable Designs, pp. 167–308. Springer, Cham (2020). https://doi.org/10.1007/978-3-030-14899-7_11

Mitchell, L., Flin, R., Yule, S., Mitchell, J., Coutts, K., Youngson, G.: Evaluation of the scrub practitioners' list of intraoperative non-technical skills (SPLINTS) system. Int. J. Nurs. Stud. **49**(2), 201–211 (2012). https://doi.org/10.1016/j.ijnurstu.2011.08.012

Nicolaides, M., et al.: Developing a novel framework for non-technical skills learning strategies for undergraduates: a systematic review. Ann. Med. Surg. **36**, 29–40 (2018). https://doi.org/10.1016/j.amsu.2018.10.005

Nicolaides, M., et al.: Team performance training for medical students: low vs high fidelity simulation. Ann. Med. Surg. **55**, 308–315 (2020). https://doi.org/10.1016/j.amsu.2020.05.042

Nirino, N., Santoro, G., Miglietta, N., Quaglia, R.: Corporate controversies and company's finan-cial performance: exploring the moderating role of ESG practices. Technol. Forecast. Soc. Change **162**, 120341 (2021). https://doi.org/10.1016/j.techfore.2020.120341

Pahl, G., Beitz, W., Feldhusen, J., Grote, K.-H.: Introduction. In: Pahl, G., Beitz, W., Feldhusen, J., Grote, K.-H. (eds.) Engineering Design: A Systematic Approach, pp. 1–25. Springer, London (2007a). https://doi.org/10.1007/978-1-84628-319-2_1

Pahl, G., Beitz, W., Feldhusen, J., Grote, K.-H.: Product planning, solution finding and evaluation. In: Pahl, G., Beitz, W., Feldhusen, J., Grote, K.-H. (eds.) Engineering Design, pp. 63–124. Springer, London (2007b). https://doi.org/10.1007/978-1-84628-319-2_3

Pessôa, M.V.P., Trabasso, L.G.: The product development system. In: Pessôa, M.V.P., Trabasso, L.G. (eds.) The Lean Product Design and Development Journey: A Practical View, pp. 3–18. Springer, Cham (2017). https://doi.org/10.1007/978-3-319-46792-4_1

Phillips, J.L.J.: The Origins of Intellect: Piaget's Theory. W. H. Freeman and Company, San Fransisco (1971)

Piaget, J.: Biology and Knowledge. The University of Chicago Press, Chicago (1971)

Pivka, M.: ISO 9000 value-added auditing. Total Qual. Manag. Bus. Excell. **15**(3), 345–353 (2004). https://doi.org/10.1080/1478336042000183406

Porter, L.J., Tanner, S.J.: The ISO9000 quality management system. In: Porter, L.J., Tanner, S.J. (eds.) Assessing Business Excellence, 2nd edn., pp. 254–283. Butterworth-Heinemann, Oxford (2004)

Pugh, S.: Total Design: Integrated Methods for Successful Product Engineering. Addison-Wesley Publishing Company, Great Britain (1991)

Rao, S.S., Ragu-Nathan, T.S., Solis, L.E.: Does ISO 9000 have an effect on quality management practices? An international empirical study. Total Qual. Manag. **8**(6), 335–346 (1997). https://doi.org/10.1080/0954412979352

Relvas, C., Ramos, A.: New methodology for product development process using structured tools. Proc. Inst. Mech. Eng. Part B-J. Eng. Manuf. **235**(3), 378–393 (2021). https://doi.org/10.1177/0954405420971228

Rodwell, C.: Engineering design management. CME (the chartered mechanical engineer): the journal of the institution of mechanical engineers (18) (1971). https://books.google.com.tw/books?id=2etIAQAAIAAJ

Sanders, M.S., McCormick, E.J.: Information input and processing. In: Human Factors in Engineering and Design, 6th edn, pp. 43–78. Mcgraw-Hill Book Company, New York (1987)

Sim, S.K., Duffy, A.H.B.: Evolving a model of learning in design. Res. Eng. Des. **15**, 40–61 (2004). https://doi.org/10.1007/s00163-003-0044-2

Simske, S.: System design optimization. In: Simske, S. (ed.) Meta-Analytics, pp. 253–271. Morgan Kaufmann (2019)

Tjosvold, D.: The conflict-positive organization: it depends upon us. J. Organ. Behav. **29**(1), 19–28 (2008). https://doi.org/10.1002/job.473

Tjosvold, D.: Cooperation and competition in restructuring an organization. Can. J. Adm. Sci. Rev. Can. des Sci. de l'Administration **7**, 48–54 (2009). https://doi.org/10.1111/j.1936-4490.1990.tb00645.x

Ulrich, K.T., Eppinger, S.D.: Product Design and Development, 5th edn. McGraw-Hill, New York (2012)

Wilpert, B.: Psychology and design processes. Saf. Sci. **45**(1), 293–303 (2007). https://doi.org/10.1016/j.ssci.2006.08.016

Yu, E., Van Luu, B.: International variations in ESG disclosure – do crossisted companies care more? Int. Rev. Financ. Anal. **75**, 101731 (2021). https://doi.org/10.1016/j.irfa.2021.101731

A Study of Traditional Culture-Based Animation Symbols in the Context of Intercultural Communication

Sheng Ye[✉] [ID]

Fuzhou University of International Studies and Trade, 28, Yuhuan Road, Shouzhan New District, Changle District, Fuzhou 350202, Fujian, China
Willye@163.com

Abstract. The process of transnational and cross-cultural communication is based on the differences of different cultural systems, and the interaction and interaction between different cultures. With the increasing frequency of cross-cultural communication, animation is an important carrier of cultural communication, a film and television expression to convey national culture and show different traditional cultures, and an important communication medium to construct different national images and cultural forms in the process of cross-cultural communication, which will promote the mutual recognition and integration of global cultures, help eliminate the alienation and divide between human cultures and even misunderstanding and hostility, and create a rich and open dialogue space for the ideal human with The formation of a 'global culture' with common interests and common value norms creates a rich and open space for dialogue. This study is dedicated to summarising the ways in which regional traditional culture can be combined with animation to help create cross-cultural animation scripts.

Keywords: Intercultural communication · Traditional culture · Animation design

1 Introduction

In the globalised environment of film and television, the phenomenon of intercultural communication is becoming more and more frequent. Like films, TV dramas and TV programmes, animation, as an important part of intercultural communication and an important carrier of cultural output, plays an irreplaceable and important role in the intercultural communication of film and television, and is an important carrier of cultural symbols, humanistic ideas, spiritual cores and values. In addition to its economic, cultural and artistic value, it also has a huge social value in today's era of new media. Not only does it play an important role in a country's external communication, but it is also an important tool for cultural diplomacy in countries around the world. Whether it is American animation or Japanese animation, while actively capturing the global market, they have always succeeded in spreading their own culture and local spirit. Although Chinese animation has made considerable progress and achievements in recent years, there are still very few works that can successfully communicate across cultures, so it has become a priority to study how to integrate traditional culture into animation works and produce animation works that are suitable for cross-cultural communication.

The purpose of this study is to summarize the creative characteristics of cross-culturally transmitted anime works from various countries, analyze the anime symbols with traditional culture in the works, and the forms of combining traditional culture with animation. Successful cross-cultural animation works produced in different countries are selected and compared with Chinese works containing traditional culture, and conclusions are drawn on how to integrate traditional culture into animation production.

2 Cross-Cultural Communication of Traditional Culture

Apart from the entertainment aspect of animation works, it can be found that animation actually carries a lot of things beyond images, such as the social life and national culture of a country. When examining how a culture spreads across national cultures in worldwide cinema, we cannot ignore animation as an important medium. Looking at cultural diffusion in the era of globalisation, we can easily find that developed countries and regions are also the central source of diffusion, not only in terms of cultural status but also in terms of information flow, and they are constantly exporting culture to lagging countries and regions by virtue of their absolute superiority. Disney animated films, for example, work mostly with traditional cultures from around the world, and have managed not only to expand their dissemination and create film and television content that is accessible to a world audience, but also to gain cultural identity in the process of translating stories across cultures. Although most of the animated works have been able to promote the intercultural transmission of local traditions and cultures, there have been some negative comments. The convergence hypothesis school of thought believes that we are all converging towards a single global culture. This has led to a certain degree of "cultural convergence" around the world, which has caused alarm and resistance in many countries.

3 Cross-Cultural Communication of Cultural Symbols in Animation Works

When it comes to cross-cultural animation works, the most famous one is Disney Animation. Since its establishment, Disney Animation has represented the highest technology of animation production for a long time and produced many classic animation works. Facing the needs of audiences and markets in different countries in the context of cross-cultural communication, Disney aims at global communication and possesses an American multicultural style in the selection and creation of story subjects. Disney takes the cultural themes of the world as its own resource base, and creates Disney animation works by summarizing and classifying stories from all over the world and selecting materials. For example, Disney's first feature-length animation Snow White was based on Grimm's Fairy Tales written by German linguists Jacob Grimm and the brothers

Wilhelm Grimm, while many subsequent animated works were based on Hans Christian Andersen's Fairy Tales written by the 19th century Danish writer Hans Christian Andersen and the Arabic folk tale collection Tales from the thousand and one nights".

The animated film "Finding Neverland," released in 2017, was produced by Pixar Animation Studios and co-produced by Walt Disney Studios and Pixar Animation Studios. The culture of the Mexican Day of the Dead is present throughout the movie, and the film is known as a true reflection of Mexican culture. The film serves both an educational and cultural purpose through its storytelling format and unique artistic style. It earned $807.8 million at the box office and received excellent scores on various review sites. The film team's portrayal of the Mexican Day of the Dead left a lasting impression on audiences in various countries, which contributed to the cultural and artistic enhancement of the film's central idea. The main points of these culturally based plots are to honor the dead family members, to remember them, and to highlight the explicit and implicit love for family to remind you to cherish the wonderful family you currently have.

The animation also has many traditional Mexican artworks, such as the skulls of many of the characters in the animation, which are made according to the calavera. Calavera is an expression of the human skull that is used in edible or decorative skulls made of sugar or clay for the Mexican Day of the Dead and the Roman Catholic celebration of All Souls Day, as shown below.

Papel-Picardo paper cuts also appear in the work. This is a Mexican folk culture decorative craft in which shapes are cut into thin paper. The traditional subjects are birds, flowers and bones. Papel-Picardo cutouts are usually reserved for special occasions such as Easter, Christmas and the Day of the Dead. On the day of the deceased's death, paper cutouts are often placed on the altar. This is usually done by stringing several paper cutouts together to form a banner. These banners can be hung throughout the street or on the walls of a room or home, as shown in the picture below.

Ballerina, a joint production of Gaumont, France and Canadian animation studio, was released in France on December 14, 2016. Set in 19th century France, the story tells the story of Felicity, who grew up in an orphanage and wants to become a real ballet dancer. In order to realize her dream, she escapes from the orphanage with her friend Victor and ventures into Paris.

In the performance of the story plot, the audience will also be attracted by the French architectural style of the animation scenes. Street scenes of the building body both to fresh, bright, modern tone and the formation of light, lively architectural form, but also the pursuit of the overall shape of the building majestic, the whole body overflowing with neo-classical French style. The most representative buildings include the Statue of Victory and the Eiffel Tower under construction, as well as the place where the main character learns to dance and finally steps on stage, the Paris Opera House. In the animation process, several traditional architectural forms such as Greco-Roman colonnade and Baroque in the Paris Opera House are perfectly restored in the animation, as shown in the picture below.

Unlike the animation works in Europe and America, Japanese animation works prefer to express the famous culture. Japan has advanced production technology and industry chain, mature business operation mode let people from all over the world understand Japan through animation. Japanese animation works are very good at portraying Japanese folk culture and shaping the storyline in line with the current popular issues, focusing on the depth of traditional culture and modern combination. Japanese animations are very diversified and cover a variety of story topics, the core of which is composed of traditional Japanese folk culture. For example, the Japanese ninja culture expressed in "Naruto" and "Nintama Rantarō" is as familiar to people of all countries as the Japanese code name, and its prototype is a kind of special warfare killer and special warfare spy produced by special training in ancient Japan, and its official name was determined in the Edo period. Ninja usually wear dark blue or dark purple clothes, because the dark blue and dark purple dress close to the color of the night sky can make the ninja less likely to be discovered by others, the animation is often so performance as shown in the picture below.

"Your Name" is also an excellent animated work that incorporates traditional culture. It ranked second in the box office of Japanese animated films, second only to Spirited Away. Its success in cross-cultural communication relies not only on beautiful graphics and clever storyline settings, but also on the flexible use of modern perspectives combined with traditional Japanese culture. The elements that appear in the story, such as shrine rituals and autumn festivals, have a strong Japanese Shinto flavor. The knotted rope, Miyamizu shrine, ritual chewing wine and other elements appearing in the film make the national elements of Japanese animation obvious. Then fused with modern storyline, the modern urban culture and traditional shrine culture are contrasted and compatible. As one of the main clues of the movie, the knotted rope plays an important role in running the plot and driving the story forward. As a figurative expression in traditional Japanese culture, the knotted rope carries the ancient Japanese understanding of primitive Shintoism. In large Japanese rituals, the shinigami tied knotted ropes in the four colors of red, white, blue and black and, by doing so, got rid of demons and prayed for peace and good fortune. In the eyes of the Japanese, this physical knotting power is with the power of God, through the knot, the power of nature can be blocked in the knot, people can knot has a spiritual power, soothe the fear of the heart, to obtain peace and health. The shape of the knotted rope is shown in the figure below.

"Your Name" reintegrates and innovates traditional Japanese culture in a modern story context, making these traditional cultural elements the catalyst that drives the plot and perfectly realizes the foreign dissemination of traditional Japanese culture.

One of the most successful Japanese animation works in terms of cross-cultural communication is Spirited Away, which has traditional Japanese cultural images as references for most of its imagery. The onijin who gets off the boat is the Kasuga god worshipped by Nara Kasuga Taisha, the river god is from the traditional Japanese mask Nohmien, and the green onijin statue is a combination of the image of the head of Rohan in Buddhism and the bushogen fire in Japanese culture, as shown in the picture below.

The success of "Spirited Away" in cross-cultural communication is not only the expression of traditional Japanese culture, but also the combination of Eastern and Western cultural symbols in the work. For example, in "Spirited Away", there are traditional

Chinese elements such as auspicious clouds, peony trays, screens, blue and white porcelain vases and pines in the "soup kitchen", Japanese elements such as various baths, kabuki, Japanese shopping streets and murals, as well as the chimney and steam train outside the main scene of the "soup kitchen". There are also symbols with typical European cultural characteristics such as the chimney and the steamy train outside the main scene "soup kitchen", the tall bookcase in the room, the mural of characters, the candelabra and the fireplace. The film carries symbols of different cultural connotations, forming a scene of cultural interplay between opposites and unity, so that audiences from all over the world can see their familiar symbols and form cultural identity when watching the film, which enhances the value of cross-cultural communication of the work.

With the development of globalization, Chinese animation is also actively engaged in cross-cultural communication, and more and more works combining traditional Chinese cultural elements with animation have entered the public eye. China began to experiment with cross-cultural dissemination of traditional cultural animation works as early as the 1940s. 1941 saw the release of the feature-length animated film "Hard fan princess" by the Chinese Wan brothers in Southeast Asian countries and Japan, in which the Chinese cultural style is reflected in many places. The shades of gray background images show the coloring techniques of Chinese ink painting. The split screen repeatedly shows the characters performing on the screen, showing the stage style of traditional Chinese opera. And the small movements of the characters convey the Chinese humorous characteristics. Finally, it succeeded in getting many positive comments from audiences in different countries.

In the Chinese animated movie "Big Fish Begonia", the costumes of the main character are the student costumes of the Republic of China period, and the hairstyle is also the "child flower head" of the Republic of China period. The costume design of the character Ling Po is based on Chinese Peking Opera costumes, and the belt on the waist and the sun pattern in the blouse have the classic Peking Opera costume characteristics, as shown in the picture below.

The scene design in the film "Big Fish Begonia" is subtly combined with traditional Chinese cultural elements, especially in the architectural design of the scenes. The design of the building in the animation is inspired by the traditional Chinese Hakka representative building "Tulou", which is the unique living place of Hakka people. From the outside, the building is cylindrical in shape, with a wall on the outside and a layer of rooms on the inside, neatly lined up. The architectural features of an earthen floor facilitate the connection between families and reflect the cohesiveness of a family, and also show the world the unique architectural art of China, as shown in the figure below.

The Chinese animation "the outcast" not only incorporates many Taoist ideas and Taoist culture, but also adds Chinese visual culture symbols of martial arts to its action design. Not only do they express various martial arts techniques through the images, but they also explain these martial arts styles in the story plot, tracing their roots and relating the mysterious martial arts techniques to China's traditional culture and philosophical thoughts, so that viewers from different countries can learn about traditional Chinese culture while enjoying various martial arts techniques, thus creating a sense of identity.

4 Summary

In order to make animation works with traditional cultural characteristics and successful in cross-cultural communication, there are two mainstream creative ideas. One is to collect stories and cultures from various countries around the world for production like Disney, and the other is to incorporate strong Japanese cultural characteristics into the expression of common world emotions like Japanese animation masters Hayao Miyazaki and Hoshikaijo. The pursuit of dreams, the importance of environmental protection, the opposition to war and other connotations that can be understood by all human beings are able to cross different cultures and languages and hit the hearts of viewers.

According to various animation review websites, it is found that the selection of traditional culture in cross-cultural works cannot be subjectively selected from one's own favorite culture, but it is necessary to create and think from the perspective of a third party, and to examine the cultural content expression of animation from the perspective of audiences who do not understand the traditional cultural background of the region, in order to avoid the wrong interpretation of the content between different cultures. Therefore, in the process of cross-cultural communication of traditional cultural animation works, it is necessary to confirm the cultural expressions in the subject matter of the works several times, combine the perspective needs of different audiences, and realize the cultural understanding in different cultural states in the form of cultural tolerance, so as to promote the animation works not to be misunderstood in the cross-cultural communication.

Many countries around the world hope to make more people understand their own culture through the cross-cultural communication of animation works, and encourage animation creators to explore more of their own special culture. For example, Chinese Tai Chi culture and various Chinese Kung Fu martial arts, or adaptations based on some literature with national characteristics, such as Shan Hai Jing and Liao Zhai Zhi Yi. Combining the cultural characteristics of the works with the expression of common human emotions will certainly move audiences from different cultural backgrounds and successfully achieve cross-cultural communication.

References

1. Salonova, A.: The role of intercultural communicative competence in the animation sector: multi-stakeholders perspectives. MS thesis. Itä-Suomen yliopisto (2019)
2. Mikidenko, N.L., Storozheva, S.P.: Animation role in ethnocultural socialization. Printed by resolution of the Presidium of the Academy of Polar Medicine and Extreme Human Ecology (APM&EH) LBC 5+ 88+ 74 I **66**, 246 (2016)
3. Zhao, Y.: Animation film Zootopia's intercultural communication's strategy. Dissertatin Doctoral dissertation, Hebei University of Economics and Business, Shijiazhuang city (2017)
4. Liu, J., Wu, J.: The elements application arts in the international communication of American animation films. Agro Food Ind. Hi-Tech. **28**(3), 3430–3432 (2017)
5. Sun, H.: On the beauty of imagery of Chinese traditional animation. In: International Conference on Education, Language, Art and Intercultural Communication (ICELAIC-14). Atlantis Press (2014)

6. Shang, L.: The application of Chinese traditional culture in the animation scene design. In: 2015 2nd International Conference on Education, Language, Art and Intercultural Communication (ICELAIC-15). Atlantis Press (2015)
7. Khalis, F.M., Mustaffa, N.: Cultural inspirations towards Malaysian animation character design. Malays. J. Commun. **33**(1), 487–501(2017)
8. Baldwin, D.L., Daubs, M.S., Ludwick, J.B.: Flashimation: the context and culture of web animation. In: SIGGRAPH Art Gallery (2006)
9. Huang, Y.: Study on the transmission of Japanese animation culture. In: 2016 2nd International Conference on Economics, Management Engineering and Education Technology (ICEMEET 2016). Atlantis Press (2017)
10. Napier, S.: Anime from Akira to Princess Mononoke: Experiencing Contemporary Japanese Animation. Springer, New York (2001). https://doi.org/10.1057/9780312299408
11. Aládé, S.M., Fọlárànmí, S.A., Ọd´ejóbí, O.A.: A model for animation of Yorùbá folktale narratives. Afr. J. Comput. ICT **8(3)**,113–120 (2015)
12. Baglay, V.: Mexican horror animation in search of national identity. Fantastic images of traditional culture and Hollywood cinematic monsters. Latin Am. **3**, 86–101 (2019)
13. Hasri, M., Hakim, U., Md Syed, M.A., Runnel, C.: Transmedia storytelling in the Malaysian animation industry: embedding local culture into commercially developed products. Atlantic J. Commun. **30**, 1–17 (2020)
14. Zang, N., Huang, X.: The application of national elements in animation costume design. In: 2019 5th International Conference on Humanities and Social Science Research (ICHSSR 2019). Atlantis Press (2019)
15. Lee, J-S.: A research of relationship between animation content and traditional folk culture: centered around Michel Ocelot's<Kirikou et la Sorcière>(Kirikou and the Sorceress) and KBS Satellite Channel's< Animentary Korean Folklore>. Cartoon Anim. Stud. 65–88 (2010)
16. Oh, D.-I.: Hayao Miyazaki's animation storytelling: aesthetics of confrontation and coexistence represented in the mythical space. J. Digit. Cont. Soc. **18**(4), 649–657 (2017)
17. Walsh, T.: Irish animation and radical memory. Place and memory in the new Ireland. Re-animating the Past, vol. **57**
18. Gang, Z., et al.: Research on Tujia nationality's brocade three-dimensional character modeling and animation integration. In: 2017 6th International Conference on Industrial Technology and Management (ICITM). IEEE (2017)
19. Worasamutprakarn, E.: The design and development of thai cultural inspiration to animation character. In: 2021 Joint International Conference on Digital Arts, Media and Technology with ECTI Northern Section Conference on Electrical, Electronics, Computer and Telecommunication Engineering. IEEE (2021)
20. Sugihartono, R.A.: Developing indonesian animation based on local culture. Bandung Creat. Movement (BCM) **4**(1) (2018)
21. Keys, J.: Doc McStuffins and Dora the explorer: representations of gender, race, and class in US animation. J. Child. Media **10**(3), 355–368 (2016)
22. Belkhyr, S.: Disney animation: global diffusion and local appropriation of culture. Études caribéennes **22** (2013)
23. Shangguan, J.: Analysis on the reasons for the intensive resonance among Mexican of the Film Coco. In: 2020 4th International Seminar on Education, Management and Social Sciences (ISEMSS 2020). Atlantis Press (2020)
24. Chen, M., Lingxuan W., Li, Q.: Condensation and dissipation on the visual processing of fear elements in animation. In: Knowledge Innovation on Design and Culture: Proceedings of the 3rd IEEE International Conference on Knowledge Innovation and Invention 2020 (IEEE ICKII 2020) (2022)
25. Peña Jr., N.M.R.: 41/Violence and Values in the Japanese Manga Naruto. The London Film Media Reader **406**

26. Shaver, T.J.: Taking the tradition out of traditional: the Shakuhachi in the Naruto Anime. Diss. University of Hawai'i at Manoa (2021)
27. Dwivedi, R.P.: Your name: a study of imagery and post-postmodernity in cinema. Cinema Stud. (2020)
28. Castiglioni, A.: From your name to Shin-Gojira: spiritual crisscrossing, spatial soteriology, and catastrophic identity in contemporary Japanese visual culture. In: Spirits and Animism in Contemporary Japan: The Invisible Empire, pp. 171–186. Bloomsbury Academic, London (2019)
29. Napier, S.J.: Matter out of place: carnival, containment, and cultural recovery in Miyazaki's "spirited away." J. Jpn. Stud. **32**, 287–310 (2006)
30. Lim, T.W.: Spirited away: conceptualizing a film-based case study through comparative narratives of Japanese ecological and environmental discourses. Animation **8**(2), 149–162 (2013)
31. Dou, G.-H.: Analysis on the traditional cultural elements of the Chinese animated film big fish & Begonia. 한국엔터텍인먼트산업학회논문지 **13**(7), 165–172 (2019)
32. Yang, K., Lee, S.-k.: A study on the traditional aesthetic characteristics appearing in the Chinese animation <Big Fish and Begonia>-focusing on three elements of Zong Baihua's artistic conceptions. Cartoon Anim. Stud. **47**, 53–79 (2017)

HCI and the Global Social Change Imposed by COVID-19

Post-COVID-19 Era Fashion Culture Perception Impacting on Beauty Consumption Behavior Change

Yang-Wen Chang[(✉)] 🆔 and Yen Hsu 🆔

The Graduate Institute of Design Science, Tatung University, Taipei, Taiwan
vincent27870352@gmail.com

Abstract. The COVID-19 epidemic has affected the daily activities of people all over the world as never before. To prevent the epidemic, most people have greatly reduced outings, especially those that require face-to-face or in groups. Beauty salons require physical consumption behavior in the store. Previously, it was an important consumption activity for many women. Moreover, the COM-B model was proposed in 2011, using ability, motivation, and opportunity as the research framework to explain human behavior. This research is aimed at members of the three-party matching APP in the beauty industry, including consumers, technicians, and shopkeepers. In the post-COVID-19 era, this study used COM-B as the framework to explore the APP user behaviors affected by capabilities, motivations, and opportunities. A total of 385 valid questionnaires were collected. This study used descriptive statistics to analyze the samples' basic data, confirmatory factor analysis to test the reliability and validity of the questionnaire, and structural analysis to verify the research hypotheses. Finally, this study validated the behavior change model of the COM-B framework and obtained significant results for both direct and indirect effects between the variables. Among them, the motivation of pursuing beauty best explains the behavior of members on the app platform. In addition, the sense of fashion culture as a moderating variable also successfully strengthened the relationship between motivation and behavior. Under the influence of the COVID-19 epidemic, the motivation of beauty and fashion culture sense still plays an important role in influencing the consumption-related behaviors of hairdressing and beauty consumers.

Keywords: COVID-19 · COM-B · Beauty APP · Fashion culture perception

1 Introduction

In early 2020, COVID-19 became a public health emergency of international concern [1], and the outbreak spread further around the world, impacting the globalized economy and the supply chain of each industry, and seriously affecting the livelihoods of countries [2]. Sudden public health events caused governments to be at a loss as to what to do with the overall economy and harm people's livelihoods [3]. Countries are actively seeking effective vaccines and preventing the spread of the epidemic [4]. Due to the

P.-L. P. Rau (Ed.): HCII 2022, LNCS 13313, pp. 215–229, 2022.
https://doi.org/10.1007/978-3-031-06050-2_16

effects of virus mutations, there is no relief from the health, economic and social crises that threaten humanity [5, 6]. Consumers, in general, are also experiencing a change in consumer behavior caused by COVID-19, which should be continuously observed [7]. Nowadays, social media is the main tool for people to get information about their lives [8]. With the COVID-19 circumstance, especially due to the psychological impact of panic consumption, it has become the norm to adjust people's consumption through social software or messaging [9].

In the post-COVID-19 era, there are many difficulties and concerns in activities that require face-to-face or group gatherings with people. For example, the consumption behavior of hairdressing needs to be carried out in physical stores, which is an important consumption item for many women. In addition to finishing their appearance, the interaction with the hairdresser in the process of consumption to the store, but also psychological expression and satisfaction. However, at the peak of COVID-19, consumers were afraid of contracting the disease and did not go to physical stores. As the epidemic eases, fashionable beauty wins out over fear of infection. People will use beauty and other methods to make themselves more confident, groom themselves with beauty salon to relieve the depression of the mood panic [10]. So during a pandemic, it is clear that the beauty function has a self-healing function [11]. During the epidemic, female consumers sought alternative ways to satisfy the perceived need for fashion culture. Secondly, during the epidemic period, people pay much attention and concern to personal, family-based epidemic prevention and public health measures [12]. Therefore, during an epidemic, people would change their consumption habits in physical beauty stores to protect themselves from gathering with other consumers. Many beauty consumers are changing their habits from physical to online appointments or in-home services [13]. However, there is little academic research on consumer behavior in the beauty industry. Based on the needs of hairdressing consumers, technicians, and industry players, the research team developed a three-party platform app for the beauty industry. The main function is to match consumer needs, providing personalized information of technicians, trend information, marketing, and promotional programs, store resources, appointments, and member interaction, etc. This study focuses on three types of members of the platform, and uses the COM-B model as the main framework to propose a mechanism that includes the ability, motivation, and opportunity to pursue beauty to influence members' platform behavior, and adds fashion culture perception as a moderating factor to explore the influencing aspects of members' behavior change.

The COM-B model is a theoretical explanation of people's behavior [14]. This flexible theoretical framework can provide a basis for changing the influences on behavior. Although COVID-19 is severely diffused, the pursuit of beauty is a human instinct. This study adopts the COM-B model as the research framework and adds a sense of fashion culture as a new construct to expand the COM-B model's moderating role to explore the consumer behavior changes of consumers using beauty media according to the characteristics of the beauty industry platform users. The samples for this study were taken from the OPENBeautiful APP three-party appointment service platform, which was supported by the Small and Medium Enterprise Division of the Ministry of Economic Affairs of Taiwan under the COVID-19 Small Business Innovation Research and Development Program. The project proposed a business model that integrates consumers, beauty technicians, and beauty stores in the beauty industry through a mobile app.

In summary, there are three main objectives of this COM-B extension model study.

1. to investigate what are the determinants of user behavior of the APP platform?
2. to investigate whether users' ability, motivation, and opportunity influence each other and their usage behavior?
3. to investigate the role of fashion culture as a moderating factor in influencing the behavior of platform users.

2   Literature Review

2.1   COM-B Theory

COM-B is a behavioral theory proposed by Michie in 2011 to explain human behavior patterns using this theoretical framework. The so-called COM-B construct is to use the established theoretical domain framework (TDF) to propose three main constructs of ability, motivation, and opportunity that influence behavior, and then propose the framework as the theoretical model basis for determining behavior according to the different research contexts [15]. The COM-B model is well suited to be applied in different contexts for a wider range of behavioral explanations, including to groups, populations, or corporate sectors [16]. In the COM-B research framework, different research domains develop different constructs that extend the theoretical domain framework and use them to predict behavior patterns in different contexts, providing researchers with additional variables that play a role such as antecedents, mediators, or moderators. Like in the application of health-promoting behavioral models to research, the social cognitive model used in the past was replaced with the COM-B model for research explanation, therefore, the interaction between the outcome of behavior (B) and the subject's capability (C) to formulate the opportunity (O) and motivation (M) of the behavior, therefore, integrating the concept of behavior change science and replacing it with a more multifaceted study of behavioral inference (Coulson, Ferguson, Henshaw & Heffernan, 2016). Thus, the concept of behavior change science was integrated and replaced with a more multifaceted study of behavioral inference [17].

The rate of transmission and infection of COVID-19 has a relatively decisive role because of the role of behavioral science, which influences the mechanisms by which people behave. Inherently, it can influence the spread of the epidemic [18]. This study proposes to modify the COM-B model to include a moderating effect by examining the factors affecting consumer behavior in the beauty industry under the COVID-19 epidemic by ability, motivation, and opportunity. The ability represents knowledge, physical and spiritual responses. Opportunity is the influence of the social environment on social resources, including the prospect of cooperative and social relationships; motivation is defined and connotes the mechanism of self-reflection and automatic instinct. Behavior is generated by the interaction of ability, opportunity and motivation [14]. Based on the research framework provided by COM-B theory, this study examines the factors influencing user behavior in the beauty industry platform, divided into ability, motivation, and opportunity. This study proposes that the ability sub-structures are knowledge and behavior regulation, the motivation sub-structures are intrinsic and extrinsic motivation, and the opportunity sub-structures are cooperative relationship and social relationship.

2.2 Fashion Culture

A sense of fashion culture is the communication of popular aesthetics, including popular culture and fashionable clothing, and is a way of communication in life [19, 20]. The tools of communication include various cultural elements of the media, driving the phenomenon of pleasure and reference to the celebrity effect [21]. Because of a need for self-information, adding some psychological motives to create a space for discussion in the media [22]. Since cultural identity brings a sense of iconic worship, it is a product of the modern fashion culture circle [23]. Evaluating the humanistic effect in the media empirically is mostly about self-providing profound reflections, provoking cultural perceptions of core values, and assessing them as the purpose of personal life [24].

The target of this study is the users of the beauty app platform, who are mostly young women pursuing fashion and expressing their own characteristics. Fashion culture sense can be defined as the pursuit of popular things and fashion. Therefore, this study assumes that the higher the sense of fashion culture of the member users of the beauty platform APP, the higher the knowledge (ability) of maintenance and behavior, the drive (motivation) to pursue self-beauty, and the demand for future establishment of relational cooperation behavior (opportunity). Therefore, it will add the sense of fashion culture dimension to the research area of COM-B expansion model adjustment.

2.3 Research Hypotheses

COM-B Capability, Motivation, Opportunity, Behavior

According to the concept of COM-B competence, which is essentially based on knowledge and behavior change, it is necessary to have the knowledge to satisfy the beauty care. Because of the motivation always seek change, the phenomenon of behavior change is considered reasonable [25]. Accordingly, summarizing the above, this study proposes hypothesis one.

H1: Beauty platform users' beauty care ability positively and significantly affects their motivation to use the platform.

In addition to the use of information technology to achieve the purpose of life and work tasks, people's perception of future cooperation opportunities on the platform will affect their inner motivation to pursue beauty [26]. This study uses the opportunity of COM-B model to explain the pursuit of fashion culture and beauty motivation, and from a customer-centric point of view, marketing opportunities must be socially relevant in order to be realized. Summarizing the above, this study proposes the following hypothesis.

H2: The opportunities for future collaboration among beauty platform users can positively and significantly influence the motivation of self-pursuit for beauty.

The COM-B model is a behavioral research framework that parses the specific behaviors (B), the capability (C), and the opportunities (O) that must be available to engage in a particular activity in order to perform a particular behavior. Motivation (M), on the other hand, is the psychologically driven desire to engage in behavioral states that contain habitual intentions [27]. The COM-B architecture is particularly strong in mediating the effect of the presence of the motor in the model. In this study, the interaction of capability, opportunity and motivation is used to study the behavior of APP users on the APP platform; that is, the capability, opportunity and motivation of member users are used to explain users' behavior [28]. In addition, members' motivation to pursue beauty plays the role of a mediating variable between capability and behavior, and between opportunity and behavior, respectively. Accordingly, summarizing the above, the following hypotheses are proposed in this study.

H3: The motivation of beauty platform users to pursue beauty will positively and significantly affect the behavior of members in using the platform.

H4: Beauty platform users' beauty maintenance ability will significantly affect members' behavior in using the platform.

H5: The future cooperation opportunity of beauty platform users will positively and significantly affect the behavior of members in using the platform.

H6: The motivation of beauty platform users to pursue beauty will have a mediating effect between their beauty care capability and their behavior of using the platform.

H7: Self-motivation of beauty platform users will have a mediating effect between future collaboration opportunities and platform usage behavior.

COM-B with the Fashion Culture Perception
In fashion culture circles, Welters and Lillethun [29] suggests the need for rich collaborative and social relationships to work together due to fashion culture sensemaking, operational and customer service needs. This study suggests that fashion sense is largely a cultural phenomenon, and that fashion sense of culture can influence the capability, motivation, opportunity, and behavior to pursue beauty. Therefore, this study suggests that when members have higher fashion sense of culture, it will strengthen the relationship between their capability, motivation, and opportunity to members' behavior on the platform. This study used the COM-B model as the basis for constructing the influence behavior construct, and therefore concluded that fashion culture sense is a reasonable phenomenon for behavior regulation [25]. Therefore, this study uses an extension of the COM-B model to increase the context of the COM-B model's fashion and cultural sense constructs as a validation for studying the various behavioral patterns of beauty app platform members. This study proposes the following hypotheses.

H8: Fashion culture perceptions of beauty platform users will have a moderating effect between their beauty care capability and their behavior of platform use.

H9: Fashion culture perceptions of beauty platform users will have a moderating effect between their self-motivation to pursue beauty and their platform use behavior.

H10: Fashion culture perceptions of beauty platform users will have a moderating effect between their future collaboration opportunities and their platform usage behaviors.

This study proposes the research model as shown below (Fig. 1).

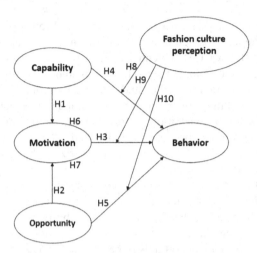

Fig. 1. COM-B extended research model.

3 Methodology

3.1 Subjects and Sampling

The samples for this study were taken from the OPENBeautiful APP three-party appointment service platform, which includes consumers, beauty stores and technicians of the platform. Members volunteered to complete the questionnaire on the platform. From August to September 2021, 385 valid questionnaires were collected from members. With a confidence level of 95% and a confidence interval of 5%, the sample size is sufficient to represent the entire membership.

3.2 Questionnaire Design

The research questionnaire design for this study consisted of two parts. One was the demographic variables, which included age, occupation, education, marital status, and income. The second part is the study construct variables, which include behavior, capability, motivation, opportunity, and fashion culture perception. The questions were measured on a seven-point Likert scale ranging from strongly disagree (1), disagree (2), somewhat disagree (3), average (4), somewhat agree (5), agree (6), and strongly agree (7), with higher scores indicating higher levels of agreement with the study variables.

Measurement
The behavioral constructs questionnaire items are based on Hsieh, Kuo, Wang, Chuang, Tsai's [30] model of PMT, the questions of health profile user behavior. Also, Wang, Huang, Yang, and Carolyn [31] provided topics such as an assessment of user behavior for social networking site users' sharing behavior. In the capability construct questionnaire, the knowledge core questions refer to Azmawani, Rahman Ebrahim, Asrarhaghighi Suhaimi Ab Rahman's [32] study of consumer perceptions of halal cosmetics on knowledge, religion, attitudes, and intentions. Then, the behavioral adjustment core questions

are based on James, Wallace & Deane's [33], research to compile three questions, for a total of five questions. Moreover, the questions of the motivation construct questionnaire were adapted from Ma, Du & Liu's [34] study of teacher-student relationships and language achievement. There are five questions developed. Also, the opportunity dimension includes the core topics of partnership and social relationships, according to Thornton, Henneberg and Naudé's [35] research. Then, five questions were adapted from McCutcheon, Lange and Houran's [36] research questionnaire on "conceptualization and measurement of celebrity worship" in the context of fashion culture perception.

3.3 Data Analysis

The data analysis methods used in this study include Descriptive Analysis, Confirmatory Factor Analysis (CFA), and Structural Equation Model (SEM). Descriptive statistics are used to organize the basic information of the sample for statistical analysis and present the data distribution of the sample. The main purpose of the validating factor analysis is to verify the reliability and validity of the questionnaire in this study and to ensure the quality of the questionnaire. The structural equation model is used to examine the research hypotheses, including model fit, path analysis, mediating effects, and validation of the moderating effects.

4   Results

4.1   Frequency Distribution

The occupation was mainly office workers with 100 people accounting for 26.0%; income was mainly 30,001–50,000 yuan with 147 people accounting for 38.2%; marriage was mainly married to 261 people accounting for 67.8%; education level was tertiary/university with 247 people accounting for 64.2%; age was mainly 31–40 years old with 132 people accounting for 34.3%. Table 1 below presents the data content.

Table 1. Frequency distribution table.

Variable		Frequency	Percent	Variable		Frequency	Percent
Occupation	Office workers	100	26.0	Marital status	Married	261	67.8
	Freelancer	49	12.7		Unmarried	124	32.2
	Self-employed	36	9.4	Education level	College/University	247	64.2
	Others	65	16.9		Graduate school上	51	13.2
	Service industry	97	25.2		Under high school	87	22.6
	Military and Civilian Personnel	32	8.3	Age	Under 20 years old	4	1.0
	Student	6	1.6		21–30 years old	30	7.8

(continued)

Table 1. (*continued*)

Variable		Frequency	Percent	Variable		Frequency	Percent
Income	100,00 -	32	8.3	31–40 years old		132	34.3
	30,000 NT dollars	82	21.3	41–50 years old		127	33.0
	30,001–50,000 NT dollars	147	38.2	Over 50 years old		92	23.9
	50,001–100,000 NT dollars	124	32.2				

4.2 Convergent Validity

Fornell and Larker [37] and Nunnally [38] pointed out that the factor loadings should be greater than 0.7, the composite reliability should be greater than 0.7, the average of variance extracted should be greater than 0.5., and Cronbach's α should be greater than 0.7. The results of this study using SmartPLS3 statistical software are shown in Table 2. The analysis of the data in this study shows that the factor loadings for each construct are greater than 0.7. The composite reliability values of all the constructs are 0.921–0.967, greater than 0.7. The average variance extractions are 0.701–0.856, greater than 0.5. The Cronbach's α values for the constructs are 0.900–0.958, greater than 0.7. Based on the above statistical data, the study has good convergent validity.

Table 2. Frequency distribution table.

Construct	Item	Factor loading	Cronbach's alpha	Composite reliability	Average variance extracted (AVE)
Capability	CAP1	0.890	0.900	0.921	0.701
	CAP2	0.904			
	CAP3	0.808			
	CAP4	0.804			
	CAP5	0.773			
Motivation	MOT1	0.908	0.956	0.966	0.851
	MOT2	0.940			
	MOT3	0.948			
	MOT4	0.933			
	MOT5	0.880			

(*continued*)

Table 2. (*continued*)

Construct	Item	Factor loading	Cronbach's alpha	Composite reliability	Average variance extracted (AVE)
Opportunity	OPP1	0.832	0.941	0.955	0.810
	OPP2	0.917			
	OPP3	0.927			
	OPP4	0.928			
	OPP5	0.893			
Behavior	BEH1	0.915	0.958	0.967	0.856
	BEH2	0.950			
	BEH3	0.942			
	BEH4	0.914			
	BEH5	0.906			

4.3 Discriminant Validity

In this study, the average variance extracted (AVE) method was used to analyze the discriminant validity of the reflective indicators. Fornell and Laker [37] showed that the average variance extraction (AVE) for each construct should be greater than the correlation coefficient between the pairs of variables to indicate the discriminant validity between the constructs. Most of the average variance extractions (AVEs) in this study are larger than the squared correlation coefficients, which indicates that this study has discriminant validity (Table 3).

Table 3. Discriminant validity

	Behavior	Capability	Motivation	Opportunity
Behavior	**0.925**			
Capability	0.460	**0.837**		
Motivation	0.473	0.482	**0.922**	
Opportunity	0.562	0.414	0.546	**0.900**

4.4 Goodness of Fit

According to scholars, a model fitness between 0.1 and 0.25 represents a small model fitness, a model fitness between 0.25 and 0.36 represents a moderate fitness, and a model fitness greater than 0.36 represents a better model fitness [39]. The model fitness of this study is 0.557, which is higher than 0.36, indicating that the study model has good fitness.

4.5 Path Analysis

Direct Effect

The results of structural model analysis, R2, and path coefficients are the main indicators to determine the goodness of the model [40]. Endogenous latent variables with R2 > 0.67 are highly explanatory, R2 > 0.33 or so indicates moderate explanatory ability, and R2 > 0.19 or so indicates weak explanatory ability [40, 41]. The results of this study showed that the R2 value of behavior is 0.393 and the R2 value of motivation is 0.377, indicating that the model has good explanatory power.

The significance check is conducted by t-test, and the larger the t-value, the stronger it is. This study uses the "bootstrapping" [40] method to analyze the t-value of the following example to discriminate. This is listed in Table 4 below.

The t-value of hypothesis H1 (Capability → Behavior) is 3.010.
The t-value of hypothesis H2 (Motivation → Behavior) is 2.039.
The t-value of hypothesis H3 (Opportunity → Behavior) is 7.138.
The t-value of hypothesis H4 (Capability → Motivation) is 4.072.
The t-value of hypothesis H5 (Opportunity → Motivation) is 7.656.

When the t-value is greater than 1.96, the hypothesis is valid because of the significance level. Therefore, H1, H2, H3, H4, and H5 all proved significant impacts. Figure 2 displays the statistical analysis results.

Table 4. Path analysis

DV	IV	Original sample (O)	Standard deviation (STDEV)	T statistics (IO/STDEVI)	P values	R^2
Behavior	Capability	0.226	0.075	3.010	0.003	0.393
	Motivation	0.154	0.076	2.039	0.042	
	Opportunity	0.384	0.054	7.138	0.000	
Motivation	Capability	0.309	0.076	4.072	0.000	0.377
	Opportunity	0.418	0.055	7.656	0.000	

Mediating Effects

The mediating effect of this study is determined by t-value and the results are shown in Table 5 below. The t-value of hypothesis H6 (Capability → Motivation → Behavior) is 1.761, less than 1.96. It means that when α equals 0.05, the result is insignificant, indicating that the mediating effect does not exist. Then, the t-value of hypothesis H7 (Opportunity → Motivation → Behavior) is 2.127, greater than 1.96. It means that when α equals 0.05, the result is significant, indicating that the mediating effect does exist (Table 6).

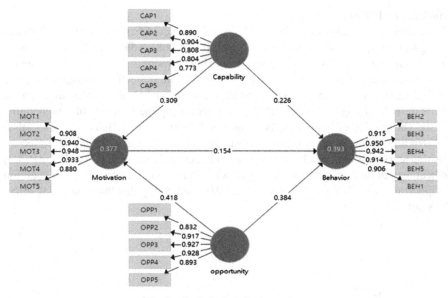

Fig. 2. Statistical analysis results.

Table 5. Mediating effects analysis

	Original sample (O)	Standard deviation (STDEV)	T statistics (|O/STDEV|)	P values
Capability → Motivation → Behavior	0.048	0.027	1.761	0.079
Opportunity → Motivation → Behavior	0.064	0.030	2.127	0.034

Table 6. Moderating effects analysis

	Original sample (O)	Standard deviation (STDEV)	T statistics (|O/STDEV|)	P values
Fashion * Capability → Behavior	0.110	0.060	1.829	0.068
Fashion * Motivation → Behavior	−0.167	0.055	3.026	0.003
Fashion * Opportunity → Behavior	0.051	0.040	1.259	0.209

Moderating Effects

The results of the analysis showed that the cross-product of Fashion and Capability had no significant effect on Behavior ($\beta = 0.110$, $P = 0.068$) indicating that there was no moderating effect. The p-value of hypothesis H8 (Fashion*Capability $\rightarrow$ Behavior) is greater than 0.05. It means that the result is insignificant, indicating that the moderating effect does not exist. Then, the cross-product of Fashion and Motivation had a significant effect on Behavior ($\beta = -0.167$, $P = 0.003$) indicating the presence of a moderating effect. The p-value of hypothesis H9 (Fashion * Motivation $\rightarrow$ Behavior) is less than 0.05, indicating that the moderating effect does exist. After that, the cross-product of Fashion and Opportunity had a non-significant effect on Behavior ($\beta = 0.051$, $P = 0.209$) indicating that there was no moderating effect. The p-value of hypothesis H10 (Fashion * Opportunity $\rightarrow$ Behavior) is greater than 0.05, indicating that the moderating effect does not exist (Fig. 3).

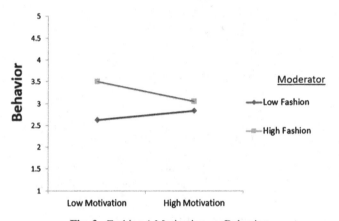

Fig. 3. Fashion * Motivation $\rightarrow$ Behavior

5   Conclusions and Recommendations

This study discusses the factors influencing the behavior of OPENBeautiful APP members under the post-COVID-19, based on the COM-B model framework, and adds the construct of fashion culture perception to the model of capability, opportunity, and motivation influencing behavior. The following conclusions were obtained.

Capability and Opportunity Positively and Significantly Influence the Motivation of Members

The results of this study showed that the score of capability on motivation was 0.309 and the score of opportunity on motivation was 0.418, both of which achieved significant positive effects. Therefore, using the platform to increase the view of beauty knowledge and increase the opportunity of cooperation between members can promote communication and activate the APP platform. In addition to matching consumers with other technicians and store members on the platform, it also strengthens the integration of resources between technicians and stores and strengthens the cooperative relationship between members. The capability and opportunity to explain the motivation also maintain a good explanation, so the design of the app can lead the user to participate in the presentation of the work and trigger the motivation to use.

The Higher the Capability, Opportunity and Motivation of Platform Users to Pursue Beauty, The Higher the Intensity of Behavior

The results of this study showed that the capability, opportunity, and motivation to pursue beauty had a significant impact on behavior with a score of 0.384. Among them, the user's perception of the opportunity has the most influence on the usage behavior. Therefore, business opportunities to enhance the business model can increase the use. For example, to increase the user's consumer membership so-called customer value, come to this APP platform can find the right designer or a good environment for their consumption. In addition, the capability, motivation, and opportunity in this study model has good explanatory power for APP behavior. Therefore, it is important to optimize and upgrade the interaction on the platform, such as encouraging technicians and store members to enhance their spending discounts or giveaways, or even linking to other profitable methods to meet member value.

The Mediating Effect of Opportunity to Influence Behavior Change Through Motivation

The results of this study found that in the extended COM-B model, opportunity affects behavior more strongly than capability and motivation, and both the direct and indirect effects hold. That is, a member's perception of future opportunities for collaboration has a twofold impact on his or her behavior on the platform. Therefore, the operation of the platform should focus on the members' perception of future cooperation opportunities. It can motivate members to be more active on the platform. For example, in the business model of creating customer value, it pays attention to the matchmaking function of resource integration and skill integration among platform members, because with the innovative information flow, business flow, gold flow and logistics, it can absorb the resources and intersection of cross-discipline and make the participation of downloading APP members higher.

Fashion Culture Perception Moderates Motivation to Influence Behavioral Relationships

This study verified the behavior change pattern of COM-B framework, and significant results were obtained for both direct and indirect effects between variables, among which the motive of pursuing beauty best explained the behavior of members on the APP platform. In addition, the fashion culture perception as a moderating variable also successfully strengthens the relationship between motivation and behavior. Under the influence of the COVID-19 epidemic, the motivation to pursue beauty and the fashion culture perception continue to play an important role in influencing the consumption-related behavior of hairdressing consumers. Therefore, this study suggested that platform operators should combine the application of popular culture or seasonal fashion products to increase the usage rate of platform users when they slide the app, and promote the fashion culture perception as an important element of the business model of the app media platform.

Future Research Recommendations
During the research process, there are many issues that cannot be explored in detail in the research content, including the three identities of consumer members, technicians, and store members. The different cultural backgrounds of platform users may have significant differences, which may lead different conclusion of APP suggestion. Moreover, in future studies, other constructs can be added to affect hairdressing behavior as antecedent variables of capability, motivation, and opportunity, such as personal attributes and Big Five personality attributes, in order to expand the application of the COM-B model and enrich empirical studies.

References

1. Liu, Y.-C., et al.: A locally transmitted case of SARS-CoV-2 infection in Taiwan. N. Engl. J. Med. **382**(11), 1070–1072 (2020)
2. Wen, Y., Zhang, T., Du, Q.: Quantifying the Covid-19 Economic Impact (2020)
3. Drummond, M.F., et al.: Methods for the Economic Evaluation of Health Care Programmes. Oxford University Press (2015)
4. Shahcheraghi, S.H., et al.: An overview of vaccine development for COVID-19. Ther. Deliv. **12**(3), 235–244 (2021)
5. Mishra, M.K.: The World after COVID-19 and its impact on Global Economy (2020)
6. Shereen, M.A., et al.: COVID-19 infection: Origin, transmission, and characteristics of human coronaviruses. J. Adv. Res. **24**, 91 (2020)
7. Mehta, S., Saxena, T., Purohit, N.: The new consumer behaviour paradigm amid COVID-19: Permanent or transient? J. Health Manag. **22**(2), 291–301 (2020)
8. Westerman, D., Spence, P.R., Van Der Heide, B.: Social media as information source: recency of updates and credibility of information. J. Comput.-Mediat. Commun. **19**(2), 171–183 (2014)
9. Makridis, C., Wang, T.: Learning from friends in a pandemic: social networks and the macroeconomic response of consumption. SSRN J. (2020). Available at SSRN 3601500
10. Linardon, J., et al.: Do body checking and avoidance behaviours explain variance in disordered eating beyond attitudinal measures of body image? Eat. Behav. **32**, 7–11 (2019)
11. Pikoos, T.D., et al.: The COVID-19 pandemic: psychological and behavioral responses to the shutdown of the beauty industry. Int. J. Eat. Disord. **53**(12), 1993–2002 (2020)
12. Gerstell, E., et al.: How COVID-19 is changing the world of beauty (2020)
13. Sheth, J.: Impact of Covid-19 on consumer behavior: will the old habits return or die? J. Bus. Res. **117**, 280–283 (2020)
14. Michie, S., Van Stralen, M.M., West, R.: The behaviour change wheel: a new method for characterising and designing behaviour change interventions. Implement. Sci. **6**(1), 1–12 (2011)
15. Howlett, N., et al.: A prospective study exploring the construct and predictive validity of the COM-B model for physical activity. J. Health Psychol. **24**(10), 1378–1391 (2019)
16. Michie, S., et al.: ABC of Behaviour Change Theories. Silverback Publishing (2014)
17. Heffernan, E., et al.: Understanding the psychosocial experiences of adults with mild-moderate hearing loss: an application of Leventhal's self-regulatory model. Int. J. Audiol. **55**(sup3), S3–S12 (2016)

18. Michie, S., et al.: Slowing down the covid-19 outbreak: changing behaviour by understanding it. BMJ (2020)
19. Kaiser, S.B., Green, D.N.: Fashion and Cultural Studies. Bloomsbury Publishing (2021)
20. Kawamura, Y.: Fashionology: An Introduction to Fashion Studies. Bloomsbury Publishing (2018)
21. Oliver, M.B., et al.: Entertainment effects: media appreciation. The International Encyclopedia of Media Effects, p. 1–8 (2017)
22. Davis, F.: Imaginary social worlds: a cultural approach. JSTOR **92**(1), 219–221 (1986)
23. Giles, D.: Illusions Immortality: A Psychology of Fame and Celebrity. Macmillan International Higher Education (2000)
24. Wirth, W., Hofer, M., Schramm, H.: Beyond pleasure: exploring the eudaimonic entertainment experience. Hum. Commun. Res. **38**(4), 406–428 (2012)
25. Grant, K.: Knowledge management: an enduring but confusing fashion. Lead. Issues Knowl. Manage. **2**, 1–26 (2015)
26. Davis, F.D., Bagozzi, R.P., Warshaw, P.R.: Extrinsic and intrinsic motivation to use computers in the workplace 1. J. Appl. Soc. Psychol. **22**(14), 1111–1132 (1992)
27. Cane, J., O'Connor, D., Michie, S.: Validation of the theoretical domains framework for use in behaviour change and implementation research. Implement. Sci. **7**(1), 1–17 (2012)
28. Stanton, J.M., et al.: Analysis of end user security behaviors. Comput. Secur. **24**(2), 124–133 (2005)
29. Welters, L., Lillethun, A.: Fashion History: A Global View. Bloomsbury Publishing (2018)
30. Hsieh, H.-L., et al.: A study of personal health record user's behavioral model based on the PMT and UTAUT integrative perspective. Int. J. Environ. Res. Public Health **14**(1), 8 (2017)
31. Wang, S.J., Huang, H.C., Yang, C.Y.S.: To say or not to say: the mediating role of psychological safety and self-efficacy on the influence of social capital on users' knowledge sharing behavior in social network sites. NTU Manage. Rev. **26**(2), 37–72 (2016)
32. Abd Rahman, A., Asrarhaghighi, E., Ab Rahman, S.: Consumers and Halal cosmetic products: knowledge, religiosity, attitude and intention. J. Islamic Mark **6**(1), 148–163 (2015)
33. James, T.L., Deane, J.K., Wallace, L.: An application of goal content theory to examine how desired exercise outcomes impact fitness technology feature set selection. Inf. Syst. J. **29**(5), 1010–1039 (2019)
34. Ma, L., Du, X., Liu, J.: Intrinsic and extrinsic value for English learning: mediation effects of self-efficacy in Chinese EFL context. Chin. J. Appl. Linguist. **41**(2), 150–168 (2018)
35. Thornton, S.C., Henneberg, S.C., Naudé, P.: An empirical investigation of network-oriented behaviors in business-to-business markets. Ind. Mark. Manage. **49**, 167–180 (2015)
36. McCutcheon, L.E., Lange, R., Houran, J.: Conceptualization and measurement of celebrity worship. Br. J. Psychol. **93**(1), 67–87 (2002)
37. Fornell, C., Larcker, D.F.: Evaluating structural equation models with unobservable variables and measurement error. J. Mark. Res. **18**(1), 39–50 (1981)
38. Nunnally, J.C.: Psychometric Theory 3E. Tata McGraw-hill Education (1994)
39. Wetzels, M., Odekerken-Schröder, G., Van Oppen, C.: Using PLS path modeling for assessing hierarchical construct models: guidelines and empirical illustration. MIS Quar. **33**, 177–195 (2009)
40. Chin, W.W.: Commentary: issues and opinion on structural equation modeling, JSTOR. MIS Quar. **22**(1), 7–16 (1998)
41. Ringle, C.M.: Gütemaße für den Partial-least-squares-Ansatz zur Bestimmung von Kausalmodellen. Univ. Hamburg, Inst. für Industriebetriebslehre und Organisation (2004)

Effects of Microblog Comments on Chinese User's Sentiment with COVID-19 Epidemic Topics

Hao He, Ziqi Guo, Jiajie Zhan, Pingfan Fan, Yihe Xia, Meng Wang, Qinwei Liu, and Zhe Chen[✉]

Beihang University, Beijing 100191, China
zhechen@buaa.edu.cn

Abstract. Social media is one of the most significant sources of information in modern people's life. Due to the large quantity of user base and public opinions, when people read a blog post, the different tendencies of comments may affect their views on the event to a certain extent. This paper, taking the COVID-19 epidemic as an example, investigated the impact of Weibo (a popular social software in China) comments on readers' sentiments. In this paper, text mining technology was adopted to collect data including the blogs and the comments under each blog, and the NLPIR-Parser platform was used to analyze the sentiment of the comments. Finally, the conclusion that the sentiments of other comments tend to follow the sentiments of the first comments was drawn. Based on the research results, this paper also gave some enlightenment on social media management and suggestions of public opinions oversight.

Keywords: Sentiment analysis · Microblog · COVID-19 epidemic · Text mining · China

1 Introduction

User behavior research is an important area of research. It aims to identify patterns of the behavior of users and to use these patterns to provide advice to developers and maintainers of products. User behavior research is of great value because of the commercial value it can bring and the guidance it can provide for product maintenance.

As an important source of information, Weibo reached 511 million monthly active users and 224 million daily active users in September 2020, according to the Weibo 2020 User Development Report [1]. Due to the large user base and the easy access to studying public opinions, a large number of user behavior studies have been conducted on Weibo. The large volume and easy accessibility of data on the microblogging platform have led to a large proportion of research using text mining which is also used by this study to collect data. In addition, there is a paucity of research analyzing the factors of commentary and sentiment, which is an innovative aspect of this study.

P.-L. P. Rau (Ed.): HCII 2022, LNCS 13313, pp. 230–240, 2022.
https://doi.org/10.1007/978-3-031-06050-2_17

This study explores the impact of microblog comments on readers' sentiments, through which the mechanisms by which microblog comments affect readers will be understood better, and the findings of this study can make practical contributions.

Microblogging has gradually penetrated people's lives. However, the study [2] shows that the level of engagement among Weibo users is generally low, with most users at a shallow stage where they only browse or occasionally reply with updates. These users rarely post, choosing mostly to view other people's tweets or comments. This makes comments on Weibo a significant influence on these Weibo users. Users often make their judgments using other users' comments when reviewing the content of their tweets. Focusing on the impact of microblog comments on users is the innovative aspect of this study.

Chinese users' posting a small number of comments is closely related to Chinese culture. In the West, people tend to be more willing to express their views on something. Chinese people, on the other hand, are more modest and tend to look internally at their own views by drawing on the views of others [3]. This makes the number of comments by Chinese users smaller and the impact of comments on internet users will be greater, so the study of comments is of some relevance.

During the COVID-19 epidemic in China, social media becomes an important means of communication and information dissemination between people who avoid meeting offline. The widespread use of Microblog has created a strong public opinion based on a large number of netizens in the event of a disaster, which, in addition to disseminating information about the disaster, also plays an important role [4] in guiding and influencing the users of microblogs and public opinions. As a result of the epidemic, there has been an increase in the number of online posts about health and epidemic prevention, and Weibo comments containing the views of the general public have a strong role [5] in guiding users' opinions. Microblog users' opinions on the epidemic will spread online, and over time, emotions will fester to form a strong subjective bias [6]. Studies have shown that Chinese netizens' attitudes towards the epidemic can be broadly divided into three stages: nervous and anxious, united and confident, and stable, while in the spatial dimension, the number of netizens commenting in the most serious areas of the epidemic is the highest and the sentiment value is the lowest [7]. This study provides new ideas for user sentiment analysis and explores the influence of comments on the sentiment of microblog users based on data mining.

2   Literature Review

2.1   Weibo Emotion

Considered as the largest social network platform in China, Weibo possesses massive users and features generating public opinions. Therefore, many domestic scholars have conducted a lot of research on user behavior and emotions on Weibo. There are many methods of estimating users' emotions, and one of them is building a sentiment attributor for Weibo user comments through grabbing comments from public safety emergencies with a crawler, and it was proposed by Chunlin Deng et al. [8]. Furthermore, Nan Li et al. (2021) built an analysis model of public opinion tendency by analyzing emojis are used in Weibo comments to judge emotion contained in the text [9]. There is another way proposed by Rujia Feng et al. (2021), which is based on the XLNet word embedding method, the Transformer's Encoder model and BiLSTM+Attention network to distinguish the emotional tendency reflected by users in microblog comments [10]. During the COVID-19 pandemic, Caihui Gu et al. (2021) firstly used the Text Rank algorithm to extract keywords from labeled texts, then conducted the textual emotion classification through three traditional machine learning methods and two neural network methods, finally analyzed the change in users' sentiment based on the annotation results of the best algorithm [11]. What's more, The Emotion Dictionary Extension Technology is worth being mentioned. It extends emotional words and highlights emotional weights from certain texts to extend emotion dictionary, aiming at analyzing text emotion through looking up extended emotion dictionary, and it's proposed by Shihong Wang [12].

2.2 Text Analysis

Text analysis can be one of the cores during the research on social media. At the same time, it's demanding for technology. There have been many researches on Weibo text. In a study of the visualization of the topic graph of Weibo public opinion based on text mining, the structural characteristics of graphs were analyzed by applying different text similarity, network optimization and text clustering algorithms [13]. Moreover, generating the character and word vectors by FastText algorithm and comparing training effect of the recurrent neural network in the bidirectional GRU, so that emotional classification of Weibo comments can be predicated [14]. In a survey investigating the public's cognition and attitude towards artificial intelligence during the COVID-19 pandemic, word-frequency analysis and topic clustering of the text were conducted, then geostatistical analysis was performed to show public opinion [15]. Besides, by selecting verbs and adjectives in the texts as the features, and the designed emotion-based method, a position weight calculation method based on featured polarity value can be put forward. With the help of SVM as the machine learning model, Weibo texts can be classified by emotions [16].

2.3 Big Data

Due to the popularity of the Internet and the advent of Web 2.0 technologies, big data analysis has recently become an important research field. In addition, the popularity and adoption of social media applications provide researchers and practitioners with a wide range of opportunities and challenges. The large number of data generated by users using social media platforms is the result of the integration of their background details and daily activities [17].

Through the analysis of big data on social media, we can get a lot of information, especially about the views and attitudes of social software users towards various news. For instance, while large volumes of Twitter data, reflecting the emotional state of the public towards COVID-19, can easily be accessed, the available data requires significant data pre-processing to minimize the inherent noises as discussed [18]. Therefore, the analysis of big data is an effective method to study the impact of social media on users.

Big data analysis provides a new tool that can match the speed of disasters, so as to help make decisions. These technologies are conducive to adaptation and can help communities become more resilient [19]. During the time of the COVID-19 pandemic, big data could be used to analyze the information on social media, to get the attitude of social software users to the COVID-19 pandemic, and to help make decisions.

2.4 Previous Research on Public Attitude to the COVID-19 Pandemic Information

The impact of the COVID-19 pandemic continues to affect people's lives. At the same time, information related to the COVID-19 pandemic has also sprung up. Besides the massive information regarding the virus is being disseminated through different print and electronic media, a flood of misinformation is also easily propagating through these sources [20]. Therefore, the information from social media influences people's attitudes toward the epidemic. The impact of media coverage and public sentiment may have a significant impact on the public and private sectors when deciding to stop certain services, including air services, which are out of proportion to real public health needs [21]. The public attitude which is easily influenced by social media has a great impact on epidemic prevention and control.

For the COVID-19 pandemic, social media can have a crucial role in disseminating health information and tackling infodemics and misinformation [22]. A lot of mixed information about the COVID-19 pandemic has sprung up on social media. The complex information makes it difficult for the public to distinguish between true and false, resulting in panic and unable to correctly grasp the actual situation of the epidemic. In this era of globalization, verifying information is the most effective way to prevent people's panic [23]. When real information has a great impact on controlling panic, people's cognition and attitude towards epidemic information are very important. Therefore, comments are an important topic to discuss in the aspect of comments affecting people's identification of epidemic information.

Besides, social media can be used as an effective way to prevent the spread of the epidemic. For instance, by analyzing Twitter data on the issue, this study [24] offers insights into the issue considering established theoretical constructs from the Health belief model (HBM) and Theory of Planned Behavior (TPB). By unpacking social media posts on a public platform, the study helps illuminate the path forward in implementing an effective COVID-19 passport system.

3   Methodology

3.1   Data Collection

Python is a mature programming tool, and this article uses Python to get the data in Microblog. The specific steps can be displayed as follow:

(1) Preparation. In order to ensure the request of obtaining the data in Microblog is accepted, fake_useragent, a Python library, is used in the code.
(2) Data searching. Choosing "the COVID-19 pandemic" as keyword to get the data from February 4th to February 6th.

(3) Data collection. the blogs, the comments under each blog, and other important information (such as forwarding, comments, thumber up) are collected.

(4) Data saving. The data will be saved as a csv file.

After obtaining microblog data about the COVID-19 pandemic, the examples of these data can be partly demonstrated in Table 1 and Table 2. The example only includes one blog which is displayed in Table 1 and some comments under this blog which is displayed in Table 2.

Table 1. Blog example

Text	Release time	Other information (forwarding, comments, thumber up)
I have stayed at home for a long time because of the epidemic, and I can go out today finally. I am in Hangzhou~	2022/2/4,22:51:38	0, 14, 33

Table 2. Comments example

Comment index	Text
1	Come on, I know that you always go out
2	I have been quarantined for almost three months because of the epidemic. I almost got depression. It's too boring
3	Can we go to the cinema together?

3.2 Data Management

The purpose of data management is to process the semi-structured and unstructured data. Python and NLPIR-Parser platform are used as tools to realize the data management, and the specific steps are displayed as follow:

Text Preprocessing. Text preprocessing is an important procedure and denoising is the first step of text preprocessing. The comment is an important indicator that this paper analyses, therefore the blogs with less than 10 comments are deleted. In addition, the unqualified data will be removed (such as repeated data, irrelevant data, advertisement, and the data lacking the important information) with the help of python and manual work. This paper set several standards for removing unqualified data, and the specific standards are as followed:

(1) Repeated data. Keep one blog if there are some same blogs in the file. Keep one comment if there are some same comments which were posted by the same user under the blog.

(2) Irrelevant data. Remove the blog and the comments under this blog that are irrelevant to the topic, COVID-19 epidemic.
(3) Advertisement. Remove the data which is an advertisement.
(4) The data lacking the important information. Remove the data lacking the information, such as the text of blog and the text of comment.

Word Segment. This paper uses jieba, a Python Chinese word segmentation module, for word segment. Jieba supports three types of word segmentation modes: accurate mode, full mode and search engine mode. Jieba builds a directed acyclic graph (DAG) for all possible word combinations based on prefix dictionary structure. In order to find the most probable combination based on the word frequency, jieba uses dynamic programming. For unknown words, jieba uses the HMM-based model. Then, the stop-words dictionary is used to filter the unimportant words.

3.3 Sentiment Analysis

The NLPIR-Parser platform is used for sentiment analysis. The NLPIR-Parser platform recognizes the emotional words and calculates the weights automatically, and this platform uses co-occurrence relationships and the strategy of bootstrapping, and it iterates repeatedly to generate new emotion words and weights. Then the platform extends the calculation of emotional words by using deep neural network, and the result can be obtained.

The NLPIR-Parser platform divides the emotion of text into positive and negative. This platform measures the emotional value of text and gives positive and negative scores. In addition, this platform can further divide the emotion of text into interest, happiness, surprise, anger, disgust and fear.

4 Results and Discussions

The results of microblog data which include the blogs and comments under each blog were combined, as follows: This study collects 3484 comments from 1915 authenticated users about the COVID-19 epidemic from February 4th to February 6th. After Text preprocessing, there are 2483 comments from 192 authenticated users about the COVID-19 epidemic from February 4th to February 6th.

4.1 Chinese Users Post a Small Number of Comments

As for the mean, median, mode, standard deviation, maximum and minimum of microblog data, the result of descriptive data analysis is demonstrated in Table 3.

The small number of comments from Chinese users is closely related to Chinese culture. In the West, people tend to be more willing to express their own views on something. Chinese people, on the other hand, are more modest and tend to look internally at their own views by drawing on the views of others. This makes the number of comments by Chinese users smaller and the impact of comments on internet users be greater, so the study of comments is of some relevance.

Table 3. Descriptive data analysis of comment under the blog

Statistical indicators	Value
Mean	14.29
Median	0
Mode	0
SD	201.53
Max	8086
Min	0

The indicators such as thumber up and forwarding are important and the descriptive data analysis is conducted. The top-ranking blogs are ranked by the number of thumber up, comments and forwarding, and these indicators play an important role in public discussion. The result is demonstrated in Table 4.

Table 4. Descriptive data analysis of thumber up and forwarding

	Thumber up	Forwarding
Mean	172.01	7.01
Median	3	0
Mode	0	0
SD	4796.42	152.91
Max	208757	6627
Min	0	0

4.2 The Cities with the Pandemic Capture Public Attention

The text of the blogs and the comments under each blog are analyzed using jieba and the most frequent terms are discovered after calculating the frequency of terms. Figure 1 shows the top-15 most frequent terms and the frequency of terms.

On February 5, 2022, after nucleic acid test, one person was diagnosed as positive case in Baise, a city in Guangxi, and after that, more positive cases were found in Baise, therefore 'Baise' and 'Guangxi' are the hot topic in the discussion of the COVID-19 epidemic. The Winter Olympics was held in Beijing from February 4th to February 6th, and it means a high level of population mobility. In addition, one person was diagnosed as positive case in Beijing On February 4, 2022. Therefore 'Beijing' was discussed. New cases each day rose to 351 in Hong Kong on February 5, 2022, and this news captures public attention, 'Hong Kong' became a hot topic. Jiayou, a Chinese vocabulary, means encouraging the people in the city facing a serious situation of the epidemic in the context of battling the pandemic, and it is translated into "Keep fighting" in Fig. 1.

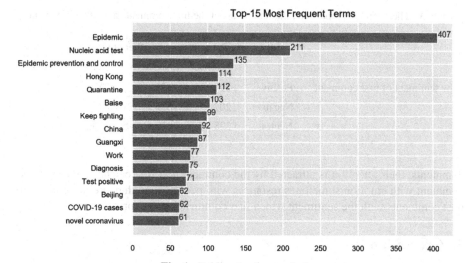

Fig. 1. Public attention analysis

4.3 The Top Comment Matters

According to the data after text preprocessing, this study conducts the sentiment analysis on the NLPIR-Parser platform to test the sentiment of text. For blogs, the result is that positive sentiments account for 53.13%, negative sentiments account for 33.85% and sentiments without obvious inclination accounts for 13.02%. For comments, the result is that positive sentiments account for 31.33%, negative sentiments account for 30.49% and sentiments without obvious inclination account for 38.18%.

The top-ranking comments under each blog are posted earlier or have a larger number of thumber up, these comments capture more attention of readers than the comments which are under these comments. According to the study of attention [25], people tend to read from top to bottom and are more likely to be influenced by the information they browse firstly. Microblog browsers post the comment under the impact of the comment which firstly catches their eyes, and it concludes that it's meaningful to study the impact of the first comment on other comments.

Under the same blog, the sentiment of the first comment influences the sentiment of other comments, and this paper studies this relationship using the NLPIR-Parser platform. The sentiments of the first comments under different blogs are divided into three classes: positive sentiment, negative sentiment and sentiments without obvious inclination, and the blogs are divided into three classes according to their first comment. The sentiments of other comments which exclude the first comment are divided in the same way. Table 5 reveals the condition of other comments' sentiment under the blogs belonging to different classes. In Table 5, "positive", "negative" and "neutral" represent positive sentiment, negative sentiment and the sentiments without obvious inclination respectively.

The sentiments of other comments tend to follow the sentiments of the first comment. In Table 5, the number of the other comments expressing the sentiment which the first comments also express is higher than the other two classes. When browsers post their

Table 5. The relationship between the sentiments of the first comments and other comments

		The sentiment of other comment			
		Positive	Negative	Neutral	Sum
The sentiment of first comment	Positive	294	221	277	792
	Negative	207	239	250	696
	Neutral	228	219	356	803

comments, their attention is attracted by the comment that first catches their eyes and comment with emotion sometimes resonates with people, then they are more likely to post comments with the sentiment which first comments also express.

5 Conclusion

This study collects the data including the blogs and the comments under each blog from Microblog. After the text preprocessing, the descriptive data analysis, public attention analysis and sentiment analysis are conducted with the help of Python and the NLPIR-Parser platform, and the main conclusions are as follows: (1) Chinese users post a small number of comments and tend to look internally at their own views by drawing on the views of others. It means that Chinese users are more likely to be influenced by comments, therefore it's meaningful to study the comments. (2) The cities where events of the COVID-19 epidemic happens capture public attention and it's a phenomenon that the public get accustomed to cheer up the person in the city with the COVID-19 epidemic online in China. (3) The sentiments of the first comments influences the sentiments of other comments which exclude the first comment, the sentiments of other comments tend to follow the sentiments of the first comment.

This study makes both academic and practical contribution. From academic perspective, this paper indicates that the sentiments of the first comments have an important impact on the sentiments of other comments which exclude the first comment, therefore it's meaningful to focus on the first comment. From practical perspective, more attention should be paid to the first comment to monitor the change of public sentiment in social media like Sina Weibo.

There still exist some limitations for this study. The main limitations are as follows: (1) Due to the limitation of data mining, there are many people who browse the blogs and don't post the comment, and the influence of sentiment on these people can't be covered. (2) Some Bloggers filter the comments in their blogs, the collected data may be incomplete. The future research directions are using the means of behavior experimentation and taking the comments filtering into consideration to conquer these two limitations.

Acknowledgement. This study was supported by the State Key Laboratory of Media Convergence Production Technology and Systems, Beijing (Grand number SKLMCPTS2020003) and Beijing Key Laboratory of Emergency Support Simulation Technologies for City Operations.

References

1. 2020 User Development Report. https://data.weibo.com/report/reportDetail?id=456. Accessed 11 Feb 2022
2. Wang, J.: Miro-Blog User'S Participation Motivation and Behavior—an Empirical Research Based on TAM. Shandong University (2010). (in Chinese)
3. Yang, Y.: The dual character of Chinese people: reserved and enthusiasm. J. Harbin Vocat. Tech. Coll. **6**, 118–119 (2012). (in Chinese)
4. Wang, Q.W., Yu, Z.H.: Research on microblog reporting and public opinion guidance of sudden disaster events – taking "Chongqing Bus falling into the river" as an example. News Dissemin. **14**, 23–24 (2019). (in Chinese)
5. Gao, Q., Tian, Y., Tu, M.Y.: Exploring factors influencing Chinese user's perceived credibility of health and safety information on Weibo. Comput. Hum. Behav. **45**, 21–31 (2015)
6. Zhang, C., Ma, X.Y., Zhou. Y., Guo, R.Z.: Analysis of public opinion evolution in COVID-19 pandemic from a perspective of sentiment variation. J. Geo-inf. Sci. **23**(2), 341–350 (2021). (in Chinese)
7. Chen, X.S., Chang, T.Y., Wang, H.Z., Zhao, Q.L., Zhang, J.: Spatial and temporal analysis on public opinion evolution of epidemic situation about novel coronavirus pneumonia based on micro-blog data. J. Sichuan Univ. (Nat. Sci. Ed.) **57**(02), 409–416 (2020). (in Chinese)
8. Deng, C.L., Zhou, S.Y., Long, Z.F.: Analysis on the emotional evolution of microblog users in emergencies based on emotional attribution theory. Sci. Inf. Res. **3**(03), 60–72 (2021). (in Chinese)
9. Li, N., Zhang, Y.H.: An analysis of web opinion combining the dynamic characteristics of emoji. J. Mod. Inf. **41**(08), 98–108 (2021). (in Chinese)
10. Feng, R.J., Zhang, H.J., Pan, W.M.: Microblog rumor detection based on sentiment analysis and transformer model. Comput. Modern. **10**, 1–7 (2021). (in Chinese)
11. Gu, C.H., Zhou, Q.: Identification research about the sentiments of Sina-Weibo users during the COVID-19 outbreak pandemic. J. Jiangsu Norm. Univ. (Nat. Sci. Ed.) **39**(04), 41–45 (2021). (in Chinese)
12. Wang, S.H.: Emotion Analysis of Chinese Microblogs Using Extended Emotion Lexicon. Nanjing University of Aeronautics and Astronautics (2015). (in Chinese)
13. Xing, Y.F., Li, Y.H.: Visualization of topic graph of Weibo public opinion based on text mining. J. Lib. Inf. Sci. Agric. **33**(07), 12–23 (2021). (in Chinese)
14. Fan, H., Li, P.F.: Sentiment analysis of short text based on FastText word vector and bidirectional GRU recurrent neural network—take the microblog comment text as an example. Inf. Sci. **39**(04), 15–22 (2021). (in Chinese)
15. Huang, N., Xiao, J., Zhang, Z.Y.: The public cognition and attitude to artificial intelligence during the COVID-19 epidemic: based on the text mining of Weibo content. Stud. Sci. Popul. **16**(05), 33–41 (2021). (in Chinese)
16. Sun, J.W., Lü, X.Q., Zhang, L.H.: On sentiment analysis of Chinese microblogging based on lexicon and machine learning. Comput. Appl. Softw. **31**(07), 177–181 (2014). (in Chinese)
17. Ghani, N.A., Hamid, S., Hashem, I.A.T., Ahmed, E.: Social media big data analytics: a survey. Comput. Hum. Behav. **101**, 417–428 (2019)
18. Chew, A.W.Z., Pan, Y., Wang, Y., Zhang, L.M.: Hybrid deep learning of social media big data for predicting the evolution of COVID-19 transmission. Knowl.-Based Syst. **233**, 107417 (2021)
19. Joseph, J.K., et al.: Chapter 16 - big data analytics and social media in disaster management. In: Samui, P., Kim, D., Ghosh, C. (eds.) Integrating Disaster Science and Management, pp. 287–294 (2018)

20. Kumar, N., Sulaiman, S.A.S., Hashmi, F.K.: An evaluation of public understanding regarding COVID-19 in Sindh, Pakistan: a focus on knowledge, attitudes and practices. J. Res. Pharm. **25**(6), 881–889 (2021)
21. Depoux, A., Martin, S., Karafillakis, E., Preet, R., Larson, H.J.: The pandemic of social media panic travels faster than the COVID-19 outbreak. J. Trav. Med. **27**(3) (2020)
22. Tsao, S.F., Chen, H., Tisseverasinghe, T., Yang, Y., Butt, Z.A.: What social media told about us in the time of COVID-19: a scoping review. Lancet Dig. Health **3**, e175–e194 (2021)
23. Lancet, T.: COVID-19: fighting panic with information. Lancet **395**(10224), 537 (2020)
24. Khan, M.L., Malik, A., Ruhi, U., Al-Busaidi, A.: Conflicting attitudes: analyzing social media data to understand the early discourse on COVID-19 passports. Technol. Soc. **68**, 101830 (2022)
25. Li, J.: Research of Webpage Visual Attention. Beijing University of Posts and Telecommunications (2017). (in Chinese)

From the Perspective of Social Design: Research on the Construction of Mass Epidemic Prevention Media System for Elderly Groups

Suihong Lan⬥, Jiaxiang Li, and Chao Zhao⁽⊠⁾

Tsinghua University, Beijing, China
{lansh21,lijiaxia21}@mails.tsinghua.edu.cn,
zhaochao@tsinghua.edu.cn

Abstract. The first case of the NOVEL CORONAVIRUS disease (COVID-19) patient appeared in China in December 2019, besides this, it spread widely with a large proportion of elderly among the newly diagnosed cases last year. To confirm whether the mass media's epidemic prevention education needs to be improved in its spread among middle-aged and elderly people, The research was conducted on 2582 Chinese people, who were asked about personal risk perception, self-efficacy, the effectiveness of protective equipment, availability of protective equipment and so on. Logistic binary analysis and logistic ordered analysis were employed to determine how favorably respondents of different age groups received epidemic prevention education, as well as predictions of implications of acceptance on epidemic prevention behavior. The results indicate that epidemic prevention education can improve individuals' ability to protect themselves in public health emergencies, also shows that the mass media's epidemic prevention education has a greater connection with individual prevention measures, but has slimmer coverage among the middle-aged and elderly, which needs to be improved. Therefore, the research suggests forward several topics which are valuable of application in the construction of the mass epidemic prevention media system while the process of combining design and sociology.

Keywords: Social design · Anti-epidemic effectiveness · Middle-aged and elderly people

1 Introduction

In December 2019, the first confirmed case of new coronavirus disease (COVID-19) was found in China, and the epidemic spread across the country speedily [1]. In addition to droplet transmission or contact transmission, there is the possibility of aerosol transmission of fecal mouth transmission [2]. Accordingly, prevention measures (such as wearing face masks, goggles, and frequent disinfection) or vaccinating are the principal ways and means of containing the epidemic [3, 4].

In recent years, there has been controversy about the effectiveness of the mass media's epidemic prevention education in terms of its effect on people's Epidemic prevention efficiency. On the one hand, some community surveys [5, 6] show that there are still some

P.-L. P. Rau (Ed.): HCII 2022, LNCS 13313, pp. 241–254, 2022.
https://doi.org/10.1007/978-3-031-06050-2_18

defects in the mass media's epidemic prevention education, but on the other, A large number of studies [7–11] have shown that there is a large connection between epidemic prevention education and personal epidemic prevention manners. The mass media's epidemic prevention education can transmit information quickly, guide social opinions and bring closer the government and the public. Furthermore, it can popularize prevention education, supervise the public, and put forward correct supervision and reflection on past events. People who are frequently exposed to the mass media's epidemic prevention education have a higher sense of self-efficacy and a more positive attitude on epidemic prevention.

In the early stage of the epidemic, Chinese mass media conducted epidemic prevention education prompt, ranging from mobile phones and TV advertisements to door-to-door education, which activated people to take prevention measures. Therefore, the epidemic has currently been brought under preliminary control. However, according to the analysis of newly confirmed cases in the past years, middle-aged and elderly people account for a large proportion of new patients with COVID-19 [12–14].

It indirectly shows that the level of acceptance of the media's prevention education by middle-aged and elderly people is relatively low, which is related to older people's lack of access to media prevention education and also their lack of enthusiasm for community activities [15].

In China, where the population is aging, middle-aged and old people are an important part of society [16], and the amount of middle-aged and elderly people will continue to increase in the next two decades [17]. Compared with young people, the use of media by middle-aged and elderly people is only limited to a small subset, that is, watching [18], and does not produce too much actual interaction, which directly results in less diversity in their use of media. Although elderly people are concerned about all kinds of information such as traveling, socializing, health, and dependence [19], their access to those kinds of information is relatively singleness. If middle-aged and elderly people can use media more often, they will have a higher level of acceptance of the media [20]. Therefore, improving the fitness of the middle-aged and the elderly in the mass media's epidemic prevention education plays a critical role in epidemic prevention education as a whole [21].

At present, the majority of the respondents in the study are the public who have received prevention education from the mass media, but there are few studies on media education among certain groups of people. This article studies several potential ways in which the mass media's epidemic prevention education affects individual behaviors by issuing a large number of questionnaires to society. A consistent relationship found between the level of acceptance of mass media education and prevention measures will support the idea. That is, the mass media's epidemic prevention education among the elderly population demands improvement. This may become a sally port in the social interaction design of middle-aged and elderly. Enriching the channels for the middle-aged and elderly to receive media propaganda and improving the degree of acceptance can provide a certain reference for the social design of the middle-aged and elderly.

2 Method

2.1 Conceptual Framework

Since the outbreak of COVID-19, the number of confirmed cases has reached more than 99,000. The domestic mass media in China have actively popularized new epidemic prevention education, which benefits the public a lot, such as increasing the perceived risk and severity [8], providing easier access to epidemic prevention education, and helping understand the benefits of prevention and the importance of self-efficacy [22]. The epidemic has been brought under preliminary control with the active epidemic prevention education from the mass media. The study is based on all provinces in China. Due to the difference in prevention education between urban and rural areas, a large number of samples are required to obtain reliable data. Since the research focuses on the relationship between media education and the prediction of personal behaviors rather than the different levels of prevention education, a questionnaire in the form of a scale was not used. A total of 2833 questionnaires were collected which 2582 were valid data.

2.2 Design of Questionnaire

The questionnaire investigation is based on a standardized questionnaire from the International Population Services Organization (PSI), which is responsible for assessing individuals' risk perception, self-efficacy, knowledge of prevention, exposure to the mass media, and knowledge of the virus.

The questionnaire contains two different types of question: behavioural and attitudinal. Answers to behavioural questions tell the researcher where an education is now and where it could be in the future. Attitudinal questions establish respondents' opinions and their perception of covid-19.

2.3 Variables

Independent variables

An urban area or rural area, age, gender, education (primary, secondary or higher). In addition, two indicators were developed to measure the accessibility of the mass media, namely television broadcasting and mobile phones. The variables measured are epidemic prevention information at low-, medium- and high-reception levels.

Dependent variables

Six of the dependent variables are based on a yes/no questionnaire. To assess the availability of protective equipment (such as face masks, goggles, alcohol, etc.), they were asked whether protective equipment could be bought; to evaluate the effectiveness of protective equipment, respondents were asked whether protective equipment was effective in preventing COVID-19 and whether the main reason for buying protective equipment was to prevent COVID-19; to measure self-efficacy, respondents were asked if they could persuade loved ones to wear protective equipment; to measure their perceptions of severity, respondents were asked if they believed COVID-19 could be cured. The questionnaire contains two ordered variable questions. In order to assess personal risk perception, the respondents were asked if they thought they might be infected with

244   S. Lan et al.

COVID-19 whether at a small, medium, or high risk. To assess their perceptions of the prevalence of COVID-19, respondents were asked whether COVID-19 in the community is "not a problem", "just a little problem", or "a serious problem".

Table 1. The sample data

	N (people)	Percentage
Gender		
Female	1566	60.7%
Male	1016	39.3%
Age		
15–25	857	33.2%
25–45	1425	55.2%
45–60	300	11.6%
Education		
Primary	263	10.2%
Secondary	2097	81.2%
Higher	222	8.6%
Residence		
City	1836	28.9%
Rural	746	71.1%

2.4 Analysis Methods

Research shows that Logistic analysis can be used as a tool to assess the association between research covariates [23]. Logistic binary analysis and Logistic ordered analysis are used to determine the level of acceptance of epidemic prevention education by different respondent groups, as well as predictions on factors impacting the level of acceptance of individual prevention measures. The sample data is shown in Table 1. The valid data is 2582 copies (n = 2582).

3 Results and Analysis

3.1 Results

In both binary regression analysis and ordered regression analysis, the last options are used as a reference. The numbers shown in the figure are multiples. N is the valid data of the survey. Models 3, 6, 11 and 12 are ordered dependent variables, so ordered analysis is used. This model is valid when the Hosmer-Lemeshow (p) is above 0.05 in the binary regression analysis. The model is valid when the parallel line test significance {SIG (p)} is above 0.05 in the ordered analysis. In the model parameter table, the significance is valid when below 0.05, and the lower the value, the higher the significance.

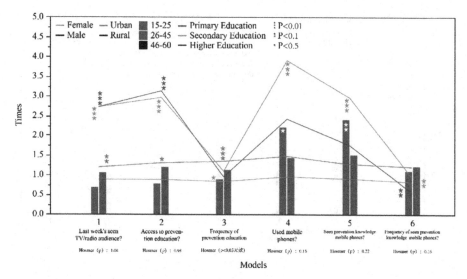

Fig. 1. Model 1–6.

Figure 1 shows last week's TV/radio audience (model 1), the number of people who had access to prevention education (model 2), the frequency of exposure to prevention education (model 3), the respondents who used mobile phones last week (model 4) and the odds ratio between the number of people who had access to prevention education (model 5) and the frequency of exposure to prevention education (model 6).

Model 1 shows that respondents with primary and secondary education are 2.74 times more likely to watch television/listen to the radio than those with higher education. Model 2 showed that respondents with primary education (3.19 times) and respondents with secondary education (2.98 times) are more likely to be exposed to epidemic prevention education on television or radio than those with higher education. Respondents living in cities are more likely to be exposed to epidemic prevention education on television or radio than those living in rural areas. And model 3 shows that urban respondents are exposed to epidemic prevention education more frequently than rural counterparts.

Model 4 shows that respondents aged 15–25 are 2.22 times more likely to use mobile phones than those aged 45–60. Respondents with elementary (2.43 times) or secondary education (3.92 times) are much more likely to use a mobile phone last week than those with higher education.

Model 5 shows that respondents aged 15–25 are 2.42 times more likely to be exposed to epidemic prevention education from their mobile phones than those aged 45–60. Respondents with secondary education are 2.97 times more likely to be exposed to epidemic prevention education on mobiles phones than those with higher education. Model 6 shows that female respondents are 0.82 times more likely to be exposed to high-frequency epidemic prevention education than male respondents. Respondents with primary education and primary education were 0.56 times more likely to be exposed to high-frequency epidemic prevention education on mobiles phones than those with higher education. The probability of being exposed to high-frequency epidemic prevention education among urban respondents is 1.21 times that among rural respondents.

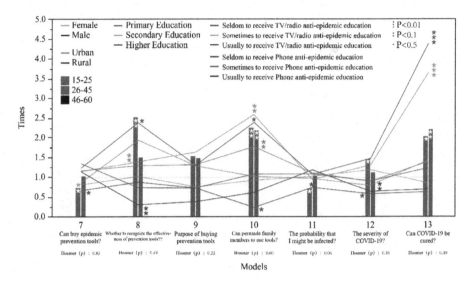

Fig. 2. Model 7–13.

In Fig. 2, Models 7–10 evaluate the impact of exposure to broadcast/television prevention education and exposure to mobile phone prevention education on the availability of protective equipment, perception of the efficacy of protective equipment, and self-efficacy. Models 11–13 assess the impact of prevention education on risk awareness and the perceived severity of COVID-19.

3.2 Analysis

3.2.1 Perception of the Availability of Protective Equipment

Model 7 shows that com-pared with males, females are more likely (0.81 times) to consider that protective equipment is difficult to purchase. Respondents aged 15–25 are more likely (0.74 times) to consider it difficult to purchase protective equipment than those aged 45–60. Respondents with low exposure to prevention education on radio and television are more likely (0.67 times) to consider it difficult to purchase protective equipment than those with high exposure to prevention education on radio and television. Respondents with medium exposure to prevention education on mobile phones are more likely (1.34 times) to believe that protective equipment can be purchased than those with high exposure to prevention education on mobile phones.

3.2.2 Perception of the Effectiveness of Protective Equipment

Model 8 shows that respondents aged 15–25 are more likely (2.53 times) to think that protective equipment is effective than those aged 45–60. Respondents with primary education (2.39 times) and secondary education (2.26 times) are more likely to consider protective equipment to be effective than those with higher education. Compared to respondents with high exposure to prevention education on mobiles phones, respondents with high exposure to prevention education on mobiles phones are more likely (0.30 times) to consider protective equipment to be ineffective. Model 9 shows that respondents with high exposure to prevention education on mobiles phones are more likely (0.30 times) to say that they would use protective equipment to prevent COVID-19 than those with low exposure to mobile phone prevention education.

3.2.3 Self-efficacy

Model 10 shows that respondents aged 15–25 (2.26 times) and those aged 25–45 (2.20 times) are more likely to persuade loved ones to use protective equipment than respondents aged 45–60. Compared to respondents with higher education, respondents with secondary education (2.58 times) and those with primary education (2.39 times) are more likely to persuade loved ones to use protective equipment, and urban respondents are more likely (1.78 times) to persuade loved ones to use protective equipment than rural respondents. Respondents with low exposure to epidemic prevention education on radio and television are more likely (0.23 times) to fail to persuade loved ones to use protective equipment. Model 11 shows that respondents aged 45–60 are more likely (0.72 times) than respondents aged 15–25 to think they are at high risk of getting infected with COVID-19. Respondents with high exposure to epidemic prevention education on radio and television are more likely (0.74 times) than those with low exposure to believe that they are at high risk of getting infected with COVID-19.

3.2.4 Risk Awareness

Model 12 shows that respondents aged 15–25 are more likely (1.47 times) to think that COVID-19 is a serious problem in the community than respondents aged 45–60. Respondents with high exposure to epidemic prevention education on radio and television are more likely (0.58 times) than those with low exposure to believe that COVID-19 is a serious problem in the community. Respondents with high exposure to epidemic prevention education on mobile phones are more likely (0.63 times) than those with low exposure to believe that COVID-19 is a serious problem in the community.

3.2.5 Perception of Severity

Model 13 shows that respondents aged 25–45 (2.22 times) and those aged 15–25 (2.05 times) are more likely than those aged 45–60 to think that COVID-19 can be cured. Compared with those with higher education, those with primary education (4.44 times) and those with secondary education (3.68 times) are more likely to think that COVID-19 can be cured.

4 Discussion and Conclusions

4.1 Research Result

The results of the study show that respondents who were more frequently exposed to epidemic prevention education had higher awareness of the availability of protective equipment, the efficacy of protective equipment, and higher self-efficacy and risk awareness, indicating that epidemic prevention education can improve individuals' ability to protect themselves in public health emergencies. The perception of the efficacy of protective equipment and self-efficacy directly represent the individual's epidemic prevention, which determines whether epidemic prevention education is in place. It can be found from the survey results that although respondents aged 45–60 have higher figures for risk awareness (models 11 and 12) and perception of risk severity (model 13), they have lower figures for the perception of the efficacy of protective equipment (models 8, 9) and lower self-efficacy (model 10), which is probably related to their lower exposure to mobile phone prevention education (model 4), which is consistent with the conclusions reached by (models 8, 9, 10). Therefore, it can be inferred from the middle-aged and elderly population in the main body of confirmed patients in this epidemic that the spread of epidemic prevention propaganda in the middle-aged and elderly population is low, which is consistent with the research hypothesis.

4.2   Based on the Above Research Results, Some Discussions on Mass Media Information from the Perspective of Social Design

Currently, most of the epidemic prevention propaganda designed by society is based on basic audiences, and BJ Hu [24] pointed out that the management of health emergencies should be more diversified. Focusing on a larger and more in-demand audience is the goal of epidemic prevention propaganda. Because individual characteristics will directly affect their acceptance of the media [25]. Therefore, in the design of the epidemic prevention propaganda society, the characteristics of the middle-aged and elderly groups should be fully considered.

Because the middle-aged and elderly groups have not received high levels of current mass media, the spread of epidemic prevention propaganda among their groups is low. Therefore, research on improving acceptance is likely to become a breakthrough in social interaction design for middle-aged and elderly groups.

The current social media propaganda characteristics for the middle-aged and elderly groups tend to be "flat", and the middle-aged and elderly groups only assume the role of "audience" in the promotion link, which does not generate more actual interactions and cannot truly enjoy the multi-functional Internet. Therefore, enriching available media functions can be the main direction of social design for middle-aged and elderly groups.

Because the physical and psychological characteristics of middle-aged and elderly groups are different from those of adolescents [26]. Therefore, they need a social design that better matches their physical and psychological characteristics (such as color, depth of field, and hearing). Physiologically, due to the gradual decline in physical functions after entering the aging stage, the psychology, sensory and life patterns of the middle-aged and elderly groups will be different from those of the young people [27]. As shown in Fig. 3, since the degree of adaptation to the depth of field will decrease with age [28], watching pictures with a small depth of field for a long time will cause visual fatigue in middle-aged and elderly people. In addition to vision, hearing can also meet the social and emotional needs of middle-aged and elderly people [29]. As shown in Fig. 4, social background and individual characteristics will directly affect their media contact characteristics. Because middle-aged and elderly groups have different growth experiences and social backgrounds, social background characteristics, knowledge, and

Fig. 3. The depth of field.

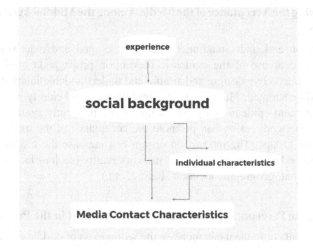

Fig. 4. The Factors of media contact characteristics.

abilities and health is the primary consideration are used in the design of epidemic prevention propaganda for middle-aged and elderly groups [30]. In addition, the media characteristics that ease of use are also important factors that affect the degree of media reception by middle-aged and elderly people [26]. Since middle-aged and elderly people face a lack of information infrastructure, the fear caused by their unfamiliarity with the Internet has also increased their difficulty in acquiring knowledge about epidemic prevention [31].

4.3 Suggestions for Improvement and Tasks in Future Social Design

The design of mass media anti-epidemic propaganda that is more in line with the physiological and psychological characteristics of the middle-aged and elderly people will greatly increase the degree of acceptance of the middle-aged and elderly people's knowledge of epidemic prevention, thereby enhancing their anti-epidemic actions. Combining the perspective of social design, mass media anti-epidemic propaganda should develop in the following directions in the design of future media characteristics:

4.3.1 Fully Consider the Individual Characteristics of Middle-Aged and Elderly People

Since most middle-aged and elderly people have presbyopia, fonts should be appropriately enlarged in visual propaganda. Contrast and messy colors will make middle-aged and elderly people visually confused, and the calm and simple color design will make them like it more. In general, warm and bright colors are more suitable. As memory declines with age, more easy-to-remember graphical expressions can be used when media propaganda to middle-aged and elderly people. And in the design, try to avoid using graphics with a small depth of field for visual expression. Emotional design can be used in psychological interactions, and more use of intentional symbols, language, and soundtracks familiar to middle-aged and elderly groups.

4.3.2 Improving the Acceptance of the Media Among the Middle-Aged and Elderly Groups

As the perception and understanding of the middle-aged and elderly groups have declined, the ease of use of the epidemic prevention propaganda media should be improved in the interactive design, and simple and understandable interface designs or prompts should be adopted. Make it easy for middle-aged and elderly people to understand and use the anti-epidemic propaganda media independently again. In addition, a higher sense of network reality can promote the acceptance of the media by middle-aged and elderly groups. The interaction design can increase the media's promotion by increasing the relevance between users' network reality (such as face-to-face friend addition, online chat, geographic location sharing, etc.).

4.3.3 Adding the Perceptual Encouragement Component in the Propaganda

The encouragement component can increase the willingness of middle-aged and elderly people to use the media. Through certain rewards, such as question and answer points, interaction, and answering questions, middle-aged and elderly groups can express respect and recognition when receiving epidemic prevention propaganda [32] to realize their self-worth needs and promote the multi-functional use of the media. Thereby increasing the use of propaganda media by middle-aged and elderly people.

Appendix: Questionnaire

Dear Sir/Madam: Hello!

It is a pleasure to contact you to participate in this survey, and thank you very much for your support and cooperation! This is an academic survey, the purpose of this survey is to explore the popularity of mass media propaganda. The survey was conducted anonymously, answering fearlessly right or wrong. At the same time, we declare: The data collected by this survey will be used for academic research only, and will only be handled by professional researchers related to this topic for overall statistical analysis, and will not involve any specific individuals. We promise that for Your answers will be kept strictly confidential. Please fill in the questionnaire according to your actual situation, do not miss the answer. The objective and truthful information you provide is critical to the validity and accuracy of the research conclusions. After completing the questionnaire, return the questionnaire to our research staff. Thanks!

1. What is your gender? [Single choice] *

   O male
   O female

2. Your age is? [Single choice] *

   O 15–24
   O 24–40
   O 40–60

3. Your qualification is [Single choice] *

   O Elementary, middle or high school
   O College, Undergraduate
   O master or above

4. Where you live now? [Single choice] *

   O Rural
   O Urban

5. Did you listen to the radio or watch TV in the last week? [Single choice] *

   O Yes
   O No

6. Have you heard about the epidemic prevention of New Coronavirus pneumonia on radio or TV? [Single choice] *

   O Yes
   O No

7. How many times do you hear epidemic prevention knowledge on radio or television in a day? [Single choice] *

   O 0–5
   O 5–15
   O 15+

8. Do you use the mobile phone? [Single choice] *

   ○ Yes
   ○ No

9. Have you seen any knowledge about New Coronavirus pneumonia in mobile phone? [Single choice] *

   ○ Yes
   ○ No

10. How many times do you browse epidemic prevention knowledge on your mobile phone in a day? [Single choice] *

    ○ 0–5
    ○ 5–15
    ○ 15

11. Can you buy protective tools (e.g. masks, goggles, disinfectant) ? [Single choice] *

    ○ Yes
    ○ No

12. Can you persuade relatives (parents or children) to take protective measures when traveling (e.g. wearing masks, goggles, washing hands frequently) ? [Single choice] *

    ○ Yes
    ○ No

13. Do you think protective tools (such as mask, goggles, disinfectant) can prevent New Coronavirus pneumonia? [Single choice] *

    ○ Yes
    ○ No

14. Do you buy protective tools (such as respirators, goggles, disinfectants) to prevent New Coronavirus pneumonia? [Single choice] *

    ○ Yes
    ○ No

15. How high do you think you might be infected with New Coronavirus pneumonia? [Single choice] *

    ○ Unlikely
    ○ Perhaps
    ○ Probably

16. Do you think New Coronavirus pneumonia is a serious problem in the community? [Single choice] *

    ○ Is a serious problem
    ○ Just a little problem
    ○ No problem

17. Do you think New Coronavirus pneumonia can be cured? [Single choice] *

    ○ Yes
    ○ No

References

1. Singhal, T.: A review of coronavirus disease-2019 (COVID-19). Indian J. Pediat. **87**(4), 281–286 (2020). https://doi.org/10.1007/s12098-020-03263-6
2. Ge, Z., Yang, L., Xia, J., et al.: Possible aerosol transmission of COVID-19 and special precautions in dentistry. Zhejiang Univ. Sci. B **21**(5), 361–368 (2020)
3. Wang, X., Zhang, X.X., He, J.J.: Challenges to the system of reserve medical supplies for public health emergencies: reflections on the outbreak of the severe acute respiratory syndrome coronavirus 2 (SARS-CoV-2) epidemic in China. BioSci. Trends **14**(1), 3–8 (2020)
4. Deng, S.Q., Peng, H.J.: characteristics of and public health responses to the coronavirus disease 2019 uutbreak in China. J. Clin. Med. **9**(2), 575 (2020)
5. Lu, X., Xie, X., Liu, L.: Inverted U-shaped model: How frequent repetition affects perceived risk. Judgm. Decis. Mak. **10**(3), 219–224 (2015)
6. Collinson, S., Heffernan, J.M.: Modelling the effects of media during an influenza epidemic. BMC Public Health 2014 **14**, 376 (2014)
7. Wilder-Smith, A., Freedman, D.O.: Isolation, quarantine, social distancing and community containment: pivotal role for old-style public health measures in the novel coronavirus (2019-nCoV) outbreak. J. Travel Med. **27** (2020). taaa020
8. Zhou, W.K., Wang, A., Fan, X., et al.: Effects of media reporting on mitigating spread of COVID-19 in the ear y phase of the outbreak. Math. Biosci. Eng. **17**(3), 2693–2707 (2020)
9. Agha, S.: The impact of a mass media campaign on personal risk perception, perceived self-efficacy and on other behavioural predictors. AIDS Care **15**(6), 749–762 (2010)
10. Di Giuseppe, G., Abbate, R., Albano, L., et al.: A survey of knowledge, attitudes and practices towards avian influenza in an adult population of Italy. BMC Infect. Dis. **36** (2008)
11. Stoecklin, S.B., Rolland, P., Silue, Y., et al.: First cases of coronavirus disease 2019 (COVID-19) in the WHO European Region, 24 January to 21 February. Eurosurveillance **25**(9) (2020)

12. Post-Traumatic Growth Experiences among COVID-19 Confirmed Cases in China: A Qualitative Study
13. COVID 19 meets changing traditional care systems for the elderly and a budding social work practice. Reflections for geriatric care in Ghana
14. Wu, J.T., Leung, K., Bushman, M., et al.: Estimating clinical severity of COVID-19 from the transmission dynamics in Wuhan, China. Nat. Med. **26**, 506–510 (2020)
15. Sanders, K., Valle, M.S., Viñaras, M., et al.: Do we trust and are we empowered by "Dr. Google"? Older Spaniards' uses and views of digital healthcare communication. Public Relat. Rev. **41**(5), 794–800 (2015)
16. He, T., Huang, C., Li, M.: Social participation of the elderly in China: the roles of conventional media, digital access and social media engagement. Telematics Inform. **48**, 101347 (2020)
17. Chen, R., Xu, P., Song, P.P., et al.: China has faster pace than Japan in population aging in next 25 years. Biosci. Trends **13**(4), 287–291 (2019)
18. Hargittai, E., Piper, A.M., Morris, M.R.: From internet access to internet skills: digital inequality among older adults. Univ. Access Inf. Soc. **18**(4), 881–890 (2018). https://doi.org/10.1007/s10209-018-0617-5
19. Netuveli, G., Blane, D.: Quality of life in older ages. Br. Med. Bull. **85**(1), 113–126 (2008). https://doi.org/10.1093/bmb/ldn003
20. Chou, M.C., Liu, C.H.: Mobile instant messengers and middle-aged and elderly adults in taiwan: uses and gratifications. Int. J. Hum. Comput. Interact. **32**(11), 835–846 (2016)
21. Bandura, A., Caprara, G.V., Barbaranelli, C., et al.: Sociocognitive self-regulatory mechanisms governing transgressive behavior. J. Pers. Soc. Psychol. **80**(1), 125–135 (2001)
22. Deng, F., Lv, J.H., Wang, H.L., et al.: Expanding public health in China: an empirical analysis of healthcare inputs and outputs. Public Health **142**, 73–84 (2017)
23. Avery, E.J., Park, S.: The influences of relationship quality with external partners and required levels of approval of messaging on crisis preparedness. Public Relat. Rev. **45**(1), 119–127 (2018)
24. Hu, B.J.: The overall review and evaluation of my country's crisis management research since "SARS"—Also on the core concept, research path and academic paradigm of crisis management. Int. Press **6**, 12–16+50 (2008)
25. Milan, Z., Ovidiu, N., Hervé, P., et al.: Enabling interoperability as a property of ubiquitous systems for disaster management. Comput. Sci. Inf. Syst. **12**(3), 1009–1031 (2015)
26. Kwon, O., Wen, Y.: An empirical study of the factors affecting social network service use. Comput. Hum. Behav. **26**(2), 254–263 (2009)
27. Marten, H., Sebastian, W., Anika, S., et al.: Touch interaction with Google Glass – is it suitable for older adults? Int. J. Hum. Comput. Stud. **110**, 12–20 (2017)
28. Vinnikov, M., Allison, R.S., Fernandes, S., et al.: Impact of depth of field simulation on visual fatigue: who are impacted? and how? Int. J. Hum. Comput. Stud. **91**, 37–51 (2016)
29. Young, R.: Remembering Bogle Chandler: an exploration of new media's storytelling potential. Dig. Creat. **25**(2), 97–112 (2013)
30. Chen, B., Shan, O.: The impact of the change in the elderly population on the demand for media contact: a predictive analysis based on the generational effect. J. Nanchang Univ. (Hum. Soc. Sci. Ed.) **3**, 153–157 +176 (2005)
31. Diana, C., Cristina, B., Ignacio, M., et al.: Teaching digital literacy skills to the elderly using a social network with linear navigation: a case study in a rural area. Int. J. Hum. Comput. Stud. **118**, 24–37 (2018)
32. Yang, C.Y., Lu, Y.M.: A piece of spring in the cold winter—the strong growth of "Happy Elderly" creates a miracle. Media **12**, 9–13 (2016)

"Do Not Touch" and "Maintaining Social Distance": A Study of the Model of Exhibition Viewing Under the Influence of COVID-19 Pandemic

Rungtai Lin[1]([✉]), John G. Kreifeldt[2], and Yikang Sun[3]

[1] Graduate School of Creative Industry Design, National Taiwan University of Arts, New Taipei City 22058, Taiwan
rtlin@mail.ntua.edu.tw
[2] School of Engineering, Tufts University, Medford, MA 02155, USA
john.kreifeldt@tufts.edu
[3] College of Art and Design, Nanjing Forestry University, Nanjing 210037, China
sunyikang120110@hotmail.com

Abstract. COVID-19 has revolutionized our lifestyle. Whether it is "Do Not Touch" or "Maintaining Social Distance", there is a need for distance. Unless COVID-19 disappears automatically, we will have to change the way we live for a long time. The distance between people and things will be maintained by physical measures to make it safer, but the psychological dimension needs to be intimate. Therefore, closing the space between people and things through emotional design (whether physical or virtual) and the shortening the distance between people and the world around them is worthy of further discussion. This paper first reviews the concepts involved, then randomly selects two typical exhibitions for analysis and discussion, and finally puts forward conclusions and suggestions. Whether the audience's experience meets expectations will determine the success of the exhibition to some extent. In the process of interaction, "touching" the real exhibits may still be unacceptable, but it can satisfy people's curiosity and innate habits in other ways. As part of a previous study, we also hope that more readers will genuinely comment on this issue.

Keywords: Do Not Touch · Social distancing · Exhibition viewing model · User experience design · Post-epidemic era

1 Introduction

Most people alive today did not experience the pandemic of the early 20th century. As a result, the impact of COVID-19 on human society is unprecedented. It has dramatically changed the way we are used to living (and will continue at least until the outbreak is completely over). Obviously, we will live with COVID-19 for a long time, and our lifestyle will need to be adjusted. As for enjoying cultural activities and experiences, we must also take a break or take other measures during pandemics. Thanks to the advances

© The Author(s), under exclusive license to Springer Nature Switzerland AG 2022
P.-L. P. Rau (Ed.): HCII 2022, LNCS 13313, pp. 255–264, 2022.
https://doi.org/10.1007/978-3-031-06050-2_19

and popularity of technology, people can visit museums online, watch live events using various apps (for example, some events are only for performers and are not open to spectators), and use virtual reality technology and equipment to interact with different exhibits, or even simulate traveling abroad. However, these eclectic experiments have failed to produce the desired results. In the same way, design and creativity face big challenges. Design has also moved from function to feeling, which has been one of the main trends in design development for the 21st century. During the pandemic, designs that bring us comfort and pleasure have become more popular, moving us away from the continuous refinement of the user experience design (UXD) model.

This article explores the following issues:

1. As COVID-19 will not end in the short term, we consider potential issues with existing design experience models, while respecting the provisions of the "New Epidemic Life Movement".
2. Whether it is "Do Not Touch" or "Maintaining Social Distance", there is a need for separation. Unless COVID-19 disappears automatically, for a long time we will have to change the way we live, and the distance between people and things created by physical measures will make it safer, but the psychological dimension needs to be more intimate. Therefore, how to draw people closer to other people and things through emotional design (whether physical or virtual) and how to establish the distance between people and the world around them are questions worthy of further discussion.

2 Literature Review

2.1 The Challenges and Emerging Values of Emotional Design Within the Context of the COVID-19 Pandemic

In the human mind, there are numerous areas responsible for what we call emotion; collectively, these regions constitute the emotional system. Don Norman suggested that the emotional system is composed of three different but interconnected levels, each of which influences our world experience in a special way. The three levels are visceral, behavioral, and reflective. The visceral level is responsible for the ingrained, automatic, and almost animalistic qualities of human emotion, which are almost entirely out of our control. The behavioral level refers to the controlled aspects of human action, where we unconsciously analyze a situation so as to develop goal-directed strategies most likely to prove effective in the shortest time or with the fewest actions possible. The reflective level is, as Don Norman stated, "…the home of reflection, of conscious thought, of learning of new concepts and generalizations about the world". These three levels, while classified as separate dimensions of the emotional system, are linked and influence one another to create our overall emotional experience of the world [1].

In *Emotional Design: Why We Love (Or Hate) Everyday Things*, Don Norman [2] distinguished three aspects, or levels, of the emotional system (i.e., the sum of the parts responsible for emotion in the human mind), which are as follows: the visceral, behavioral, and reflective levels. Each of these levels or dimensions, while heavily connected and interwoven in the emotional system, influences design in its own specific way.

2.2 "Do Not Touch!" or "Do Not Touch?": The Interplay, Experience, and Cognition Between Individuals and Exhibits

A warning sign at art museums and galleries around the world reads: "Do not touch the artwork." There is no need to demonstrate that art is protected from damage caused by touch. In terms of aesthetic experience, however, "Do Not Touch" is a cruel warning, as unacceptable as implementing a "Do Not Watch" warning beside the "Mona Lisa".

In Fig. 1, we see that the photos that people take with their smartphones or cameras may not be ideal. Even if you move to the front of the crowd, there is still a distance between you and the painting, including the piece of glass in front of the painting. However, perhaps we can explain it this way: people prefer to make up for the barrier of physical space through the camera. During the pandemic, "Do Not Touch" seems to be better expressed without emphasis because of the need to maintain some social distance and minimize unnecessary "contacts".

Fig. 1. Leonardo da Vinci, *Mona Lisa*, Louvre, Pairs, France. [Obviously, most people take photos that are more useful to record that they have visited this world-famous painting.]

However, from the audience's point of view, visual viewing alone is not enough to satisfy curiosity; there is always the subconscious impulse to reach out to touch, whether or not you can touch the "feeling". Consequently, "touching" is the instinct of people to experience the world further. We have artists to satisfy our vision, musicians to meet our hearing, five-star celebrity chefs to satisfy our taste in our daily lives, and even designer perfumes to challenge our sense of smell, but who will satisfy our need for touch? We often say that humans recognize things through the experiences of their five senses and use rich words to describe what they see, what they hear, the pleasant sounds of heaven, the fascinating smells they hear, and the delicious mountains they taste, but there are not enough words to describe the feeling of touch.

A famous and interesting artwork installation named Rain Room is shown in Fig. 2. It allows visitors to the installation to walk through a downpour without getting wet [3]. Motion sensors detect visitors' movements as they navigate through the darkened space, becoming "performers in this intersection of art, technology, and nature". It is not difficult to find that people are in contact with virtual rainwater in various ways!

Fig. 2. Hannes Koch and Florian Ortkrass, *Rain Room*, Random International, the Barbican, London, UK, 2012. [The viewer raises his head and stretches out his hands to feel the contact between man and nature.]

Obviously, after the COVID-19 pandemic, it may be difficult for people to view and interact with art in a similar way. It is true that this can be developed to an extent by limiting the number of people and wearing masks, but its sense of experience will definitely be reduced. Compared with the traditional way of viewing, this way of interacting with the work can bring a deeper feeling to the audience. Therefore, it is necessary to think further about how we can continue during the pandemic.

2.3 Immersive Experience Powered by Technology: A Feasible Measure

While online exhibitions are nothing new, for most people, the feeling of virtual viewing may not be ideal. In addition to factors such as equipment, people are accustomed to coming face-to-face with exhibits, even as mentioned earlier: people want to "touch" exhibits. A similar situation can be confirmed by the relationship between e-books and physical books.

Recently, VR (Virtual Reality), AR (Augmented Reality), SR (Substitutional Reality), and MR (Mixed Reality) have become increasingly sophisticated, and more people can use the above technologies to achieve a better experience [4–6]. Some recent studies have pointed out that through digital technology, we can shorten the gap between a virtual painting and a physical one; however, we must still improve the design of the object size and the interaction in the VR context so that a virtual exhibition can be as impressive as a physical one [7]. Thanks to these proven technologies, people can complete the viewing experience without leaving their homes, or, even if they are on the spot, they can watch it "without contact" and maintain a certain social distance from others. While this approach may be uncomfortable, it can improve security.

This study does not focus on technology, so the above four techniques will not be discussed in this section. It is important to stress that we need to make good use of these technologies and not be overly dependent on or even kidnapped by them because the ultimate goal is to start from the perspective of human nature and bring the audience as beautiful an experience as possible during this special period.

3 Method

3.1 Process

This study was conducted in the following way:

1. The relevant concepts and problems were clarified through the literature review.
2. Two typical exhibitions were selected for analysis and discussion.
3. An exhibition experience model framework was constructed that was suitable for the post-pandemic era. This framework will be further validated in subsequent studies.

3.2 Stimulus

We randomly selected two typical exhibitions as stimuli for discussion (Table 1). In order to allow readers to better understand these two exhibitions, we also attached relevant video links. Figures 3 and 4 show screenshots of some of the exhibitions. If the reader has not seen the exhibitions before, we highly recommend that you gain a more comprehensive understanding of them by watching the film when time permits.

Table 1. Stimulus.

Case	Brief description
Case 1 The First VR Experience of the Mona Lisa [8-10]	The Louvre will present the museum's first VR experience, in partnership with HTC VIVE Arts, which will bring to life the story of the *Mona Lisa*, da Vinci's most famous masterpiece.
Case 2 Van Gogh: The Immersive Experience [11-13]	The exhibition is on a global tour. Van Gogh: The Immersive Experience is all digital, hands free, and perfect for our socially distant world. Its rich content is suitable for a wide audience, including families, school groups, couples, and seniors. In addition to a spacious central area where Van Gogh's works stretch floor-to-ceiling, the experience includes separate galleries that chronicle his life, technique, and influence thru informative panels, larger than life re-creations and engaging interactives.

Fig. 3. VR experience of the *Mona Lisa*.

Fig. 4. Van Gogh: the immersive experience.

4   Analysis and Discussion

4.1   Analysis of Case 1: The First VR Experience of the Mona Lisa

Obviously, as shown in Fig. 1, there are always large numbers of spectators in front of this world-famous painting. As tourists, we use our cameras to take pictures of this rare and precious moment and even ask others to take a picture of themselves with this painting. However, not everyone has plenty of time to make their way through the crowds. Also, assuming that the Louvre does not allow visitors to take pictures, we venture to guess that many people may not come back.

From the viewer's standpoint, we all want to get as close to the painting as possible, even if in fact there is still a great distance between us. In addition, after the outbreak began, such a dense crowd clearly increased the risk of infection. Thanks to the advancement of technology, the Louvre launched a service that not only allows people to see the painting up close, but also to travel through time and space, enter the painting, and experience a richer context.

Please recall how you visited the exhibition: we will ask the organizer for a brochure or read the instruction card next to the exhibit. It is true that most people do not understand the technical terms in the manual, but this does not prevent them from interpreting the exhibits according to their own experience. In the digital age, in order to reduce the waste or pollution problems caused by printing, these manuals have become QR Codes that people can scan with smart devices to read the manual online. In the wake of the COVID-19 pandemic, this model also eliminates unnecessary contact. However, although this method is convenient, we remain skeptical about whether it will help the viewing experience. The reasons are as follows:

1. Affected by the epidemic, we have had to reduce non-essential outings. Even in countries or regions where the outbreak is slowing down, we are still at risk of being infected by asymptomatic infected people. In such a situation, in addition to challenges to our health, the quarantine policies implemented by many countries or regions will also cause us great inconvenience. Therefore, watching the exhibition online may be a good choice.
2. In addition to digitizing exhibits, models such as Case 1 are becoming more popular in museums or galleries than in the past. Their success lies in allowing the viewer to participate in the work and even interact with the characters in the work. This is far more interesting than simply looking at the work and reading the captions.

However, it should be noted that not all museums have this capability. The development of this software requires a monetary investment and consideration of whether it meets the needs of most people. At the same time, for the viewer, whether viewing an exhibition or a painting is worth buying a not-so-cheap device is also one factor to consider.

4.2   Analysis of Case 2: Van Gogh: The Immersive Experience

Van Gogh's life was short, but he moved forward despite adversity, and his story was as wonderful as his paintings. I have communicated with many friends with non-artistic backgrounds and found that many of them are as familiar with Van Gogh as professional artists. They go online to retrieve Van Gogh's life story, and they are impressed by Van Gogh's unrestrained brushstrokes and pulsating tones and give them high praise.

In fact, the proportion of artists in the entire population is not high, and the people who view their works are often those who do not have an artistic background. These people may not be professional, and the simpler and more unpretentious the description, the likelier they are to appreciate the essence of the art. Table 2 excerpts some audience feedback [14]; more content can be found on the official website. Almost all the visitors have given a very high evaluation. Because of the limitations, we were unable to interview those who were visiting the site, but both the photos from the scene and the official release of the film are shocking.

It seems that when people walk through the progressive field, everything around them becomes Van Gogh's art, as if they are literally walking into a beautiful painting. For the first time, the brushstrokes and tones are very close to them, and although virtual, this whole-body "interaction" (touching) can offer each visitor a different experience.

Table 2. Feedback from some audiences.

Name & Data	Brief description
rose.ghould – SASKATOON Published on: 10/26/2021	One of the most beautiful experiences I've ever had the privilege to experience.
Zaïde Masich - SASKATOON Published on: 11/02/2021	Definitely one of the coolest, most immersive experiences I've attended!
Laurae Klassen – SASKATOON Published on: 11/05/2021	It was an amazing show, absolutely loved every second of it!
Louise Gust - SASKATOON Published on: 11/08/2021	We went yesterday and were awed and amazed. The experience of being immersed in Imagine Van Gogh was incredible.
katiedora7 – BOSTON Published on: 12/22/2021	I got to see #ImagineVanGogh and now I would like to live inside this exhibit.

4.3 Discussion

Owing to the impact of the epidemic, the physical distance between people must be widened, which also affects their interaction with the world around them. To be honest, just as with e-books, I do not like to view exhibitions online.

As some studies have pointed out, when we look at a work of art, we are more concerned about how we feel after seeing it. In other words, can we experience some kind of touch from the exhibits? Such an experience may only be possible by meeting the work face-to-face. If there are two cases like the one selected in this article, I would love to experience them.

Based on the literature review and the discussion of the two cases, we proposed a model of exhibition viewing that is suitable for the post-epidemic era. The brief description is as follows:

1. **Select the appropriate display method for exhibits in different categories.** Relatively speaking, a painting may be more suitable for display in a virtual way. As for other types of exhibits, such as sculptures, crafts, clothing, etc., 3D or even 4D experiences can also be realized through technology. However, if conditions permit, it is still recommended to use a combination of physical and virtual displays.

2. **Examine the rationality of the presentation method according to the characteristics of the potential audience.** With the continuous improvement in living standards, people's need for a spiritual level is increasing. People visit various exhibitions in their spare time, and most of these people are not professional critics or artists. Therefore, how to highlight the meaning of the exhibits in the simplest way and how to allow the audience to visit easily and freely have become topics that the organizer or artist must consider. For example, some information related to the exhibition (which can be non-physical) can be distributed in advance, or the interaction between visitors and the work (of course, not the original) can be allowed in a specific area to increase the viewer's interest. In this way, even if the official exhibition adopts the online mode, it can still create a good experience.

3. **Excavate the value beyond the exhibition itself.** In the past, many exhibitions launched peripheral goods. In addition to the daily necessities, limited-edition foods were also made available. Because of the impact of the epidemic, these activities have had to be cancelled temporarily. So, is it possible to offer the visitors a food box? Or can we make good use of online shops so that viewers can experience the habits of the past? In these special times, if you can more closely consider the needs of the audience, you will likely inspire good feelings.

4. **Lower the bar for technology and equipment.** If the audience wants to spend a lot of money to buy viewing equipment, it will greatly reduce their participation. Because these devices may not be universal, once the exhibition is over, they will not be usable. Therefore, it is necessary to promote further cooperation between organizers and technology manufacturers to introduce affordable, general-purpose virtual viewing devices to consumers.

5 Conclusions and Recommendations

While it is unfair to say that the emergence of COVID-19 has given humanity an opportunity to reflect on past ways of life and examine the problems that exist, in terms of our viewing and interaction with works of art, this is an opportunity to take a more comprehensive look at exhibition patterns such as those mentioned above: Is this a more acceptable experience for the viewer? For presenters, does such a model help to spread their creative ideas? For organizers and critics, it is possible to think about how to expand such a model.

The core of the above question is whether we actually put the needs of the audience (people) first? No matter what viewing method is adopted, whether the audience's experience meets expectations will determine the success of the exhibition to some extent. In the process of interaction, "touching" the real exhibits may still be unacceptable, but it can satisfy people's curiosity and innate habits in other ways.

Although unrelated to the issues this article considers, we would like to point out that the needs of those with visual impairments must also be considered. For them, "touching" is probably the most important way they experience the world. Fortunately, some organizers have begun to pay attention to the needs of this special group when viewing works of art, and this will become an aspect of our follow-up research.

References

1. Norman's Three Levels of Design. https://www.interaction-design.org/literature/article/norman-s-three-levels-of-design. Accessed 10 Jan 2022
2. Norman, D.: Emotional Design: Why We Love (or Hate) Everyday Things. Basic Books, New York (2003)
3. Rain Room. https://en.wikipedia.org/wiki/Rain_Room. Accessed 10 Jan 2022
4. Home - 3DPhotoWorks, https://3dphotoworks.com/. Accessed 10 Jan 2022
5. Popoli, Z., Derda, I.: Developing experiences: creative process behind the design and production of immersive exhibitions. Museum Manage. Curatorship **36**(4), 384–402 (2021). https://doi.org/10.1080/09647775.2021.1909491
6. What Is an Immersive Experience? https://www.lifewire.com/what-is-an-immersive-experience-4588346#:~:text=An%20immersive%20experience%20is%20the,you%20are%20actually%20in%20another.&text=According%20to%20Wikipedia%2C%20an%20immersive,reality%2C%20this%20holds%20doubly%20true. Accessed 10 Jan 2022
7. Lin, C., Chen, S., Lin, R.: Efficacy of virtual reality in painting art exhibitions appreciation. Appl. Sci. **10**(9), 3012 (2020). https://doi.org/10.3390/app10093012
8. The Mona Lisa in virtual reality in your own home. https://www.louvre.fr/en/what-s-on/life-at-the-museum/the-mona-lisa-in-virtual-reality-in-your-own-home. Accessed 10 Jan 2022
9. Mona Lisa: Beyond the Glass in Virtual Reality, https://www.youtube.com/watch?v=41J0nZcjw_U. Accessed 10 Jan 2022
10. Mona Lisa: Beyond the Glass at The Louvre I HTC VIVE ARTS, https://www.youtube.com/watch?v=Au_UpzhzHwk. Accessed 10 Jan 2022
11. Van Gogh Exhibition: The Immersive Experience. https://vangoghexpo.com/. Accessed 10 Jan 2022
12. Van Gogh: The Immersive Experience. https://www.youtube.com/watch?v=dZkQSjZYsgc. Accessed 10 Jan 2022
13. Beyond Van Gogh: The Immersive Experience. https://www.youtube.com/watch?v=Lxmh5m8hm8g. Accessed 10 Jan 2022
14. What people are saying about us. https://www.imagine-vangogh.com/exhibition-reviews/. Accessed 10 Jan 2022

Going Cashless? How Has COVID-19 Affected the Intention to Use E-wallets?

Han Wei Wong[1] and Andrei O. J. Kwok[2]([⊠]) [iD]

[1] Sunway University Business School, Sunway University, Petaling Jaya, Selangor, Malaysia
[2] Department of Management, School of Business, Monash University Malaysia, Subang Jaya, Selangor, Malaysia
andrei.kwok@monash.edu

Abstract. The COVID-19 outbreak has accelerated the use of technology among consumers. Given the perceived health risks associated with using cash, this study aims to investigate the behavioral intention of Malaysians to use e-wallets during the pandemic. How has the pandemic affected consumer adoption of e-wallets? Drawing on the Technology Acceptance Model, a survey of 212 users was conducted to determine how three specific factors (trustworthiness, reliability, and perceived health risk) drive the intention of consumers to use e-wallets. The findings offer insights into the social impact of e-wallets as an innovative form of technology.

Keywords: Mobile payment · Digital transaction · Trustworthiness · Reliability · Perceived health risk · Technology acceptance model

1 Introduction

The COVID-19 outbreak could be a catalyst for the widespread adoption of innovative technologies. During the pandemic, the Malaysian government has encouraged the public to adopt e-wallets for the payment of purchases as they are regarded as far safer than paying by cash. Since e-wallets offer contactless payments, using them may protect consumers against COVID-19 [1]. The Malaysian government adopted the contactless payment method to pay out a subsidy of RM50 to every individual qualified to receive it under the Penjana Economic Recovery Plan initiative [2]. The subsidy is electronically deposited into the most popular and commonly used e-wallets in Malaysia, such as Touch 'n Go eWallet, GrabPay, Boost, Maybank Pay, and Alipay. In this context, we seek to investigate how three specific factors (trustworthiness, reliability, and perceived health risk) drive the intention of consumers to use e-wallets.

An e-wallet is a medium or application that allows users to make monetary transactions via smartphones or websites. Money (value) can also be loaded into an e-wallet from an individual's bank account using an electronic funds transfer (EFT) or debit card, or from an individual's credit card [3]. Additionally, an e-wallet mobile application provides access to food deliveries, bill payments, ride-hailing, and online purchases linked to merchants. This financial innovation has resulted in monetary transactions shifting away from the traditional use of cash.

P.-L. P. Rau (Ed.): HCII 2022, LNCS 13313, pp. 265–276, 2022.
https://doi.org/10.1007/978-3-031-06050-2_20

E-wallets have rapidly gained user acceptance given the ease with which payments can be transacted via mobile applications [4]. E-wallets are widely accepted in Malaysia due to the increasing preference for cashless transactions that offer consumers convenience and efficiency [1]. Cash payments at physical stores are gradually being replaced by scanning a QR code using a smartphone linked to an e-wallet. In recent years, studies have slowly integrated the "trust" variable into the TAM model. The model is insufficient as originally conceived to assess and describe technology related to the financial sector, such as internet banking [5]. Despite the extensive studies on the effect of perceived usefulness and perceived ease of use on e-wallet acceptance, studies are lacking on factors such as trustworthiness, reliability, and perceived health risks that are driving the shift towards e-wallet adoption during the COVID-19 pandemic [6–8].

2   Theory and Hypothesis Development

2.1   The Technology Acceptance Model

In this study, we validate the two typical elements of the Technology Acceptance Model (TAM). These elements are the perceived usefulness (PU) and the perceived ease of use (PEOU) of technology [9, 10]. Several scholars have indicated that the intention to use a technology or innovation is relevant to PU and PEOU due to their direct relationship with technology acceptance behavior. For example, Garrett et al. [6] found that users were highly likely to change their approach to transactions and accept online banking in place of mobile payments because convenience is a critical factor. A positive relationship has been demonstrated between the PEOU and PU of mobile payment systems on one hand, and the behavioral intention to use them (IU) on the other [11].

A positive relationship between PU and IU has been observed among users who intend to use smartphones when they find the technology useful [12]. A similar relationship has been observed regarding online technologies such as e-learning, e-books, and online travel services [13–15]. Therefore, based on the findings in the existing literature, the following hypothesis was developed:

H1: There is a positive relationship between PU and the consumer's intention to use e-wallets.

Meanwhile, past studies have demonstrated a positive relationship between PEOU and PU [16]. PEOU has also been found to correlate positively to PU because when users have extensive experience using e-wallets, they will find e-wallets useful as their knowledge can be applied effectively. Amoako-Gyampah [17] indicated that when users perceive that a system is easy to use, they are more likely to perceive that the system is useful to them. Furthermore, in a recent study, Caffaro et al. [18] identified a positive relationship between PEOU and IU. Therefore, hypotheses 2 and 3 were developed as follows:

H2: There is a positive relationship between PEOU and PU.
H3: There is a positive relationship between PEOU and IU.

2.2 Trustworthiness (T)

Trust is a fundamental element that facilitates the success of interpersonal relations and transactions, as its central role is to regulate social interactions [19]. Trust in technology focuses on "what it is about technology that makes the technology itself trustworthy, irrespective of the people and human structures surrounding the technology [20]." According to Yang et al. [21], trust in innovation is based on information supplied by service providers. The extent to which trust is built with users significantly influences acceptance intention. Lu et al. [22] examined e-wallet use in China, demonstrating that trust influences a user's intention to adopt an e-wallet, whereby users who regard a payment system as trustworthy display a higher level of intention to use it.

On the other hand, Hoffman et al. [23] posited that a lack of trust could lead to low engagement. According to Becerra and Korgaonkar [24], users tend to avoid online transactions that demonstrate low trustworthiness. Liébana-Cabanillas et al. [4] found that tech-savvy users are more likely to exhibit higher trust in online applications so they are more likely to adopt e-wallets and trust the payment system. Hence, when users develop trust in an online payment system, they will acknowledge that the mobile payment system can provide the service they expect [8]. Therefore, hypothesis H4 is posited as follows:

H4: There is a positive relationship between the trustworthiness of an e-wallet and the intention to use it.

2.3 Reliability (R)

Reliability refers to the expectation that a form of technology will operate with consistency and certainty [20]. In the context of e-wallet use, Liébana-Cabanillas et al. [25] found that a lack of reliability was a significant factor preventing e-wallet adoption in Spain. Ramadan and Aita [7] demonstrated that mobile payment reliability has a positive relationship with trustworthiness, directly affecting users' intentions to adopt e-wallets. As such, the reliability and trustworthiness of a mobile payment system are interrelated. Therefore hypotheses 5 and 6 were developed as follows:

H5: There is a positive relationship between the reliability of an e-wallet and its trustworthiness.
H6: There is a positive relationship between the reliability of an e-wallet and the intention to use it.

2.4 Perceived Health Risk (PHR)

Angelakis et al. [26] found that banknotes used in traditional cash payments were highly likely to be contaminated, with up to 88% of banknotes being contaminated with microorganisms due to the circulation of the notes. The use of banknotes is one of the easiest ways through which diseases can spread, as scholars have proven that human influenza viruses can survive on banknotes and thereafter be transferred to other objects or their surroundings. Contact with such objects would contaminate a person's hands with viruses and create a public health risk [26, 27]. Although banknotes can be regarded as a medium through which diseases are transmitted, few studies have analyzed the relationship between the perceived health risks of using e-wallet applications compared to using banknotes, and how this might affect the intention to use e-wallets. Hence, the final hypothesis was developed:

H7: There is a positive relationship between perceived health risk and the intention to use an e-wallet.

2.5 Age as a Moderator

Based on the existing literature, we predicted that age would moderate the relationship between PU, PEOU, trustworthiness, reliability, and perceived health risk on one hand, and the intention to use an e-wallet (IU) on the other. For example, given the preference for convenience and utility, PU tends to influence those in lower age groups more, while PEOU tends to motivate those in higher age groups [28]. Likewise, Natarajan et al. [29] found that those in lower age groups perceived usefulness as necessary for their use of shopping applications, while those in older age groups generally emphasized the ease of use and the trustworthiness of these applications. The conceptual framework of this study is illustrated in Fig. 1.

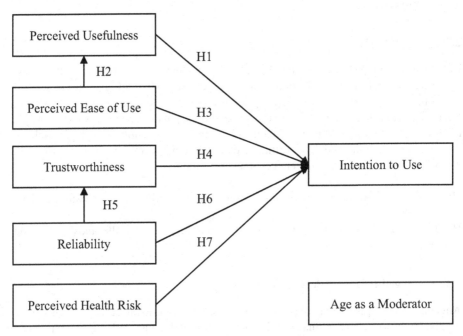

Fig. 1. Conceptual framework

3 Methodology and Data Analysis

3.1 Data Collection

An online survey based on the measurement items in Table 1 was randomly administered to 212 individuals in Malaysia, 110 of whom (51.9%) were female. The age breakdown of the respondents was as follows: 32.5% of respondents (69) were 18 to 24 years old, 33.0% of respondents (70) were 25 to 39 years old, and 34.4% of respondents (73) were 40 to 55 years old.

A seven-point Likert scale with values ranging from 1 (strongly disagree) to 7 (strongly agree) was used instead of a five-point Likert scale to capture data with a higher degree of sensitivity and a greater range to provide better accuracy [30].

3.2 Data Analysis

Table 1 presents the results of an analysis performed using Cronbach's alpha. As the composite reliability values were all greater than 0.7, they were deemed reliable for use in the analysis.

Table 1. Measurement instrument.

Construct	Items	Cronbach's alpha
Perceived Usefulness (Adapted from Liébana-Cabanillas et al. [14])	Using an e-wallet could help me make purchases I usually make on the internet/social networks	.91
	Using an e-wallet could increase the efficiency of making my purchases on the internet/social networks	
	Using an e-wallet for my purchases on the internet/social networks could increase my productivity	
	In general, an e-wallet could be useful for me to make purchases on the internet/social networks	
Perceived Ease of Use (Adapted from Liébana-Cabanillas et al. [14])	Interaction with the e-wallet is clear and understandable	.96
	Interaction with the e-wallet does not require mental effort	
	I think it is easy to get the e-wallet to do what I want to do	
	I think this is a useful e-wallet for making small purchases on the internet/social networks	
	In general, the e-wallet is easy to use	
Trustworthiness (Adapted from Liébana-Cabanillas et al. [14])	I think that the e-wallet will keep the promises and commitments that it makes	.96
	The e-wallet is trustworthy	
	I would qualify the e-wallet as honest	
	I think that the e-wallet is responsible	
	In general, I trust the e-wallet	

(continued)

Table 1. (*continued*)

Construct	Items	Cronbach's alpha
Reliability (Adapted from Dabholkar et al. [31])	Performs the service right the first time	.91
	Providing services on time that it is promising to do so	
	Availability of customer service	
	Error-free transaction and record	
Perceived Health Risk (Adapted from Liao et al. [32])	I believed that the e-wallet can protect me against COVID-19	.87
	I believe that it will help to protect my family or friends against COVID-19 if I adopt an e-wallet	
	I believe that using an e-wallet instead of cash can reduce my risk of contracting COVID-19	
Intention to use (Adapted from Merhi [33])	I intend to continue using e-wallets in the future	.94
	Given that I have access to e-wallets, I intend to use them	
	It is likely to continue using e-wallets in the future	

Table 2. Bivariate correlations.

	M	SD	1	2	3	4	5	6	7
Gender	1.52	0.50							
Age	2.02	0.82	−.06						
PU	5.36	1.41	.06	.10					
PEOU	5.37	1.65	.06	−.02	.53**				
T	4.73	1.74	−.03	−.11	.08	−.03			
R	5.00	1.63	−.01	.05	.56**	.46**	.26**		
PHR	5.37	1.30	−.01	.03	.15*	.03	.16*	.22**	
IU	4.87	1.60	−.01	−.23**	.46**	.42**	.32**	.41**	−.02

**. *Correlation is significant at the 0.01 level (2-tailed).* *. *Correlation is significant at the 0.05 level (2-tailed).*

Correlations among the variables were tested and are shown in Table 2.

Table 3 presents the results of the regression and mediation analyses performed using PROCESS (v.4.0) from Hayes [34] by holding gender and age as constants. The independent variables were regressed to determine the variance inflation factor (VIF) value in the collinearity analysis. All the variables demonstrate tolerance values above 0.2 and VIF levels below 5, indicating no multicollinearity issue [35, 36].

Table 3. Regression and mediation analysis.

Variables	Tolerance	VIF	Effect	β	se	t	p	Boot SE	Boot LLCI	Boot ULCI	Decision
PU → IU	.58	1.72	Direct	.42	.08	5.57	.00				H1 supported
PU → PEOU	.99	1.02	Direct	.45	.05	8.99	.00				H2 supported (partial mediation)
PU → PEOU → IU			Total	.41	.06	6.88	.00				
PU → IU			Indirect	.19				.05	.11	.28	
PEOU → IU	.66	1.52	Direct	.22	.07	3.30	.00				H3 supported
T → IU	.88	1.14	Direct	.17	.06	3.01	.00				H4 supported
R → T	1.00	1.00	Direct	.28	.07	3.96	.00				H5 supported
R → T → IU			Total	.46	.06	8.02	.00				(partial mediation)
T → IU			Indirect	.05				.02	.01	.10	
R → IU	.59	1.71	Direct	.42	.06	7.08	.00				H6 supported
PHR → IU	.94	1.07	Direct	-.16	.07	-4.41	.00				H7 supported

*$p < 0.10$; **$p < 0.05$; ***$p < 0.01$

Table 4 presents the results of a moderation analysis performed to identify whether gender and age had any moderating effects on the variables. Gender showed no moderating effect but age had a significant effect on the relationship between PU ($p < .001$) and IU, PEOU ($p < .00$) and IU, T ($p < 0.05$) and IU, and R ($p < .001$) and IU. Age, however, did not significantly affect the relationship between PHR ($p > .05$) and IU.

Table 4. Moderation analysis.

Independent Variable × Moderating factor	p
Perceived Usefulness × Gender	.96
Perceived Ease of Use × Gender	.12
Trustworthiness × Gender	.52
Reliability × Gender	.84
Perceived Health Risk × Gender	.85
Perceived Usefulness × Age	.00***
Perceived Ease of Use × Age	.00***
Trustworthiness × Age	.05**
Reliability × Age	0.00***
Perceived Health Risk × Age	.30

*$p < 0.10$; **$p < 0.05$; ***$p < 0.01$

4   Discussion of the Findings

The results shown in Table 3 demonstrate that all hypotheses H1, H2, H3, H4, H5, H6, and H7 are supported. Consistent with the existing literature, PU and PEOU were found to be crucial factors that influence a user's intention to use e-wallets. There were positive relationships between PU and IU and between PEOU and IU, thus supporting hypotheses H1 and H3. As expected, the empirical evidence suggests that Malaysians intend to use e-wallets because they found them useful when making purchases, especially during the COVID-19 pandemic. Furthermore, H2 was supported, proving that PEOU positively influences PU. E-wallets that are easy to learn and control and that provide clear and understandable instructions offer a positive user experience that helps users become proficient in using them. As a result, users find e-wallets useful.

4.1   The Effect of Trustworthiness (T) on Intention to Use (IU) E-Wallets

Past studies have found that the integration of trust, as one of the determinants of the intention to use mobile payments, has a positive and significant relationship with UI [8, 37]. The current findings were consistent with these studies, as there was a positive relationship between T and IU, thus supporting hypothesis H4. User age was found to moderate the relationship between T and IU, as respondents in the younger age groups agreed that applications that induced greater trust would stimulate their intention to accept the technology and use e-wallets [29].

4.2   The Effect of Reliability (R) on Intention to Use (IU) E-Wallets

A positive relationship was found between R and T. This corresponds with the result of Greenberg et al.'s [38] study that affirmed a positive relationship between R and R. When users acknowledge that an e-wallet system is reliable, their level of trust will increase.

The findings also show a positive relationship between R and IU, supporting H6. The positive correlation between R and IU showed that user confidence using e-wallets was enhanced after the system had worked effectively the first time. Thus, the results were consistent with the past study of Ramadan and Aita [7]. It is not surprising that users would look for e-wallet services that are less error-prone and that offer better service availability and performance [39]. Furthermore, as Tsai et al. [40] evidenced, a system's reliability involves the ability of the organization to provide consistent service to its users. E-wallet applications with minimal errors would enhance the user experience, thus increasing the intention to use these applications.

Moreover, customer service availability is crucial. When users encounter an issue with their e-wallet, they tend to seek help from a customer service touchpoint. Quick customer service response time leaves users with a positive impression and builds a stronger connection with the e-wallet application. Notably, the surge in e-wallet adoption and use during the pandemic caused some systems to crash. Therefore, firms offering e-wallets must anticipate and have a plan in place to mitigate such issues and ensure the best user experience possible.

Age was found to have a moderating effect on R as each generation defines reliability differently. Respondents in the younger age groups might emphasize technological reliability, perhaps prioritizing e-wallet applications that react quickly and do not crash when an instruction is requested, whereas older age groups may tend to emphasize better customer service [41].

4.3 The Effect of Perceived Health Risk (PHR) on Intention to Use (IU) E-Wallets

To assess user perceptions of the health risks they face, PHR can determine the influence of the pandemic on the intention of users to adopt e-wallets. Research has shown that viruses such as COVID-19 can be transmitted through contact with inanimate objects [42] as the fluid droplets in viruses spread through sneezing or talking. This can easily cause cash to become contaminated. The adoption of e-wallet offers an alternative to the use of case and can reduce the transmission of the virus. Thus, H7 was supported, because a negative yet significant relationship exists between PHR and IU. Furthermore, the results show that age does not moderate PHR or intention to use e-wallets, suggesting that users, regardless of their age, have adopted e-wallet applications to reduce the possibility of contracting COVID-19 from handling cash that may be contaminated with it.

4.4 Managerial Implications

These findings provide three notable implications for managers. First, e-wallet providers must create e-wallet applications that are secure from cyber threats. Since sensitive personal information such as identity and banking or credit card details must be provided to set up and fund e-wallet accounts, such information must be kept private and robustly protected from exposure, theft, and misuse. Second, e-wallet providers must ensure that their services are reliable and work as promised. The ICT infrastructure underpinning their e-wallet services must therefore be capable of supporting a large volume of simultaneous transactions that may result from movement restrictions associated with pandemics and natural disasters. Third, e-wallet providers must provide a service that is easy to use and that comes with highly responsive customer service cross-channel touchpoints that users can access if they have questions, need help, or have problems using the service.

4.5 Theoretical Implications

Existing studies have focused on how PU and PEOU, as part of the TAM model, contribute to e-wallet adoption [7, 8, 11]. However, this study also investigates whether reliability, trustworthiness, and perceived health risks are factors that influence the acceptance of e-wallets. This has been lacking in previous empirical studies. Notably, our study extended the TAM model has been extended with the addition of these three factors. Specifically, trustworthiness would facilitate users' acceptance of technology [43]. Despite the limited research on reliability and PHR, both these factors contribute to one of the critical factors that establishes relationships with e-wallet adoption among diverse age groups. Thus, in discussing trustworthiness, reliability, and PHR, this study has contributed to bridging the theoretical e-wallet gap.

5 Conclusion

This study aimed to examine the intention to use e-wallet applications during the COVID-19 outbreak. Our research assessed the factors that facilitate e-wallet adoption in Malaysia. Each factor was analyzed to identify whether it affected e-wallet use during the pandemic. These factors include perceived usefulness, perceived ease of use, trustworthiness, reliability, and perceived health risk. The direct and indirect effects of these factors were also assessed with respect to the acceptance of e-wallets. In summary, a direct relationship was found to exist between trustworthiness, reliability, and perceived health risk on one hand, and intention to use e-wallets on the other. Additionally, reliability affected trustworthiness such that an e-wallet with a high degree of reliability would generate higher trustworthiness in the application resulting in a greater intention to use e-wallets among the study's subjects.

References

1. Teng, S., Khong, K.: Examining actual consumer usage of E-wallet: a case study of big data analytics. Comput. Hum. Behav. **121**, 106778 (2021). https://doi.org/10.1016/j.chb.2021.106778
2. RM50 e-wallet credit to encourage contactless payment I New Straits Times. https://www.nst.com.my/news/nation/2020/06/598242/rm50-e-wallet-credit-encourage-contactless-payment
3. Bagla, R., Sancheti, V.: Gaps in customer satisfaction with digital wallets: challenge for sustainability. J. Manage. Dev. **37**, 442–451 (2018). https://doi.org/10.1108/JMD-04-2017-0144
4. José Liébana-Cabanillas, F., Sánchez-Fernández, J., Muñoz-Leiva, F.: Role of gender on acceptance of mobile payment. Ind. Manage. Data Syst. **114**, 220–240 (2014). https://doi.org/10.1108/imds-03-2013-0137
5. Alalwan, A., Dwivedi, Y., Rana, N., Lal, B., Williams, M.: Consumer adoption of Internet banking in Jordan: examining the role of hedonic motivation, habit, self-efficacy and trust. J. Finan. Serv. Mark. **20**, 145–157 (2015)
6. Garrett, J., Rodermund, R., Anderson, N., Berkowitz, S., Robb, C.: Adoption of mobile payment technology by consumers. Fam. Consum. Sci. Res. J. **42**, 358–368 (2014)
7. Ramadan, R., Aita, J.: A model of mobile payment usage among Arab consumers. Int. J. Bank Mark. **36**, 1213–1234 (2018). https://doi.org/10.1108/IJBM-05-2017-0080
8. Zhou, T.: Understanding the determinants of mobile payment continuance usage. Ind. Manage. Data Syst. **114**, 936–948 (2014). https://doi.org/10.1108/IMDS-02-2014-0068
9. Davis, F.: Perceived usefulness, perceived ease of use, and user acceptance of information technology. MIS Quart. **13**, 319 (1989). https://doi.org/10.2307/249008
10. Davis, F., Bagozzi, R., Warshaw, P.: User Acceptance of computer technology: a comparison of two theoretical models. Manage. Sci. **35**, 982–1003 (1989). https://doi.org/10.1287/mnsc.35.8.982
11. Kim, C., Mirusmonov, M., Lee, I.: An empirical examination of factors influencing the intention to use mobile payment. Comput. Hum. Behav. **26**, 310–322 (2010). https://doi.org/10.1016/j.chb.2009.10.013
12. Joo, J., Sang, Y.: Exploring Koreans' smartphone usage: an integrated model of the technology acceptance model and uses and gratifications theory. Comput. Hum. Behav. **29**, 2512–2518 (2013). https://doi.org/10.1016/j.chb.2013.06.002

13. Baker-Eveleth, L., Stone, R.: Usability, expectation, confirmation, and continuance intentions to use electronic textbooks. Behav. Infor. Technol. **34**, 992–1004 (2015). https://doi.org/10.1080/0144929X.2015.1039061
14. Li, H., Liu, Y.: Understanding post-adoption behaviors of e-service users in the context of online travel services. Inform. Manage. **51**, 1043–1052 (2014). https://doi.org/10.1016/j.im.2014.07.004
15. Lin, W., Wang, C.: Antecedences to continued intentions of adopting e-learning system in blended learning instruction: a contingency framework based on models of information system success and task-technology fit. Comput. Educ. **58**, 88–99 (2012). https://doi.org/10.1016/j.compedu.2011.07.008
16. Liu, Z., Ben, S., Zhang, R.: Factors affecting consumers' mobile payment behavior: a meta-analysis. Electron. Commer. Res. **19**(3), 575–601 (2019). https://doi.org/10.1007/s10660-019-09349-4
17. Amoako-Gyampah, K.: Perceived usefulness, user involvement and behavioral intention: an empirical study of ERP implementation. Comput. Hum. Behav. **23**, 1232–1248 (2007). https://doi.org/10.1016/j.chb.2004.12.002
18. Caffaro, F., Micheletti Cremasco, M., Roccato, M., Cavallo, E.: Drivers of farmers' intention to adopt technological innovations in Italy: the role of information sources, perceived usefulness, and perceived ease of use. J. Rural Stud. **76**, 264–271 (2020). https://doi.org/10.1016/j.jrurstud.2020.04.028
19. Ortega Egea, J., Román González, M.: Explaining physicians' acceptance of EHCR systems: An extension of TAM with trust and risk factors. Comput. Hum. Behav. **27**, 319–332 (2011). https://doi.org/10.1016/j.chb.2010.08.010
20. Mcknight, D., Carter, M., Thatcher, J., Clay, P.: Trust in a specific technology. ACM Trans. Manag. Inf. Syst. **2**, 1–25 (2011). https://doi.org/10.1145/1985347.1985353
21. Yang, C., et al.: Analyzing drivers' intention to accept parking app by structural equation Model. J. Adv. Transport. **2020**, 1–11 (2020). https://doi.org/10.1155/2020/3051283
22. Lu, Y., Yang, S., Chau, P., Cao, Y.: Dynamics between the trust transfer process and intention to use mobile payment services: a cross-environment perspective. Inform. Manage. **48**, 393–403 (2011). https://doi.org/10.1016/j.im.2011.09.006
23. Hoffman, D., Novak, T., Peralta, M.: Building consumer trust online. Commun. ACM. **42**, 80–85 (1999). https://doi.org/10.1145/299157.299175
24. Becerra, E., Korgaonkar, P.: Effects of trust beliefs on consumers' online intentions. Eur. J. Marketing. **45**, 936–962 (2011). https://doi.org/10.1108/03090561111119921
25. Liébana-Cabanillas, F., Leiva, F., Fernández, J.: Examining merchants' refusal to adopt mobile payment systems in Spain. Smartphones Appl. Res. Persp. (2017). https://doi.org/10.5772/intechopen.70284
26. Angelakis, E., et al.: Paper money and coins as potential vectors of transmissible disease. Future Microbiol. **9**, 249–261 (2014). https://doi.org/10.2217/fmb.13.161
27. Thomas, Y., et al.: Survival of influenza virus on banknotes. Appl. Environ. Microbiol. **74**, 3002–3007 (2008). https://doi.org/10.1128/AEM.00076-08
28. Assaker, G.: Age and gender differences in online travel reviews and user-generated-content (UGC) adoption: extending the technology acceptance model (TAM) with credibility theory. J. Hosp. Market. Manag. **29**, 428–449 (2019). https://doi.org/10.1080/19368623.2019.1653807
29. Natarajan, T., Balasubramanian, S., Kasilingam, D.: The moderating role of device type and age of users on the intention to use mobile shopping applications. Technol. Soc. **53**, 79–90 (2018). https://doi.org/10.1016/j.techsoc.2018.01.003
30. Joshi, A., Kale, S., Chandel, S., Pal, D.: Likert Scale: explored and explained. British J. Appl. Sci. Technol. **7**, 396–403 (2015)

31. Dabholkar, P., Thorpe, D., Rentz, J.: A measure of service quality for retail stores: scale development and validation. J. Acad. Market. Sci. **24**, 3–16 (1996). https://doi.org/10.1007/bf02893933

32. Liao, Q., Cowling, B., Lam, W., Fielding, R.: Factors Affecting intention to receive and self-reported receipt of 2009 pandemic (H1N1) vaccine in Hong Kong: a longitudinal study. PLoS ONE **6**, e17713 (2011). https://doi.org/10.1371/journal.pone.0017713

33. Merhi, M.: Factors influencing higher education students to adopt podcast: an empirical study. Comput. Educ. **83**, 32–43 (2015). https://doi.org/10.1016/j.compedu.2014.12.014

34. Hayes, A.: Introduction to Mediation, Moderation, and Conditional Process Analysis, 2nd edn. Guilford Publications (2017)

35. Hair, J., Anderson, R., Babin, B., Black, W.: Multivariate Data Analysis. Cengage, Australia (2019)

36. Kock, N., Lynn, G.: Lateral collinearity and misleading results in variance-based SEM: an illustration and recommendations. J. Assoc. Inf. Syst. **13**, 546–580 (2012). https://doi.org/10.17705/1jais.00302

37. Chandra, S., Srivastava, S., Theng, Y.: Evaluating the role of trust in consumer adoption of mobile payment systems: an empirical analysis. Commun. Assoc. Inf. Syst. **27** (2010). https://doi.org/10.17705/1cais.02729

38. Greenberg, R., Li, W., Wong-On-Wing, B.: The effect of trust in system reliability on the intention to adopt online accounting systems. Int. J. Account. Inf. Manag. **20**, 363–376 (2012). https://doi.org/10.1108/18347641211272740

39. Zo, H., Nazareth, D., Jain, H.: End-to-end reliability of service oriented applications. Inform. Syst. Front. **14**, 971–986 (2011). https://doi.org/10.1007/s10796-011-9308-y

40. Tsai, M., Wu, H., Liang, W.: Fuzzy decision making for market positioning and developing strategy for improving service quality in department stores. Qual. Quant. **42**, 303–319 (2006). https://doi.org/10.1007/s11135-006-9047-1

41. Chau, V., Ngai, L.: The youth market for internet banking services: perceptions, attitude and behaviour. J. Serv. Mark. **24**, 42–60 (2010). https://doi.org/10.1108/08876041011017880

42. Ather, A., Patel, B., Ruparel, N., Diogenes, A., Hargreaves, K.: Coronavirus disease 19 (COVID-19): implications for clinical dental care. J. Endodont. **46**, 584–595 (2020). https://doi.org/10.1016/j.joen.2020.03.008

43. Rauniar, R., Rawski, G., Yang, J., Johnson, B.: Technology acceptance model (TAM) and social media usage: an empirical study on Facebook. J. Enterp. Inf. Manag. **27**, 6–30 (2014). https://doi.org/10.1108/JEIM-04-2012-0011

Design Education in Post-pandemic Age: Examining the Roles Digital Platforms Play in Collaborative Design Activities

Yuhan Zhang[✉]

Faculty of Education, University of Cambridge, Cambridge, UK
yz691@cantab.ac.uk

Abstract. Due to the experimental and collaborative nature of design activities, studio-based teaching and learning have always been a central part of design education. It is perceived that knowledge is primarily obtained through the act of designing, which encompasses not only verbal conversation with other humans but also real-time material interactions with each person's physical environment. However, since the global COVID-19 pandemic, design students, educators, and institutions around the world have had to quickly adapt to working and collaborating on digital platforms such as Zoom, Microsoft Team, etc. At the same time, there has been a lack of understanding of what these digital platforms can do in collaborative design activities. The study presented in this article aims at exploring the effects of digital platforms on real-time collaborative design activities with a focus on object handling and communication, which are key elements of studio-based interactions. The participant in this study was invited to finish a small collaborative task which entailed building a paper toy with the researcher on Microsoft Teams. It was discovered that apart from facilitating the communication between the participant and the researcher, the digital platform was continuously regionalising, de-regionalising, and re-regionalising the space in the rooms the researcher and participant were working in. This characteristic of the digital platform opens new doorways to studying the roles technologies play in design education that embraces the contextual nature of pedagogical practices in the changing environment of the 21st century.

Keywords: Online design education · Digital platforms · Design pedagogy · Post-pandemic

1 Introduction

Due to the experimental and collaborative nature of design activities, studio-based teaching and learning have always been a central part of design education. Students are usually expected to communicate with each other and their tutors in the form of tutorials and informal discussions on a regular basis. Presenting ideas in audio-visual forms is also seen as an essential practical skill design students seek to develop during their studies. Knowledge is primarily obtained 'through the act of designing', which encompasses

P.-L. P. Rau (Ed.): HCII 2022, LNCS 13313, pp. 277–285, 2022.
https://doi.org/10.1007/978-3-031-06050-2_21

not only verbal conversation with other humans but also real-time material interactions with each person's physical environment [12]. The emphasis on face-to-face communication and real-time object manipulation differentiates design education from other academic disciplines and makes it difficult to be moved into an online environment [6]. While subjects like business management and accounting are embracing the growth of technology, design education displays a relatively slow pace in making its teaching and learning online. In an internet search for American Graphic Design Bachelor programmes, it was found that only five institutions provide online degrees, compared to the number of 61 schools giving online Bachelor's degrees in accounting [6]. However, since the global COVID-19 pandemic, design students, educators, and institutions around the world have had to quickly adapt to working and collaborating through online platforms such as Zoom, Skype, Microsoft Team, etc. Although communicating online is not a new concept for design practitioners, there has been a lack of comprehensive understanding of the roles these digital platforms play in collaborative design activities. Moreover, with the complexity and intelligence of digital technologies growing every day, it is concerning that we have not yet developed new theoretical and methodological tools to engage with the increasingly digitalised environment. In this article, I would like to present the approach I have adopted from Karen Barad's new materialist framework to set up my research which explores the roles digital platforms can play in collaborative design activities. I will start by looking at how digital platforms are conceptualised in existing studies and discuss the potential limitations of their approaches. Then I will introduce Barad's approach to the human-technology relationship and explain why her theory is relevant to studying digital platforms in our current environment. Finally, I will present how my study was carried out and discuss the outcomes as well as the potential pathways it opens for design research and design education research communities.

2   Literature Review

2.1   Moving Away from the Instrumental Conceptualisation of Digital Platforms

Since the beginning of the 3rd millennium, academics have investigated the impact digital technologies have on collaborative design activities in different areas with various focuses [5, 7–9, 11, 13]. Despite the range of design fields and methodological approaches covered in these studies, a few recurring patterns can be found in the conceptualisation of digital platforms. Most studies mentioned above assume that digital platforms are instrumental tools that humans use to aid one or more aspects of their design processes. This could be seen in the terms they use such as 'Information Communication Technology' or 'ICT' which implies that digital technology exists to serve the purpose of facilitating communication between humans in co-located design processes [5]. Studies based on this premise tend to give digital technology a pre-determined assistant role to play and focus on making inquiries around how humans think and behave in a digitally-mediated environment. This approach allows researchers to conduct interview studies and discourse analysis which are believed to reflect what is happening in people's minds. However, such a notion of human-digital-technology being a user-used relationship is facing challenges today. As a result of the rapid technological advancement accelerated by the COVID-19 pandemic, the ontological status of our reality is blurring the boundary between the 'human' and 'nonhuman' [10]. The traditional worldview where human is superior to materials and environments is inadequate as both human and nonhuman entities are now intrinsically enmeshed with one another [3]. It is suggested that we need to respond to the agencies of all these 'nonhuman' players as much as it does to humans to better understand our rapidly changing environment [4]. I would like to add that it is an important step for us researchers to take since how we define the human-technology relationship has a substantial impact on the information we can find out about the effect digital technology has on design activities while conducting studies. When we confine the meaning of digital platforms to a pre-determined instrumental purpose such as transmitting verbal information, we are simultaneously limiting the roles that human designers can perform outside of being users of that function. Both humans and digital platforms have properties that allow them to react to their environment in different ways that form their collaboration, which cannot be reduced to one operating another. Treating digital platforms as tools whose agencies happen to coalesce with humans' intentions has the potential to constrain our vision of both human and technological capabilities, which is clearly contradictory to our goal of further developing design in light of the expanding human-technology interaction in 21st-century education. A new approach to researching the engagement of digital platforms in design that releases the potential meanings of digital platforms and humans from being trapped in each other is in urgent need.

2.2 Revisiting Human-Technology Relationship with Karen Barad's Theory

New materialists like Karen Barad rejects the traditional approach to the human-technology relationship applied by existing studies that are based on the idea of human and nonhuman being pre-existing entities that control or manipulate each other. Instead, she offers a radical philosophical framework in which various phenomena in the world are seen as being co-constituted by human and nonhuman entities [2]. In the new materialist worldview she developed, 'intra-action' is used instead of 'interaction' [1]. While inter-action implies pre-existing entities with independent agencies, intra-action means that agency emerges from within the relation between bodies, not outside of it [2]. Following Barad's train of thought, we can see that the capacity of what humans and technology are able to do together in a collaborative activity is not a result of any of them manipulating each other, but emerges within their continuous encounter with one another as well as other human and nonhuman elements in space. Barad's theory allows us to jump outside of the pre-determined roles we set for digital platforms to play and start to explore the dynamic connection between all human and nonhuman elements that make up our design space, whether that be co-located studios, workshops or even bedrooms, like many of us have experienced during the pandemic. In light of Barad's ideas, I designed a study that moves away from human-centred narrative to exploring the possible roles digital platforms can play in human-involved activities. Here it is worth pointing out that by moving away from human-centred narrative I do not mean to disadvantage humans in design activities. In fact, it offers a good opportunity for researchers to discover opportunities for human designers to engage with digital platforms in innovative ways that can potentially enhance their performances. This will be further unpacked in later sections where I will discuss the findings of my research.

3   Problem Conceptualisation and Methodology

3.1   Barad's Diffractive Methodology

As discussed previously, understanding design activities in the context of growing technological integration requires the adoption of a new philosophical perspective that treats all entities, humans or nonhumans, as always intra-actively part of the making up of the design space. This philosophical perspective must also be reflected in the methodological approach, which means the human researcher must also be considered as a co-constitutor of the phenomenon under investigation. This makes Barad's diffractive methodology the most suitable approach to answering the research question of my study which is: What roles can digital platforms play in collaborative design activities from a more-than-human perspective? The idea of diffraction is developed based on the famous double-slit experiment in which the ontological nature of light is co-constituted by the research apparatus used in the study [2]. Barad extends the notion of research apparatus from physical measuring instruments to including the intention, the materiality of and the method used by the researcher. Adopting diffractive methodology allows researchers to develop methods where researchers can place themselves in the intra-active relations to provoke reactions from all human/nonhuman elements in a collaborative activity.

3.2   Moving from Interview to Intra-view

Based on Barad's diffractive methodology and the idea of intra-action, I developed an innovative method called 'intra-view'. Unlike interviews that primarily focus on collecting responses from humans with pre-existing positions such as the interviewer and interviewed, intra-view implies a process of non-hierarchical mutual becoming. This means that the researcher is simultaneously the intra-viewer and intra-viewed, co-creating and reacting to the relations between and among all elements involved in the study, including human participants, the digital platform used as well as everything else in the space where the collaborative design activity takes place.

3.3   Research Set-up and Data Collection

The participant recruited for my study is a university student doing a degree in Urban Design. Since the pandemic started in 2020, she has been doing her learning, designing, and researching almost entirely online, including completing the final year of her undergraduate degree as well as the first year of her Master's Degree remotely. The name of the participant is not included in the study for the purpose of anonymity. In order to ensure safety for both the researcher and participant, no face-to-face interaction took place throughout the duration of this study. The participant was invited to finish a small task which entailed building a paper toy with the researcher on Microsoft Teams which is an information communication software that allows people located in various parts of the world to see each other's faces and close surroundings and has real-time interactions. Both the researcher and participant were designers and were asked to keep their workplace normal and no special preparation work was needed. During the study, they both sat in front of the desk they usually worked on and kept their laptops at their usual positions, and had all the common design tools like pencils, markers, scissors, cutting mats in their rooms.

The whole meeting was roughly an hour long and was recorded audio-visually using a double- perspective filming system, which included Microsoft Team's built-in recording function which captured what was shown on the participant and researcher's screens during the intra-view as well as a camera filming them from the side. The researcher had a notebook and a pen next to her laptop using which she took observational and reflective notes during the intra-view (Fig. 1).

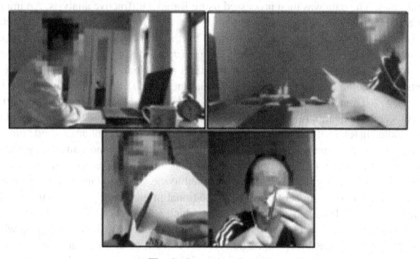

Fig. 1. Intra-view Set-up

The intra-view started with an unstructured conversation around the kind of activities the participant normally did on digital platforms like Zoom, Skype, Microsoft Teams, and what her general feelings were working with this kind of technology as a design student. This was to (1) get her more relaxed and open about talking about things related to digital platforms; (2) act as a warm-up activity to get the researcher and participant used to interacting with each other on Teams. After having an interesting chat where the participant shared some stories and her struggles working online as a designer, it was time for the collaboration task. The task was to build a 3D paper model collaboratively from a 2D drawing prepared before the meeting using a piece of paper, scissors and glue stick. The task required some light cutting, folding, thinking, comparing, and a lot of discussion between people. It was for both the researcher and the participant to decide how exactly the work was going to be split between them and how each part of the model can be made and put together remotely while they were in two different rooms.

There was a flexible time limit of 40 min and no assessment at the end of the task. The outcome of the task was not measured or judged in any kind of way. The participant was also allowed to stop and finish the activity at any time if she felt like it was an impossible task to complete. Luckily although there were more puzzles than certainty, more questions than answers, the task was finished successfully. At the end of the intra-view, there was a 5-min reflection period where the researcher and participant discussed their thoughts and feelings as well as some unexpected insights based on their professional practices.

4   Data Analysis and Findings

4.1   Diffractive Analysis

The data collected from the intra-view included video clips, transcripts, and observational notes. The data was then processed using Barad's diffractive analysis. An important aspect of the diffractive analysis is to move away from only perceiving the activity through the words and expressions said by the participant, but also through the researcher's experience of intra-actively being part of the ongoing task. Drawing the researcher's attention to the intra-actions made it possible to reveal how different elements in the collaborative tasks existed in relation to each other in the duration of the intra-view. All material intra-actions were equally significant regardless of being part of human's communicational intentions or not. Almost all objects included in the videos were studied in terms of how their status was facilitated by other nonhumans and humans.

Take the participant's screen as an example, it had a static and quite stable spatial relation to the desk and other objects on the desk thanks to gravity and the surface friction co-provided by the desk. It was attached to the vertical plate of her laptop in a firm way that made it subject to a smooth rotational motion in reference to the surface plane of her desk. It had a very small weight which was a relief for the flatness of the desk but also indirectly contributed to the degree of vibration the desk was having when the laptop volume was turned up. The screen was of a certain size and shape which allowed it to act as a stable visual navigator for the participant that directly co-drew her body posture with the materiality of the chair, her slippers, and the floor, etc. The screen also contributed to the distance between itself and the participant sitting on the chair. The usual position of the screen also affected the amount and direction of light arrived at the areas close to the screen and created rectangular shadows implying that 'this area maybe not be a great desk space to do drawing and cutting'. It can also display certain visual information that had functional meanings to humans and indicate what they can do with it. It also created a sense of work or a sense of relaxation when it displayed different visual-audio abilities. Also, according to the participant, what could be done with the screen had an accumulating effect that changed the meaning of her desk, her bedroom, and even her bed to her in the past few months. The screen was made of a material that was stronger than the air and weaker than some objects in the workspace like scissors and penknives. The immediate surrounding area of the screen thus became a dangerous area the scissors needed to avoid having an encounter with. There are much more connections that can be made as the relations that the screen was in were like a huge net, each growing and merging into other networks. The screen was constantly joining and leaving intra-actions, creating new ones and re-connecting old ones in the flow of time. These human-human/human-nonhuman/nonhuman-nonhuman intra- actions related to each other and co-created all the movements the participant and researcher were making during the task. As the data analysis process went on, more and more of these relations were revealed and a few patterns started to emerge.

4.2 Mediated Sensations

One major challenge in the collaboration was that the participant and the researcher could not directly sense the physicality of each other's material in hand and their surroundings. If they were in the same space, communicating the physical parameters of an object could easily be done by passing the object from one person to the other. The way the object performs its materiality such as sensations of weight, softness, ductility, elasticity is through direct intra-action with the materiality of the human. In a digital environment, however, the physical properties of an object had to be transferred to senses that can be captured by the digital platform to be communicated. Take the piece of paper they were using as an example: to check if the participant and the researcher were using the same type of paper, they could only sense the material when it encountered other objects and created visual/audio signals that could be transmitted by Microsoft Teams. These signals included their facial expressions while folding the paper, the sound made when the paper was being cut by scissors and rubbed by humans' hands, the creases on folded papers, the roughness of cutting edges, etc. When it comes to properties like sizes and shapes, the team members had to look for reference objects to check whether their workpieces ended up aligning in size and shape. They ended up using their student ID card as references and each pressed their component firmly against their student card to figure out the geometrical relation between them (Fig. 2).

Fig. 2. The participant and the researcher trying to match the shapes and sizes of their paper parts by showing each other the relative distance between the bottom of their parts and the bottom of their student IDs

Here, the shapes and sizes of their pieces were converted into the distances between their edges and the edges of the cards. This kind of mediation in sensations appeared continuously in the collaboration and provoked ways of using everyday objects that people could not have imagined in face-to-face collaboration. It was both a challenge in interaction and a door to exploring innovative ways of using ordinary objects in design activities.

4.3 Regionalisation, De-regionalisation and Re-regionalisation

Another major discovery was that the space in the rooms where the researcher and participant worked was continuously being regionalised, de-regionalised, and re-regionalised by the digital platform throughout the activity. The regionalisation process in which different parts of the room facilitated different types of sensory communications to take place was largely achieved by the various physical parts of the device that supported the running of the digital software. The regionalising process emerged at the times when any of the collaborators changed the main type of information the platform was carrying. For instance, when they started to cut their shapes from paper, a necessity of keeping track of what each other was making emerged. Both of them lifted their hands, scissors, and papers and tried their best to keep in that position throughout their cutting process. In situations like this when the conversation required them to exchange the visual properties of the product they were building, such as dimensions, angles, and shapes, the area of the room covered by their webcams became the region in which they had to stay in to carry on the communication. Later on in the task, the communicative focus switched from visual to other senses such as sound, the space was re-regionalised and facilitated a new sphere of physical movement each collaborator could make. For instance, when the researcher left her desk to look for her student ID card, the conversation between them was still happening. Since the researcher told the participant before she left her desk what she was going to do, the communicative requirement changed and the participant did not need to have the researcher's head on her screen. The only need the researcher had was to not get too far away from her laptop so that her voice was still within the area covered by the audio recording system of her laptop. As the communicative requirement changed, the regionalisation dissolved and no longer restricted her body movements in the way it did before. This is a unique characteristic of online collaboration, as in offline interactions the participant would share the vision of the researcher's desk and her surroundings. All sensations would be directly accessed, whereas in digitally mediated interactions, the physical space they were in was constantly being regionalised, de-regionalised, and re-regionalised by the digital platform.

5 Conclusions and Future Design Education

It can be concluded that digital platforms are far more than facilitators of human-human interaction, but play an active role in collaborative design activities. For design educators and researchers, the regionalisation, de-regionalisation, and re-regionalisation phenomenon can open some potential opportunities embedded in the use of digital technologies in online design education. Firstly, the reconfiguration of room space by the digital can be referenced while developing digital design studio layouts for online teaching and learning. Secondly, design educators could take this phenomenon as an advantage and interact with students in a new way that guides students to explore new ways to use digital devices and interact with their surroundings. Finally, this study has potentially set up a new pathway to studying the roles technologies play in design education that takes into account the increasingly blurred boundary between humans and technology in the changing environment of the 21st century.

References

1. Barad, K.: Posthumanist performativity: toward an understanding of how matter comes to matter. Signs: J. Women Culture Soc. **28**(3), 801–831 (2003)
2. Barad, K.: Meeting the Universe Halfway: Quantum Physics and the Entanglement of Matter and Meaning. Duke University Press, Durham (2007)
3. Braidotti, R.: The Posthuman. Polity Press, Cambridge (2013)
4. Chappell, K.: From wise humanising creativity to (posthumanising) creativity. In: Creativity Policy, Partnerships and Practice in Education, pp. 279–306. Palgrave Macmillan, Cham (2018)
5. Chulvi, V., Mulet, E., Felip, F., García-García, C.: The effect of information and communication technologies on creativity in collaborative design. Res. Eng. Design **28**(1), 7–23 (2016). https://doi.org/10.1007/s00163-016-0227-2
6. Fleischmann, K.: Online design education: searching for a middle ground. Arts Humanit. High. Educ. **19**(1), 36–57 (2020)
7. García-García, C., Chulvi, V., Royo, M.: Knowledge generation for enhancing design creativity through co-creative virtual learning communities. Think. Skills Creat. **24**, 12–19 (2017)
8. Hart, J., Zamenopoulos, T., Garner, S.: The learningscape of a virtual design atelier. Compass: J. Learn. Teach. **2**(3), 1 (2011)
9. Kratzer, J., Leenders, R.T.A., Van Engelen, J.M.: Managing creative team performance in virtual environments: an empirical study in 44 R&D teams. Technovation **26**(1), 42–49 (2006)
10. Łapińska, J.: Creativity of human and non-human matter interwoven: autonomous sensory meridian response videos in a posthuman perspective. Creat. Stud. **13**(2), 336–350 (2020)
11. Leenders, R.T.A., Van Engelen, J.M., Kratzer, J.: Virtuality, communication, and new product team creativity: a social network perspective. J. Eng. Tech. Manage. **20**(1–2), 69–92 (2003)
12. Smith, D., Hedley, P., Molloy, M.: Design learning: a reflective model. Des. Stud. **30**(1), 13–37 (2009)
13. Tang, H.H., Lee, Y.Y., Gero, J.S.: Comparing collaborative co-located and distributed design processes in digital and traditional sketching environments: a protocol study using the function–behaviour–structure coding scheme. Des. Stud. **32**(1), 1–29 (2011)

Association of Knowledge with COVID-19 Vaccine Hesitancy Under Emergency: A Nationally Study in China

Chunpeng Zhu[1]($\boxtimes$), Jiayan Liu[1], Yanfeng Liu[2], and Hao Tan[1]

[1] Emergency Science Joint Research Center, Hunan University, Changsha, China
chunpengzhu@hnu.edu.cn
[2] Million Education Group, Cambridge, UK

Abstract. Identifying and understanding the hesitancy degree of public COVID-19 vaccine in emergency may be helpful to the dissemination of vaccine-related public health information. Through a survey among the adult population of Chinese mainland (N = 1080) after the COVID-19 vaccine was approved for mass vaccination, it is found that although more than 80% of the public (87.8%) have a low hesitancy attitude towards COVID-19 vaccine, a considerable number of people still have a medium hesitancy and a high hesitancy attitude towards COVID-19 vaccine (the middle hesitancy rate is 9.8% and the high hesitancy rate is 2.4%). By multiple logistic regression, the subjective and objective knowledge levels of medium-high hesitancy group and low hesitancy group in COVID-19 vaccine were compared. The results showed that there were significant differences in subjective and objective knowledge levels between medium-high hesitancy group and low-hesitancy group in COVID-19 vaccine. Compared with those with low hesitancy, those with medium and high hesitancy have lower subjective knowledge level and objective knowledge level. The influence of subjective knowledge level on public vaccine hesitancy is significantly greater than that of objective knowledge. In addition, through multiple linear regression, the study found that the information channel had a significant impact on the public's subjective and objective knowledge. Receiving vaccine information from television, web pages, health professionals, health departments can promote subjective knowledge and objective knowledge, while receiving vaccine information from family and friends reduces subjective knowledge and objective knowledge. Considering the geographical location of the population in this study, the research results in this paper cannot be extended to the public in other countries. However, the method used in this paper is helpful for researchers to understand the hesitancy degree of COVID-19 vaccines in other places and its relationship with the public knowledge level of COVID-19 vaccines.

Keywords: COVID-19 vaccine hesitancy · Subjective knowledge · Objective knowledge · Information channel

1 Introduction

COVID-19 reached a global pandemic in March 2020. As of January 11th, 2022, COVID-19 has caused 308,458,509 infections and 5,492,595 deaths around the world [1]. At

P.-L. P. Rau (Ed.): HCII 2022, LNCS 13313, pp. 286–297, 2022.
https://doi.org/10.1007/978-3-031-06050-2_22

present, various countries have adopted policies to delay the spread of COVID-19, such as physical isolation, but these measures can't improve the immunity of the public, and the public still faces the risk of infection. At present, it is generally believed that promoting a sufficient proportion of the global public to vaccinate against the COVID-19 and build a collective immune barrier is the most effective way to restore the world to the state before the COVID-19 virus pandemic [2].

However, studies have shown that there are still some groups of people who are reluctant to receive vaccines. In the June 2020 study, Lazarus et al. surveyed 13,426 people in 19 countries to determine potential vaccine acceptance rates and analyze factors that affect the acceptance of the COVID-19 vaccine. Among them, 71.5% of respondents reported that they are likely to be vaccinated against COVID-19, but still 14.2% were neutral and 14.2% said they would not be vaccinated against COVID-19 [3]. Not everyone is willing to be vaccinated, which is commonly known as vaccine hesitancy. Vaccine hesitancy is defined as "delay in acceptance or refusal of vaccines despite availability of vaccine services." according to the research of World Health Organization's SAGE Working Group on Vaccine Hesitancy. As early as the 1960s, vaccine hesitancy has emerged as an academic topic, and researchers in scientific fields such as public health have conducted extensive research on it and produced some theoretical or empirical results [4, 4]. In 2019, the World Health Organization listed vaccine hesitancy as one of the top ten global health threats [6]. The hesitancy of the COVID-19 vaccine may reverse the efforts made by governments and people around the world to prevent and control the epidemic, and should be paid attention to by researchers.

Knowledge level is an important factor affecting public behavior, which has been confirmed in the research of Pieniak et al. [7]. Among the factors affecting the hesitancy of the COVID-19 vaccine, the level of knowledge is also an important decisive factor. Previous studies have shown that the level of knowledge about vaccines affects the probability of professionals to vaccinate themselves, and also affects the probability of professionals to recommend vaccines to patients. The findings of Martinello et al. on the determinants of influenza vaccination among nurses show that knowledge is an important factor influencing vaccination decisions. The higher the nurse's vaccine knowledge, the higher her own vaccination rate and the more willingness to promote influenza vaccine to her patients [8]. Knowledge level is a relatively complex psychological concept, and researchers generally divide knowledge level into subjective knowledge level and objective knowledge level. Subjective knowledge level refers to people's self-judgment of knowledge level in a certain field; objective knowledge level reflects people's actual knowledge ability in a certain field [9]. It should be noted that subjective and objective knowledge levels may have different effects on public attitudes. In previous studies, the level of subjective knowledge has been shown to be a strong predictor of public vaccine hesitancy, that is, the public's self-judgment about vaccine knowledge affects their decision to vaccinate. For example, Matthew et al. have found that public anti-vaccine attitudes are positively correlated with overconfidence [10]. Thus, increased levels of subjective knowledge are likely to increase anti-vaccine attitudes and generally increase the degree of public vaccine hesitancy. Objective knowledge can also have an impact on vaccine hesitancy, and in a study of specific populations such as the elderly, a lack of objective knowledge of influenza and vaccines was found to hinder vaccine uptake [11]. Lack of relevant knowledge about vaccines and vaccine-prevented diseases may lead to insufficient or biased public understanding of disease risks, the importance of vaccination, and vaccine risks, which will undoubtedly increase the public's vaccine hesitancy. At the same time, different types of knowledge may also influence public attitudes. In a study of climate change, researchers found that the more people knew about the causes of climate change, the more worried they were. However, the more that is known about the physical characteristics of climate change, the more negative or no significant impact it has on people's concerns [12].

After the COVID-19 vaccine began to be vaccinated around the world, some articles on the public's knowledge of the COVID-19 vaccine appeared. For example, Abdelhafiz et al. assessed the knowledge and attitude of the Egyptian public towards the COVID-19 vaccine through questionnaires [13]; Similarly, Reuben et al. also used a semi-structured questionnaire to measure the level of COVID-19 vaccine knowledge among the Nigerian public [14]. However, these studies only measured the public's objective knowledge level, did not involve the public's subjective knowledge level, nor did they study the relationship between the public's vaccine hesitancy and the public's knowledge level. With the comprehensive development of vaccination work, it is of great practical significance to carry out research on the relationship between public vaccine hesitancy and the public's subjective and objective knowledge levels. Therefore, this study intends to measure the subjective knowledge level and objective knowledge level of the public, and study their relationship with vaccine hesitancy. At the same time, this research intends to study the information channels that affect the public's knowledge level, so as to provide an effective way to change the public's subjective and objective knowledge level.

The latest research results show that there is still a considerable part of the public who are hesitant or rejecting the COVID-19 vaccine, so it is necessary to focus on researching and solving this problem [15–18]. Therefore, it is imperative to begin to understand the level of knowledge among vaccine hesitant group, and to use the findings to improve the status quo and facilitate global vaccination against Covid-19. To achieve these goals, we formulated three research objectives. First, the study determined the proportion of different levels of hesitancy in the Chinese adult population over the course of the survey. Then, we explored the influence of subjective knowledge level and objective knowledge level on different hesitant groups. Finally, the study determined the impact of different information channels on the subjective and objective knowledge levels. Research on information channels can help public health commissioners understand how to effectively adjust the transmission of health behavior information to effectively change the public's knowledge of vaccines level.

2   Method

2.1   Participant

The researchers conducted a nationwide survey of public COVID-19 vaccine hesitancy and knowledge from August 25, 2021 to August 27, 2021. A questionnaire on COVID-19 vaccine hesitancy and knowledge level was distributed through Baidu's survey platform. Adult respondents in mainland China were asked to complete the questionnaire anonymously. The questionnaire included the measurement of COVID-19 vaccine hesitancy, the measurement of public knowledge, and a survey of information channels. The questionnaire can effectively understand the public Vaccine hesitancy and level of knowledge.

The total sample covered citizens over the age of 18 from 31 provinces (autonomous regions/municipalities) in mainland China, and the study successfully recovered a total of 1098 questionnaires. In order to ensure the quality of the paper questionnaire filling and the validity of the answers, this study sets the attention detection question according to the attention detection method of Frankie et al. in the questionnaire survey [19]. And the samples that failed the attention detection were excluded. Finally, some questionnaires were removed according to whether the respondents answered the questions completely, and finally 1080 valid samples were obtained.

2.2 Vaccine Hesitancy

The degree of vaccine hesitancy for the Covid-19 vaccine was measured by five-item questions [20], all of which asked respondents to rate their responses using a 5-point scale. The first four project questions are vaccine safety evaluation: "Do you think the covid-19 vaccine is safe"; Vaccine effectiveness evaluation: "You think the COVID-19 vaccine is effective"; Level of trust in vaccine information: "You trust the information you receive about COVID-19 vaccinations"; and the purpose of the vaccination: "You are vaccinated just to be able to go to school or work", Answers to this section of the question range from "strongly disagree" to "strongly agree". Finally, we ask respondents about their overall hesitancy: "In general, how much do you think you are hesitant about getting vaccinated against COVID-19?", Answers to this part of the question range from "not at all hesitant" to "very hesitant". In this study, the response scores of vaccine safety, vaccine effectiveness, and vaccine information trust were coded from strongly agree (0 points) to strongly disagree (4 points), while the purpose of vaccination was reverse-coded to strongly agree (4 points) to strongly disagree (0 points), and respondents' overall hesitancy section was coded as "not at all hesitant" (0 points) to "very hesitant" (4 points). After summarizing the total scores of the 5 questions, it is divided into three vaccine hesitancy levels: low hesitancy (0–8), medium hesitancy (9–12), and high hesitancy (13–20) [21].

2.3 Knowledge Level

The measurement of knowledge level is divided into subjective knowledge level part and objective knowledge level part to comprehensively measure the knowledge level of respondents. First measure the level of subjective knowledge, asking respondents: "How would you rate your knowledge of the COVID-19 vaccine?" Responses to this question were scored using a 7-point Likert scale, ranging from "very unknown" (1 point) to "very well understood" (7 points) [22]. Afterwards, the study used nine items to measure respondents' objective knowledge level. These questions come from the Q&A section on the official World Health Organization website. This part is divided into states, causes, and consequences according to the nature of the problem. Each nature uses several item topics to examine the objective knowledge of the COVID-19 epidemic and/or the COVID-19 vaccine. The types of questions in this part are multiple-choice questions, and the answer is a specific response to the question or a non-true or true question. If the answer is correct, it will be counted as 1 point, and if the answer is incorrect or the answer is "don't know", it will be counted as 0 point. The total score of objective knowledge level is the total score of 9 items. For the convenience of analysis, the research reassigns the scores of subjective knowledge level and objective knowledge level to 0–5 points according to the percentage.

2.4   Information Channel

In the information channel section, participants were asked, "Where did you learn about the COVID-19 vaccine?" Participants were given seven choices: TV, Newspaper/Magazine, Web, Family/Friends, Health Professional, Health Department, Social Media. (1 = received information from this source, 0 = not received information from this source).

2.5   Sociodemographic

The sociodemographic variables used in this study were derived from existing evidence directly related to vaccine hesitancy. The questions involved gender, age, highest level of education, and income. Based on the guidelines for forming age categories from Chinese census data, we classified ages from ten years to ten years (eg 30–49, 40–49). According to the principle that the COVID-19 vaccine requires people to be over 18 years old when the research is carried out, we divide the minors into 0–18 years old.

2.6   Analysis Strategy

The analytical strategy consists of three elements related to the research objectives. First, the proportion of people who were classified as "low hesitant", "moderate hesitant" and "high hesitant" in the sample for the study period was calculated. Second, we performed multiple logistic regression analyses to determine the relationship between subjective knowledge, objective knowledge, and public vaccine hesitancy ratings. The medium hesitant group and the high hesitant group were combined into one group, which was compared with the low hesitant group on the variables of subjective knowledge and objective knowledge, and some demographic factors were also involved in the analysis. Subsequently, the study reassessed the model using the medium hesitant group as a reference category to determine the differences in subjective and objective knowledge levels between medium and high hesitant subjects. All associations between predictors and standard variables were expressed as adjusted odds ratios (AORs) with 95% confidence intervals. (i.e. adjust all predictors for all other covariates in each model). Third, the study used multiple linear regression to evaluate the impact of different information channels on the subjective and objective knowledge levels, and the impact of demographic factors on the subjective and objective knowledge levels was also incorporated into the model.

3 Result

3.1 Objective 1: Overall Situation of Vaccine Hesitancy in Mainland China

In this study, 87.8% (95%CI = 85.8%, 89.7%) of the respondents were low hesitant, 9.8% (95%CI = 8.0%, 11.6%) were moderately hesitant, 2.4% (95%CI = 1.5%, 3.3%) were high hesitancy. Among them, the middle-high hesitancy group accounted for 12.2%, accounting for about one-eighth of the total number. This conclusion supports the view that nearly one in eight Chinese public may not receive the COVID-19 vaccine on time or not be able to receive.

3.2 Objective 2: Knowledge Level Characteristics of Different COVID-19 Vaccine Hesitant Groups

The study first compared the knowledge level of the middle-high hesitant group with the low-hesitant group. Table 1 shows the full results from multiple logistic regression. It can be seen from Table 1 that compared with the low hesitancy group, the middle-high hesitancy group is more likely to have a lower subjective knowledge level ($e^{-1.059}$ = 0.683). That is to say, the middle-high hesitant thinks that they have less knowledge about the COVID-19 vaccine. Objective knowledge also showed the same trend, the middle-high hesitancy group was more likely to have a lower level of objective knowledge ($e^{-0.381}$ = 0.683). The middle-high hesitant group had less knowledge about the status, definition and reasons of vaccines. The comparison of regression coefficients shows that the subjective knowledge level has a greater impact on the degree of public vaccine hesitancy than the objective knowledge level, and is a key factor in identifying public vaccine hesitancy. In the model, gender, age, monthly income and education level did not have a significant effect (P > 0.05).

Second, we compared the high and medium hesitant groups. In the study sample, the high hesitant group was more likely to have a lower level of subjective knowledge than the medium hesitant group ($e^{-0.853}$ = 0.426). For the objective knowledge level, the model showed that the direction was consistent, that is, the high hesitant group may have a lower objective knowledge level than the medium hesitant group, but this effect was not statistically significant (P > 0.05). At the same time, the regression coefficient also shows that the influence of subjective knowledge on the degree of hesitancy is greater than that of objective knowledge. Similarly, gender, age, monthly income, and education level were not significant in differentiating vaccine hesitancy (Table 1).

Overall, subjective knowledge had a significant effect on distinguishing between medium-high and low hesitancy groups, and high and medium hesitancy groups in vaccines. Objective knowledge played a significant role in distinguishing between medium-high hesitant from low hesitant, but this effect was no longer significant in distinguishing vaccine high from medium hesitant. At the same time, with the increase of hesitancy level, the public's subjective knowledge level and objective knowledge level show a downward trend. The influence of subjective knowledge level on the public vaccine hesitancy level has always been greater than that of objective knowledge level. These all suggest that improving the level of subjective knowledge is the key to reducing the degree of public vaccine hesitancy.

Table 1. Multiple logistic regression of vaccine hesitancy and knowledge level.

Independent variable	Medium-High vs Low		High vs Medium	
	B	Exp(B)	B	Exp(B)
Subjective knowledge	−1.059*** (0.134)	0.347	−0.853** (0.260)	0.426
Objective knowledge	−0.381** (0.134)	0.683	−0.083 (0.302)	0.920
Gender (Female)	−0.053 (0.208)	0.948	−0.010 (0.481)	0.990
Age	0.042 (0.185)	1.043	0.628 (0.411)	1.87
Monthly income	0.125 (0.130)	1.133	−0.314 (0.304)	0.731
Education level	0.123 (0.183)	1.131	0.659 (0.461)	1.933
Constant	2.095* (0.857)		−1.317 (1.942)	
Chi-sqr	85.950		101.220	
Prob > chi	0.000		0.000	
N	1080			

*P < 0.05. **P < 0.01. ***P < 0.001; Gender is a male-referenced categorical variable.

3.3 Objective 3: Influence of Different Information Channels on Subjective and Objective Knowledge of Vaccines

In this section, we study the impact of different information channels on the public's subjective and objective knowledge. People who have received information about vaccines from TV (Coef = 0.129), newspapers and magazines (Coef = 0.151), websites (Coef = 0.131), health professionals (Coef = 0.262) and health departments (Coef = 0.187) have a higher subjective knowledge level, while the knowledge about vaccines obtained from family, friends and social media has no effect on the subjective knowledge level of the public (P > 0.05). At the same time, we observed the significant influence of monthly income and education level on subjective knowledge. The higher the monthly income, the higher the subjective knowledge (Coef = 0.110). The higher the education level, the higher the subjective knowledge (Coef = 0.120). At the same time, by comparing the regression coefficients, it can be found that the information channels that have the greatest impact on subjective knowledge are health professionals, health departments, newspapers and magazines, web pages, and television.

In terms of objective knowledge, those who have received vaccine information from television (Coef = 0.140) and health departments (Coef = 0.194) have higher objective knowledge. Received vaccine information from newspapers and magazines (Coef = −0.100), family and friends (Coef = −0.098) reduced the public's objective knowledge. Different from the influencing factors of subjective knowledge, web pages and health professionals that had a positive effect on the subjective knowledge level no longer had any influence on the objective knowledge level of the public (P > 0.05). We also observed the promotion effect of education level on objective knowledge, that is, the higher the education level, the higher the objective knowledge (Coef = 0.120). At the same time, age also has a positive effect on objective knowledge. With the increase of age, the public is more likely to have a higher level of objective knowledge (Coef = 0.148). By comparing the regression coefficients, it can be seen that the information channels that have the greatest impact on the level of objective knowledge are the health department, television, newspapers and magazines, family and friends.

Table 2. Multiple linear regression between knowledge level and information channel.

Independent variable	Subjective knowledge		Objective knowledge	
	Coef	95%CI	Coef	95%CI
Information channel				
Television	0.129^{**}	0.044, 0.215	0.140^{**}	0.056, 0.225
Newspapers and magazines	0.151^{**}	0.054, 0.248	-0.100^{*}	$-0.196, -0.005$
Web page	0.131^{**}	0.043, 0.219	0.054	$-0.033, 0.142$
Family and friends	-0.013	$-0.096, 0.069$	-0.098^{*}	$-0.180, -0.017$
health professionals	0.262^{***}	0.172, 0.351	0.066	$-0.023, 0.154$
health department	0.187^{***}	0.093, 0.281	0.194^{***}	0.101, 0.287
social media	-0.026	$-0.110, 0.058$	0.034	$-0.049, 0.117$
Gender (Female)	0.003	$-0.082, 0.088$	$-.038$	$-0.122, 0.046$
Age	0.024	$-0.052, 0.101$	0.189^{***}	0.113, 0.265
Monthly income	0.110^{***}	0.057, 0.163	0.001	$-0.051, 0.054$
Education level	0.120^{**}	0.044, 0.197	0.148^{***}	0.072, 0.223
Constant	2.305^{***}	1.966, 2.644	2.447^{***}	2.111, 2.783
Model statistics	$F(11, 1068) = 13.610; P < 0.001; R^2 = 0.123$		$F(11, 1068) = 8.480; P < 0.001; R^2 = 0.080$	

$^{*}P < 0.05.$ $^{**}P < 0.01.$ $^{***}P < 0.001$; Information channels are categorical variables, and each information channel is based on that has not received vaccine information from the information channel.

In general, we observed that information channels such as television, web pages, health professionals, and health departments promote both subjective and objective knowledge, while receiving vaccine information from family and friends reduces both subjective and objective knowledge. Although some of these factors were not statistically significant. At the same time, we observed significant effects of age, monthly income, and education level on both subjective and objective knowledge. Among them, education level has a significant role in promoting both subjective and objective knowledge.

4 Discussion

4.1 Vaccine Hesitancy and Knowledge Level

In the research sample, although more than 80% of the public (87.8%) reported low hesitancy for the COVID-19 vaccine, a considerable proportion of the public still reported medium and high hesitancy for the COVID-19 vaccine (the rate of medium hesitancy was 9.8% and High hesitancy rate 2.4%). These findings are similar to other estimates of China's Covid-19 vaccine studies, such as a recent study of public attitudes toward Covid-19 vaccines, which showed that of the 1,879 respondents who received the vaccine, 52.2% hoped to receive it as soon as it became available. While others (47.8%) will delay vaccination until they can confirm the safety of the vaccine [23]. The hesitancy status for covid-19 vaccines is also the same as for other types of vaccines. For example, in a survey of 2,124 caregivers of children under the age of 6, 60% expressed hesitancy about getting vaccinated. Among those who were hesitant, 26% sometimes expressed doubts about vaccinating their children, 31% delayed vaccination, and 3% refused to receive a particular vaccine [24]. As a result, there is a general hesitancy among some people to get any form of vaccine.

Regarding the level of knowledge, the study found that compared with those with low hesitancy, the level of subjective knowledge and objective knowledge of those with medium-high hesitancy were lower, and their awareness of the epidemic status and harm of COVID-19 epidemic was less. This is partly different from the study by Matthew et al. Specifically, the research on the level of subjective knowledge is at odds with Matthew's opinion on the level of subjective knowledge and attitudes towards vaccines [10], and Fernbach's views on the level of subjective knowledge and attitudes towards GM foods [22], However, the research on the objective knowledge level part is consistent with their view. Matthew and Fernbach et al. believed that disapproval attitude was positively correlated with overconfidence of knowledge level and negatively correlated with objective knowledge level. The data in this paper found that individuals with lower levels of subjective knowledge and objective knowledge were more likely to have medium-high hesitancy in the COVID-19 vaccine. Our results may be because the COVID-19 epidemic is a public health emergency, and the COVID-19 vaccine is a newly developed vaccine. The public has not had enough time and channels to fully understand the epidemic and vaccine, which reduces the public's subjective knowledge level, there is no overconfidence phenomenon.

Additionally, we can observe that the subjective knowledge level has a greater impact on the vaccine hesitancy level than the objective knowledge level. In addition, subjective knowledge has a significant effect in identifying the low hesitant group and the middle-high hesitancy group, the middle-hesitant group and the high-hesitancy group. While objective knowledge has a significant effect in distinguishing low-hesitant from medium-high hesitant, this effect is no longer significant when distinguishing medium-hesitant from high-hesitant. This may have two inspirations for us. First, the publicity policy should not only improve the public's objective knowledge level, but also focus on improving the public's subjective knowledge level, that is, Let the public increase their awareness of "their knowledge of the new crown vaccine", which is even more important than improving the public's objective knowledge of vaccine and epidemic. Second, there should be different priorities for the public with different levels of hesitancy. For the medium hesitant group, improving subjective knowledge and objective knowledge has a positive effect on promoting the lowering of the hesitant level. For the high hesitant group, improving subjective knowledge is obviously a more important direction when objective knowledge does not play a role in distinguishing between hesitant and high hesitant. We emphasize that for the high hesitant group, we should focus on improving their subjective knowledge level, so as to effectively reduce their degree of hesitancy.

4.2 Knowledge Level and Information Channel

In terms of information channels, we observed the effects of multiple information channels on subjective and objective knowledge. In short, we observed that information channels such as television, web pages, health professionals, and health departments promote both subjective and objective knowledge. Among them, television, health professionals, and health departments are relatively authoritative information channels, which shows that authoritative information channels are still an important way for the public to obtain vaccine knowledge and improve their own awareness of vaccine knowledge. Web pages also play a positive role in improving public knowledge, and should also be given the attention of relevant publicity policies. Receiving vaccine information from family and friends reduces both subjective and objective knowledge, which may be because the circle of friends has less authority. The information spread among family and friends may be mixed with some rumors or misinformation, so receiving information from family and friends has a negative impact. We emphasize that the government needs to strengthen and guide the public to obtain more relevant information from television, web pages, health professionals, and health departments, and control rumors, and spread positive information about vaccines, so as to increase the chances of vaccine hesitant people being exposed to correct information about vaccines. In addition, we also observed that some information channels show an opposite trend for subjective and objective knowledge levels: receiving vaccine information from newspapers and magazines increases the public's subjective knowledge, but limits the growth of the public's objective knowledge. This may be related to the inherent properties of newspapers and magazines: the accuracy of information disseminated by newspapers and magazines can generally be guaranteed, but their frequency of publication is low. Compared with other information channels with real-time characteristics, newspapers and magazines may have less effect on improving objective knowledge. Receiving vaccine information from social media did not increase the public's objective knowledge and subjective knowledge, which reminds us that the use of new information channels such as social media to spread information about epidemic and vaccines still requires further research.

On this basis, three sociodemographic factors are significantly correlated with the public's subjective and objective knowledge levels: age, education, and income. The older public has more objective knowledge. This suggests that older people may be more concerned with information about epidemic and vaccines than younger people. The more educated the public, the higher both subjective and objective knowledge. People with higher monthly incomes are more likely to think they are more knowledgeable about vaccines. The demographic characteristics found in this study have important practical implications. Based on these demographic characteristics, public health information can be targeted more precisely to groups that are more likely to have lower subjective and objective knowledge, that is, younger age, lower education, and lower income groups. Compared with general publicity, targeted and precise publicity has better cost-effectiveness.

4.3 Research Limitations

These findings should be interpreted in light of several limitations. First, this study employed a random sampling method when recruiting samples via the Internet, although this is a cost-effective method that allows for rapid collection of large samples. However, due to the limitations of online samples, this method inevitably suffers from sampling bias, and can't reach some people who can't access the Internet, such as some elderly people. Second, the current study is limited to one country, and the extent to which the findings can be generalized to other countries in the world is unknown. Crucially, many other countries must obtain estimates of the general population's degree of COVID-19 vaccine hesitancy. Identify the relationship between public vaccine hesitancy and knowledge levels in the country and improve its public information to maximize vaccine uptake. Despite these limitations, our findings provide important evidence on the degree of Chinese general public hesitancy about COVID-19 vaccine and its relationship to knowledge levels. We provide these findings with the hope that it will underscore the importance of understanding the level of knowledge that drives COVID-19 vaccine hesitancy and how to leverage various information channels to maximize the positive impact of public health information.

References

1. Data from the World Health Organization's Covid-19 Epidemic Dashboard. https://covid19.who.int/
2. Yang, J., et al.: Can a COVID-19 vaccination program guarantee the return to a pre-pandemic lifestyle? medRxiv (2021)
3. Lazarus, J.V., et al.: A global survey of potential acceptance of a COVID-19 vaccine. Nat. Med. 27, 225–228 (2021)
4. Dubé, E., et al.: Vaccine hesitancy: an overview. Hum. Vaccin. Immunother. 9(8), 1763–1773 (2013)
5. Bish, A., et al.: Factors associated with uptake of vaccination against pandemic influenza: a systematic review. Vaccine 29(38), 6472–6484 (2011)
6. MacDonald, N.E., SAGE Working Group on Vaccine Hesitancy: Vaccine hesitancy: definition, scope and determinants. Vaccine 33, 4161–4164 (2015)
7. Pieniak, Z., Aertsens, J., Verbeke, W.: Subjective and objective knowledge as determinants of organic vegetables consumption. Food Qual. Prefer. 21(6), 581–588 (2010)
8. Martinello, R.A., et al.: Correlation between healthcare workers' knowledge of influenza vaccine and vaccine receipt. Infect. Control Hosp. Epidemiol. 24(11), 845–847 (2003)
9. Raju, P.S., et al.: Differential effects of subjective knowledge, objective knowledge, and usage experience on decision making: an exploratory investigation. J. Consum. Psychol. 4(2), 153–180 (1995)

10. Motta, M., et al.: Knowing less but presuming more: Dunning-Kruger effects and the endorsement of anti-vaccine policy attitudes. Soc. Sci. Med. **211**, 274–281 (2018)
11. Lau, J.T., et al.: Prevalence of influenza vaccination and associated factors among community-dwelling Hong Kong residents of age 65 or above. Vaccine **24**(26), 5526–5534 (2006)
12. Shi, J., Visschers, V.H., Siegrist, M., Arvai, J.: Knowledge as a driver of public perceptions about climate change reassessed. Nat. Clim. Chang. **6**(8), 759–762 (2016)
13. Abdelhafiz, A.S., et al.: Knowledge, perceptions, and attitude of Egyptians towards the novel coronavirus disease (COVID-19). J. Commun. Health **45**(5), 881–890 (2020)
14. Reuben, R.C., Danladi, M.M., Saleh, D.A., Ejembi, P.E.: Knowledge, attitudes and practices towards COVID-19: an epidemiological survey in North-Central Nigeria. J. Commun. Health **46**(3), 457–470 (2021)
15. İkiışık, H., Sezerol, M.A., Taşçı, Y., Maral, I.: COVID-19 vaccine hesitancy: a community-based research in Turkey. Int. J. Clin. Pract. **75**, e14336 (2021)
16. Castellano-Tejedor, C., Torres-Serrano, M., Cencerrado, A.: Unveiling Associations of COVID-19 vaccine acceptance, hesitancy, and resistance: a cross-sectional community-based adult survey. Int. J. Environ. Res. Public Health **18**(23), 12348 (2021)
17. Cerda, A.A., García, L.Y.: Hesitation and refusal factors in individuals' decision-making processes regarding a coronavirus disease 2019 vaccination. Front. Public Health **9**, 1–10 (2021)
18. Maraqa, B., Nazzal, Z., Rabi, R., Sarhan, N., Al-Shakhra, K., Al-Kaila, M.: COVID-19 vaccine hesitancy among health care workers in Palestine: a call for action. Prev. Med. **149**, 106618 (2021)
19. Kung, F.Y.H., et al.: Are attention check questions a threat to scale validity? Appl. Psychol. **67**(2), 264–283 (2018)
20. Opel, D.J., et al.: Validity and reliability of a survey to identify vaccine-hesitant parents. Vaccine **29**(38), 6598–6605 (2011)
21. Amin, A.B., et al.: Association of moral values with vaccine hesitancy. Nat. Hum. Behav. **1**(12), 873–880 (2017)
22. Fernbach, P.M., et al.: Extreme opponents of genetically modified foods know the least but think they know the most. Nat. Hum. Behav. **3**(3), 251–256 (2019)
23. Jiang, R.: Knowledge, attitudes and mental health of university students during the covid-19 pandemic in china. Child Youth Serv. Rev. **119**, 105494 (2020)
24. Du, F., Chantler, T., Francis, M.R., Sun, F.Y., Hou, Z.: The determinants of vaccine hesitancy in china: a cross-sectional study following the changchun changsheng vaccine incident. Vaccine **38**(47), 7464–7471 (2020)

Intercultural Design for Well-being and Inclusiveness

Case Study on the UI Design of Health Management Apps for Patients with Hypertension Based on User Need

Liyan Cao^(✉) (ID)

Graduate School, Industrial Design, Hongik University, 94 Wausan-ro, Mapo-gu, Seoul 04066, Korea
caoyan7604670@gmail.com

Abstract. Hypertension is one of the most common chronic diseases, which needs long-term detection, management and treatment, Hypertension has brought a great burden to patients' life. Hypertension health management is a pressing issue for people with hypertension. Fast, effective and comfortable hypertension management has become a key consideration for designers. This paper analyzes and studies a variety of health management apps for patients with hypertension. It aims to provide effective basic information of UI design for the development of new hypertension self-management apps.

This paper adopts the methods of literature investigation, interview investigation and case comparative analysis. In order to understand the characteristics and needs of older, middle-aged and adolescent patients with hypertension. Through the investigation of the information structure of the functions used in the app and the five elements of layout, color, icon, font and chart in the GUI design, combined with the deep access survey results, this paper analyzes the advantages and disadvantages of the UI design of the three apps.

The study found that: all three apps were more suitable for adolescents and middle-aged hypertensive patients in terms of information structure and GUI design. In general, the user classification is not clear across apps, and the content of the information structure is inconsistent with the functional needs of the patient groups. In terms of GUI design, the difficulty of identifying and obtaining information is also different. The UI design of hypertension health management apps should be carried out according to the characteristics and requirements of different patient groups.

Keywords: User needs · Hypertension · Health management app · Case studies

1 Introduction

1.1 Background and Purpose

Hypertension is a common and frequently-occurring disease in the world [1], which is one of the most common chronic diseases, and needs long-term monitoring, management and treatment. It is easy to cause damage and pathological changes of important organs such as brain, heart and kidney, and lead to serious diseases such as stroke, myocardial infarction and renal failure, which affect patients' labor ability and quality of life, and even die, and seriously threaten human health [2]. Age is an important factor causing hypertension, and the aging of the population leads to the increase of hypertension patients. According to epidemiological investigation, the incidence of hypertension in the elderly in the world is about 55% [3]. In addition, some bad living habits and eating habits in today's society, as well as various pressures, have also caused an increase in the incidence of hypertension, and patients with hypertension are becoming younger and younger. In 2015, there were more than 1.1 billion patients with hypertension in the world, and there were more patients with blood pressure-related diseases [4]. It is estimated that by 2025, the incidence of hypertension in the world will increase by 30% on the existing basis [5]. According to the "Report on Nutrition and Chronic Diseases of Chinese Residents (2015)" released by the Information Office of the State Council on June 30th, 2015, the number of hypertension patients in China is 270 million, of which the prevalence rate of hypertension among residents over 18 years old has reached 25.2%, and the prevalence rate of hypertension increases significantly with age [6]. On April 7th, 1978, the World Health Organization and the International Society for Federation of Cardiology decided to designate May 17th as "World Hypertension Day", which aims to arouse people's attention to the prevention and treatment of hypertension [7]. Health management of hypertension is an urgent problem for patients with hypertension. Fast, effective and comfortable hypertension management has become a key consideration for designers. The design of health management app is constantly innovating, and the market demand for functional requirements and interface design of hypertension health management app is getting higher and higher. The use of different hypertension management APPs was analyzed. The purpose is to provide effective basic information for user interface design for developing a new hypertension self-management APP.

1.2 Scope and Method

This paper adopts the methods of literature investigation, interview investigation and case comparative analysis. Through literature investigation, we know the definition of hypertension, the reasons of hypertension, the symptoms and hazards of hypertension. In order to understand the characteristics and needs of hypertensive patients of three different age groups, 20 subjects were selected from adolescent, middle-aged and old-aged hypertensive patients by using the method of interview investigation in quantitative analysis. According to the criteria of download volume, score and comprehensive function, three hypertension health management APPs were selected as research objects in Apple App Store, which are Smart Blood Pressure, Songaree Blood Pressure and Blood Pressure++. For the patients, this paper analyzes the use function and interface design of three different hypertension management APPs based on the comprehension, readability, fatigue, intuition and coherence of information such as layout, color, icon, text and chart. Through the careful investigation of the information structure of the functions used in APP and the five elements of layout, color, icon, font and chart in GUI design, the advantages and disadvantages of its APP interface design are analyzed combined with the investigation results of deep access.

2 Investigation and Analysis of Patients with Hypertension

The method of interview survey was used to conduct in-depth interview survey on hypertensive patients of different ages, and analyze the characteristics and needs of different hypertensive patients. In order to do a good job of investigation and analysis, it is necessary to understand the definition, classification, reasons, symptoms and hazards of hypertension.

2.1 Definition and Classification of Hypertension

(1) Definition and classification of hypertension

Hypertension refers to a clinical syndrome characterized by increased systemic arterial blood pressure (systolic blood pressure and/or diastolic blood pressure) (systolic blood pressure $\geq$ 140 mmHg, diastolic blood pressure $\geq$ 90 mmHg), which may be accompanied by functional or organic damage of heart, brain, kidney and other organs [8].

Hypertension has become a major global public health problem, and the definition and classification of hypertension are slightly different in different countries around the world. The specific grades of hypertension are shown in Table 1 [9]:

Table 1. Hypertension grading in each guideline clinic

Hypertension grade	Systolic pressure (mmHg)		diastolic pressure (mmHg)
2017 new guidelines for hypertension in the United States			
Grade 1 hypertension	130–139	And/or	80–89
Grade 2 hypertension	$\geq$140	And/or	$\geq$90
New blood pressure guidelines for universities in Europe 2018, China 2018, and Japan 2019			
Grade 1 hypertension	140–159	And/or	90–99
Grade 2 hypertension	160–179	And/or	100–110
Grade 3 hypertension	$\geq$180	And/or	$\geq$110
2020 new International Guidelines for Hypertension			
Grade 1 hypertension	140–159	And/or	90–99
Grade 2 hypertension	$\geq$160	And/or	$\geq$100

At present, normal blood pressure (SBP < 120 mmHg and DBP < 80 mmHg), normal high value [SBP 120–139 mmHg and/or DBP 80–89 mmHg] and hypertension [SBP $\geq$ 140 mmHg and/or DBP $\geq$ 90 mmHg] are used to classify blood pressure levels in China. The above classification is applicable to adults of any age over 18 years old [10].

Hypertension in China is defined as measuring blood pressure in clinic three times on different days without using antihypertensive drugs, with SBP $\geq$ 140 mmHg and/or DBP $\geq$ 90 mmHg. SBP $\geq$ 140 mmHg and DBP < 90 mmHg were isolated systolic hypertension. The patient has had hypertension in the past and is currently using anti-hypertensive drugs. Although the blood pressure is lower than 140/90 mmHg, it should still be diagnosed as hypertension [10]. The classification of blood pressure in China is shown in Table 2:

Table 2. Blood pressure level grading

Grade	SBP (mmHg)	DBP (mmHg)
Normal blood pressure	<120 And	<80
Normal high value	120–139 And/or	80 –89
Hypertension	≥140 And/or	≥90
Grade 1 hypertension (mild)	140–159 And/or	90–99
Grade 2 hypertension (moderate)	160–179 And/or	100–109
Grade 3 hypertension (severe)	≥180 And/or	≥110
Isolated systolic hypertension	≥140 And	<90

(2) Hypertension classification

Clinically, hypertension can be divided into primary hypertension and secondary hypertension [11].

Essential hypertension is an independent disease with elevated blood pressure as its main clinical manifestation and unclear etiology, accounting for more than 90% of all hypertensive patients [12].

Secondary hypertension is also called symptomatic hypertension. The etiology is clear in this kind of disease. Hypertension is only one of the clinical manifestations of this disease, and blood pressure can rise temporarily or persistently. Patients with secondary hypertension have higher risk of cardiovascular disease, stroke and renal insufficiency, and the etiology is often neglected, which results in delayed diagnosis.

2.2 Reasons, Symptoms and Harm of Hypertension

There are many reasons of hypertension, but at present, medicine has not fully recognized the reasons of hypertension. Some hypertension diseases are caused by a single reason, and some hypertension diseases are caused by various reasons. The factors related to hypertension have been found, such as heredity, age, diet, region, mental stress, smoking, obesity, drugs, diabetes and so on [13]. Among them, heredity, age, region and drugs are uncontrollable factors, while diet, mental stress, smoking, obesity, diabetes and other factors can be regulated and controlled by self-management methods such as living habits, drugs and exercise.

Different hypertensive patients have different symptoms and reactions. The most typical symptoms are: no symptoms, dizziness, headache, irritability, palpitation, insomnia, inattention, memory loss, limb numbness, bleeding (epistaxis, fundus hemorrhage, cerebral hemorrhage, etc.) [13].

The harm of hypertension not only reasons many diseases, but also is prone to pathological changes. The most common diseases are coronary heart disease, heart failure, cerebrovascular diseases (cerebral hemorrhage), kidney diseases, retinopathy and so on [14].

2.3 Characteristics of Patients with Hypertension

Hypertensive patients are divided into elderly hypertensive patients, middle-aged hypertensive patients and adolescent hypertensive patients according to their age. Hypertensive patients of different ages have different cognition, regulation and control of hypertension because of their different physiology and psychology. Through literature investigation and interview investigation, the characteristics of hypertensive patients are summarized as follows.

(1)   The characteristics of elderly patients with hypertension
①   The incidence rate is high

The incidence of hypertension among the elderly is very high, which is the main group of hypertension patients. Data show that the prevalence rate of hypertension among people aged $\geq$ 60 in China reached 58.9% in 2012, an increase of about 20% compared with 2002 [15].

②   The adjustment ability decreases

With the increase of age, the physiological function of the elderly gradually declines, which easily affects their blood pressure regulation ability and body arterial elasticity. The ability to regulate blood pressure decreases, and it is easy to cause repeated increases in blood pressure due to factors such as diet, regional environment, emotional and mental stress, smoking and drinking [16]. The elasticity of large arteries of the body decreases, the stiffness of arteries increases, and severe arteriosclerosis is easy to occur [17].

③   Hypertension has many complications [18]

Among hypertensive patients, elderly hypertensive patients are more likely to cause hypertension complications than other age groups, and there are many complications. Among the related complications, 39.8% were complicated with diabetes mellitus, 51.6% with hyperlipidemia, 52.7% with coronary heart disease, 19.9% with renal insufficiency and 48.4% with cerebrovascular disease [19].

④   Feeling powerless about hypertension

Hypertension is a high-risk chronic disease, which takes a long time to self-manage and the cure rate is extremely low. Slight relaxation in management and control may cause other complications or aggravate the degree of hypertension, and endure physiological pain, mental torture and family economic burden caused by hypertension while suffering physiological degradation. It is easy to lead to mental stress, loss of confidence and even depression of the elderly. For the long process of hypertension management, elderly hypertensive patients will have a deep sense of powerlessness.

⑤ Insufficient cognition of hypertension [20].

During the investigation, it is found that the elderly have great deficiencies in their understanding of hypertension, which are mainly manifested in two aspects: Firstly, they have insufficient understanding of the reasons of hypertension, and there are many reasons for hypertension, so they need to pay attention to these inducements at all times in the process of hypertension management. Secondly, there is insufficient understanding of the symptoms of hypertension. Different degrees of hypertension have different symptoms, and different patients have different symptoms because of their different physical qualities.

⑥ Lack of attention to hypertension

Patients with hypertension do not respond most of their lives, which easily gives the elderly patients an illusion of their own health, so there will be bad behaviors such as not taking antihypertensive drugs on time, taking too much sodium salt, and being too excited. When blood pressure rises and there are obvious symptoms, antihypertensive drugs will be taken continuously.

⑦ Misunderstanding of antihypertensive drugs

There are many kinds of antihypertensive drugs. Not only do different degrees of hypertension take different antihypertensive drugs, but even patients with the same degree of hypertension need to take different antihypertensive drugs because of their own medical records and physical factors. Many patients often consult the surrounding hypertensive patients directly when the antihypertensive drugs they take have adverse reactions, poor antihypertensive effects or need to change antihypertensive drugs because of taking certain antihypertensive drugs for a long time without consulting professional doctors. These hypertensive patients are easy to take antihypertensive drugs that are not suitable for themselves.

If you don't follow the doctor's instructions, the patient will automatically reduce the number and dosage of antihypertensive drugs. Give up taking antihypertensive drugs even when blood pressure is normal.

⑧ The utilization rate of sphygmomanometers and related management design products is low.

Through the investigation of elderly patients with hypertension, it is found that the utilization rate of sphygmomanometer is very low, and blood pressure is measured only when the body has dizziness, headache, fatigue, palpitation and other symptoms. Sometimes, even if the blood pressure is high, the symptoms of patients are not obvious, which often does not attract attention and does not measure blood pressure. When the symptoms are obvious, the degree of hypertension has worsened and even caused other complications. Most design products of hypertension management have many functions and poor guidance. It is difficult for elderly patients to use these products because of presbyopia, which leads to low utilization rate of design products of hypertension management.

(2) Characteristics of middle-aged hypertensive patients
① Lack of cognition of hypertension [20].
Most of the middle-aged hypertensive patients suffer from hypertension for a short time, and there are many and difficult knowledge about hypertension, so it is very difficult to fully understand its contents in a short time.

② Insufficient attention to hypertension
Middle-aged people work every day, even need to stay up late to work overtime when they are very busy, take care of their children in life, and neglect their own health. Therefore, the busy life leads to neglect of the monitoring and management of hypertension.

③ Misunderstanding of antihypertensive drugs
Similar to elderly hypertensive patients. There are many kinds of antihypertensive drugs. Not only do different degrees of hypertension take different antihypertensive drugs, but even patients with the same degree of hypertension need to take different antihypertensive drugs because of their own medical records and physical fitness factors. Many patients buy and take antihypertensive drugs directly because of the good effect of antihypertensive drugs taken by patients they know around them without consulting professional doctors, so these patients are easy to take antihypertensive drugs that are not suitable for themselves.

In addition, middle-aged patients also do not follow the doctor's instructions, and patients automatically reduce the number and dosage of antihypertensive drugs. Even give up taking antihypertensive drugs when blood pressure is normal.

④ The utilization rate of sphygmomanometer is low
Middle-aged people are busy with their work and need to do housework and take care of their children, so they are measured once every many days. In addition, blood pressure will be measured frequently when the body has dizziness, headache, fatigue, palpitation and other symptoms. In ordinary life, people would forget to measure blood pressure.

⑤ High utilization rate of relevant management design products
Because the utilization rate of sphygmomanometers is low when busy at work, middle-aged patients often use watches that monitor blood pressure from time to time or use blood pressure management APP to download software to record and manage their own blood pressure and learn more about hypertension.

(3) The characteristics of adolescent hypertension patients
① Lack of cognition of hypertension [20].
Hypertension and its related contents are many, and the technical terms are obscure, which is difficult for non-professional medical workers to understand.

② Insufficient attention to hypertension
Teenagers blindly think that they are strong, and they don't pay attention to hypertension because they don't know enough about it.

③ Misunderstanding of antihypertensive drugs

There is no need to take antihypertensive drugs in the primary stage of hypertension, and life intervention can be used, but many patients take antihypertensive drugs immediately after confirming hypertension. Similar to middle-aged and elderly patients. There are many kinds of antihypertensive drugs, and they don't know about drugs, so they take drugs recommended by others directly, but don't take antihypertensive drugs suitable for themselves. Do not follow the doctor's instructions and take medicine on time.

④ The utilization rate of sphygmomanometer is low

There are no adverse symptoms in ordinary life, so I often forget to measure blood pressure.

⑤ High utilization rate of relevant management design products

Watches that monitor blood pressure from time to time and APP software for blood pressure management have a high utilization rate, which can always know the blood pressure status and is small and convenient to carry, so more related management design products are used for teenagers.

2.4 Needs Analysis of Hypertensive Patients

Different age groups have different needs, so the elderly, middle-aged and adolescent patients with hypertension were investigated and analyzed. 10 adult hypertensive patients (adolescent patients and middle-aged patients) and 10 elderly hypertensive patients were selected as interviewees to conduct in-depth interview investigation to understand the needs of hypertensive patients of different ages.

(1) The needs of elderly hypertensive patients [20]
① Can answer the question of hypertension at any time

The elderly have weak memory and are easy to forget. They don't need to remember a lot of knowledge about hypertension, and can answer questions and provide help for the elderly patients at any time. It can explain hypertension test results and data analysis for elderly patients in a simple way and solve the problem that the elderly have insufficient understanding of hypertension and their own hypertension degree.

② Become a "obedient"

There is no need for elderly patients to record their daily blood pressure, medication and diet. According to their own physical condition, they are recommended to adjust their blood pressure and remind them to take medication every day, which can solve the misunderstanding of antihypertensive drugs and the neglect of hypertension.

③ Don't measure blood pressure every day

Under the condition of not affecting the life of the elderly, it can automatically transmit the blood pressure measurement results every day, automatically record the information synchronously, and does not need to measure with a sphygmomanometer every day, which can solve the problem of low utilization rate of sphygmomanometer and related management design products.

(2) The needs of middle-aged patients
① Can answer the question of hypertension at any time
Middle-aged people have many responsibilities and great work pressure. They also need to be able to help them answer the problem of hypertension at any time, explain their own hypertension degree to middle-aged patients in a concrete and easy-to-understand way, and reduce the memory burden of middle-aged people, which can solve the problems of middle-aged people's insufficient understanding of hypertension and their own hypertension degree and wrong understanding of antihypertensive drugs.

② Targeted blood pressure management methods
According to the life rhythm and working status of middle-aged hypertensive patients, we can recommend targeted management methods, which can solve the problem of neglecting hypertension.

③ Don't measure blood pressure every day
It can automatically input blood pressure measurement results every day, and record information automatically and synchronously without using sphygmomanometer to measure every day, which can solve the problem of low utilization rate of sphygmomanometer.

(3) The needs of adolescent hypertensive patients
① Can answer the question of hypertension at any time
Teenagers have heavy academic burden and lack curiosity and interest in boring knowledge of hypertension. They also need to be able to help them solve hypertension problems at any time, which can solve the problem that young people have insufficient understanding of hypertension and their own hypertension degree.

② Targeted blood pressure management methods
It can recommend targeted management methods according to their own life rhythm and learning status, which can solve the problem of neglecting hypertension.

③ Don't measure blood pressure every day
It can automatically input blood pressure measurement results every day, and record information automatically and synchronously without using sphygmomanometer to measure every day, which can solve the problem of low utilization rate of sphygmomanometer.

3   Cases Investigation and Analysis

3.1   Case Investigation and Analysis

The investigation object of the case is the related hypertension management APP. According to the download volume, score and comprehensive function, three hypertension health management APPs were selected as the research objects in Apple App Store, namely Smart Blood Pressure (SmartBP), Blood Pressure++ (Hypertension Tracker) and Songaree Blood Pressure. The specific contents are shown in Table 3.

Table 3. Survey objects

APP	Smart Blood Pressure（SmartBP）	Blood Pressure ++ （Hypertension Tracker）	Songaree Blood Pressure
logo			
score	4.3 points	4.2 points	5 points
Down loads	10000+	10000+	1000+
Methods	Can connect to Apple Watch	Can connect to Apple Watch	Use alone
Function	It can be connected to Apple Watch, blood pressure recorded manually or automatically synchronized through Apple Health, blood pressure charting, data analysis, sharing blood pressure information with doctors and other functions.	It can be connected to Apple Watch, blood pressure recorded manually or automatically synchronized through Apple Health, data analysis charts, data analysis, alerts and other functions.	Blood pressure, medication, diet, weight, diagnosis and other management functions, blood pressure chart, reminder function
Features	Reasonable layout, strong icon guidance, easy to use and understand, multi-functional	Simple layout, easy to use, few functions	Well laid out, easy to use, multi-functional

Through the investigation and analysis of the information structure of the functions used in APP and the five elements of layout, color, icon, font and chart in GUI design, this study analyzes the advantages and disadvantages of its APP interface design [21] combined with the investigation results of deep access.

(1) Information structure analysis

From the information structure point of view, the information structures of Smart Blood Pressure (Smart BP) and Songaree Blood Pressure in Figs. 1, 2 and 3 are similar, and they are all composed of three-level information structures from blood pressure, analysis, diet, drugs, shared icons to corresponding pages on the main information screen. Similar information structure enables users who use APP for the first time to easily find the desired information, which provides convenience for users to manage blood pressure. Although the information structure of Blood Pressure++ (Hypertension Tracker) is also composed of three-level information structure, the information structure and function are simpler than those of the previous two APPs from the main information screen through blood pressure, analysis and shared icons to the corresponding pages. In addition, Smart Blood Pressure and Blood Pressure++ can be connected with Apple Watch, which can synchronize blood pressure information from time to time and understand blood pressure trends in more detail. Songaree Blood Pressure needs to manually enter blood pressure values.

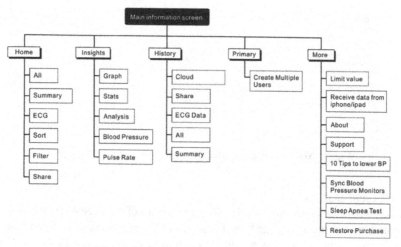

Fig. 1. Main information structure of Smart Blood Pressure

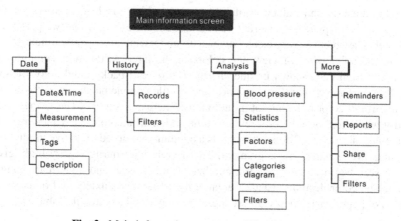

Fig. 2. Main information structure of blood pressure++

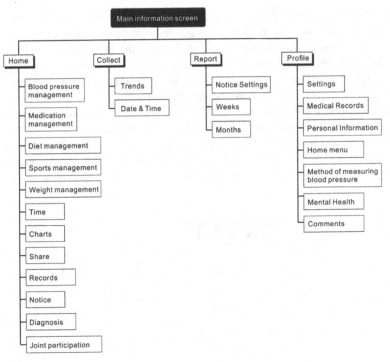

Fig. 3. Main information structure of Songaree Blood Pressure

(2) GUI design analysis

From the layout factors (as shown in Table 4), the layouts of the three APPs are obviously different. Although the homepage layout structure of Smart Blood Pressure and Songaree Blood Pressure is the same, they are divided into three parts: Header, Body and Footer, but the layout of Smart Blood Pressure is clearer, and it can be operated quickly even if it is used for the first time. The layout of Songaree Blood Pressure is somewhat vague in the classification and induction of information, which can lead to misunderstand. Although the home page layout structure of Blood Pressure++ only has two parts: Body and Footer. The layout is very clear, and easy to understand and operate quickly.

From the color point of view, the colors of the three APPs are harmonious and unified, and each has its own unique charm. The overall background color of Smart Blood Pressure adopts comfortable gray, and a little complementary color is used to make its overall color rich and not monotonous. The background of Blood Pressure++ is boldly white, and only blood pressure, time and chart are colored. That's neat. The overall color of Songaree Blood Pressure is a combination of red to orange gradient and white, and most icons also use gradient. The overall color purity is very high, giving people a very warm feeling. A large number of red is used, and a gradual change is adopted. The color design is easy to enlarge the irritability, anxiety and other uneasy emotions of hypertensive users, and reduces their goodwill towards it (Table 5).

Table 4. Layout analysis

APP	Smart Blood Pressure	Songaree Blood Pressure
Layout	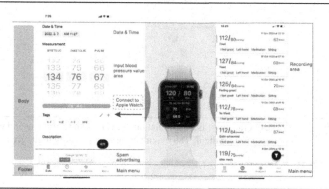	
Features	The layout structure of the home page is divided into three parts: header, body and footer. It is very clear and easy to understand, and easy to operate quickly.	The layout structure of the home page is divided into three parts: header, body and footer. There is some ambiguity in the classification and categorization of information, which can lead to misunderstandings.

APP	Blood Pressure ++
Layout	
Features	The layout structure of the homepage is divided into two parts: Body and Footer, which are clear and easy to understand, and easy to operate quickly.

Table 5. Color analysis

APP	Smart Blood Pressure	Blood Pressure ++
Color		
Features	The background color is a light blue-gray, and the symmetrical two function options in the home page use a complementary color of blue and orange. Most of the function options are in blue. The overall color is comfortable and harmonious.	The overall color is white, only the blood pressure value, time and the chart are colored, very simple.

APP	Songaree Blood Pressure	
Color		
Features	The overall color is a combination of red to orange gradient and white, and most icons also use gradient. The overall color purity is very high, giving people a very warm feeling.	

From the Icon design (as shown in Table 6), among the icons of the three APPs, there are icons with the same meaning, but their designs are completely different. For example, the Home icon of Smart Blood Pressure uses the graphics of the house, and the graphics and text content are in harmony. However, the Home icon in Songaree Blood Pressure is the same as its logo, so it is difficult to identify and easily misunderstand because it can't connect the meaning of words in the graphics. In addition, the graphics in the Insights icon of Smart Blood Pressure adopt column chart and broken line trend graphic elements, which makes it easy for users to know that the icon is mainly for data analysis of blood pressure, while the Analytics icon in Blood Pressure++ has a flower shape as a whole. From the matching degree of text meaning and graphic elements, the Insights icon of Smart Blood Pressure is easier to understand. The remaining icons are very easy to understand, some are common icons, and some icons have a high degree of matching between text and graphic elements.

Table 6. Comparative analysis of icons

APP	Smart Blood Pressure	Blood Pressure ++
Icon		
Features	The overall icons are annotated with graphics and text to convey icon information to users, deepen their memory, and guide their operations. To emphasize the information, some icons use bright colors to attract users' attention.	Apart from the logo, few graphics are used, only the navigation icon at the bottom of the app home page. Colors use black and gray.

APP	Songaree Blood Pressure	
Icon		
Features	A large number of icons are used in the APP, and the overall icons are very guiding and clearly express the meaning of the icons. Multiple colors are used to distinguish the different icons, while gradient colors are used to make the icons more prominent and not monotonous. For hypertensive patients, the use of multiple colors provides emotional comfort. However, some icons are not related to text annotations, so it is easy to misuse them without text annotations, such as the icon Home.	

From the chart analysis (as shown in Table 7), Songaree Blood Pressure mainly uses line chart and pie chart to analyze hypertension. The three colors in the line chart respectively represent the trend of systolic blood pressure, diastolic blood pressure and pulse for one week. Pie chart is an analysis chart of the results of blood pressure measurement during a week. Different color areas represent the proportion of different degrees of hypertension, for example, red is the proportion of dangerous hypertension. Songaree Blood Pressure's analysis of two charts is clear and understandable. Blood Pressure analysis of Blood Pressure++ mainly adopts the form of dot chart with straight lines. Although the colors representing systolic blood pressure, diastolic blood pressure and heart rate are marked with dots, there are lines and dots in the chart, and the dots are dense and similar in color, which not only looks very troublesome, but also is difficult to understand. In addition, there is no label in FACTORS chart, which makes it difficult to understand. Three kinds of charts are selected in Smart Blood Pressure, among which blood pressure chart analysis is a polyline chart representing systolic blood pressure and diastolic blood pressure in two colors, which is simple and easy to understand. In order to better understand the blood pressure, the systolic blood pressure was analyzed separately, and the columns of different colors respectively represented the proportion of different blood pressure degrees using the commonly used column chart. The last kind of Sinus Rhythm analysis chart is not a common chart, so it is difficult to understand, but the generated chart and supplementary instructions can be shared with doctors, and the contents of the chart can be understood by doctors.

From the font design point of view, it is found that all menus use bold type without pen strokes, which is easy to identify when reading information through the text in the above chart. In order to show the primary and secondary content and the consistency with the layout, the font size, thickness and other changes are appropriately adjusted to increase the sense of design.

By taking the comprehension, readability, fatigue, intuition, coherence and other information of layout, color, icon, text, chart and other information as analysis criteria, a comparative analysis is made (as shown in Fig. 4). Smart Blood Pressure has the best GUI design, and the five elements of layout, color, icon, chart and font are designed harmoniously and uniformly. In the GUI design of Blood Pressure++, except color design, the other four element designs are slightly worse than the other two APPs. Songaree Blood Pressure's icon and chart design is simple and easy to understand, which is superior to the other two APPs.

3.2 Case Analysis Results

The three APPs have their own advantages and disadvantages in information structure and GUI design. After comparative analysis, the design of Smart Blood Pressure is worth learning from. Its information structure helps users solve difficult problems through layout optimization, icon guidance, color and font size distinction and emphasis, and through chart analysis and doctor interaction. Even though the information structure is complex and there are many contents, users can still find the required contents quickly. The information structure of Songaree Blood Pressure is similar to that of Smart Blood Pressure, but the layout distribution of Songaree Blood Pressure is a bit messy, there are overlapping parts between titles, there are many kinds of colors, a large number of red is

Table 7. Comparative analysis of charts

APP	Songaree Blood Pressure	Blood Pressure ++
Charts		
Features	Mainly uses line chart and pie chart to analyze hypertension. The three colors in the line chart respectively represent the trend of systolic blood pressure, diastolic blood pressure and pulse for one week. Pie chart is an analysis chart of the results of blood pressure measurement during a week. Different color areas represent the proportion of different degrees of hypertension.	Blood Pressure analysis mainly adopts the form of dot chart with straight lines. Although the colors representing systolic blood pressure, diastolic blood pressure and heart rate are marked with dots, there are lines and dots in the chart, and the dots are dense and similar in color, which not only looks very troublesome, but also is difficult to understand. In addition, there is no label in FACTORS chart, which makes it difficult to understand.

APP	Smart Blood Pressure	
Charts		
Features	Among the above three charts, the blood pressure chart analysis is a line chart with two colors representing systolic and diastolic blood pressure respectively, which is simple and easy to understand. In order to better understand the blood pressure, the systolic blood pressure was analyzed separately, and the columns of different colors respectively represented the proportion of different blood pressure degrees using the commonly used column chart. Sinus Rhythm analysis chart is not a common chart, so it is difficult to understand.	

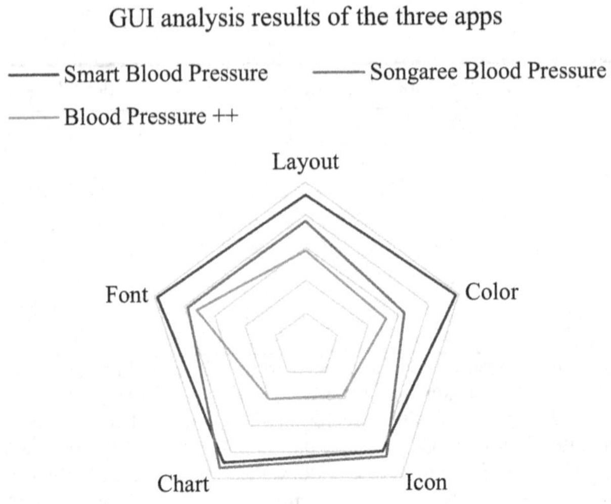

GUI analysis results of the three apps

——— Smart Blood Pressure   ——— Songaree Blood Pressure

——— Blood Pressure ++

Fig. 4. GUI analysis results of the three APPs

used, and a gradual change is adopted. The color design is easy to enlarge the irritability, anxiety and other uneasy emotions of hypertensive users, and reduces their goodwill and utilization rate. Although the design of icons and charts is easy to understand, it still can't make up for the problems caused by layout and color. The information structure of Blood Pressure++ is simpler than that of the previous two APPs. However, there are very few icons and lack of guidance to information. The overall color is mainly white, and the use of color is less, which reduces the distinction and emphasis. Large-scale text information is easy to produce fatigue, which reduces users' curiosity and interest in reading information. In addition, in the chart analysis diagram, the labeled information is inconsistent with the graphic information, and the graphic information is confused and difficult to understand.

The five elements of information structure and GUI design are mutually optimized and promoted. The information structure improves the user's goodwill through the optimization of layout, the guidance of icons, the readability of charts, the distinction of colors and fonts, and the role of emphasis and explanation.

4   Conclusion

From the perspective of patients, we investigate and analyze three APPs: Smart Blood Pressure, Songaree Blood Pressure and Blood Pressure++. Combined with the needs of elderly, middle-aged and adolescent hypertensive patients, we find that each app is more suitable for adolescent and middle-aged hypertensive patients in terms of information structure and GUI design. All personal information needs to be entered manually, and users who use Apple Watch can synchronize the measurement data to APP. These operations are cumbersome and a burden for elderly hypertensive patients. Because of the problem of vision loss, the elderly use APP for a long time, which increases their fatigue and reduces their demand for products. Although the use of Smart Blood Pressure can help teenagers and middle-aged hypertensive patients not to measure blood pressure every day, it has a certain degree of management, but it cannot completely match the needs of teenagers and middle-aged hypertensive patients, and the satisfaction is still relatively low.

From the research results, the users of hypertension management APP are not clearly distinguished, and the content of information structure is inconsistent with the functional needs of patient groups; Middle-aged and elderly patients account for the majority, followed by middle-aged and adolescent patients; Different patient groups have different characteristics and different functional requirements. In GUI design, the difficulty of identifying information and obtaining information is also different. The interface design of hypertension health management APP should be carried out according to the characteristics and needs of different patient groups.

References

1. Li, P., Qu, H., Cang, Y.: Care and health guidance for hypertension. Xinjiang J. Tradit. Chin. Med. **30**(4), 113–114 (2012)
2. Yan ZhaoStud, on risk prediction and control decision of hypertension management. Donghua University (2020)
3. Ruining lv, Current status of geriatric hypertension research. Dietary Health Care 291–292 (2019)
4. Zhang, M.: Design and research of home sphygmomanometer based on emotional sustainability design theory. Southeast University (2018)
5. Kearney, P.M., Whelton, M., Reynolds, K., et al.: Global burden of hypertension: analysis of worldwide data. Lancet **365**(9455), 217–223 (2005)
6. Lingyun Ding, he analysis on the association of hypertension and depression and their epidemic status among middle-aged and elderly in China. University of South China (2018)
7. World Hypertension Day (May 17). Shanghai J. Preventive Med. **31**(5), 384 (2019)
8. Du, Y.: Lecture on hypertension (2017)
9. Guo, X., Cai, G.: Interpreting and reflecting on the latest national and international guidelines for the management of hypertension. Chin. J. Kidney Dis. Invest. (Electron. Ed.) **10**(1), 1–7 (2021)
10. The Revision Committee of the Chinese Guidelines for the Prevention and Control of Hypertension, Chinese Guidelines for the Prevention and Treatment of Hypertension 2018 Revised Edition, Cardiovascular and cerebrovascular disease control. Prevention Treatment Cardio_Cerebral_Vascular Disease **19**(1), 1–44 (2018)
11. Wang, L.: Research on the Relations between Cognitive Emotion Regulation, Quality of Life, Anxiety and Depression in Hypertensive Patient, Hangzhou Normal University (2015)
12. Kasper, E., Braunward, A., Fauci, D., Jameson, J.: Harrison's Principles of Internal Medicine, 16th edn, pp. 1596–1614 (2006)
13. Wu, Z., Huo, Y., Wang, W., Zhao, L., Zhu, D., et al.: Education guidelines for hypertensive patients in China. Chin. J. Hypertens. **21**(12), 1123–1149 (2013). https://doi.org/10.16439/j.cnki.1673-7245
14. Symptoms of high blood pressure, Early signs and symptoms of hypertension, Disease inquiry, 39 Disease Encyclopedia
15. China Association of Gerontology and Geriatrics Specialized Committee on Cardiovascular and Cerebrovascular Diseases, Chinese expert consensus on the diagnosis and treatment of hypertension in the elderly (2017 edition). Chin. J. Internal Med. **56**(11), 885–893 (2017)

16. Hypertension branch of Chinese Geriatric Society, Guidelines for the management of hypertension in the elderly in China 2019. Chin. J. Mult. Organ. Dis. Elderly **18**(2), 81–106 (2019)

17. Aronow, W.S., Fleg, J.L., Pepine, C.J., et al.: ACCF/AHA 2011 expert consensus document on hypertension in the elderly: a report of the American College of Cardiology Foundation Task Force on Clinical Expert Consensus Documents developed in Collaboration with the American Academy of Neurology, American Geriatrics Society, American Society for Preventive Cardiology, American Society of Hypertension, American Society of Nephrology, Association of Black Cardiologists, and European Society of Hypertension. J. Am. Soc. Hypertens. **5**(4), 259–352 (2011)

18. Hu, D., Liu, M., Guo, Y.: Chinese expert consensus on the diagnosis and treatment of hypertension in the elderly (2011 Edition). Chin. J. Front. Med. (Electronic Version) 31–39 (2012)

19. Chinese Society of Geriatrics Hypertension Branch, Chinese expert consensus on blood pressure management in the elderly. Chin. J. Cardiovasc. Med. **20**(6), 401–409 (2015)

20. Cheng, X.: The predictors of self-management behavior in patients with hypertension based on Health Ecological Model. Shandong University (2014)

21. Li, M.: Development Evaluation Model for Improving the Usability of Smart Home App GUI Design, Chungnam National University Daejeon, Korea (2020)

Assessing the Needs of Mobility Solution for Older Adults Through Living Lab Approach: An Experience Report

Borui Fang[1] ⓘ, Chun Yong Chong[2](✉) ⓘ, Pei-Lee Teh[3] ⓘ,
and Shaun Wen Huey Lee[4] ⓘ

[1] School of Business, Monash University Malaysia, Subang Jaya, Selangor Darul Ehsan,
Malaysia
bfan0005@student.monash.edu
[2] School of Information Technology, Monash University Malaysia, Subang Jaya,
Selangor Darul Ehsan, Malaysia
chong.chunyong@monash.edu
[3] School of Business, Monash University Malaysia, Subang Jaya, Selangor Darul Ehsan,
Malaysia
teh.pei.lee@monash.edu
[4] School of Pharmacy, Monash University Malaysia, Subang Jaya, Selangor Darul Ehsan,
Malaysia
shaun.lee@monash.edu

Abstract. Staying mobile is the key to ensuring high quality of life for older
adults. With the impact of the COVID-19 pandemic, the ability to live and move
around independently becomes more critical for the most aging society. While
several efforts have been made to invest in mobility solutions to help improve
older adults' mobility, there is still a lack of good practice and guidelines for
developing such a niche Information Technology (IT) solution. In this paper, we
report our experience of using Living Lab, a design science approach, to assess
and capture the needs of mobility solutions for older adults. A semi-structured
interview involving 25 older adults was conducted. We identified interesting and
practical requirements/functionalities from the participants that might be otherwise overlooked if we followed the traditional software development process. The
participants provided valuable feedback to help improve our mobility solution in
two main areas, mainly the design and functionality of the application. The findings from this case study can potentially be applied for future work that attempts
to address similar problems in the same domain.

Keywords: Mobility solution · Older adults · Living lab · Experience report

1 Introduction

1.1 Challenges in Mobility of Aging Population

With age, the functional ability to move around freely and independently might be
degraded. Research has concluded that older adults' quality of life is highly correlated

P.-L. P. Rau (Ed.): HCII 2022, LNCS 13313, pp. 321–336, 2022.
https://doi.org/10.1007/978-3-031-06050-2_24

with their mobility, regardless of whether it is confined to their home, short-distance travel, or long-distance travel [1]. Maintaining a good amount of mobility allows older adults to live independently while having self-autonomy of their personal care and well-being [2, 3]. With the COVID-19 pandemic, the reduction of old-age dependences calls for mobility solutions that cater to older adults across different mobility contexts, including strategies that would encourage its adoption among older adults in order to realize its promised benefits for seamless and sustainable aging.

With the rapid and widespread adoption of mobile technologies, various mobile solutions that improve individuals' mobility have been proposed (i.e., e-hailing services), but they are generally meant for millennials who are more familiar and comfortable with the use of I.T. technologies [4]. The work by Khor et al. [4] discussed that the usage of e-hailing services among individuals between 55–64 years old in Malaysia is merely 5.1%, indicating modern mobility solutions might not be able to cater to the requirements of older adults and hence hinder the realization of sustainable aging.

This proves that mobility solutions for the general public are not always suitable for older adults due to their low technology adoption. As such, there is an urgent need to develop suitable mobility solutions that specifically cater to older adults' needs, especially those that might face some level of cognitive frailty, to overcome the issue of sustainable and independent aging.

However, common best practices in developing mobile applications for older adults are still in their infancy, largely due to unclear user requirements [5, 6]. For example, developers are likely to incorrectly assume older adults' requirements during the software development phase. Ultimately, when the end user's needs are not captured correctly, it will cause unintended barriers for older adults to adopt this kind of mobility solution.

This study aims to explore the perceptions among older adults in Malaysia regarding using digital mobility solutions to improve their mobility through a qualitative study. Information and data gathered will then be used to propose a system design of mobility solution that enables older adults to interact with assistive technologies to guide and recommend the optimal transportation solutions to reach their intended destination.

2   Literature Review

2.1   Mobility Challenges in Older Adults

One of the key elements to reduce old-age dependency is the independent ability for older adults to move beyond their home, which frequently entails using some form of transportation [7]. Driving a personal vehicle has been proven to be one of many older adults' most preferred transportation methods [8]. However, the ability to drive may not be feasible in the long run, especially when the cognitive ability of older adults deteriorates due to age-related complications [9].

More importantly, given the prominent role of mobility in maintaining health and quality of life in the pursuit of seamless and sustainable aging, it is crucial to address the mobility issues faced by older people holistically. Therefore, this study considers mobility issues within and beyond the home in urban and non-urban areas. In addition, several studies have attempted to determine factors that influence mobility and maximize mobility as people age [9].

The work by Atoyebi et al. [10] discussed the main mobility challenges among older adults, which include human (personal factors), the desired activity (mobility), assistive technology (mobility devices), and context (physical and social environmental factors). The authors discussed the importance of mobile technologies to improve the wayfinding capabilities for older adults to get around the community and lower down the barrier to engage in social activities. However, they found that very limited research focuses on IT that cater specifically to older adults' needs. One of the suggestions made by the authors is to develop better technologies and mobile apps to improve the travel experience for older adults, especially for those who are using mobility devices (wheelchairs).

2.2 Living Lab Approach for Software Development

For the mobile application to be effective for older adults, it should be customized and tailored to the special needs and requirements well suited for the intended population (older adults). One approach for such tailored interventions is the **Living Lab** approach [11, 12]. The living lab is a concept of a collaboration between multiple participants, including the software developers, end-users, and stakeholders, to best represent their needs [12]. It is a user-centered and innovative activity where all the involved stakeholders actively participate in the software development lifecycle. The apps are conceptualized, designed, prototyped, tested, and developed jointly. The living lab approach helps capture the technical and social-technical needs of end users and other stakeholders in a proactive way, which is different from traditional software development methodologies.

The living lab approach has been found to have contributed positively to identifying and addressing vulnerable groups' health needs in a study conducted by Kim et al. [13]. On the other hand, Swinkels et al. [14] highlight how the living lab approach helped identify important lessons learned on adopting electronic health in primary health care.

To summarize, the main advantages of using a living lab approach include the possibility of understanding all the key enablers and negative impacting factors from all the stakeholders early in the software development phase. Furthermore, the information can potentially be used to improve software developers' level of understanding regarding mobility solutions for older adults.

3 Research Methodology

3.1 Initial Conceptualization

The work by Andria et al. [15] outlines the process involved in the living lab approach:

- Co-creation involves a wide range of stakeholders (crowdsourcing) and gathers diverse views, constraints, and knowledge to visualize scenarios and concepts related to the subject matter.
- Exploration: engage and explore all potential stakeholders at the early stage of software development to discover different use case scenarios, usages, and behavior of end-users in real environments.
- Experimentation: frequent prototyping, collect data, improve design iteratively with real end-users.

- Evaluation: perform user acceptance testing, assessing social-economic aspects and social cognitive aspects of the solution to reveal new concepts from different views potentially.

Co-creation and Exploration

In this research, we started by using the "Co-creation" and "Exploration" stages, where we performed a preliminary qualitative study through semi-structured in-depth telephone interviews to understand the needs of mobility solutions (mobile app) among older adults, as shown in Fig. 1.

Researchers and Other Stakeholders: We performed a few series of round table discussions with academics from Monash University Malaysia, Monash University Australia, Swinburne University of Technology Sarawak Campus, University of Malaya, Universiti Putra Malaysia, and Universiti Kebangsaan Malaysia, who are experts in the field of gerontology, I.T. adoption, mobile app development, and transportation. We also discussed with two care companion service providers in Malaysia. Their feedback is taken into consideration to identify the initial sets of requirements.

Older Adults: Phone interviews were conducted to elicit requirements from older adults. Note that telephone interviews were chosen due to the impact of COVID-19 lockdowns, where we are unable to conduct face-to-face interviews. In addition, we also conducted several brainstorming and discussion sessions with the involved researchers, research assistant, students, and their family members to come out with different use case scenarios for the mobile application.

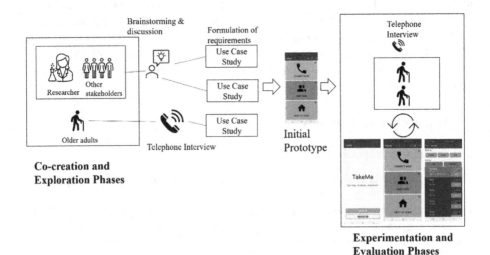

Fig. 1. Adopted living lab approach to assess the need for mobility solutions for older adults in Malaysia

Based on the results from the first phase of the living lab approach, we managed to identify the following lists of requirements:

1. Two main users type; older adults and volunteers: the target end-users for this mobility solution are older adults who wish to travel for various purposes. On the other hand, we aim to position the mobility solution as a crowdsourced application where people can offer help voluntarily. As such, we define users who offer help to older adults as "volunteers".
2. Allow the older adults to choose the assistance needed: different users might have different needs, depending on the situation and context. Hence, the mobile solution will need to provide a feature to choose the type of assistance required.
3. The provision of assistance for volunteers is important in the app design. For example, an individual volunteer can choose their services, such as voice calls, messaging, general guidance, wayfinding, or fetching older adults from their homes.
4. Ability to meet at home: older adults who wish to travel and cannot move independently might want to meet with the volunteers at their homes.
5. Ability to talk/chat: verbal guidance can be provided to users based on the different needs (such as translation, social needs, etc.).
6. Ability to meet at designated point: older adults can choose to meet the volunteer at a chosen destination, such as hospitals if they have an issue locating a specific clinic.

Experimentation and Evaluation

We then developed the first version of the prototype on the Android platform based on the initial requirements. The mobile app, called TakeMe, was developed as the first proof-of-concept. Figures 2 and 3 are some of the screenshots of the app.

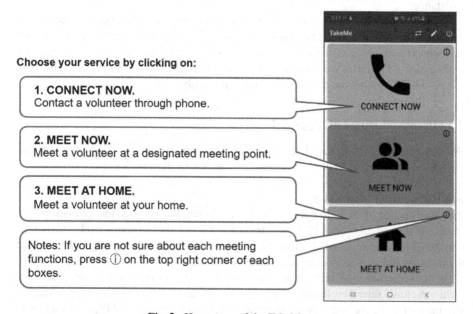

Fig. 2. Homepage of the TakeMe app

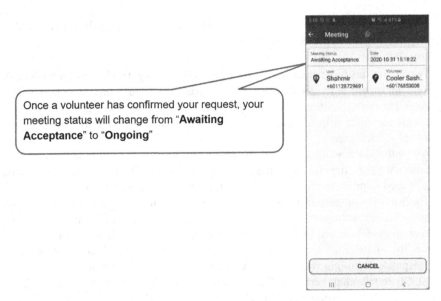

Fig. 3. Screenshot of awaiting acceptance from the volunteer, once a request is made

Figure 2 shows the app's main functionality, where users can choose to 1.) Connect Now, 2.) Meet now, or 3.) Meet at Home user interface is designed with simplicity in mind, and the chosen font size is big enough to improve readability.

Figure 3, on the other hand, shows the page after the older adults initiate a help request. Volunteers can then look at the pending requests and either accept or reject the assistance.

The above is the first version of the prototype for the researchers to understand the needs of stakeholders and end-users. The initial prototype helped better understand the context and easier visualization of the workflow and real case study. Based on the first version of the app, we reiterated the Living Lab approach by engaging with more stakeholders to gather the requirements more precisely.

3.2 Iterative Living Lab Approach

We went through the Living Lab approach again with a more thorough requirement elicitation approach after developing the first version of the TakeMe app.

Semi-structured Interviews

This study is part of larger longitudinal cohort research. We analyzed the semi-structured interview data of 25 older adults aged 60 years old and above for this study. The semi-structured interview was used because it was the most appropriate method to understand the mobility needs of older adults to ensure the highest validity of results [16] and adhere to the "Co-creation and Exploration" phase of the Living Lab approach. Additionally, the semi-structured interview listed specific questions related to the overall topic to ensure it was on track and gave interviewees more space to share their insights [17]. The study was approved by Monash University Human Research Ethics Committee (Review Reference Number: 2020-23698-51013). Considering the younger generation out-migrating from rural areas that reduced the local service provider [18], we intended to recruit participants from both rural and urban areas to identify the different mobility needs between these regions and combine those needs in our mobile application development process. The participants were recruited from two-channel: 1) the main participants from Transforming Cognitive Frailty into Later-Life Self-Sufficiency (AGELESS) Longitudinal Study Cohort, 2) the new participants were recruited from advertisements, non-government organizations (NGOs), community centers in purposive sampling. AGELESS is a five-year longitudinal study involving Malaysian residents aged 60 years and over. This study has emerged by merging two studies on aging among Malaysians called the MELoR and TUA studies which were conducted between 2013–2016.

The researchers developed, reviewed, and revised a semi-structured interview guide. Some participants were older generations who could not speak English, and therefore Chinese and Malay language interview guide was provided and proofread by the native speakers. The following categories were included in the interview guide: (1) the perception towards our mobility application after watching the demo video, (2) the preference and opinion of the current transportation mode, such as Grab (e-hailing service in Malaysia), train, and Bus Rapid Transit (BRT), (3) the feedback of our mobility application's features, interface, and accessible, (4) opinion and advice about the willingness of older adults adopt the technology. Figure 4 illustrates the interview procedure and the purpose of these questions.

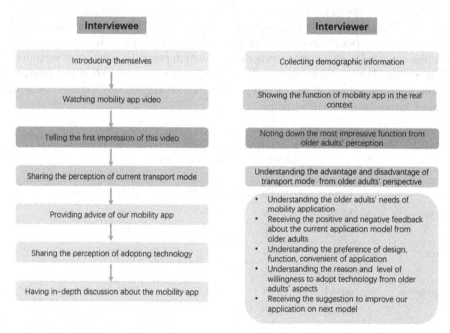

Fig. 4. The procedure and purpose from the semi-structured interview guide

Data Collection. The team prepared a walkthrough video demo to help the older adults understand the core functionalities of the mobility solution. The participants were given the video link prior to the interview process.

One author (PLT) conducted the initial individual interviews to test whether the semi-structured interview guide was feasible and adjusted some questions after interviews. This pre-test interview was also conducted in three languages to test whether the translated questions are straightforward in the actual context to eliminate ambiguity from participants to answer the question. Then the research assistant, based on the practical interview guide to conduct the individual interview by telephone or zoom. The interview took around 45 to 60 min.

The participant has been informed of the rights to leave the interview before the data is stored in our database. Verbal consent was required from the interviewee.

Data Analysis. The interview was recorded and be transcribed after the interview by a native speaker to ensure accuracy. Once the transcript has been stored in our database, the original recording file will be deleted. All the transcription work are performed using Microsoft Word and the coding done on NVivo. The theme of coding will be: (1) the needs of older adults to have a mobility solution, (2) the current transport mode they used, (3) perception of wayfinding, carrying stuff, and volunteer service, (4) the extent of willingness to accept this mobile solution, (5) the preferred design such as button, font size, and color, (6) the recommendation provided by participants to improve the functionalities of the mobile app.

Results. We developed the first version of the prototype based on the basic requirements and needs from the initial 104 interview data in phase one. Detailed information about the phase one interview can be found in this paper [19]. For this study, we analyzed 25 samples collected in phase two to gather feedback to improve the subsequent version of the prototype. The minimum age was 60, and the maximum age was 86. All participants shared their perceptions of our prototype and provided suggestions for improvement. Table 1 shows the profile of participants.

Table 1. Profile of participants

	Items	Frequency ($n = 25$)	Percentage (100%)
Gender	Male	9	36%
	Female	16	64%
Area	Urban	14	56%
	Rural	11	44%
Age group	60–64	8	32%
	65–74	13	52%
	75–84	2	8%
	>85	2	8%

We structured the inputs from the participant into a few main categories below, including preferred design elements, perception of wayfinding functionalities; recommendation for other services; preferred mode of transportation; perception, and willingness to adopt the TakeMe application. We conducted several rounds of brainstorming and discussion to further improve the mobility solution by incorporating the participants' feedback.

Preferred Design Elements

Interviewers showed the interface design for the participants. Fifteen participants shared their perceptions about the current font size used in the app. Three participants regarded the current font size as standard and could read it easily. For example, participant T005 mentioned, "The font size is normal. Not very big, not very small." T036 indicated, "It is easy to read." However, most participants suggested that the font size could be bigger. T004 reported that "Because now my eyesight is fading, so everything small we will find it difficult to read." T006 proposed that "Maybe double up the size of the newspaper? Will it be better?" T049 commented that "I think as we are older, the font a bit bigger is better. We are old, and we cannot see well."

The TakeMe logo was designed in blue and white, our theme color. Therefore, the functions buttons were blue, and the other pages were in a white background with black font. Eleven participants shared their opinion about our current design in color aspects. All of them were satisfied with the color matching. For example, T002 said, "I think it is okay. When we see it, it is clearer." T033 added, "the blue is pretty good." On the other hand, two participants, T003 and T028, suggested contrasting colors because the older adults may not have strong visibility to distinguish colors, especially grey, red, and green.

Nine participants reported their preference for the button operation approach. Six of them shared that they prefer the tap method as the tap button is more accessible (T007). Moreover, only one participant preferred to swipe the button given her user experience in answering calls from the iPhone. Interestingly, one participant (T028) proposed the integration of voice command, enabling users such as people with Parkinson's disease to use their voice to operate the app. Two participants (T049 and T083) who were not tech-savvy disliked having multiple buttons on the app interface.

Perception of Wayfinding Functionality; Recommendation for Other Services

Additionally, the participants were asked to comment on the prototype's features that they liked and disliked. We divided the app features into two parts: Volunteer and Navigation in the nodes. Twenty-one participants stated that they thought the volunteer service was helpful and liked it. For instance, T006 said, "Yes (the volunteer service is useful), especially those who live alone, I think it is. I mean, those are children who are working, no pay leave or those who have a lot of their children, but all overseas or other places." T028 also excited about the function and expressed that "(the volunteer service) to them (lonely older adults) out for lunch or something like that. That is good." These participants regraded this service was helpful for those alone aging population. Another group of participants thought this service was helpful because they would be too shy to keep seeking assistance from friends or neighbors. T001 mentioned that "if not (volunteer service), they are at a loss they do not know searching for who, you or neighbor knows *relative? People may not be free to help you, you see, but when you call the volunteer. The volunteer service is free, right?" "Consequently, the older generations did not need to stay at home every day and went out with volunteers, which would make the senior citizens happy (T049, T055)".*

By contrast, only four participants regarded the volunteer service as unhelpful. For example, T082 was concerned about the safety of picking up service, *"Yeah. (I was) sent to the home. Yeah. And especially totally alone, it can be quite dangerous."* Additionally, one participant stated that *"It is more convenient for me to drive to buy it myself. What to buy, we ourselves are more psychologically prepared. (T031)"* Lastly, the last two participants did not want to rely on and bother volunteers, as the volunteer may not be available. For instance, T033 mentioned that *"Maybe that volunteer, he lives far away or something, of course it is not reasonable if you ask him to hurry up to pick you up and help you get things. You can call, as if it is easy for you in Kuala Lumpur, you can call Taxi one by one or just pick you up. Do not bother to call the volunteer, but this volunteer may not be available, and there is no way for him to come, right? I think so. (T033)".*

The second function we discussed was navigation and wayfinding. Eight participants mentioned they were looking forward to this service, and only one participant reported he was not satisfied with it. The main reason for those who liked this function was that there were more options to compare the distance and price to obtain the information. For example, T004 said, *"That makes us independent, then we do not have to ask. You can just look at the app, and the app will guide you how to go to a place, how cheap you take, the fastest whatever."* T036 mentioned that *"I think, to me, it's (the navigation service) more information more informative. Actually, when you want to go somewhere, like apply your location, you want to know more yeah more information."* Although most of the participants liked this service, one participant came up with the opposite argument that this transportation option may be useless. T028 explained that *"You choose the best one for me lah. I just follow. You see, look the numbers are so small. What is 3.2 km, seven minutes, 5.6 km nine minutes? You get what I mean or not? You confuse everybody. Just take the average one and select for... you pre-screen, you filter for them, because this is... this is not... the... the what, what? Just say this," we have already selected. This is best for the seniors. "That is all."*

After we gathered the comments from the existing function, we also encouraged the participants to express what other services they expect in the next version of the prototype.

Some suggestions have been proposed to improve the TakeMe app. Firstly, three participants desired that two volunteers provide service depending on the situation. For example, T003 suggested that *"Sometimes the volunteer, if you check on you, need two people to help. One to drive one to help to bring the patient down and all that. You need two people to help, one is not sufficient."* T028 also mentioned that *"Some people are wheelchair-bound. You cannot have one person, one driver, you know? You have one driver and one companion so that you know, you... you have to assist the person."* Apart from that, some participants discussed the basic requirements for volunteer selection. For instance, T004 hopes that the volunteer can provide digital assistance. T007 hoped that the volunteer could speak in various languages. T080 demanded that the volunteer provide counseling services to reduce the stress when the older generations stay alone. One of the most insightful requirements was given by T082, who expressed that *"we prayed the volunteer to have compassion have a passion for helping people and having a compassion to help people not just to get as fun like that."* T082 also mentioned that *"it might be good to send the same people to see if they are available so that they are familiar with the people who are coming forward to help. Especially with the very old people, they like to see a familiar face rather than strangers all the time."*

T001 and T003 considered that some older generations are non-literate, which means they could not read the instruction and understand the button. Thus, they expected a voice message for older adults to understand the button. For example, T001 said, *"I think that by reading Chinese and maybe the words they may not be able to be able to read all the words, but when you read it out to them, read it out to them, that will be better. You see, they may not know how to read the 10 words in the sentence, but when you read it out, they will understand. I think it should be read out."*

In addition, more than six participants advised that there should be helpful guidance for them. For example, T001 suggested that there should be an introduction of how to use the app to ask whether those users need help or guidance. Then, it should be better to provide someone to teach them. This teaching process could be conducted via video conferencing or through face-to-face sessions. T004 came up with a different approach to guide the user, such as there would be a short video to guide them step by step, as T004 explained, *"Because the short short videos, separate videos are very easy. Then if anything you want to see, you go to that particular video, no need from the start on functions like that. Our comprehension is not that fast. So pace needs to go a bit slower. So that we can comprehend and then there must be a way to transfer that to a written thing. Like one do this, two do it. It's easier for us, then we'll take a screenshot."* Lastly, T006 and T007 believed that many older generations would be willing to learn about it if there were face-to-face teaching sessions. Consequently, the aging population received the confidence and understand how to use it the next time.

Preferred Mode of Transportation

The participants were asked about what transportation mode they usually used. We coded their option in four nodes: motorbikes or bicycles, e-hailing or taxi, public transport, and private car.

Four participants mentioned they rode bicycles or motorbikes when they went for short distances, and their relatives would fetch them to farther places. For example, T048 said, *"When you go shopping to buy things, you can ride a motorcycle like this."* Moreover, T032 mentioned that *"I just use a bicycle. The bicycle is for closer places, and my husband will fetch if we are going further."* However, only one participant rode motorbikes anywhere because public transportation is inconvenient in rural areas. T055 explained that *"Grab (e-hailing service in Malaysia) is not in the coverage area for our kampung (village). The train is a bit far. The nearest train station is about 15 km. So we go everywhere around with a motorcycle."*

The eight participants told us they sometimes adopted e-hailing or taxis. The main reason might be that the payment method is convenient. Some of the reasons why the participants chose e-hailing or taxis are because 1.) they cannot drive to unfamiliar places by themself, 2.) lack of parking spots in the city center, or 3.) during emergency conditions. For instance, T006 said, *"I used I have Grab (e-hailing service in Malaysia) also, I have TouchNGo (e-wallet)."* T027 explained, *"Grab. It is mostly myself. I go alone. I never used to drive to places that I am not familiar (with). I always drive at pathways where I am familiar. Go to work, come back. And certain places I know very well I will drive. If I am not confident of the way, I will take a taxi or Grab."* T083 also said, *"Whenever I go to a place, parking is a problem like a city center, I will take public transport by taxi or even the MRT."* Then, T080 mentioned that *"if I really have a problem then I will use Grab, not public transport. I do not mind paying more."* Lastly, T080 was excited about the convenience of Grab, *"So far quite convenient, convenient and easy you know, it is easy, you just text and certain time they come and pick you up and send you, I'm surprised it's very convenient for Grab."* By contrast, some participants explained that they seldom adopted e-hailing or taxis due to the price. For example, T004 mentioned that *"I do not use Grab because I cannot afford to pay the Grab. That will be more alternative."* T075 said that *"Taxi, Bawang cars. It's just that the cost is high."* Additionally, one participant told us that e-hailing services have poor coverage in rural areas. For instance, T048 shared that *"Because there is no Grab for a small place on our site, but there is one in Johor Bahru because I have seen it. We do not seem to have it here."*

Seven participants said they took public transport, such as Bus, Light Rapid Transit (LRT), or train. Most of them explained that the senior citizen discount, convenience, and speed attracted them. For instance, T003 introduced that *"we used the free bus, then you can use the Mass Rapid Transit (MRT), Light Rapid Transit (LRT) all half price."* T005 also mentioned that *"I used to go by myself and take a train or the bus, sometimes I record the cab, but my Kelana Jaya LRT is nearby."* Additionally, T082 mentioned that public transports such as LRT were faster and safer than taxis or drive-by themselves, *"I prefer LRT taxi because of the traffic jam outside. I do not know what the condition is outside, the situation. So LRT, I know, is very fast one way down. When I prefer LRT straight faster and save time and is safer than a taxi, to be honest with you."*

Lastly, twelve participants mentioned that they drive independently, the most preferred transportation mode. The freedom of self-driving was one of the preferable factors, *"Yes, I do drive around. Like going to Klang, my son's place. Or I am going to Taiping. I normally prefer to drive there because mobility is so (…) you are more flexible when you can plan (T004)."* Meanwhile, some participants used to take public transport, but they choose to drive now to minimize human-to-human contact due to COVID-19 pandemic, *"Yeah, I drive or… I lived just in front of the LRT station last time before Movement Control Order. I either drive or if I go to the town center. I will use the LRT. If not, I drive. Now, like now, since the Movement Control Order, I only drive (T028)."* Moreover, for those who could not drive the car by themselves, their relatives would fetch them to the hospital, shopping mall, or farther places. The two participants said that *"my husband will fetch if we are going further (T032). Likewise, my husband will fetch me from the hospital (T034)."*

Perception and Willingness to Adopt TakeMe Application

At the end of the interview, most of the participants understood the functions and services provided by TakeMe. Six participants said they would adopt it immediately because they enjoy these volunteer and wayfinding services, but they need to learn how to use the application. *"Yes, I will use it. But I have to learn. It seems like we are getting older, it's not like we can do it at a glance. You have to learn how to use it at the end (T033)."* For example, T003 said, *"I will definitely use it. It is very, very useful provided as I say that there are enough volunteers to join this app to give free service." "Yeah, because sometimes you need to find things around ways to find things, you know (T036)." "We are single. So if I need help, I need a volunteer to come and help me. Yeah, so I need a volunteer to help because I stay alone (T049)."* Lastly, T083 shared, *"I do not need to search for things. Take me around, and it is okay. Yeah. Okay, then when I need it, I will use it straight away."*

At the same time, seven participants would use TakeMe when they needed it. Most of the participants explained that they are still mobile and independent. They believe that they will adopt TakeMe if they can no longer move around independently. For instance, T030 explained that *"I have the support of my daughter, just in case next time when I am all alone, maybe and I am not so mobile. Yeah, I may use it."* Likewise, T004 mentioned, *"By myself, I would want to be myself. But when it comes to a stage where I am unable to do it myself, then my first option will be to depend on the app."* By contrast, four participants had different reasons to adopt TakeMe when they needed it. T032 and T033 explained that *"It depends on the situation, uh, if it means that in case the car breaks down, there are still other things that would come to mind about this TakeMe."* T082 shared that *"If it is easy to use, I would use it what motivate me to use it when I am lazy to drive. Yeah, when is too, too heavy traffic outside. I do not want to drive. If the distance is too long, it is not safe for me to drive. I rather use this the one who knows the way I will be very happy that he knows the way whereas I do not know the way."*

Conversely, four participants stated that they would not use it. The first participant explained that *"I would not use it because I got a Grab to use that is the easiest (T027)."* The second participant mentioned, *"so I do not think it is necessary. It is more convenient for me to drive to buy it myself. If we have to pay, I will not use it. Because where I go, if I have money, I will arrange where I want to go. This experience is more pleasant. (T031)."* The third participant considered TakeMe a good application, but T047 did not want to try and use the app. Lastly, T075 was worried about her safety, as she mentioned, *"(I) did not know who was with her. (I) will not know where (I) will be brought to be sold away."*

4   Refined and Proposed Design

The findings from the several rounds of interviews and discussion gave useful insights into our proposed mobility solution design, TakeMe. In terms of the look and feel of the user interface, our proposed solution must be 1.) easy to learn, 2.) simplistic in terms of design and color choice, and 3.) easy for older adults with potential eyesight impairment to read the contents of the application. Therefore, apart from the list of basic features listed in Sect. 3.1, we have added the following new features in the revised version:

1. Mode of transport recommendation: users who can navigate on their own tend to find it hard to decide on the best mode of transportation in terms of cost and travel time. As such, we implement a comparison feature where once the users provide the

destination, they can compare the different modes of transportation depending on the traveling method: by car, public transport, and e-hailing services, as shown in Fig. 5. As a result, the improvement was made based on participants T001, T006, and T028.

2. A variety of assistant categories were provided to end-users: from the interview, we realized that in some instances, the assistance sought by the older adults is not just wayfinding, but more general assistance such as carrying heavy items, parking a car, or simple verbal assistance. As such, we have implemented those features, as shown in Fig. 5. The improvement was made based on participants T003, T004, and T028.

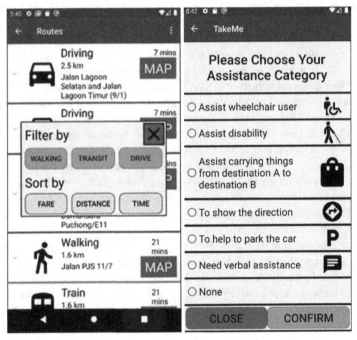

Fig. 5. Mode of transportation comparison; selecting the type of assistance required

All in all, the overall workflow of the proposed mobility solution, TakeMe, is shown in Fig. 6. The end users (older adults) will first request assistance through the TakeMe app. The request will then be stored on a cloud server (Google Firebase). When there is an active request, the information will be fetched and displayed on the volunteer's homepage. The volunteer can then choose to accept or reject the active requests. The TakeMe app will act as the main interface between the end-users and the volunteers.

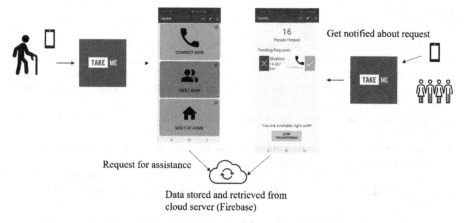

Fig. 6. General workflow of the proposed TakeMe app

5 Conclusion

Population aging is unavoidable, and the living arrangements of older adults require immediate attention from government sectors worldwide. However, due to its niche market, the software requirements and best practices in developing mobile solutions for older adults are not widely explored in the current literature. This study contributes to a better understanding of the mobility challenges faced by older adults and their user requirements for a mobility app. We adopted the living lab design science approach, which helped us uncover the needs from the end user's perspective. With the engagement of the end-users and stakeholders in the software development life cycle, we gained fresh insights into the age-friendly technological design in the pursuit of developing a seamless mobility solution for older users.

There are two limitations to this study. First, data was collected in Malaysia and hence, the results reported in this work might not be generalized to a wider population. Future research can include other countries to solicit different views from older adults. Second, the findings of this study were based on qualitative data. Therefore, we will assess the effectiveness of the mobility app more objectively through field experiments. We will observe the actual actions when older adults interact and use the mobile app.

Acknowledgment. The authors wish to thank the Ministry of Higher Education, Malaysia, for sponsoring this research project under the Long-Term Research Grant Scheme [(LR005-2019, GOV-000047) LRGS/1/2019/UM//1/1]. Special thanks to Desmond Wong, Mun Hong Tai, Muhammad Hakimi, Mohammed Junaid, and Elizabeth Lee for their software development and data collection assistance. The TakeMe app received the Consolation Prize in the Innovative Ageing Conference (iAGE 2021), organized by the Malaysian Invention and Design Society (MINDS) and the Gerontological Association of Malaysia.

References

1. Madhushri, P., Dzhagaryan, A., Jovanov, E., Milenkovic, A.: An mHealth tool suite for mobility assessment. Information **7**, 47 (2016)
2. Boschmann, E.E., Brady, S.A.: Travel behaviors, sustainable mobility, and transit-oriented developments: a travel counts analysis of older adults in the Denver, Colorado metropolitan area. J. Transp. Geogr. **33**, 1–11 (2013)
3. Loe, M.: Aging Our Way: Lessons for Living from 85 and Beyond. Oxford University Press, New York (2011)
4. Anggriawan, R.: E-hailing transportation and the issue of competition in Indonesia. Indones. Compar. Law Rev. **2**, 56–66 (2019)
5. Wildenbos, G.A., Peute, L., Jaspers, M.: Aging barriers influencing mobile health usability for older adults: a literature based framework (MOLD-US). Int. J. Med. Inform. **114**, 66–75 (2018)
6. Poh, Z. et al.: What do users like about smart bottle? Insights for designers. In: Rau, P.L. (eds.) Cross-Cultural Design. Culture and Society. HCII 2019. LNCS, vol. 11577, pp. 325–336. Springer, Cham (2019). https://doi.org/10.1007/978-3-030-22580-3_24
7. Myers, A., Cyarto, E., Blanchard, R.: Challenges in quantifying mobility in frail older adults. Eur. Rev. Aging Phys. Act. **2**, 13–21 (2005)
8. Dickerson, A.E., et al.: Transportation and aging: an updated research agenda to advance safe mobility among older adults transitioning from driving to non-driving. Gerontologist **59**, 215–221 (2019)
9. Foley, D.J., Heimovitz, H.K., Guralnik, J.M., Brock, D.B.: Driving life expectancy of persons aged 70 years and older in the United States. Am. J. Public Health **92**, 1284–1289 (2002)
10. Atoyebi, O.A., et al.: Mobility challenges among older adult mobility device users. Curr. Geriatr. Rep. **8**(3), 223–231 (2019). https://doi.org/10.1007/s13670-019-00295-5
11. Kim, Y., Lee, H., Lee, M.K., Lee, H., Jang, H.: Development of a living lab for a mobile-based health program for Korean-Chinese working women in South Korea: Mixed methods study. JMIR Mhealth Uhealth **8**, e15359 (2020)
12. Grundy, J., Abdelrazek, M., Curumsing, M.K.: Vision: improved development of mobile ehealth applications. In: 2018 IEEE/ACM 5th International Conference on Mobile Software Engineering and Systems (MOBILESoft), pp. 219–223. IEEE (2018)
13. Kim, J., et al.: Living Labs for health: an integrative literature review. Eur. J. Pub. Health **30**, 55–63 (2020)
14. Swinkels, I.C.S., et al.: Lessons learned from a living lab on the broad adoption of eHealth in primary health care. J. Med. Internet Res. **20**, e83 (2018)
15. Andria, G., et al.: A novel approach for design and testing digital m-health applications. In: Proceedings of the 2015 IEEE International Symposium on Medical Measurements and Applications (MeMeA) pp. 440–444. IEEE (2015)
16. Brankaert, R.G.A., den Ouden, P.H.: The design-driven living lab: a new approach to exploring solutions to complex societal challenges. Technol. Innov. Manag. Rev. **7**, 44–51 (2017)
17. Tharenou, P., Donohue, R., Cooper, B.: Management Research Methods. Cambridge University Press, Cambridge (2007)
18. Porru, S., Misso, F.E., Pani, F.E., Repetto, C.: Smart mobility and public transport: opportunities and challenges in rural and urban areas. J. Traffic Transp. Eng. (English Edition) **7**, 88–97 (2020)
19. Tang, K.F., Teh, P.-L., Lim, W.M., Lee, S.W.H.: Perspectives on mobility among older adults living with different frailty and cognitive statuses. J. Transp. Health **24**, 101305 (2022)

Elderly Life Inquiry Toolkit: Empathy Expanding in Elder-Friendly Technology Design

Yi Liu and Fang Zhong[✉]

Tsinghua University, Beijing 10084, China
Zhocngfang@mail.tsinghua.edu.cn

Abstract. ICTs have become deeply ingrained in social life. Design for elder-friendly technology is gaining traction in China to reduce obstacles for older people's access to smart gadgets and services. Designers must increase their awareness of heterogeneous images of the old and elder technology usage in everyday life to create technological solutions that are meaningful to the aging population. Young designers encounter empathetic difficulties in design practice due to a lack of experience with aging, qualitative research abilities, and training. This research proposed a human-centered Elderly Life Inquiry toolkit to bridge this gap. The toolkit establishes a qualitative research framework of 'Exploration-Interaction-Reflection,' together with thematic guidelines, to assist young designers in engaging with the elderly utilizing various empathy techniques. It enhances designers' empathy for older adults in everyday life, develops qualitative research abilities, and incorporates insights into designs. According to a series of empirical experiments and prototyping involving young student designers and older participants, the qualitative research method of face-to-face intergenerational communication is more suited to Chinese elders' social preferences. This research demonstrated the process of developing the toolkit and the potential of the research techniques during the COVID-19 outbreak. At last, we emphasize the importance of supporting young designers to engage with diverse older adults, valuing the creativity of multidisciplinary participants, and focusing on the relationship between older life and technology for empathy in technology design.

Keywords: ICTs · Elderly · Empathy · Design research · Prototyping

1 Introduction

As China, with the world's largest elderly population, has entered a moderately ageing society, ICT-based technological devices and services are seen as one of the most effective alternatives to address the challenges of ageing and to promote social inclusion [1]. Similar to the EU's 'ICT for Ageing Well' initiative [2], China had started developing new technology-based products and services to meet the elderly's needs since 2012 when the concept of 'Smart Senior Care' was first introduced [3]. However, during the COVID-19, many older people were unable to achieve essential functions such as online medical appointments and access to the latest pandemic prevention information on their own because of insufficient use of smartphones, and not everyone can benefit from technology

© The Author(s), under exclusive license to Springer Nature Switzerland AG 2022
P.-L. P. Rau (Ed.): HCII 2022, LNCS 13313, pp. 337–352, 2022.
https://doi.org/10.1007/978-3-031-06050-2_25

[4]. To solve the enormous challenges of older people's inability, fear, and reluctance to use technology, in December 2020, the Chinese government promoted top-down information accessibility and age-friendly modification action. In China, however, the concept and scope of elder-friendly technology design are unclear, and design practices are primarily based on universal design specifications to redesign the interface and content of Internet service and mobile applications. Designers and older adults have limited participation and ownership in the design process.

With active ageing policies providing the worldwide policy framework for addressing age-related concerns [5], what older people want to do, what they can do, and the chance to do the things they like are critical to sustaining health and well-being in later life [6]. Several recent studies have shown that technology designers should pay greater attention to older people's willingness and daily lives. According to Elisa et al., technology should be employed as a resource to supplement the skills of aging in everyday objects and situated settings [7]. It requires designers to be aware of age-related human factors [8], has qualitative research skills that provide insight into the relationship between older people and technology in the complexity of social contexts, and bring the elderly's knowledge to the co-design process [9, 10]. Young designers in their twenties and thirties are constrained by their empathic horizons due to differences in age, background, culture, experience, education, and other characteristics [11]. It became challenging to design products and services appropriate for the traits and experiences of older people without ageing. Current industrial product design education is beginning to realize the need to foster qualitative research capabilities in young design students and empathy for the elderly [12, 13]. Ethnographic research techniques in Western socio-technical environments offer innovation in technology design [14].

In the context of China's increasing aging and rapid growth of ICTs, this paper presents an overview of the notion of elder-friendly technology design and research gaps, as well as reflections on the field's essential qualitative research techniques. The Elderly Life Inquiry toolkit results from empirical research and prototyping in a Chinese social context to understand how older adults use technology in everyday life and address the difficulties of empathy faced by young designers. It concludes with suggestions on how to conduct design research when designing elder-friendly technologies in the post-pandemic future that enhance young designers' empathy.

2 Related Works

2.1 Design for Elder-Friendly Technology

In China, 'elder-friendly technology' is a concept discussed in various fields in late 2020, so there is no widely accepted definition of the term. Translated by the authors, it means the process that technology is applicable and adapted to the ageing to ensure the quality of life of the elderly in their old age. China's latest policy states that the scope of elder-friendly technologies includes high-frequency activities and service scenarios in the lives of the elderly, such as the use of technological terminal products, access to Internet information, participation in digital literacy training [14]. In this paper, we consider 'Smart Senior Care,' 'Internet+ Ageing' and 'Smart community service,' which ICT-based (including the Internet, 5G, artificial intelligence, big data, cloud computing,

Internet of Things, etc.) [4, 15], are also significant parts of elder-friendly technology. To better understand the scope of this term, we attempt to classify it (see Table 1). Above all, China's fundamental goal of elder-friendly technology is human-centered, respecting older adults' lives across online, offline, domestic, and social life.

Table 1. Classification of elder-friendly technology

Categories	Examples
Personal smart terminal	Mobile smart devices, smart assistive devices, smart wearables devices, smart households, smart robots, etc.
Internet services and mobile applications	Mobility, healthcare, shopping, food ordering, housekeeping, socializing, entertainment, etc.
Community-based smart senior services	Emergency assistance, biological indicators testing, health management, telemedicine, security monitoring, life maintenance, etc.
Smart social welfare services	Time bank, caring network, third Age University, disaster relief assistance, spiritual comfort, etc.

Elder-friendly technology emphasizes the balance between technologies, the social environment, the autonomy of older people, and the participation of multiple actors from government, the market, society, families, and older people [16].To some extent, this concept is similar to Gerontechnology. Designers work with technical engineers and social workers to provide products, services, and environments to create a better life for older people, with user-centered, multidisciplinary, cross-disciplinary user engagement [17]. Nowadays, it has become a consensus to improve digital inclusion and user experience by involving older people in the technology design process and providing technical support to meet contextual scenarios' dynamic needs [18]. However, the adoption of both technology devices and services to support older people's lives has been low and has a pattern of deficits [19]; Giaccard et al. based their reflections on Gerontechnology and proposed that 'technologies as resources that can complement the ageing competencies of older people and adapt in a variety of ways, rather than merely complementing and preventing cognitive and physical decline [7]'. The structured transfer of the needs, aspirations, aesthetics, creativity, and wisdom of everyday life of older people into projects is an important way of promoting technology designed for active, pleasurable, and resourceful ageing [7, 20]. The experience of Western countries in designing ICTs for older people is of great relevance to China today. We consider that elder-friendly technology design is not just about finding technical solutions to specific problems but about discovering what to accommodate the elderly's values.

In China, design for elder-friendly technology is still in its early stages. Sensory compensation strategies were employed by Ping et al. to allow the elderly to be physically and psychologically more willing to use intelligent products [21]. Lin et al. investigated the trend of intelligent kitchens and recommended design methods based on functional requirements, interactive behaviors, and emotional experiences for the elderly [22]. Jin-hua et al. was indicated to improve the elderly's motivation to adopt smart healthcare and senior care technologies by increasing product aesthetics, interactive interfaces, and service content [23]. Alibaba Design released its Age-Friendly Design Guide, with technical suggestions in nine categories, including text size, contrast, expression, color, and interactive operation. Beyond the technical factors that determine the usability, older people's daily needs and meanings have an impact on their understanding and imagination of technology, primarily affecting their technology usage behavior and experience [24]. Elderly-friendly technology design should account for age-related declines in abilities and the emotional, cultural, social factors. As a result, when confronted with the mixed environment of physical life and the digital world, technology design should pay more attention to the elderly's everyday life and grasp the complexity between their lives and technology from a holistic viewpoint.

2.2 Empathy Techniques in Design for Elder-Friendly Technology

When older people are the target users of design solutions, it is difficult to make more appropriate design decisions since designers typically lack experience with ageing, necessitating empathy to comprehend others [25]. Empathy in the design field is 'the intuitive ability to identify with other people's thoughts and feelings - their motivations, emotional and mental models, values, priorities, preferences, and inner conflicts [26].' Empathic design helps empathizer improve the ability to identify empathee thoughts and feelings through a range of design methods and tools [27], providing insight for positive design action. When designing new technology solutions for older people, designers often use ethnographic qualitative research methods to increase awareness of older users' usability, inclusivity, sensitivity to enhance empathy [28]. Based on Deana McDonagh's classification of empathy techniques [26], we present an incomplete summary of qualitative research methods frequently used to increase empathy in technology design for older adults (see Table 2).

Table 2. Qualitative research methods for elder-friendly technology design

Empathy techniques	Methods
Designers engage directly with elderly users (research)	Participant observation, interview, focus group, mapping, shadow, perceptual walking, etc.
External researcher conducts user research and feeds data back to the designer (communication)	Storytelling, visualizing, cultural probes, visual diary, photovoice, personas, scenarios, storyboards, design fiction, etc.
Designer simulates user to gain their own experience (ideation)	Simulating, role-playing, experience prototype, capabilities loss simulation suites, etc.

Direct engagement with older people for empathic experiences requires designers to have qualitative research skills. In addition, it requires time to build trust with elderly participants or costs for professional recruitment. For example, the Interval Research

Corporation project involved an interdisciplinary team of anthropology, sociology, computer science, and design researchers working on technology innovations for elderly customers, using interviews, ethnographic observations, shadow, persona, storyboarding, prototype iteration, and informance design to conduct long-term research. They propose a 'ask, observe, perform' qualitative research framework that applies to all stages of design technology for older people [29]. Because older people's attitudes and intentions to use technology are almost invisible in all aspects of their lives, many studies cannot be conducted directly due to privacy, cultural, and other practical constraints. Bill Gaver et al. worked on how information technology supports older people to increase their social participation in their communities by using the cultural probe to record their daily behavior by taking photos, drawing, collaging, and noting. The designers ultimately provide local community-centered technological solutions inspired by elder participants' indescribable feelings, preferences, and aesthetic appeal reflected in the toolkits materials [30]. Soud Nassir et al. take into account the cultural customs of the Saudi Arabian and use visual diaries and social chat software to gain information about the elderly' daily life [31]. The University of Cambridge's Engineering Design Centre has produced digital personas to help designers understand older people in digital products who are less technologically competent due to prior technology experience, motivation, and attitudes. Besides, designers use simulating suites that limit hearing, vision, and manipulation to create a simulated user experience is the most cost-effective way to gain empathy. Deana McDonagh et al. applied the five-stage empathic experience framework of receptivity, discovery, immersion, connection, and detachment to a transport design course, using various methods to help students increase their empathic horizons towards older and vulnerable people [12, 32].

According to the research, empathetic design techniques require designers to be sensitive, insightful, motivated and have specific training resources. Young designers are unfamiliar with the strategies that may involve older people in their studies, necessitating a more rigorous research process. Cultural probes and visual diaries, for example, were developed predominantly in Western social contexts. There is little evidence that they can be used effectively in the Chinese societal context. Brief experiential and virtual immersions are superficial, generating emotional empathy rather than cognitive empathy [33]. How can we help Young Chinese designers develop empathy for elderly adults and overcome elder-friendly technology design's technological product-centric limits? The authors demonstrate the development of the qualitative research toolkit 'Elderly Life Inquiry' and reflections in the next section.

3 Methods and Toolkits Development Process

This paper adopts a participatory research approach to increase the overall understanding of the phenomenon, gain multiple perspectives and information, engage with a wide range of participants at different stages [34, 35]. The toolkit's development went through three stages: initial research, prototyping and iteration, implementation, and evaluation, resulting in a prototype booklet and digital interactive version of the toolkit. All field studies were conducted with research ethics informed consent and signed consent of the participants.

3.1   Initial Research

The authors engaged as a researcher in three research projects related to the use of technology by older people in Beijing, China (see Table 3). The initial research goal was to obtain a wide knowledge of research processes conducted by different researchers with the elderly. The authors focus on research activity contents, techniques, obstacles, and subjective perspectives through photographic recording, participant observation, interviews, and self-reflection. Although these studies were not directly related to the technology design, feedback on research activities from young researchers and older adults in the field studies was universal.

Table 3. Information of initial research

Projects	Time	Researchers	Participants	Sample	Data collection
Smart senior care demand survey	Winter 2020	N = 3, sociology and design students	N = 9	Probabilistic and non-probabilistic	Questionnaire survey, interviews, ethnographic observations
Design for elder-friendly tech workshop	Spring 2021	N = 8, student designers	N = 12	Open, non-probabilistic	Focus groups, participant observations
Digital literacy training for the elderly	Spring 2021	N = 24, volunteers	N = 18	Open, non-probabilistic	Questionnaire survey, participant observations

Reflections Based on Elder Participants

- Each participant's understanding and demands about technology-related concepts differed widely. Quantitative study approaches such as surveys that lacked contextual context could not describe the elements that drove technology use. Participants stated that matching their experiences, feelings, and requirements with the Likert scale used in the questionnaire to represent satisfaction, attitudes, and frequency of use of technology items is challenging.
- They are more cautious when speaking in a multi-participant situation (both online and offline) and more likely to communicate their thoughts in a one-on-one chat.
- When older are increasingly experiencing physiological and cognitive declines such as deteriorating vision and aging hand joints, independent reading and writing can be challenging. In addition, when they are not clear about the objectives and tasks of the research activity may also affect their willingness to participate in the research.
- Many social events for elderly people were restricted due to the pandemic, so participants enjoyed the chance to engage with young people and felt grateful to be 'cared for' and 'beneficial to society.'

Reflections Based on Young Researchers

- They lack opportunities and experiences interacting with older people and thus are more nervous during direct interaction.
- Young designers are more conscious of the subtle technology operational behavior than other specialist researchers. They tend to assess and imagine participant behavior more from personal capabilities, preferences, and use norms, with certain stereotypes of older people.
- Limited by the specific research tasks, researchers lack the curiosity and willingness to understand older people and their lives.

3.2 Prototyping and Iteration

Initial research has found that informal interviews and participant observation provide a more contextual understanding of older people's real-life experiences and are more appropriate for Chinese older people's social preferences. Researchers with extensive research experience prefer this informal and loose research style. In contrast, research methods such as questionnaires and structured interviews, based on the scripted framework, are more accessible for young student designers to apply in practice due to the precise research tasks and operational approaches. As a result, after considering the merits and drawbacks of many methods in practice, the toolkit's original version was designed as an intuitive booklet to assist young designers in developing empathy for older people and their circumstances through direct engagement. The toolkit's content extends from a personal introduction about the older participant to life scenarios related to technology. Each theme has several sub-questions for the toolkit's user to lead a dialogue with the older participant. 'Describe your daily routine and indicate when and where you use technical product or service?' for example, is one of the questions in 'My Day.' Older folks can freely express themselves by sketching or attaching stickers instead of writing. After the research, the toolkit's user can give the booklet to the elder participants as a souvenir. In addition, the toolkit includes an informed consent form.

Table 4. Information of prototype testing

Time	Testers	Participants	Sample	Data collection
Spring 2021	N = 2, student designers	N = 2	Non-probabilistic	Semi-structured interview, participant observations

Prototype testing was affected by the lockdown of COVID-19, which made it challenging to facilitate open recruitment for multi-sample testing. Two graduate students in industrial design used the prototype toolkit separately (Tester A and Tester B, see Table 4). Before and after testing, the authors and testers had online meetings to discuss the toolkit's usage and review the research experience. Tester A invited her 81-year-old grandfather, who lives in the countryside to participate. At the beginning of the research, she mentioned that it was unclear what specific issues were of concern in older life. Following the toolkit's tips, she explored several topics with her grandfather. During the testing, she discovered that the most significant reason participant utilized the Internet to relieve loneliness and keep up with grandkids from afar seemed to be to meet emotional demands. She found that the elder had his technology strategies, such as carrying a lightweight phone without internet access while using another smartphone to check the news in the WiFi environment at home. Participants write down phone numbers, account information, and passwords on paper and keep them in smartphone cases (see Fig. 1). Reviewing the research experience, Tester A identified the importance of designing technology for older people to ensure cyber security, reduce the risk of misuse and enhance their confidence in using technology. With the toolkit's support, Tester A found that the elderly could actively participate in the research and that she had a better understanding of grandfather's needs, concerns, and expectations. She suggested that the toolkit could add provocative open-ended questions rather than directly asking about specific usage pain points.

Fig. 1. Tester A's empathy may have developed as she identified and described the distinctive qualities of older people utilizing technology items. She began to focus on how design could respond to older adults' preferences (Private data has been hidden).

Tester B reported that when conducting the research with her 85-year-old grandmother, it was difficult to explain the background and purpose of the research activity clearly. The 'self-portrait' in the toolkit was a good ice-breaker and gradually interested the participant. However, as the participant had no experience of using the Internet directly in daily life, some of the questions in the toolkit emphasized scenarios of older people using technology, making her feel irrelevant to herself and gradually lose patience. Tester B found that the participant was most excited when the conversation moved on to her relatives, old friends, and neighbors, specifically mentioning the community activities she'd like to attend. The elder participant was unwilling to sketch and complete the booklet independently, and the tester filled in almost all of the blanks (see Fig. 2). In addition, she noted that other family members and caregivers were present during the investigation that affected participants' responses. It was not easy to identify whether the older people were telling the truth or not.

The authors found that the young student designers had begun to develop their understanding and reflections on older people's lives, their relationship with technology, and even subtle psychological and behavioral patterns through the use of the toolkit. Based on feedback, we refined the prototype toolkit and produced the Elderly Life Inquiry

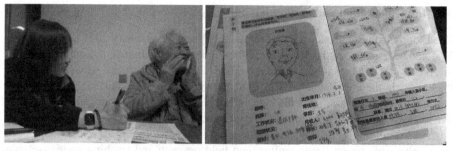

Fig. 2. Tester B became more sensitive to the emotional changes of the elderly and the surroundings, which assisted her in synthesizing the older participant's responses and actions to gain a deeper understanding (Private data has been hidden)

Toolkit (see Fig. 3). That includes a background introduction and instructions for using the toolkit, divided into a research booklet for the researcher and an interaction booklet for both participants, with adjustments to the layout, fonts, colors, and copy content. The booklet simplifies the topic of technology while emphasizing concerns relevant to older people's daily lives. The Elderly Life Inquiry toolkits offer more guidance for tool users on observing situations and feelings, such as "What was the participant's emotional state during the research?" 'How did it change?' Increasing users' sensitivity and insight contextual factors.

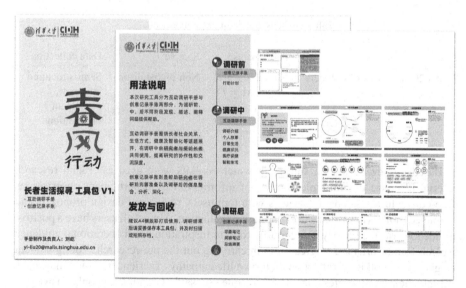

Fig. 3. The Elderly Life Inquiry toolkit's introductory page includes the study objectives and background, research methodology, and toolkit usage description.

3.3   Implementation and Evaluation

The Elderly Life Inquiry toolkit was released online on 27 January 2021 for free download and access. The authors organized the toolkit as a qualitative research tool in the pre-phase of a co-curriculum program entitled 'Design for inclusive service system for the elderly in the Post-Pandemic Era.' The positioning of the toolkit in the educational curriculum is to immerse students in the context of ageing and acquire specific qualitative research skills to create empathetic experiences of older people's lives around them. Later on, designing technological products and services solutions for older people. All inter-university contact occurs online, and field research and teaching stages are split among the universities. Before beginning the pre-phase, the authors held an online meeting with all participating teachers and student designers on the Tencent Meeting platform to discuss the social background of ageing, the co-curriculum, and the use of the Elderly Life Inquiry toolkit. The majority of the toolkit users were senior undergraduates, including 17 postgraduate students and 1 Ph.D. student. The students arranged their research plans and user recruitment in distributed. Since they were living at home during the winter vacations, elder participants were primarily grandparents, parents, elderly relatives, and neighbors of young student designers (see Table 5). Young student designers took images and scanned the completed toolkits into electronic files utilizing online forms after qualitative research on the elderly. According to the 8–10-week co-curriculum, the three universities have created 41 design proposals oriented on elder-friendly technology design in total.

Table 5. Information of implementation

Time	Users	Participants	Sample	Data collection
Winter 2020	N = 150, student designers	N = 160, Aged 52–87, M = 71	Non-probabilistic	Semi-structured interview, participant observations

Based on several design studies in which toolkits were used as crucial research material [36], we use multiple sources of information from participant observations of co-curriculum sessions, interviews with tool users, reviews of design proposals and completed toolkits as evidence for qualitative evaluation. Almost all users have a positive attitude towards the Elderly Life Inquiry Toolkit. Inspirational and operational guidance research frameworks are of great help in carrying out the pre-research. Young student designers use toolkits to reflect on their own life empathy experiences, which may carry over into their future professional work. As one user said, 'Grandma can only answer the phone on her phone. It's not that she doesn't have enough money to get a smartphone; rather, she is incapable of adapting to technological progress. Technology has made them incompetent in the familiar surroundings of their lives. I want to support older people and empower them to do the things they find curious.'

The imaginative ways in which the young designers utilize and adapt the toolkit go beyond the creator's vision, demonstrating their need for toolkit flexibility and customization. Someone adapts the toolkits based on individual research interests, such as adding shopping, socializing, travel, and personal items pages; others express research evidence and insights in the form of maps, photos, hand-drawn sketches, etc. (see Fig. 4). By analyzing these creative usages from young designers, the authors have increased the understanding of the design research demands of users and the life of older people in different social contexts. Furthermore, the toolkit's utilization in the educational curriculum exceeded expectations, for example, some groups used the toolkits as inspiration material for brainstorming; the tool to evaluate scenarios and prototypes for alignment with the needs and values of older people throughout the ideation stage. The authors and teachers summarize key findings from the all finished Elderly Life Inquiry toolkits and share research insights with all students at the end of the pre-research.

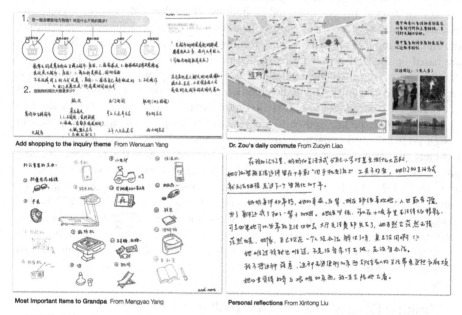

Add shopping to the inquiry theme From Wenxuan Yang   Dr. Zou's daily commute From Zuoyin Liao

Most Important Items to Grandpa From Mengyao Yang   Personal reflections From Xintong Liu

Fig. 4. Users have made creative adaptations to the toolkit's layout, content, and format.

According to the young student designers, discussing research findings allowed them to better compare and supplement their own empathic experiences with the research insights of others. It was more advantageous for them to expand their understanding of older individuals' typical and unique traits. Furthermore, some of the incomplete toolkits suggested that the toolkits' usefulness may be related to where the elder participants lived, their computer literacy, and health status. For example, young designers reported that when they engaged older people living in rural areas with limited digital literacy or multiple chronic illnesses, particularly cognitive impairment like Parkinson's, were difficult based on the content guidance in the toolkit to conduct the research. As a result, students prefer to adopt more direct, less verbal research techniques such as shadowing and working with those vulnerable elderly to understand their lives. The evaluation of the Elderly Life Inquiry toolkit's application revealed that a single qualitative research technique or toolkit is difficult to adapt to a wide range of settings, design phases, and elder scenarios. Young designers might improve their qualitative research capabilities and research interests in real-world circumstances with toolkits that give thematic action guidelines, clear research frameworks, illuminating inquiry questions, flexible research formats, and the sharing of research insights.

This paper focuses on a reflective description of the toolkit development process and empathy techniques rather than a detailed discussion of the design proposal. Reviewing the final design proposals, allowed us to glimpse how the toolkit might assist in enhancing the image of older people in designs and provide more scenarios for technological applications and human-centered development in design goals. The students expanded the 'abstract' image of older people by refining their physical and mental capacities, hobbies and talents, living environment, digital literacy, health condition, and other attributes to depict their diverse life situations and aspirations. These depict the many life conditions and demands of the elderly who are excellent, vital, frail, off-grid, living alone in the city or rural, offering more possibilities for technology applications. Some of the proposals are based on the rich emotional needs and the ingenuity of the elderly. For example, the community space co-construction service system employs technology to integrate repairs in the community so that the elderly can maintain the community environment, alleviating the elderly's sense of loss after retirement. It allows more people to discover the value of older people and build a community atmosphere of mutual help. Several design proposals also consider extreme users' physical and mental abilities, such as technical support for older people who do not have any digital device. Several design proposals consider extreme users' physical and mental limitations, such as technical assistance for the elderly who do not have access to a digital device. By combining qualitative research findings into designs, we believe that applying the Elderly Life Inquiry toolkit in practice helps young designers expand their empathy visions for enhancing their general grasp of the diversity of older persons and the complexities of ageing. It encourages young designers to create elder-friendly technology by focusing on what matters to the elderly themselves.

4   Results: Elderly Life Inquiry Toolkit

Based on the toolkit's development and evaluation, this article delivers an interactive version of the Elderly Life Inquiry applet with the functions to edit and share information. Users may access the WeChat applet via their smartphones instead of installing a mobile application. This applet may be used to care for the elderly and perform participatory qualitative research on ageing concerns by design students or anyone in their everyday life. 'Exploration-Interaction-Reflection' are the three components of the Elderly Life Inquiry applet (see Fig. 5). It enables users to acquire qualitative research capabilities and establish a more flexible process of empathetic experience in daily situations.

- Exploration: This section presents multidisciplinary information about ageing to assist users in understanding the complexity and variety at the macro, meso, and micro levels

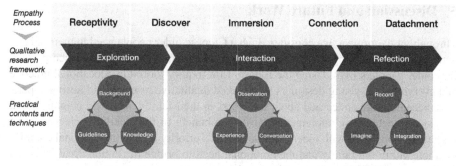

Fig. 5. The Elderly Life Inquiry applet creates a qualitative research framework that allows users to shift between the older person's life and the designer's perspective, bringing insight into the designs; this framework is also aligned with the process of developing empathy in empathic design [12, 26]

to build an active ageing perspective. Furthermore, providing qualitative research techniques and considerations with older adults assists users in taking action for inquiry research.

- Interaction: This module provides users with practical research techniques in the form of thematic inquiry cards, allowing them to gain further understanding about the elderly. Personal stories, lifestyle, social engagement, intelligent living, and health were the five topics of most concern to older adults. Each inquiry card includes enlightening questions and action tasks for 'observation-conversation-experience,' which guide the user through a multi-sensory immersion in the circumstance to sympathize with the elderly's daily lives. 'Observation' instructs users to pay attention to information regarding older individuals' physical and mental health, behavior, and living environment, such as 'Check out the accessibility of the community environment and service where She/He resides'. 'Conversation' focuses on encouraging meaningful dialogue that develops narratives about participants' past, present, and future lives, such as 'Share your favorite activities and why' and 'Imagine what life would be like with a robot in the home.' In some circumstances, users get more actively involved in others to form a deeper connection. The 'Experience' section contains several tasks that can be conducted with the participants, such as 'Try using another's phone with permission and see what happens.' Users are not required to complete all of these inquiry cards, and they can mix and match to accommodate their purposes. Users may also utilize the 'quick note' functions during the interaction stage to capture their thoughts and feelings.
- Reflection: This component pulls toolkit users away from the lives of older people and puts them back in their own shoes. The toolkit includes generating elderly personas and insight cards by taking notes, looking back, picturing. That helps Incorporate research findings into the subsequent design research or innovation process.

5 Discussion and Future Work

Throughout the project, we considered what Chinese older people need in their old age and what techniques might assist design practitioners in making technology incorporated into older people's lives. Using the Elderly Life Inquiry toolkit in educational practice and everyday life, young designers who lacked qualitative research and ageing experience became more concerned about the elders in their family, relatives, neighbors and considered technology implementation for the benefit of the elderly. Such qualitative research is consistent with older Chinese people's priority on intergenerational communication within the family and the emotional need to bridge the digital divide through pre-figurative [37]. The Elderly Life Inquiry applet is more suited to various scenarios in distributed research. It can effectively broaden the study sample's variety by allowing designers to directly connect with older adults in rural and vulnerable as part of an empathetic experience.

There is no denying that the COVID-19 pandemic has erected more barriers to researchers entering the lives of older people to undertake research, demanding new types of research methodologies and technologies to support future research [9]. This article creates a hybrid online-offline distributed design research to allow stakeholders from various backgrounds to apply the Elderly Life Inquiry toolkit in their work and everyday life. We want to continue to improve the toolkit based on user input and data analysis under the notion of active ageing and human-centered approaches. It might bring together actors from many generations and disciplines to share their ingenuity experiences through participatory research, storytelling, and co-design, similar to an open-source platform that is instructive, flexible, and interactive. It might be used to assist young designers in incorporating empathy for a diverse group of people into the professional design practice and creating age-friendly contexts. As young designers who have used the Elderly Life Inquiry toolkits put it, 'The primary goal of elder-friendly design technology should not be to entice older adults to become digital geeks. Since the merging virtual and traditional physical worlds are inevitable, technology design should be compatible to their ideal lifestyles.'

Acknowledgments. This work was supported by the Scientific Research Institute of Tsinghua University as part of the 'Design of an inclusive service system for the elderly in the Post-Pandemic Era' (Research number is 20203080033) under the Open Collaboration for International Research Cooperation Spring Wind Foundation. We want to thank all the participants in this study, especially the older participants, community workers, and young students who used toolkits. We are particularly grateful to the teaching teams of Professor Qian Xiaobo from Jiangnan University and Professor Zhang Jun from Hunan University for their strong support for this research, who participated in the co-curriculum program. We are thankful to the China-Italy Design Innovation Hub at Tsinghua University for doing the project known to a broader audience.

References

1. Peng, D., Wenting, H.: Internet and life of older adults: challenges and opportunities. Popul. Res. **45**(03), 3–16 (2021)

2. EU: Overview of the European strategy in ICT for Ageing Well (2010)
3. Jiane, S., Zhixiong, Z.: Research on 'internet plus' based aged service model and its development path. J. Soc. Sci. Hunan Normal Univ. **48**(03), 46–53 (2019)
4. Meng, W.: The positioning, deficiencies and development measures of Smart Senior Care in China. Theory J. (03), 143–149 (2021)
5. WHO.: Active ageing: a policy framework. World Health Organization (2002)
6. Lak, A., Rashidghalam, P., Myint, P.K., Baradaran, H.R.: Comprehensive 5P framework for active aging using the ecological approach: an iterative systematic review. BMC Public Health **20**, 33 (2020)
7. Giaccardi, E., Kuijer, L., Neven, L.: Design for resourceful ageing: intervening in the ethics of gerontechnology. In: 2016 Design Research Society Conference (DRS 2016), Brighton, UK, 27–30 June 2016 (2016)
8. Harrington, C.N., Koon, L.M., Rogers, W.A.: Design of health information and communication technologies for older adults. In: Sethumadhavan, A., Sasangohar, F. (eds.) Design for Health, pp. 341–363. Academic Press (2020)
9. Carlo, S., Bonifacio, F.: Elderly, ICTs and qualitative research: some methodological reflections. In: Gao, Q., Zhou, J. (eds.) HCII 2021. LNCS, vol. 12786, pp. 3–20. Springer, Cham (2021). https://doi.org/10.1007/978-3-030-78108-8_1
10. Ostrowski, A.K., Harrington, C.N., Breazeal, C., Park, H.W.: Personal narratives in technology design: the value of sharing older adults' stories in the design of social robots. Front. Robot. AI **8**, 716581 (2021)
11. McDonagh-Philp, D., Denton, H.G.: User-centred design and the focus group: developing the student designer's empathic horizons (2000)
12. McDonagh, D., Osmond, J.: Developing empathy for older users in undergraduate design students. Des. Technol. Educ. Int. J. **23**, 24–39 (2018)
13. Woodcock, A., McDonagh, D., Magee, P., Ball, T., Iqbal, S.: Eexpanding horizons: engaging students with empathic thinking (2019)
14. Endter, C.: Design for elderly–a meeting point for ethnography and usability. i-com **15**, 17–26 (2016)
15. General Office of the State Council of the People's Republic of China: Solutions to effectively address older people's difficulties in using smart technology. http://www.gov.cn/gongbao/con tent/2020/content_5567747.htm. Accessed 31 Dec 2021
16. Li, C., Qin, L., Qingqing, Q.: Research on the construction of the wisdom community endowment service system. Popul. J. **38**(03), 67–73 (2016)
17. Wahl, H.W., Fänge, A., Oswald, F., Gitlin, L.N., Iwarsson, S.: The home environment and disability-related outcomes in aging individuals: what is the empirical evidence? Gerontologist **49**, 355–367 (2009)
18. Righi, V., Sayago, S., Blat, J.: When we talk about older people in HCI, who are we talking about? Towards a 'turn to community' in the design of technologies for a growing ageing population. Int. J. Hum. Comput. Stud. **108**, 15–31 (2017)
19. Subasi, O., Malmborg, L.: Ageing as design culture. Nordes 1 (2013)
20. De Angeli, A., Jovanovic, M., McNeill, A., Coventry, L.: Desires for active ageing technology. Int. J. Hum Comput Stud. **138**, 102412 (2020)
21. Ping, Z., Xiaomin, D.: Research on interaction design of intelligent products for the elderly under compensatory mechanism. J. Graph. **39**(04), 700–705 (2018)
22. Lin, L., Fangyu, L., Zheng, L.: Development trend and oriented design of intelligent kitchen under the background of active aging. Packging Eng. 1–19 (2020)
23. Jinhua, D., Jingyan, Q.: Senior-friendly design of smart health care products and research methods for elderly users. Packging Eng. **42**(06), 62–68 (2021)

24. The Institute of Sociology of the Chinese Academy of Social Sciences, Tengyun, and Research Centre for National Survey and Big Data: Research Report on the Internet Life of the Middle Aged (2018)
25. Seïler, N.R., Craig, P.: Empathetic technology. In: Tettegah, S.Y., Noble, S.U. (eds.) Emotions, Technology, and Design, pp. 55–81. Academic Press, San Diego (2016)
26. Kouprie, M., Visser, F.S.: A framework for empathy in design: stepping into and out of the user's life. J. Eng. Des. **20**, 437–448 (2009)
27. McDonagh, D.: Empathic research approaches to support the designer: a supra-qualitative research for designing model. Design Issues (2006)
28. Newell, A.F., Gregor, P., Morgan, M., Pullin, G., Macaulay, C.: User-sensitive inclusive design. Univ. Access Inf. Soc. **10**, 235–243 (2011). https://doi.org/10.1007/s10209-010-0203-y
29. Dishman, E.: Designing for the new old: asking, observing, and performing future elders, design. In: Design Research: Methods and Perspectives, pp. 41–48. The MIT Press, Cambridge (2003)
30. Gaver, W., Dunne, A., Pacenti, E.: Design: cultural probes. Interactions **6**, 21–29 (1999)
31. Nassir, S., Leong, T.W.: Conducting qualitative fieldwork with ageing saudis: a visual diary. In: Proceedings of the 2018 Designing Interactive Systems Conference, Hong Kong, China, pp. 427–439. Association for Computing Machinery (2018)
32. Battarbee, K.: Co-experience: understanding user experiences in interaction. Aalto University (2004)
33. Martingano, A.J., Hererra, F., Konrath, S.: Virtual reality improves emotional but not cognitive empathy: A meta-analysis. Technol. Mind Behav. (2021)
34. Tracy, S.J.: Qualitative Research Methods: Collecting Evidence, Crafting Analysis Communication Impact. Wiley, Hoboken (2019)
35. McIntyre, A.: Participatory Action Research. Sage Publications, Thousand Oaks (2007)
36. McKinnon, H., Sade, G.: Exploring the home environment: fusing rubbish and design to encourage participant agency and self-reflection. Des. Stud. **63**, 155–180 (2019)
37. Yuqiong, Z.: The digital divide and pre-figurative: a quantitative study of the 'silent revolution' within the family. Mod. Commun. (J. Commun. Univ. China) **36**(02), 117–123 (2014)

Improving Smartphone Reading Experience for Middle-Aged and Elderly Users: The Effect of Font Size, Line Spacing and Stroke Weight

Yongsheng Lu[(✉)], Hui Li, Nan Chen, and Yujie Shi

Baidu (China) Co., Ltd., Beijing, People's Republic of China
{luyongsheng,lihui15}@baidu.com

Abstract. Aging and digitization are two major trends in modern society, resulting in a rapid increase in the number of middle-aged and elderly smartphone users. Research into these user's mobile reading experience has significant value in industry application, as well as social value. Based on the subjective experience evaluation and eye movement data of 60 Chinese adults aged 50–70 years, we investigated the impact of different font sizes, line spacing, and stroke weight on the smartphone reading experience of Chinese characters in three typical scenarios: searching, overview reading, and long-text reading. Results show that font size has a significant impact on reading experience in all scenarios. Line spacing and stroke weight have different impacts in different reading scenarios. Line spacing has a significant effect on long-text reading (such as the news details page), while stroke weight has a significant impact on search scenarios (such as news headlines). Bold type fonts can highlight key information on a page with multiple levels of information. This study also identifies the optimal font size, line spacing and stroke weight for different scenarios and different levels of information. This is the first study that provides smartphone application developers with design specifications for optimal font size, line spacing and stroke weight in different scenarios for middle-aged and elderly Chinese users. These findings can be utilized to improve the reading experience of Chinese news apps in a comprehensive manner.

Keywords: Reading experience · Font size · Line spacing · Stroke weight · Middle-aged and elderly users · Chinese news apps design

1 Introduction

Due to the declining fertility rate and continuous improvement of living and medical conditions, population aging has become a global trend. According to data from the United Nations, in 2010, individuals aged 50 and above accounted for 20.6% of the global population. This number reached 24.2% in 2020 [21]. The degree of population aging is more significant in China. In 2009, individuals aged 50 years and above accounted for 28.5% the population, and in 2019, the number reached 33.4% [20]. With the development of smartphone technology, an increasing number of middle-aged and elderly users in China are beginning to experience a more convenient life. The percentage of netizens aged 50 and above has almost tripled, from 9.2% in 2015 to 26.3% in 2020 [2, 3]. Considering the changes in the age distribution of Internet users, we define middle-aged and elderly users as those who are aged 50 and above in this study. The rapid increase of middle-aged and elderly smartphone users has also resulted in great challenges for software developers, as smartphone apps need to be upgraded to adapt to deterioration in eyesight, hearing, response, judgment, and control of older users. With these efforts, smartphone apps can help middle-aged and elderly users to better integrate into the digital society.

Due to aging, the eyesight of middle-aged and elderly users inevitably declines [18]. The impact of aging on eyesight has been an important research topic that attracted attention. Previously, scholars have found that, compared with young users, middle-aged and elderly users face more difficulties in reading Chinese characters, such as slow reading speeds, long gaze times, additional backtracking, more frequent skipping of words, and difficulties reading Chinese characters with more strokes (9 strokes or more) [1, 14, 17, 23]. This type of vision loss results in different demands compared to young users, for example, older users require larger font size and line spacing than younger users [9, 25] and more contrasting colors [4].

Therefore, it is important to study the font size, line spacing, and stroke weight, to determine what is suitable such that middle-aged and elderly people are able to read effectively on their smartphone. This subject also has important industrial applications and social significance. Research results can provide more normative references for developing and designing smartphone apps suitable for the aging population, so as to help middle-aged and elderly users to read text on their smartphones with better experience.

This paper proceeds as follows. Section 2 reviews previous academic research on the influence of font size, line spacing, and stroke weight on the reading experience of middle-aged and elderly users, and outlines the novelty of this study, which we investigated three typical reading scenarios using smartphone news apps (search, overview reading, and long-text reading). Section 3 introduces the research methods and Sect. 4 analyzes the results for the different scenarios. Section 5 discusses the results of each reading scenario, and analyzes how the results differ from previous studies. Finally, Sect. 6 draws the conclusions.

2   Related Studies

The majority of previous studies on digital reading have focused on analyzing the influence of font size and line spacing. However, their conclusions vary, owing to the use of different experimental equipment and types of reading tasks (representing different reading scenarios and reading strategies).

Rello, Pielot, and Marcos [19] studied the impact of different font sizes on fixation duration, text comprehension, and legibility evaluation for subjects aged 14–54 years using personal desktop computers (screen size: 17 in., pixel resolution: 1024 × 768), and concluded that fonts larger than 18pt are more suitable for text-intensive websites. Liu, Yu, and Zhang [15] studied the easy-to-read Chinese font size, with 19- to 26-year-old college students using personal desktop computers (screen size: 22 in., pixel resolution:

1680 × 1050). Through search tasks, the influence of different font sizes on search time, number of characters found, and correct response rate of the target Chinese characters was analyzed. Results found that a font size of 12–14pt has superior legibility, but a larger font size (16pt) will actually reduce legibility. When compared with a computer, the suitable font size for digital reading on a smartphone is significantly smaller. For example, Darroch et al. [4] used a personal digital assistant (PDA, a handheld computer with a screen size of 4.0 in. and pixel resolution of 640 × 680) to study 61- to 78-year-old users reading English articles. After collecting users' objective reading data and subjective evaluations for different font sizes, this research concluded that 9–12pt was a suitable font size for the handheld device. Hou et al. [7] used a smartphone (screen size of 5.5 in. and pixel resolution of 1920 × 1080) as an experimental device to analyze users' experience when reading Chinese articles and to study the impact of font size and line spacing on the perceived usability, comfort, and recognition of users. Participants were aged 57 to 70, and the results concluded that 10.5–15pt was the most suitable font size for them to read on a smartphone. In comparison to Darroch's research, Hou believed that a higher resolution and a larger screen could change the requirements, such as larger font sizes, of middle-aged and elderly users.

Wang et al. [24] studied the impact of different line spacing on Chinese reading performance and readability for middle-aged and elderly users (average age: 66 years old; standard deviation: 11), using 2px (≈1.1 times), 4px (≈1.3 times), 6px (=1.4 times) and 8px (≈1.5 times) line spacing and a fixed font size of 15 * 15px (8pt). Results found that an increase in line spacing significantly increased the readability of text, with a line spacing of 8px (≈1.5 times) having the highest readability; however, the study did not observe an upper limit of line spacing. Hou's research [7] selected three different line spacings, 1.0, 1.2, and 1.4 times. The results showed that larger line spacing improved the usability for middle-aged and elderly users, with a line spacing of 1.4 being the best of the options studied; however, from the perspective of comfort, a line spacing of 1.2 was preferred.

Previous studies have not yielded a uniform conclusion for the impact of stroke weight on reading experience, hence this field requires further research. Zhang et al. [28] confirmed that the outline of appropriately bolded fonts was more distinctive and can improve the recognition speed and accuracy of Chinese characters. Wang [22] explored the impact of five font styles (bold, underline, character border, italics, and shadow) on the visual search results for Chinese characters. The results showed that a bold font type resulted in the fastest visual search speed and the highest accuracy. In a study by Fang et al. [5], participants searched for target words initially presented in a news interface. The aim of their research was to study the influence of bold, regular, and fine font types on the efficiency of visual searches in different information density and graphic structure environments. The results concluded that the fine font had the highest degree of recognition and could improve the user's visual recognition efficiency.

Most of the aforementioned studies did not take into account the differences between various smartphone reading scenarios. Additionally, their experimental scenarios differed significantly from real-life usage scenarios. Therefore, these studies cannot be effectively applied to improve the smartphone reading design for middle-aged and elderly users. For example, Liu [15] and Darroch et al. [4] both selected the search scenario for their experimental task. In both of these studies, users were given the task of finding a target word in a passage. A real-life search scenario would not be limited to finding a target word, and would also involve extracting useful content to solve a specific problem. Hou's research [7] deduced the recommended font size and line spacing for different scenarios based on the characteristics of different experience indicators, and his experimental task was a long-text reading scenario. As the reading patterns and motivations of users differ between smartphone reading scenarios, it is necessary to study the characteristics of various scenarios. This can ensure that the results are more comprehensive and have a greater applicability, to provide a set of design specifications for text and its layout that covers multiple reading scenarios, to design age-appropriate smartphone applications.

With regard to the classification of reading scenarios, Huang, Rau, and Liu [10] believed that when users read text on smartphone devices, they have only two reading modes: intensive reading and fast browsing. Moreover, users have different requirements for the readability of fonts in different modes. Yuan [27] highlighted that users' information search modes on social media include search, browsing, tracking, encounter, and inquiry. Research by Li et al. [13] and Liu et al. [16] compared two modes of visual search and visual browsing when people use the Internet. They defined visual search to be when users find the required information on the Internet purposefully, and visual browsing to be when users do not have a clear goal and freely browse and view information. Additionally, they suggested that a visual search relies on top-down attention control.

In summary, to address the lack of systematic analysis of different smartphone reading scenarios in the existing research of middle-aged and elderly users, this study analyzed three reading modes for news apps: searching, overview reading, and long-text reading. "Searching" refers to a user using a search engine on a smartphone to purposefully find the required information from the search result page. overview reading refers to when users freely view information on a news page and select a title of interest. This is the state before a user clicks on the title of interest. long-text reading refers to the scenario where users enter into a specific news page of interest and browse the detailed content. This study analyzes the impact of font size, line spacing, and stroke weight on the reading experience of middle-aged and elderly users in the three types of scenarios listed above, and presents the optimal font size, line spacing and stroke weight for each scenario to provide detailed guidelines for smartphone app developers for the text layout design for different scenarios.

3   Methodology

This research includes three separate experiments to study the effects of different font sizes, line spacing, and stroke weight on the reading experience of Chinese news apps in three different scenarios: search reading, overview reading, and long-text reading.

3.1   Subjects

There were 60 subjects in this study, equally distributed between the three experiments, with 20 users in each experimental group, as shown in Table 1. All participants were middle-aged and elderly users in China, aged between 50 and 70 years old, with an average age of 61.9 years (standard deviation 6.0). There were 29 males and 31 females. All participants had normal vision or normal vision after correction, an education level of junior high school or above, and the ability to read news articles.

Table 1. Experimental groups and the corresponding number of subjects.

Experimental group	Research scenario	Number of subjects
Experiment 1	Search scenario: search results	20
Experiment 2	Overview reading scenario: news list	20
Experiment 3	Long-text reading scenario: news details	20

3.2 Experimental Environment and Setup

The experiment was carried out in an indoor environment, with common indoor lighting. The test equipment was a Huawei P30 (screen size: 6.1 in.; pixel resolution: 1080 × 2340). The brightness of the screen was automatically adjusted before the experiment, according to the lighting in the room, then the automatic adjustment function was turned off so that the background brightness was fixed at this suitable level. SMI-ETG2w eye-tracking glasses were used to track participants' eye movements.

3.3 Independent and Dependent Variables

Independent Variables. There are three independent variables in this study: font size, line spacing, and stoke weight. To ensure the scientific validity and practical applicability of the research results, the level of independent variables was selected based on past research results and consultations with design experts in the industry. The specific scope in different scenarios are outlined in Table 2.

Font Size. In this study, both pixel (px) and point (pt) were used as the measurement units of font size. Px is the unit used in smartphone applications, and was used as a reference when making the experimental materials. Pt is the absolute unit for text layout, which made the research results scalable and applicable to different mobile devices. The following equation was used to covert between pt and px[1]:

$$Font\ size\ (pt) = font\ size\ (px) \times 72/actual\ PPI \qquad (1)$$

Previous studies have not reached a consistent conclusion on the optimal font size for middle-aged and elderly users. Therefore, the range of font sizes studied in this research was based on Hou's study [7], which is the most relevant research to our study. Hou's research showed that when the font size was larger than 12.75pt, the improvement of usability and visual comfort was limited. Huang's research [11, 12] also confirmed that

---

[1] *PPI of the test equipment in this study was 422 px/in.*

increasing font size affects reading efficiency, and that it does so because the text length of small fonts is shorter, which means that the scrolling distance of users is shorter, and the required reading time is shorter. The font size range selected in this study is smaller than Hou's research. We selected font sizes of 66px(11.26pt), 72px(12.28pt), and 81px(13.82pt) for the title and text. There were no previous studies related to the font size of the abstract in the search scenario, so that the font sizes of the abstract in this study were 48px, 54px, or 60px, selected based on the experience of design experts. The abstract font size was appropriately adjusted according to the title font size.

Line Spacing. According to previous research experience [7, 24], to meet the demand of reading comfort for middle-aged and elderly users, the line spacing should be 1.2 times or larger. Therefore, the minimum line spacing for each experiment was 1.2 times. The maximum line spacing increased as the text content increased. The maximum headline spacing was less than the maximum line spacing of the summary, which was less than the maximum line spacing of the long text. Thus, line spacing of 1.2, 1.3, and 1.4 times were selected for titles of search scenario and overview reading scenario, while 1.2, 1.4, and 1.6 times were selected for abstract in the search scenario. And 1.2, 1.4, and 1.7 times were selected for long text.

Stroke Weight. The title was divided into two categories: bold and non-bold.

Table 2. Independent variables in three smartphone reading scenarios.

Scenarios		Experiment 1: Search scenario		Experiment 2: Overview reading scenario	Experiment 3: Long-text reading scenario
		Title	Abstract	Title	Long text
Font size	Pt	11.26/12.28/13.82	8.19/9.21/10.24	11.26/12.28/13.82	11.26/12.28/13.82
	Px	66/72/81	48/54/60	66/72/81	66/72/81
Line spacing	Times	1.2/1.3/1.4	1.2/1.4/1.6	1.2/1.3/1.4	1.2/1.4/1.7
Stroke weight		Bold/non-bold	–	Bold/non-bold	–

Experience Indicators (Dependent Variables). The dependent variable combined subjective user experience evaluation data and objective eye movement data (as outlined in Table 3). The dimensions of the subjective evaluation included finding key information, clarity, comfort, and satisfaction, which were measured using the Likert 5-point scale. In the search scenario and overview reading scenario, users want to find important content or content of interest quickly, so we selected finding key information as one of the reading experience indicators. And finding key information has not been investigated in previous studies; therefore, study of this indicator is in great demand. Clarity and comfort are commonly used dimensions for studying a user's text reading experience, and satisfaction is a typical indicator that reflects user experience. The objective data included blink frequency, pupil diameter variability, and reading speed, which were directly measured using an eye tracker. Blink frequency and pupil diameter variability are highly correlated with users' cognitive load. Blink frequency has a significant negative correlation with the occupancy of a user's cognitive load. When a user is at a high cognitive load, their blink frequency tends to be lower, and when the user is at a low cognitive load, their blink frequency tends to be higher [6, 8]. Pupil diameter variability has a significant positive correlation with the occupancy of a user's cognitive load. When the user is at a high cognitive load, they tend to show a higher pupil diameter variability, and when the user is at a low cognitive load, they show a lower pupil diameter variability [6, 26] (Table 4).

Table 3. Reading experience indicators (dependent variables).

Indicator type	Measurement method	Indicator	Definition
Subjective evaluation data	Likert 5-Point Scale	Finding key information	The ease of finding the important content or content of interest
		Clarity	Whether the text is presented clearly
		Comfort	Feeling comfortable and not tired, awkward, or depressed
		Satisfaction	The overall satisfaction with the font size, line spacing, and stroke weight on the current page
Objective eye movement data	SMI-ETG2w eye-tracking glasses	Reading speed	Words read per second
		Blink frequency	Times the participant blinks per second
		Pupil diameter variability	–

3.4 Materials

Experiments 1 and 2 adopted a 3 × 3 × 3 orthogonal experimental design (see Tables 5 and 6). According to the orthogonal experimental design L9 (34), nine combinations of font size, line spacing, and stroke weight were designed. Experiment 3 used 3 × 3 repeated measurement experimental design (see Table 7). All experiments required participants to read 9 formal texts and 1 test text, i.e., a total of 10 tasks.

Table 4. Experience indicators (dependent variables) measured in three research scenarios.

Experimental groups & research scenarios	Subjective variables	Objective variables
Experiment 1 (Search scenario: search result page)	Degree of difficulty finding key information Clarity Comfort Satisfaction	Reading speed Blink frequency Pupil diameter variability
Experiment 2 (Overview reading scenario: news list page)	Degree of difficulty finding key information Clarity Comfort Satisfaction	Reading speed Blink frequency Pupil diameter variability
Experiment 3 (Long-text reading scenario: news details page)	Clarity Comfort Satisfaction	Reading speed Blink frequency Pupil diameter variability

Table 5. Orthogonal experimental design $L_9(3^4)$ of experiment 1 (search scenario).

Task	Title				Abstract		
	Font size (px)	Line spacing (times)	Line spacing (px)	Stroke weight	Font size (px)	Line spacing (times)	Line spacing (px)
Test task	66	1.3	86	Non-bold	48	1.6	58
Formal task 1	66	1.2	79	Bold	48	1.2	58
Formal task 2	66	1.3	86	Bold	48	1.4	67
Formal task 3	66	1.4	92	Non-bold	48	1.6	77
Formal task 4	72	1.2	86	Non-bold	54	1.2	65
Formal task 5	72	1.3	94	Bold	54	1.4	76
Formal task 6	72	1.4	101	Bold	54	1.6	86
Formal task 7	81	1.2	97	Bold	60	1.2	72
Formal task 8	81	1.3	105	Non-bold	60	1.4	84
Formal task 9	81	1.4	113	Bold	60	1.6	96

Table 6. Orthogonal experimental design $L_9(3^4)$ of experiment 2 (overview reading scenario).

Task	Font size (px)	Line spacing (times)	Line spacing (px)	Stroke weight
Test task	66	1.3	86	Bold
Formal task 1	66	1.2	79	Bold
Formal task 2	66	1.3	86	Non-bold
Formal task 3	66	1.4	92	Bold
Formal task 4	72	1.2	86	Non-bold
Formal task 5	72	1.3	94	Bold
Formal task 6	72	1.4	101	Bold
Formal task 7	81	1.2	97	Bold
Formal task 8	81	1.3	105	Bold
Formal task 9	81	1.4	113	Non-bold

Table 7. Repeated measures design of experiment 3 (long-text reading scenario).

Task	Font size (px)	Line spacing (times)	Line spacing (px)
Test task	66	1.3	86
Formal task 1	66	1.2	79
Formal task 2	66	1.4	92
Formal task 3	66	1.7	112
Formal task 4	72	1.2	86
Formal task 5	72	1.4	101
Formal task 6	72	1.7	122
Formal task 7	81	1.2	97
Formal task 8	81	1.4	113
Formal task 9	81	1.7	138

Experiment 1 (Search Scenario). Ten search keywords with strong comprehensiveness and relating to diverse topics were chosen from categories common to middle-aged and elderly users (such as news, medical treatment, and people), and were presented as 10 separate tasks. The layout of each result list page was identical and contained 12 results. The comprehensive difficulty of each task, as assessed by experts, did not significantly differ.

Each task simulated a real-world search scenario, and subjects were asked to complete the experiment according to the following procedure. First, subjects clicked on any area on the cover page to access the search input (transition) page. Then, they clicked on the search button to access the search result page. Finally, the subjects were asked to read through the search results page from beginning to end, and find the answer to the question on the search input page. If the reading material was not fully displayed on one screen, the subject could scroll down to read the whole content. Examples of these materials are shown in Fig. 1.

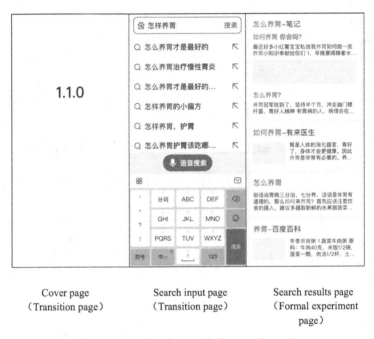

Cover page   Search input page   Search results page
(Transition page)   (Transition page)   (Formal experiment
                                                            page)

Fig. 1. Example of materials for experiment 1.

Experiment 2 (Overview Reading Scenario). One hundred and twenty titles were selected from current social affairs, international news, food, music, knowledge, and other content commonly read by middle-aged and elderly users. All titles were combined into 10 news list pages, with 12 headlines per page. Each news list page was used as an individual experimental task. The comprehensive difficulty of each task, as assessed by experts, did not significantly differ.

Each task simulated an overview reading scenario, and subjects were asked to complete the experiment according to the following procedure. First, subjects clicked on any area on the cover page to access the refresh (transition) page. Then, they refreshed the page to access the news list page. Finally, the subjects were asked to read through the news list page from beginning to end and find the titles that interested them. If the reading material was not fully displayed on one screen, the subject could scroll down to read the whole content. Examples of these materials are shown in Fig. 2.

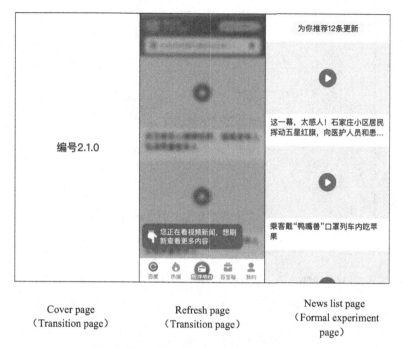

编号2.1.0

为你推荐12条更新

这一幕，太感人！石家庄小区居民挥动五星红旗，向医护人员和患…

乘客戴"鸭嘴兽"口罩列车内吃苹果

您正在看视频新闻，想刷新查看更多内容

百度　热搜　陪伴电台　百宝箱　我的

| Cover page (Transition page) | Refresh page (Transition page) | News list page (Formal experiment page) |

Fig. 2. Examples of materials for experiment 2

Experiment 3 (Long-Text Reading Scenario). Ten articles with 260 characters from the news, health, and wellness, and other content commonly read by middle-aged and elderly users were selected as 10 separate experimental tasks. The comprehensive difficulty of each task, as assessed by experts, did not significantly differ.

Each task simulated a long-text reading scenario, and subjects were asked to complete the experiment according to the following procedure. First, subjects clicked on any area on the cover page to access the overview (transition) page. Then, they clicked on the blue title to enter the news page (the long-text reading page). The subjects were asked to read through the long-text reading page from beginning to end and understand the main idea of the article. If the reading material was not fully displayed on one screen, the subject could scroll down to read the whole content. Examples of these materials are shown in Fig. 3.

3.5 Experimental Procedure

The experimental procedure was the same for all three experiments. Before the experiment started, the subjects with myopia and presbyopia were fitted with appropriate lenses so that they could participate in the experiment with normal vision. Subjects were not limited to a uniform viewing distance in this experiment, but were allowed to adjust to a comfortable viewing distance based on their own preferences, as in Huang's [11] experiment. This was to make the experiment as close to an actual smartphone usage

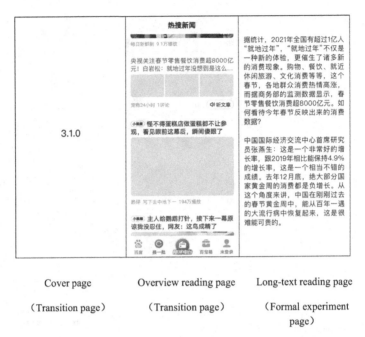

Cover page	Overview reading page	Long-text reading page
(Transition page)	(Transition page)	(Formal experiment page)

Fig. 3. Examples of materials for experiment 3.

scenario as possible. However, each subject was asked to keep their viewing distance fixed during the experiment, so that the entire experiment was completed under the same conditions.

Subjects first completed one test task, and then nine formal tasks. The nine formal tasks for all experiments were designed in Latin squares to balance the order of presentation.

In each task, eye movement data were measured after the subjects entered the formal experiment page and the data collection stopped when the eye trajectory showed that the last word was read.

After each task, the subjects were asked to answer reading comprehension questions and complete subjective evaluation questionnaires. To avoid putting a large cognitive load on middle-aged and elderly subjects, the reading comprehension questions were not multiple-choice questions with fixed correct answers. Open questions were adopted by asking the subjects what useful or interesting content they found in the different reading scenarios, to ensure that the subjects completed the experiment in a state that resembled their actual daily usage.

To avoid fatigue effects, participants had 2 min of rest between each task. Each participant took approximately 1 h to complete the full experiment.

4 Results

As the data did not satisfy the assumption of normal distribution, a non-parametric test was used to study the impact of different font sizes, line spacing, and stroke weight on the subjective evaluation data of user experience and objective eye movement data.

4.1 Experiment 1: Search Scenario

The results of non-parametric tests and range analyses are illustrated in Tables 8 and 9, respectively. The results of the Kruskal-Wallis test indicate that font size had a significant impact on the clarity of the search title ($p < 0.05$). Furthermore, the pairwise comparison test showed that 81px was significantly more clear for middle-aged and elderly users than 66px ($p < 0.05$). Range analysis found that a title size of 81px resulted in a better user performance in finding key information, clarity, comfort, and satisfaction. Stroke weight had a significant impact on title search satisfaction ($p < 0.05$), and a bold search title resulted in significantly higher satisfaction levels. Compared with average values, it was found that middle-aged and elderly users have a more positive evaluation of 1.4 times line spacing for finding key information, clarity, and better performance in reading speed, but have a more positive evaluation of 1.2 times line spacing for comfort and satisfaction.

Font size had a significant impact on finding key information, clarity, comfort, and satisfaction ($p < 0.01$, $p < 0.001$, $p < 0.01$, and $p < 0.01$, respectively), but had no significant impact on the eye movement data. Participants rated a font size of 60px significantly higher than 48px for finding key information, clarity, comfort and satisfaction ($p < 0.01$, $p < 0.001$, $p < 0.01$, and $p < 0.01$, respectively), and significantly higher than 54px for clarity ($p < 0.05$). Based on the range analysis, a line spacing of 1.2 times resulted in improved clarity, comfort, and satisfaction, as well as blink frequency and pupil diameter variability.

Table 8. Kruskal-Wallis test for the influence of font size, line spacing and stroke weight on the reading experience in the search scenario.

Reading experience	Search engine results page titles			Search engine results page abstracts	
	Font size	Line spacing	Stroke weight	Font size	Line spacing
Finding key information	.300	.858	.810	.007**	.837
Clarity	.047*	.711	.582	.000***	.815
Comfort	.563	.940	.275	.002**	.691
Satisfaction	.251	.874	.040*	.004**	.432
Reading speed	.557	.360	.523	.557	.360
Blink frequency	.858	.693	.250	.858	.693
Pupil diameter variability	.917	.670	.480	.917	.670

*$p < 0.05$; **$p < 0.01$; **$p < 0.001$.

Table 9. Orthogonal experimental range analysis: the influence of font size, line spacing, and stroke weight on the reading experience in the search scenario.

	Search engine results page titles			Search engine results page abstracts	
	Font size	Line spacing	Stroke weight	Font size	Stroke weight
Finding key information					
K1 mean	4.46	4.52	4.57	3.93	4.20
K2 mean	4.58	4.55	4.52	4.24	4.16
K3 mean	4.62	4.59	–	4.42	4.23
Excellence level	81	1.3, 1.4	Bold	60	1.6
Range analysis	0.15	0.07	0.05	0.49	0.08
Clarity					
K1 mean	4.45	4.54	4.60	3.95	4.32
K2 mean	4.58	4.59	4.56	4.27	4.22
K3 mean	4.72	4.62	–	4.61	4.28
Excellence level	81	1.3, 1.4	Bold	60	1.2
Range analysis	0.28	0.09	0.04	0.66	0.10
Comfort					
K1 mean	4.32	4.41	4.43	3.78	4.12
K2 mean	4.36	4.35	4.30	4.10	4.00
K3 mean	4.47	4.39	–	4.35	4.12
Excellence level	81	1.2, 1.4	Bold	60	1.2, 1.6
Range analysis	0.15	0.06	0.13	0.58	0.12
Satisfaction					
K1 mean	4.39	4.41	4.44	3.85	4.17
K2 mean	4.27	4.35	4.26	4.12	4.05
K3 mean	4.47	4.37	–	4.32	4.07
Excellence level	81	1.2	Bold	60	1.2
Range analysis	0.20	0.05	0.18	0.47	0.12
Reading speed (words/s)					
K1 mean	10.29	10.63	9.61	10.20	10.09
K2 mean	9.76	10.13	11.09	10.57	9.53
K3 mean	10.26	9.55	–	9.35	10.50
Excellence level	81	1.2	Bold	54	1.6
Range analysis	0.54	1.08	1.47	1.22	0.97

(continued)

Table 9. (*continued*)

	Search engine results page titles			Search engine results page abstracts	
	Font size	Line spacing	Stroke weight	Font size	Stroke weight
Blink frequency (times/min)					
K1 mean	10.29	10.63	9.61	10.75	11.02
K2 mean	9.76	10.13	11.09	10.14	10.63
K3 mean	10.26	9.55	–	10.78	10.01
Excellence level	81	1.2	Bold	60	·1.2
Range analysis	0.54	1.08	1.47	0.63	1.01
Pupil diameter variability					
K1 mean	−1.38	−1.38	−1.38	−1.38	−1.38
K2 mean	−1.39	−1.39	−1.41	−1.40	−1.39
K3 mean	−1.40	−1.40	–	−1.40	−1.40
Excellence level	81	1.2	Bold	60	1.2
Range analysis	0.01	0.01	0.02	0.01	0.02

Notes: K1 refers to the mean of the sum of the experimental results corresponding to level 1 in any column.

4.2 Experiment 2: Overview Reading Scenario

In the overview reading scenario, font size had a significant impact on the clarity of a list of news headlines, as perceived by middle-aged and elderly users ($p < 0.05$; Table 10). The pairwise comparison test showed that the clarity of text was rated significantly higher for title font sizes of 81px and 72px than that of 66px ($p < 0.05$ for all comparisons). Based on the data of range analysis in Table 11, a title font size of 72px was positively evaluated for finding key information, however a title font size of 81px performed better in terms of clarity and comfort (blink frequency). 1.4 times line spacing performed better for finding key information, clarity, and comfort. Bold characters performed better than non-bold characters for all indexes.

4.3 Experiment 3: Long-Text reading Scenario

In the long-text reading scenario, font size had a significant impact on the satisfaction of middle-aged and elderly users in long-text reading ($p < 0.05$, Table 12). A pairwise comparison test on font sizes found that among 66px, 72px, and 81px, satisfaction was significantly higher for 66px than 81px ($p < 0.05$). Additionally, line spacing had a significant impact on the clarity of long-text reading in middle-aged and elderly users

Table 10. Kruskal-Wallis test of font size, line spacing, and stroke weight on the reading experience in the overview reading scenario.

Reading experience	News list page titles		
	Font size	Line spacing	Stroke weight
Finding key information	.273	.591	.421
Clarity	.043*	.421	.293
Comfort	.488	.574	.728
Satisfaction	.817	.746	.103
Reading speed	.668	.432	.348
Blink frequency	.998	.669	.704
Pupil diameter variability	.763	.663	.835

*$p < 0.05$; **$p < 0.01$.

Table 11. Orthogonal experimental range analysis: the influence of font size, line spacing, and stroke weight on the reading experience in the overview reading scenario.

	Font size	News list page titles	
		Line spacing	Stroke weight
Finding key information			
K1 mean	4.02	4.09	4.20
K2 mean	4.28	4.17	4.11
K3 mean	4.22	4.26	–
Excellence level	72	1.4	Bold
Range analysis	0.26	0.17	0.09
Clarity			
K1 mean	4.16	4.31	4.43
K2 mean	4.48	4.41	4.33
K3 mean	4.55	4.47	
Excellence level	81	1.4	Bold
Range analysis	0.39	0.16	0.09
Comfort			
K1 mean	4.06	4.07	4.21
K2 mean	4.24	4.24	4.15
K3 mean	4.27	4.26	–
Excellence level	72	1.4	Bold
Range analysis	0.22	0.19	0.06

(*continued*)

Table 11. (*continued*)

	Font size	News list page titles	
		Line spacing	Stroke weight
Satisfaction			
K1 mean	3.97	4.00	4.12
K2 mean	4.09	4.04	3.91
K3 mean	4.09	4.11	–
Excellence level	72	1.4	Bold
Range analysis	0.13	0.11	0.21
Reading speed (words/s)			
K1 mean	4.30	4.26	4.29
K2 mean	4.25	4.15	4.16
K3 mean	4.18	4.33	–
Excellence level	72	1.4	Bold
Range analysis	0.12	0.18	0.13
Blink frequency (times/min)			
K1 mean	14.34	14.96	15.38
K2 mean	15.58	16.14	14.88
K3 mean	15.73	14.54	–
Excellence level	72	1.4	Bold
Range analysis	1.39	1.60	0.50
Pupil diameter variability			
K1 mean	−1.36	−1.38	−1.37
K2 mean	−1.38	−1.34	−1.36
K3 mean	−1.35	−1.37	–
Excellence level	72	1.4	Bold
Range analysis	0.03	0.04	0.00

Notes: K1 refers to the mean of the sum of the experimental results corresponding to level 1 in any column.

($p < 0.05$, Table 12). A further pairwise comparison test showed that among the three types of line spacing (1.2, 1.4, and 1.7 times), the satisfaction was significantly higher for 1.7 and 1.4 times than that of 1.2 times ($p < 0.05$ for all comparisons). The range analysis found that when a line spacing of 1.4 times was used, the clarity, comfort, and satisfaction scores, and the blink frequency, were the highest (see Table 13).

Table 12. Kruskal-Wallis test of font size, line spacing, and stroke weight on the experience in the long-text reading scenario.

Reading experience	Long-text reading page body text	
	Font size	Line spacing
Clarity	.843	.046*
Comfort	.190	.176
Satisfaction	.048*	.564
Reading speed	.862	.111
Blink frequency	.870	.900
Pupil diameter variability	.652	.987

* p < 0.05.

Table 13. Orthogonal experimental range analysis: influence of font size, line spacing, and stroke weight on reading experience in the long-text reading scenario.

	Long-text reading page body text	
	Font size	Line spacing
Clarity		
K1 mean	4.37	4.21
K2 mean	4.44	4.53
K3 mean	4.41	4.48
Excellence level	72	1.4
Range analysis	0.07	0.31
Comfort		
K1 mean	4.11	3.84
K2 mean	4.10	4.14
K3 mean	3.80	4.03
Excellence level	72	1.4
Range analysis	0.31	0.29
Satisfaction		
K1 mean	4.11	3.82
K2 mean	4.04	4.06
K3 mean	3.71	3.98
Excellence level	66	1.4
Range analysis	0.40	0.24

(*continued*)

Table 13. (*continued*)

	Long-text reading page body text	
	Font size	Line spacing
Reading speed (words/s)		
K1 mean	4.60	5.13
K2 mean	4.94	4.85
K3 mean	5.00	4.56
Excellence level	66	1.4
Range analysis	0.40	0.57
Blink frequency (times/min)		
K1 mean	10.61	10.50
K2 mean	11.68	10.86
K3 mean	9.73	10.66
Excellence level	66	1.4
Range analysis	1.95	0.36
Pupil diameter variability		
K1 mean	−1.30	−1.32
K2 mean	−1.33	−1.34
K3 mean	−1.35	−1.33
Excellence level	66	1.4
Range analysis	0.05	0.02

Notes: K1 refers to the mean of the sum of the experimental results corresponding to level 1 in any column.

5 Discussion

This study examined the influence of font size, line spacing, and stroke weight on the experience of middle-aged and elderly users for the Chinese characters read on smartphones. The results confirmed that subjective ratings can more sensitively measure changes of the smartphone reading experience than objective eye movement measurement, which is consistent with the findings of previous studies. However, we highlighted a new finding that has not been outlined in previous research. In addition to the font size, line spacing and stroke weight had varied effects in different scenarios; hence, all of these features need to be analyzed in the context of specific scenarios. Table 14 and Fig. 4 show the optimal ranges of font size, line spacing, stroke weight, and examples of text layout designs for different scenarios, respectively.

5.1 Impact of Font Size on Reading Experience

Font size has a significant impact on the reading experience in each scenario. Changing the font size can significantly improve clarity, comfort and satisfaction for middle-aged and elderly users.

According to the collected data, the optimal font size for the search scenario title was 13.82pt (81px), for the overview reading title was 12.28pt (72px) or 13.82pt (81px), and for the long-text reading body text was 11.26pt (66px). These results indicate that for a title, especially for a scenario where the title and the lower-level information are displayed together, middle-aged and elderly users expect a larger font size to highlight the title information. In the long-text reading scenario, a larger font was not considered to be superior. The appropriate font size for middle-aged and elderly users was slightly smaller than the font size for both the search scenario and overview reading scenario. This confirms the results of Huang's research [11, 12], in that larger fonts take up more space and lengthen the text, negatively impacting the reading experience. The optimal font size concluded from this study (11.26pt) is smaller than that in Hou's [7], who found that 12.75–15pt was more suitable for middle-aged and elderly users to read long texts in a smartphone application. Hou's research used articles that were approximately 200 characters long. A font size of 81px with 1.4 times line spacing occupies approximately one screen length. In this study, all articles in the long-text reading scenario were longer, with approximately 260 characters, and occupied approximately 1.3 screens with the font size and line spacing mentioned above. In this study, middle-aged and elderly users were more likely to feel the impact of larger fonts in terms of screen display efficiency and reading speed.

5.2 Impact of Line Spacing on Reading Experience

The impact of line spacing varied in different scenarios, and line spacing had a greater impact on the reading experience in the long-text reading scenario. This is demonstrated by the fact that changes in line spacing of long-text reading significantly affected the changes in the perceived clarity by middle-aged and elderly users. However, this pattern was not observed in the search or overview reading scenarios. For the long-text reading scenario, the comfort of 1.4 times line spacing was significantly higher than that of 1.2 times, and the average value for clarity, comfort, and satisfaction was higher for a line spacing 1.4 times than that of 1.7 times. In this study, larger line spacings were investigated compared to previous studies. Results indicated that the optimal range for line spacing in long-text reading scenarios on smartphone apps for middle-aged and elderly users is between 1.4–1.7 times, and that bigger or smaller line spacing than this would not be conducive to the reading experience.

5.3 Impact of Stroke Weight on Reading Experience

The bold stroke weight had a significant impact on the satisfaction of the search title but had no significant impact on the reading experience of the overview reading title. This shows that bolding titles in pages with high information density or with multiple information levels plays an important role in highlighting important information (such as titles) and improving the reading experience; however, it has no significant impact on the reading experience of pure title pages (such as news list pages).

Table 14. Optimal ranges of font size, line spacing and stroke weight for the different reading scenarios on smartphone apps.

Scenarios		Search scenario		Overview of reading scenarios	Long-text reading scenario
		Title	Abstract	Title	Long text
Font size	pt	13.82	10.24	12.28/13.82	11.26
	px	81	60	72/81	66
Line spacing	Times	1.4	1.2	1.4	1.4–1.7
Bold		Bold	–	Bold/non-bold	–

Search scenario

(Title: 13.82pt, 1.4 times line spacing. Abstract: 10.24pt, 1.2 times line spacing; bold.)

Overview reading scenario

(Title: 12.28pt; 1.4 times line spacing; bold.)

Long-text reading scenario

(Long- text: 11.26pt; 1.4 times line spacing; non-bold.)

Fig. 4. Examples of optimal font size, line spacing, and stroke weight for typical reading scenarios on smartphone apps.

6 Conclusion

In the context of population aging and digital life, the smartphone reading experience for middle-aged and elderly users is a subject with important industrial applications and social implications, particularly for a country such as China that has a large and increasing proportion of middle-aged and elderly people. Based on objective eye movement measurement and the subjective feedback results from 60 Chinese middle-aged and elderly users, aged 50–70, this study analyzed the impact of font size, line spacing and stroke weight on reading experience in typical smartphone reading scenarios. This is the first study to systematically analyze the effect of font size, line spacing and stroke weight in different scenarios of Chinese news apps for middle-aged and elderly users. The results can provide software developers with a set of layout design specifications that are suitable for middle-aged and elderly users. For mobile reading scenarios in other languages, our study also outlines a novel method to determine the optimal font size, line spacing and stroke weight for users in different realistic scenarios.

The results found that font size has a significant impact on the experience of reading on a smartphone in each of the scenarios, for middle-aged and elderly users. For different scenarios and information densities, different font sizes should be used. It is recommended that the font size of the title be 12.28–13.82pt, and the font size of the body of a long piece of text be 11.26pt. Compared with previous research, this study discovered that line spacing and stroke weight have different impacts in different scenarios. Line spacing has a significant impact on the long-text reading experience, in which 1.4 to 1.7 times line spacing is recommended, but no impact on the other scenarios was investigated. Bolding can highlight key information in multi-level information pages (such as the title in a search result page), thereby improving satisfaction, but it does not have a significant impact on the reading experience of a page with a main title (such as a list of news titles).

Acknowledgements. We would like to thank all subjects for their participation in this study.

References

1. Cheng, H.Y.: Effects of font size and spacing on Chinese reading the newspaper material in urban low-age senior citizens. Tianjin Normal University, Tianjin, China (2015)
2. China Internet Network Information Center: The 37th China statistical report on internet development. http://www.cnnic.net.cn/hlwfzyj/hlwxzbg/201601/P020160122469130059846.pdf. Accessed 31 Jan 2022
3. China Internet Network Information Center: The 47th China statistical report on internet development. http://www.cnnic.net.cn/hlwfzyj/hlwxzbg/hlwtjbg/202102/P020210203334633480104.pdf. Accessed 31 Jan 2022
4. Darroch, I., Goodman, J., Brewster, S., Gray, P.: The effect of age and font size on reading text on handheld computers. In: Costabile, M.F., Paternò, F. (eds.) INTERACT 2005. LNCS, vol. 3585, pp. 253–266. Springer, Heidelberg (2005). https://doi.org/10.1007/11555261_23
5. Fang, H., Chen, Y.C., Zhao, Y., Li, X.H., Wei, Q.: The influencing mechanism of information design elements of mobile news platform on visual search efficiency. Libr. Inf. Serv. **63**(22), 58–67 (2019)
6. Guo, X., Tian, J.J., Hu, Z.G., Li, Q.: Impact of illumination on visual fatigue and brain arousal during written variable reading times. Packag. Eng. **39**(04), 164–169 (2018)
7. Hou, G.H., Dong, H., Ning, W.N., Han, L.H.: Larger Chinese text spacing and size: effects on older users' experience. Ageing Soc. **40**(2), 389–411 (2020)
8. Hou, G.H., Ning, W.N., Dong, H.: Research on older user's experience in digital reading from a cognitive load perspective. China J. Inf. Syst. **20**(1), 15–26 (2018)

9. Hsiao, C.Y., Wang, M.J., Liu, Y.J., Chang, C.C.: Effects of Chinese character size, number of characters per line, and number of menu items on visual search task on tablet computer displays for different age groups. Int. J. Industr. Ergon. **72**(7), 61–70 (2019)
10. Huang, D.L., Rau, P.L.P., Liu, Y.: Effects of font size, display resolution and task type on reading Chinese fonts from mobile devices. Int. J. Ind. Ergon. **39**(1), 81–89 (2008)
11. Huang, S.M., Li, W.J.: Format effects of Traditional Chinese character size and font style on reading performance when using smartphones. In: 2017 International Conference on Applied System Innovation (ICASI), pp. 1239–1242. IEEE, NewJersey, USA (2017)
12. Huang, S.M.: Effects of font size and font style of Traditional Chinese characters on readability on smartphones. Int. J. Industr. Ergon. **69**(1), 66–72 (2019)
13. Li, M., Zhong, N., Lv, S.F.: Exploring visual search and browsing strategies on web pages using the eye-tracking. J. Beijing Univ. Technol. **37**(05), 773–779 (2011)
14. Li, L., et al.: Establishing a role for the visual complexity of linguistic stimuli in age-related reading difficulty: evidence from eye movements during Chinese reading. Atten. Percept. Psychophys. **81**(8), 2626–2634 (2019). https://doi.org/10.3758/s13414-019-01836-y
15. Liu, N., Yu, R., Zhang, Y.: Effects of font size, stroke width, and character complexity on the legibility of Chinese characters. Hum. Factors Ergon. Manuf. Serv. Industr. **26**(3), 381–392 (2016)
16. Liu, W., Zhao, Y.F., Li, J.Z.: User visual behavior on different layouts of photo sharing website using the eye-tracking. J. Beijing Univ. Posts Telecommun. (Soc. Sci. Ed.) **16**(1), 18–24 (2014)
17. Liu, Z., Tong, W., Su, Y.: Interaction effects of aging, word frequency, and predictability on saccade length in Chinese reading. PeerJ **8**(4), 8860 (2020)
18. Lu, J.H., Wang, X.Y.: Research on the vision health status of Chinese elderly people and its social, economic and healthy determinants: based on the Chinese longitudinal healthy longevity survey data 2014. Popul. Dev. **24**(04), 66–76 (2018)
19. Rello, L., Pielot, M., Marcos, M.C.: Make it big! The effect of font size and line spacing on online readability. In: Proceedings of the 2016 CHI Conference on Human Factors in Computing System, pp. 3637–3648. Association for Computing Machinery, New York (2016)
20. National Bureau of Statistics of China: Annual Data (Population data from sample survey). //data.stats.gov.cn/easyquery.htm?cn=C01. Accessed 31 Jan 2022
21. United Nations: World population prospects 2019. https://population.un.org/wpp/. Accessed 31 Jan 2022
22. Wang, H.F.: Influence of highlighting, columns, and font size on visual search performance with respect to on-screen Chinese characters. Percept. Mot. Skills **117**(2), 528–541 (2013)
23. Wang, J., et al.: Adult age differences in eye movements during reading: the evidence from Chinese. J. Gerontol. B Psychol. Sci. Soc. Sci. **73**(4), 584–593 (2016)
24. Wang, L., Sato, H., Rau, P.L.P., Fujimura, K., Gao, Q., Asano, Y.: Chinese text spacing on mobile phones for senior citizens. Educ. Gerontol. **35**(1), 77–90 (2008)
25. Wu, H.C.: Electronic paper display preferred viewing distance and character size for different age groups. Taylor Francis **54**(9), 806–814 (2011)
26. Yan, G.L., Xiong, J.P., Zang, C.L., Yu, L.L., Cui, L., Bai, X.J.: Review of eye-movement measures in reading research. Adv. Psychol. Sci. **21**(4), 589 (2013)
27. Yuan, H.: Research on consumer's information-seeking behavior in social media. Wuhan University, Wuhan, China (2013)
28. Zhang, L.N., Zhang, X.M., Chen, X.Y.: The legibility research of Chinese font and font structure. Chin. J. Ergon. **20**(03), 32–36 (2014)

Research on the Gamification Design of Family Early Intervention Products for Children with Autism Based on the Peak-End Rule

Ximeng Lu, Jinjie Li, Kesi Zhu, and Yun Liu

Xiamen Academy of Arts and Crafts, Fuzhou University, Xiamen, China
liuyun525@fzu.edu.cn

Abstract. Early family intervention is an important part of the effective treatment of children with autism. In order to improve the experience of early intervention in the family of autistic children and improve the effectiveness of the intervention, based on the effective connection between the peak-end rule and gamified thinking, a design study of auxiliary products for early intervention in the family of autistic children is carried out. Research through user interviews, in-depth observations, video archives and other methods to clarify user needs at peak and endpoints, and select appropriate driving forces according to the octagonal behavior analysis method, convert demand points into product functions, and combine the basic steps and core design of gamification. According to the characteristics, a high-quality and efficient family early intervention plan for children with autism is proposed, and finally the feasibility and effectiveness of the product are evaluated by the octagonal behavior analysis method. The results show that the product under this design method can enable children to receive targeted, efficient and interesting treatment, and provide families who cannot afford the expensive treatment the opportunity to enjoy a fair and high-quality education.

Keywords: Autism · Family early intervention · Peak-end rule · Gamified product design · Octagonal behavior analysis

1 Introduction

Autism Spectrum Disorder (ASD), referred to as autism, autism disorder. In recent years, the prevalence of autism has continued to rise, ranking first among children with mental disabilities in my country, and the need for intervention and treatment has increased accordingly. And the analysis of medical clinical and educational research shows that family early intervention is an important link in the effective treatment process, and how to help parents effectively carry out intervention treatment in the family environment is an urgent question. Gamification design includes the octagonal behavior analysis method and peak-end law. It has the characteristics of "education and learning" and is widely used in the field of education. Applying gamification design to rehabilitation intervention training can reduce the boringness of related training to a certain extent level, so that autistic children and parents have a higher willingness to participate in the family early intervention.

This study focuses on the growth of children with autism. Based on the family environment, based on the peak-end rule and children's cognitive behavior, this study explores the research method of gamification design for family-centered early intervention and treatment products for children with autism.

2 Background

2.1 Family-Centered Early Intervention for Children with Autism

Parents are the closest people to children with autism, and they play a vital role in the growth and development of children with autism. For children, a good family environment can have a positive impact on children, and it is also true for children with autism. Children with autism will stay at home most of the time. Parents are the closest people to the children and they are willing to Unconditionally give children all the care and support, in a warm and loving environment, it is easier for autistic children to open the closed inner world, so the family is a vital part of the rehabilitation of autistic children. The traditional institution-centered early intervention treatment is not the best solution. Several scientific experiments and studies at home and abroad have proved that family-centered early intervention can significantly improve the social and cognitive abilities of children with autism. Looking at international trends, intervention training for children with autism is gradually turning to "family-centered".

2.2 Peak-End Rule

The Nobel Prize-winning psychologist Daniel Kahneman proposed the Peak-End Rule (see Fig. 1) and found that the author's memory of the experience is determined by two factors: the peak (whether positive or negative) moment and the end moment. It has nothing to do with the length of experience time and the proportion of good or bad feelings in the whole experience. This law is based on the characteristics of people subconsciously summarizing the experience. The "peak" and "end" are actually the so-called critical moment MOT (Moment of Truth, the most shocking and influential management concept and behavior mode in the service industry). At present, the Peak-End Rule has been widely used in the field of economic management, and preliminary explorations have also been made in the field of design. Enhancing the peak experience of products in product design and improvement will help consumers get a deeper memory and enhance consumer loyalty to the brand. [2] Hong Xinhui of Fuzhou University performed the experience of children's atomization therapy based on the peak law. The design study also demonstrated the feasibility of the Peak-End Rule in the application of product design.

2.3 Gamified Thinking

Gamification refers to the method of integrating game thinking and game mechanics in a non-game environment to guide users to interact and use. The pioneer of gamification, Yu-kai Chou, proposed in "Gamification Actual Combat" that gamification is the

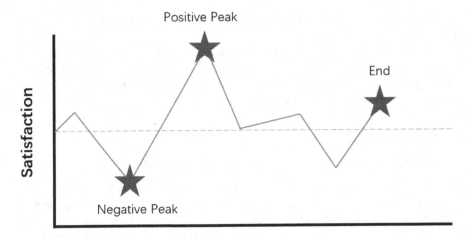

Fig. 1. Peak-end rule

clever application of interesting and attractive elements in the game to the real world or producer activities. Yu-Kai Chou calls it "People-oriented design". Based on people's psychological changes, behavioral motivation and sense of participation, the entire system is optimized and constructed based on ensuring basic functions and performance. In just a few years, gamification has reached the tipping point of society. From education, work, marketing, parenting to sustainable development, and even healthcare and scientific research, gamification has penetrated almost every aspect of the author's life. In the process of traditional intervention, children cry and do not cooperate. Parents often force their children to complete the corresponding tasks to complete the corresponding training (see Fig. 2), but this does not achieve the expected training effect. The game-based design model also stimulates designers' design inspiration and innovation consciousness, to break the inherent thinking and find a game-based design method that drives the early intervention of autistic children's families.

Fig. 2. Real shots of the training process

3 Methods to Improve Product Service Experience Based on the Peak-End Rule

To maximize the peak parameters of the "Create Peak Experience" knob, to improve user experience, you should start with the peak point of the experience, sort out all the peak points in the complete service link, confirm the key peak points, and eliminate the negative key peak points, Strengthen the positive peak point and the end of the experience, and ultimately bring more quality products and services to users.

3.1 Identify and Confirm Peak Nodes

Peak nodes in the user experience process can also be regarded as touchpoints in the experience process. Jacob Schneider proposed in the book "Service Design Thinking" that the identification tools of touchpoints include service travel, situational communication, expected value diagrams, diagrams of stakeholders, and other tools. Service travel is a method of fully recording the service travel experience through video, audio, or notes through the personal experience of the whole set of services; situational communication is the in-depth understanding of stakeholders in the form of interviews; diagrams of stakeholders are summarized and sorted out, Clearly show the characteristics of the participants. In practice, one or more of these tools can be selected according to the needs, and the goal is to carefully identify all peak points in the experience process. During the service process, many different peak points will occur. Use the user travel graph peak method to visualize all peak points, identify the key peak points, and focus on the experience optimization of the key peak nodes at the end to improve product usage. Effective methods for efficiency and experience.

3.2 Eliminate Negative Peaks and Optimize the Experience of Positive Peaks and Endpoints

After identifying many peak experience nodes, the author can improve the overall user experience by optimizing the nodes. However, due to a large number of peak nodes, optimizing each peak node is a huge project, and people will according to the peak moment, It is the best or worst moment and end to judge the quality of an experience. Therefore, we must give priority to weakening the negative peak nodes, improving the performance of negative key nodes, and reducing the negative impact it brings. Weakening the negative key nodes can only enable users to get a not bad user experience. To bring users a memorable and pleasant experience, the experience of the positive key nodes should be further improved. The higher the positive peak, the more obvious the positive effect. In addition, the endpoint of the user experience is another important factor in the impression service experience. Improving the endpoint experience will also greatly improve the overall quality of the experience.

4 Methods to Improve and Enhance the Peak User Experience Based on Gamification Thinking

4.1 Analyze the Eight Core Drivers of Gamification

There are one or more core driving forces behind all human behaviors. This driving force will affect a series of decisions and behaviors of people. Yu-kai Chou has concentrated on studying the gap between motivations and summed up the eight-core driving forces of gamification: epic meaning and sense of mission, sense of progress and accomplishment, and creativity. Empowerment and feedback, ownership and ownership, social influence and relevance, scarcity and desire, unknown and curiosity, loss and escape psychology. Its specific explanation is shown in the figure (Fig. 3). In addition, there is a core driving force hidden behind the scenes: feeling, which refers to the enjoyment of the body. Through an in-depth understanding of these driving forces, combined with the characteristics of the target user, the main driving force and auxiliary driving force are selected, and different driving forces are used to simulate user behavior at each stage. Not only can the peak user experience be improved in a scientific gamification way, but it may also stimulate the user's subjective initiative and allow the user to achieve the designer's preset target behavior.

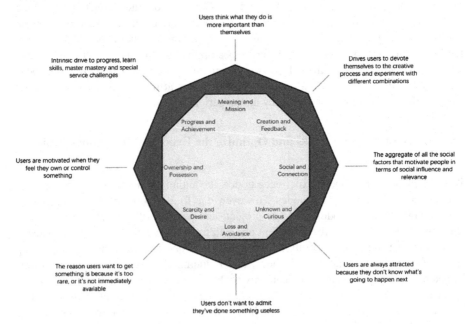

Fig. 3. Eight core driving forces and their specific explanations

4.2 Gamification Design Framework of Octagonal Behavior Analysis

As mentioned earlier, the eight-core driving forces of gamification are selected and focused based on user characteristics to promote user behavior. This is a summary of

Yu-kai Chou's octagonal behavior analysis framework (see Fig. 4), but these driving forces do not exist independently but have common points. It can be roughly divided into two categories: left brain (external tendencies) and right brain (internal tendencies) core driving forces. The core driving force of the right brain is placed on the right side of the octagon. It is the core driving force that focuses on creativity, self-expression, and sociology, and is connected to intrinsic motivation-that is, there is no need for any goals or rewards, and things are rewards; left brain The core driving force is placed on the left side of the octagon, connected with logic, calculation, and ownership, and relies on extrinsic motivation-being motivated by what you want to obtain. The upper part of the octagon is a positive motivation, and the lower part is a relatively negative motivation. Therefore, there are two techniques for using core driving force: the technique of using the upper core driving force extensively is called "white hat gamification", and the technique of using the bottom driving force is called "Black Hat Gamification". Use octagonal behavior analysis to explore step by step. (1) Analyze the advantages and disadvantages of the product experience from the perspective of motivation, and conduct a lot of analysis, thinking, testing and adjustment of the experience. (2) Use octagonal behavior analysis to understand the changes of players in the whole process (3) Consider the types of different players, and study the motivation of different people in different stages of experience. Improve the peak experience of the product through the hierarchical exploration of the octagonal behavior analysis method.

For children with autism, their way of thinking is different from that of normal children. Therefore, a specific analysis should be carried out according to their specific circumstances.

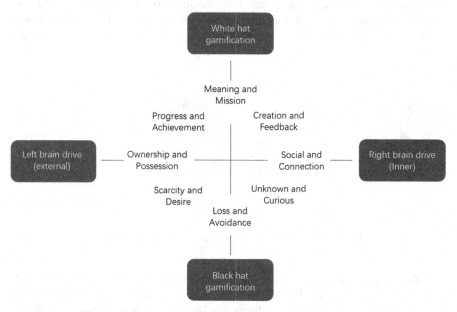

Fig. 4. Eight core driving forces and their specific explanations

5 Gamification Design Practice of Family Early Intervention Products for Children with Autism Based on the Peak-To-End Law

Carrying out family-centered intervention is an inevitable choice for the rehabilitation of children with autism or other developmental disabilities. However, most of the current intervention products are children's universal toys, which are weakly targeted, and most of the traditional interventions are only for training purposes. The psychological needs and the user experience of children with autism and their parents are ignored. This research explores the gamification design method to carry out the following practices, to help parents effectively carry out intervention treatment in the family environment, to improve the fun and entertainment of intervention training for children with autism, and to enhance the user experience of the participants—children and parents.

5.1 Identify and Confirm the Peak Point of Family Early Intervention Training for Children with Autism

Due to the particularity of autism, the intervention involves the joint participation of children with autism and their parents, so it is necessary to fully observe and explore the needs of the two in the training process before starting the design.

First, the rehabilitation training process of children with autism was observed through field research, and 10 parents of autistic children who received the early intervention were selected for situational communication, discussing personal information, and their satisfaction points, concerns and feelings about the overall intervention experience. Learning more about the pain points and emotional needs of this group from the communication. Based on this, the corresponding user portraits are summarized and summarized (see Fig. 5).

Fig. 5. User portraits of parents and children with autism

In the process of intervention training, for autistic parents, there are mainly the following problems. (1) Parents have insufficient awareness of autism, and family training lacks professional guidance. (2) It is difficult to keep consistent with the way of family training programs and institutions, which leads to confusion in the thinking of children with autism. (3) Parents want to get feedback on intervention treatment too early, but the period of intervention treatment is long, and it is impossible to get obvious effect feedback in a short period.

For children with autism, the main problems are: (1) Most of the children with autism are not very active in the intervention training, and even rely on their parents, sitting on the ground or lying on the ground, which seriously affects the intervention. (2) There are no identical children with autism in the world, and it is difficult for existing resources (families and institutions) to formulate a targeted training plan for each child.

Secondly, based on field research, the peak points are identified by the combination of service travel and situational communication. The entire intervention journey for children with autism is divided into three stages: before the intervention, during the intervention, and after intervention (see Fig. 6).

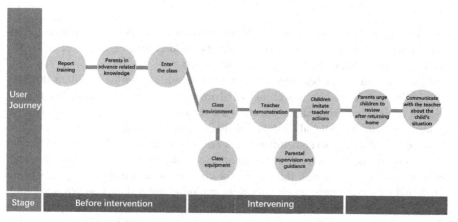

Fig. 6. User journey diagram of intervention training

The peak point experience is then quantified by the Likert method (see Fig. 7), allowing respondents to subjectively assign the peak point experience: very good 2 points, relatively good 1 point, average 0 points, relatively poor - 1 point, very poor - 2 points, the importance of the peak point is measured by the level of the final score. Finally, the positive key peak point, negative key peak point and final moment peak point of intervention training for children with autism were clarified.

Finally, gamification design is used to improve the positive peak key point and the final moment peak point and eliminate the negative key peak point.

5.2 A Gamified Design Framework Using Octagonal Behavior Analysis to Optimize the Peak Experience of Products for Children with Autism

According to Yu-Kai Chou, founder of the Octagonal Behavior Method, a framework for gamification design, "Almost every successful game is underpinned by a certain core driving force, which influences a series of behavior and decision-making." But this framework does not apply to children with autism. Therefore, it is necessary to summarize a set of octagonal behavior analysis methods suitable for autistic children

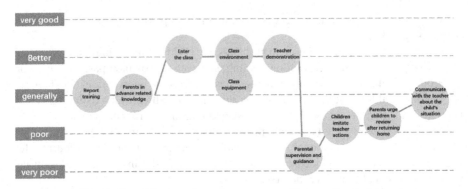

Fig. 7. Quantification of user journey map of intervention training

according to the characteristics of autistic children, and to clarify how to apply different driving forces to stimulate the behavior of autistic children (see Fig. 8), to optimize the peak experience of products for children with autism.

There are differences between children with autism and normal children in terms of creativity and feedback, as well as social interaction and connection. For normal children, social interaction and connection are themselves a reward for them. But for children with autism, not only do they dislike social interactions, but there are also social barriers. This is also something that needs to be overcome. Therefore, additional rewards must be used to motivate this behavior. Secondly, for normal children, unknown and curiosity are very normal things, but for children with autism, their interests are narrow and they don't have much interest in exploring novel things. When designing, you can start with their interests to circumvent this problem. This kind of people like light and sound, through these things, to stimulate their interest in exploration, so that this matter becomes an interesting thing, and there is no need for extra rewards.

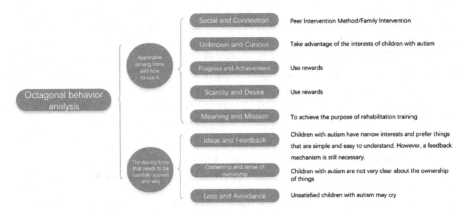

Fig. 8. Applying different driving forces to stimulate the behavior of children with autism

In summary, for children with autism, it is necessary to motivate them to participate in and cooperate with the behavior of games as much as possible. When selecting the driving force, it is necessary to consider whether the reward can drive him to cooperate with the progress of the game based on the characteristics of the child with autism. If not, consider changing the driving force or reward.

6 Design Practice of Autism Rehabilitation Training Products Based on Family Gamification

6.1 Product Design Based on Home Gamification

To verify the feasibility of the family gamification intervention method, based on the octagonal behavior analysis method and the peak-end law, a product including online and offline ends was designed. The basic design process is shown in the figure (see Fig. 9).

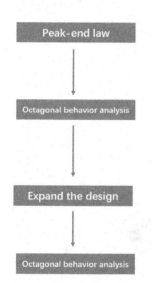

According to the survey, analyze the process of traditional training methods (shadow training), and clarify user needs at peak and end points

Use the octagonal behavior analysis method to select the appropriate driving force to enable the user to perform a specific operation to meet the user's needs. To achieve the purpose of optimizing positive peaks and eliminating weak negative peaks by meeting user needs

According to the characteristics of children with autism, a set of octagonal behavior analysis methods suitable for children with autism are specified. Based on this, design a game plan suitable for children with autism

According to the characteristics of children with autism, design a game plan suitable for children with autism

Fig. 9. Design flow

Through the investigation, six needs of children with autism in rehabilitation training were summarized: 1. social needs/motor needs. 2. arousal interest. 3. create atmosphere. 4. touch training. 5. personalized training. 6. hope for progress. Then, the collected and sorted requirements are converted into product functions, and the appropriate driving force is found according to the octagonal behavior analysis method so that users are willing to cooperate to achieve the design purpose (see Fig. 10). The final verification found that in the preset functions, except for "double cooperation", other functions do not require additional rewards to make the game go smoothly (Fig. 11).

Features	Need	Driving force analysis	Do you need additional rewards (see Figure 8)
Double teamwork	Social needs /exercise exercises	Social and Connection, Mission and Meaning	Yes
Flowering	Arouse interest	Unknown and Curiosity, Progress and Achievement	No
Light /Sound	Create an atmosphere	Unknown and Curious	No
Color /Material	Create an atmosphere /Touch training	Unknown and Curiosity, Meaning and Mission	No
Secondary development	Personalized training	Ideas and Feedback, Socializing and Feedback	No
Data feedback	Hope for progress	Ideas and Feedback	No

Fig. 10. Function point conversion and driving force analysis

Fig. 11. A gamification product which is named "Chase the Light"

The converted function was applied to the product, and after several improvements, a product called "Chasing Light" was finally designed to alleviate the social fear of autistic children. The three main functions of the product are as follows:

(1) The game of "Double Dance" (see Fig. 12). The multi-player cooperation method is adopted. After setting the number of participants in the game, the game is played cooperatively. The light is used as the driving force of the unknown and curious to attract children to step on it. Stomp on to make a complete piece of music. After children complete social interaction, they can get small gifts from automatic opening and closing mechanical flowers as reinforcements for social games.

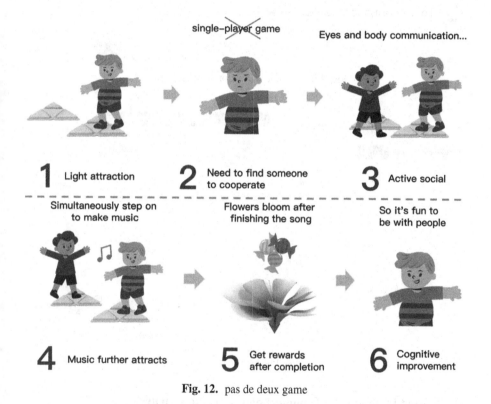

Fig. 12. pas de deux game

(2) User secondary creation (see Fig. 13). According to the intervention plan for children with autism at different stages, users can create secondary creations in a modular way on the mobile phone, which is more suitable for the needs of children of different ages and situations.

(3) App online recording. While the child is training, the product will record the child's data, transmit it to the App, visualize the training data, and generate a child evaluation report to feedback to the parents according to the evaluation standards of the China Disabled Persons' Federation (see Fig. 14).

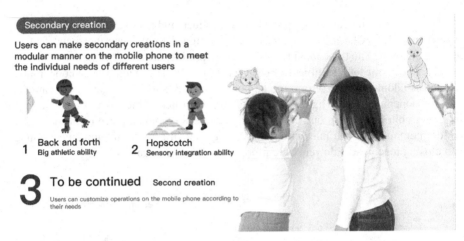

Fig. 13. Secondary development function

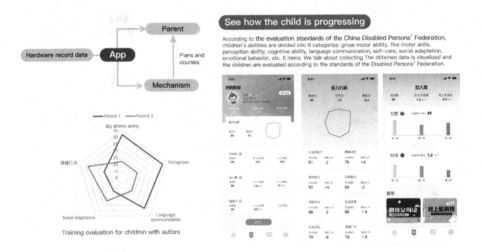

Fig. 14. Data feedback

6.2 Product Function and Gamification Correlation Analysis

To verify that the improved product has a higher degree of correlation with gamification, the opinions of 5 game product experts were solicited, and a full-point system was adopted to collect the scores of each game product expert on the correlation of the various indicators of the product, and based on their scores Create a ten-point system for each indicator (see Table 1).

Table 1. The correlation between improved products and gamification.

Evaluator serial number	1	2	3	4	5	Average
Meaning and mission	9.3	8.1	8.8	7.8	8.2	8.4
Progress and achievement	5.4	6.2	7.4	6.8	6.7	5.4
Creation and feedback	9.2	9.8	9.1	8.8	8.9	9.2
Ownership and possession	7.2	6.5	6.9	7.3	8.1	7.2
Social and connection	4.9	5.3	6.4	6.1	5.7	4.9
Scarcity and desire	8.5	8.2	7.9	7.5	7.6	8.5
Unknown and curious	5.5	4.5	6.2	7.1	7.2	6.1

Set traditional autism rehabilitation therapy toys as the control group, and let the five game product experts re-score all aspects of the octagonal analysis method corresponding to the traditional toys, conduct a control group test, and make a ten-point system based on their scores (see Table 2).

Table 2. The correlation between traditional products and gamification.

Evaluator serial number	1	2	3	4	5	Average
Meaning and mission	4.3	5.1	6.4	6.8	7.2	6.0
Progress and achievement	5.8	5.7	3.4	4.4	4.5	4.8
Creation and feedback	7.2	5.4	6.1	8.0	7.5	6.8
Ownership and possession	8.5	7.5	7.4	7.0	7.6	7.6
Social and connection	1.2	2.2	2.5	3.8	2.9	2.5
Scarcity and desire	6.9	7.8	6.8	7.2	5.5	6.8
Unknown and curious	5.6	6.4	3.9	4.2	5.3	5.1

comparison (see Fig. 15), the average scores of the 5 experts on the products show that, except that the data on ownership and ownership are slightly lower than those of traditional rehabilitation products, the improved products are better in epic significance and sense of mission, progress and achievement, creativity The seven aspects of empowerment and feedback, social influence correlation, scarcity and desire, unknown and curiosity are significantly higher than traditional rehabilitation products. In general, the correlation degree between the modified product and the octagonal analysis method is significantly better than that of the traditional product.

6.3 Product Usability Assessment

10 autistic children in the rehabilitation of Blue Pole Star in Xiamen City, Fujian Province were selected, and through the control experiment, the traditional product

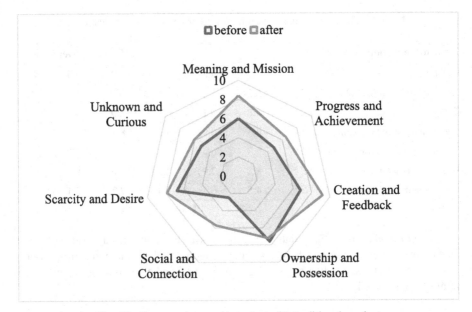

Fig. 15. Compare improved product with traditional product

and the improved product were respectively subjected to the before and after control intervention. In the same period, the number of negative behaviors before and after the intervention of 10 autistic children was recorded, and the reduction value was calculated. The experimental verification is shown in (see Table 3).

Table 3. Compared gamification intervention with traditional intervention, the reduction value of negative behaviors.

	Traditional intervention (times)	Gamification intervention (times)	Decrease value (%)
Repeated behavior	30	18	40.0
Crying	18	14	22.2
Waving arms	12	6	50.0
Looking around	41	32	22.0
Average	25	18	33.5

At the same time, the number of positive behaviors of 10 children with autism before and after the intervention was recorded, and the increased value was calculated. The experimental verification is shown in (see Table 4).

Table 4. Compared gamification intervention with traditional intervention, the increased value of positive behaviors.

	Traditional intervention (times)	Gamification intervention (times)	Value added (%)
Physical contact	35	52	48.6
Communication	4	9	125.0
Eye contact	12	21	75.0
Average value	17	27	82.9

According to the collected data, the statistics of negative behaviors of gamification intervention products are significantly lower than that of traditional intervention products, and the intervention effect of positive behaviors is significantly higher than that of traditional products. The experimental results show that the family gamification intervention treatment method using the combination of the octagon analysis method and the peak law is significantly better than the traditional intervention method, which proves the feasibility of combining family gamification and autism rehabilitation intervention.

7 Conclusion

The application of Peak-End Rule and gamification design framework in autistic children's products is an attempt to cross-integrate psychology, behavioral design and other disciplines for product design to improve user experience. In the process of research, the user's peak experience is taken as the starting point. By identifying peak points and confirming key peak points, combined with the game design framework of octagonal behavior analysis, negative key peak points are eliminated, positive peak points and endpoints are optimized to improve the user experience, and finally combined with products for early family intervention in children with autism. The design scheme verifies the feasibility and effectiveness of improving the user experience of the product based on the Peak-End Rule and the Gamification design. The design of special children's education products provides certain experience, reference and guidance significance. At the same time, innovative design and exploration of autism-related treatment product service systems, so that children can receive efficient treatment, comply with the seventeen sustainable development goals of the United Nations, and provide families in areas that cannot afford expensive treatment costs or lack corresponding medical resources with fair and quality education.

Acknowledgments. This work was financially supported by the 2021 College Student Innovation and Entrepreneurship Training Program of Fuzhou University (202110386031). We sincerely thank every teacher in rehabilitation institutions, children with autism and their parents who have helped us in the process of writing the thesis.

392   X. Lu et al.

References

1. Morris, P., Weglarz Ward, J.M., Hailey, R.: Love: preparing families of young children with autism spectrum disorder for formal school settings. Interv. Sch. Clin. **2** (2020). https://doi.org/10.1177/1053451220928968
2. Meindl, J.N., Delgado, D., Casey, L.B.: Increasing engagement in students with autism in inclusion classrooms. Child. Youth Serv. Rev. **111** (2020). https://doi.org/10.1016/j.childyouth.2020.104854
3. Chen, M.: Evention case analysis and study of art therapy for children with preschool autism. China Acad. Fine Arts (2016). (in Chinese)
4. Li, H., Li, X., Xu, M.: Research on the design strategy of adjuvant treatment for children with autism. Sci. Technol. Wind (2019).https://doi.org/10.19392/j.cnki.1671-7341.201914199 (in Chinese)
5. Wolff Jason, J., Dimian Adele, F., Botteron Kelly, N., Joseph, P.: A longitudinal study of parent-reported sensory responsiveness in toddlers at-risk for autism. J. Child. Psychol. Psychiatry Allied Discipl. **60**(3), 314–324 (2019). https://doi.org/10.1111/jcpp.12978
6. Xiang, H.: Research on the design of auxiliary products for children with autism under early family intervention. The Hubei University of Technology. https://doi.org/10.27131/d.cnki.ghugc.2020.000725. (in Chinese)
7. Jeanine, K., Linda, S., von Korflesch Harald, F.O.: Revealing the theoretical basis of gamification: a systematic review and analysis of theory in research on gamification, serious games and game-based learning. Comput. Hum. Behav. (prepublish) **125** (2021). https://doi.org/10.1016/J.CHB.2021.106963
8. Santos, A.C.G., et al.: The relationship between user types and gamification designs. User Model. User-Adap. Inter. **31**(5), 907–940 (2021). https://doi.org/10.1007/s11257-021-09300-z
9. Cui, X.: Application of RDI-interpersonal development intervention therapy in social training for autistic children. Modern. Educ. **35**, 310–311(2018)
10. Chou, Y.: Game-Based Actual Combat. Huazhong University of Science and Technology Press, Wuhan (2017). (in Chinese)
11. Li, C., Bao, Y.: Application of peak end law in user experience research. Art Des. Theor. Edn. **06**, 179–181 (2011). (in Chinese)
12. Hong, X., Zhan, X.: Research on the design of improving children's atomization therapy service experience based on the law of peak and end. Design **3**, 42–44 (2018). (in Chinese)
13. Zhang, B.: Analysis of the elements of gamification design in the practical applications of design. Int. J. Educ. Econ. **4** (2018)
14. Helena, R., et al.: Regul-A: a technological application for sensory regulation of children with autism spectrum disorder in the home context. Int. J. Environ. Res. Public Health **19** (2021)
15. Wang, M., Zhai, H.: Evaluation method and application of product design for rehabilitation training of children with autism based on AHP and TOPSIS method. J. Graphol. **3**, 453–460 (2021). (in Chinese)

Exploring the Derivation of Artistic Intervention in the Community from the Perspective of Elderly Creativity

Fu-Chi Shih[1,2(✉)] and Shu-Hsuan Chang[2]

[1] Department of Arts and Design, National Tsing Hua University, Hsinchu City 300, Taiwan
fuchi@mx.nthu.edu.tw
[2] Department of Industrial Education and Technology, National Changhua University of Education, Changhua City 500, Taiwan
shc@cc.ncue.edu.tw

Abstract. The imbalance of Taiwan's population structure in the past ten years or so has been mainly caused by such factors as a low birth rate, an extended average age of death, etc. In 2018, Taiwan's population including and over 65 years of age accounted for more than 14% of the total population, which already reached the international norm for an aging society. And it is estimated that Taiwan will become a super-aged society in 2025 with the 20% elderly population ratio criterion. However, at present (in 2022), most rural areas in Taiwan have already entered the development dilemma of a super-aged society. Taking Hengshan Township, Hsinchu County as an example, according to the demographic data of December 2021, the population including and over 65 years of age already reached 23.66% of its total population. The imbalance of population structure is one of the factors leading to the decline of the said area. This article will take the said village as a research case, and use the "art" as a medium of message passing and communication to explore how to let art intervene in the community and life of the elderly people and activate their vitality and creativity against the existing facts of population aging. Therefore, this research mainly adopts the methods of literature analysis and action design research to aim at transforming the elderly's life experience and emotional attachment to the land into artistic expressions through the planning of curricular activities of art practice, so that the elderly may have opener minds and problem-solving skills to face the physical, psychological and environmental changes brought about by the old age. This is hoped to arouse by art their sense of happiness in the life-long learning and LOHAS. The research recommends that art infiltrates the living environment of the elderly to reproduce their value and emotional connection to the local community, and hence the environmental taste of aesthetically peaceful housing may be cultivated and sculpted.

Keywords: Elderly · Creativity · Artistic intervention · Aesthetically peaceful housing · Environmental taste

P.-L. P. Rau (Ed.): HCII 2022, LNCS 13313, pp. 393–405, 2022.
https://doi.org/10.1007/978-3-031-06050-2_28

1 Introduction

According to the data on the National Development Council's population projections inquiry system, Taiwan had a population including and over 65 years of age accounting for more than 14% of the total population in 2018, becoming an "aged society", and it is predicted that such a population will exceed 20% in 2025, which will make Taiwan enter the "super-aged society". People including and over 65 years of age are generally regarded as elderly. In the face of the increasing elderly, we need to explore their psychologies and care for their lives. Therefore, this research, prompted by the local revitalization and via the planning of the art curricular activities, regards "artistic intervention" as an important factor in establishing the community's environmental taste. In addition to improving the external hardware space, it is more important to build the internal mental space formed by the emotional connection to the land. It is hoped that the elderly will contribute their value under the existing demographic structure of the community. For that reason, the purpose of this research is threefold: 1. to construct the community aesthetics and cultural character by means of the elderly participation in community art activities, 2. to show their creative energy through their works, and 3. to promote their sense of achievement in self-affirmation and their sense of happiness in the living environment.

In the life experience of the elderly, the lifelong learning concept is hoped to make the elderly residents in the local community re-recognize the beauty of the daily life environment in such an atmosphere. Therefore, the "art" becomes a medium in message passing and communication in order to build the "environmental taste of aesthetically peaceful housing" as our vision. This research is carried out by the method of literature data and case analysis. All of these--the aesthetic life and community patterns, the creativity and environmental taste, the educational perspectives on experiential learning and lifelong learning, the aesthetics, and other literature related to this research—form the discussion basis for the case studies. And through the application of action design research methods, in the process of participating in the implementation, the scheme designed for implementation in the field is adjusted in a rolling manner according to the problems faced by the actual situation.

2 Literature Discussion on Artistic Intervention and Elderly Teaching

2.1 Aesthetic Life and Community

The Industrial Revolution began in the 1760s and set off the first wave of industrial upgrading. At the same time, it also created capitalist industrialization. A large number of mechanically produced items made people who were concerned about the quality of life feel a crisis. Against such a time and space background, the emphasis on the beauty of the essence of craftsmanship made Ruskin, J. (1819–1900), a social thinker and an artist as well, become a promoter of the spirit of the Arts and Crafts Movement. In addition, Morris, W (1834–1896) personally advocated and championed handicraft technology revival. Although a large number of factory-made items and rapid consumption power made the mechanical production of the advancing times have no turning back, they also made possible the beginning of the so-called design concept. Therefore, Ruskin and Morris brought to the Arts and Crafts Movement a new wave of thought, as the life aesthetics of artistic value-added design mentioned by Hara, K. (in 2003), which embodied the joy of creating the most suitable objects and environment, or the joy of living in it, in the life objects or environmental landscapes [1]. In this regard, art and design can add beauty to life and the environment, and exploring the sense of beauty has been one of the important topics in modern aesthetics. Where does the sense of beauty come from? As Read, H. (in 1931) explained that the forms, proportions, etc. of the things we see bring us a certain sense of pleasure [2].

Art intervention in the space has produced a series of experiments and discussions. It has flourished in modern art since World War II. Artists were no longer just using media to create forms of expression. Among other things, there were creations that focused on issues such as social development, living environment, etc. And the exhibition was extended also from the refined model of art museums and galleries to the public space in society. Lacy, S. (in 1994), explained what constituted a new genre of public art in which it is not just a visual form of art, but a work that combines the efforts of artists and the people [3].

In the past one or two decades, the development of art intervention in the space in Taiwan has achieved similar results as community space beautification, but because of the unique and diverse expressions of art, it is not limited to a single mode of space beautification, but also includes the spirit of experimentation and innovation for the most part. In Hong, Y.Z.'s study (in 2013), taking Tugou Village, Houbi District, Tainan as an example, the Development Association of this community started from improving the living environment in rural areas in 2002, and it was integrated in 2004 with the cooperation of the Graduate Institute of Architecture of Tainan National University of the Arts. At the end of 2012, the Tugou Rural Art Museum was established to incorporate the entire countryside as its scope [4]. The above-mentioned case of Tugou Rural Art Museum has the same direction as the current discussion in the local revitalization to use value-added art to create local vitality, bringing aesthetics into community life. Through the practice of art and design and on the basis of companionship, a relationship of mutual trust is formed. Through the connection of people, things and objects, the aesthetic feeling can be subtly integrated into the living environment and field atmosphere. Just as Yamazaki, R. (in 2018) discussed the general policy of Japanese community design, he used the design concept of the uncreated objects to clarify the importance of participation by the owner of each space because the environment will change due to human factors [5].

2.2 Creativity Environment and Taste

Creativity is an external display of imagination, and they are closely related, but not of the same concept, as Finke, Ward, & Smith (in 1992) in the essay "Creative Cognition: Theory, Research, and Applications" explored the mode of creativity generation and explained, "the previous stage of the production process is the expression of imagination, that is, the imagination in the early stage of creativity [6]." However, whether creativity is as susceptible to the influence of environment as imagination, Amabile (in 1996) further expanded the creativity component model she developed by adding the influence of the social environment and context on the creative behavior and emphasized the aspect of the interaction between creativity archetype and environment [7]. Later, the scholar Bröckling (in 2006) divided creativity into six different fields, rather than a description that a single product design was related to art. The concept of one of the fields clarified that creativity was problem-solving and a concrete expression that was able to solve the challenges faced in a novel and appropriate manner [8]. Therefore, Huang, B.R. (in 2011) mentioned the connection between creativity and the environment, indicating that the formation of creativity was the accumulation of the interaction between the organization, adaptation, and the external environment, thereby effectively promoting the methods and possibilities for individuals to generate insights beyond the field [9]. As explained above, the elderly with the experience accumulated due to the challenges of the living environment have abundant creative energy.

In contemporary art, the explorations of the natural environment, ecological appearance, climate change, and other issues, whether in Taiwan's iconic Taipei Art Awards or the International Biennale, are a form of artistic expression used by many creators to convey certain messages to viewers. From the perspective of creators, using works to care about social development, the motivation of such art creation is just like Zheng, L.L. (in 2020) asked what good design is that should be from the convenience of life to the design of the sustainable environment, the design behavior that can stitch up these commercial and non-commercial design [10].

In fact, whether it is seen from different angles such as society, politics, psychology, etc., good design will actually be discussed continuously. In today's diverse society, many professionals in different fields are concerned about the changes in the appearance of the environment, and in the wave of local revitalization, Jian, Z.Z. (in 2020) aimed at creating sustainable development links with the local characteristics. As a result, craft creators who enjoy a beautiful relationship between life and people, with their own professionalism and design ideals, become the key persons in the development of local creativity [11]. Because of the satisfaction and fulfillment of hands-on production, and the interaction with others, such creators enrich the inner emotion of life connection and enhance the happiness of environmental taste.

However, according to the research discussion of Nelson and Simmons (in 2003), the word taste in the environmental taste does not narrowly point to the difference between high and low or the distinction between good and bad but focuses on the positive emotions of subjective perception, which, immersed in the ability developed by positive and pleasant experiences, can be used as an indicator for regulating positive emotions [12]. Bryant (in 2003) pointed out "in each person's life experience, savoring is the belief that opens the individual to the positive experience, and what cognitive or behavioral responses to each person's ability to savor are the individual's expression before, during, or beyond the occurrence of positive events [13]." Therefore, in the follow-up study of Bryant (in 2007), it is more precisely stated that savor or taste is the awareness of positive emotions and conscious attention. It is self-focused attention to inner thoughts feelings and perceptions, and the tendency to have more direct interaction with inner experience [14]. Therefore, on the basis of the above-mentioned research on the perception of positive psychological energy, scholars Quoidbach, Berry, Hansenne, and Mikolajczak (in 2010) further interpreted the taste. Taste is to focus on the moment, but it may also be people who are immersed in inner feelings at the moment or memories in the past. Being immersed in positive experiences may upgrade or predict people's positive emotions [15]. Smith and Hollinger (in 2015) went a step further by showing that taste could even predict psychological well-being and improve life satisfaction [16]. Later, Layous, Kurtz, Chancellor, and Lyubomirsky (in 2018) emphasized that happiness could be increased by letting taste guide individuals have more connections and controls in their lives with others [17].

Living environment refers to a wide range of wording. According to the World Health Organization, it includes both the physical environment and the human environment. It demonstrates that the human living environment is required to emphasize both internal and external needs [18]. Today, through the concerns of art creators on the environment and scholars' related arguments on taste research, the cultural and economic content of the research field will determine the appearance of the artistic expression, allowing the residents of Hengshan to see through the visual observation and arouse their sensibility in memory so that they will emphasize and improve their living environment. And then through the planning of participatory art activities, art practice courses will be used to evoke their local cultural memory and to build a consensus on Hengshan environmental protection. The focus of such learning is not to emphasize the expression of art forms, but to cultivate the attitude of life and to pursue positive energy, which is the embodiment of environmental taste.

2.3   Experiential Learning and Lifelong Learning

Taiwan officially entered an aged society in 2018, that is, the so-called population including and over 65 years of age was 3.31 million, accounting for 14% of the total population. Both the Statistics Department of the Ministry of the Interior and the Directorate-General of Budget, Accounting, and Statistics of the Executive Yuan also consider people including and over 65 years of age as the elderly or "silver-haired people". However, life after retirement is the beginning of another stage of learning. To avoid the situation of rapid physical or psychological degeneration and to encourage the learning motivation of the elderly, the Ministry of Education has cooperated with local governments since 2008 to combine local organizations and civil associations for the establishment of the "Senior Citizens Learning Centers" in various townships and cities for the elderly to learn locally. In 2010, the "Universities for Seniors" were further promoted by combining the high-quality campuses and teachers of colleges and universities. In recent years since 2018, it has also trained qualified self-directed senior leaders to set up the "Self-directed Senior Learning Groups", which plan appropriate learning activities and prepare the public for future old-age life from the viewpoint of preventive education. From an educational point of view, such active preparations will turn the concept and make the elderly a resource rather than a social burden [19].

Dewey, a well-known American educational scholar, stressed: "education is the reorganization or transformation of experience". There is a common pattern in different experiences, and the outline of this common pattern is determined by the fact that each experience is a result of an interaction between an organism and some part of the world in which it lives. [20] Therefore, the silver-haired learning in the art course activities has been full of "tempered" or seasoned life experience. This advantage in time is more abundant and valuable as age grows. Like the concept of lifelong education, the fact of lifelong learning has also existed in the process of historical and cultural development. In modern times, the concept of lifelong learning emerged rapidly and was generally accepted, and became the basis of education reform and planning and training system. The reason for this had something to do with such terms as lifelong education, recurrent education, and continuing education which had been broadly used and generally accepted. Especially in today's 21st century, because of medical advances, the average human lifespan has been extended, so the tasks of the life course need to be redistributed. The continuous extension of midlife backward makes people's economic life and occupational activities last for longer periods of time. Likewise, educational activities are also extended to the back end of old age. Learning is not the exclusive right of a certain stage of life, but they need at every stage of life [21].

The needs faced at different stages in the life course of the silver-haired people are the same as the hierarchy of needs postulated by Maslow (in 1943) from basic physiological needs, safety needs, love, and belonging needs, esteem needs, and self-actualization needs [22]. And Healy (2016) highlighted Maslow's hierarchy of human motivations, where the emergence of one need often depended on the prior satisfaction of another need. He pointed out that behavior was almost always determined by biology, culture, and situations [23].

3   Case Study Analysis of Elderly Learning in Hengshan Township

3.1   Elderly Mobilization for Arts and Crafts Course Activities

"Hengshan is beautiful and livable from village to village" is one of the blueprints drawn in the 2019 Hengshan Living Aesthetics Village Revitalization Project, aiming at activating the elderly, because, in the data collection of the pre-work, it was accurately found that Hengshan Township, located on the edge of Hsinchu City and Zhubei City, had a population structure that lacked economic productivity. As of May 2021, the proportion of the elderly population (65 years old and above) in Hengshan Township had risen to 23.14%. It was hoped that the curriculum planning of entering the community through art would connect the emotions and fun of residents' life, and generate a collective consciousness of empathy as a group for the co-creation and co-prosperity of the environment because the elderly could meet to create and play art together, and the process of creation would be gamified. Scholar Winnicott, D. advocated that no matter adults or children, creativity could only be achieved in playing, that is, when people have the ability to play, they will have creativity, which can stimulate the energy of personal imagination and creativity [24].

However, it is the "people" that matter most in making up a community. For example, Mattessich defines a community as a group of people living in the same geographically defined area, forming social and psychological connections with each other and with the place in which they live [25]. It can be seen that the mutual interaction between the people living in the same area of so-called geographical division affects the appearance of the community. Perhaps it is in the group chat, which is held between the elderly men and women in the neighborhood and spurred and stirred by the project staff on the spot, that the community network and relationship are established. It is the planning staff's winning affections and trust of local people that help to seek, through the process of dialogue and communication, a consensus among the people of different backgrounds, and to create an issue of silver-haired LOHAS learning and development in a community environment.

The experience of every old resident can be a living encyclopedia of Hengshan. In the development of the industry, whether it is the decline of the cement or forestry industry, and after this process of rising and fall, the wisdom and value of the old man need to be re-affirmed in different forms, as Dewey emphasizes that the connotation of thinking in experience injects experimental intelligence into experience, so that experience itself has the potential for self-regulation and improvement, and trusting experience will not become blind obedience. Instead, it produces the pursuit of progress, so the experience is not only a matter of the past but also has a forward-looking future [20]. Therefore, through artistic activities, the silver-haired people have greater energy to exert their creativity, gain a sense of accomplishment, and affirm themselves. Under the development of such positive energy, art is used to connect the stories of the life experience of the silver-haired people.

3.2 Creative Process Through Chitchat

Focusing on the art courses of the Residents LOHAS Team, each participating senior is guided to give full play to the wisdom of their personal life and the perception of the daily environment, and to play art by hands. To make "artistic community activities", the first step in this research field is to open again the iron gate of Jiuzantou Railway Station, which was previously unmanaged and abandoned for a long time, and invite neighbors to come to clean it up and revitalize the use of its space. This will also beautify its environment, successfully transforming this into a composite space, planning artists to stay during weekends, so as to shape the unique station attractions with the artistic flavor of Neiwan Branch Line. And the first Residents LOHAS Team will be set up for weekdays at Jiuzantou Railway Station and Xiaoyang Pottery Studio located in Shaking Village will be invited to plan short-term (six weeks) pottery plate design and production courses in these two different spaces. This pottery course is not produced in a general form, but will be linked to the follow-up activity of the Residents LOHAS Team, called "Jiuzantou, Interesting Memories through Art", so that the silver-haired students can use the pottery plates they designed and made to dress up their home-made goodies. In the one-person-one-dish form, local residents will get together through food and beautiful utensils, showing that residents will share with each other the beauties of life in their own homes.

In addition to seeking art professionals from outside the countryside, the teachers of the Residents LOHAS Team also began to think about how to find teachers from the elderly in the area. According to the literature and history survey data, Hengshan was also a place where bamboo brooms were produced before. One of the on-the-spot visits to the local people revealed that Xu, Z.H., former head of Dadu Village, had made bamboo brooms before. On such occasions, he was invited to give a special workshop on "Bamboo Broom Research Laboratory". And this is also, when discussing the curriculum planning at the beginning, to avoid making local residents think that a curriculum is just a superficial form of activities put into practice by outsiders, so it is possible to find elders from the community who have rich craftsmanship and industrial production capabilities here and make them teachers. Although the elders of the Residents LOHAS Team will be humble and tactful at the beginning, the actual lecturing and demonstrations in the classroom have shown the value of experience and the energy of creativity, and it also has shown that the elderly may help each other and learn together. At the same time, it also evokes the connection of the residents' memories of the times, allowing each other to review the changes in their hometowns, past and present. In addition, the "Bamboo Broom Laboratory" also cooperates with the students of the master's program of the Department of Arts and Design of Tsinghua University, interpreting the spirit of the times of traditional manufacturing through the students' innovative art forms. It also has displayed the value-added art energy, allowing residents to watch art being integrated into the community, presenting the material, and shaping aesthetics of the space installation.

3.3   The Space and Spirit of the Community

Zeng, X.Z. (in 2007) pointed out "when a project enters a community, the number of participating locals is one of the keys to the success or failure of the promotion of community plan activities. Other keys include community organization operation and mobilization, spatial imagination, problem awareness, and whether in the future the project will be able to operate independently and improve itself. And these things that need to happen in the field cover the thematic explorations of people, culture, geographical environment, industry, and landscape [26]." Therefore, when art enters a community, it is not a matter of design related to substantive activities or landscape, but a consideration of the spatial concept, because the community does not refer to the regional area of the geographical location, so the local space is not only a container but also contains the flow of time and the movement of history, that is, the so-called context of the historical evolution and cultural development.

In his book, Tally, R. mentioned that Jameson put forward the concept of "cognitive mapping" in his postmodernist article as early as 1984. In a certain aspect, it refers to the efforts of a subject who tries to determine his own position in a complex social organization or spatial environment. It is like an individual walking in an unfamiliar city trying to acquire a concrete sense of place, that is, the connection of this place to other places on his mental map. This conceptualization process demonstrates that cognitive mapping is a key method for overcoming the anxiety of being lost, which is at the most urgent level of everyday life and also at the more philosophical or existential level of inquiry [27]. Looking comprehensively at the dialectics of space discussion related to the cognitive mapping, mentioned by Jameson in literature, there is a certain connection with the space explored by local revitalization, including how to develop locally characteristic industries, etc. In essence, we must start from the fundamental space development through art to map in many different ways the real and imagined spaces in the eyes and minds of the artists. And then the local residents will also participate in a broader project of their local space mapping.

Therefore, from the overall construction of the community to the development of cultural and creative industries and to the current local revitalization, Taiwan has also improved from a simple beautification of the environment to a perception of a spiritual level. After the artists entered the community, they managed the environment with artistic expression, exploring local characteristics and resources, and reinterpreting and redesigning the space. They perfectly intervened in the community with art, improved the environmental atmosphere, and created environmental taste. This type of expression has escaped the one-way and narrow thinking of the past. It is not just the appearance of visual objects placed in public spaces, but also incorporates many aesthetic theories and aesthetic education into art activities and courses that the general public participates in. By so doing, a new type of model is formed, which will describe the situations of the new chapter of the story for the place. As mentioned by Tally in his work, Lawrence, an English novelist, and literary critic discussed the "spirit of place" that meant the gods who guard a particular place and even guide and control the minds of people living in that place [27].

4 Discussion

4.1 The Value of Elderly Creativity

Creativity comes from the interaction between systems consisting of three elements, namely a culture with symbolic rules, people who bring new things into the symbolic realm, and academic experts who recognize and determine the invention. Therefore, Csiksentmihalyi has conducted an in-depth analysis of the characteristics of creative people and what creativity is through interviews with 91 extraordinary people in the past five years. One of the three conditions for this interview list is that the subjects must be at least 60 years old. This is consistent with the opinion that there is a certain trend in silver-haired creativity mentioned in this article. Generally speaking, the term creativity can be taken literally as some mental activity or an idea that takes place in the mind of some particular person, but this may be only in a narrow sense, as explained in Csiksentmihalyi's book. Creativity does not occur in people's minds but is the result of the interaction of individual thinking and social culture. It is a systemic rather than an individual phenomenon. And precisely because human beings are different from other animals in that they have the mind to think, everyone is creative. And because creativity enriches human life, learning is made to be more efficient and productive. The operation of creativity is to solve problems, but the problems may originate from such aspects as personal experience, professional field requirements, social expectations, etc. [28]. Therefore, despite that the skills needed by silver-haired people in life have slowed down, and that the physiological functions gradually have declined, their mental abilities are increasing day by day. The crystallized wisdom accumulated from their older life experiences for deductive thinking and logical reasoning needed to face problems shows the value of the silver-haired people for local revitalization.

4.2 The Value Community's Expectations and Losses in Art

Overall community building was introduced into Taiwan in 1994, emphasizing independent development goals such as local perspectives, community awareness, etc. In recent years, the "urban and rural features" and "rural regeneration" under the cultural and environmental conservation policies have emerged locally. All kinds of cultural festivals are based on the local awareness of cultural management, local industry, environmental symbiosis, etc., and give rise to social activities of different types and scales [29]. When art intervenes in the expression of space, the boundaries of form are gradually blurred. Through the perception of the external naked eye, the artist internalizes by the mind's eye the concerns of the natural ecological environment, social development, and even the transfer of political power to express the form of art on appropriate materials. However, in order to prevent artists from becoming only representatives of rights and discourse rights, becoming monolingual others in the community, and losing the opportunity for language to function in both directions, it is necessary to make good use of the contingency traits of art by allowing them to enter the community and make possible the mutually-subjective interactive mode [30]. Artistic intervention in the space should not be regarded as pure art for discussion, but a kind of countermeasure for either a response or consensus, which is obtained from group life experience or public issues on the appropriate occasion and problem awareness, and based on concrete artistic behavior [29]. Under such a consensus, in the use of artistic methods to intervene in local development plans, the participation of residents in design and discussion plays a key factor in concept communication and action strategies. In addition to the architecture, landscape design, and other hardware facilities set in the space, the course activities of participatory art will cultivate the environment tastes and upgrade the spiritual-level environmental perception for the residents.

5 Conclusion

5.1 Elderly Learning - to Arouse by Art LOHAS for Life

Elderly learning is the last stage in the practice of lifelong education. Community education is a way of lifelong learning for community residents. They not only have the ability to learn but also have the ability to teach [31]. Like the field and object studied in this article, elderly learning is like the lifelong learning of community residents, and the teacher-student relationship between the lecturer and the learner is one that is the opener, more democratic, and more participatory. Therefore, with the elderly as the main target, both the method of artistic intervention and art courses and activities are used to bring together the elderly to meet the upcoming super-aged social environment with positive learning energy, so that they will live with a healthy mindset for lifelong happiness as the goal in order to build a community with a high-level consensus on aesthetic life settlement awareness.

With the lapse of time, changes in the environment, and changes in the social and demographic structure, the silver-haired people's living needs such as food, clothing, housing, transportation, education, and entertainment will change in accordance with the aging and degeneration of their bodies. However, the elderly are not a burden, but a creative force that can solve problems. As Cai, W.F. (in 2021) describes the process in which individuals as they age will develop, enhance, and integrate their unique neural, emotional, intellectual, and psychological potentials up to optimal states. Through the accumulation of time and experience, the elderly are a kind of living wisdom, and such wisdom is also the expression of developmental intelligence. As shown in the field studied in this article, the life experience and wisdom of the elderly are a kind of feelings rooted in the land and attached to the community, which is an important part of the community of life where the community thrives and survives [32]. As the article emphasizes: the elderly, with their rich life experience, through artistic methods, are helped to retain their creativity and visualize it, so that the old age may also be full of energy for learning and growth, and may further create an aesthetic quality of life and unique value in the environmental taste.

5.2 Aesthetically Peaceful Housing - to Sculpt the Community's Environmental Taste

Hengshan, less than half an hour drive away from Hsinchu City center, has the geographical advantage, potential, and development opportunity on the edge of the city to become an urban sub-land, due to its close proximity to Hsinchu City, Zhubei, and other places with growing populations. As a consequence, although Hengshan faces the dilemma of population structure and development, it is more convenient in space than in other towns. Therefore, in the future development considerations, as Kinoshita (2018) emphasized, the key to local activation is to do things differently from other places, through which it can gradually accumulate and create a new industrial structure [33]. As far as long-term economic benefits are concerned, although the silver-haired people are of a less economically productive group, through the value-added of artistic expression and the spirit of aesthetic education, it will become a consensus of the residents to create unique artistic and humanistic characteristics specific to Hengshan and to establish a talent pool in the field of art and design for the local area. Both non-locals and locals are attracted by the abundant artistic energy and environmental taste. When people travel, they will drive the energy and potential of local vitality.

In the research results of this article, the art and design courses are brought into the activities of the Hengshan's Residents LOHAS Team, so that art may enter the community and meet, communicate, share and identify with the silver-haired life circle to form a common-good learning environment for displaying the value of the elderly creativity, by which the environmental taste of aesthetically peaceful housing may be built up, as shown below (Fig. 1).

By means of artistic design actions, we will activate the elderly life circle and construct the responsibility of environmental awareness and social care. The art courses and activities designed for the locality, through the creative energy displayed by the participation of the elderly, will activate the local traits, form a sense of community aesthetics from the daily living environment, construct local emotions, and, from local individuals to the field of the crowd, build a sense of identity with the local environmental taste so that the aesthetic life can truly enter the elderly group. Zeng, X.Z. (in 2009) described dwellings types that under the appearance of human life and environment [34]. This study extends the concept of the dwelling style by using art to intervene in the community for the aesthetic housing environment to enhance the spiritual level of life perception. This becomes the important conclusion of this paper. In the case analyses, we anticipate that the development vision of future Hengshan's aesthetically peaceful housing for environmental taste will highlight the value of the elderly and passing down

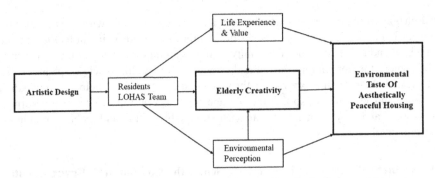

Fig. 1. The process to sculpt the environmental taste of aesthetically peaceful housing.

from generation to generation, and regard aesthetically peaceful housing as the core of sustainable development in the research field of this paper.

References

1. Hara, K.: Design of Design (Huang, Y.W. Trans.). 1st edn. Pan Zhu Creative Co., Ltd., Taipei (2005). (Original work published in Japan in 2003)
2. Read, H.: The Meaning of Art (Liang, J.Y. Trans.). 2nd edn. p. 23. Yuan-Liou Creative Co., Ltd., Taipei (2011). (Original work published in 1931)
3. Lacy, S.: Mapping the Terrain: New Genre Public Art (Wu, M.L., etc. Trans.). 1st edn. p. 27. Yuan-Liou Creative Co., Ltd., Taipei (2004). (Original work published 1994)
4. Huang, Y.Z.: The village is the Art Museum, and vice versa: a narrative analysis of Tainan Tugou Rural Art Museum. Modern Art J. **26**, 5–35 (2013)
5. Yamazaki, R.: Community Design No Jidai-Jibuntachi de "Machi" Wo Tsukuru (Zhuang, Y-X. Trans.). 1st edn. Faces Publications, Taipei (2018). (Original work published in 2012)
6. Finke, R.A., Ward, T.B., Smith, S.M.: Creative cognition: Theory, Research, and Applications. The MIT Press, Cambridge (1992)
7. Amabile, T.M.: Creativity in Context: Up to the Social Psychology of Creativity, 1st edn. Westview Press, Boulder (1996)
8. Bröckling, U.: On Creativity: a brainstorming session. Educ. Philos. Theory **38**(4), 513–521 (2006)
9. Huang, B.R.: The educational practice of creativity and its limits. J. Educ. **26**, 79–99 (2011)
10. Zheng, L.L.: Ordinary Social Design – An Exhibition of Objects Selected by a Wayward Sociologist, 1ST edn., p. 240. Shuangxi Publishing, New Taipei City (2020)
11. Jian, Z.Z.: Accompanied by craftsmen to recall memory with crafts and recover oneself from skills. Taiwan Crafts **78**, 26–31 (2020)
12. Nelson, D.L., Simmons, B.L.: Health psychology and work stress: a more positive approach. In: Quick, J.C., Tetrick, L.E. (eds.) Handbook of Occupational Health Psychology, pp. 97–119. American Psychological Association, Washington (2003)
13. Bryant, F.: Savoring Beliefs Inventory (SBI): a scale for measuring beliefs about savouring. J. Ment. Health **12**(2), 175–196 (2003)
14. Bryant, F.B., Veroff, J.: Savoring: A New Model of Positive Experience. Lawrence Erlbaum Associates Publishers, New Jersey (2007)
15. Quoidbach, J., Berry, E.V., Hansenne, M., Mikolajczak, M.: Positive emotion regulation and well-being: comparing the impact of eight savoring and dampening strategies. Person. Individ. Differ. **49**(5), 368–373 (2010)

16. Smith, J.L., Hollinger-Smith, L.: Savoring, resilience, and psychological well-being in older adults. Aging Ment Health **19**(3), 192–200 (2015)

17. Layous, K., Kurtz, J., Chancellor, J., Lyubomirsky, S.: Reframing the ordinary: Imagining time as scarce increases well-being. J. Posit. Psychol. **13**(3), 301–308 (2018)

18. You, H.Z., Xu, Z.H.: Study on the Living Environment Development of Ageing Society. Architecture and Building Research Institute, Ministry of the Interior, New Taipei City (2013)

19. Senior Learning Network Homepage, https://moe.senioredu.moe.gov.tw/. Accessed 3 Jan 2022

20. Lin, X.Z.: Experience and Education: An Interpretation of John Dewey's Philosophy of Education, 1ST edn. Shita Bookstore, Taipei City (2007)

21. Huang, F.S.: The Significance, Origin, Development and Implementation of Lifelong Learning. (Published in: Lifelong Learning and Educational Reform, pp. 1–32) Shita Bookstore, Taipei City (1996)

22. Maslow, A.H.: A theory of human motivation. Psychol. Rev. **50**(4), 370–396 (1943)

23. Healy, K.: A theory of human motivation by Abraham H. Maslow (1942). Br. J. Psychiatr. **208**(4), 313–313 (2016)

24. Winnicott, D.: Playing and Reality. (Zhu, E.L. Trans.). 1st edn. PsyGarden Publishing, Taipei City (2009)

25. Mattessich, P., Monsey, B.: Community Building: What Makes It Work – A Review of Factors Influencing Successful Community Building. 1ST edn. Amherst H. Wilder Foundation, Minnesota (1997)

26. Zeng, X.Z.: Rethinking Community Participation in Taiwan: The Concept and Practice of 'Participation' in Community Architecture. (Published in: Art and Public Sphere: Working in Community, pp. 34–61) Yuan-Liou Creative Co., Ltd., Taipei (2007)

27. Tally Jr., R.: Spatiality. (Ying, F. Trans.). 1ST edn. Peking University Press, Beijing (2021)

28. Csiksentmihaly, M.: Creativity. (Du, M.C. Trans.) China Times Publishing, Taipei City (1996)

29. Lin, Z.M.: Taiwan Public Art I: Theory of Black Public Art, 1st edn. Sunny & Warm Publishing, New Taipei City (2017)

30. Chen, H.Y.: Land Texture and Social Ethics. (Published in: Public Art in the Community, pp. 20–39) Tainan University of the Arts, Guantian Township (2009)

31. Lin, Z.C.: Lifelong Learning and Community Education. (Published in: Lifelong Learning and Educational Reform, pp. 181–239) Shita Bookstore, Taipei City (1996)

32. Cai, W.F.: Growing Old with Art-playing: Theory, Practice and Case Sharing of Art Therapy for the Elderly, 1ST edn. Business Weekly Publishing, Taipei City (2021)

33. Kinoshita, H.: Local Revitalization: 28 Survival Wisdoms of Sightseeing, Specialty Products, and Local Brands. (Zhang, P.Y. Trans.). 1ST edn. First Press & Hiking Culture Publishing, New Taipei City (2018)

34. Zeng, X.Z.: From His Space to Where We Are - Rethinking the Production Theory of Public Space. (Published in: Public Art in the Community, pp. 6–19) Tainan University of the Arts, Guantian Township (2009)

Design Education for Students with Disabilities: A Technical Graffiti Course in a High School

Fu-Hsuan Su[✉] and Yen Hsu

The Graduate Institute of Design Science, Tatung University, Taipei, Taiwan
d10917009@ms.ttu.edu.tw

Abstract. The emotional turmoil in the learning process can affect the overall outcome of learning, especially for students with disabilities, where negative emotions are often the biggest factor affecting learning outcomes. Therefore, this study uses a technical graffiti class in a special education senior secondary school as the research context to explore how students with disabilities solve practical problems in learning and overcome frustration and anxiety in the process of facing a new environment. The main objective of this study is to develop a design course for students with disabilities. Based on the concept of positive psychology, the curriculum is designed to motivate learners to learn positively, to encourage students to overcome their fears, and to express themselves in order to increase their willingness to learn. In this study, a contextual action research approach was adopted to build positive emotions through skill learning and color creation. Then, through experiential training and education, students were able to simulate the workplace application of their learning. The findings of this study revealed that there is a close correlation between learning outcomes and positive teaching. The curriculum planning and design in special education were discussed, reviewed, revised, and agreed upon in collaboration with the researchers, resulting in learning outcomes that are in line with the aims of the curriculum design, including contextual education, skills learning, and the color expression techniques project, which enhance learners' thinking skills and build their self-confidence.

Keywords: Positive psychology · Positive emotions · Contextual action research · Special education · Graffiti

1 Introduction

1.1 Motivation and Objective

In recent years there has been a great deal of research into the application of psychology to teaching and learning, with many scholars applying the concept of positive psychology (Fredrickson 1998) to students learning a particular skill. In particular, the role of positive emotions in positive psychology has led to new perspectives on educational approaches (Fredrickson 2001). In the field of special education, many studies have focused on the development of teaching planning and design skills, but less on the influence of emotions on learning. This study adopts positive psychology concepts to design a contextual course for special education students, incorporating the emotional response of color, to stabilize students' emotions and enhance their willingness to learn.

Martin Seligman is the father of positive psychology and his research promotes positive psychology as a scientific field of study, encompassing the effects of emotions such as positive psychology, resilience, learned helplessness, depression, optimism, and pessimism. Then, positive emotions are not only beneficial to healthy human development, but also help prevent disease (Fredrickson and Joiner 2002). Moreover, positive emotions promote decision-making, productivity, creativity, social integration, and pro-social behavior in the workplace (Fredrickson and Joiner 2002). Nevertheless, positive emotional environments help organizations to perform at their best and sustain a positive impact over time (Bagozzi et al. 2003). In addition, positive emotions contain a sense of love and happiness and have the value of enhancing interest in learning. In short, the importance of positive emotions in helping learners cannot be overlooked.

The study was designed to stimulate learners' interest in learning through positive emotions and to help children deal with negative emotions during the learning process. Students will also learn color expression techniques through graffiti creation to enhance their self-confidence. The main research objectives are as follows.

1. To design a course that is suitable for special education high school learners through the concept of positive psychology to induce positive emotions in learners.
2. By using the contextual course on graffiti creation, skills learning, and color expression techniques to stimulate learners' thinking skills and build their self-confidence

2 Literature Review

2.1 The Value of Positive Psychology

In Fredrickson and Joiner's (2002) study, positive emotions were found to have a positive effect in triggering upward emotions in a spiral manner. In research, learners are encouraged to discover new ideas through a particular activity. In other words, a process of creative exploration that fosters the development of the learner's brain while building physical, emotional, and intellectual capacity. In addition, learners can build self-confidence as they develop positive emotions. Moreover, positive emotions generate broadening attention and cognition, as well as creative thinking, which induces positive thinking. In this study, the creation of color perception is used; the learner's color perception is fed back to the learner to express the emotions of the moment. It would help researchers to distinguish between positive and negative emotions by looking at the colors created by students.

Positive psychology is the field that studies how people can feel happy and demonstrates the validity and legitimacy of positive interventions (Lee Duckworth et al. 2005). American psychologist Martin E. P. Seligman studies positive subjective experiences and explores how positive psychology can be used to help people lead good lives. Moreover, positive psychology is not just about living a pain-free life, but about living a happy and fulfilling life, advocating a positive attitude towards the many psychological phenomena that people experience. In addition, positive psychology stimulates the positive qualities and strengths inherent, actual or potential, in each individual. The existence of positive psychology is necessary, not for people to live without illness or pain, but to live happily ever after.

Positive thinking interventions (Creswell 2017) have been identified over the past two decades as having a positive impact on health, cognition, and emotions. There has been much research in this area in medicine and academia in recent years. It is also a major reform of psychology. In a study by Junjie (2008), two contrasting phenomena were identified between traditional psychology and positive psychology. Traditional psychology is problem-centered; positive psychology focuses on the development of the whole person. Positive psychological development has a direct impact on learners' emotional well-being. On the other hand, positive psychology can eliminate deferred negative emotions (Gable and Haidt 2005). Psychological interventions focused on increasing personal well-being and facilitating learning development (Lee Duckworth et al. 2005).

2.2 Color, Perceptual Psychology

The psychology and application of color have been used in many empirical studies and reports. The psychological effects of color and the perceptual associations of color are all part of positive psychology (Junjie 2008). For example, adding color to teaching is effective in enhancing learning (Xueli 2013). The positive effects of color psychology and perceived color on human psychological functioning (Elliot and Maier 2014). In Bayesian perceptual psychology, perceptual constancy is the ability to perceive a property or physical surface as a constant, mediating the color of retinal stimuli caused by that surface, which is transmitted to the brain to produce different perceived emotions. To varying degrees, human vision displays many constants of attributes, including size, shape, position, color, depth and motion, perceptual accuracy, and truthfulness (Burge 2010). When color perception is incorporated into the planning of teaching design, it is possible to observe changes from the blending of colors to the production of shapes, from a state of personalized perception to a state of psychological mood in a state of perceptual representation, and then to physical expression. Like Frege's theory of sensation in philosophy (Perry 1977), it is a clear expression of perception and the presentation of the spirit of thought. According to Frege, an idea does not have to be a complete word or sentence, but can also be expressed through shapes or movements and colors.

2.3 The Influence of Color on Educational Design

Researchers have used color psychology theory to explore the effects of perceived color on human psychological functioning (Elliot and Maier 2014). During the perception process, the learner displays the mental emotion of the color (Elliot and Maier 2007). Color is an element of design that has a profound psychological, emotional and physical response (Gaines and Curry 2011). Studies have shown that students with attention deficit and hyperactivity disorder and autism are more sensitive to perceptions in the learning environment. Students with physical disabilities have enhanced sensory responses and visual processing skills (Freed and Parsons 1997). Research has found a correlation between color and disabled students, demonstrating the impact of color theory on people. Early research has found that color perception has a physiological and psychological effect on human responses, including changes in mood and attention (Otto and Askov

1968). Moreover, Pett and Wilson (1996) incorporated color research into the design of teaching materials. Then, Gaines and Curry's (2011) explored the impact of color on learning and behavior in the classroom. This type of research confirms that color not only affects the mind, physiology, emotions, and attention but also the learner's brain. Because the message of color is transmitted to the brain through the eyes, the brain releases certain hormones that make the mind clear. Furthermore, the impact of color is not only visual, as color wavelengths are absorbed by the skin and the color of the learning environment has an impact on learners' emotions (Soma 2013). Many studies have looked at the impact of color on teaching and learning (Amarin and Al-Saleh 2020; Gaines and Curry 2011; Grangaard 1995) and have used color to achieve positive learning outcomes when planning teaching and learning designs.

3   Research Method

3.1   Contextual Action Research

Action research originated in 1940 when Kurt Lewin, a German experimental psychologist, published a paper on action research in 1946 and is known as the father of action research. Action research is about adopting the perspectives of people in problem situations after problems have been identified and proposing practical solutions while promoting social science goals (Altrichter et al. 2002). This type of research takes a professional practice approach, collecting data for analysis on a cyclical basis, planning, acting, observing, and reflecting during a research cycle, and adjusting solutions flexibly as problems change. Action research is applied to real-world situations rather than artificial experimental research, with the main focus on solving practical problems. Contextual action research is valued in educational research methods and is also known as action learning. The data and documents collected are highly effective in educational curriculum planning (Stringer 2008) and are conducive to action-oriented educational experiments (Corey 1953).

3.2   Research Framework

This study adopts an action research approach to teaching by selecting the Taoyuan Special Education School as the study context. Action research is a holistic approach to problem-solving rather than a single method of collecting and analyzing data. It, therefore, allows for the use of different research tools alongside the project, in a qualitative research paradigm approach that includes: keeping a research journal, document collection and analysis, participant observation records, questionnaires, structured and unstructured interviews, and case studies.

3.3 Research Process

1. Exploratory research

In this study, criteria were developed for assessing students based on the records of the previous year's special education architectural painting course. This excludes students with abnormal behavior, including those who are easily distracted by external factors, those who are too active, those who are not in control, and those who have poor initiative skills. The target population of this study was students with multiple disabilities from a Taoyuan Special Education School. The criteria used to select the students for this study were: initiative, endurance, work speed, work quality, communication skills, equipment knowledge, time perception, functional numeracy, functional writing, lifting and carrying, and abnormal behavior. Ten students were selected for this study.

2. Identification of research themes

Research Theme 1: The benefits of color in course planning and design.
Research Theme 2: How architectural painting skills can help specialized students in their transition to society.
Research theme 3: How to improve and overcome the psychological barriers to skills acquisition for learners.

3. Research process

The research process is as the following Fig. 1.

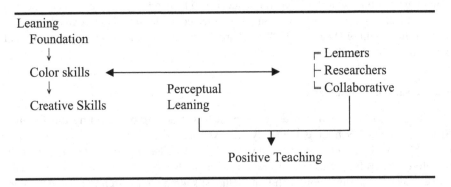

Fig. 1. Research process.

Positive teaching takes basic painting skills, color skills, and creative skills as basic teaching, and observes learners' reactions. Researchers hope to find out how to improve and overcome learners' psychological barriers to skill learning. Learning basic skills can easily make learners feel frustrated. It is hoped that the use of bright colors can arouse learners' interest, and guide creation to improve learners' interest in learning. Through researchers and co-researchers, pre-teaching observation, evaluation stability and active ability are better. High learners, conduct this research, this research is carried out with the method of action research, taking special education senior high school, the physical and mental state as the learning object, using positive teaching, imitation teaching, researcher and co-researcher in teaching. Observing and discussing, collecting data to analyze the learning effect of students; the psychological characteristics of people with multiple physical and mental disabilities are sensitive and meticulous, and the individual perception and feedback of the learners are reflected and corrected during the research process.

4. Course design

The structure of the course design is as the following Fig. 2.

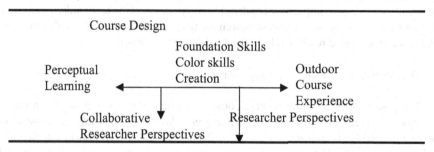

Fig. 2. Course design.

After confirming the research direction and research process steps, the curriculum design is carried out. This research course is designed from the first stage of painting basic skills learning, the second stage of color skills to color, and the third stage of creation; it is carried out horizontally in the course, and the perception learning and outdoor practice courses are intercepted in each process. Collaborate with the researcher's point of view and researcher's inspection to observe the psychological reaction of the learner's experience process. The completion of painting works must start with basic skills. Before color skills and creation, basic skills must be implemented. Each teaching course includes: learners Learning status, collaborating researchers' viewpoints, and researcher's review. During the research period, the researcher is also a teacher, responsible for observation, interviews, data collection, discussing with the collaborating researcher's viewpoints and other teachers, and focusing on the observation and discussion content. For future curriculum design and teachers engaged in similar research as a reference.

3.4 Research Context and Participants

Taoyuan Special Education School was established on July 1, 1992, and has a history of 30 years. The students are junior and senior high students with a moderate, severe, profound intellectual disability or with multiple impairments. The school is committed to the integration of general education and special education program, diversified functional development, and comprehensive services for students with special needs. Moreover, it has established the Painting Skills Development Class to provide special education students with an additional functional skill option. The course contains an individual classroom, equipped with real working conditions, good lighting and ventilation, special tools for painting, and the necessary items for learning. The students in this class were selected in terms of personality traits, initiative skills, and less deviation in emotional expression.

3.5 Data Collection and Analysis

This study uses the action research method to record learners' learning outcomes, their perceptual responses to color, and their reactions when faced with frustration during the teaching process. This study adopts a diverse approach to data collection, including teaching content and observation records. The information and records collected were analyzed to provide a comparative result of the perspectives of different individuals, such as students, co-researchers, and co-research analysts. The following data collection and analysis are presented respectively to reach an objective consensus.

1. Transcripts of researcher teaching course

The researcher's teaching diary recorded the curriculum design, teaching methods, teaching ideas, and contexts in which lessons take place, including teacher-student interactions, student-student interactions, collaborative researcher-student interactions, and researcher-colleague interactions and discussions as events occur. Also, it recorded learners' perceptual feedback, including emotional responses and reactions.

2. Teacher and collaborative researcher perception confirmation

Observe and record what is happening in the students' learning process, including good learning, poor learning, or particular status anomalies, and discuss, criticize and advise with critical friends. The participants include two critical friends, two senior high school teachers, and two professional painters in the construction industry.

3. Photos of the learning process and the finished work

The researcher is also the educator in the classroom. The study recorded students' learning situations. The observations in detail through photographic records provided the researcher with better information. The teacher will explain the content before taking photographs. When the students begin to work, the teacher will take photographs. Finally, the students' work will be photographed.

3.6 Study Reliability and Validity

Corey (1953) used action research to improve traditional education and to promote more effective practice. Then, Susman and vered (1978) demonstrated the scientific value of action research in their study. Moreover, Masters (1995) proposed three models of action research: the technical, practical, and emancipatory models. In addition, Holter and Schwartz-Barcott (1993:301) also discussed three types of action research studies, including technical collaboration methods, interoperability methods, and enhancement methods. Also, McKernan (1991:16–27) listed three types of action research: Type 1: scientific-technical view of problem-solving; Type 2: practical deliberative action research; Type 3: critical emancipatory action research. A scientific-technical view of problem-solving in which a specialist or group of specialists use their skills to carry out action research and promote improvement in practice. Alternatively, by engaging learners to develop a specialism from practical or internship courses, such as research, researchers, and practitioners' perspectives identify potential problems and bring learner course content closer to the workplace (Stringer and Aragón 2020).

1. Reliability

The reliability of qualitative research in educational research can be used as a criterion for assessing the quality of research. Reliability should be verifiable, transferable, and reliable (Berends 2006). One of the most important basic research methods in social science is the survey of a sample of individuals, groups, or organizations (Armstrong et al. 1997). The main aim of pragmatic educational research is to understand and acquire practical knowledge, which has a substantial impact on the development of educational research. The main benefit of a practical approach to educational research is that it facilitates informed and reflective decision-making by educational practitioners (Biesta and Burbules 2003).

2. Validity

This study used triangulation (Wilson 2014) to collect data, observation records, and research teaching logs. A cross-checking approach was used to verify the consistency of the study. The researcher was responsible for the collection, observation, and analysis of the data, the analysis with the co-teachers, and the initial evaluation after discussion and analysis with the painting course instructors. The tri-partite collaboration provides input and facilitates reflection and reflexivity in order to examine validity.

4 Action Research Findings

The study begins with a fun conversation to ease learners' anxiety when they are first learning. When a learner is occasionally disturbed from concentrating or has unusual behavioral patterns, the first step is to address the learner's negative emotions through conversation, care, and advice. Because learners with multiple impairments, mainly intellectual, are low to think and express themselves. The observer needs to check the verbal and written content of the expression several times to ensure that the perception and feedback are similar. In this case, as learners are mostly emotionally sensitive, the feedback of learners is the same when negative or positive comments are given by the instructor. Students are more sensitive than regular students and have less contrast in expressing negative emotions and more contrast in expressing positive emotions.

Learners' basic painting skills and basic skill creation, and color blending skills and color creation are clearly divided into two types of learners who are satisfied with the results of their painting skills, depending on their hidden personality.

1. "Positive" Teaching

In this study, the same content was taught in two ways during the painting session. Repetition is a curriculum designed for learners to enhance memory learning and to overcome the memory component of intellectual disability. After the first instructional explanation, the major concern is the learner's emotional response, using metaphorical stories or conversations to guide the learner out of negative emotions. The context of the communication content can engage learners or be interpreted as leading them towards positive thinking and building positive attitudes to learning. In addition, the content is taught by way of demonstration, so that learners can observe and learn at close range, increasing the opportunities for interaction with the teacher and between students and classmates. In addition, the first three weeks of the course focus on tool awareness, basic tool handling, and clay sharpening. At the beginning of a course, learners can easily become emotional, cautious, or timid when faced with a new environment, course, and teacher. Unlike normal children who are bashful in their encounters with others, learners with multiple disabilities, especially those with intellectual disabilities, are more sensitive than normal learners and are easily frustrated in their learning. The researcher should then provide positive emotional guidance to the individual based on the observed learning.

Situation 1: Learner Code 2–02.
Teacher: After listening to what the teacher has just taught you, do you understand?
Student: I don't know how to do it, teacher.
Teacher: Why can't you concentrate? Is it because you didn't sleep well last night?
Student: I couldn't put the tape on properly. (learner shows frustration)
Teacher: We can't do it, that's why we are learning. It will be fine after a few times of trying. You will be very happy. Look at your tape, it is only this section that is loose. The tape is not reusable, so just peel it off and use a new one.

Situation 1: Guiding learners through positive language expressions
The learners receive messages of encouragement from the teacher and do not give up even if they cannot put up the stickers properly. After a full lesson of practice, the learners were happy to show the teacher the results of their learning.

Scenario 2: Learner Code 2–07
Teacher: You have not taped this side properly, the tape cannot be reused.
Student: No expressive language.
Teacher: Do you want me to teach you again?
Student: There is no expressive language. (Learner appears frustrated, suppresses facial expressions, and is upset. looks at the teacher with wide eyes and asks you to teach him again with strong eyes).
Teacher: Slow down the teaching and give individual instructions.

(Look at the edge and press down with the fingertips, gently press down before moving on to the next section.)

Situation 2 is unusual in that the learner is not good at verbal expression and has less flexibility in physical functioning due to multiple barriers. In the first three weeks of foundation exercises in the pre-course, he was all in a state of emotional stress. The researcher repeated the individual instruction in the same way during the three weeks, and the learners' emotional state subsided after three weeks. In the following lessons, the learner smiled and stopped staring at the teacher with wide eyes. The learner was able to observe the movements of other students.

2. "Simple" teaching

There are four assessment items in the domestic technician's skills test, namely viscosity determination of coatings, color mixing, coating work, and calculation of coating area. The basic techniques used in painting include surface preparation, coating filler grinding, priming, and top coating. On this basis, the foundation skills course is taught and repeated every week. Individual guidance will be given according to the individual's learning speed and learning details during the course.

Scenario 3: Learner Code 2–03 (Stage 1)
Teacher: The tape you put on is not sticky and the tape cannot be reused.
Student: How can I do?
Teacher: You should re-tape the untaped section.
Student: Aaah! Aaah! Is that right, teacher? (The learner repeats the tape carefully, making frustrated noises from time to time. The learner's body is not working flexibly, feeling frustrated and tense, sweating)。
Teacher: Take your time and let the most handsome teacher teach you how to have fun with the tape after you finish taping the edges.

In Scenario 4, students with multiple disabilities have poor physical performance and are clearly not controlled by their brain in terms of physical flexibility, but they are able to think and express themselves well. Learners are still reluctant to leave the class at the end of the break and insist on completing this stage of their learning. After three weeks of basic lessons, the student was unable to use his fingers flexibly and was constantly shaking his hands to relieve the stiffness of his fingers. Foundation courses need to overcome congenital physical inflexibility and the pace of teaching will not be adjusted to suit the individual's condition. In the lesson planning and design, the tape creation course is designed to build learners' confidence in their creative work, geometric patterns as a principle of tape creation. The learners were able to express their emotions to the teacher after the three-week course, and their state of mind changed during the tape creation course.

Scenario 4: Learner Code 2–03 (Stage 2)
Student: Teacher, can I put my name on the sticker?
Teacher: Of course, you can! This is creative work.
Student: Yeah, I want to put my name on it, can I do that? Can I do it?

Teacher: Yes, you can! You can post a brand like Tsang Kee Mochi.
Student: Ah! Will the teacher do that? I didn't think about it. (no longer nervous)
Teacher: Come on, everyone wants to see what you've put up.

Scenario 5 follows on from the second stage of creative teaching, in which learners have fun creating their own name on a piece of tape after positive language. The emotional reactions expressed are very happy, and even the physical expressions are clearly encouraging. The frustration of practicing taping was overcome in the creation of this work. When the work is posted with the learner's own name, the learner shows full confidence.

Scenario 5: Learner Code 2–03 (Stage 3)
Student: Teacher, look, I've done it. (The learner calls the teacher to come and see his work)
Teacher: You have really put up the branding.
Student: No teacher, I put my name on it.
(He is smiling happily and showing his work to the students around them).

The Foundation Course repeats the basic skills and exercises each week so that learners and follow-ups no longer show anxiety about taping.

Scenario 6: Learner Code 2–10
Student: Teacher, can you teach me. (The learner walks silently to the back of the researcher and whispers.)
Teacher: Yes, let's go over to your table.
Student: No words, quietly waits for the teacher.
Teacher: The researcher demonstrates the movements.
Student: No expressive language and very focused on taping.
(Learner is not visibly agitated and only wants to do the job well)
Teacher: Repeat the demonstration again.
Student: Concentrates on practice (All students leave the class but the student is still practicing quietly).

The learner in Context 6 shows an active desire to know and learn, which is rarely the case in special education painting skills instruction. The learner in this teaching situation is sensitive and responds to perceived emotions. The learner is a tall, stout man with a very delicate mind and is considerate of others. The researcher, the co-researcher, and the teacher discussed the same point of view and expected the same perceptual experience as this learner in the creative curriculum. After practicing twice as long as the others, he performed poorly at the beginning of the lesson but has improved since then. He occasionally smiles happily during class. At the end of class, he stands quietly in the corridor looking at the classroom still in a mood of achievement and anticipating the arrival of the class bell.

3. "Color" Teaching

Color can convey imagery and emotion, communicating directly with people's thoughts. Color mixing techniques include learning the principles and logic of color matching, understanding the variety of color types and techniques derived from the three primary colors.

Situation 7: Learner Code 2–06
Teacher: Use the tools you have at hand in the colors you like, there are no rules about what to use. Just use what you like.
Student: I just want this one.
Teacher: How many more colors can you choose?
Student: This one. (point to the color he chooses)
Teacher: Yes, you are free to choose.

The study of color has never stopped in the academic field, and color perception has become common sense. The learners can convey their emotions through color and their choice of color is usually monochrome. Most of the learners are introverted, not good at expressing themselves verbally and make their color choices through their subconscious mind after receiving teaching information. Most of them prefer to express themselves in a single color and do not like disorderly colors. The learners use paint tools such as brushes, squeegees, and sponges to demonstrate their own skills and attributes. Figure 3 shows two monochrome pieces.

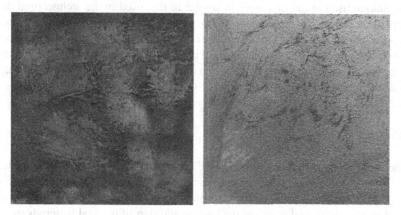

Fig. 3. Two monochrome pieces.

Situation 8: Learner Code 2–08
Teacher: Use the tools you have at hand in the colors you like.
Just use what you like.
Students: You can choose a few.
Teacher: How many do you like?

Figure 4 shows two pieces of student work.
Color creation is a part of the formal fine art curriculum as a representational technique, while in painting it is a part of the modeling category. It is mainly used in special wall designs. The teaching design is open-ended and does not use general techniques to teach creativity, allowing the learner complete freedom to express the purest expression

Fig. 4. Two multi-colored works.

of the mind. The majority of learners in this study were introverted and rarely expressed themselves verbally in the learning process. For introverted students, the content of the communication process is based on listening instead of verbal expression in learning. The technique used in the first work is similar to that used in the architectural design industry. Researchers, co-researchers, and educators who have discussed and examined this work agree on the professional quality of the work. The students who have received an art education course, or trainees who have been taught by masters in the field, may not have the same level of technique. When interest is aroused, learners' desire to learn is heightened, and such inexpressive learners listen and watch, presenting a more focused approach to learning.

4. "Creative" Teaching

There are many different techniques of expression. The use of painted materials allows learners to become accustomed to them, to enjoy them, and to fall in love with the pleasure they can bring. The creative practice guides learners through the use of clay, color, technique, and more, as well as the addition of unusual materials to create a completely different art form. Learners are stimulated by the novelty of incorporating new materials into their skills.

Situation 9: Learner Code 2–04.

Teacher: Use the tools you have at hand in the colors you like, there are no rules about what to use. Just use what you like.

Student: I want to choose as many as I can.

Teacher: That's fine! How many do you like?

In addition, if the learner has an active personality, likes to talk to people and express what he or she wants to do, can communicate clearly in words and is keen to help with the preparation of materials, and has his or her own ideas after receiving instruction in the color creation course, no individual guidance is required. However, due to their active nature, they need to be given emotional stability to balance the excitement after their interest in learning has been aroused. In this study, the students' creative skills were above the expected level, and the colors chosen were dark blue with grey to represent their emotional reactions to the inner turmoil. Figure 5 demonstrates another two pieces of students' works with active personalities

Fig. 5. Another two multi-colored works.

Situation 10: Learner Code 2–07
Teacher: Use the tools you have at hand according to your favorite colors, there are no rules about what to use. Just use what you like.
Students: OK (nod and gesture).

In addition, the students have a lively personality, but in the process of communication, if something does not go their way, they do not express their unhappiness in words, but instinctively react to it with their facial expressions. The following photos are the results of the learners' work in Figs. 6, 7, 8, 9, 10, 11, 12, 13, 14.

Fig. 6. Creating outcomes of learner 2–01

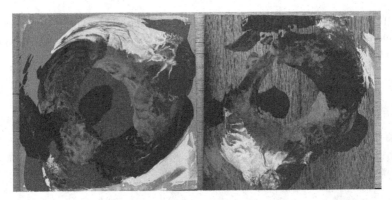

Fig. 7. Creating outcomes of learner 2–02.

Fig. 8. Creating outcomes of learner 2–04.

Fig. 9. Creating outcomes of learner 2–05.

Fig. 10. Creating outcomes of learner 2–06.

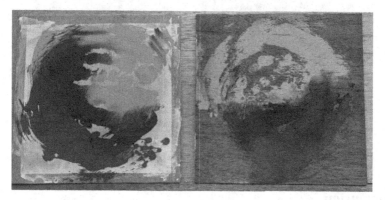

Fig. 11. Creating outcomes of learner 2–07.

Fig. 12. Creating outcomes of learner 2–08.

Fig. 13. Creating outcomes of learner 2–09.

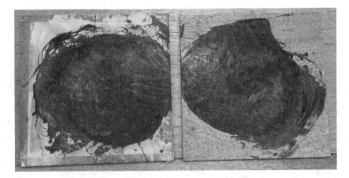

Fig. 14. Creating outcomes of learner 2–10.

5   Conclusion

This study uses positive psychology to enhance the learning outcomes of special education students in painting. This research has shown that by encouraging students to create freely, guided learning and using the psychological effects of color, students become less frustrated in the learning process and more willing to take the initiative to learn. Positive emotions are extremely helpful to students in the learning process, which in turn affects the effectiveness of learning. Before designing this course, we analyzed the students' learning data and concluded that the biggest problem of this course is the lack of understanding of professional skills and lack of self-confidence. Negative emotions would result from an apparent resistance to being exposed to new things. This study aims to balance students' negative emotions towards learning by incorporating positive psychology into the curriculum to increase willingness to learn and enhance learning effectiveness. These experimental results have proven that the application of positive psychology and color in the design of curriculum in special education is effective in enhancing students' learning outcomes and self-learning intentions. Although this experiment was only used to teach architectural painting to special education students, the redesigned curriculum can be incorporated into other special education programs.

Action research is a continuous process of discussion and revision during the implementation of the curriculum. After reflection, innovative curriculum adjustments are made to match the needs of the teaching content and to decide on the most appropriate content for the learners, and the researcher reflects on the professional skills of the teachers after the action research.

1. Teacher-student interaction

This study focuses on the researcher's perception of the learners' emotional responses to the learning process. In collaboration with the researcher's perception of the content through examination and discussion to confirm the consistency of perception, the perceived feedback to the learners contains non-positive priming.

2. Teaching Methods

The researcher's use of color, creativity, and positive emotion in teaching emphasizes priming more than basic skills, and learners are easily misled to overlook the importance of basic skills.

3. Teacher beliefs

Positive beliefs immerse the researcher in the teaching. When the learner holds up the work and says "Do you like my work, teacher?" This action plants a seed in the researcher's perception of the importance of the teacher's beliefs about teaching to the learner, and the importance of sharing the results with the learner.

References

Altrichter, H., Kemmis, S., McTaggart, R., Zuber-Skerritt, O.: The concept of action research. Learn. Organ. (2002)

Amarin, N., Al-Saleh, A.A.-S.: The effect of color use in designing instructional aids on learners' academic performance. J. e-Learn. Knowl. Soc. **16**(2), 42–50 (2020)

Armstrong, D., Gosling, A., Weinman, J., Marteau, T.: The place of inter-rater reliability in qualitative research: an empirical study. Sociology **31**(3), 597–606 (1997)

Bagozzi, R.P., Dholakia, U.M., Basuroy, S.: How effortful decisions get enacted: the motivating role of decision processes, desires, and anticipated emotions. J. Behav. Decis. Mak. **16**(4), 273–295 (2003)

Berends, M.: Survey methods in educational research. In: Green, J.L., Camilli, G., Elmore, P.B. (eds.) Handbook of Complementary Methods in Education Research, pp. 623–640. Lawrence Erlbaum Associate (2006)

Biesta, G.J., Burbules, N.C.: Pragmatism and Educational Research. Rowman & Littlefield, Lanham (2003)

Burge, T.: Origins of Objectivity. Oxford University Press, Oxford (2010)

Corey, S.M.: Action Research to Improve School Practices. American Psychological Association, Washington, DC (1953)

Creswell, J.D.: Mindfulness Interventions. Annu. Rev. Psychol. **68**(1), 491–516 (2017). https://doi.org/10.1146/annurev-psych-042716-051139

Elliot, A.J., Maier, M.A.: Color and psychological functioning. Curr. Dir. Psychol. Sci. **16**(5), 250–254 (2007)

Elliot, A.J., Maier, M.A.: Color psychology: effects of perceiving color on psychological functioning in humans. Annu. Rev. Psychol. **65**, 95–120 (2014)

Fredrickson, B.L.: Cultivated emotions: parental socialization of positive emotions and self-conscious emotions. Psychol. Inq. **9**(4), 279–281 (1998). https://doi.org/10.1207/s15327965 pli0904_4

Fredrickson, B.L.: The role of positive emotions in positive psychology: the broaden-and-build theory of positive emotions. Am. Psychol. **56**(3), 218 (2001)

Fredrickson, B.L., Joiner, T.: Positive emotions trigger upward spirals toward emotional well-being. Psychol. Sci. **13**(2), 172–175 (2002)

Freed, J., Parsons, L.: Right-Brained Children in a Left-Brained World. Fireside Books, New York (1997)

Gable, S.L., Haidt, J.: What (and why) is positive psychology? Rev. Gen. Psychol. **9**(2), 103–110 (2005)

Gaines, K.S., Curry, Z.D.: The inclusive classroom: the effects of color on learning and behavior. J. Fam. Consum. Sci. Educ. **29**(1) (2011)

Grangaard, E.M.: Color and Light Effects on Learning (1995)

Lee Duckworth, A., Steen, T.A., Seligman, M.E.: Positive psychology in clinical practice. Annu. Rev. Clin. Psychol. **1**, 629–651 (2005)

Masters, J.: The history of action research. first published (1995)

Otto, W., Askov, E.: The role of color in learning and instruction. J. Spec. Educ. **2**(2), 155–165 (1968)

Perry, J.: Frege on demonstratives. Philos. Rev. **86**(4), 474–497 (1977)

Pett, D., Wilson, T.: Color research and its application to the design of instructional materials. Educ. Tech. Res. Dev. **44**(3), 19–35 (1996)

Soma, K.: Colour and its effects in interior environment: a review. Int. J. Adv. Res. Sci. Technol. **2**(2), 106–109 (2013)

Stringer, E.T.: Action Research in Education. Pearson Prentice Hall, Upper Saddle River (2008)

Stringer, E.T., Aragón, A.O. Action Research. Sage Publications, London (2020)

Susman, G.I., Evered, R.D.: An assessment of the scientific merits of action research. Adm. Sci. Q. **23**, 582–603 (1978)

Wilson, V.: Research methods: triangulation. Evid. Based Libr. Inf. Pract. **9**(1), 74–75 (2014)

Xueli, M.: Research on improving the educational performance of digital color art in educational technology majors. Henan Normal University (2013)

Junjie, H.: A new paradigm of psychology-on positive psychology. In: Friends of State Religion (2008)

Image Preference of Intelligent Voice Assistant for the Elderly Based on PAD Emotion Model

Lei Wu[(⊠)] and Min Chen

School of Mechanical Science and Engineering, Huazhong University of Science and
Technology, Wuhan 430074, People's Republic of China
`lei.wu@hust.edu.cn`

Abstract. Explore the design theory framework of mental model and behavior
of intelligent voice assistant for the elderly and provide corresponding design
pathway and theoretical models for the current interaction design. The independent variables were three kinds of visual images of voice intelligent assistant:
quasiphysical image, abstract image and personification image, and two kinds of
dialogue relationship (equal tone and upper and lower tone). The dependent variable were the elderly's perception of the interface of intelligent voice assistant, the
influence mechanism of PAD affective model under different dialogic mood was
studied quantitatively. Conclusion through the statistical analysis of PAD emotion
model measurement data, the characteristics and rules of intelligent voice assistant
image design for the elderly were obtained, which can be applied to the field of
intelligent voice assistant design for the elderly, and play a supporting role in the
design of mental model and behavior design theoretical framework.

Keywords: PAD emotion model · Elderly people · Intelligent voice assistant ·
Image preference · User experience

1 Introduction

According to the number of aging populated in china is 255 million, accounting for about
17.8% of the total population, indicating that china has comprehensively entered an aging
society [1]. With the development of big data analysis and cloud computing in artificial
intelligence technology, intelligent voice interaction technology is gradually mature,
and the development of the industry has rapidly entered the stage of scene application.
Intelligent voice technology has witnessed rapid development in the fields of mobile
intelligent terminals, vehicle-mounted voice interaction, intelligent wearable products
and smart home, among which key technologies include speech recognition technology,
natural language understanding and speech synthesis technology. At present, in view of
the aging population of voice intelligent products are mainly used in health monitoring
and safety emergency, life companion, and information communication field, such as
intelligent dressing equipment, intelligent hand ring, intelligent blood pressure meter,
but most of these speech technology, simply use the speech, and no visual image, less
consideration were given to the psychological needs of the elderly. In the retirement

P.-L. P. Rau (Ed.): HCII 2022, LNCS 13313, pp. 425–435, 2022.
https://doi.org/10.1007/978-3-031-06050-2_30

life, the social role of the elderly has changed significantly, and they feel at a loss for a lot of leisure time, resulting in anxiety and loneliness, and increasing demands for active participation in information interaction. Intelligent voice assistant can effectively reduce the complexity of the operation interface of the elderly, increase the interest of human-computer interaction, and improve the willingness of the elderly to use intelligent products. Based on the image of aging populations intelligent voice assistant preference research, using PAD emotion model, an experimental evaluation of intelligent voice assistant image be implemented, get effect factors and laws on the influence of aging populations intelligent voice assistant, for older people life better in informatization and has important significance in digital information fairness.

2 Literature Review

In the field of intelligent voice assistant research, Chai (2021) studied the image of the vehicular cartoon voice assistant and analyzes the cartoon voice assistant from five dimensions of recognition, effect, communication, design sense and affinity. It was concluded that among the five dimensions of cartoon voice assistant image, that had an absolute advantage in affinity, but there was a serious problem of image homogenization [2]. Zhang (2020) investigated the influence of intelligence level on consumers' willingness to use AI voice assistant and analyzed the mediating role of trust as well as the moderating role of individual innovation and usage scenarios [3]. Ke (2019) made comparative analysis and researched on the intonation and display interface of the smartphone voice interaction system and summarized the problems of the existing voice assistant [4]. Zhang (2019) summarized the problems in the standardization research of intelligent terminal voice assistant and gave relevant suggestions [5]. Li (2018) conducted factor analysis on the design elements of the speech system and obtained the evaluation system of the smartphone speech system design, provided relevant guidance for the logical design of the speech system [6]. Jia (2018) found out the factors affecting the voice interaction between the elderly and smart speakers from their experience of smart speaker products, including wake word, voice role and dialogue content [7]. Li (2019) explored the overall development of voice interaction technology and the main features of key voice interaction technologies, studied the evaluation methods of AI voice interaction technology, and sorted out the status of the standard of voice recognition technology [8].

In the field of intelligent human-computer interaction for the elderly, Wang (2021) explored the design of short video learning APP for the elderly by investigating their acceptance of short video learning [9]. Teng (2020) took intelligent companion products of the elderly as the research object, adopted the Kano model, and took the elderly living alone as the target users to design a multi-mode interaction mode between the elderly living alone and the accompanying robot [10]. Hu (2017) from the perspective of the composition of China's aging population, put forward the population trend and relevant policy recommendations for aging population [11]. Zhang (2019) analyzed the key literatures, hot areas, research institutions and measurement methods of interface usability research for elderly users at home and abroad through comprehensive analysis of relevant literatures in recent 10 years and using Cite space software and CNKI measurement visualization analysis tool. It provides important guidance for the elderly to integrate into the internet world, improve their interaction design level and stimulate their interest in participating in the internet [12]. Zhang (2020) conducted a quantitative analysis and research on the user experience factors of elderly users in view of the change in the characteristics of elderly users, as to grasp the factors that affect the initiative of elderly users in using products, as to improve the product satisfaction of elderly users [13]. Yu (2019) developed a research tool and experimental framework to help designers and researchers think and explore the behavior pattern of human-intelligence communication. Researchers can manipulate experimental subjects through the speech module, visual module and motion module of the experimental platform, observe the responses of the subjects and draw relevant experimental conclusions [14]. Qin (2021) introduced linguistic theories and specific methods into design research, providing new improvement ideas for the specific practice of conversational speech interaction [15]. Wang (2020) studied the active interaction of agents in the smart home environment. Studies show that users' experience in using smart home products will significantly affect their preference for active style of conversational agent [16].

Based on the above literature analysis, it can be concluded that in the field of intelligent voice assistant interaction at present, scholars pay more attention to the interaction and technical factors of intelligent voice assistant, and some research achievements have been made. However, studies on the image of intelligent voice interaction for the elderly are still scarce. Therefore, from the perspective of vulnerable groups of the elderly, this paper studies the preference of the elderly for the image of intelligent voice assistant based on the analysis method of PAD emotion model, as to build a theoretical framework for the subsequent design.

3 Experiment Method

3.1 Intelligent Voice Assistant Image Classification

Intelligent voice assistant is an intelligent image agent assisting human-computer interaction interface. Through intelligent interaction mode of intelligent dialogue and instant question and answer, it helps to improve the interactive behavior between users and agents. After statistical analysis, the mainstream intelligent voice interaction images can be divided into three categories: (1) Quasiphysical image: for example, the image of Xiaoou in Oppo color and the image of Flyme creek in Meizu. The image features are as follows: most intelligent voice assistants are mainly shaped like the image of the microphone. In most cases, monochromatic colors are used, and a few colorful colors are used. The shape style tends to be two-dimensional flat. (2) Abstract image: For example, apple's latest Siri image, Huawei's xiaoyi image, etc. Image modeling features: fluid irregular modeling, full sense of halo, smooth moving effect, rich and changeable colors. (3) Personification image: such as NOMI image of NIO and Wiki image of Ideal car. Image modeling features: The appearance can be combined with the company's IP image, and more abundant expressions can be made in different scenarios, robot modeling is mostly used, as shown in Fig. 1.

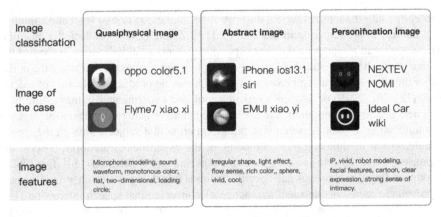

Image classification	Quasiphysical image	Abstract image	Personification image
Image of the case	oppo color5.1 Flyme7 xiao xi	iPhone ios13.1 siri EMUI xiao yi	NEXTEV NOMI Ideal Car wiki
Image features	Microphone modeling, sound waveform, monotonous color, flat, two-dimensional, loading circle;	Irregular shape, light effect, flow sense, rich color,, sphere, vivid, cool;	IP, vivid, robot modeling, facial features, cartoon, clear expression, strong sense of intimacy.

Fig. 1. Classification and characteristics of different intelligent voice assistant

The PAD emotional model consists of three independent dimensions: Pleasure (P), Arousal (A) and Dominance (D) [17]. In the PAD emotion model, pleasure refers to an indicator that measures a user's emotional state. For example, "joy", "happy" and other positive emotions belong to positive emotional states. At this point, P is positive if P is taken as the horizontal coordinate and 0 is set as the equilibrium point. On the contrary, when there are negative emotional states such as "sadness" and "depression", the P value is negative. Arousal (A) is an indicator of the user's neurophysiological activation level and degree of excitement. When "surprise" or "accident" occurs in the user's mood, it is the state of high excitement. A is taken as the horizontal coordinate and 0 is set as the equilibrium point. This time, the value of A is positive. When the mood is "boring", it belongs to the state of low excitement, and A value is negative this time. Dominance (D) can be understood as the strength or weakness of users' control over external situations or others, which can be used to distinguish whether emotional states are caused by individual subjectivity or by the influence of objective environment. When the emotion reflects the user's strong dominance and control over the outside world, D is taken as the longitudinal coordinate and 0 is set as the equilibrium point, and D value is positive. If it has weak control over the outside world and is affected, the D value is negative. In this study, the spatial emotion model established from the three dimensions of PAD is used to measure the emotional experience of users using intelligent voice assistant, as shown in Fig. 2.

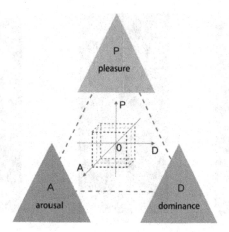

Fig. 2. Spatialization of PAD emotion model

3.2 Preparation of Experimental Materials

Through screening and analyzing the image of mainstream intelligent voice assistant on the market, such as Siri, Oppo, Nio, Nomi, Wiki, etc., combined with in-depth interviews with 8 experts in design and psychology (working years > 15 years), The main factors that affect the cognition of intelligent voice assistant among the elderly are the image characteristics and dialogue relationship of intelligent voice assistant.

In this experiment, the image features and dialogue relations of intelligent voice assistant are taken as independent variables. The image features of intelligent voice assistant can be divided into three experimental levels: quasiphysical image, abstract image and personification image. The dialogue relationship of intelligent voice assistant is divided into two experimental levels, equal tone and upper and lower tone. The dependent variable of the study was the measurement data of the PAD emotion model of intelligent voice assistant in the elderly population.

According to the above definition of experimental independent variables, intelligent voice assistant can be divided into S1 (quasiphysical image), S2 (abstract image) and S3 (personification Image). Considering the acceptance and familiarity of the image of intelligent voice assistant among the elderly, S1 (quasiphysical Image) selected the microphone with metal texture to design the shape, S2 (abstract image) select abstract wave form, S3 (personification Image) select robot form. In conversation, equal tone refers to the equal address between the intelligent voice assistant and the elderly users, which is called "equal". Upper and lower tone refers to the master-servant relationship between intelligent voice assistants and the elderly. To ensure the effectiveness of the experimental sample, 10 elderly people were invited for pre-test. After several rounds of screening and discussion, the image stimulus material of intelligent voice assistant was finally developed, as shown in Fig. 3.

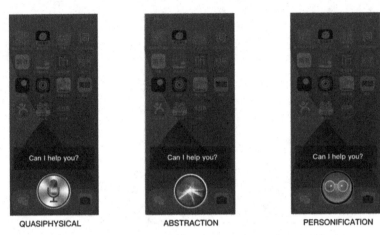

QUASIPHYSICAL   ABSTRACTION   PERSONIFICATION

Fig. 3. Experimental study of intelligent voice assistant image stimulus

3.3 Experimental Subjects

A total of 80 elderly were recruited, including 17 (21.25%) under 60 years, 50 (62.50%) between 60 and 74 years, and 13 (16.25%) between 75 and 89 years old. Among them, 43 (53.75%) were male and 37 (46.25%) were female. All subjects had normal visual acuity or corrected visual acuity, no color blindness or color weakness, and no history of mental illness. All subjects participated in the experiment voluntarily.

4   Experiment Data Analysis

Experimental tasks: subjects were randomly presented with 6 different combinations of intelligent voice assistant image features and dialogue relations (2 kinds of dialogue relations:equal tone and upper and lower tone*3 kinds of image features: quasiphysical image and abstract image and personification image, 6 stimuli in total), and the scores of the subjects on the PAD emotion model scale (1–5) were measured.

A total of 80 valid data were collected in this experiment. SPSS23.0 was used for data reliability analysis, and the Cronbach's α coefficient value of experimental data was 0.83, indicating that the experimental data had good consistency and met the statistical requirements for further analysis. The experimental task tested the combination of six different intelligent voice assistant image features and dialogue relations. According to the experimental data, W1-2 (quasiphysical image + upper and lower) has the highest pleasure score and gives the highest psychological pleasure to the elderly users. W1-2 (quasiphysical + upper and lower) had the highest score in arousal, which led to the highest psychological arousal in the elderly. W2-1 (abstract + equal) has the highest dominance score. Overall, W1-2 (quasiphysical + upper and lower) = 3.84, with the highest comprehensive score.

According to the data analysis of the experiment, the score of equal tone and upper and lower tone was analyzed from three dimensions of pleasure, arousal and dominance. In the design of quasiphysical image, the score of upper and lower tone is higher than that of equal tone, while in the design of abstract image and personification image, equal tone is rated higher than upper and lower tone. The possible reason is that in the face of the image of quasiphysical, based on the existing experience of objects being used in real life, the conversational tone of upper and lower tone can significantly stimulate the control psychology of the elderly. Studies have shown that the use of upper and lower tone can significantly enhance the confidence, sense of need and sense of self-worth of the elderly, so it can effectively reduce the tension in intelligent voice interaction and improve the willingness to use intelligent voice assistant. However, when the quasiphysical image acts as an equal tone to carry out speech dialogues, it seriously conflicts with the existing empirical cognition of the elderly population. In the existing cognition, the simulated object is often an inanimate object that is used and manipulated. If the equal tone is changed in the voice interaction, the elderly will have resistance and reduce their willingness to use intelligent voice assistant. In the face of the intelligent voice assistant of abstract image and personification image, the elders are in the emotional state of loneliness and sense of loss for a long time, while equal tone just provides appropriate information exchange and psychological companionship, catering to the emotional needs of the elderly. Therefore, the equal tone score is higher than the upper and lower tone score.

Experimental data show that the image combination of quasiphysical + upper and lower is more suitable for the elderly. When the elders use intelligent voice assistant, the combination of this type of image dialogue can better improve the pleasure and emotional activation of the elderly when using intelligent voice assistant, as shown in Table 1.

Table 1. Intelligent voice image score based on PAD emotional model

	Pleasure		Arousal		Dominance	
	AVG	SD	AVG	SD	AVG	SD
W1-1	3.57	1.32	3.51	1.28	3.63	1.23
W1-2	3.80	1.28	3.94	1.12	3.79	1.19
W2-1	3.80	1.16	3.74	1.23	3.86	1.15
W2-2	3.62	1.33	3.50	1.34	3.81	1.22
W3-1	3.61	1.38	3.71	1.38	3.65	1.33
W3-2	3.51	1.37	3.54	1.35	3.64	1.28

Further statistical analysis was conducted, the preference of the intelligent voice assistant image (male and female) as the main body factor. The 2 * 3 subject interaction analysis of the intelligent voice assistant image was performed. The results of S1 (quasi-physical image), S2 (abstract image) and S3 (personalization image) showed that the main effect of gender was significant, $F(1,15) = 7.26, p < 0.05, \eta = 0.34$; The main effect of image preference was significant, and the adjusted F value of Greenhouse-Geisler method was $F(1.26, 17.34) = 14.32, P < 0.05, \eta = 0.54$. In terms of gender, elderly women give higher scores to S3 personification voice assistant, and their comprehensive scores are significantly higher than those of elderly men. In addition, the interaction of gender * image preference was not significant, and the F value was $F(1.38, 24.75) = 8.25, P > 0.05$, as shown in Fig. 4.

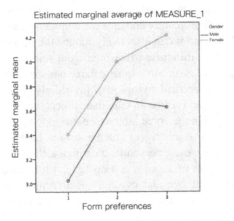

Fig. 4. Line chart of analysis of variance with interaction within the subject

5 Design Strategy

It can be concluded from the research conclusions in the above section that, without considering the dialogue relationship, the abstract image of intelligent voice assistant has the highest evaluation for the elderly, followed by personification image and quasiphysical image. However, after joining the conversation relationship, W1-2 (quasiphysical + upper and lower) has the highest pleasure score; W1-2 (quasiphysical + upper and lower) has the highest activation score, and W2-1 (abstract + equal) has the highest dominance score. It is found that the combination of upper and lower tones in quasiphysical image has higher evaluation, but personification image and abstract image have higher evaluation in equal tone. Overall, The score of W1-2 (quasiphysical + upper and lower) is 3.84, which has the highest comprehensive score and is most suitable for the intelligent voice assistant combination image expected by the elderly population.

Through the above research, it is found that the design of quasiphysical image is closer to the physical modeling, which makes the intelligent voice assistant have better recognition and familiarity, and can effectively reduce the cognitive load of the elderly. Its shape and motion effect are often seen in science fiction movies, so it has an advantage in showing AI intelligence properties and design trends. Intelligent voice waveform animation shows listening state when playing, which is easy for users to understand. However, abstract image will weaken the affinity of intelligent voice assistant image, which is not conducive to the emotional appeal of the elderly. Personification image design can be combined with different facial expressions, and the needs of different interactive scenes change. However, overly complex facial expressions will make it difficult for elderly people to identify. In conclusion, in the image design of intelligent voice assistant, the design of intelligent voice assistant using quasiphysical image, combined with the dialogue relationship of upper and lower tone, can better stimulate the positive emotional response of the elderly, as shown in Fig. 5.

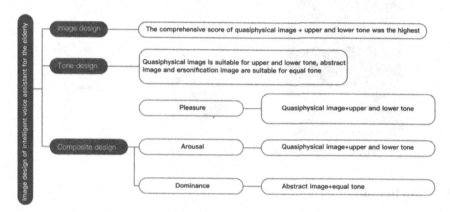

Fig. 5. The design strategy of intelligent voice assistant for the elderly

Taking social apps for the aged as practical design cases, design case practice and usability evaluation are carried out. In the past, social apps usually have complicated interface information, which makes it difficult for the elderly to operate and master how to use them. Intelligent voice assistant can effectively assist the elderly in task operation. According to the foregoing research conclusions, elderly people score the highest comprehensive score for the familiar combination of quasiphysical image + upper and lower, and this combination can well improve emotional pleasure and arousal of elderly people when they use APP. Therefore, the color palette of intelligent voice assistant image adopts blue and yellow, which is easy to be recognized by the elderly. The classic analogical contour of the microphone is adopted to reduce the cognitive and memory burden of the elderly, and at the same time, the appropriate ring gradual change effect is combined. Compared with the traditional flat shape, the design of intelligent voice assistant uses light and shadow effect to make the design more scientific and three-dimensional, which is more in line with the preferences of the elderly. See Fig. 6 for details.

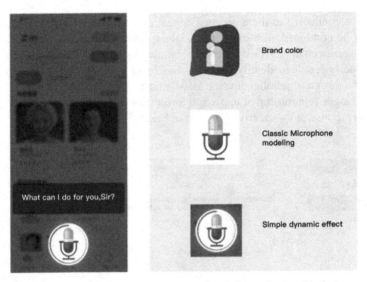

Fig. 6. Design case of intelligent voice assistant for the elderly

6   Conclusion

Intelligent voice assistant is an intelligent image agent to assist the elderly human-computer interaction interface, which can effectively improve the interaction between the user and the agent. This paper conducts research on the image preference design of intelligent voice assistant in the elderly population, uses PAD emotion model to conduct experimental psychological evaluation on the image of intelligent voice assistant, and obtains the key factors and rules that affect the intelligent voice assistant in the elderly population, and verifies them through practical cases. The conclusion is of great significance for the elderly to better integrate into the information life and digital information fairness. In the follow-up study, intonation, motor efficiency and other factors of intelligent voice assistant for the aged will be further studied.

Acknowledgments. The research supported by the youth foundation for humanities and social sciences of ministry of education of China, humanized design of intelligent mobile products for the elderly based on inclusive theory (20YJC760105).

References

1. Zhao, H.: The General Office of the State Council issued the "13th Five-Year Plan for the Development of National Undertakings for the Aged and the Construction of the Old-age Care System". China Civil Affairs 21 (2017)
2. Chai, R., Sun, M.: Research on the impact of intelligence level on consumers' intention to use AI voice assistant. Industr. Des. **01**, 30–31 (2021)
3. Zhang, Y., Fang, X., Lv, W.: Research on the influence of AI voice assistant intelligence on consumers' willingness to use. Shanghai Manag. Sci. **42**(04), 11–15 (2020)

4. Ke, R., Gao, D.: Current situation and development of mobile phone voice assistant user experience. Inner Mongolia Coal Econ. **15**, 216–218 (2019)
5. Zhang, D., Yang, T., Sha, T.: Research on standardization of intelligent terminal voice assistant. Guangdong Commun. Technol. **39**(12), 10–15 (2019)
6. Li, H., Hou, W., Chen, X.: Design evaluation system of smart phone voice system based on factor analysis. Packag. Eng. **39**(16), 42–49 (2018)
7. Jia, G.: Research of AI speaker voice interaction design for the aged. South China University of Technology, Guangzhou (2018)
8. Li, W., Zhu, Y.: Research on AI voice interaction technology and evaluation. Inf. Commun. Technol. Policy (12), 83–87 (2019)
9. Wang, M., Zeng, F.: Research on the design of short video learning app for the elderly based on user acceptance. Packag. Eng. 1–14 (2021)
10. Teng, Y.: Research on the design of elderly accompanying intelligent products based on user experience. Harbin University of Science and Technology, Harbin (2020)
11. Hu, J.: Current situation, trend and suggestions of population aging in China. China Econ. Trade Guide (12), 59–62 (2017)
12. Zhang, K., Zhang, T.: Interface usability for the elderly users in the past 10 years. Packag. Eng. **40**(24), 217–222 (2019)
13. Zhang, Z., Zhang, L., Li, Y.: Priority of mobile product interface based on feature classification of the elderly. Packag. Eng. **41**(18), 249–257 (2020)
14. Yu, Z., Yuan, X.: Design of active communication experimental platform for intelligent products. Zhuangshi (06), 62–63 (2019)
15. Qin, J., Wang, Y.: Dialogue-based voice interaction system in high/low-context. Packag. Eng. **42**(10), 85–91 (2021)
16. Wang, E., Yuan, X., Li, S.: Proactive interaction design of conversational agent for smart homes. J. Graph. **41**(04), 658–666 (2020)
17. Jang, N., Li, R., Liu, C.: Application of PAD emotional model in user's emotional experience evaluation. Packag. Eng. 1–9 (2021)

An Innovative Guidance for Outdoor Fitness Equipment Design

Fucong Xu[1], Xinyue Guo[1], Jiayu Pan[1], Langyue Deng[1], and Yu-Chi Lee[2(✉)]

[1] South China University of Technology, Guangzhou, China
[2] Ming Chi University of Technology , New Taipei City, Taiwan
liyuchi1113@gmail.com

Abstract. Improving the well-being of older people has become a prior policy of many countries and international communities. A community with outdoor fitness equipment (OFE) near a residence is an ideal place to work out, especially for seniors with limited mobility. However, there are few studies concerning the connection between the elderly and OFE, and lack of guidance information on the improvement and development of OFE. This study took the connection between the elderly and OFE as an entry point to conduct the research. First, we built a preliminary understanding of the psychological and physical characteristics of the elderly through relevant articles and then collected relevant data on the current status of OFE. The main research method was methodological triangulation model consisting of user observation, intercept survey, and focus groups. In the process, we preliminarily analyzed the situation of the elderly using OFE, and adopted an innovative design method, the deconstruction stage of the Vision in Product (ViP) design method, to extract a series of context factors about the future development and construction of OFE. Finally, based on the analysis result of the methodological triangulation model, the study built the guideline for the future construction of OFE, which can be a reference for subsequent research and design.

Keywords: Outdoor fitness equipment · Methodological triangulation · ViP design method · Elderly

1 Introduction

It is estimated that by 2050, the number of individuals aged over 60 will reach 210 million. The aging problem is particularly prominent in China under the influence of the large aging population and the rapid aging rate. In response to worldwide aging populations, many efforts have attempted to improve the well-being of elderly, and research has focused more on the meaning of the "good life" in older age [1]. China also issued the policy of "Healthy China 2030 Program Outline" in 2016, supporting people to carry out fitness activities nationwide and realizing "healthy aging" with fitness as the starting point [2].

Adequate physical activity plays an irreplaceable role in public health and disease prevention, but activity frequency and intensity levels are low in older populations, with

P.-L. P. Rau (Ed.): HCII 2022, LNCS 13313, pp. 436–448, 2022.
https://doi.org/10.1007/978-3-031-06050-2_31

only 25% of people over 65 receiving recommendations for physical activity guidelines [3]. Furthermore, sedentary behavior and lack of physical activity are particularly prominent among the elderly. To this end, local governments promote the health and mobility of elderly by creating outdoor spaces for them to engage in physical activity [4]. In addition, by analyzing the logistic regression model for predicting park use, it can be concluded that the distance between residence and outdoor exercise site is positively correlated with the frequency of exercise in the park. For example, people who live within a mile of a park are four times more likely to visit the park once a week or more, and exercise 38 percent more per week on average than people who live farther away [5]. Thus, communities equipped with outdoor fitness equipment (OFE), located near the place of residences, are ideal fitness venues, especially for seniors with limited mobility.

With the popularity of OFE, there is an increasing variety of exercise equipment to choose from, but little guidance on how to choose the right equipment for the elderly. Despite the availability of OFE for seniors, little research has considered older adults' perceptions and experiences with using this equipment. Whether OFE meets the needs of the elderly, and the details of its use are still unclear [6]. Therefore, this study aims to provide an innovative guidance for OFE design to better meet the fitness needs of the elderly.

2 Background Research

2.1 Characteristics of the Elderly

Considering that the elderly is a special group, it is necessary to analyze the characteristics of the elderly and OFE.

On the physiological level, the elderly demonstrate the main characteristics of sensory, memory, and motor decline; On the psychological level, the elderly show decreased psychological security, weakened adaptability, inferiority, loneliness and emptiness, desire to realize the value of the body; Most of them are very willing to participate in outdoor activities and have a strong demand for outdoor leisure places [2].

2.2 Development Status of OFE

This study analyzes common OFE on the market in-depth and is summarized in Table 1.

2.3 Problem Between the Elderly and the OFE

Numerous studies have shown that OFE is widely used and increasing rapidly in China, South Korea, Spain, Portugal, the United States and other countries [6]. In addition to fitness, stretching and rehabilitation, it helps maintain mental health and social connections with family, friends and other users in the community [6–8].

With the increasing popularity of OFE, there is a variety of sports equipment to choose. However, according to the research report, for the elderly user group, OFE still

Table 1. Analysis of common outdoor fitness equipment (OFE) on the market

No	OFE Models	Pictures	Descriptions
1	Air walker		Hold the armrests and step on the pedals, then alternately move the feet back and forth.
2	Back massager		1. Hold the armrest with both hands, then massage up and down to exercise. 2. Hold the handle with both hands and press the waist to the massage wheel, then move the body left and right.
3	Horizontal bar		Keep the body vertical, then pull the body up until the top of your chest is at the same level as the horizontal bar, then slowly lower back to the starting position.
4	Flat walker		Hold the handle tightly with both hands, stand with feet on the pedals, and swing the feet back and forth naturally to perform a walking exercise.
5	Upright exercise bike		Keeping the body slightly forward, straighten the arms, tighten the abdomen, and make the legs parallel to the beam of the bike, maintain the coordination of the knees and hips to grasp the riding rhythm.
6	Parallel ladders		1. Bend the buttocks and hang vertically: hold the horizontal bar with both hands, and then hang up vertically when the elbows are raised; 2. Walk with hands: hold the bar with both hands and move forward alternately.
7	Shoulder wheel		Keeping the legs in a horse stance, then hold and press the surface of the wheel with both hands and turn in the same or opposite direction.

has the following major problems: equipment iteration is too slow [9]; human-computer interaction is unclear [10]. The structure and effect are not obvious; emotional design is insufficient; the equipment is not suitable for the elderly [11].

3 Methodological Triangulation Model

3.1 Data Collection Methods

According to Kathryn Whitenton [12], the definition of Triangulation is the practice of using multiple sources of data or multiple approaches to analyzing data, to enhance the credibility of a research study. Methodological triangulation is a common approach in studies of user experience. Triangulation approaches can be claimed to lead to higher confidence in results and also to uncover unexpected results [13]. Focusing on quantitative research, qualitative research and expert analysis, triangulation typically involves examining data from observing, interviews, focus group, or other sources [14]. Hence, user observation, intercept survey and focus group were conducted in this study to gather information about how people use the OFE, what motivates them to use it, and how satisfied they are with it.

3.2 Observation and Intercept Survey

The fieldwork began with the user observation in three residential areas in first-tier and second-tier cities, including Country Garden in Foshan, Qi Fu Village in Guangzhou, and Lijiang Garden in Guiyang. We used an observation instrument called System for Observing Play and Recreation in Communities (SOPARC) to obtain direct information on community park use, including relevant concurrent characteristics of parks and the users [15]. Afterwards, we conducted the intercept survey following these steps: (1) selecting a representative sample of people who use the equipment. (2) conducting interviews with these users. (3) collecting data on the performance and satisfaction of the items and analyzing the results of the survey.

3.3 Focus Group

Focus group method was applied to organize a series of small groups (normally 5–10 members) where people are asked to provide feedback on the OFE. The major members include two elderly women and two elderly men randomly recruited from the intercept survey, a community manager, a manufacturer, an ergonomics expert and a host. The specific implementation process is as follows: (1) having participants try out OFE (to get real-time user feedback). (2) conducting a focus group that has enough space and short sessions in a duration (0.5h each time, twice). (3) organizing participants to complete their tasks and provide feedback. (4) analyzing the data collected through the process.

3.4   Results

The results can be summarized as follows: (1) The demand for public fitness equipment has always existed, manufacturer and community property both hope to integrate with new technology to keep up with the trend of the times. (2) Development costs and testing costs are major factors hindering the development of fitness equipment. (3) There are no norms or principles and device design guidelines on outdoor fitness equipment that keep pace with the times. (4) Current fitness equipment has a weak or no connection between the community property and residents.

According to the research results, we found that the problems were no longer just from the relation between the elderly and OFE, the user populations or scenarios involved in the study had gradually become more extensive with the development of society in the past 10 years. From the research statistics of user experience design studies by Ingrid Pettersson [13], those used 4 or more methods in empirical study, the majority (75%) of them pursued an exploratory user study. Hence, we also agreed with Vermeeren et al. [16] that it was not a cause in itself to add more methods, but careful consideration of combining the right method is the key. Therefore, based on the methodological triangulation model, the study added a context-driven design exploration called Vision in Product (ViP) design method.

4   ViP Design Method

The Vision in Product (ViP) design method [17] shows a different approach to design for values of OFE, the designer is stimulated to understand the future context of the product to be designed. In the ViP design method, users in future context cannot be interviewed, but the method does emphasize the importance of understanding people and is human-centered design in mind. The ViP design method required the designers to explicitly state what they want to offer people in this future context. This represented the designer's own belief that the design should be valuable to prospective users. Therefore, although the statement was based on deep context research, the responsibility for design rested entirely on the designers, who should perceive and take responsibility for anticipating the value of their design in the future environment [18].

In order to construct the existence form of OFE in a future context, the study described how we applied ViP design method to the research and the final vision factors we collected during the exploration. The first half of the ViP design method is called the deconstruction stage, which is the principal part of this study (see Fig. 1). It required examining a product, thinking about the past's design context, and how designers consciously or unconsciously incorporated various contextual factors into the design.

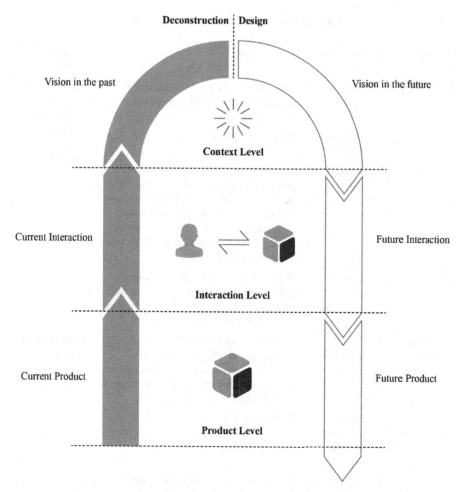

Fig. 1. The main research framework of ViP design method.

4.1 Deconstruction Phase (1): Product Level

In the deconstruction of the product level, the product is generalized, can be a service or touchable, any artificial object can be deconstructed. While deconstructing, the designers need to understand that the product has qualities, some of which are design qualities given by the designer, and some called static qualities are from the product itself. The process is difficult for novice designers, and it requires more observation and practice. In this process, we had identified 19 questions and answers to help excavate for the product qualities of OFE from five dimensions: appearance, component structure, using process, daily status, and development. The question reference come from the "(ViP design method): A Guidebook for Innovators" written by Hekkert et al. [19]. The specific process of deconstruction Phase (1) is listed in Table 2.

Table 2. Deconstruction phase: product level

Dimensions	No	Questions	Descriptions	Product qualities
Appearance	1	How big was it?	Generally, it was a little wider than the user. Different types of models were different in size	• Bicolor or tricolor • Vivid and highly saturated • Rigid
	2	What did it look like?	It had a lot of round pipes	
	3	What color was it?	Usually, within 2–3 colors, the movable part used a conspicuous color (typically yellow). The immovable part used a color that was relatively integrated into the environment, which was darker and less conspicuous. And the handle part of some devices used black	
	4	Did it have any decorations?	If the color was decoration, it can be described as no decoration, and not well integrated into the environment, more like a separate area or space	
Component structure	5	What material was it made of?	The main body was a cold-rolled steel plate or pipe, usually the outer layer was electrostatically sprayed. ABS or plastic was used as protection parts, and stainless steel was used to link components	• Mechanical • Formalistic
	6	What components were it made of?	Immovable brackets and fixed feet, movable discs or pendulums, graspable bars, or handles	
	7	How are the different components connected?	The main body was smoothly welded, and bolts connected the movable components for reinforcement	
Using process	8	Did it look pleasant?	Serious, ordinary, without special interest, unpretentious, traditional	• Lively • Vivid
	9	What emotional qualities did it have?	Express a relaxed and entertaining sense of leisure exercise—no pressure and intensity of fitness	
	10	What about the environment surrounding it?	The space was usually separated by some large soft cushions, which is generally a place where people often gather for socializing or physical exercise. And the equipment was placed around them	

(continued)

Table 2. (*continued*)

Dimensions	No	Questions	Descriptions	Product qualities
	11	How does the light hit its surface?	Outdoors, direct sunlight, wind and rain	
Daily status	12	How it worked?	Guided the user to move or rotate different components, or provided spatial space for support and suspension	• Simple • User-friendly • Public
	13	What kind of usage did it conform to?	Used it to complete low-difficulty and low-intensity repetitive fitness movements	
	14	What convenience did it have?	Usually placed in an open space Simple and accessible It can be used by multiple people at the same time The job was done through physical action, with no electricity Quality of entertainment	
	15	How long was the service life?	Used in normal conditions, it can generally be used for eight years	
	16	What damage did long-term use bring?	The surface paint was easy to be scratched while using. Rainy or wet weather caused the steel to rust, and the connected components could not rotate smoothly, and the paint wore out and fell off	
Development	17	Have any changes since the outset of OFE?	With the intelligent development, it realized the technology of charging and discharging It also has the function of showing the effect of exercise, the structure added solar baffles The shape and color also improved a little bit	• Relatively unprogressive • Inattentive
	18	How did it evolve?	Followed the development of social technology much more slowly than other products	
	19	Was the product still improving?	There were improvements, but more of them were additional functions, appearance changed, application scenarios changed, but the using steps were unchanged	

By deconstructing the current OFE at the product level, we refined several static qualities, which helped analyze the user's interaction process in the next stage.

4.2 Deconstruction Phase (2): Interaction Level

Designers need to perceive the interaction between users and products from existing products, and are responsible for describing the interaction process. Interaction qualities describe the attributes that designers give to the products, as well as how the product was presented and used. This stage requires designers to observe the people interacting with the product and analyze the user and product as a whole. The analysis material came from Soho and the user observation stage when we photographed some typical scenarios of the elderly using OFE. In the analysis process, we mainly observed and described the state of the elderly while using the product, the internal or external connection between the elderly and the OFE, and the surrounding environment. Also, the static qualities from deconstruction Phase (1) were called. The specific process of deconstruction Phase (2) illustrates in Table 3.

Through analysis and induction, the above interaction qualities about OFE were brainstormed and extracted. It was also found that although the elderly had good acceptance and contact with OFE benignly, there was an invisible barrier between users' communication, especially under the requirements of COVID-19 epidemic prevention. OFE was a community-based facility, but the communication and connection between people were rarely and weakly reflected in the analysis. Setting a single user and a product as a whole, such a single unit in the perspective of OFE area, was more lonely, independent, and isolated. We also found that the elderly were inclined to communicate and contact with the children around them. This phenomenon went against the original intention of the community OFE construction. To sum up this stage, we added the word "Isolation", "Disconnection" and "Incommunicable" to the interaction qualities of OFE extracted above.

4.3 Deconstruction Phase (3): Context Level

The vision considered by the ViP design method was not only the current user environment of the product, but also what users valued, their behavior, their aesthetic pursuits, etc. The designer must consider all factors that were relevant to the design. At this stage, designers naturally analyzed down from the interaction level, and only need to find out the reasonable concepts of the designers at that period. The reasonable result of this stage could be used to participate in the factors collection stage as a series of vision factors, which could also be the follow-up design guidance. Thus, it allowed other designers to redefine the design domain in a more innovative way. The specific analysis process was shown in Table 4.

In the next step of this stage, the root cause of some design problems was usually found, and it is more dependent on the designer's experience and thinking ability. According to the static product qualities and interaction qualities deconstructed from the first and second level, through continually questioning, we extracted a series of mappings of views and ideas, which were also contextual factors. These contextual factors can be

Table 3. Deconstruction phase: interaction layer

No	Photos	Descriptions	Interaction Qualities
1		The elderly in the photo was calm and relaxed when using OFE. The user and the product looked like brothers and partners. The morning sunlight made the overall atmosphere look harmonious.	•Partner •Cooperation
2		The elderly in the photo held his head high and full of energy when using OFE. The product was like a capable guard behind the user, and he felt energetic to strike forward.	•Adaption •Obedience
3		The elderly in the photo was very cozy and relaxed when using OFE. The user and the product were like old friends who had known each other for a long time. Having tea and chatting activities were daily routines in their spare time.	•Companion
4		The elderly in the photo was leaning on the OFE, and the user let the product support the body's weight, showing mutual support and trust between each other.	•Support •Reliance
5		The elderly in the photo was slightly struggling to use OFE, and the product looked like an obstacle that the user needed to overcome and challenge.	•Discourage
6		The elderly in the photo was serious and conscientious when using OFE. There seemed to be a competition between the user and the product. The red and yellow color of the product also rendered a tense atmosphere.	•Challenge

Table 4. Deconstruction phase: context level (designer's past opinions)

No	Questions	Related brief background
1	Why did the designer design this product?	Improving the quality of living for people in the community and national fitness is the requirement of the development of society Strengthening the construction of community entertainment and sports facilities has become a national policy The designers at that period wanted to increase the connection between people in the community and pay attention to the physical and mental health of the elderly living alone in the community
2	In what context (world view) are the product qualities and interaction qualities I described reasonably?	A sustainable community that cares about people's livelihood The caring group should include all kinds of family members living in the community, especially the children and the elderly Everyone can live in harmony in this area
3	How did the designer in that period understand people's needs and motivations?	Because of various technical limitations at that period, the previous understanding of the designers may be that the opportunity to go out for a walk or do some outdoor activities are valuable for people who often stay at home It was much better, especially for the elderly who need to accompany, need someone to talk with
4	Why are products the way they are now? (People's behavior)	User's cognition at that period: An acceptable amount of outdoor physical exercise through a low-risk and low-difficulty approach
5	Why are products the way they are now? (People's aesthetic pursuits)	User's aesthetic cognition at that period: The aesthetics of middle-aged and elderly people generally tended to brighter, more visible, and identifiable colors Many mainstream children's toys at that period were also brighter than the present

used as the basic viewpoints and ideas to be formed first for designers who were on improving the OFE related job. The specific process and results are as follows (Table 5).

Table 5. Deconstruction phase: context level (contextual factors)

Product qualities	Interaction qualities	Contextual factors
• User-friendly • Public	• Partner • Companion	1. People want to lower the barriers on physical training People who lack company in the community can have a place to connect with others while doing some outdoor activities
• Rigid • Mechanical	• Discourage • Challenge	2. Some people want to capture attention or be appreciated through some difficult actions or activities in front of others
• Simple • User-friendly	• Cooperation • Obedience	3. People want to make sure that their physical training is reliable and can be controlled by themselves
• Lively • Vivid	• Support • Partner • Cooperation	4. People see the product as a lively, welcoming friend of their own, with which they support and live in harmony

5   Conclusion

In this paper, we applied a main research method of user experience (methodological triangulation model) and an innovative design method (ViP design method) to provide an innovative design guideline of OFE based on the elderly needs. In the results of methodological triangulation model, the improvement of OFE involving multiple stakeholders was confirmed. According to the contextual factors from ViP design method, the design guideline statements could be 1) The center of design needs to focus on a space, environment, or a system rather than simple improvement of equipment; 2) The design should use some supplements or service that is not rigid and uncompromising, not necessarily fitness equipment, to enhance the communication and connection between people in the community; 3) An emotional connection like close friends or partners should be developed between the design and users and 4) The difficulty of using the new design should be low.

Acknowledgements. This study would like to extend our gratitude to the support of the 2021 Guangdong Innovation and Entrepreneurship Training Program for College Students Project No. S202110561230.

References

1. Ku, P.-W., Fox, K.R., McKenna, J.: Assessing subjective well-being in chinese older adults: the chinese aging well profile. Soc. Indic. Res. **87**, 445–460 (2007). https://doi.org/10.1007/s11205-007-9150-2
2. Zeng, X., Liao, Y., Wu, Q.: Study on the design strategy of outdoor fitness equipment for elderly users. In: 2020 International Conference on Artificial Intelligence and Electromechanical Automation (AIEA) (2020). https://doi.org/10.1109/aiea51086.2020.00106
3. Australian Bureau of Statistics: Australian health survey: physical activity, 2011–12 (2013)
4. Levinger, P., Panisset, M., Parker, H., Batchelor, F., Tye, M., Hill, K.D.: Guidance about age-friendly outdoor exercise equipment and associated strategies to maximise usability for older people. Health Promot. J. Austr. **32**, 475–482 (2020). https://doi.org/10.1002/hpja.367
5. Cohen, D.A., McKenzie, T.L., Sehgal, A., Williamson, S., Golinelli, D., Lurie, N.: Contribution of public parks to physical activity. Am. J. Public Health **97**, 509–514 (2007). https://doi.org/10.2105/ajph.2005.072447
6. Chow, H.: Outdoor fitness equipment in parks: a qualitative study from older adults' perceptions. BMC Public Health **13** (2013). https://doi.org/10.1186/1471-2458-13-1216
7. Stride, V., Cranney, L., Scott, A., Hua, M.: Outdoor gyms and older adults - acceptability, enablers and barriers: a survey of park users. Health Promot. J. Austr. **28**, 243–246 (2017). https://doi.org/10.1071/he16075
8. Furber, S., Pomroy, H., Grego, S., Tavener-Smith, K.: People's experiences of using outdoor gym equipment in parks. Health Promot. J. Austr. **25**, 211 (2014). https://doi.org/10.1071/he14038
9. Hu, Z.Y.: A systematic study on products for the elderly to improve their ability to live independently - from the perspective of ADL VALS and hierarchy of needs theory. Mod. Bus. Trade Ind. **01**, 102–103 (2014)
10. Zhang, Y.F.: Research on the design of community fitness equipment based on the social needs of the third age group. Industr. Des. **04**, 121–122 (2017)
11. A-Reum, S., Eui-Tay, J.: Sign system design guideline of outdoor fitness equipments for seniors. J. Korea Contents Assoc. **19**, 271–279 (2019). https://doi.org/10.5392/JKCA.2019.19.09.271
12. Kathryn, W.: Triangulation: Get Better Research Results by Using Multiple UX Methods. https://nngroup.com/articles/triangulation-better-research-results-using-multiple-ux-methods/
13. Pettersson, I., Lachner, F., Frison, A.-K., Riener, A., Butz, A.: A Bermuda triangle? In: Proceedings of the 2018 CHI Conference on Human Factors in Computing Systems, Paper 461, pp. 1–16 (2018). https://doi.org/10.1145/3173574.3174035
14. Salkind, N.: Encyclopedia of Research Design. Encyclopedia of Research Design, vol. 1 (2010). https://doi.org/10.4135/9781412961288
15. McKenzie, T.L., Cohen, D.A., Sehgal, A., Williamson, S., Golinelli, D.: System for observing play and recreation in communities (SOPARC): reliability and feasibility measures. J. Phys. Act. Health **3**, S208–S222 (2006). https://doi.org/10.1123/jpah.3.s1.s208
16. Vermeeren, A.P.O.S., Law, E.L.-C., Roto, V., Obrist, M., Hoonhout, J., Väänänen-Vainio-Mattila, K.: User experience evaluation methods. In: Proceedings of the 6th Nordic Conference on Human-Computer Interaction Extending Boundaries - NordiCHI 2010 (2010). https://doi.org/10.1145/1868914.1868973
17. Hekkert, P.: Vision in Product Design: A Guidebook for Innovators. BIS, Amsterdam (2014)
18. Vermaas, P.E., Hekkert, P., Manders-Huits, N., Tromp, N.: Design methods in design for values. In: Handbook of Ethics, Values, and Technological Design, pp. 1–19 (2014). https://doi.org/10.1007/978-94-007-6994-6_10-1

Effects of Exergames Intervention on Older Adults: A Review

Yunlong Xu and Runting Zhong[✉] [iD]

School of Business, Jiangnan University, Wuxi 214122, China
zhongrt@jiangnan.edu.cn

Abstract. With the number and proportion of aging populations growing rapidly around the world, new forms of exercise such as exergames have been introduced and popularized in daily activities. This review highlights the potential benefits of exergames as an exercise platform for older adults. The purpose of this review is to explore the physical and mental effects of exergame use on older adults and to compare the differences between single-player and multiple-player interaction, traditional and new exercise modes and young and old age. Searches were conducted in Science Direct and Web of Science for articles published from 2013 to 2021 in journals and proceedings. In the 22 articles reviewed, we found that the most common exergame device is the Xbox Kinect, followed by the Nintendo Wii™. Exergame interventions were mostly set at 30 to 50 min, 2 or 3 times per week for 6 or 8 weeks. In addition, the sample size is relatively concentrated between 20 and 50. The experiment was conducted in a single-group pre-post design (no control group) or pre-post control group design (at least one control group). In many studies, exergames were found to have a positive effect on physical activity, cognitive function and sociability, as well as improving their mood and attitudes toward exergames, although a few studies found no significant effects. Especially in the home environment or in situations where older adults are unable to leave the house for some reason, exergames can be used as an alternative to traditional exercise and have a positive impact on the physical and mental health of older adults.

Keywords: Exergames · Older adults · Exercise · Review

1 Introduction

With the number and proportion of aging populations growing rapidly around the world, new forms of exercise such as exergames have been introduced and popularized in daily activities. These trends present both opportunities and challenges for older adults to exercise with exergames. These exergames, also known as active video games (AVGs) or exercise video games (EVGs), include platforms such as the Nintendo Wii™ and Xbox 360 Kinect, as well as dance simulation products. Popular exergames include the Nintendo Wii™, Just Dance, Xbox Kinect and Ring Fit Adventure [1]. Unlike traditional video games, exergames not only promote physical movement, but also strength, balance

P.-L. P. Rau (Ed.): HCII 2022, LNCS 13313, pp. 449–460, 2022.
https://doi.org/10.1007/978-3-031-06050-2_32

and flexibility activities [2]. In addition to providing immediate audio and visual performance feedback, exergames can also provide motivational messages such as bonuses and encouraging reviews, which make game activities more fun and interactive [3]. Studies have proved that exergames offer a relatively cheap, convenient, easy and fun way to exercise at home [4, 5]. Nevertheless, early results suggest that exergames are acceptable, enjoyable and safe for home use [6–9].

According to the World Health Organization, populations are aging faster than ever [10]. Between 2020 and 2030, the proportion of the world's population aged over 60 will increase by 34%. With further aggravation of the aging population, it is important to explore the potential opportunities and challenges for the elderly with regard to using exergames. This article reviews the literature on the use of exergames in the elderly. The purpose of this review is to explore the physical and mental effects of exergames on the elderly and to compare the differences between single-player and multiple-player interaction, traditional and new exercise modes and young and old age. We reviewed 22 studies of exergames in older adults and the devices that are currently available for exergames. This study aims to answer the following questions: (1) What exergame devices are currently available for older adults; (2) what are the physical and mental effects of exergames on older adults; and (3) what are the similarities and differences in the effects of exergames between the young and the old, exergames and traditional exercise and single-player and multiple-player interactions?

2 Method

Searches were conducted in Science Direct and Web of Science for articles published from 2013 to 2021 in journals and proceedings. Search keywords included exergame, intervention, exercise video game and older adults. At the same time, the cited literature and related literature were collected to look for additional studies (snowball method). The inclusion criteria were: (1) sample consisting of healthy adults older than 18 years; (2) journals and proceedings including a technology-based intervention; and (3) published in English between 2013 and 2021. The exclusion criteria were (1) a sample targeting children and teenagers under 18 years or adults with diseases; (2) literature reviews; (3) literature not published in English; and (4) literature that could not be downloaded.

Titles and abstracts were screened independently and in duplicate by the authors to determine their relevance to this review. Then, the authors reviewed all eligible studies. Data were extracted from study characteristics, such as device, number and age of participants, independent variables and dependent variables. The authors discussed the interpretation of study characteristics until a consensus was reached. Indicator measurements, study design and gender uniformity of participants preclude the use of quantitative methods, such as meta-analyses. Thus, this review provides a narrative description of eligible studies.

3   Results

3.1   Study Characteristics

This review includes 22 studies. Group sample sizes range from 9 to 170 and sample sizes range from 9 to 337. As can be seen from Fig. 1, studies with a sample size of 20 to 30 were the most common and 20 studies had a sample size of less than 100. The sample size is relatively concentrated in the range from 20 to 50. Long-term intervention trials were conducted in 14 of the 22 studies. The mean duration of intervention was 7 weeks and the standard deviation was 3.37 weeks, ranging from 1 to 12 weeks. The intervention duration was 6 weeks in 5 studies and 8 weeks in 3 studies (see Fig. 2). As for the frequency of intervention, there were four studies with interventions once a week, six studies twice a week, three studies three times a week and one study five times a week. The shortest intervention time was 5 to 10 min [11], the longest was about 180 min [12] and the most frequent intervention time was 30 min (n = 5). There were 12 studies with an intervention time between 30 and 50 min, accounting for 85.71%. Exergame interventions were mostly set at 30 to 50 min, 2 or 3 times per week for 6 or 8 weeks.

The main characteristics of the included studies are shown in Table 1, including device, number and age of participants, independent variables and dependent variables. The main devices used were the Nintendo Wii™ (n = 5) and Xbox Kinect (n = 14), but VR (n = 1), video games (n = 1) and MoviLetrando (n = 1) were also used. Exergames users are generally divided into two groups: one using them for gaming and the other for exercise. Chen et al. found that exercise-primed participants used the exergame system for significantly longer than game-primed participants [13]. The potential impact of campaigns that promote health emphasizes the dual purpose of exergames (play and exercise) compared to gamifying health behaviors. One study found that physically active older adults performed better than sedentary older adults after exergame interventions [14].

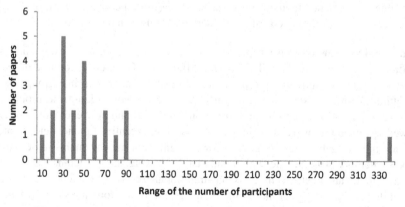

Fig. 1. Distribution of the number of participants in the reviewed papers

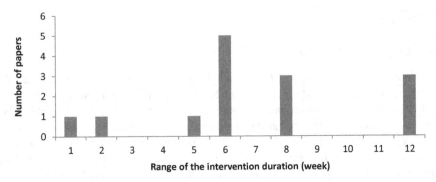

Fig. 2. Distribution of the intervention duration in the reviewed papers

3.2 Summary of Findings in Previous Research

The findings of previous research are summarized under eight headings: older vs. younger age groups, traditional vs. new exercise type, single player vs. multiplayer, attitude, physical activity, cognitive function, sociability and mood. The variables studied in this review are shown in Table 2.

Older vs. Younger Age Groups. Differences in the effects of technology-based interventions between older and younger user groups have been found in a number of studies. Chua et al. found that game enjoyment was only important for older adults in developing positive intergenerational perceptions, but not for youths who participated in the video-game group [16]. Osmanovic and Pecchioni pointed out that sharing exergames fostered relationships and connections while generating positive emotions for both generations [17]. Nguyen et al. found that playing exergames helped to maintain happiness levels in young people [27]. At the same time, Zangirolami-Raimundo et al. also found that exergames helped to alleviate depression in older adults [14].

In general, playing exergames can improve the communication between the old and the young and enhance their feelings, especially in older people. In addition, playing exergames improves the moods of both older and younger individuals.

Traditional vs. New Exercise Types. Many studies have compared exergames with traditional exercise to find similarities and differences. Chua et al. found that participants in the video-game group reported more positive changes in intergroup anxiety and attitudes toward exergames than participants in the non-video-game group [16]. After 12 weeks of intervention, both traditional physical and new exergame exercises showed significant improvements in overall cognition, executive function and attention, but only the exergame exercise group showed significant improvements in verbal and working memory [19]. Naugle et al. found that Wii boxing and Wii tennis led to greater increases in fun and positive emotions than traditional exercise [20]. Gonçalves revealed that while participants spent more time on moderate-to-vigorous physical activities in exergames than in traditional activities, they also expended less energy and thus exercised at a lower intensity but for a longer duration [23]. Compared with traditional exercise, the balance ability of those in the exergame group showed significant changes after the

Table 1. Summary of reviewed papers

Reference	Device	Number and age of participants	Independent variable	Dependent variable
[11]	Microsoft Kinect	102 G: 70.93 (6.51) 100 G: 73.72 (5.48) 117 G: 72.39 (6.55)	Play type (play with peers, youths or along)	Attitude toward exergames; sociability; positive affect and negative affect
[15]	Nintendo Wii™	19 M: 22.5 (5.5) 17 F: 21.5 (2.3)	Single and dual player; gender	Positive and negative affect; subjective vitality; intrinsic motivation
[16]	Nintendo Wii™	37 Y: 16–19 37 O: 60–89	Video-game condition; non-video-game condition	attraction; intergroup anxiety; attitude towards the other age group; game enjoyment
[17]	Video Game	17 Y: 18–22 19.99 (1.22) 9 O: 58–71 64.78 (3.46)	Younger playing with older; older playing with family	Habits; preferences; motivations; outcomes of video game play
[18]	3-dimensional VR	29 Y: 23.2 (2.1)	AVR group; SVR group; Control group	Physical activity; motion sickness; game experience; recognition memory
[19]	Kinect system	25G: 76.6 (9.0) 21G: 83.8 (5.1)	Exercise type	Cognitive function; brain activation
[20]	Nintendo Wii™ and Wii Fit™	11G: 20.18 (0.87) 11G: 20.72 (1.19)	Intensity of exercise; exercise type	Percentage of heart rate reserve; rate of perceived exertion; enjoyment; positive and negative affect schedule
[13]	Xbox Kinect	44 Y: 26.5 (7.1)	Intention framing (gameplay or exercise); feedback (health or no health)	Perceived exertion; energy expenditure; positive affect; duration of session

(*continued*)

Table 1. (*continued*)

Reference	Device	Number and age of participants	Independent variable	Dependent variable
[21]	Microsoft Kinect	31 G: 75.91 (6.00) 26 G: 76.00 (7.43) 32 G: 73.06 (9.38)	Age; play type (playing with an elderly person, adolescent or alone)	Social anxiousness; sociability; loneliness
[22]	Microsoft Kinect	317 O: 72.76	Play type (playing with an elderly person, youths or alone)	Motivation; attitude; sociability; loneliness; intergenerational perception
[23]	Microsoft Kinect V2 sensor	31 O: 67.5 (4.6)	Exercise type	Physical activity; physical exertion
[24]	Microsoft Kinect for Xbox 360	10 G: 68.71 (64.09–74.84) 10 G: 67.54 (62.08–76.75)	Exercise type	Overall balance ability
[25]	Nintendo Wii™	30 Y: 23.7 (3.7)	Exercise type	Heart Rate; blood pressure
[26]	Xbox 360 Kinect™	42 G: 71.5 (4.7) 48 G: 71.3 (6.1)	Exercise type	Balance; functional walking; quality of life
[27]	Xbox 360 Kinect™	170 G: 21.99 (1.97) 167 G: 22.01 (2.29)	Exercise type; user characteristics	Happiness
[28]	Xbox 360 Kinect™	32 G: 70.84 (4.53) 34 G: 70.76 (5.60)	Exercise type	Perceptive cognitive; physical function
[29]	Microsoft Kinect	29 O: 76.97 (7.34)	Exercise type	Cognitive function; gait characteristic; mobility performance; fear of falling; fall frequency
[30]	Xbox 360 Kinect	9 O: 71.9 (5.7)	pre- and post-test	Cognitive function; blood samples
[31]	Xbox Kinect	29 G: 84.7 (7.4) 36 G: 85.5 (7.2)	Exercise type	Physical activity; mobility

(*continued*)

Table 1. (*continued*)

Reference	Device	Number and age of participants	Independent variable	Dependent variable
[32]	Xbox 360 Kinect	16 O: 69.13 (2.6)	Game software	Weight shifts; muscle activity; maximal consecutive blocks; intrinsic motivation
[12]	Nintendo Wii™	27 G: 70.78 (8.37) 25 G: 73.56 (8.88)	Play type (single-player or multiple-player)	Social support; loneliness; depression
[14]	MoviLetrando	41 G: 69.37 (5.56) 42 G: 74.17 (8.6)	User characteristics	Physical activity; mood

Note: Y: young, O: old, G: group, AVR: active virtual reality, SVR: sedentary virtual reality.

Table 2. Variables reported in enrolled studies

Variables	References
Older vs. younger age groups	[14, 16, 17, 27]
Traditional vs. new exercise type	[16, 19, 20, 23–26, 28, 29]
Single-player vs. multiple-player	[11, 12, 15, 21, 22]
Attitude towards exergames	[11, 22]
Physical activity	[18, 23, 28, 31]
Cognitive function	[18, 19, 28, 30]
Sociability	[12, 21, 22]
Mood	[11, 12, 15, 20–22, 27]

intervention [24]. However, Silva et al. found no significant difference between exergame training and traditional training conditions [25]. Similar results were reported in studies by Karahan et al., Ogawa et al. and Moreira et al. [26, 28, 29], while Moreira et al. found that both exergames and traditional exercise have different focuses. For example, exergame training may be a better choice for improving cognitive performance while traditional training may be the better option for improving physical performance [28].

In summary, both exergames and traditional exercise have an effect on adults, but the effect of exergames is more pronounced than that of traditional exercise, such as intergroup anxiety and attitudes toward exergames [16], fun and positive emotions [20], balance ability [24] and cognitive performance [19, 28]. In addition, some studies reported that there was no significant difference between exergames and traditional exercise [25, 26, 28, 29].

Single-Player vs. Multiple-Player. Many studies have considered the effects of multi-person interactions. Three studies used three play types to carry out their experiments: playing alone, playing with peers and playing with younger people [11, 21, 22]. After exergame interventions, older adults' attitudes toward exergames, their perceptions of younger people and sociability significantly increased, while levels of loneliness significantly decreased [22]. The level of sociability in the elderly-elderly condition is significantly higher than in the elderly alone and the elderly-youth condition [21, 22]. In addition, the elderly-youth condition showed a lower level of loneliness compared to the elderly alone and elderly-elderly condition [21, 22]. While there was no significant difference in the changes in positive emotions among different play types, those who played alone showed a greater decline in negative emotions than those who played with peers and younger people [11]. Two studies used single-player and multiple-player exergame interactions [12, 15]. Studies found that elderly people who participated in multiple-player exergames had lower levels of loneliness compared with those who participated in single-player exergames and that the incidence of subthreshold depression was further reduced [12], but there were no significant differences in energy expenditure or psychosocial outcomes for single-player and multiple-player exergame [15].

In conclusion, multiple-player interactions show more positive effects, including sociability, social anxiety and loneliness. Playing alone showed a greater decline in negative emotions [11], but multiple-player exergames led to lower levels of loneliness and higher sociability [12, 21, 22].

Attitude Towards Exergames. Older adults' attitudes toward exergames improved after exergame interventions. Zheng et al. found that attitudes toward exergames were associated with two types of emotions (negative and positive emotions) after six weeks of playing exergames and that sociability can mediate such relationships [11]. Older adults' attitudes toward exergames increased after six weeks of play [22]. Both studies used a five-item scale [33] to assess attitude towards exergames. Each item is a one-word description (e.g., beneficial, pleasant) to capture how older adults feel about playing exergames at least once a week for the following month. In the current study, this scale showed good internal consistency on both pretest and posttest data (Cronbach's α = 0.94; Cronbach's α = 0.96).

Physical Activity. Using exergames leads to people spending more time exercising and increases levels of physical activity, but one study showed no such relationship. Sousa pointed out that exergames induced more time spent on physical activity [18]. This result also appeared in the study by Gonçalves et al., who found that participants spent more time doing moderate-to-high intensity physical activity during the exergame than during regular exercise and burned less energy, so the workout was less intense but lasted longer [23]. In addition, Moreira et al. found that participants' physical function significantly increased after the intervention [28]. However, Taylor et al. pointed out that there was no significant difference in physical activity levels between the baseline and following the intervention [31].

Cognitive Function. Cognitive function improved significantly after exergame interventions, or at least some domains of cognitive function improved. Participants in the exergames group showed greater improvements in overall cognitive function than those in the physical exercise group [19, 28]. Sousa found that AVR can induce better boundary cognitive performance [18]. Cavalcante et al. found that participants' overall cognitive function did not change before and after the intervention, but improved in the language domain [30].

Sociability. Sociability improved significantly after exergame interventions. Xu et al. found that participants' social anxiety and sociability improved significantly after exergame interventions [21, 22]. While social support was not affected by play types, a significant relationship was found between social support, loneliness and depression in the context of exergames [12].

Mood. Exergames can help to reduce loneliness and depression and improve the mood of older adults. There was a significant decrease in loneliness after exergame intervention [12, 21, 22]. The results of Zheng et al. showed that playing exergames can lead to an increase in positive emotions and a decrease in negative emotions over time [11]. Mackintosh et al. pointed out that men reported higher levels of negative emotions and stress than women for both single-player and dual-player exergames [15]. Naugle et al. found a greater increase in positive emotions in Nintendo Wii™ boxing and tennis than in traditional exercise [20]. Nguyen et al. found that playing exergames helped to maintain happiness levels and prevent them from falling [27]. Maintaining happiness was more significant among participants who were trying to control their weight, but there was no difference between highly optimistic and less optimistic participants [27]. Li et al. noted that depression improved significantly after the intervention [12].

4 Discussion and Conclusion

Many of the studies in this review were conducted within the last 10 years, showing that exergames as a form of exercise for older adults is still in its infancy. Depending on the product and device used, players can participate in a variety of exergames, with Nintendo Wii™ and Xbox Kinect being the most frequently used exergame platforms. Simple and single movements are recommended for older people because of their impaired physical and cognitive condition [34]. Therefore, exergame intervention trials in older adults should use simple and single movement exergames.

Different study designs and outcome measures have been used in the exergame intervention. The study designs were broadly divided into two categories: (1) a single-group pre-post design (no control group); and (2) a pre-post control group design (at least one control group). The control group received either no intervention or other interventions, such as traditional exercise or multiple-player interactions. The first design can investigate the effectiveness of the exergame intervention using a smaller sample size. However, it lacks the ability to compare the effectiveness of exergames with traditional exercise. Exergame interventions were mostly set at 30 to 50 min, 2 or 3 times per week for 6 or 8 weeks. Of course, different test populations (young people, old people, healthy people, patients), sample sizes and study designs affect the length and frequency of the experiment. In most studies, the exergames intervention lasted for longer than 4 weeks and less than 12 weeks. In addition, the sample size is relatively concentrated in the range from 20 to 50. In terms of the outcome measures of exergame interventions, most studies use subjective scales to measure outcomes. Only a few studies have used instruments to objectively measure some of the indicators [20, 25, 29, 30, 32], such as gait test, blood samples and surface electromyography (EMG).

Exergames show the following limitations as an alternative to physical exercise. First, most existing exergame technologies are not tailored for older adults, meaning that they lack sufficient skills to handle new interactive technologies [35]. Most exergames are designed primarily for the entertainment of young people, rather than for exercise or rehabilitation in older adults. Some exergames only focus on the fun of the exergame, thus ignoring the exercise nature of the exergame; these exergames are therefore not suitable for older adults to exercise. In addition, another current issue with exergames is the amount of space required for activities and long periods of staring at a screen, which can limit the player's movements and create other aspects of fatigue, such as visual fatigue.

This review outlines the potential benefits of exergames as an exercise platform for older adults. Technology regarding exercise has gained increasing attention and using exergames may be a viable option and acceptable for older adults. In many studies, exergames were found to have a positive effect on physical activity, cognitive function and sociability, as well as improving the mood and attitudes toward exergames, although some studies have found no significant effect. In addition, these exergames can be played individually, with others, or even virtually. The wide selection of exergames offers players a personalized experience based on their interests and skills, thereby reducing barriers and increasing participation in exergames. The relatively low motion sickness score suggests that exergames do not cause severe motion sickness [18]. Therefore, exergames can be an effective way for older adults to exercise and serve as an alternative to traditional exercise. Especially in a home environment or in situations where older adults are unable to leave the house for a specific reason, exergames can be used as an alternative to traditional exercise and have a positive impact on the physical and mental health of older adults.

Acknowledgement. This study is supported by the National Natural Science Foundation of China 72101100.

References

1. Comeras-Chueca, C., et al.: Assessment of active video games' energy expenditure in children with overweight and obesity and differences by gender. Int. J. Environ. Res. Public Health **17**(18), 6714 (2020). https://doi.org/10.3390/ijerph17186714
2. Oh, Y., Yang, S.: Defining exergames and exergaming. In: Proceedings of Meaningful Play, pp. 1–17 (2010)
3. Agmon, M., Perry, C.K., Phelan, E., Demiris, G., Nguyen, H.Q.: A pilot study of Wii Fit exergames to improve balance in older adults. J. Geriatric Phys. Therapy **34**, 161–167 (2011)

4. Goble, D.J., Cone, B.L., Fling, B.W.: Using the Wii Fit as a tool for balance assessment and neurorehabilitation: the first half decade of "Wii-search." J. Neuroeng. Rehabil. **11**, 12 (2014). https://doi.org/10.1186/1743-0003-11-12
5. Warburton, D.E.R.: The health benefits of active gaming: separating the myths from the virtual reality. Curr. Cardiovasc. Risk Rep. **7**, 251–255 (2013). https://doi.org/10.1007/s12170-013-0322-0
6. Forsberg, A., Nilsagård, Y., Boström, K.: Perceptions of using videogames in rehabilitation: a dual perspective of people with multiple sclerosis and physiotherapists. Disabil. Rehabil. **37**, 338–344 (2015). https://doi.org/10.3109/09638288.2014.918196
7. Plow, M., Finlayson, M.: Potential benefits of nintendo Wii Fit among people with multiple sclerosis: a longitudinal pilot study. Int. J. MS Care **13**, 21–30 (2011). https://doi.org/10.7224/1537-2073-13.1.21
8. Prosperini, L., Fortuna, D., Giannì, C., Leonardi, L., Marchetti, M.R., Pozzilli, C.: Home-based balance training using the Wii balance board: a randomized, crossover pilot study in multiple sclerosis. Neurorehabil. Neural Rep. **27**, 516–525 (2013). https://doi.org/10.1177/1545968313478484
9. Robinson, J., Dixon, J., Macsween, A., van Schaik, P., Martin, D.: The effects of exergaming on balance, gait, technology acceptance and flow experience in people with multiple sclerosis: a randomized controlled trial. BMC Sports Sci. Med. Rehabil. **7**, 8 (2015). https://doi.org/10.1186/s13102-015-0001-1
10. World Health Organization. https://www.who.int/news-room/fact-sheets/detail/ageing-and-health
11. Zheng, H., Li, J., Salmon, C.T., Theng, Y.-L.: The effects of exergames on emotional well-being of older adults. Comput. Hum. Behav. **110**, 106383 (2020). https://doi.org/10.1016/j.chb.2020.106383
12. Li, J., Theng, Y.-L., Foo, S.: Play mode effect of exergames on subthreshold depression older adults: a randomized pilot trial. Front. Psychol. **11**, 552416 (2020). https://doi.org/10.3389/fpsyg.2020.552416
13. Chen, F.X., King, A.C., Hekler, E.B.: "Healthifying" exergames: improving health outcomes through intentional priming. In: Proceedings of the SIGCHI Conference on Human Factors in Computing Systems, pp. 1855–1864. Association for Computing Machinery, New York, NY, USA (2014)
14. Zangirolami-Raimundo, J., et al.: Contrasting performance between physically active and sedentary older people playing exergames. Medicine **98**, (2019). https://doi.org/10.1097/MD.0000000000014213
15. Mackintosh, K.A., Standage, M., Staiano, A.E., Lester, L., McNarry, M.A.: Investigating the physiological and psychosocial responses of single- and dual-player exergaming in young adults. Games Health J. **5**, 375–381 (2016). https://doi.org/10.1089/g4h.2016.0015
16. Chua, P.-H., Jung, Y., Lwin, M., Theng, Y.-L.: Let's play together: effects of video-game play on intergenerational perceptions among youth and elderly participants. Comput. Hum. Behav. **29**, 2303–2311 (2013). https://doi.org/10.1016/j.chb.2013.04.037
17. Osmanovic, S., Pecchioni, L.: Beyond entertainment: motivations and outcomes of video game playing by older adults and their younger family members. Games Culture **11**, 130–149 (2015)
18. Sousa, C.V., et al.: Active video games in fully immersive virtual reality elicit moderate-to-vigorous physical activity and improve cognitive performance in sedentary college students. J. Sport Health Sci. (2021). https://doi.org/10.1016/j.jshs.2021.05.002
19. Liao, Y.-Y., Chen, I.-H., Hsu, W.-C., Tseng, H.-Y., Wang, R.-Y.: Effect of exergaming versus combined exercise on cognitive function and brain activation in frail older adults: a randomised controlled trial. Ann. Phys. Rehabil. Med. **64**, 101492 (2021). https://doi.org/10.1016/j.rehab.2021.101492

20. Naugle, K.E., Naugle, K.M., Wikstrom, E.A.: Cardiovascular and affective outcomes of active gaming: using the nintendo Wii as a cardiovascular training tool. J. Strength Cond. Res. **28**, 443–451 (2014)

21. Xu, X., Li, J., Pham, T., Salmon, C., Theng, Y.-L.: Improving psychosocial well-being of older adults through exergaming: the moderation effects of intergenerational communication and age cohorts. Games Health J. **5**, 389–397 (2016). https://doi.org/10.1089/g4h.2016.0060

22. Li, C., Li, J., Pham, T., Theng, Y.-L., Chia, B.: Promoting Healthy and Active Ageing through Exergames: Effects of Exergames on Senior Adults' Psychosocial Well-Being. Presented at the (2018)

23. Gonçalves, A.R., Muñoz, J.E., Gouveia, É.R., Cameirão, M., Bermúdez i Badia, S.: Effects of prolonged multidimensional fitness training with exergames on the physical exertion levels of older adults. Vis. Comput. **37**(1), 19–30 (2019). https://doi.org/10.1007/s00371-019-017 36-0

24. Yang, C.-M., Chen Hsieh, J., Chen, Y.-C., Yang, S.-Y., Lin, H.-C.: Effects of Kinect exergames on balance training among community older adults: a randomized controlled trial. Medicine **99**, e21228 (2020). https://doi.org/10.1097/MD.0000000000021228

25. Silva, E., Lange, B., Bacha, J., Pompeu, J.E.: Effects of the interactive videogame nintendo Wii sports on upper limb motor function of individuals with post-polio syndrome: a randomized clinical trial. Games Health J. **9**, 461–471 (2020)

26. Karahan, Y.A., Tok, F., Taskin, H., Kucuksarac, S., Basaran, A., Yildirim, P.: Effects of exergames on balance, functional mobility, and quality of life of geriatrics versus home exercise programme: randomized controlled study. Central Eur. J. Public Health **23**, S14–S18 (2015). https://doi.org/10.21101/cejph.a4081

27. Nguyen, H.V., Huang, H.-C., Wong, M.-K., Yang, Y.-H., Huang, T.-L., Teng, C.-I.: Moderator roles of optimism and weight control on the impact of playing exergames on happiness: the perspective of social cognitive theory using a randomized controlled trial. Games Health J. **7**, 246–252 (2018). https://doi.org/10.1089/g4h.2017.0165

28. Moreira, N.B., Rodacki, A.L.F., Costa, S.N., Pitta, A., Bento, P.C.B.: Perceptive-cognitive and physical function in prefrail older adults: exergaming versus traditional multicomponent training. Rejuven. Res. **24**, 28–36 (2021). https://doi.org/10.1089/rej.2020.2302

29. Ogawa, E., et al.: Effects of exergaming on cognition and gait in older adults at risk for falling. Med. Sci. Sports Exerc. **52**, 1 (2019). https://doi.org/10.1249/MSS.0000000000002167

30. Cavalcante, M.M., et al.: Exergame training-induced neuroplasticity and cognitive improvement in institutionalized older adults: a preliminary investigation. Physiol. Behav. **241**, 113589 (2021). https://doi.org/10.1016/j.physbeh.2021.113589

31. Taylor, L., Kerse, N., Klenk, J., Borotkanics, R., Maddison, R.: Exergames to improve the mobility of long-term care residents: a cluster randomized controlled trial. Games Health J. **7**, 37–42 (2018). https://doi.org/10.1089/g4h.2017.0084

32. Willaert, J., de Vries, A., Tavernier, J., Van Dieen, J., Jonkers, I., Verschueren, S.: Does a novel exergame challenge balance and activate muscles more than existing off-the-shelf exergames? J. NeuroEng. Rehabil. **17**, (2020). https://doi.org/10.1186/s12984-019-0628-3

33. Stephen L. Crites, Jr., Fabrigar, L.R., Petty, R.E.: Measuring the affective and cognitive properties of attitudes: conceptual and methodological issues. Person. Soc. Psychol. Bull. **20**, 619–634 (1994). https://doi.org/10.1177/0146167294206001

34. Gao, Y., Mandryk, R.L.: GrabApple: the design of a casual exergame. In: Anacleto, J.C., Fels, S., Graham, N., Kapralos, B., Saif El-Nasr, M., Stanley, K. (eds.) ICEC 2011. LNCS, vol. 6972, pp. 35–46. Springer, Heidelberg (2011). https://doi.org/10.1007/978-3-642-24500-8_5

35. Sonderegger, A., Schmutz, S., Sauer, J.: The influence of age in usability testing. Appl. Ergon. **52**, 291–300 (2016). https://doi.org/10.1016/j.apergo.2015.06.012

Let the Camera Eat First? Engaging the Older Adults' Reflection and Sharing About Food Photograph to Enhance Wellbeing

Hsiu-Ping Yueh[1] , Long-Jing Hsu[2], and Weijane Lin[1(✉)]

[1] National Taiwan University, No. 1, Sec. 4, Roosevelt Road, Taipei 106319, Taiwan
vjlin@ntu.edu.tw
[2] Indiana University Bloomington, Myles Brand Hall, Suite E226, 901 E. Tenth Street,
Bloomington, IN 47408, USA

Abstract. With the increased interest in older adults' technology use, and with the understanding the association between ICTs use and well-being, it is important to further explore older adults' technology use in other life contexts than communication. This study focused on the diet scenario and aimed to assess their needs and performances of using food photographs with a current food diary app. The methodology of design-based research (DBR) was adopted, using the methods and instruments of qualitative in-depth interviews, diaries, and focus group interviews. It was found that taking food photographs could improve well-being for the older adults. The preliminary findings suggested that participants were more mindful of their food and were highly involved during the sharing session.

Keywords: Gerontechnology · Food photograph · Older users

1 Introduction

The rise of Information and Communication Technology (ICT) has inexorably shifted how the older adults used technology for communication in their daily lives. In the U.S., 33% of social media users ages older than 50 years said it would be hard for them to give up social media [1]. In Taiwan, over 90% of people aged 50 and above had frequent access to instant message services, and over 80% of them used Internet phone calls [2]. As shown here, technology was inevitably part of the older adults' life. And just like the younger generation, there were also significant individual differences in ICTs and social media uses among older users. These differences in behavioral patterns engendered controversies on the effect of ICT on well-being. A local survey in Taiwan suggested that the more frequent older users in social media may have a higher possibility of odd being lonely [3]. Similar studies conducted in Canada [4] asserted digital media could be overwhelming and wasting time to the older adults, while they also perceived positive feelings such as the sense of control, independence, safety, stronger social network and connection. [5] supported that the positive feelings encouraged older adults' communication through technology, which could provoke awareness and performance of health,

© The Author(s), under exclusive license to Springer Nature Switzerland AG 2022
P.-L. P. Rau (Ed.): HCII 2022, LNCS 13313, pp. 461–471, 2022.
https://doi.org/10.1007/978-3-031-06050-2_33

and even raise self-efficacy and relieve stress [6] that resulted in better mental well-being [7–9].

Despite the contradictions on the effect of ICT, the approaches to ICT with food are auspicious. Previous studies found that participants have a better understanding of nutrients consumed with food diary [10], accurately record their dietary intake [11], and help them balance emotions and thoughts while creating a sense of empowerment and control in their life [12]. Additionally, irritable bowel syndrome patients were better at eliciting their eating goals through a photo-based food diary [13]. However, the previous studies have rarely investigated older generations. With the increased interest in older adults' technology use, and with the understanding the association between ICTs use and well-being, it is important to further explore the technology use in more life contexts other than communication. Therefore, this study focused on the diet scenario and aimed to assess their needs and performances of using food photographs with a current food diary app. The methodology of design-based research (DBR) was adopted, using the methods and instruments of qualitative in-depth interviews, diaries, and focus group interviews. Through the investigations of older adults' use contexts, this study is expected to provide empirical support for older users' diet technology, and contribute to the research communities of diet and gerontechnology studies.

2 Literature Review

2.1 Association Between ICT Use and Well-Being

One of the major concerns for the older population is deterioration in one's well-being. Well-being is a term derived from subjective well-being (SWB), is a subjective definition of quality of life, on how a person defines what a good life and can be measured with several pleasant emotion, whether they are engaging with interesting activity, experiencing pleasure, and satisfaction with their life [14]. In other words, to have good well-being is relevant to being happy, good subjective well-being, and psychological quality of life [15].

People's well-being decrease as they age. First, the rates of chronic illness, such as high blood pressure, high cholesterol, or diabetes, increased tremendously during middle age [16]. And as people get older, they lost their independence and mobility due to the decline in their mental and physical health. As a result, it became harder for people to engage with others [17, 18], and thus decreased wellbeing. The problems worsen as they face deaths in their family and friends [19]. Nevertheless, a change in job and status may also affect one's well-being. Although there was no effect on well-being for voluntary retirement, an individual who retired involuntary and prefers to work more would result in negative well-being [20]. Therefore, it is important to explore ways that can enhance the older adults' wellbeing.

Using ICTs is a solution to increase good social relationships and have a good level of social engagement [6, 21–23]. ICTs include mobile phones, computers, and the Internet [24]. Recent attention has investigated the provision of how technologies may impact older adults' well-being. ICT was beneficial for human society by helping people overcome geographical and time barriers [6] and communicate more with one another. It led to satisfaction on social needs, a sense of control, independence, feeling of safety, strengthen the social network, stay connected [4], and provoke better health behaviors [5]. It also raised feelings of control and self-efficacy and relieved stress [6]. And could lead to better mental well-being and reduction in depression [7–9, 25]. Overall, ICT was beneficial for the older adults' quality of life (QoL) [24]. With the myriad of ICT studies, this paper aimed to tackle the ICT with the lens of food.

2.2 Food and the Historical Setting for the Taiwanese Older Adults

The importance of food photograph is embedded with the idea of "food" itself. Food is not only for nutrition and survival, but it also encompasses culture, memory, and history. It is related to cooking or preparing meals, eating or sharing a meal, with friends, family, or work colleagues. For example, eating at home is an important process within the kinship network, it allows the coherence and solidarity for the family, and is an opportunity for every individual to be emotionally and socially attached [26]. According to [27], food is "a highly condensed social fact": it is a topic and location for social discourse that can mobilize people's emotions and experiences. A person's food choice represents their culture and social environment [28]. Food represents who we are, where we came from, and what we want to be.

Food for the older adults in Taiwan changes as they age. Baby Boomers have experienced and adapted themselves to changes throughout their life [29, 30]. They were born after World War II when Taiwan undergoes a postwar transformation, when time is hard, even for a bowl of rice to eat. During this time, the Chinese government established the "regulations for implementation on economical movement," taking away the civic resources for military use, people have to practice savings on their food and were not allowed to eat more than one dish and soup per meal in the restaurant [31]. Similar to the early 20th century, scarcity in food made food the center of their life, people greet one another by saying "Have you had your bowl of rice?". As Taiwan entered the industrial state, the society got wealthier with better education and mobility, government policy change, and migration from mainland China [32]. This migration brought new dishes to the local communities, with the emergence of cuisines from mainland China with indigenous material, known as the "Military Dependent Villages Food". Next, they have experienced the U.S. Aid between 1951 and 1965, where western cuisine come in. Finally, as industrialization come in, agricultural production resulted in abundance of food [33], from then to today. From this history, these baby boomers have experienced changes in the food, the history, the culture as they age, and is inevitably different from the younger generations today. Yet, past literature has not explored ways on how the Baby Boomers use ICT under "food."

2.3 Food Photograph

Food photographs were emerging on ICT applications. It appeared on sites that target visual presentations such as Instagram and Pinterest instead of text-based systems [34]. Instagram has 1 billion monthly active users, 500 million photos uploads per day, and 4.2 billion likes per day (Instagram.com/press). Not only this, YouTube has lots of information on food and diet [28].

Specifically, people take food photographs for many reasons. The literature reviewed that taking photographs before was similar to performing a ritual [35] that increase people's enjoyment in the food [10]. When photographs are taken, food act as a symbolic content, connecting the producer and the audience which further represent the culture in the real social world [34]. The camera operator can choose what to capture their experience according to their tastes and intent and share it with the audience. Foods are also like artifacts people chose, to be displayed on the social media exhibition. People choose how to be displayed as a form of impression management [36]. In the twenty-first century, nouveau rich share aestheticized food to show social prestige with high culture capital; nowadays 'foodies' share photographs of food show others their food taste [34], indicating that not only for visualization, but food could also be a tool of storytelling.

Food photographs could be a reminder for a person to share their story. Through storytelling, the teller could share history, transfer information, and create a connection to the listener [37, 38]. Stories were able to create bonds and social support [39] and also cultivate and reveal family identity [40]. Specifically, food stories were able to spread the needs, values, and principles, communicate knowledge, and provide attention [41]. Food stories also revealed the food environments and dietary behaviors of each individual [42]. Overall, sharing one's stories has many benefit on individuals and relationships.

When photographs are taken regularly, it becomes journaling. Previous studies supported that older adults' journaling could promote skills development, enhance employability, and reflect life events and friendships [43]. Photographic food records can resemble a food diary and can be used to accurately record their dietary intake [11]. As people take food diary, they were more aware of their food choice [10], be able to identify environmental cues for unwanted behaviors [44], evoke memories, and increase people's engagement with health promotion [45]. Moreover, in the process of writing and naming experiences, participants understand their own experiences in a clear and organized way and can balance emotions and thoughts while having a sense of empowerment and control in their life [12]. However, not much research on food diary was done on older adults and was therefore one of the core purposes of this study.

3   Methodology

This study used the design-based approach (DBR) that developed from our previous studies to design and develop the technological interventions for the older adults [46] in order to find the theoretical and practical implications of food and food photographs on older adults. This DBR was done with two iterations (see Fig. 1) that were constructed by semi-structured interview and focused group interview.

The first iteration was a one-on-one semi-structured interview with open-ended questions about social media use and production of food photographs of late middle-age adults. Semi-structured interviewing were useful for the researcher to discover in-depth, subtle differences to make explanations and arguments on the specific topics Specifically, the authors assessed the user's needs (the importance of food and application) with the theoretical conjecture. For the second iteration, the theoretical conjectures were refined to interpret and analyze the available apps, and the Recovery Record app was selected (see Fig. 2). Participants were instructed to take food photographs, describe and

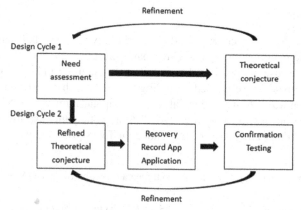

Fig. 1. Research framework of this study

record their feelings and experience through a selection of words or written words on their mealtime environment, 3 times per day, for one week with their mobile phones. Step by step instructions was printed out and instructed vocally to the participants. Artificial accounts were created for a record to further analyze. The mealtime environment could include both food and friends. Questions on the app include "How are you feeling overall," "Which feelings are you experiencing," "who did you eat with," and "where did you eat." Participants were asked to jot down any other comments and were also allowed to take any other pictures during their snack time. Only photos of food for regular mealtimes were coded for the study.

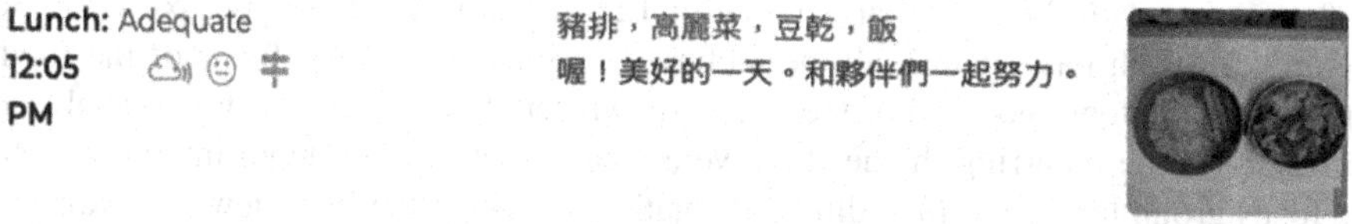

Lunch: Adequate   豬排，高麗菜，豆乾，飯
12:05 🔔 ☺ ♉ 喔！美好的一天。和夥伴們一起努力。
PM

Fig. 2. Excerpt from the food diary APP illustrating a photograph of a meal and comment

At the end of the two-week photography period, the participants met together to discuss the pictures for testing confirmation. Before the group interview, each individual selected the three most significant or liked the most photographs to discuss with the group. And they also wrote a brief survey based on the photographs taken in the past week (3 questions for each picture) and experiences (23 questions) to elicit responses. The survey was based on the evaluation survey by [47] with other self-made questions on naming themes and labeling the pictures according to the themes they identified.

During this group interview, participants discussed the selected meaning of the photographs, what they saw and how they interpret. Individuals shared their personal stories and experiences about the meal, taking food photographs, and everyone's opinion on their overall experience, their acceptability in terms of adoption and uses, and efficacy with the app use.

3.1 Participants

The participants (N = 6) were recruited on a voluntary and snowball basis. The three criteria for participation were (1) age: participants must be born between the year 1946 and 1965, (2) ever use of social media, and (3) ever taken food photographs. The participant characteristics were labeled according to the order they were interviewed, and basic information was summarized in Table 1. Participants number 2 to 5 were recruited to continue with our research voluntarily. All four participants use the application to record their food diary and all of them attended the focus group interview.

Table 1. Demographics and social media use of participants (N = 6)

No	Gender	Occupation	Social media use	Participated in food diary app and focus group
1	F	Securities specialist	Line, Facebook	
2	F	High school teacher	Line	v
3	F	High school teacher	Line	v
4	M	Administrative civil servant	Line, Facebook	v
5	F	High School teacher	Line, Facebook	v
6	M	Repairman	Line, Facebook	

3.2 Data Analysis

In the session with the food diary, a total of 122 meals were taken (approximately 30 pictures for each participant), all the pictures were taken with the focus of the food. Among the photographs, 110 of them include written diaries. The diary was analyzed according to the recurring themes that were created with the in-depth interviews and the focus group interview. In addition, thematic analysis of the interviews was done to analyze the themes from the diary and the note itself.

4   Preliminary Findings

4.1   Older Users' Perception of Food Photograph

The participants reported familiarity and frequent accesses of using social media such as Line and Facebook to stay in contact with their friends, family, co-worker, and sometimes client. Almost all of them acknowledged the importance of photographs, including food photographs, for them to share and connect with people. Participants used photographs as a center of topics on ICT to bond with other people. The connection could be a wide social network, such as posting on Facebook, or intimate one on one, such as instant messaging Line. The idea of sharing on ICT was beneficial for the connection of people who currently not living or not enjoying the moment with them. Photographs were used because were easier for the receivers to interpret. It could express the care and love from the sender and where they would expect the same love and feedback. It could be an initiator of topics to share about what is happening in their lives, to stay connected, and a sense of belonging and happiness. This initiator could result in a short and casual conversation online and offline. It could help the participants maintain and facilitate their relationships while helping them to improve their well-being. This initiator could be everything from special occasions to anything simple as day-to-day context.

And the participants would take pictures on special occasions such as family gathering and trips as the facilitator pictures for discussion. For instance, several participants mentioned how they had Line Chat groups with their families, where the family members would share their photographs of scenes, artifacts and portraits to keep a record and share special moments in their lives. The examples above showed the importance of photographs on ICT for the participant's lives. It was the tool to share their excitement, happy emotions, habits, and joy with their friends and family. And through sharing, they would gain feedback on the maintenance of relationships and an even better feeling when responding.

However, participants possessed quite different views toward sharing food photograph. Some were affected by their childhood memories and historical background. As mentioned earlier, when the participants were small, food was scarce, and dining out was a luxury than a necessity. Three participants (P1–P3) talked about their apathy in food as "*I think the food is brought to eat. Even if it's beautiful I still have to eat it. So for those on beautiful dishes, I don't want to keep it. I think this is because when we are small, we are taught to be practical, eat is to eat, eat is delicious*" (P2). While other 2 younger participants (P4, P6) were more mindful of the eating moments and emotions. They mentioned the satisfaction and happiness when they were eating as "*After eating the food, I will feel very happy and very satisfied*" (P4).

Despite the lack of interest in daily foods, the participants take food photographs during special occasions. It was the focus and something that stands out from the daily routine. Food played a role in the participants' social lives and celebrations. These participants captured the moment with a photo of food to share with their close friends, and also keep informed about the special meal and moments in life. And it could remind them of the essence of the bonds and ties or the moments that they have shared. Five of the six participants took food photographs when they were at a restaurant. Restaurants were different from ordinary meals because of their atmosphere, special garnishing, the way the meal was served, or the taste of the food. The participants mentioned: "*When we are out during a big meal… when the dishes are different from others, and will be happy to take photos and share them. Or when we dine in the hotel, the dishes used are different from others, and are made very beautiful*" (P4). More conservative food photo sharer like P3 took photo in special occasions: "*Sometimes during special occasions you will learn something special. For example, I learn something special from the Internet, maybe I will take the picture, such as pumpkin rice noodle or shrimp floss or three cup chicken. Something extraordinary. And then after I made it, will take photo and share it with other people. Usually with garnish, will take photo, and then tell everyone, this is new dish I made today*" (P3).

4.2 Participants' Uses and Evaluation of the Food Diary App

The participant's views changed subtly after taking photos meal by meal and jotting down their feelings albeit the participants hold different views about the food for daily lives. From the 70 entries of the 110 related to daily lives, many take special care from their mundane lives.

To begin with, the participants acknowledged nutritional value in their meals. When we asked the participants to name themes and label the pictures of the food photographs, one participant distinguished the photographs to levels of starch, while another participant separates the pictures into white flour, rice, whole grain, brown rice. Similarly, one of the participants emphasized the nutritional concept of two of the entries in the app.

The surrounding environment was also mentioned. To write something down for the experiment, the participants opened their sensations to connect with the living environment with the food. The elicited sensations and happenings included the weather during the day, work, home, exercise, health condition, and emotions. Several participants showed the food photograph with their life diary, recoding information such as the interaction with the family members, reflection or memory of the childhood and daily routine, making one simple food photograph mingle with their jobs, personal life and relationships.

Cooking or preparing meals was brought up as a memorable experience of their lives. Particularly, the categorizing of the photograph of P3 was evident, which she distinguished her meal by who cooked it. Cooking was an activity to be shared with ties during the process and creates "a sense of achievement" as she mentioned. This sense of achievement also arises from a connection that was unique to every family. It was the taste of the food that bonds the family together. The sense of achievement elevated when the food was shared with other people with a positive response. It was one of the highlights and excitements during the focus group interview when participants shared photographs of husband, wife, daughter, or self-made dishes. For example, when P5 proudly presents the beef noodle cooked by his wife to the group, the group even went to deep conversation into how to make the most delicious fried egg in the world when P5 showed his lunch box, proving that not only feeling good, food could be the center of social discourse and improve well-being.

As for usability, four of the participants agreed that the app was easy to use, especially on the functions of taking photographs, recording food, and emotions. The reminder was supportive and recommends the future application have the same functions. Next, mindfully taking it was also beneficial in helping them recall the mundane food they ate in the previous week. Moreover, they think the time spent on the app was acceptable. Participants reported that they have changed their behavior when using the Recovery Records App. Half of the participants report that there was a difference in how they use the Recovery Records App when alone compared with the public. Half of the participants changed their behavior and ate foods they normally do not eat. Half of the participants agreed that the app changes their social behavior and dietary behavior.

The changes in behavior also paralleled with what the participants discussed during the focus group interview. When participants gather together to discuss the food, they would compare what they eat with other participants, and reflect on the meal they had is "*too monotonous*" (P5). P5 was aware that she has not prepared the meal as hard as the old days when she cook for the kids, so she consciously search new recipes and cook for herself. On the other hand, despite the similarity in the food, participant 3 noted that "Slowly, I found myself with more connection with the food, and a little more interest in myself" (P3). Moreover, by constantly keeping track of their emotions during meals, participants realize the importance of emotions during eating, to reflect on my own feeling (P3), and learn to calm down (P2). Also, some participant changed their habit of eating to create a better environment when dining.

5 Conclusion

This study demonstrates the importance of photographs on ICT and evaluates the Recovery Record app as a potential to increase their well-being. The findings offered critical insights into the essence of the literature of photographs, food, and food photographs. The study also provides applicable guides to the future development of food diary applications for older adults. In general, photographs could recall memories and share locally and remotely. When the participants see the pictures, they remembered the valuable time they spent with their friends and families. This process showed how photographs can become a topic for conversation and help people to bond with their ties. Despite the benefits of sharing photographs, some participants were not aware of the food they eat day to day life. Therefore, we wondered what would happen if the participants repeatedly taking food photographs and focused on sharing with other participants offline. Four participants experienced taking photographs with the Recovery Records App for two weeks.

After the intervention, the participants were more aware of their happening surrounding them, and several themes emerged. First, they were more aware of the food nutrient that provides basic human safety and basic nutritional values. Despite the triteness for everyday food, participants were more focused and opened their sensations when they were eating. The diary entries focused on changes in weather or driving from home to work were. Nevertheless, our participants reflected on their positive emotional change with a sense of gratitude. This hence proved the benefit of the app on the increase in well-being. This is in line with the past finding that food diary increased people's awareness of food choice [10], environmental cues for unwanted behaviors [44], such as negative emotions from television shows, an increase in people's engagement with health promotion [45].

The preliminary results suggested that older adults became more mindful of the food they are eating, even in their daily lives. And the participants were happy when they talked about food and stories of their lives when they were showing their food pictures. Along the process, they talked about their needs, values, and principles and could create a connection with others. The participants were satisfied and improved on their overall well-being. Overall, the use of the food diary app was an appropriate technique to record one's feelings and emotions and together the people can elicit better well-being.

References

1. http://www.pewinternet.org/2018/03/01/social-media-use-in-2018/

2. Concil, N.D.: Survey report on digital opportunities for individual households in 108. In: Concil, N.D. (ed.) National Development Council, p. 545. Taipei: Taiwan (2019)
3. Chang, C.: The 2016 Taiwan communication survey (phase one, year five): risk and disaster communication. National Chengchi University (2016)
4. Quan-Haase, A., Williams, C., Kicevski, M., Elueze, I., Wellman, B.: Dividing the grey divide: deconstructing myths about older adults' online activities, skills, and attitudes. Am. Behav. Sci. **62**, 1207–1228 (2018)
5. Hunsaker, A., Hargittai, E.: A review of Internet use among older adults. New Media Soc. **20**, 3937–3954 (2018)
6. Leist, A.K.: Social media use of older adults: a mini-review. Gerontology **59**, 378–384 (2013)
7. Cotten, S.R., Ford, G., Ford, S., Hale, T.M.: Internet use and depression among older adults. Comput. Hum. Behav. **28**, 496–499 (2012)
8. Cotten, S.R., Ford, G., Ford, S., Hale, T.M.: Internet use and depression among retired older adults in the United States: a longitudinal analysis. J. Gerontol. Ser. B Psychol. Sci. Soc. Sci. **69**, 763–771 (2014)
9. Sims, T., Reed, A.E., Carr, D.C.: Information and communication technology use is related to higher well-being among the oldest-old. J. Gerontol. B Psychol. Sci. Soc. Sci. **72**, 761–770 (2017)
10. Zepeda, L., Deal, D.: Think before you eat: photographic food diaries as intervention tools to change dietary decision making and attitudes. Int. J. Consum. Stud. **32**, 692–698 (2008)
11. Higgins, J.A., et al.: Validation of photographic food records in children: are pictures really worth a thousand words? Eur. J. Clin. Nutr. **63**, 1025 (2009)
12. Barak, A., Boniel-Nissim, M., Suler, J.: Fostering empowerment in online support groups. Comput. Hum. Behav. **24**, 1867–1883 (2008)
13. Chung, C.F., et al.: Identifying and planning for individualized change: Patient-provider collaboration using lightweight food diaries in healthy eating and irritable bowel syndrome. In: Proceedings of the ACM Interact Mob Wearable Ubiquitous Technology, vol. 3 (2019)
14. Diener, E.: Subjective well-being. The science of happiness and a proposal for a national index. Am. Psychol. **55**, 34–43 (2000)
15. Medvedev, O.N., Landhuis, C.E.: Exploring constructs of well-being, happiness and quality of life. PeerJ **6**, e4903 (2018)
16. Chang, R.C.-S., Lu, H.-P., Yang, P.: Stereotypes or golden rules? Exploring likable voice traits of social robots as active aging companions for tech-savvy baby boomers in Taiwan. Comput. Hum. Behav. **84**, 194–210 (2018)
17. Giummarra, M.J., Haralambous, B., Moore, K., Nankervis, J.: The concept of health in older age: views of older people and health professionals. Aust. Health Rev. **31**, 642–650 (2007)
18. Nicholson, N.R., Jr.: Social isolation in older adults: an evolutionary concept analysis. J. Adv. Nurs. **65**, 1342–1352 (2009)
19. Klinenberg, E.: Social isolation, loneliness, and living alone: identifying the risks for public health. Am. J. Public Health **106**, 786–787 (2016)
20. Bonsang, E., Klein, T.J.: Retirement and subjective well-being. J. Econ. Behav. Organ. **83**, 311–329 (2012)
21. Bloom, I., et al.: What influences diet quality in older people? A qualitative study among community-dwelling older adults from the Hertfordshire Cohort Study UK. Public Health Nutr. **20**, 2685–2693 (2017)
22. Rowe, J.W., Kahn, R.L.: Successful aging. Gerontologist **37**, 433–440 (1997)
23. Lin, W., Chen, H.-C., Yueh, H.-P.: Using different error handling strategies to facilitate older users' interaction with Chatbots in learning information and communication technologies. Front. Psychol. **12** (2021)
24. Jacqueline, D., Martin, K., Paul, F., Daniel, L.: Effects of digital engagement on the quality of life of older people. Health Soc. Care Community **25**, 1679–1703 (2017)

25. Escobar-Viera, C.G., et al.: Passive and active social media use and depressive symptoms among United States adults. Cyberpsychol. Behav. Soc. Netw. **21**, 437–443 (2018)
26. Hunt, G., Fazio, A., MacKenzie, K., Moloney, M.: Food in the family bringing young people back in. Appetite **56**, 394–402 (2011)
27. Appadurai, A.: Gastro-politics in Hindu South Asia. Am. Ethnol. **8**, 494–511 (1981)
28. Holmberg, C.: Adolescents' food communication in social media. In: Encyclopedia of Information Science and Technology, 4th edn. IGI Global, Hershey (2017)
29. Pruchno, R.: Not your mother's old age: baby boomers at age 65. Gerontologist **52**, 149–152 (2012)
30. Yu, H., Miller, P.: Leadership style - the X generation and baby boomers compared in different cultural contexts. Leadersh. Organ. Dev. J. **26**(1), 35–50 (2005)
31. Chen, S.H., Shao, J.H.: 'Have you had your bowl of rice?': a qualitative study of eating patterns in older Taiwanese adults. J. Clin. Nurs. **21**, 2–10 (2012)
32. Katz, P.R.: Religion and the state in post-war Taiwan. China Q. **174**, 395–412 (2003)
33. Liu, T.C.: The process of industrailization in Taiwan. Dev. Econ. **7**, 63–80 (1969)
34. McDonnell, E.M.: Food porn: the conspicuous consumption of food in the age of digital reproduction. In: Bradley, P. (ed.) Food, Media and Contemporary Culture: The Edible Image, pp. 239–265. Palgrave Macmillan, London (2016)
35. Vohs, K.D., Wang, Y., Gino, F., Norton, M.I.: Rituals enhance consumption. Psychol. Sci. **24**, 1714–1721 (2013)
36. Hogan, B.: The presentation of self in the age of social media: distinguishing performances and exhibitions online. Bull. Sci. Technol. Soc. **30**, 377–386 (2010)
37. Banks-Wallace, J.: Talk that talk: storytelling and analysis rooted in African American oral tradition. Qual. Health Res. **12**, 410–426 (2002)
38. Fabius, C.D.: Toward an integration of narrative identity, generativity, and storytelling in African American elders. J. Black Stud. **47**, 423–434 (2016)
39. Johnson, J.K., et al.: Exploring the effects of visual and literary arts interventions on psychosocial well-being of diverse older adults: a mixed methods pilot study. Arts Health **13**(3), 263–277 (2020)
40. Saksono, H., Parker, A.G.: Reflective informatics through family storytelling: self-discovering physical activity predictors. In: Proceedings of the 2017 CHI Conference on Human Factors in Computing Systems, pp. 5232–5244. Association for Computing Machinery, Denver (2017)
41. Mossberg, L., Eide, D.: Storytelling and meal experience concepts. Eur. Plan. Stud. **25**, 1184–1199 (2017)
42. Belon, A.P., Nieuwendyk, L.M., Vallianatos, H., Nykiforuk, C.I.J.: Perceived community environmental influences on eating behaviors: a photovoice analysis. Soc. Sci. Med. **171**, 18–29 (2016)
43. Shepherd, C.E., Aagard, S.: Journal writing with Web 2.0 tools: a vision for older adults. Educ. Gerontol. **37**, 606–620 (2011)
44. Staiano, A.E., Baker, C.M., Calvert, S.L.: Dietary digital diaries: documenting adolescents' obesogenic environment. Environ. Behav. **44**, 695–712 (2011)
45. Pettinger, C., et al.: Engaging homeless individuals in discussion about their food experiences to optimise wellbeing: a pilot study. Health Educ. J. **76**, 557–568 (2017)
46. Lu, M.H., Lin, W., Yueh, H.P.: Development and evaluation of a cognitive training game for older people: a design-based approach. Front. Psychol. **8**, 1837 (2017)
47. Rollo, M.E., Ash, S., Lyons-Wall, P., Russell, A.W.: Evaluation of a mobile phone image-based dietary assessment method in adults with type 2 diabetes. Nutrients **7**, 4897–4910 (2015)

Author Index

Printed in the United States
by Baker & Taylor Publisher Services